The Metamorphosis of Criminal Justice

RECENT TITLES IN

STUDIES IN PENAL THEORY AND PHILOSOPHY
R. A. Duff, Michael Tonry, General Editors

Retributivism Has a Past
Has It a Future?
Edited by Michael Tonry

Punishment, Participatory Democracy, and the Jury
Albert W. Dzur

Just Sentencing
Principles and Procedures for a Workable System
Richard S. Frase

Popular Punishment
On the Normative Significance of Public Opinion
Jesper Ryberg and Julian V. Roberts

Taming the Presumption of Innocence
Richard Lippke

Sentencing Multiple Crimes
Edited by Jesper Ryberg, Julian V. Roberts, and Jan W. de Keijser

Playing Fair
Political Obligation and the Problems of Punishment
Richard Dagger

Hate, Politics, Law
Critical Perspectives on Combating Hate
Edited by Thomas Brudholm and Birgitte Schepelern Johansen

Criminal Law in the Age of the Administrative State
Vincent Chiao

Punishment and Citizenship
A Theory of Criminal Disenfranchisement
Milena Tripkovic

Beyond Punishment?
A Normative Account of Collateral Restrictions on Offenders
Zachary Hoskins

The Metamorphosis of Criminal Justice

A Comparative Account

JACQUELINE S. HODGSON

OXFORD
UNIVERSITY PRESS

OXFORD
UNIVERSITY PRESS

Oxford University Press is a department of the University of Oxford. It furthers the University's objective of excellence in research, scholarship, and education by publishing worldwide. Oxford is a registered trade mark of Oxford University Press in the UK and certain other countries.

Published in the United States of America by Oxford University Press
198 Madison Avenue, New York, NY 10016, United States of America.

CIP data is on file at the Library of Congress
ISBN 978-0-19-998142-7

1 3 5 7 9 8 6 4 2

Printed by Integrated Books International, United States of America

Contents

Preface

This book has been a long time in the making, interrupted by other projects and research collaborations that were simply too interesting to pass up. As a study, it is an attempt to tell at least part of the story of how criminal justice values, in England and Wales and in France, have altered in fundamental ways. Our court processes and our treatment of accused persons and victims have become a facsimile of justice, in which courts and legal actors are increasingly absent and legal procedures are increasingly routinized and bureaucratic. Crime has become a core political issue, and governments have sought to demonstrate their "tough on crime" credentials with short-term and sometimes disastrous policies. At the same time, as a result of expanded cross-border police and judicial cooperation through the European Union and, through the Council of Europe, the European Court of Human Rights' response to increasing national challenges to the expansion of fair-trial rights, there has been a countercurrent of strengthened procedural rights for suspects and accused persons. The ways in which jurisdictions have embraced or resisted these transnational norms illustrate the wider process values they cherish.

I have been helped in the writing of this book by a great many people and institutions—by the British Academy and the Leverhulme Trust in awarding me a fellowship that marked the start of this project, and by Warwick Law School for granting me research leave and supporting me in the lengthy process of writing. Particular thanks to Victor Tadros, who has encouraged me from start to finish and propped me up with untold amounts of coffee, as well as, most importantly, being a good friend. I could not have asked for a better series editor than Antony Duff, who has been patient and encouraging in equal measure. The staff at Oxford University Press have been helpful and efficient at every stage of the process. Much of my research has been collaborative, and mention is made throughout the book of the many colleagues across Europe with whom I have had the pleasure of working and from whom I have learned so much, but I also want to thank them formally here—especially Ed Cape and Taru Spronken and the various teams of researchers at the University of Maastricht. A host of colleagues have also been exceptionally generous with their time, reading and commenting on some or all of the draft manuscript, and I am grateful for their wise and sensible suggestions: Antony Duff, Stewart Field, Juliet Horne, Layla Skinns, Laurène Soubise, Victor Tadros, Miles Trent, and Thomas Weigend. I am also indebted to Jo Harwood, Laurène Soubise and Catherine Vincent for research assistance at various points in this project.

I argue in the book that criminal justice is in a kind of perpetual metamorphosis, its endpoint ever changing. For the same reason, this has made it a difficult project to draw to a close. There is always more to add. But now is a good time to stop, as the UK is poised to leave the European Union and the next chapter unfolds.

Overview

The focus of this book is the potentially radical and fundamental changes that are taking place within criminal justice in Britain and in France and the ways that these are driven by wider domestic, European, or international concerns. The criminal justice process in England and Wales has been undergoing something of a metamorphosis, moving away from established adversarial values, rules, and practices, in many instances eroding what were once regarded as core rights and freedoms in the name of efficiency, security, and justice to victims. What is at the end of this process is unclear. There is no single coherent model or framework, no obvious direction of travel, no unifying objective, but, rather, a set of responses to issues and imperatives arising at different points in time—ranging from the crisis in confidence around miscarriages of justice in the 1980s and 1990s, to the rise of law and order politics, the preoccupation with risk and efficiency that took hold in the 1990s, the accelerated security-driven agenda after the events of 9/11, and the austerity measures applied across the public sector in the wake of the 2008 financial crisis. France, too, is experiencing a shift away from the more judicially centered procedures and values that have characterized the inquisitorial tradition, in favor of measures promoting efficiency, security, and a justice system that is more responsive to the needs of victims. Like England and Wales, there is no clear direction of travel or underpinning rationale, but a series of uncoordinated and often politically driven changes that, taken together, undermine procedural integrity and process values. At the same time, the European Court of Human Rights (ECtHR) and the European Union (EU) have promoted pan-European fair-trial and due process standards, challenging some of the more repressive domestic trajectories of criminal justice and influencing national reforms.

By adopting a comparative approach with France, whose inquisitorially rooted criminal justice process is different from that of England and Wales, this study explores the nature and reach of these various trends, the ways in which they challenge and disrupt criminal processes and values, the contrasting responses that they provoke, and what this tells us about the similarities and differences between procedural traditions. In both jurisdictions, the opportunity for rigorous testing of the accusations against the accused—whether through public trial or pretrial judicial investigation—has all but disappeared. Due process and fair-trial guarantees have become subordinate, altering the core functions of criminal justice professionals in sometimes fundamental ways and distorting the criminal process balance between effective investigation and prosecution, on the one hand, and the protection of the presumption of innocence, on the other. Preoccupations with prevention, securitization, and a managerialist form of bureaucratic efficiency that has been likened to the "McDonaldization" of criminal justice have been elevated to the objectives against which criminal justice success is measured.[1]

Through a comparative analysis of these fundamental changes across two contrasting jurisdictions, the study explores the ways that criminal justice traditions continue to be shaped in different ways by broader policy and political concerns, and the ways in which different systems adapt, change, and distort when faced with (sometimes conflicting) pressures domestically and externally. This comparative lens also illuminates the ways that, in England and Wales and in France, different procedural values may serve to structure or limit reform, and so work to facilitate or resist change. The book also seeks to understand the extent to which these changes are part of a wider shift (or shifts) in criminal justice stemming from domestic and European agendas, or whether they are restricted to context-specific areas and to key historical moments such as the perceived crisis in criminal justice that led to the Royal Commission on Criminal Justice in 1991, or the raft of legislative measures following the terrorist attacks in the United States and then Europe in the twenty-first century. It considers how procedural values both determine, and are impacted by, these shifts and what, if anything, is the endgame—are criminal processes endlessly adaptable, or are there core features and structures that must and will remain?

Underpinning these transformations in criminal process and policy in Britain and in France has been the increasing politicization of criminal justice. The treatment of crime has taken on far greater electoral importance in recent decades, as politicians across the political spectrum compete to be tough on crime, embracing the politics of law and order and a form of penal populism in which the risks of harm are portrayed as ever greater and multiplying, requiring increasingly punitive responses in order to keep the public safe. Where criminal justice was once a key battleground between left and right, we now see consensus on more repressive policies that has taken the heat out of political debate, but at the expense of fairness and integrity in the criminal justice system. The result of this relative political unity is an almost universal ideology of crime control embedded within politics and able to flourish virtually unopposed, leading to an explosion in legislative reform. In both jurisdictions, the continued addition of new measures has created an undisciplined mass of criminal law and procedure, lacking the coherence and guiding principles of any single clear procedural model. Powers, procedures, and offenses have been added to criminal codes and

[1] Ritzer (2004); Bohm (2006).

statute books without any rationalization, creating complex and sometimes contradictory structures of criminal law and procedure.

Increasingly, criminalization is preventive and linked to forms of risk management rather than the acts and intentions of the accused. Procedures are simplified, rationalized, and made cheaper by removing due process protections considered too costly in terms of time and resources. Exceptional powers legislated following terrorist attacks in Europe, and in France in particular, are also finding their way into states' ordinary common law in unplanned-for ways. Weaker judicial guarantees tolerated in the context of what were understood to be short-term measures have become part of a more permanent agenda of securitization. Running counter to this, ECtHR decisions and EU measures together represent a developing and increasingly interlinked body of pan-European norms and practices that seek to develop certain procedural safeguards and guarantees. However, while these legal decisions and measures can encourage some alignment as well as strengthening of standards, their differential and often reluctant implementation within domestic legal systems further contributes to procedural incoherence at the national level.

The book is organized into four parts. The first part explores procedural values and traditions, together with broad domestic and European trends in criminal justice, before discussing the ways that the roles of prosecution (Part 2) and defense (Part 3) have been reshaped in different ways in both jurisdictions. The final part considers how systems within different procedural traditions adapt to address, or at least provide a remedy for, systemic flaws that produce wrongful convictions and, in particular, the part that the defense is able to play in these procedures. A good deal of this project is informed by my own empirical research conducted over three decades, focusing principally on England and Wales and France, but also, in collaboration with European colleagues, several broader comparative studies examining Scotland, the Netherlands, Italy, Belgium, and Poland.[2] Reference is made to other jurisdictions at various points in the discussion where pertinent—principally European, but occasionally the United States—to highlight more strongly particular aspects or trends in procedural practices, but the focus of this study is firmly on England and Wales and on France. These two are often treated as paradigmatic examples of procedures rooted in the adversarial and inquisitorial traditions and so serve as ideal and contrasting comparators.

Part 1 of the book addresses the nature of the criminal justice traditions of England and Wales and France, and the broad policy and legislative trends

[2] These studies have explored criminal investigation, prosecution, and defense work, as well as the workings of the Criminal Cases Review Commission, and chapters 7, 9, and 10 draw explicitly on, and include examples from, this body of empirical data.

of recent decades, many of which have been common to both jurisdictions. Chapter 1 begins with a discussion of the ways that we understand the terms "adversarial" and "inquisitorial," before going on to stress-test them in a number of ways. First, it looks at how the values and practices of different criminal procedural traditions have been impacted by a procedure that has become ubiquitous within criminal justice: the practice of plea bargaining. Then, from an external perspective, the analysis explores what might be considered the key tenets of adversarial procedure as understood by those seeking to adopt it, often as part of a wider process of legal or political change. The discussion then shifts to international criminal justice's potential as a form of laboratory for criminal procedure. The chapter considers why, and the extent to which, the procedural traditions developed in international courts and tribunals have adopted procedures and legal actors reflecting the values of one system or another. The chapter closes with a discussion of the major influence of European criminal justice, as developed through ECtHR decisions and EU measures. Although the product of the national jurisdictions that make up the Council of Europe and the EU, European legal decisions and instruments also challenge and reshape those jurisdictions and so are resisted by states at various points. They are at once a reflection of and a challenge to the jurisdictions from which they are created. Developed further in Part 3, the analysis explores the extent to which European transnational norms can reflect or recalibrate broadly adversarial and inquisitorial procedural values. Chapters 2 and 3 then provide a detailed consideration of some of the broad trends that have shaped criminal justice in recent decades, moving it away from the values of procedural fairness as differently expressed in the two traditions, to a form of bureaucratic managerialism and securitization that has built on discourses of efficiency, risk, and preventive justice. In this, the treatment of the threat of terrorism has been central both as a strand of exceptional criminal procedure with new offenses, limited safeguards, and expanded police powers, and in the influence this has had on ordinary criminal law and procedure.

Parts 2 and 3 focus on the changing roles and practices of prosecution and defense domestically, comparatively, and in the European context, exploring the ways in which they have been reshaped by law-and-order politics and contemporary managerialism, and how this re-forming of functions serves to illuminate the values and commitments that motivate contemporary criminal procedure. These functions have much in common across jurisdictions but are situated within procedural traditions that understand and structure the roles of legal actors in different ways. Common challenges such as the drive for greater efficiency, the implementation of European norms strengthening suspects' rights, or the expansion of police and judicial powers in the investigation of terrorism produce different legislative and judicial responses, as they are operationalized within the context of contrasting legal traditions with differently allocated rights and responsibilities.

The treatment of the prosecution in Part 2 challenges the effectiveness of efficiency measures that have refocused prosecutors away from legal decision-making informed by their professional skills, training, and autonomy. The emphasis on standardization and speed has led to the delegation of tasks to nonprofessionals and the diversion away from trial and prosecution of large numbers of minor offenses, producing measurable outputs but casting prosecutors more as managers than as lawyers. Part 3 looks at the defense role and the centrality of custodial legal advice in particular, as the pretrial process takes on ever greater importance with the gradual disappearance of the public trial. Despite the growing emphasis on what happens during this initial phase of investigation, France and other states in the inquisitorial tradition have resisted the strengthening of the role of the defense lawyer in advising suspects detained and questioned by the police. An examination of how states have adjusted to these new expectations, including the implementation of the EU directive on legal assistance for suspects in police custody, shows how the role of the prosecutor in overseeing police investigation and detention becomes a site of resistance in inquisitorial traditions. Police and lawyers across both legal traditions also struggle to adapt—to imagine this new proactive defense function and to work toward promoting it through training and changing their professional ideology and mindset.

Part 4 examines how criminal processes have responded to the more direct challenges to procedural values posed by wrongful convictions. Although small in number, miscarriages of justice reveal not only human error and malpractice, but also more systemic flaws reflecting weaknesses in the procedures of investigation and trial. How does a system respond when its legal procedures and personnel are shown to have failed? Both France and England and Wales have experienced wrongful convictions as a result of the tunnel vision of those responsible for criminal investigation, be they police, prosecutors, or judges. France has responded by adjusting aspects of its procedure, albeit in fairly limited ways, making it more collegial and accusatorial (or *contradictoire*, as it would be described),[3] while England and Wales have introduced a system of inquisitorial postconviction review, operated by an independent body, the Criminal Cases Review Commission (CCRC). This study examines what these changes mean for our understanding of procedural values—how inquisitorial and adversarial (or accusatorial) values fare in the aftermath and correction of wrongful convictions,

3 "Accusatorial" tends to refer to the separation of investigation and prosecution and a greater role for the parties, stopping short of the party-driven character of the adversarial model in which the parties are responsible for the collection, selection, and presentation of evidence at trial. The French term *contradictoire* expresses the process of debate, where both prosecution and defense are able to state their arguments before a decision is made.

how they become mixed, and how they might coexist in the same system. It also considers the impact of these adjustments on the role of those charged with overseeing and challenging the prosecution account—the investigating judge and the defense lawyer. How is the judicial function in France changed by a more collegial process of decision-making and by the strengthening of the criminal defense lawyer's role? And what role might the criminal defense lawyer properly play in the inquisitorial CCRC review, given that the party-based adversarial process resumes if the case is referred to the Court of Appeal?

Throughout, the analysis aims to understand the nature of the two criminal justice processes and the extent to which the major shifts that have taken place have maintained or retreated from the core values of the adversarial and inquisitorial traditions; or whether these values have become obfuscated by the politically driven nature and excess of criminal legislation to which police, prosecutors, lawyers, and courts are subjected and must continually adapt. While procedural traditions are often lost in the rhetoric of policy reform, as well as in the practices of law, they continue to have value as benchmarks against which we might evaluate criminal justice. Recent decades have seen major shifts in criminal procedure, often undercutting, ignoring, or explicitly criticizing the guiding principles and values on which criminal justice processes are understood to rest. Yet while defense rights, judicial protections, or principles of proportionality and reasonableness continue to be attacked and diminished, they are also used to justify more punitive measures and to clothe them in the legitimacy of due process. Furthermore, despite the decreasing hold that broadly adversarial and inquisitorial principles of criminal justice have in each jurisdiction, no alternative models have emerged. Indeed, both France and England and Wales consider periodically the potential advantages of one another's criminal justice systems in the course of commissions and enquiries, only to reject them in a ritualistic affirmation of existing principles and procedures. The result seems to be a kind of perpetual metamorphosis, away from procedural values of justice, truth, and fairness, guided by more politically powerful considerations of efficiency, security, and prevention.

Abbreviations

AG	attorney general
CCRC	Criminal Cases Review Commission
CM	commission member (CCRC)
CPP	*code de procédure pénale*
CPS	Crown Prosecution Service
CRM	case review manager (CCRC)
CRPC	*comparution sur reconnaissance préalable de culpabilité* (French guilty plea procedure)
CSM	Conseil supérieur de la magistrature
DPP	Director of Public Prosecutions
EAW	European Arrest Warrant
ECHR	European Convention on Human Rights
ECtHR	European Court of Human Rights
EIA	early investigative advice
ENM	Ecole nationale de la magistrature
EU	European Union
GAV	*garde à vue*
ICC	International Criminal Court
ICTY	International Criminal Tribunal for the former Yugoslavia
IGSJ	Inspection générale des services judiciaires
JLD	*juge des libertés et de la détention*
PACE	Police and Criminal Evidence Act 1984
PSOR	Provisional Statement of Reasons (explaining CCRC intention to reject)
RCCJ	Royal Commission on Criminal Justice (1993, chair, Viscount Runciman)
SOR	statement of reasons (explaining CCRC decision to refer)

Glossary of French Legal Terms

à charge, à décharge. For and against the culpability of the suspect.

avocat. Lawyer. The defense lawyer is an *avocat*, with a distinct professional training and status from the prosecutor, the procureur, who is part of the *magistrature*.

chambre de l'instruction. Division of the court hearing appeals against decisions of the *juge d'instruction*.

commission rogatoire. The *juge d'instruction* may delegate formally certain acts of investigation to the police, through the issuing of a *commission rogatoire*. This must be carried out according to the provisions set out in Articles 151 and 152 CPP.

comparution immédiate. Under Article 395 CPP, if the procureur considers that the case is ready to be tried, the accused can be brought before the court immediately under the procedure of *comparution immédiate*. This procedure is currently available for offenses punishable by between six months' and ten years' imprisonment.

comparution sur reconnaissance préalable de culpabilité **(CRPC).** The guilty plea procedure.

composition pénale. A financial or other sanction imposed by the prosecutor as an alternative to trial.

Conseil constitutionnel. The main judicial functions of this body are to judge the constitutionality of legislation and international treaties, to supervise elections, and to judge any litigation resulting from elections.

Conseil supérieure de la magistrature. The governing body of the judiciary.

contradictoire. Hearing arguments from both sides before coming to a decision.

contravention. The lowest category of criminal offenses.

contrôleur général des lieux de privation de liberté. Independent commissioner overseeing all places of detention.

correctionalisation. Charging a lesser offense to ensure trial in the *tribunal correctionnel*, avoiding the more length and costly *instruction* and trial in the *cour d'assises*.

cour d'appel. Hears, as a retrial, appeals from the *tribunal de police* and the *tribunal correctionnel*.

cour d'assises. Criminal court that hears the most serious cases (*crimes*), which are tried by three judges and six lay jurors. Since June 2000, there has been a right of appeal to a differently constituted *cour d'assises* with nine jurors.

Cour de cassation. Hears appeals on a point of law. Exceptionally, it can act as a full appeal court if there is new factual evidence that suggests a prima facie judicial error in the original trial.

crime. The most serious category of criminal offenses.

délégués du procureur. Lay officers, typically retired police, who administer alternatives to prosecution.

délit. The middle-ranking category of criminal offenses.

détention provisoire. The period of custody during the *juge d'instruction*'s investigation, or between successive hearings before the court.

échevinage. Judgment by a mixture of lay and professional judges.

enquête de flagrance. Police investigation of recently committed offenses (now defined as up to sixteen days after the offense was committed). The police enjoy wider powers in this type of investigation.

enquête préliminaire. The ordinary police investigation.

erreurs judiciaires. Miscarriages of justice.

fonctionnaire. A civil servant.

garde à vue. The period of police detention of suspects and, formerly, witnesses.

gendarme. Military police officer.

groupes locaux de traitement de la délinquance. Multiple agency group (from police, local politics, education, customs, licensing, etc.) headed by the public prosecutor, designed to tackle local criminality.

information. Investigation to be carried out by the *juge d'instruction*.

injunction thérapeutique. Therapeutic order (for the treatment of drug or alcohol addiction, or sexual offending, for example).

instruction. The process of investigation by the *juge d'instruction*.

juge de l'application des peines. The *magistrat* responsible for the execution of the court's sentence.

juge délégué. The *magistrat* responsible for determining whether to place a person in *détention provisoire*, a post introduced in the January 1993 reform, abolished in the August 1993 reform.

juge délégué aux victims. Judge that was created in 2008 to assist victims affected by the penalty imposed (e.g., where the offender should pay the victim compensation, in cases of mediation, etc.).

juge de proximité. Lay judge dealing with minor affairs (created in 2003, ceasing to exist in 2017).

juge des enfants. *Magistrat* specializing in juvenile justice. She has wide powers to investigate and to put in place educational measures.

***juge des libertés et de la détention* (JLD).** The judge responsible for granting bail and deciding on measures that restrict liberty (e.g., extending detention for questioning in police custody in terrorism or organized crime investigations).

***juge d'instruction*.** The *magistrat* responsible for investigating more serious cases through the procedure known as *instruction*.

***juge du siège*.** The "sitting" judiciary (trial judges, JLD, *juges d'instruction*, etc.) who are independent of the minister of justice, in contrast to the standing judiciary (the prosecutors).

***magistrat*.** A judge or public prosecutor.

***magistrature*.** The career-trained judiciary that includes the standing judiciary (the Parquet) and the sitting judiciary (the *juge d'instruction* and the trial judge).

***maison de la justice et du droit*.** Administers alternatives to prosecution, tasked with improving access to justice locally (e.g., they host lawyers for pro bono legal advice, as well as arbitration/mediation services for civil disputes. Probation officers can also offer appointments here).

***mediation pénale*.** Mediation in criminal cases.

***ordonnance pénale*.** A simplified procedure for minor offenses, such as motoring offenses, in which the prosecutor invites the judge to sentence without a full hearing.

Parquet. The collective name for procureurs, also known as the *ministère public*.

***partie civile*.** The civil party, or victim.

***politique pénale*.** Criminal justice policy.

préfet. Representative of central government at the local level.

procureur. The public prosecutor, also a *magistrat*.

***procureur général*.** Senior prosecutor at the appeal court level.

***rappel à la loi*.** Alternative to prosecution for minor offenses, a warning.

***taux de réponse pénale*.** Response rate (used to measure effectiveness of prosecutors in bringing prosecutions or alternatives to trial).

***traitement en temps réel*.** Dealing with cases in real time.

***tribunal correctionnel*.** Hears middle-ranking criminal cases (*délits*) that comprise the majority of criminal cases. Three judges may sit, but less serious cases (about half of those heard) are tried by a single judge.

***tribunal de grande instance*.** The court of first instance.

***tribunal de police*.** Hears minor offenses (*contraventions*).

The Metamorphosis of Criminal Justice

PART 1

CRIMINAL JUSTICE TRADITIONS AND TRENDS

1
Perspectives on Adversarial and Inquisitorial Criminal Procedure

In order to understand the nature of core features of adversarial and inquisitorial processes in a more applied and dynamic way, as well as the conditions in which they continue to evolve, this introductory chapter examines the two traditions through a variety of perspectives and contexts. Beginning with a discussion of adversarial and inquisitorial models, the chapter considers the organizing principles around which the criminal procedures of England and Wales and of France are structured. This is not a static picture, as systems mingle with and borrow and retreat from one another, sometimes in profound ways, over time. The chapter then examines a particular and widespread example of system borrowing and adaptation: the guilty plea. It sets out the development of plea bargaining in England and Wales, which might be seen as either epitomizing adversarial values (as a party-led process) or subverting them (avoiding the key trial moment through an incentivized or negotiated admission), before considering how a range of criminal justice processes from the inquisitorial tradition have sought to adapt their procedures to common demands for the avoidance of a contested trial. What we see is the development of a range of plea and sentence agreement models and abbreviated trial procedures, reflecting different core institutional and process values. In France, for example, an admission may trigger the offer of a lower sentence in exchange for the accused forgoing trial, but this is a very different procedure from that in England and Wales. The process is regulated by the prosecutor, whose judicial status serves to prevent proceedings descending into the kind of crude bargaining or persuasion that is more familiar in England and Wales and the United States.

An interesting feature of modern adversarialism is its appeal to jurisdictions wishing to reform their legal and political structures away from inquisitorial values and practices. The chapter considers adversarialism from this more external standpoint, including the features that make it attractive to those seeking legal and political change. Associated with individual rights, fairness, and transparency, the adversarial model has an appeal to systems seeking to move away from a more state-dominated process, or the concentrations of power that can lead to corruption. This perhaps explains why we do not see the converse trend of adversarial traditions seeking to transform their criminal process to the

The Metamorphosis of Criminal Justice. Jacqueline S. Hodgson, Oxford University Press (2020).

DOI: 10.1093/oso/9780199981427.001.0001

inquisitorial tradition. However, through these processes of transformation and reform, we also see the different ways in which the aspirations of criminal justice rhetoric are distorted by the broader legal and political contexts in which it operates. As a newly created system, international criminal justice provided the opportunity to adopt an existing model, or to create something hybrid or sui generis. It has taken aspects of both traditions, and their strengths and limitations are highlighted in new ways by the very different demands presented in the context of international tribunals. Even in its infancy, international criminal justice has adapted, countenancing plea bargains with those accused of international crimes.

Finally, returning to the legal, social, and political forces that shape the evolution of procedural traditions, the chapter turns to contemporary pan-European influences on criminal procedure and the development of common criminal justice values and standards of fair trial. Although European institutions are not immune to efficiency concerns, both the decisions of the ECtHR and EU measures have sought to promote common standards of procedural fairness and effective safeguards for accused persons in ways that run counter to domestic trends that tend to favor managerialism and security over the rights of the individual. However, the success of these measures depends in part on countries' willingness to implement change, which in turn reflects the extent to which different procedural values are able to fit together. As with other criminal justice narratives and drivers of reform, the different ways in which processes of criminal justice seek to incorporate, adapt, or avoid these broader European norms illuminate underlying process values and offer a dynamic perspective on the development of legal systems. For example, the accusatorial interpretations of fair-trial rights by the ECtHR are frequently resisted by France as inappropriate to its criminal procedure, despite its adoption of the principle of *contradictoire*.[1] And although enthusiastic in its support of EU criminal justice arrangements to share intelligence, criminal records, and other information, the UK has operated a selective approach around mutual recognition, operating on the basis that it is not part of any measures unless it decides explicitly to opt in. How these EU measures of which Britain is a part (such as the European Arrest Warrant) as well as the various forms of institutional cooperation that are currently part of UK law will operate post-Brexit, however, is unclear.

[1] The principle of *contradictoire* refers to the requirement that the accused should have the opportunity to know of, and to respond to, the accusations against her—not only at trial, but also during the investigation, bail hearings, etc. It also incorporates the notion of equality of arms. This is perhaps closer to accusatorial (which generally refers to the separation of the investigation and prosecution, and a greater role for the parties to be heard) than adversarial (which generally reflects a greater role for the parties in shaping and arguing the case—in the investigation, selection, and presentation of evidence).

A. Adversarial and Inquisitorial Criminal Procedure

We use the labels "adversarial" and "inquisitorial" to describe different procedural models of justice.[2] They are, of course, just that—procedural models that represent a set of guiding principles or ideal types, not descriptors that lend themselves to the strict classification or taxonomy of legal systems. They neither describe nor are reflected in the criminal procedure of any single jurisdiction.[3] Rather, we can identify organizing principles and features within criminal justice systems that tend to reflect these models and ideal types.[4] For example, adversarialism is typically represented as a party-driven contest with a passive adjudicative judicial role, whereas the inquisitorial model is characterized by a more centralized state enquiry. Other features, such as the lay jury, the use of oral testimony, or the role of the defense, might typically be ascribed to one model or another, but it is more difficult to state with confidence that these are intrinsically adversarial or inquisitorial features.[5] Jurisdictions evolve over time, and those within the same legal family adapt in different ways depending on historical, social, and political factors. Most inquisitorially rooted procedures no longer have a *juge d'instruction*, for example, and adversarially rooted procedures have a professional prosecutor function.[6] The guiding ideas or principles of a procedural model can be identified, along with the related features (such as oral or written procedure) that they typically influence and shape, but modern legal systems are mixed. When looking at contemporary criminal justice systems, they are better understood in more complex and contextual ways, as legal traditions or cultures, reflecting a set of values and practices grounded in particular historical or ideological contexts that change over time. Procedural models retain explanatory force, however, in conveying the roots of a legal system, its organizing principles and values, and so the kinds of considerations that might govern reform in order to maintain some degree of internal coherence.[7]

[2] These are the two models that I explore in this study—there are of course other models and systems, such as the Soviet-influenced socialist systems in Central and Eastern Europe, the Communist Party inquisitorial Chinese model, as well as traditional and informal systems of justice. See, generally, Vogler (2005); on Eastern Europe, Cape and Namoradze (2012); on China, Mou (2017).

[3] I do not intend here to set out a history of legal systems or models. This is done far better elsewhere. See, e.g., Esmein (1913); Salas (1991); Spencer (2002); Vogler (2005).

[4] See further Hodgson (2005: 26–32). On the features of criminal procedural models see Damaška (1973). For a discussion of the place of rights, fairness, and truth-finding in the theory of the American adversary trial, see Goodpaster (1987).

[5] See also Jackson (2005); Field (2009).

[6] The *juge d'instruction* represents the centralized judicial investigation often thought to typify inquisitorial procedure, which is now replaced by the police and prosecution functions in most instances. Adversarial procedure is understood to be party centered, but a professional prosecutor, representing the state, the people, or the Crown (not the victim), is now more typical.

[7] For a discussion of the categorization of inquisitorial and adversarial distinctions, see Langer (2014).

Some commentators reject the existence or the value of these models in understanding criminal procedure. Summers, for example, has challenged the utility of these two models on the grounds that they lack descriptive precision, do not reflect current systems, and tend to conceal differences between procedures grouped within the same procedural family or tradition.[8] It is certainly true that procedural models are not reflected in current systems, most of which have evolved through a history of borrowings and would describe themselves as "mixed" albeit rooted in a particular model. But this perhaps overstates the purpose of models. We do not understand systems by placing them within strictly defined categories, but by analyzing them in a more contextual and historical way.[9] Summers also argues that the adversarial and inquisitorial labels mask the existence, historically, of a more unified European procedural model—the Austrian jurist Vargha's concept of an "accusatorial trinity" of prosecution, defense, and impartial trial judge—which is drawn on by the ECtHR in its development of fair-trial principles. The idea of this accusatorial trinity has some attraction as a way of looking at modern criminal procedures. They certainly tend to share accusatorial features in that they separate the phases of investigation and prosecution and allow the defense some role, but important differences remain. While adversarial-type procedures allow the parties to define the scope of the investigation and trial, this remains largely state-centered in inquisitorially rooted procedures. Judicial impartiality is also understood in different ways: while active judicial questioning is the norm within the inquisitorial tradition, it is generally seen to undermine impartiality in adversarial procedures. By focusing on the trial, this analysis also takes insufficient account of the defining role played by the pretrial enquiry, especially in inquisitorial-type procedure where the defense has little or no role even today.

In discussing criminal procedures here, I acknowledge that both the contemporary French system and that in England and Wales are more properly described as mixed systems, reflecting values and procedures that might be understood as belonging within both traditions. The roots and guiding ideas of these processes are, however, different and they are best understood as located within broadly adversarial or inquisitorial traditions. An adversarial process is characterized typically by responsibility for the investigation, selection, and presentation of evidence lying with the two parties to the case, the accuser and the accused. Trial is based on oral evidence presented before an impartial and relatively passive judge, often, but not necessarily, with a lay jury delivering the

[8] Summers (2007).

[9] See further Field's (2009) critique of Summers's approach. Drawing on Glenn's concept of legal tradition, Field argues that "the concept of 'legal tradition,' if understood in a sociologically complex way, may offer an alternative means to make use of the adversarial/inquisitorial distinction which can accommodate, acknowledge and even explain some of the difficulties in classification" (2009: 369).

verdict. In England and Wales, while criminal procedure does not rest on a centralized state-defined enquiry in the inquisitorial tradition, neither are cases organized around the victim and the accused as the two opposing parties. The role of accusation is passed first to the police and then to the public prosecution service (the Crown Prosecution Service, CPS), and most accused persons are legally represented. A fully contested trial with live oral evidence presented to a jury is the exception—guilty pleas and alternative forms of case disposal being the norm—and while most cases are determined by laypeople, these are magistrates rather than a jury.[10]

However, it might still be considered a broadly adversarial procedure, given the police monopoly on carrying out the investigation that will form the prosecution case, unsupervised by any central judicial authority; the rights of the accused to conduct her own investigation; the relatively partisan role of the prosecutor (rather than a more neutral "ministry of justice" function); the place of the trial, with live oral evidence as the ultimate forum for case disposal (and admissibility at trial continuing as the governing feature of what will be accepted as evidence); the passive and trial-based role of the judge; and the fact that avoidance of trial is only with the consent of the accused (albeit that consent may be obtained with the aid of powerful incentives). However, as we will see in the chapters that follow, these roles are becoming blurred, as judges take on a disciplinary role in ensuring pretrial case management; as an increasingly centralized and regulated prosecution service advises on police investigations and is responsible for aspects of case disposition; and as defense lawyers are increasingly coopted into the managerialist goals of the system with ever-decreasing resources available to them. These developments move the criminal process further away from the guiding ideas and values of the adversarial tradition.

An inquisitorial process is characterized by an active, centralized (state or judicial) enquiry, rather than a party-led process. There is greater emphasis on the pretrial phase as an active site of fact-finding, and in a pure inquisitorial model, the same person is responsible for the investigation, prosecution, and trial of the accused; the case is dealt with in secret and on the basis of written evidence. In effect, the inquisitorial pretrial model is predominantly a single-party enquiry: the accused is simply a witness in the overall investigation and so there is no expectation that she conduct her own enquiries in order to present an equal and opposite case to that of the prosecution. This places a great deal of trust, power, and responsibility in the hands of one person, to act neutrally, without favoring either

[10] The magistrates' court is the lower court, where lay magistrates (or in some instances a legally qualified district judge) are advised by a legally qualified clerk. The magistrates decide on issues of fact and law (on advice), determining bail, evidence issues, guilt, and sentence. The Crown Court consists of a judge, who is typically a senior barrister, and a lay jury of twelve. The jury decides only on the guilt of the accused. Sentence is determined by the judge.

party. In this model the guarantee of fairness resides in the integrity of the investigator, rather than in the process of trial.

French criminal procedure sits within the broad inquisitorial tradition: the pretrial phase remains heavily centralized and the court places much reliance upon the dossier of written evidence gathered by the judge—or increasingly the prosecutor, who also enjoys a judicial status. The functions of investigation, prosecution, and case disposition have been separated out, but the legal actors responsible (the prosecutor, investigating judge, and trial judge) share a common training and status as *magistrats*, providing a historical continuity and giving rise to what some have termed a form of judicial corporatism that undermines the guarantees implied by the separation of roles and in which the defense remains firmly the professional outsider.[11] At trial, the judge is empowered to take on a more proactive role, calling and interrogating evidence, rather than relying exclusively on that selected by the defense and prosecution. In practice, the prosecution case dominates and judicial interrogation of the case is largely symbolic, especially in the rapid trial procedures, discussed subsequently.

In this way, the influence of inquisitorial values and ideals is still clearly visible in modern French procedure. There have been some reforms, designed to promote the rights and participation of the accused, but these are limited in scope, designed to assist and complement, rather than to challenge, the centralized judicial function. For example, suspects may have a lawyer present during police questioning, but the legal adviser's role is limited to one of passive observer. Those under investigation by the *juge d'instruction* are permitted to request acts of investigation and to access the case file, but this affects only a tiny minority of accused: over 97 percent of investigations are carried out by the police, under the authority of the prosecutor rather than the *juge d'instruction*, where the accused enjoys no such opportunities.

Criminal procedures are not true to a single adversarial or inquisitorial ideal in theory or in practice, but evolve over time and are subject to a range of influences. Legal traditions constitute a series of historical borrowings between jurisdictions, a "procedural exchange" and adaptation that continues today.[12] Typically, features imported from other systems are not simply grafted on or transplanted, but are adapted to the culture and *mentalité* of the host procedure. For example, the appearance of the English jury in French criminal trials at the end of the eighteenth century introduced an accusatorial feature into an otherwise inquisitorial procedure, over which the judiciary had enjoyed almost complete control. However, the unwelcome independence of lay jurors was soon

[11] See Hodgson (2005: 65–85) for a discussion of the development and separation of investigation, prosecution, and case disposition. On the defense as professional outside, see Hodgson (2002a).

[12] Spencer (2002: 3).

tempered by the inclusion of professional judges sitting as part of the jury.[13] The English jury model was also found to be unsuitable in other respects and so the judiciary again found ways to assert their influence. In 1808, the French judge was, like her English counterpart, tasked with providing a résumé to sum up the evidence at the close of the trial. However, "[T]he English respect for the impartiality of the judge has never gained a foothold in France and as time passed the summing up came to be regarded as a final address for the prosecution, delivered from the bench, and one to which the accused could not reply."[14] This practice was finally abolished in 1881 when the Republicans gained parliamentary control, to which the judiciary once again responded by including in the judge's interrogation of the accused "much that he formerly said in the summing up."[15] The attempted introduction of lay adjudication as a more democratic form of justice could not displace the centrality and the strength of the judiciary at the heart of the French criminal process.[16]

An example of a borrowing in the other direction is the public prosecutor, now a feature of all European criminal procedures. In the 1980s, England and Wales borrowed the continental idea of the public prosecutor, which was already well established in Scotland through the office of the procurator fiscal. But unlike countries such as France, Belgium, and the Netherlands, where the prosecutor has a judicial or quasi-judicial status and is responsible for the investigation as well as the prosecution of crime, the CPS is staffed by lawyers and is underpinned by a strict separation between investigation and prosecution in which the police remain autonomous, accountable to neither a prosecutor nor a judge. Although providing a centralized and more uniform prosecution function, it is unsurprising that the crown prosecutor does not mirror her European neighbors, but has developed to fit within a different legal procedural tradition; there is no culture of judicial investigation in England and Wales, where the judge's role is entirely separate from the parties and limited to the trial. The CPS is also shaped in part by the motivation for its establishment. Following recommendations of the Royal Commission on Criminal Procedure in 1981, it was introduced as a necessary response to inconsistent police prosecution practices, and so prosecution independence from the police investigation was considered paramount.[17]

[13] Nineteenth-century French advocates were required to argue eloquently to counter the pro-prosecution bias of the inquisitorial judges. See Fischer Taylor (1993: 9–10, 14, 53–55).

[14] Garner (1916: 271).

[15] "It must be admitted that the French are not entirely consistent when they forbid the judge to sum up because of his want of impartiality yet allow him to participate actively in the trial through the interrogatory." Garner (1916: 272).

[16] See also the example of Italy, discussed subsequently, whose resistance to adversarial reform has resulted in the retention of inquisitorial safeguards, resulting in a slow and cumbersome criminal process, whose procedures are ill-adapted to the effective investigation and trial of criminal cases.

[17] Prior to the establishment of the CPS, the police had employed their own "prosecuting solicitors" in some cities, but these lawyers were bound to act on the instructions of their police client and

Some commentators characterize the two traditions of adversarial and inquisitorial procedure as not just borrowing concepts, but converging toward a common middle ground.[18] Others reject this thesis as an oversimplification, as "impossible on account of the fact that the differences arising between the common law and civil law *mentalités* at the epistemological level are irreducible."[19] Might European supranational norms provide some degree of harmonization around, for example, fair-trial requirements?[20] In modern European criminal justice systems, in addition to individual procedural models, the idea of fairness is seen increasingly as an overarching goal of criminal procedure. Article 6 of the ECHR sets a common "fair trial" baseline, which extends from the pretrial investigation and includes the right of the accused to access an effective defense, to hear and to challenge the evidence against her, and to be able to participate effectively in a public trial.[21] Although the margin-of-appreciation doctrine acknowledges that a fair trial is achieved in varying ways across jurisdictions, reflecting the values and approaches of different traditions, the approach of the ECtHR has been to equate fair trial with a more accusatorial or adversarial procedure. This is criticized as failing to acknowledge sufficiently that the emphasis is different, for example, as between systems that depend on a pretrial judicial role and those whose primary site for the testing of evidence is at trial. Legal traditions adopt different methods of achieving the same goal: for example, both adversarial and inquisitorial traditions would claim justice through a process of legal fact-finding as their overarching objective.[22]

so unable to make independent prosecution decisions. Roles continue to develop and evolve over time, and the gap between the phases of investigation and prosecution has narrowed in England and Wales in order that the CPS might have some earlier influence on the nature of the evidence investigated; conversely, a greater separation between police and prosecutor has been urged in France in order to promote greater independence between the functions. Hodgson (2005); Beaume (2014).

18 E.g., Markesinis (1994). Jackson and Summers argue that while the adversarial and inquisitorial labels have some value in identifying procedural traditions and describing how legal actors understand their practices, "the dichotomy is increasingly unhelpful in describing actual systems of justice and as a heuristic tool for gauging whether or not systems are converging" (2012: 8). Jackson (2005) argued earlier that the ECtHR has given rise to a sui generis rights-based model of participation. See also *SC v. UK* (60958/00) 15 June 2004 on the defendant's right to "effective participation." It is also notable that while adversarial concepts are being adopted and adapted within inquisitorial traditions, the reverse is not generally true.

19 Legrand (1996: 62). See also Hodgson (2005: 8–9).

20 See Arnold (2016) and the contributions therein.

21 The ECtHR is inconsistent on whether a fair trial requires all of these elements (such that breaching one amounts to an Article 6 ECHR breach), or some combination (such that less of one and more of another might ensure compliance with Article 6 ECHR). See Goss (2014).

22 See Damaška (1973). Jackson (1988) has also argued that, despite the differences in procedural tradition, the two models are rooted in a common epistemological tradition of fact-finding using the classic scientific method of proof. He considers a dialectic method of legal fact-finding would better address the evidential gap between claims and the evidence we have for making them. "Because the evidence that is appealed to will necessarily be selective, it seems important to explain not just *why* a particular conclusion is arrived at but *how* it was arrived at . . . if we gain support for the procedures, then we are entitled to have more confidence in the conclusion . . . reached." Jackson (1988: 563).

In England and Wales, where the prosecution and defense cases are presented to a lay judge or jury at trial, fairness is an established principle in order to guide the layperson's evaluation of evidence in a way not considered necessary where cases are handled by professional, career-trained judges.[23] But the right of the accused to hear and test out the evidence, as well as to have the opportunity to counter it with a defense case, is at the heart of the ECHR concept of fair trial. Influenced by the jurisprudence of the ECtHR, in France, this is now encapsulated by the term *contradictoire*,[24] the principle by which the accused must have the opportunity to hear and to challenge the evidence against her. EU measures have now added more normative detail to some aspects of what constitutes a fair trial, setting out the information that should be provided to suspects and what is required to ensure effective defense assistance, for example.[25]

Although these developments are significant, trials remain very different across countries. Principles and procedures are adapted and applied through the existing legal cultural tradition.

> Even textually identical rules acquire a different meaning and produce different consequences in the changed institutional setting. The music of the law changes, so to speak, when the musical instruments and the players are no longer the same.[26]

In France, inquisitorial values continue to dominate: greater credibility attaches to the dossier of evidence presented by the prosecutor (seen as the product of a judicial enquiry) than that of the accused; it is of central importance and is evidence on which the accused can be convicted, without the necessity for live witnesses and cross-examination.[27] The judicial role also remains central in the legal imagination: measures that have cast the trial judge in a passive role have been held to be unconstitutional. The principle of *contradictoire* does not intrude unduly into the detail of criminal procedure, having little impact in the majority of investigations, and any broader shift toward a more accusatorial procedure has been rejected.[28]

Fairness as a unifying, overarching principle toward some form of convergence of European systems seems unlikely, as the ECHR margin of

[23] This might include rules on admissibility such as those under sections 76 and 78 of PACE.

[24] This is set out in the preliminary article to the Code de procédure pénale, CPP.

[25] See EU Directives 2012/13/EU on the right to information in criminal proceedings and 2013/48/EU on the right of access to a lawyer in criminal proceedings, discussed in Blackstock et al. (2014: chap. 1).

[26] Damaška (1997: 839–840).

[27] To get a sense of this in practice, see generally Raymond Depardon's 2004 documentary film *10th District Court*.

[28] Most recently by the Beaume Commission. Beaume (2014).

appreciation is broad, allowing considerable variation in how ECtHR decisions are interpreted and applied at the national level, precisely to take account of the variety of legal methods and traditions. It is a process designed to achieve compatibility with Convention standards, not convergence. The permitted latitude in applying ECHR standards, together with the different ways in which fairness is understood to be achieved, mean that a uniform standard of fairness is unlikely, and the standard of fairness itself can be diluted. EU legislation, in contrast, is more targeted and prescriptive, requiring states to transpose EU measures directly into national law.[29] The objective here, however, is not to unify systems, but to strengthen trust in one another's legal systems, in order to promote confidence in effective cooperation.[30] In particular, if citizens and evidence are to be exchanged between Member States, it is essential that states have trust in the effectiveness of one another's criminal procedure, including the fair-trial safeguards in place.

The place of the victim in these different systems is also instructive when thinking about procedural models. Although originally the accuser who set in motion the adversarial process in England and Wales, she now lacks any formal standing, despite measures such as the Code of Practice for Victims of Crime: the parties are the state and the accused. The victim has no rights in the process, no ability to mandate investigation or prosecution, and standards of fairness relate to the accused, not to the alleged victim.[31] In countries such as France and Belgium, in contrast, the victim may be a party to the case along with the prosecutor and the accused, and may claim compensation at the criminal trial hearing. More significantly, she may request acts of investigation and effectively force the police to follow lines of enquiry supporting her account. In some instances, it has been the persistence of victims' lawyers that has led to the evidence needed for a successful prosecution. During the investigation of the French *juge d'instruction*, the victim is a party to the case along with the accused and the prosecutor and enjoys similar rights to access the file and request acts of investigation. Yet, bolstered by the overarching standard of the right to a fair trial, systems tend to center on the rights of the accused. This means that when interests conflict—for example, the witness's desire not to testify in front of the accused, as against the accused's right to hear and challenge the evidence against her—it is the rights of

[29] Although the EU has not yet acceded to the ECHR, the EU Charter of Fundamental Rights is an autonomous source of EU law and must be read in light of the ECHR.

[30] Although the rhetoric of the EU centers on trust and cooperation, it too is concerned to streamline criminal justice processes across Europe.

[31] Victims now have the right to seek a review of a decision not to prosecute, following *R v. Christopher Killick* [2011] EWCA Crim. 1608. See guidance available at https://www.cps.gov.uk/legal-guidance/victims-right-review-scheme. See also The Code of Practice for Victims of Crime [Ministry of Justice (2015)].

the accused that will prevail, in order to respect the presumption of innocence and ensure a fair hearing.[32]

Although legal systems do not appear to be converging, either across procedural models or in the pursuit of common values, they do share common concerns. It is in the response to these concerns—be they around security when faced with new terrorist threats, European standards of fairness, or efficiency in a context of managerialism and cuts to public spending in many countries—that we understand better the underlying values of criminal justice. In some instances, countries are attracted to similar solutions, but refracted through different procedural lenses, they play out through national systems in a variety of ways. The guilty plea and resulting abbreviation of the trial, whether as a result of plea bargaining or other means, is one such example. An examination of the variety of ways in which trial is avoided helps us to understand some of the guiding principles and ideas of a legal tradition as they operate in a more dynamic and applied way.

B. Reading Plea Bargaining and Admissions of Guilt into Adversarial and Inquisitorial Procedure

One of the most pressing concerns across domestic, and now international, legal systems is the need to reduce both cost and delay. Processes of criminal justice are unable to live up to their own rhetoric, with the criminal trial becoming something of a luxury in an environment of managerialist efficiency coupled with increased criminalization: "[T]he full adjudicative process is everywhere in decline."[33] This has resulted in the growth of a range of abbreviated criminal trial procedures, many of which hinge on the offer of a sentence reduction in exchange for an admission from the accused.[34] This has emerged from within the adversarial tradition, where party control of the issues is the norm, though commentators disagree as to whether it is an expression of adversarialism,[35] or

[32] This may be resolved through shielding measures, such as giving evidence via a video link. On the implementation of the EU Victims Directive 2012/29/EU see Bahr and Melum (2017).

[33] Damaška (2004: 1019). Or, as the title of Weigend (2006a) has expressed it, "Why Have a Trial When You Can Have a Bargain?" For an account of trial avoidance in various jurisdictions, see Thaman (2010).

[34] There are various modes of incentivizing an admission. Plea bargains offer a reduced sentence or range of charges, in exchange for a guilty plea, sometimes coupled with an abbreviated court procedure. Sentence bargaining focuses on a reduced sentence and charge bargaining, a reduced charge—both in exchange for a guilty plea. Sentence canvassing is where the judge is asked to give an indication of the maximum sentence discount to be awarded on a plea of guilty.

[35] Feeley (1982) and Langbein (1979) argue that the accused's ability to negotiate followed the stronger position that she came to have at trial at the end of the nineteenth century, making the outcome of trials less predictable and negotiation more appealing for all concerned. For a historical account of the rise of adversarialism, see also Langbein (2003).

its negation.[36] However we characterize the guilty plea, the need for simpler and faster modes of case disposition has been recognized across Europe.[37]

There are important differences, however, in these procedures as they operate in different jurisdictions. While the phenomenon of "negotiated justice" has saturated the US criminal system[38] and, to a lesser extent, that of England and Wales, procedures in many European countries operate as a simple exchange—a lower sentence where there is an existing admission. There is no negotiation with the prosecutor, no persuasion in order to extract an admission. Instead, sentence discounts are structured through guidelines or a fixed mandatory discount. In Spain, for example, defendants receive a mandatory one-third sentence discount when they plead guilty. The charges are not negotiated, and the incentive, the sentence discount, remains fixed—there is no negotiation.[39] This contrasts with the US system, where bargained justice has become so entrenched that criminal justice is described as a contractual arrangement governed by the state prosecutor in which all procedural protections are waived under the threat of (Supreme Court sanctioned) sentence coercion, including, occasionally, the threat of death.[40]

These approaches reflect different process values underpinning the allocation of roles and responsibilities. In each system, accused persons who admit their guilt are offered some benefit or incentive, but jurisdictions within the inquisitorial tradition may be less comfortable with party-driven agreements, preferring legislative and judicially determined outcomes to those negotiated with a prosecutor. More adversarial procedures, on the other hand, are at pains to maintain the judicial role as independent of, and separate from, any party-based agreement prior to trial. Both procedural models struggle to make sense of the consequences attached to an admission of guilt: although expressed in system terms as an appropriate sentencing response to expressions of remorse

[36] McConville and Marsh, in contrast, argue that the pressure on defendants to plead guilty is "intended to replace, in whole or in part, the promise of adversary justice" (2014: 216) by a judiciary that is complicit and holds a deep-seated mistrust of the jury.

[37] Recommendation R (87) 18 of the Council of Europe Committee of Ministers (1987) encouraged countries to make use of discretionary prosecution and to adopt summary, simplified, and out-of-court procedures for mass and minor offenses, in order to combat delay and to simplify the workings of criminal justice.

[38] In the United States, 95 percent of cases are resolved without the need for a trial. As Justice Anthony Kennedy in the US Supreme Court case of *Missouri v. Frye* 566 U.S. 134 (2012) expressed it: plea bargaining "is not some adjunct to the criminal justice system; it *is* the criminal justice system" (citing Scott and Stuntz [1992: 1912]). This is aggravated by the practice of charge stacking—when the prosecutor stacks up all possible charges so that the defendant faces a huge sentence and so is further pressured into accepting a plea deal.

[39] Sixty percent of cases are dealt with through this procedure. This does not mean that the accused will not feel pressured to plead guilty, however. For a troubling example, see an account of one Spanish case (Flavia Totoro) reported by Fair Trials International, available at https://www.youtube.com/watch?v=RUIT1V3S3Gg&feature=youtu.be.

[40] *Brady v. United States* 397 U.S. 742 (1970). See Scott and Stuntz (2012); Elm et al. (2015).

and admissions of guilt, trial avoidance is in fact about maximizing the efficiency of criminal case management.[41] We see this in the evolving regulation of plea bargaining and case management in England and Wales, and more starkly in the United States, where judicial neutrality in plea bargaining has all but been abandoned.

In England and Wales, plea bargaining was not widely acknowledged in the 1970s, though research suggested that it was widely practiced[42] and the Court of Appeal in the *Turner* judgment issued guidelines for the very limited extent to which sentence canvassing was permissible.[43] The *Turner* rules, as they came to be known, only allowed trial judges to give an indication of the type of sentence (for example, a fine) that would be imposed whatever the plea. They were not to give a specific indication of the sentence that a guilty plea would attract, nor to indicate that one sentence would be imposed after a guilty plea and a more severe one imposed after a contested trial: this would amount to improper pressure to plead guilty. Research showed that these rules were not adhered to either by counsel or by judges;[44] sentence discounts were an integral part of charge bargaining, especially in the Crown Court,[45] where barristers enjoy access to trial judges.[46]

The practice of awarding sentence discounts for guilty pleas was placed on a legislative footing in 1994, but this did not address the sentence-canvassing issue.[47] Following the recommendations of the Royal Commission on Criminal Justice (1993) and the Auld Review (2001) to move away from the *Turner* rules,[48] the defense lawyer in "either way"[49] offenses in the magistrates' court may now ask the bench for an indication of whether or not a custodial sentence is likely should the accused plead guilty and the case be tried summarily.[50] Although

[41] Whatever the procedural tradition or rhetoric, it is clear that confessions are central to criminal justice systems. Some older studies in the United States have also doubted the extent to which caseloads are the real reason for trial avoidance. See Mather (1979); Schulhofer (1984).

[42] Although often denied, plea bargaining was alive and well in England and Wales in the 1970s. See Baldwin and McConville (1977).

[43] *Turner* (1970) 2 WLR 1093.

[44] See Zander and Henderson (1993: 145).

[45] See, e.g., McConville et al. (1994).

[46] See the comments of the Court of Appeal in *Goodyear* (2005) EWCA Crim. 888 (discussed later) at para. 31: "Prior to *Turner*, it was not unusual for counsel to be seen (often separately from their solicitors) by the trial judge in his chambers, and for the judge to tell counsel his view of the sentence which would follow an immediate guilty plea."

[47] S.48 of the Criminal Justice and Public Order Act 1994. See now s.144 Criminal Justice Act 2003. In determining sentence, the court must take account of when the accused indicated their intention to plead guilty and in what circumstances.

[48] The RCCJ proposed an indication of sentence after a guilty plea; Auld also favored an indication of the possible sentence after a contested trial.

[49] "Either way" offenses are those that may be tried either summarily in the magistrates' court or on indictment in the Crown Court.

[50] Schedule 3 of the Criminal Justice Act 2003.

there is no legislation addressing the Crown Court position in the same way, the plea and case management hearing requires the judge to ensure that the defendant understands that credit will be given for a guilty plea and to ascertain what steps have been taken to resolve the case without trial.[51] The anxiety to avoid improper pressure on the accused to plead guilty, expressed so forcefully in *Turner*, appears to be less of a concern in an environment where case management is designed to avoid the contested trial.

In 2005, the judicial part played in plea negotiations was made yet more explicit when the Court of Appeal in *Goodyear* abandoned the *Turner* rules, ruling that a sentence indication for a guilty plea could be given in open court with both parties present and would be binding on future judges, though as with *Turner*, no indication of the sentence following trial was to be given.[52] Discussion of the sentence that might be imposed following a plea of guilty could be initiated by a request from the defense lawyer (with a signed request from the client), or, more controversially, the judge could prompt such a request in open court, in line with her wider responsibilities for efficient case management. This creates an obvious risk that the accused will feel pressure to plead guilty, especially when the suggestion comes from the judge. This is not recognized in the legal guidelines, which simply seek to reassert the impartiality of the judge by underlining that responsibility for determining (or at least expressing) guilt in practice rests primarily with the defense lawyer, not with the court.[53] Provision for the judge to be proactive in encouraging the defense to canvas sentence on a plea of guilty challenges the generally passive role of the judge and the principle that she should play no part in shaping the case on which she will adjudicate and pass sentence.

Systems that have moved to a more adversarial procedure have also embraced plea bargaining as a necessity. Italy (discussed further subsequently) has adopted a range of abbreviated procedures following its shift to a more adversarial criminal process. The testing of evidence through live witnesses is much more time-consuming than a dossier-based trial, and so abbreviated procedures were recognized as necessary from the very outset.[54] Like several other Eastern European states whose systems were influenced heavily by the Soviet Union,

51 Criminal Procedure Rules 2005 and the Practice Direction on Criminal Case Management.

52 *Goodyear* (2005) EWCA Crim. 888. The court noted (at para. 54) that the judge is in no position to evaluate the sentencing position once all the evidence has been aired at trial and so would be likely to err on the side of the maximum likely. This in turn would create a greater discrepancy between this and the sentence proposed on a guilty plea, and so increase the pressure on the defendant to plead guilty.

53 The Bar Standards Board Written Guidelines (2004), para. 11.5, allow defendants to plead guilty who profess their innocence. It can no longer be said that a guilty plea is a judicial confession or an acceptance, on the part of the accused, of the truth of the allegation.

54 There is a system of plea bargaining in place in Poland, though conversely, it is considered a more adversarial procedure, where the court's role is limited, and likely to shorten proceedings. See Jasiński and Kremens (2019: para. 117–118).

Bulgarian criminal procedure gradually became more adversarial under the influence of the jurisprudence of the ECtHR and the legal reforms following the collapse of the communist regime in 1989. However, since 2005, the emphasis has shifted from building fair-trial rights to ensuring efficiency, promoting shortened and expedited trial procedures and plea bargaining.[55]

Inquisitorially rooted systems have also sought to adapt their procedures in order to aid the more efficient disposal of cases, but within this more judge-centered model, the concept of a plea bargain is problematic.[56] Inquisitorial procedure represents a more centralized enquiry into the truth, in which trial issues are not determined ultimately by the parties, but by the court.[57] This has led to a variety of adaptations, in which the accused makes an admission or a confession (such as the German *Verständigung*), rather than entering a formal guilty plea.[58] This can be characterized as shortening the trial rather than avoiding it completely,[59] but this, of course, depends on how one understands the term "trial." In England and Wales, and in the United States, going to trial is generally understood as the process of contesting the prosecution case and entering a plea of not guilty. However, even in uncontested cases, the court continues to exercise a judicial function in ensuring the voluntary nature of the guilty plea and the legal sufficiency of the charges. In practice, in adversarial systems this is delegated to the defense lawyer, but an indication of ambivalence as to guilt by the accused may yet lead the court to reject the plea. In this sense, any disposition of the case by a judge in court is properly understood as a trial.[60] In countries rooted in the inquisitorial tradition, without a formal plea procedure, the concept of trial refers more unequivocally to any court disposition of the case, as the judge understands herself to be determining the verdict whatever the evidence of the accused.

The development of features such as jury trial, guilty pleas, or the office of public prosecutor at particular moments in time can be the product of a variety of factors, some planned and some opportunistic. In assessing the emergence of plea bargaining in Germany, Weigend (2008) attributes the change in approach to the more active role developed by defense lawyers. He describes their increasing inventiveness and confrontational character, after reform in the 1970s

55 See Grozev (2012).

56 Other formal procedures include the *conformidad* in Spain and the *confissão* in Portugal. For wider discussion of plea bargaining in a comparative context, see Hodgson (2015).

57 E.g., the predecessor of the 1999 *composition pénale* (described later) was the *injonction pénale*, created in 1994 as an alternative measure to prosecution. It was subsequently struck out by the French constitutional council, the Conseil constitionnel, on the grounds that it eliminated the judge's role, effectively turning the procureur into a judge by allowing her to hand down a sentence.

58 See para. 257c German Code of Criminal Procedure; Langer (2004).

59 See Damaška (2004: 1026).

60 The ECHR concept of trial also refers to any determination of the criminal charges.

allowing defendants to avoid trial, also opened up communications between prosecution and defense, as well as the possibility that cases could be settled by the parties, rather than by the court.[61] In contrast to the judicial reluctance to be seen to be part of any negotiations in England and Wales, the German variant on plea bargaining sees the defense lawyer negotiating directly with the judge rather than the prosecutor, making the judge the dominant player, reflecting the broader and more judge-centered inquisitorial tradition within which negotiations take place, what Delmas-Marty (2008) has termed the "legal grammar" of a system. Moreover, judicial involvement is not equated here with greater pressure on the accused to provide an admission. Rauxloh (2011) suggests that this is a function of the greater autonomy of defendants facing economic and environmental charges (those most often subject to bargaining), whose background is closer to that of the judiciary than the marginalized members of society involved in more routine criminal offenses. The explanation may more plausibly lie in the social status and procedural expertise of the "elite" lawyers to which these more wealthy defendants have access. These factors perhaps explain why Germany is alone among the more inquisitorial traditions in practicing plea bargaining in serious as well as less important cases. Britain and the United States, on the other hand, employ plea bargains across the whole spectrum of criminal offenses.

The absence of a statutory framework for plea bargaining in Germany until very recently has allowed lawyers to develop the practice more freely, unconstrained by the requirement to adhere to wider procedural principles.[62] When, in 2013, the German Constitutional Court examined the constitutionality of the 2009 statute, it first commissioned an empirical study of the operation of the legislation, which surveyed 190 criminal court judges, sixty-eight prosecutors, and seventy-six criminal defense lawyers.[63] The findings demonstrate the dominance of existing informal procedures over those more recently set out in law,[64] as well as evidence of the same fault lines seen in adversarial procedure—a tendency toward overreliance on the prosecutor's version as constituting the facts

[61] Legislation in 1974 permitted suspects to avoid prosecution by paying money to the victim, a charity, or the state—see para. 153a Strafprozessordnung. Like France, there is no formal system of pleas. These are agreements to concessions in exchange for admissions. See Weigend and Turner (2014: n. 1). Coupled with the pressure of prosecuting complex and lengthy cases relating to drugs and economic crime, the prospect of shortening proceedings became increasingly attractive. See also Rauxloh (2011).

[62] In 2005, the Grand Panel of the Federal Court of Appeals declared negotiated judgments to be compatible with the German criminal justice system, but this still lacked any legislative basis until the reform of 2009, the constitutionality of which was upheld by the German Constitutional Court in 2013. Rauxloh (2011); Weigend and Turner (2014).

[63] Karsten Altenhain, Frank Dietmeier, and Markus May, *Die Praxis der Absprachen in Strafverfahren* (2013), described in Weigend and Turner (2014).

[64] Fifty-nine percent of the judges questioned admitted that in more than half of the cases where a negotiated agreement was reached, the statute protocols were not complied with; in 30 percent of cases the defendant was not told that the court could withdraw from the agreement.

of the case and so the guilt of the accused. In a judicial restatement of the proper function of the court (as we saw in *Goodyear* in England and Wales, and in the French constitutional council's decision relating to guilty pleas, discussed later), the Constitutional Court reminded the trial court of its mandate to investigate the substantive truth in order to determine guilt.[65] The courts both develop and participate in plea bargaining, while at the same time serving as an authority to ensure its justification.

In France too, a range of accelerated or abbreviated procedures have been introduced in an attempt to combat delay and the growing caseload of the courts, as well as alternatives to prosecution that allow the parties to agree on the case outcome and sentence.[66] For example, the *composition pénale* allows the procureur (the public prosecutor) to propose in writing a range of measures to an accused who admits the offense,[67] from fines to restrictions of movement and association.[68] The suspect is told that she may consult with a lawyer before deciding whether to accept the proposal, and the agreement is validated by the court after speaking to the offender and to the victim if it considers it necessary. If the offender complies, there is no trial—though the fact of the *composition pénale* is recorded on the person's criminal record. For the procureur, this is an important way of dealing rapidly with offenses such as assault, theft, criminal damage, or driving with excess alcohol;[69] defense lawyers, however, argue that it is difficult for the accused to refuse and so it does not represent a real choice.[70] Furthermore, the procureur may propose such a measure to the suspect held by the police during the *garde à vue*,[71] which risks putting further pressure on those detained in police custody to confess. This procedure has strengthened the role of the procureur, and while it remains different from plea bargaining (containing no provision for negotiation), it attaches a particular legal significance to the accused's confession.

In 2004, France went further and introduced a form of sentence bargaining in which the case is brought before the court as a form of guilty plea—a radical

[65] Weigend and Turner (2014) note the court's willingness to impose constitutional constraints on practice—condemning fact bargaining and forbidding appeal waivers to form part of the negotiation.

[66] These are described in more detail in chapter 5, discussing the impact this has on the prosecution role in particular.

[67] Under Arts. 41-42 and 41-43 CPP. In 2001 there were around fifteen hundred *compositions pénales*; by 2009 the number had risen to seventy-three thousand (Ministère de la justice et des libertés [2010]) and has remained consistent at around 5 percent of prosecutable offenses. Ministère de la justice et des libertés (2017).

[68] Pradel (2002: 211) notes that while these are punitive measures that sanction an offense, they are not technically regarded as a "sentence." They are not given by the court, and the terminology is slightly different: a fine is an *amende*, whereas this provides for an *amende de composition*; community service is *travail d'intérêt général*, but this provides for unpaid work, *travail non rémunéré*.

[69] The range of offenses covered is described as *la délinquance urbaine* or *la délinquance de masse*.

[70] See, e.g., *Le Monde*, 21 January 2004.

[71] The *garde à vue* is the period of detention of the suspect in police custody.

reform in a criminal procedure that has never had a formal system of guilty or not guilty pleas. Known as *comparution sur reconnaissance préalable de culpabilité* (CRPC), the guilty plea procedure may be proposed by the prosecutor, the accused, or her lawyer, and the sentence proposed may not exceed one year's imprisonment or half of the maximum sentence for that offense.[72] Legal representation of the accused is mandatory; the confession and the sentence offer must be made in the presence of the lawyer who has immediate access to the case file, and the accused is allowed a delay of up to ten days to decide whether to accept the offer.

This new procedure has significant consequences for the role of legal personnel.[73] The prosecutor discusses the proposal directly with the accused; the defense lawyer is asked to agree the sentence; and the judge is required to confirm or reject that sentence in court. This procedure is more party centered than judge centered and therefore is seen as relating more easily to an adversarial process.[74] It requires both defense and prosecution to engage in a pretrial agreement, and judge and prosecutor to share power in case disposition. As a *magistrat* (a judicial officer), the French prosecutor has a broader role than her counterpart in more adversarial systems: in practice she may not represent the elevated neutrality of a judge as understood within Anglo-American procedure, but she is less driven toward the attainment of a guilty plea.[75] If the defendant has made a clear admission, the prosecutor will propose a sentence, which the defense lawyer may seek to reduce further, or adapt to the specific circumstances of the accused. But if the accused is not content to admit the offense, there is no question of persuasion or negotiation; the case will simply be listed for ordinary trial. This is an important difference from adversarial plea bargaining. The French model rests on a factual admission and the prosecutor's role in carrying out the verification that the court might otherwise do; it is not about a plea as a procedural mechanism, which is a separate decision and may not be underpinned by a factual admission. In this way, the CRPC can be seen as a guilty plea procedure, shortening court proceedings, but it is not a process of bargaining around either plea or admission.[76] Any negotiation will be around the specifics of the sentence—never around the plea itself.[77] While plea bargaining has become the

72 See Arts. 495-497–495-516 CPP. In 2006 there were 51,028 CRPCs out of 1.5 million prosecutable offenses (Ministère de la justice et des libertés [2007]); in 2008 there were 56,326 CRPCs out of 1.5 million (Ministère de la justice et des libertés [2009]), rising to 87,733 out of 1.4 million in 2016 (Ministère de la justice et des libertés [2017]).

73 See Hodgson (2005: 59–61).

74 The victim's consent is not required for this procedure, and she may still claim compensation as *partie civile* just as in an ordinary criminal trial.

75 For a discussion of the French *magistrat* roles, see Hodgson (2005: 65–85).

76 See the empirical observations of the CRPC procedure in action in Soubise (2016: 237–248).

77 Observations of CRPC meetings between prosecutor, defense, and the accused were cooperative and nonconflictual. Soubise (2016); Hodgson and Soubise (2016b).

norm in Anglo-American procedure, it is still regarded with some suspicion in France.[78] On the other hand, unlike in England and Wales, it is the procureur who proposes the sentence (as she does in ordinary court proceedings), which is a significant role given that nearly two-thirds of those subject to a CRPC receive a prison sentence (either immediate or suspended).[79]

Although the prosecutor does not engage in negotiation over plea or charge, the possibility of a reduced sentence may nevertheless serve to encourage the accused to make an admission. However, as we have seen in adversarial models, where the accused's own representative becomes captive to wider system goals, the agent of persuasion is not the prosecutor, but the defense lawyer. In a recent empirical study that included the provision of legal advice to suspects in French police stations, lawyers varied in their expertise and experience of criminal work, but common to all cases was reference to the possibility of a sentence discount for a guilty plea.[80] Crucially, suspects were told of this during their first consultation with their lawyer, before being interrogated by the police and on the basis of very little evidence disclosure.

Perhaps the most striking feature of this procedure, given the proactive judicial role that is often understood to characterize inquisitorially rooted systems, is the very limited power of the judge: she can only accept or reject the sentence proposed by the parties—she has no power to amend it. The Conseil constitutionnel (like the German Constitutional Court described previously) squares the passive judicial role imposed in this procedure with the constitutional and inquisitorial procedural ideal of a judge-led trial by requiring the judge to do more than rubber-stamp the proposal. This is reinforced by the Ministry of Justice circular, which emphasizes the differences between this procedure and the "Anglo-Saxon guilty plea" in which primacy is given to the confession, rather than to the truth.[81] The circular describes the judge as being responsible, as she is with any criminal case, for verifying the guilt of the accused and the legal sufficiency of the charges. She must also ensure that the accused's consent has been given freely, with full understanding of the consequences, and that the sentence is appropriate. If she is not satisfied on any of these counts, or there are other reasons that she considers make such a disposal inappropriate, she should reject the proposal.

Like the judgments described previously, the circular is designed to reinforce the legitimacy of the CRPC and to counter any suggestion that the procedure

[78] Although significant, the CRPC procedure accounts for only 18 percent of cases dealt with in the *tribunal correctionnel*. Ministère de la justice et des libertés (2017).

[79] Around 63 percent of people subject to CRPCs receive a prison sentence (either immediate or suspended), and in 85 percent of cases this is for six months or less; 27 percent receive a fine, and 7 percent community service work. Houllé and Vaney (2017).

[80] Blackstock et al. (2014).

[81] Circular CRIM 04-12 E8 of 2 September 2004.

undercuts the court's role in determining guilt. In practice, however, the procedure will operate very much like a "traditional" guilty plea.[82] It would be counterproductive in practical terms if it did not reduce the court's role and so the time taken to dispose of the case.

The structure of the guilty plea procedure leaves no space for the court to interrogate the accused's motivation or her character, no possibility for the court to individualize the sentence to fit the offender. This is in marked contrast to cases not dealt with under the CRPC procedure, where the court will be concerned to understand something of the accused's character as part of its function in trying to reintegrate the offender into society.[83] It is perhaps ironic that in borrowing this procedure from more adversarial procedures (where pre-sentence reports would provide some personal information), the French model has concurrently removed its more individualized justice function.[84]

Is plea bargaining a consequence of adversarialism, or its negation? It is designed to remove cases from trial and so prevent the defendant from testing out the case against her, relieving the prosecutor of the requirement to discharge the burden of proof in a public courtroom and allowing weak cases to go unchecked. In this way, the adversarial ideal of live evidence tested before a judge and jury is frustrated. From the inquisitorial standpoint, plea bargaining allows the parties to determine the verdict and sentence for the most part, weakening the truth-finding judicial function. As an expression of party control, the guilty plea reflects adversarial values; it is the parties' decision to withhold the case from the court's fact-finding, not that of a central investigator.[85] Bargained justice is not part of either tradition, but it undercuts the core tenets of each, representing neither party control (as incentives remove free choice), nor oral procedure, nor judicial independence, as judges are increasingly drawn into the management of cases toward a guilty plea. Neither does it represent a truth-seeking judicial role, where parties agree on an outcome for the judge to rubber-stamp. What it does engender is a form of privatized and secret justice, in which the evidence is neither heard nor tested and the roles of legal actors are subverted in many instances.

This brief look at the ways in which bargaining and admission-based procedures have been translated into nonadversarial legal cultures provides a

[82] Of course, as noted earlier, the court in England and Wales is not bound to accept the defendant's plea either. If it appears involuntary or if the charges appear to be legally insufficient, the court may reject the plea.

[83] On sentencing functions in France see Hodgson and Soubise (2016b).

[84] Delage (2005).

[85] Countries from the inquisitorial tradition tend to favor confessions rather than a guilty plea, so that the judicial trial role in uncovering the truth is reduced, but not eliminated.

recent example of borrowing concepts across legal procedures, but also illustrates the ways that imported practices are adapted to local conditions. This next section considers borrowing and adaptation in the context of wholesale and systematic procedural reform.

C. From Inquisitorial to Adversarial: An External Perspective

In some instances, change has gone beyond mere borrowing, and whole procedures have been imported into (or imposed upon) countries,[86] and then adapted to local conditions. Along with Napoleon and his army, the Napoleonic code spread through Europe and Russia during the nineteenth century; English criminal procedure was imported briefly by the French revolutionaries at the end of the eighteenth century, but was ultimately abandoned; and more recently, Italy, China, several Central and Eastern European states and large parts of Latin America have undergone major procedural changes toward an adversarial procedure. In the case of jurisdictions whose processes of criminal justice reflected the Soviet model prior to the collapse of the Soviet Union, their adoption of more adversarial principles of criminal procedure is attributed in part to their accession to the ECHR and the need to comply with new fair-trial standards.

> All have had to grapple with the challenges inherent in changing their system from one where the primary allegiances of the police, prosecutors, judges and even lawyers, was to the state, to one that reflects, at least in principle, the characteristics of a liberal democracy which demands an independent judiciary and a less powerful role for prosecutors.[87]

In exploring the shifts in our own criminal process, it is perhaps instructive to examine how adversarial procedure is defined from without. What does it mean to move toward a more adversarial procedure? What attracts countries to adversarialism and what features are viewed as key to such a transformation? And how important are existing legal cultures in promoting or undermining the success of major system change, and creating new hybrid procedures?

[86] Vogler (2005) describes, for example, how inquisitorial procedure was abused for the political ends of Hitler and Stalin.

[87] Cape and Namoradze (2012: 409). For similar concerns re China, see Mou (forthcoming).

(i) Italy

The transformation of Italian criminal procedure from its inquisitorial roots to a more adversarial process was fraught with difficulty. The shift to adversarialism introduced profound changes to the judicial function that went to the core of the Italian inquisitorial tradition. The judiciary is a powerful institution within the Italian legal system, and its strength and influence were felt in the force of its resistance to reform. After being challenged in Italy's three highest courts, only a constitutional amendment finally ensured that the legislation introducing a more party-centered procedure could be applied in full.

Italy's criminal procedure was based on the French *code d'instruction criminelle* of 1808. This underpinned the 1930 Italian code of criminal procedure—described as a "relic from the Fascist era"—with a heavy emphasis upon the pretrial judicial investigation.[88] Reforms in the 1970s allowed the defense the opportunity to challenge or contradict the evidence gathered and presented, and live witnesses were permitted at trial. However, this was undermined in practice by the trial judge's access to the case dossier, which continued to serve as the real evidential basis of the case. As Illuminati explains:

> The trial simply functioned as a control on what had been previously decided . . . merely an occasion for the "official reading" of the record formed during the investigative stage . . . in most cases the witness was asked to simply "confirm" the statements given to the investigating judge.[89]

Italy's shift to an adversarial procedure began in 1988. It sought not to replicate existing procedures such as those in England and Wales or the United States, but to adapt its own criminal process through the incorporation of adversarial principles drawn from those systems. These were thought to protect better the values inherent in the 1948 Constitution, such as the right to effective defense counsel and the separation of the prosecution and judicial functions.[90] The result is a mixed system, underpinned by adversarial values. So, while evidence is now presented and tested by the parties in place of the judge, in line with adversarial procedure,[91] the victim continues to have the right to participate in the proceedings through counsel, in line with inquisitorial jurisdictions. In contrast to procedures such as those in Britain and the United States, a lay jury was not introduced into the Italian criminal process, though in the most serious crimes

[88] Marafioti (2008).
[89] Illuminati (2005: 568).
[90] Illuminati (2005: 570, 572).
[91] Pizzi and Montagna (2004: 435–437).

there are mixed panels of laypeople and professional judges, as there are in France.

The thrust of the 1988 reform was to reduce the power of the judge by shifting responsibility for the investigation, presentation and testing of evidence away from a central judicial power, to the two parties, prosecution and defense. Previously, evidence gathered during the investigation was admissible at trial;[92] under the new procedure this was not permitted, ensuring a strict separation between the investigation and trial phases and respect for the principles of orality and immediacy.[93] Witnesses were required to testify before the court, and the defendant could cross-examine them and present her own evidence, preventing the judge from placing any reliance on the dossier of evidence produced by the prosecutor. However, features of the inquisitorial procedure remain.[94] Trials are before a professional judge or a mixed panel of professional and lay judges; the judge may still introduce evidence at trial; the principle of legality means that prosecution is mandatory, that is, it is not within the prosecutor's discretion;[95] and the prosecutor remains under a duty to supervise the police investigation and to gather both incriminating and exculpatory evidence.

The move away from an inquisitorial to an adversarial procedure was no simple matter. It represented a major legal, political, and cultural shift that took over a decade to establish itself, requiring constitutional as well as legislative reform in order to overcome the force of judicial resistance. The procedural reforms impacted most profoundly on the judicial function: once the main protagonist, enjoying power across all stages of the criminal process, the judge was expected to step aside in favor of the newly enhanced role of the parties. The judiciary was not prepared for this and it was not well received. It challenged the core nature of their role and appeared to introduce a more lengthy and inefficient trial procedure. Thus, despite legislation that was designed to bring about clear change, the new procedure continued to be interpreted in a way that corresponded more closely to the old inquisitorial tradition. Exceptions to the principle that only evidence heard in court should found the basis of a conviction were expanded, as was the limited power of the judge to introduce evidence in court.[96] A major blow came in 1992, when the Constitutional Court struck down a number of key provisions of the reform, its reasoning demonstrating a clear

92 Pizzi and Monatgna (2004: 434).

93 Illuminati (2005: 571).

94 See also Illuminati (2010).

95 Though see Caianiello (2016) for a discussion of how discretionary ways of working have found their way into the prosecution function. Like orality and the jury trial in adversarialism, the principle of legality is something associated with more inquisitorial procedures, but in fact prosecutorial discretion has long been a feature of the French (and Dutch) criminal process.

96 The Constitutional Court heard more claims in the first years after the reform than in the preceding four decades. Illuminati (2005: 574).

underlying inquisitorial ideology and adherence to the supremacy of the truth-seeking function of the judge.[97] This was then compounded by legislative reform allowing reliance on evidence gathered during the investigation.[98]

In 1997, parliament legislated to restore the adversarial process, but again this was thwarted by the interpretation of the Constitutional Court. The only solution was to amend the constitution to make more explicit the values of adversarial procedure. This was done in 1999 and was known as the "fair-trial reform." In 2001, the code of criminal procedure was amended to restore the adversarial procedure and in particular, the inadmissibility of out-of-court statements and the importance of the opportunity to cross-examine witnesses. These changes were upheld by the Constitutional Court, placing the trial at the center of criminal proceedings and finally confirming the clear separation between investigation and trial.

Marafioti argues that the existing legal culture and practice has not been displaced fully by the reforms. The judiciary has continued to dominate the process and has expanded its power to call witnesses such that this can no longer be considered exceptional.[99] This is justified as serving the overarching truth-seeking function of the court, but in practice, "it has had the effect of counter-balancing weaknesses in the prosecution case and reversing the onus on it to prove its case."[100] Dissatisfied with the exclusionary rules of evidence and time limits for trial, prosecutors have also resorted to using written evidence at trial, and the extension of time limits has become the norm rather than the exception.

As we know, jurisdictions with established adversarial procedures rarely invoke the full trial process. The introduction of improved procedural defense rights seems immediately to trigger the establishment of procedures through which these rights can be waived. Italy too has put in place various expedited procedures, or "special proceedings," in order to make caseloads more manageable; the original plan was that 20 to 40 percent of cases would be dealt with under one of these special proceedings, making space for the remainder to be dealt with through an adversarial trial.[101] In exchange for a reduced penalty, these procedures eschew the lengthy process of an adversarial trial in favor of

97 Illuminati (2005: 574); Pizzi and Montagna (2004: 450–457).

98 The justice system was under particular pressure to deal with organized crime at this time; Borsellino and Falcone, two prosecutors investigating the Mafia in Sicily, had been assassinated. Illuminati (2005: 575); Pizzi and Montagna (2004: 457–459).

99 Marafioti (2008: 93–94) attributes this to the fact that the judge (rather than a jury) is responsible for the verdict and so finds it difficult to respond only to what the parties choose to present. One might also pose an opposite psychology, whereby the adversarial judge might want to seek to control the evidence in order to influence the jury, given that she has no role in determining the verdict.

100 Marafioti (2008: 93).

101 Delays in criminal proceedings are a problem that has long blighted Italy, as evidenced by its numerous violations of Article 6(1) ECHR.

a decision based on the case file.[102] This has had some success, but defendants continue to experience long delays, with a huge backlog of cases and inadequate resources invested in the criminal justice process. Used in around 15 percent of cases, the *patteggiamento*[103] allows the accused to agree a penalty reduction of up to one-third with the prosecutor (with a maximum of five years' imprisonment), and this is reviewed by the judge.[104] In the *giudizio abbreviato*, or abbreviated trial, the accused can again obtain a penalty reduction of one-third for any level of offense if she agrees to be tried on the basis of the pretrial file. This is used in around 10 percent of cases. And for more minor offenses, the prosecutor may request *procedimento per decreto penale*, or "proceedings by penal decree." In this procedure, the judge determines the case in the absence of the parties, solely on the basis of the case dossier, and imposes a fine that is half the legally established minimum. The accused is not obliged to accept this—she may challenge the sentence and may request a trial.

It is interesting that this was an important part of the 1988 reform to an adversarial procedure in Italy, but in Anglo-American procedures, such measures are often seen as subverting the adversarial ideal. In Italy, the requirement for the parties' consent is crucial in understanding the measures as adversarial rather than inquisitorial. In France too, the recent guilty plea and sentence bargain procedure is located within the adversarial tradition because it depends on the agreement of the parties rather than the judge. This underlines the point that it is less the absence of a trial that undermines adversarialism, than the absence of choice or control of the case on the part of the accused.[105] Decades of research in Britain and the United States demonstrates that plea bargaining is not generally experienced as a "bonus" for those who have already made admissions of guilt and make a positive choice to forgo trial, so much as a threat or negative incentive in order to ensure that an admission is obtained.[106]

The introduction of more accusatorial features into the criminal procedures of countries such as France and Italy often focuses on moving away from the "trial-by-dossier model." Yet, although the guilty plea procedure in England and Wales is generally characterized as forgoing a contested trial, it is in fact a decision to be sentenced on the basis of the court (i.e., the prosecution) file, to accept guilt on

[102] There are also abbreviated procedures such as the *giudizio immediato* in which the prosecutor must bring formal charges within ninety days of the crime being registered. The case will then go directly to trial, omitting the preliminary hearing.

[103] In the Italian code it is called *applicazione della pena su richiesta delle parti*, or the application of punishment on the request of the parties. Pizzi and Montagna (2004: 438).

[104] This is different from plea bargaining in that there is no charge bargaining (Pizzi and Montagna [2004: 438–445]) and this does not require a guilty plea (Illuminati [2005: 579]).

[105] It might be argued that even without explicit incentives, the power imbalance between the state and the accused limits the defendant's freedom of choice within adversarial practice.

[106] Discussed in Hodgson and Roberts (2010); Hodgson (2015).

the facts as presented by the prosecution. In many ways this is of even greater significance in England and Wales, in theoretical terms, than in a jurisdiction such as France. The French model proceeds on the basis that the dossier is a broad judicial or judicially supervised enquiry, bringing together exculpatory as well as incriminating evidence and, in the more serious cases, allowing contributions from the victim and the accused. In England and Wales, however, it is simply a police-constructed prosecution file, with no defense or other input. The guilty plea in England and Wales is a simple admission to the police case.

(ii) Latin America

Across Latin America too, criminal justice reform has been toward more adversarial procedures, but in contrast to Italy, this has been part of a more profound political shift associated with the strengthening of human rights, democracy, and the rule of law.[107] At the forefront of this, and perhaps the most successful in terms of radical and effective change, has been Chile.[108] Up until the 1990s, Latin American criminal justice was characterized by the arbitrary behavior of the state; the ability of the elite to operate effectively outside the law; and the huge challenge posed in dealing with organized crime and violence.[109] The judiciary was in no position to take on these issues.[110] Widely regarded as being weak, ineffective, and lacking in political independence, judges served as a tool for the executive and the military to employ for their own ends.[111] In many countries, such as Colombia, the endemic corruption of the police and military, together with low judicial salaries and professional standing, left judges virtually powerless to resist the bribery and threats of the drug lords.[112]

[107] This also characterizes the impetus for change in Eastern European states such as Bulgaria, Georgia, Lithuania, Moldova, and Ukraine following the fall of the communist regime. Georgia, in particular, has adopted an adversarial criminal procedure, including jury trial. See Cape and Namoradze (2012). In Poland, the shift to a more adversarial process was short-lived. Within a year of its coming into force, the newly elected right-wing government restored the former inquisitorial procedures. See also Jasiński and Kremens (2019).

[108] See, e.g., Véliz (2012); Cooper (2008). Riego (2008) emphasizes the importance to Chile's success in establishing a proper system of judicial management, which utilized the expertise of nonlawyers. Civil protestors in 2019 argued for more fundamental changes to the constitution in order to bring about real political change.

[109] Domingo and Sieder (2001: 151–152).

[110] See Garcia (1998); Prillaman (2000).

[111] Lawyers Committee for Human Rights (2000). This report addresses Bolivia, but is typical of many Latin American countries. Nagle (2000: 349) describes the judiciary in Latin American states as a "Cinderella" to the executive and legislature.

[112] Nagle (2000: 361–364). This is summed up in the choice presented to judges of "silver or lead" (*plata o plomo*) by the all-powerful international drug lords.

The judicialization of politics[113] and the creation of an independent judiciary were seen as key components in the transition away from various forms of military dictatorships and internal armed conflicts, toward democracy and respect for the rule of law.[114] An increased emphasis on the protection of human rights formed the basis for the political agenda of new governments, and the reform of criminal justice was central to this.[115]

The dominant procedural model across Latin America was the inquisitorial system inherited from the Spanish and Portuguese colonization of the Americas, itself based on the procedure developed by the Catholic Church in Europe.[116] The sole aim of this process was the extraction of the truth, due process rights being largely irrelevant. This centralized, secret, and written procedure, in which the accused has few or no rights to participate, is described as having "a pre-democratic logic, in which subjects do not have any rights or at the very least have rights that are subordinate to general interests of the State."[117] The accusatorial model, in contrast, has been regarded as able to provide the necessary basic due process protections, and in particular, respect for the presumption of innocence and the right to a defense.[118] It is also seen to offer the potential for greater efficiency than the lengthy written procedures and mandatory prosecution that characterize inquisitorial procedure—somewhat in contrast to the perceived efficiency gains of greater resort to written procedure in England and Wales.

The defining feature of the Latin American inquisitorial procedures from the early nineteenth to late twentieth centuries was the central role of the judge. She was responsible for the investigation and mandatory prosecution of offenses, developing the facts at trial, determining the verdict and the sentence. Pretrial detention was lengthy, indiscriminate, and virtually systematic,[119] used as a means of obtaining a confession or anticipating the sentence, given the absence of a

[113] See, e.g., Sieder et al.'s (2005) book of that name. A host of international organizations have had a stake in this process. See, e.g., Salas (2001: 24–25).

[114] And these wider political goals of democracy and the rule of law were, in turn, regarded as necessary to the process of Latin America undergoing the kind of economic reform it desired and for which, crucially, aid was on offer. Nagle (2000: 349–350). She goes on to say that "judicial reform became the target that both the executive branch and the judicial branch worked together to bring about in order to stimulate economic development and investment" (355–356).

[115] Riego and Vargas (2003: 2).

[116] Langer (2007: 637–638). See also Nagle (2000) for a historical account of colonial Latin American justice.

[117] Riego and Vargas (2003: 3). It is interesting that most former state-socialist systems also operated under a form of inquisitorialism in which the pretrial was key, with trials being staged as formalized, political events. Since the collapse of the USSR, these states have undergone a range of reforms—some in an adversarial direction, but most maintaining a strong investigation and trial role for the judiciary. See Vogler (2005).

[118] See, e.g., Goodpaster (1987) for a discussion of the adversarial trial not only as means of ensuring fairness in the process of truth-finding, but also as protecting the individual from the possible abuse of government power and resources.

[119] Langer (2007: 629).

presumption of innocence.[120] As the procedure was written and secret, the accused did not always get to see the charges or the evidence against her. In this highly bureaucratic system, junior staff made many decisions on behalf of the judge, resulting in a lack of public trust in the system.[121] The absence of any form of counterbalance to the judicial investigation led to an inevitable conviction bias on the part of the police and the judiciary. Riego and Vargas describe the proceedings thus:

> There is no trial as such, but an accumulation of proceedings which, step by step, give rise to a decision, giving probative value to the evidence gathered during the investigation without submitting it to confrontation in an open debate.[122]

It is easy to see how such a concentration of power, coupled with a lack of political independence, might have a corrupting effect on the justice process and an inability to act as any kind of restraint on political and military power.[123]

Beginning in the early 1990s, the adversarial reforms away from (sometimes extreme forms of) inquisitorialism vary in degree from country to country,[124] but at their center is the removal of the judge's stranglehold on the entire criminal process. Instead, just as with Italy, responsibility for directing the criminal investigation,[125] formulating the charges, and discharging the burden of proof to demonstrate the guilt of the accused has passed to the public prosecutor's office.[126] And unlike the former system, prosecutorial discretion allows for weak

[120] Riego and Vargas (2003: 3).

[121] Véliz (2012: 1365).

[122] Riego and Vargas (2003: 3). The Lawyers Committee for Human Rights (2000: 10) describes the procedure in Bolivia as one where "all phases of trial were captured only in documents whose flow and distribution the judges and court secretaries controlled."

[123] See Loveman (1993). This is aggravated further by the low pay and status of police and judges, which makes them an easy target for intimidation and bribery by organized criminals in the drugs trade. See, e.g., Nagle's (2000: 361–363) account of Venezuelan judicial corruption. The highly political nature of the criminal process in China also produces a prosecution service and a judiciary lacking in independence. See McConville et al. (2011); McConville and Pils (2013); Mou (forthcoming).

[124] For more detail on when new accusatorial codes of criminal procedure were adopted in each jurisdiction, see Langer (2007: 631).

[125] This separation of the investigation and judgment phases was an important part of the dismantling of the inquisitorial model in which a single authority was responsible for the investigation, prosecution, trial, and sentence of an accused. There are parallels with France, where under the *grande ordonnance* of 1670, these functions were dominated by a single individual, the *lieutenant criminel* (Esmein [1913]). These roles came to be redistributed, with a formal separation of investigation and trial in Napoleon's *code d'instruction criminelle*. (Discussed in Hodgson [2005: 68–72].) In England and Wales, there is a further degree of separation, that between investigation and prosecution, which has been seen as an important part of prosecutorial independence.

[126] In Chile, this required a constitutional amendment to create the office of public prosecutor. The Ministerio Público was created in 2000.

cases to be filtered out, making caseloads more manageable. The use of pretrial detention is also regulated and limited. Evidence must be presented in court in order that it can be debated and challenged, and the defense is given rights of disclosure as well as of legal counsel.[127] The judge no longer has a pretrial role, and at trial it is for the parties to set the parameters of the case; the judge's function is purely adjudicatory rather than investigatory, being required to make an impartial determination on the culpability of the defendant. The secrecy of the trial proceedings has also been removed. Evidence is presented orally and in public, making judges accountable for their decisions.[128] These radical changes in the role and function of various legal personnel have necessitated and been supported by professional training and the development of codes of professional ethics,[129] and there is apparently widespread support for the reforms, according to public surveys conducted in 2004 and 2006.[130]

However, while the structure of criminal procedure is radically different, it takes more than legislation to bring about the kinds of legal cultural change needed for an effective shift from the old inquisitorial mentality to a more proactive adversarial defense role in particular. There are potentially two hurdles to overcome. First, the gap between rhetoric and reality in the criminal process is well understood.[131] Changes in the law are only the first step, and it can take years before practice reflects the aspirations of the text of the law. This is especially problematic where the legal actors concerned do not "buy in" to the reforms, failing to recognize their importance or seeing them as contrary to their interests.[132] Second, this difficulty can be compounded in the case of norms derived externally—either through supranational standards, or legal transplants from other jurisdictions. Legal norms are often interpreted differently when refracted through the lens of another legal procedural tradition and culture, making it difficult to guarantee changes in practice. In the case of defense practice, the risk is that the law gives the appearance of due process while masking the lawyer's role in legitimating the process and so leaving the accused with less, rather than more, protection. In Chile, the focus has been on reforming prosecution and judicial practice, the defense function attracting less attention and so remaining under-theorized. Although central to the adversarial shift away from a judge-dominated procedure, the rights of the accused to challenge the

[127] The public defender office, the Defensoria Penal Pública, was created in 2001. See King (2017).

[128] In some countries, such as Bolivia, the "democratization" of criminal justice has also extended to the use of juries. See Véliz (2012) for a discussion of the reforms in Chile.

[129] Véliz (2012).

[130] Riego (2008: 347–348).

[131] See discussion in Hodgson and Mou (2019).

[132] This was evident, for example, in the reluctance of both police and defense lawyers to accept the reforms contained in PACE 1984. See McConville et al. (1991); McConville and Hodgson (1993); Blackstock et al. (2014).

prosecution case and present a defense have not been embraced by defense lawyers who remain passive in their acceptance of the state's case. Lacking either a clearly defined mission or any criteria of success, the defense role has not evolved sufficiently from its inquisitorial past and serves mainly to legitimate the process.[133]

The initial success of the reforms in general terms has also been contested. In 1998, despite judicial reforms, on average 70 percent of prisoners in Latin American jails were awaiting sentence.[134]

> The data showing a dramatic rise in incarceration in Chile after the adoption of the adversarial system suggest that a formal change in the structure of adjudication is of limited value in meaningfully protecting the interests of those involved in the criminal justice system.[135]

The extent to which such radical changes in criminal procedure were a strictly necessary part of democratic and economic reform in Latin America has also been contested by a number of authors, especially in Latin America. Nagle, herself a former Colombian judge, comments:

> To placate the first world countries sending aid their way, Latin American countries have played the judicial reform game to a dextrous effect, bringing in millions of dollars to the judiciary that would otherwise be unavailable from internal sources.[136]

In this way, "the Latin American judiciaries have fuelled a lucrative consulting industry in the United States."[137]

Jensen and Heller question whether financial and human resources have been used effectively given the questionable incentives offered to reformers and the

133 This was the case with poor lawyering practices in England and Wales in the 1980s and 1990s and more recently in ensuring that EU states implement measures requiring the provision of effective legal advice to suspects in police custody. See also King (2017: 861–870).

134 "[T]he picture of success depicted by judicial reform professionals completely contrasts [*sic*] the one painted by Human Rights watchdogs." Nagle (2000: 346).

135 King (2017: 836). Although starting to decline, the prison population increased from 33,050 to 54,628 between 2000 and 2010 (from 215 per 100,000 of population, to 320). Between 1990 and 1995 it remained stable at around 22,000. King (2017: 871).

136 Nagle (2000: 346).

137 Nagle (2000: 346). She is similarly cynical about the motivations of these foreign consultants: "In support of democracy in Latin America, court consultants and organizations who butter their bread with justice reform Requests for Proposals (RFP), jump at any opportunity to win contracts from government agencies tasked with carrying out the policies of the United States. And in the off chance that there is not a particular problem to be fixed, one can easily be manufactured by either government officials of the United States seeking personal enrichment through foreign aid, or abroad by over-enthusiastic NGO[s] in need of justifying the salaries of senior staffers." (2000: 347).

inadequate knowledge of how legal systems might be strengthened.[138] It is also ironic that despite the documented failure of the American system to operate along its own adversarial principles (characterized instead by bargained justice and mass incarceration), it is being exported so enthusiastically as a model procedure. Others are also critical of the ill-informed and ethnocentric approach of American lawyers to earlier legal reforms in Latin America: "American legal assistance was inept, culturally unaware, and sociologically uninformed. It was also ethnocentric, perceiving and assisting the third world in its own self-image."[139] This sentiment is echoed by Nagle:

> Judicial reform projects benefit the armies of highly compensated consultants and NGOs whose existence depends to large measure on judicial reform projects more than the programs benefit the targeted institutions. There is also something very disingenuous about judicial reform projects run by United States citizens who have little if any legal training, familiarity with the continental law system, language facility, and cultural orientation to the countries in which they go to work. This, in addition to little, if any, accountability for the quality of work being done, and no way of knowing if project staffers are being hood-winked by unscrupulous or corrupt Latin American judicial officers.[140]

Muñoz offers a different perspective, describing the American influence on the reforms in Chile as the product of a kind of "local-international interaction."[141] Beginning with Juan Enrique Vargas and Cristián Riego, a number of critical legal scholars, some educated in the United States, played a key role in influencing the content of the reform proposals.[142]

> [O]nce the parliamentary discussion was underway the initial project went through some changes, and elements from the Anglo-American world were added. . . . These contributions came during the same period that part of the team began studying in the United States and incorporating elements from the Anglo-American model of criminal justice in their consultancies during the parliamentary discussion.[143]

[138] Jensen and Heller (2003).

[139] Gardner (1980: 9). See also Mattei (2003), who, in positing a theory of imperial law, sees a more profound agenda at work. He argues that the American adversarial legalism "cannot be seen as a mere feature of American law, but is actually the fundamental philosophy of globalization." Mattei (2003: 390 n. 27).

[140] Nagle (2000: 378).

[141] Muñoz (2011: 113).

[142] After a postgraduate degree at Yale in 1982, Correa Sutil became dean of the Diego Portales Law School, opening it up for the study of human rights and judicial modernization. Vargas and Riego were soon appointed.

[143] Muñoz (2011: 122). These were the contributions of Mauricio Duce and Andrés Baytelman.

What is interesting, however, is the extent to which inquisitorialism has been seen as the tool of dictatorship, and adversarialism the natural procedural model for a modern democracy. One commentator who might question this characterization is Langbein, who has long been an advocate for inquisitorial procedure. He has criticized the turn taken by English criminal procedure in the eighteenth century, when the use of defense counsel grew dramatically in the face of increasingly zealous and partisan prosecutions and a weak and passive judiciary that was apparently powerless to intervene.[144] This marked the beginning of the professionalization of justice and a move away from the testimony of the defendant being central to the trial. He argues that a better response would have been to strengthen the judiciary, who at that time served at the Crown's pleasure and so lacked both independence and impartiality. This would enable judges to tackle the excessively partisan and at times dishonest courtroom practices of the prosecution directly, thus obviating the need for increased legal representation. A stronger judiciary would also be better placed to take control of the pretrial process, ensuring a greater degree of neutrality in both investigation and prosecution. The political agenda of the time favored equality between the defendant and the Crown, and so what ultimately became an escalation of adversarial procedure was equated with a more democratic process; Langbein, however, argues that a judge-centered model would have better served the interests of justice and prevented the silencing of the accused in favor of the prosecutorial burdens of production and proof.[145]

The Latin American experience of the judge-centered model, operating within a particular political culture, however, is one that has facilitated dictatorships and military regimes; the move to a more adversarial process is equated with the democratization of justice and a break with the old regime.[146] In post-Revolutionary France too, a strongly inquisitorial procedure was associated with the oppressive nature of the ancien régime.[147] An accusatorial procedure was introduced after the French Revolution, but after only twenty years it was replaced with a modified and less draconian version of the old inquisitorial system. An alternative solution in Latin America might have been to strengthen the independence and professional status of the judiciary in order that the justice system could function effectively, rather than jettisoning it altogether in favor of

144 Langbein (2003).

145 See also the historical accounts of Landsman (1990) and Beattie (1986, 1991).

146 One might wonder, for example, if the progress made in Chile would continue if a right-wing head of state came to power. In Poland, for example, the newly established adversarial process was replaced by the former inquisitorial structure following the election of a right-wing government. Only time will tell the extent to which reforms are institutionally entrenched and independent of the politics of those in power.

147 This refers to the legal and constitutional period under the monarchy, preceding the French Revolution in 1789.

a procedure "for which no regional precedent, historical context, or experience exists."[148] It is perhaps not that one procedure is inherently better than another, but rather, the context (especially the political context) in which it operates can serve quickly to distort its aspirations.[149] The truth-seeking neutrality of the judicial enquiry can become a political tool cloaked in legality, unable to be challenged by those accused;[150] the party-centered procedures of adversarialism can facilitate a conviction-oriented process that discourages and even penalizes the exercise of due process rights.

D. International Criminal Justice

The establishment of the United Nations ad hoc international tribunals (such as the International Criminal Tribunal for the former Yugoslavia, ICTY) and the permanent International Criminal Court (ICC) has created the possibility of developing new types of criminal justice that do not conform entirely to existing models.[151] There is much debate as to whether a more adversarial or more inquisitorial structure is best suited to the objectives of international criminal justice,[152] or whether it requires something altogether different. This new context provides a kind of laboratory for the analysis of adversarial and inquisitorial procedures, their claimed benefits, the legal cultures within which they are grounded, the extent to which convergence is possible,[153] and the relationship between the objectives of a criminal process and the best means of their achievement.[154]

Most commentators describe the ad hoc tribunals and the ICC as being established within a predominantly adversarial model (perhaps unsurprisingly, given the common-law background of those responsible for drafting the procedures) with defense and prosecution teams responsible for the investigation and presentation of evidence, and a trial with live witnesses before a fairly passive judge.

148 Nagle (2000: 358).

149 More broadly, on the limitations of transitional justice in Latin America, see Roht-Arriaza (2019). She argues that forced displacement and attacks on human rights and environmental activists continue; that the region is one of the most violent in the world; and that political corruption continues.

150 See empirical accounts of Chinese criminal justice by Mou (forthcoming); McConville and Pils (2013); McConville et al. (2011).

151 For a reflection on the achievements and future challenges of international law see Drumbl (2013).

152 Ambos (2003) notes the ardent loyalty shown by the French and the Americans to their respective procedures. See Vasiliev (2014) for an analysis of the inquisitorial paradigm as it relates to the Extraordinary Chambers in the Courts of Cambodia.

153 Pizzi (2006) argues that the experience of the ICTY shows the myth of convergence.

154 For a discussion of the ways that inquisitorial and adversarial procedural variants have been adapted to administrative procedure in different jurisdictions, see Jacobs et al. (2011).

In the case of the ICTY, an adversarial process was necessary to try to allay fears that the tribunal was politically driven and would achieve little: a procedure that relied upon the benevolence of the state would not engender the necessary trust.[155] Subsequent reforms[156] have increased the role of the judge and placed more reliance on written evidence, and so have been understood as drawing more on the inquisitorial tradition.[157] Some favor this refinement as producing a more effective hybrid system based on the two procedural traditions;[158] others argue for a more decisive move toward civil-law procedure, considering it more efficient and better suited to the task of trying international crimes.[159]

Langer argues that in relation to the ICTY, the reforms represent a move not so much to civil-law procedure, as to the judicial management of what remains a basically adversarial, party-led process.[160] This in turn requires the judge to ground her role within a particular framework; judicial control of the proceedings has not brought efficiency gains in relation to guilty pleas (as discussed subsequently) and Langer and Doherty's own preliminary research suggests that managerial judicial reforms in the ICTY have lengthened rather than shortened both trial and pretrial proceedings.[161] The accused's free choice of defense counsel was an important part of the initial adversarial process, giving the accused a voice with which to challenge accusations.[162] The hope was that this would increase the legitimacy of the tribunal in the eyes of the public and of the accused. As fully adversarial procedures were curtailed, so was the right to waive defense counsel. Combs argues that while this was part of the drive to expedite procedures and to ensure the use of better-quality defense counsel, it also demonstrated the ICTY's confidence in adopting procedures that would have been unthinkable in the early years, when its very legitimacy was in question.[163]

Perhaps such changes have been possible within the relatively short history of international criminal justice because it lacks a legal history or culture on which to draw in the development of its processes and the roles of its legal actors. It

[155] Combs (2012: 325–327).

[156] With very few judgments and an increase in the number of those accused, delay became a major issue. Langer (2005: 869–870).

[157] Ambos (2003); Kay (2004).

[158] E.g., Ambos (2003).

[159] Pizzi (2006). The way in which the advantages of civil-law procedure are presented as almost self-evident ignores all that we know about the myth of the single disinterested investigator and the importance of some coordinate checks on power.

[160] Langer (2005). Jackson (2009) also argues for an active judicial management model, which seeks to maintain the benefit of party investigation, with an active pretrial judicial role.

[161] Langer and Doherty (2009).

[162] The role of defense counsel here is different from that in domestic proceedings: defendants may not be seeking an acquittal, but to voice their version of events, or to attack the legitimacy of the tribunal and its proceedings. Combs (2012: 373–376) argues that the notion of counsel proficiency and independence is rather different in the context of the ICTY.

[163] Combs (2012).

has no "legal grammar" to guide its legislation and judicial interpretation.[164] Lawyers are required to overcome their national procedural loyalties[165] to try to devise an international criminal procedure that is fit for purpose. But with the number of accused increasing, international criminal justice is not immune from the pressure to reduce cost and delay.[166] And just as with domestic systems, once these become the drivers for reform, procedural incoherence and role conflict follow. Human rights standards and procedural integrity may be traded for system efficiencies.[167] Is the prosecution a neutral Ministry of Justice function, or a partisan party in the case? Is this a judge-dominant procedure or a party-led one? The development of the guilty plea procedure provides an example of this clash of legal procedural cultures.

What, if any, is the role for guilty pleas in this context? In terms of process objectives, this will silence witnesses and victims; in terms of procedure, it is party driven and excludes the court from the finding of guilt. Provision is made for an "admission of guilt procedure" in which the accused enters a plea of guilty and then proceeds to sentence, but the court has not interpreted this within an adversarial framework. Instead, it has sought to retain an active role in ensuring the fairness and validity of the plea, as well as taking account of victim testimony in sentencing. Following the Erdemović trial in the ICTY, four requirements were established for a valid guilty plea: the plea must be voluntary, informed, and unequivocal, and there must be sufficient factual basis for the crime and the defendant's participation in it. What makes this different from the adversarial understanding of a guilty plea is the court's continuing active responsibility for the determination of guilt. The court is not bound by the plea agreement made by the parties; neither is it constrained to rely only on the facts as agreed by them. In short, the guilty plea becomes "a mere confession" in the way understood within inquisitorial traditions, where the judge is accustomed to playing a more active and interventionist fact-finding role. Given the mass production of guilty pleas in England and Wales and the United States, concern to ensure the genuine and voluntary nature of such a plea is understandable. In the Erdemović trial, defense representation was inadequate and the plea appeared to be equivocal: the accused admitted killing civilians, but under duress. But even where defendants offer a straightforward plea of guilty, the court's diligence in ensuring that it

164 Delmas-Marty (2008).

165 The extent to which they have been successful in this is debatable. Ambos (2003) includes some interesting anecdotes of French (p. 5) and American (p. 9) reactions to the perception that procedures were too adversarial or too inquisitorial.

166 Langer (2005: 869–870). As well as the usual issues of reducing the number of people in custody awaiting trial, the ICTY needed to speed up procedures in order retain its credibility and international support. See also Jackson and Summers (2012: chap. 5).

167 McIntyre (2003).

meets the four requirements may become counterproductive. Ambos describes a case in East Timor when the accused

> was so intensely questioned by a three judge panel of civil lawyers . . . that he finally gave up trying to convince the judges, especially the African one, that he indeed made the plea in a voluntary, informed and unequivocal way . . . the plea was not accepted and the trial continued in the ordinary manner for quite a long time.[168]

If guilty pleas in international courts are problematic, how much more so is the prospect of plea bargaining? Damaška suggests that while a nonnegotiated admission may increase the legitimacy of international justice, the ICC's dependence on the international community for its legitimacy may make plea bargaining less attractive, given the desire for a public airing of the issues and the unpalatable prospect of "[n]egotiated acts of self-conviction [that] escape the public glare and can thus be exploited by enemies of international justice in order to foment suspicion of improper manipulation of defendants for political or other purposes."[169]

International criminal justice differs from the domestic in all kinds of ways—in the gravity of the crimes it examines and its objectives (which extend beyond mere findings of guilt) as well as its procedures and jurisdiction.[170] There are legal and bureaucratic problems posed for both prosecutors and defense teams in the investigation of international crimes. Obtaining witness evidence can be problematic, as governments may be reluctant to cooperate, and the court has no power to compel them to produce evidence. In the ad hoc tribunals such as the ICTY, the court is the final arbiter on whether the state's national security interests outweigh the need of the court to receive the evidence. Obtaining such evidence in the ICC is likely to be more difficult, as this decision rests with the national state.[171] It should also be noted that in the domestic setting, national security issues tend to arise between the defense and the state authority. In the international justice context it is more likely to be an issue between the prosecution

[168] Ambos (2003: 18). He argues that that "the 'over-regulation' of the guilty plea undermines its very purpose, namely to shorten proceedings" (2003: 17), but compare Turner and Weigend (2013), who point to a range of advantages in the conduct and outcome of guilty pleas.

[169] Damaška (2004: 1031). See also the example of Biljana Plavšić, who accepted a plea bargain at the ICTY, only to renounce her guilt after early release, discussed in Turner (2017: 220).

[170] On plea bargaining and international justice, see further Turner (2017). There are also practical difficulties particular to the international nature of the offenses and the tribunals, such as the linguistic and cultural differences in the evidence gathered and the difficulties in translating these into the two official languages of the court, English and French. Cryer (2006).

[171] Under Article 72 of the Rome Statute, the court may draw adverse inferences as to the (non) existence of a fact as may be appropriate in the circumstances. For a critique of this rule see Schabas (2006).

and the state authority. The defense team faces particular difficulties because they may be gathering evidence several years after the prosecution investigation, when documents may be lost or destroyed and memories have faded. And, as in most domestic legal systems, the defense is structurally disadvantaged both materially and in terms of its limited powers, with no institutional equivalent of the official Office of the Prosecutor.[172] Some argue that this makes an inquisitorial method the obvious choice; a single enquiry will maximize the information obtained and the defense can benefit from full disclosure.[173] This, of course, assumes that the prosecutor is a neutral figure, motivated to collect all relevant evidence, including that which is helpful to the defense. This seems unlikely given the generally adversarial structure within which the prosecutor's role is drawn.[174] She is given an adversarial role, but the court has subsequently developed disclosure rules predicated upon an inquisitorial "minister of justice" understanding of her function—an understanding that McIntyre suggests has been shown to be misplaced.[175] The result, she argues, is that the defense suffers from a real inequality of arms, despite the court's claims to respect fair-trial standards.

This is a real point of tension. Are procedures established for and within the domestic criminal justice setting appropriate for international criminal trials, given the very different nature of the offenses, the accused, and the victims? These are not single acts against single victims, but crimes that have been perpetrated systematically, often through political structures, resulting in mass victimization. Discrepancies between the power and status of offenders and their victims are on a scale not contemplated in national trials. Damaška has argued that concerns of fairness, therefore, might more appropriately be constructed around the interests of the victims rather than the perpetrator.[176] McDermott refutes this, suggesting that other interest-holders should not be seen as having rights deriving from their status as an actor in the trial proceedings, in the way that the right to trial without delay has been extended to victims,[177] and fair-trial rights have been held to apply to the prosecutor as well as the accused.[178]

[172] McIntyre (2003).

[173] E.g., Pizzi (2006).

[174] Langer (2005) sees this as managerial judging, but even this needs an overarching framework within which to operate, a legal grammar.

[175] McIntyre (2003). She describes several instances of prosecutors denying knowledge of material subsequently found to be in their possession. See also Jackson (2009: 34–35).

[176] "In short, some departures by international criminal tribunals from domestic standards of fairness can be justified, given their *sui generis* goals, the complexity and atrocity of crimes they process, and the innate weaknesses of these tribunals. And while it is true that only the defendant has the right to fair trial, the determination of what this right entails does not exclude consideration of the needs generated by the distinctive environment of international criminal justice, including consideration of the interest of other procedural participants affected by this environment." Damaška (2011: 380).

[177] McDermott (2013: 166).

[178] McDermott (2013: 168). For more in-depth treatment of fairness in international criminal trials see McDermott (2016).

Another function of the international tribunals is to establish an accurate account of what happened and to provide victims with the opportunity to tell their stories.[179] It might be argued that domestic trials also have a role in producing a legally recognized truth that goes beyond the simple adjudication of guilt. A public trial in which the issues can be fully aired may be especially important to victims of assault (especially crimes of sexual violence) and the families of homicide victims. This highlights a failing of modern adversarial procedure, in which, when coupled with efficiency concerns, its party-centered nature (in which, ironically, the victim is not a party and has no formal role) can militate against the public provision of justice. Practices such as plea bargaining and the current emphasis on noncourt disposals result not in a public, but in a privately negotiated justice. In the international justice sphere, the legal truth to be established is more complex. The court is not dealing with a single offense, but often a series of events understood through the actions of a political or military regime and a defendant whose first priority may not be acquittal. This poses a different challenge for the conduct of the trial and a stronger motivation to establish an accurate account in order to prevent politically motivated historical revisionism. On the other hand, plea bargaining in some major domestic cases has resulted in evidence helping to convict the co-accused, as well as the discovery of additional crimes and suspects in "supergrass"-type cases. This would enhance the court's ability to produce an accurate historical record.

Is an adversarial trial best suited to allowing victims[180] and witnesses to tell their stories and to establish a factual record? Even without practices such as plea bargaining, adversarial procedure does not favor the spontaneous and unfettered accounts of witnesses; cross-examination and the evidential constraints on trial testimony are likely to limit testimony to issues that go to the guilt or innocence of the accused. Inquisitorial procedure avoids this, but the heavy reliance on written evidence can again undercut the ability of the court to produce a full public account, and there are particular concerns about the accuracy of written witness statements in the international justice context.[181] There are also additional major practical challenges to overcome in trying cases in The Hague that relate to events that took place on another continent.[182] However,

[179] This in turn raises the question of whether the court is engaged in retributive or restorative justice.

[180] Victims had few concrete rights under the statutes of the ad hoc tribunals, but the Statute of Rome permits victims to be legally represented and to be heard.

[181] See Jackson (2009: 31).

[182] In the international context, courts are faced with the practical difficulties of how to select witnesses to testify before the court, sometimes from thousands of people who may have been victims of a series of crimes; how to enable witnesses in another continent to appear at the Hague; and how to guarantee their safety.

the legal procedural framing of legal actors is as important as the legal rules that define their role. Modern procedures with an inquisitorial tradition have public trials with live witnesses in line with ECHR fair-trial standards, but crucially, this operates through a legal culture within which the judge plays an active role. Accordingly, witness testimony that is guided by the trial judge may produce a more accurate account than that elicited by the interested parties.[183] A strong judicial steer at trial is also likely to be necessary in order to prevent defendants from hijacking the procedure and turning it into a show trial in which they play the (often televised) lead performance.

Our view of the most effective legal procedure, as well as the role of legal personnel, will be determined in part by our view of the proper objectives of a criminal process. If the promotion of peace is one objective of international criminal justice, this may be a factor to be taken into account in the prosecutor's exercise of her discretion. Similarly, if justice for victims is an objective, she may choose to prosecute lesser crimes that have impacted on a greater number of people over more grave offenses that affect only a few. This is no easy exercise. The precise scope of international criminal justice objectives is unclear and contested. Damaška has argued that international criminal justice has too many goals—justice for victims, procedural fairness, establishing an official history of events, deterrence, and so on. Rather than trials that promise what cannot be achieved, he favors focusing on a single objective, that of moral teacher. This would enable the court to prioritize fairness as a procedural goal, but in a way more suited to international criminal justice, without being caught up in the more polarized adversarial context. Such an approach would be more conducive to what he considers the paramount and overarching socio-pedagogical function of the court.[184] The court as moral teacher is a more normative approach, and while it has the appeal of transcending procedural differences, it may introduce a new set of differences in opinion.

International criminal justice is different from national systems in many respects, but its procedural evolution, especially around guilty pleas and plea agreements, is influenced in part by its mixed civil- and common-law judicial composition. Turner and Weigend, for example, point to the significance of the ICTY presidency passing to a judge from a US federal district court (where over 95 percent of convictions were obtained through guilty pleas) in the development of guilty pleas and plea bargaining, as a means of increasing the tribunal's efficiency. However, judges from a civil-law background were more skeptical of a procedure that sat less comfortably with their experience working in the inquisitorial tradition. They did not feel obliged to accept plea agreements, and imposed

[183] See also Pizzi (2006).
[184] Damaška (2011).

sentences on defendants that were higher than those negotiated by the parties, diminishing the appeal of plea bargains to defendants.[185]

E. Human Rights and Europe

An important factor influencing contemporary European criminal procedures is the growing body of pan-European law around criminal justice. Running as something of a countercurrent to the discourses of efficiency, managerialism, and security that continue to preoccupy domestic criminal justice is that of procedural fairness at the European level. The due process rights of suspects and accused persons have been developed by the ECtHR as an essential part of the right to a fair trial under Article 6 ECHR,[186] reinforced by the EU's focus on legislation strengthening procedural safeguards.[187] This is not to say that efficiency and security are not their concern: the European Arrest Warrant was agreed immediately following the terrorist attacks of 9/11 in order to make extradition more efficient. But rather, in contrast to criminal procedures at national level, there is considerable emphasis on the effectiveness of fair-trial rights when discussed at the European level. And while these supranational European bodies are made up of representatives of the states that created them,[188] they are sufficiently independent of single national state interests to pose challenges, sometimes unwelcome, to domestic legal arrangements.[189] The variety of legal procedural traditions and cultures that exists within these two Europes (that of the EU and

[185] Turner and Weigend (2013: 1378).

[186] More than 40 percent of ECtHR judgments since 1959 have considered possible violations of Article 6 ECHR. See European Court of Human Rights, Overview 1959–2016, at 6, available at http://www.echr.coe.int/Documents/Overview_19592016_ENG.pdf.

[187] These include the right to information, to an interpreter and translator, to legal assistance, and to legal aid—as well as a measure to strengthen the rights of victims. See the more detailed discussion of ECtHR fair-trial rights and EU measures in Blackstock et al. (2014: 1–35). Also the Victims Directive 2012/29/EU.

[188] The Council of Europe and the ECtHR are made up of representatives from signatory member states. ECtHR judges are elected by the Parliamentary Assembly of the Council of Europe from lists of three candidates provided by each country. As judges, they do not represent the interests of their state, but must remain impartial. For more information on the role and functioning of the ECtHR see http://www.echr.coe.int/Pages/home.aspx?p=home&c=. The EU has a parliamentary process run by democratically elected member state representatives, a rotating EU presidency, and a court (the Court of Justice of the European Union, CJEU) made up of one judge per member state, agreed on by national governments. The CJEU sits in Luxembourg, and its judges are assisted by nine advocates general whose role is to present opinions on the cases brought before the court. This must be done publicly and impartially. For a brief overview of the work of the CJEU see http://europa.eu/about-eu/institutions-bodies/court-justice/index_en.htm.

[189] For an analysis of the politics and motivations of the ECtHR, see Voeten (2008), who notes that while not politically motivated in the geopolitical sense, ECtHR judges have clear policy preferences on the development of human rights. For discussion of the impact on court rulings of threats of non-compliance with the ECJ (European Court of Justice, now known as the CJEU), see Carruba, Gabel, and Hankla (2008).

that of the Council of Europe) inevitably means that some decisions and legislative measures are not well received, perceived as a poor fit with national systems. France, for example, often expresses concern that Article 6 ECHR is interpreted in a way that casts fair-trial rights in adversarial terms, producing ECtHR rulings that fail to appreciate the safeguards provided by the various judicial roles in French criminal procedure.[190] This is perhaps a fair comment: Article 6 ECHR was drafted by UK lawyers, reflecting the more active defense role of adversarial procedure, rather than the truth-seeking responsibility of the court in the inquisitorial tradition. France has sought to address this tension between different procedural values by incorporating the principle of *contradictoire* into its criminal process.[191] In essence, this refers to the right to know the case against you, and to have the opportunity to challenge or respond to accusations or decisions affecting your rights and liberties, in front of a judge.

A key difference between the Council of Europe and the European Union is the nature of states' obligations to comply with the legal norms of these bodies. The ECtHR has a supervisory jurisdiction, ensuring national compliance with Convention norms. It has no real enforcement mechanism through which to implement its judgments, and states are able to resist enacting the necessary changes that flow from an unfavorable decision of the court—sometimes for many years. The UK's resistance for more than a decade to removing the blanket ban on prisoner voting following the decision of *Hirst v. UK* is a case in point. This also demonstrates the sometimes fragile political balance within the Council of Europe. Afraid, perhaps, that the UK would withdraw from the Council completely, the court became less and less robust in its requirements for compliance with *Hirst* and, ultimately, after years of political brinksmanship, the Council declared itself satisfied with a UK measure that saw only a handful of prisoners released on license being enfranchised.[192] States may also

[190] There are various ways in which the judicial nature of the Parquet has been challenged—for example, in authorizing detention and questioning (*Medvedyev v. France* [3394/03] 29 March 2010), and in advising judges at appeal. There has also been long-standing resistance to making provision for a stronger right to custodial legal advice, discussed in detail in chapter 6.

[191] In addition to specific changes to criminal procedure (see Hodgson [2005: 34–38]), France has sought to incorporate the ethos of Article 6 into its criminal process by introducing a new preliminary article to its code of criminal procedure in June 2000, setting out the principle of *contradictoire* as a governing principle across all aspects of its criminal process. The opening sentence is "La procédure pénale doit être équitable et contradictoire et préserver l'équilibre des droits des parties." This applies at trial and during the pretrial process—in pretrial detention hearings, for example.

[192] *Hirst v. UK (No. 2)* (74025/01) 6 October 2005. The balance between law and politics and between the legislature and the judiciary is complex. At the same time as the executive stated publicly that the ECtHR had overstepped its jurisdiction in the sphere of domestic political rights and that it would never give prisoners the vote, a Parliamentary Committee was set up to examine the question and make recommendations, and the Council of Europe was assured that action would follow—though not until after the 2015 general election. See Hodgson and Roach (2017). In December 2017 the UK government announced a compromise, which would see prisoners who had been released on temporary license or home detention curfew now entitled to vote. This would allow around one hundred currently disenfranchised prisoners to vote. Despite the incredibly meager nature of the UK's

be slow to recognize the implications for their own legal arrangements of ECtHR judgments addressed to another state, but which set a benchmark with wider application, such as the role of the prosecutor as judicial officer[193] and the extent to which the right to counsel should be available.[194] As well as focusing on specific criminal procedures, the court has also strengthened aspects of fair-trial rights in ways that challenge broader domestic policy around efficiency and managerialism.[195] The EU is a very different body. While the ECtHR considers cases once national proceedings are complete and remedies have been exhausted, the EU has legislative powers to produce measures that, once transposed into national legislation, must be enforced directly in national courts and a court, the Court of Justice of the European Union (CJEU), that can impose fines for noncompliance. This means that citizens can seek a remedy at the point at which a right is breached, rather than having to wait for all national proceedings and remedies to be exhausted—providing a more powerful incentive to ensure systematic compliance. However, as discussed subsequently, the effectiveness of EU measures will also depend on the more detailed way in which they are implemented within different criminal procedures.[196]

The ECHR is now more than half a century old, established as part of a postwar settlement in which European jurisdictions set out to protect fundamental rights through mutually agreed standards developed by a legal process with supranational jurisdiction. The Convention has been added to and amended, and there now exists a substantial jurisprudence developed by the ECtHR.[197] The relationship between signatory states and the ECtHR is complex and at times uncomfortable. Those founding members of the Council of Europe who drafted the ECHR understood this as "merely a Europeanisation of their own particular national practices of civil rights and 'libertés publiques' . . . an external measure

concession, the Council of Europe said it was satisfied with the package. https://www.theguardian.com/politics/2017/dec/07/council-of-europe-accepts-uk-compromise-on-prisoner-voting-rights. See comment at https://warwick.ac.uk/newsandevents/expertcomment/uk_compromise_on/.

[193] See *Medvedyev v. France* (3394/03) 29 March 2010, discussed in Hodgson (2010), and *Moulin v. France* (37104/06) 23 November 2010. Both are discussed further in chapter 4.

[194] *Salduz v. Turkey* (36391/02) 27 November 2008, discussed in detail in chapter 6. See, e.g., *Cadder v. HM Advocate* [2010] UKSC 43, in which Scotland considered that suspects in its jurisdiction did not require the assistance of counsel during police custody. The Netherlands claimed at first that as Salduz was a minor, the decision applied only to juvenile suspects.

[195] Alt and le Theule (2011) argue that the ECtHR provides an important ethical-judicial framework to protect the trial process from excessive managerialism.

[196] See discussion in chapter 7 of the various ways in which custodial legal advice has been implemented. The EU institutions also monitor implementation. See, e.g., the European Implementation Assessment report prepared for the European Parliamentary Research Service on implementation of the Victims Directive (2012/29/EU) available at http://www.europarl.europa.eu/RegData/etudes/STUD/2017/611022/EPRS_STU(2017)611022_EN.pdf.

[197] The Convention came into force in 1953 and the ECtHR was introduced in 1959. Citizens of the members of the Council of Europe have a right of individual petition to the court.

for an external threat."[198] They were undoubtedly not expecting it to gain such momentum as a living instrument, which would then place their own justice systems under scrutiny. Having crafted an instrument in their own image to some extent, jurisdictions such as the UK and France did not expect to be disciplined by their own creation. The margin-of-appreciation doctrine provides some latitude in the manner in which jurisdictions organize their criminal procedure to give effect to Convention rights. This makes more workable a system in which the judgment of the ECtHR relating to one jurisdiction also applies to the legal systems of forty-six other member countries of the Council of Europe, where the rights and responsibilities of legal actors are shared out differently.[199] But there is also a tension here between legitimate procedural differences in the provision of a fair trial, and a failure to comply with Convention rights.

States also have different constitutional arrangements for giving effect to ECtHR decisions. Countries such as France and the Netherlands adopt a monist approach to international treaties, placing decisions of the ECtHR above their own national laws, even where incompatible with the national constitution.[200] The UK adopts a dualist approach and the ECHR is given domestic effect through the Human Rights Act 1998, section 2 of which requires courts and tribunals "determining a question which has arisen in connection with a Convention right [to] take into account any . . . judgment . . . of the European Court of Human Rights." However, the UK courts have maintained their own supremacy in this, emphasizing the importance of judicial dialogue in the development of European Convention law. In *R v. Horncastle and others*, the UK Supreme Court had to decide whether a conviction based "solely or to a decisive extent" on the statement of a witness that the accused could not cross-examine, amounted to a breach of his right to a fair trial under Article 6 ECHR.[201] English law will, exceptionally, admit the evidence of a witness who is unavailable to testify, but the jurisprudence of the ECtHR has been to find this a breach of the defendant's right to a fair trial.[202] However, the Supreme Court expressed the view that there is room for dialogue between the ECtHR and national courts:

> The requirement to "take into account" the Strasbourg jurisprudence will normally result in this Court applying principles that are clearly established by

[198] Madsen (2004: 57–58).

[199] Although technically, judgments apply only to the state against which the case is brought, they have more general application through the jurisprudence that develops around ECHR rights.

[200] In Germany, the ECHR has the same status as ordinary laws, and so it must be applied directly in the national courts. It ranks below the German Constitution, and so is treated as an interpretive aid by the Federal Constitutional Court. ECtHR decisions must be taken into account by German courts when applying German law.

[201] (2009) UKSC 14.

[202] In particular see *Al-Khawaja and Tahery v. UK* (26766/05 and 2228/06) 20 January 2009.

> the Strasbourg Court. There will, however, be rare occasions where this court has concerns as to whether a decision of the Strasbourg Court sufficiently appreciates or accommodates particular aspects of our domestic process. In such circumstances it is open to this court to decline to follow the Strasbourg decision, giving reasons for adopting this course. This is likely to give the Strasbourg Court the opportunity to reconsider the particular aspect of the decision that is in issue, so that there takes place what may prove to be a valuable dialogue between this Court and the Strasbourg Court.[203]

This was well received by the ECtHR, which upheld the Supreme Court's decision and adjusted its ruling on the inadmissibility of hearsay, agreeing with the UK judges that it should not be applied in an inflexible way.[204]

Partly as a result of the growing number of EU police and judicial cooperation measures with implications for suspects and accused persons,[205] the EU has engaged in a program of measures guaranteeing the procedural rights of suspects through directives with direct applicability across the EU.[206] This includes the right to information in criminal proceedings,[207] the right to interpretation and translation,[208] and the right to access to legal counsel.[209] These safeguards are all fundamental to the right to a fair trial under Article 6 ECHR, but the EU directives define their scope in more precise detail, and in contrast to the ECtHR's margin-of-appreciation doctrine, the directives prescribe legislative change at the national level in order to approximate the laws of Member States. If individuals believe that these directives have been breached, they can rely on the EU measure directly before the national court, making enforcement quicker, simpler, and more effective. The legislative process of the EU means that the directives have been produced after lengthy periods of discussion between Member State representatives, informed by assessments of the impact that the reforms are likely to have on different aspects of the legal process of each Member State—including the financial implications. The closer involvement of Member State political representatives is likely to result in greater "buy-in" from those states, in

203 *R v. Horncastle and others* [2009] UKSC 14 at para. 11.

204 See *Al-Khawaja and Tahery v. UK* (26766/05 and 22228/06) 15 December 2011, in which the strict rule against hearsay was adjusted, and *Horncastle v. UK* (4184/10) 16 December 2014, where this was applied.

205 Evidence, records, and intelligence are all shared in various ways.

206 After various failed attempts, the so-called Roadmap developed under the Swedish presidency of the EU in 2009 set the path for reform. See discussion in chapter 6.

207 Directive 2012/13/EU.

208 Directive 2010/64/EU.

209 Directive 2013/48/EU. Also, the strengthening of the presumption of innocence and the right to be present at trial (Directive 2016/343/EU); the right to legal aid (Directive 2016/1919/EU); and, recognizing the particular vulnerability of children, the directive on procedural safeguards for child suspects and accused in criminal proceedings (Directive 2016/800/EU).

contrast to the scope for claims of nonapplicability raised under the margin-of-appreciation doctrine.

The harmonizing effect, and indeed objectives, of EU measures should not be overstated, however. First, directives do not apply to all Member States. Shaped by concerns around national sovereignty and a resistance to EU involvement in domestic policy, after the 2009 Lisbon Treaty merged police and judicial cooperation in criminal matters into the main EU framework, with qualified majority voting and initiatives subject to the supranational institutions of the EU, the UK negotiated a block opt-out option in 2014.[210] This meant that it would only opt in to criminal justice matters if it explicitly chose to do so—a choice that it immediately exercised by rejoining thirty-five measures later the same year. The UK's general approach has been to opt in to measures around police and prosecution cooperation, most notably the European Arrest Warrant (EAW), but in general, to refuse to adopt measures for the provision of procedural safeguards.[211] Other states have also adopted this selective approach. Denmark has opted out of borders, asylum, immigration, and justice policies; the UK, Poland, and the Czech Republic secured exemptions from the Charter of Fundamental Rights; and Denmark opted out of Europol, following a referendum on the issue.

Second, the successful implementation of directives is determined in part by the nature of the various domestic criminal procedures within which they are put into practice. The cornerstone of EU criminal justice cooperation is the principle of mutual recognition, whereby the legal decisions of one Member State are recognized and acted on by another Member State, in the same way that it would implement a decision from its own courts. This enables Member States to implement safeguards and procedures within the scope of their own procedure, without having to agree on detailed and identical processes and personnel. This is the essence of the EAW, for example. Instead of a lengthy political process of extradition, the EAW is a universal judicial procedure that enables requests from a Member State for the surrender of an individual for prosecution or sentence to be acted on with the minimum of formality.[212] The success of this broad mutual recognition approach, however, is also part of its weakness. Directives risk having a differential impact across Member States, as they continue to depend to some extent on the

210 For discussion of the impact of the UK's decision to opt out, see Mitsilegas, Carrera, and Eisele (2014).

211 The UK also opted into the EU Victims Directive 2012/29/EU, which established minimum standards on the rights, support, and protection of victims of crime. States were required to implement the directive by 15 November 2015. The European Protection Order was also adopted by the UK and transposed into law in 2014. This seeks to protect victims by giving effect to restrictions placed on an accused both pre- and posttrial.

212 For broader discussion, see Hodgson (2011). The EAW was proposed one week after the New York attacks of 11 September 2001. One of the first UK requests under the EAW procedure resulted in the successful return from Italy of Hussain Osman, suspected of attempting to blow up a train on the London Underground at Shepherd's Bush on 21 July 2005.

individual procedures in place.[213] For example, the role of victims is very different across European jurisdictions. In England and Wales, the victim has no formal standing; in France, by constituting herself as *partie civile*, she may participate in the investigation and claim damages for the harm suffered as a victim of crime. The implementation and impact of the Victims Directive, therefore, will vary as between states.[214] The detail within some directives—such as how private lawyer-suspect consultations should be organized, or the remedies for breach of directive rights—is often left to states to determine. This results in different practices and the stronger enforcement of rights in some jurisdictions than in others.[215]

Underpinning procedures that depend on mutual recognition is the existence of mutual trust in the legal systems and processes of EU Member States. If Member States are to share intelligence and information with one another,[216] conduct investigations on behalf of another state,[217] or surrender their citizens into the custody of another Member State, it is vital that they are able to trust one another's systems of criminal justice to protect the rights of accused persons and victims, and to conduct criminal investigations with integrity. All EU states are members of the Council of Europe and so are bound by the ECHR, but the increased obligations arising from EU police and judicial cooperation demand greater reassurances that citizens will be treated fairly when prosecuted or sentenced elsewhere.[218] This motivated the EU procedural safeguards for suspects and accused persons, designed to ensure that fair-trial protections were given meaningful effect across the EU. If a French citizen is surrendered to Italy, for example, the French authorities will want to have confidence that their citizen will be treated fairly. Brexit poses a huge challenge to this, as it moves in the opposite direction—away from mutual trust and recognition and toward what are likely to be clumsy and inferior bilateral agreements.[219]

[213] See the discussion of EAW procedures, for example, in Hodgson (2011).

[214] See DG Guidance Document related to the transposition of Directive 2012/29/EU, which states: "Since the formal role of victims in criminal proceedings varies significantly between Member States, the implementation of these Articles will be different to some extent and influence the particular procedural consequences and the extent of the rights of the victims set out in this Directive" (2013: 4), at http://ec.europa.eu/justice/criminal/files/victims/guidance_victims_rights_directive_en.pdf.

[215] For discussion of the different remedies in EU states for breach of the right to counsel, see Soo (2018).

[216] Establishing alerts under the Schengen Information System; sharing intelligence through Europol; sharing fingerprints of asylum seekers said to be "irregular" through Eurodac; exchanging fingerprint and DNA records or car registrations through the EU Prüm Convention; the European Criminal Records Information System (ECRIS); the Passenger Name Records (PNR) Directive, agreed after the Paris attacks; and sharing evidence through the European Investigation Order.

[217] Under the European Investigation Order.

[218] See general discussion of the emergence of an EU defense agenda in Hodgson (2011).

[219] For example, extradition with non-EU countries follows a political, rather than judicial, procedure. Determined by the secretary of state, such cases take three times as long on average and cost four times as much, according to the CPS (see House of Lords European Union Committee

Security cooperation with the EU is fundamental to mutual trust and recognition and was one of the government's four overarching objectives in Brexit negotiations. However, the thirty-five measures immediately opted back into post-Lisbon, considered vital to the national interest and the security of UK citizens, are in jeopardy as a result of Brexit. Access to information and intelligence sourced through EU databases is described by the senior national coordinator for counterterrorism policing in the Metropolitan Police Service as "mission critical";[220] access to the Schengen Information System is described as "an absolute game-changer for the UK" by the National Crime Agency.[221] However, the UK's ability post-Brexit to continue to benefit from criminal cooperation measures such as the EAW and intelligence sharing through Europol remains unclear unless assurances of equivalent data protection and safeguarding are in place and some oversight and accountability role for the CJEU is agreed.[222] As a non-EU Member State the UK will not be able to request the return of those it seeks to prosecute, for example, but equally, individuals residing in the UK wanted by the other twenty-seven Member States will not be able to be extradited through the EAW.[223]

Although separate, the ECHR has been extremely influential in the development of human rights protection in the EU. All EU Member States have acceded to the ECHR, and, accordingly, the Convention forms part of the shared legal values and principles that the CJEU will take into account in its own decision-making. It has done this since at least the 1970s, moving from the earlier more restrained language of "drawing inspiration from the common constitutional traditions of Member States" to direct references to the rights guaranteed under

[2016: para. 136]). The major high-profile cases of Gary McKinnon (wanted by the United States for hacking) and Khaled Al Fawaaz (an alleged associate of Osama bin Laden) took six and fourteen years respectively.

220 House of Lords European Union Committee (2016: para. 86).

221 House of Lords European Union Committee (2016: para. 89).

222 For discussion of some of the UK's post-Brexit issues, see Davidson (2017); Mitsilegas (2016). Furthermore, without a seat at the table, the UK will be unable to influence the development of measures, policies, and institutional structures of cooperation that are fundamental to the safety of UK citizens. For example, after the Paris attacks, the European Commission proposed extending the exchange of criminal records information to third-country nationals. Proposal for a Directive amending Council Framework Decision 2009/315/JHA as regards the exchange of information on third country nationals as regards the European Criminal Records Information System (ECRIS) and replacing Council Decision 2009/316/JHA, COM(2016) 7 final.

223 This is significant. According to National Crime Agency statistics there were just 3 extradition requests to the UK in 1962, 19 in 1973, and in 2003, the year before the EAW came into force, there were 114. Numbers have steadily increased under the EAW procedure, rising sharply in recent years to 14,279 requests made to the UK in 2015–16. France, Germany, Italy, Poland, and Romania account for around half of all requests. The UK made 241 requests to other Member States. https://nationalcrimeagency.gov.uk/who-we-are/publications?search=May+2016&category%5B%5D=4&limit=20&tag=&tag=.

the ECHR,[224] and many of the ECHR guarantees are now also contained (and specifically referenced) in the EU's own Charter of Fundamental Rights. The two systems will be more closely intertwined if the planned accession of the EU to the ECHR is ever agreed upon. However, the CJEU has so far rejected this idea, because as a contracting party to the ECHR, EU law and institutions would be subject to the scrutiny of the ECtHR. It is hoped that accession would ensure greater confluence of the two jurisdictions, especially given the ECtHR's recent success in drastically reducing its case backlog,[225] though the impact on individuals' right to seek redress is unclear given the preponderance of cases brought to the EU by large companies rather than individuals. For its part, the CJEU would not be able simply to take account of the ECHR, as it does currently, but would be required to determine the hierarchical status of the ECHR within the EU legal order.[226] National courts would continue to be key in applying the decisions of the CJEU and the ECtHR, and so determining their scope, but under post-accession arrangements, there would be new scope for a human rights judicial discourse between the CJEU and the ECtHR as part of the "on-going process in which European systems of human rights protection become increasingly interwoven and interlocked."[227] There is also a risk that accession might bring confusion and uncertainty. The Court of Justice has rejected the draft agreement for accession on the grounds that it lacked sufficient protection of the EU's specific legal arrangements and the court's exclusive jurisdiction. The EU has stated repeatedly that it remains committed to accession, but it is likely to be a lengthy process.[228] It is likely, therefore, that the UK's exit from the EU will also have implications, even if only indirectly, for its relationship with the ECHR.

[224] See, e.g., Case 11/70, *Internationale Handelsgesellschaft mbH v. Einfuhr- und Vorratstelle für Getreide und Futtermittel* (1970) ECR 1125, in which this principle was accepted; Case 4/73 *Nold* (1974) ECR 491; and more recently, Case C-60/00 *Carpenter* (2002) ECR I-6279, in which the applicant's right to family life under Article 8 ECHR was recognized as "among the fundamental rights which . . . are protected in Community law" (para. 41). See also Maduro and Azoulai (2010).

[225] The court has been very successful in reducing its backlog in recent years. It has a new section of the court dedicated specifically to filtering cases, and while still focusing on the more complex issues in its judgments, it now joins together cases raising the same issue. So, in 2013, it delivered 916 judgments, but these concerned 3,659 applications. It decided a total of 93,397 applications (compared with 87,879 in 2012; 52,188 in 2011) and at the end of 2013, had 99,990 applications pending (compared with 128,100 at the end of 2012; 151,600 at the end of 2011).

[226] Eckes (2013: 284).

[227] Eckes (2013: 285).

[228] After nearly three years of discussion, a draft agreement between the forty-seven members of the Council of Europe countries and the EU Commission was produced in 2013. The CJEU was asked to comment on whether the agreement was compatible with the EU treaties, and in its judgment in December 2014, the court said that it was not. (See CJEU Press Release 180/14, 18 December 2014, Opinion 2/1.) There are clearly major issues that remain to be ironed out, including the coordination of interpretations of the EU Charter and the ECHR and how the EU as a contracting party cannot realistically be treated in the same way as a single country. The Commission has included accession in its work program in 2016 and 2017.

These supranational systems of rights and justice have much to recommend them as an additional grounding force in what is sometimes a battle at state level between the judiciary and the legislature (or in reality, the government) in defining the scope and meaning of fundamental rights. Yet even here we see the schematics of efficiency, streamlining, and caseload management creeping in, in ways that threaten to undermine the universality of protection offered, especially to the most vulnerable. The ECtHR continually emphasizes the importance of rights being "practical and effective" and not simply "theoretical and illusory," but it risks falling foul of its own standards when cases are summarily dismissed without any judicial consideration of the extreme contexts in which they took place or the difficulties applicants face in pursuing domestic remedies.[229]

Domestic legal systems' concern with efficiency also conflicts with ECtHR jurisprudence and EU measures that seek to strengthen defense rights as part of the overall fair-trial guarantee. This has been felt especially strongly in inquisitorially rooted jurisdictions such as France, where ECtHR decisions and the recent EU directives providing procedural safeguards for suspects require the strengthening of defense rights.[230] These changes are seen as procedurally alien to French criminal procedure, introducing an additional layer of complexity considered unnecessary given the judicial protections in place—in theory at least.[231] Furthermore, these externally driven reforms have been added to existing procedures in a piecemeal way without any restructuring of the overall balance of rights and responsibilities as between legal actors or legal procedures. The growing complexity of criminal procedure is often lamented by legal actors and has been the subject of various reviews in France.[232] In its consideration

[229] Drawing on recent examples of applicants to the ECtHR whose families have been murdered during political conflict, sometimes by state security forces themselves, Tickell argues that the strict application of time limits from the point at which domestic remedies have been exhausted is potentially grossly unfair. Where applicants lack the means to pay for legal representation and the state responsible for investigating (and even committing) the crime is obfuscating the investigation process, it seems inappropriate to accuse applicants of negligence or of lacking due diligence. "There are serious questions about whether the Court's peremptory tone in these decisions is appropriate, given their tragic circumstances, the prima facie violations of fundamental rights they disclose and the understandable challenges faced by marginalised and economically disadvantaged applicants doing their best to navigate complex national and international legal proceedings . . . It may be considerably more challenging for inexpert, unadvised applicants to produce complete cases within four-months, where the effectiveness of domestic remedies is unclear and the issues have not been analysed in national courts." Tickell (2015: 212–213)

[230] It is also a result of the lengthy and bureaucratic style of many EU directives, not just those relating to defense rights. See, e.g., the Victims Directive 2012/29/EU, which contains seventy-two paragraphs of recitals (the preamble explaining the reasons for the contents of the directive).

[231] Jackson (2016b: 183) attributes resistance to custodial legal advice to "an unwillingness across Member States and legal traditions alike to embrace a particular vision of active defence participation that would disturb the management of cases in the pre-trial phase of criminal procedure."

[232] For example, the Truche Commission (1997); Léger Commission (2009).

of the transposition of EU measures into national law, for example, the 2014 Beaume Report for the French Ministry of Justice did not address head-on the need to restructure or recalibrate the responsibilities of different legal actors, but proposed instead to simplify proceedings so that the same degree of written formality was not required in all cases. However, ensuring the fairness of procedures and the effective protection of defense rights is more, rather than less, labor intensive, and care must be taken not to allow concerns with "simplification" and "efficiency" to undermine the spirit of the defense reforms.[233]

The ways in which rights are interpreted differently by the courts of the two Europes (the ECtHR and the CJEU) may also pose challenges to the promotion of uniform protections across European states and may even serve to restrict them. Given that EU directives providing procedural safeguards to suspects have their basis in the rights set out in the ECHR, the courts will have regard to ECtHR decisions when interpreting these measures.[234] However, directives do not simply replicate Convention protections: they provide additional detail and are designed to provide rights, remedies, and safeguards that are the same as or greater than those set out in the Convention. The danger is that if the Strasbourg jurisprudence does not keep pace with these additional rights, reliance on decisions of the ECtHR may, paradoxically, have the effect of restricting unduly the scope of the procedural protections provided by EU measures.

In the case of *Ibrahim and others v. UK*, the ECtHR retreated from its robust approach to the exclusion of evidence obtained from suspects denied custodial legal advice, expressed in *Salduz*.[235] If national courts interpret the directive on access to counsel alongside developing ECtHR jurisprudence, without daring to go beyond this, there is a risk not only of conflicting approaches, but also the weakening of EU protections. The effectiveness of EU measures depends

[233] Illuminati (2005: 578) argues that the shorter dossier-based inquisitorial system is seen as more efficient than the adversarial system of trial scrutiny: "[T]he inquisitorial system is cheaper and quicker as it solves the issues of guilt with a single investigative effort." In the UK, a more inquisitorial model of justice has been proposed as a way of saving money and as being more efficient. See, e.g., the Toynbee Hall think piece reported by *The Guardian* at https://www.theguardian.com/law/2018/aug/02/adopt-inquisitorial-criminal-justice-system-in-uk-charity-urges.

[234] All of the directives emanating from the Roadmap contain nonregression clauses (so that they do not have the effect of limiting the rights provided for by the ECHR) but also require that they be interpreted in the light of the ECHR and the jurisprudence of the ECtHR. For example, recital 6 of the directive on custodial legal assistance (2013/48/EU) provides that "strengthening mutual trust requires detailed rules on the protection of procedural rights and guarantees arising from . . . the ECHR. It also requires, by means of this Directive . . . further development within the Union of the minimum standards set out in . . . the ECHR."

[235] Applications 50541/08, 50571/08, 50573/08, and 40351/09, ECtHR 13 September 2016.

on recognition of their autonomy in developing fair-trial rights, allowing interpretations that surpass those of the ECHR. Without this, EU measures lose their force and become ineffective. For example, in May 2016, the Estonian Supreme Court rejected the argument that the directive on the right to information in criminal proceedings provided greater protections for the suspect than had the ECHR. Considering it an acte clair, the court followed the (more restrictive) jurisprudence of the ECtHR.[236]

[236] Soo (2017: 341–345). She attributes this in part to the national court's difficulty in accepting the autonomy and supremacy of EU law in the area of criminal procedure (2017: 342). Discussed in more detail in chapter 6.

2

The Demise of Procedural Fairness

Systems of criminal procedure evolve over centuries, responding to social, legal, political, and economic developments, as well as more historically fixed phenomena such as political revolution, terrorist attacks, or miscarriages of justice. The beginning of what would eventually become the English system of jury trial, for example, can be traced back to the decision of the church in 1215 to condemn trial by ordeal—a practice that had been the official mode of trial in Western Europe for centuries. Neither are procedures shaped by a single power or body: the legislature, the judiciary, legal and political cultures, international treaties and obligations, and the practices that develop through the everyday workings of the courts and the criminal justice system, all combine in different measure to influence the continuing development of systems and practices of criminal procedure. In Germany, for example, as in England and Wales, lawyers and judges had long practiced forms of plea bargaining before this was formalized into statute. The politics of criminal justice also plays a part, whether in the competitive rhetoric of recent decades around being "tough on crime," or in the positioning of different government ministries in the development of policy. In France, the balance struck between fair-trial rights on the one hand, and security and repression on the other, has at times depended on which ministry is sponsoring the legislation: stronger procedural rights for the accused and fair-trial principles of equality of arms were promoted through the justice minister's legislation in 2000, only to have core protections removed or undermined by subsequent reforms enacted at the behest of the interior minister.[1]

In recent years, we have seen a variety of common trends reflected in criminal justice discourse across Europe and beyond. Preoccupations with managerialism, efficiency, security, dangerousness, and the prevention of risk pervade the arrangement of our processes of criminal justice, manifested through a variety of mechanisms for the avoidance of trial, the avoidance even of a full investigation, and the rapid disposal of cases. Values of procedural fairness are disappearing from view, replaced by a form of administrative crime control and

[1] For example, the police were, for the first time, required to inform suspects of their right to silence under the 2000 reform, but this was repealed in March 2003 in the interior minister's *loi pour la sécurité intérieure*. This reflects, in part, the tension in the balance of responsibilities, but also the change in government from that led by the Socialist Party's Lionel Jospin to the right-wing Raffarin administration in 2002.

The Metamorphosis of Criminal Justice. Jacqueline S. Hodgson, Oxford University Press (2020).

DOI: 10.1093/oso/9780199981427.001.0001

the elevation of security concerns. Typically, the prosecutor finds herself at the center of things, diluting otherwise judicial procedures and responsible for the disposition as well as the prosecution of cases. Police powers have also increased, justified through a narrative of justice for victims, designed to attract the empathy and support of voters, but in practice providing victims with few concrete improvements. Increased crime control has been rebranded as freedom through security.[2] From terrorism to knife crime, from the sexual exploitation of children to antisocial behavior, successive governments have sought to demonstrate that they can deliver on crime.

Setting the scene for the discussion of particular criminal justice actors and the shifts in criminal procedural traditions and practices, this chapter and the next sketch briefly some of the broad trends in criminal justice in recent decades, reflecting on the changes in process values that they have encouraged in England and Wales and France. This chapter considers the ways in which values of procedural fairness were strengthened in the two criminal justice traditions during the late twentieth century, and how these have subsequently been eclipsed by broader concerns with managerialism, efficiency, and crime control, as both France and England and Wales move inexorably toward what might be described as an administrative system of criminal justice. The next chapter develops this further, exploring how these trends facilitated the concepts of prevention, security, and the management of risk, and their reflection in our criminal procedures, as well as criminal law.

A. Procedural Fairness

Accusatorial characteristics are an essential feature of a fair trial under Article 6 ECHR,[3] and a number of jurisdictions across the world have adopted or adapted a more adversarial approach with a view to strengthening the independence and fairness of their criminal processes. The presumption of innocence and standards of fairness as between the parties are of paramount importance within the adversarial tradition, and there is strong resistance from academics,

[2] For example, in 2002, the French interior minister, Nicolas Sarkozy, described security as a "fundamental right and the most important freedom." Article 1 of Loi No. 95-73 du 21 janvier 1995 d'orientation et de programmation relative à la sécurité. Also see the presentation of the Projet de loi pour la sécurité intérieure to the conseil des ministres, 23 October 2002. This idea is rather like Packer's (1968) crime control model in which the repression of criminal conduct guarantees social freedom.

[3] As well as the separation of the prosecution and judicial functions, an accusatorial procedure implies a greater role for the defense in knowing the nature of the prosecution case and being able to respond to it. Adversarial procedure goes further still in placing responsibility for the collection, selection, and presentation of evidence with the parties. In this way, it reflects more profoundly the nature of the pretrial process as well as the trial.

civil rights organizations, lawyers, and others when these core due process values come under threat.[4] Yet, in England and Wales, adversarialism is a procedural value rarely celebrated by ministers (or even judges) as producing fairness and balance in the criminal process. Instead, it is often portrayed as an unhelpful procedural complexity benefiting the accused, undermining the effectiveness of the investigation, and clogging up the courts. Yet if we look back several decades, we see a rather different narrative to the procedural reforms of that time and, most strikingly, a strong narrative around fairness in the judicial pronouncements in miscarriage of justice cases.

In England and Wales, the Royal Commission on Criminal Procedure (RCCP), chaired by Sir Cyril Philips, was established after the wrongful conviction of three youths for the murder of Maxwell Confait. Reporting in 1981, the commission made recommendations that were designed to prevent the kinds of system failures that had characterized the Confait affair, in which vulnerable suspects were pressured to make false confessions, with no available legal advice, no appropriate adult present, and no independent check on the police decision to prosecute. The report was underpinned by clear adversarial principles, while also recognizing the need for a pragmatic approach to produce a "fair, open, workable and efficient" criminal justice process.[5] It resulted in two major pieces of legislation: the Police and Criminal Evidence Act 1984 (PACE) and the Prosecution of Offences Act 1985, which established the Crown Prosecution Service (CPS). In many ways, these reforms and the case law of this period represent the high point of modern adversarial criminal procedure in Britain, in their aspirations at least.[6]

The stated aims of PACE were to strike a clear balance between the rights of the suspect and the powers of the police. Thus, while the authority of the police was strengthened, defense rights were also placed on a statutory footing in order to go some way to counterbalance this increase in police power. The statutory right to custodial legal advice, free at the point of delivery, was perhaps the most important reform in this respect. Section 58 PACE provided for private lawyer-client consultations and permitted suspects to have their lawyer present during the tape-recorded police interrogation. Vulnerable suspects were to be assisted by an appropriate adult, and the detention of all suspects was to be overseen by the custody officer, a police officer unconnected with the case, responsible for the suspect's welfare during detention—including the administration of the suspect's

[4] See, for example, the scale of the response to the recommendations in the RCCJ's 1993 report, e.g., three prominent edited collections: Field and Thomas (1994), McConville and Bridges (1994), and Walker and Starmer (1999).

[5] RCCP (1981) para. 10.1.

[6] For a historical perspective on the development of the adversarial trial see Langbein (2003), and on the defense role in particular see Hodgson (2005: 105–112).

rights—as well as ensuring that detention is conducted within the statutory custody time limits.

However, in practice, these adversarial aspirations were not met. The police found ways to circumvent the regulation of their powers, preferring their tried-and-tested practices and avoiding the safeguards set out in PACE,[7] such that suspects' experience of custody was more akin to a closed inquisitorial process in which they were unable to participate. Defense lawyers, or more often the clerks they sent in their place, failed to engage in active defense, serving only to legitimate the process by providing the illusion of due process protections for the accused.[8]

The Prosecution of Offences Act 1985 established the first independent centralized prosecution service in England and Wales,[9] the CPS, removing the decision to prosecute from the police to an independent lawyer, and so separating out the investigative and prosecution roles. The RCCP aimed to ensure greater uniformity of prosecution decision-making and a degree of legal objectivity, to ensure that weak cases were not brought before the courts. The introduction of a public prosecutor represented a radical change, with the possibility of a more "Ministry of Justice" function, as enjoyed by prosecutors in inquisitorially rooted systems. In practice, it proved harder to establish CPS independence from the police.

Although the realities of criminal justice practice were some way from the adversarial ideals set out in the legislation, the rhetoric of the law aspired to empower the defense and to regulate aspects of policing in a way not seen in subsequent reform.[10] This contrasts starkly with contemporary criminal justice rhetoric of ever-increasing police powers and the co-opting of the defense toward the managerialist imperatives of system efficiency. There is no room for the idealism of adversarial values of fairness in today's criminal process.

In addition to statutory reform, a stronger adherence to adversarial values can also be detected in some sectors of the judiciary at this time. In the decade following PACE, the appeal courts set down a number of decisions that reinforced the integrity of the criminal process as an adversarial procedure. In particular, they recognized the disadvantages experienced by accused persons who face a police and prosecution service that is better resourced and better equipped in terms of legal investigative powers. A series of cases made clear that, in order to

[7] Bottomley et al. (1991); Dixon et al. (1990); McConville et al. (1991).

[8] McConville and Hodgson (1993); McConville et al. (1994). After the implementation of a training and accreditation program, standards improved considerably (Bridges and Choongh [1998]), though the general picture of defense lawyering remains bleak. See generally Newman (2013) and, re legal aid cuts, Flynn and Hodgson (2017).

[9] The Scots have long had a procurator fiscal in charge of prosecutions.

[10] The Human Rights Act 1998 is perhaps the only exception, offering greater potential for the assertion of rights in all areas.

reduce the obvious inequality of arms, the prosecution had a duty to disclose all material gathered during the investigation, including that which might undermine its case. In the infamous Birmingham Six case,[11] the court stated:

> A disadvantage of the adversarial system may be that the parties are not evenly matched in resources. . . . But the inequality of resources is ameliorated by the obligation on the part of the prosecution to make available all material which may prove helpful to the defence.[12]

All unused material was to be preserved unless it was incapable of having an impact on the case or there were good reasons for withholding the evidence.[13] The test of relevance was not one for the prosecution, but ultimately, for the court.[14] In several high-profile miscarriages of justice, the prosecution had withheld material that would have been helpful to the defense and wholly undermined the prosecution; it was only when this evidence was finally uncovered that those wrongly convicted were freed. As the Court of Appeal stated, "[I]n our adversarial system in which the police and the prosecution control the investigatory process, an accused's right to disclosure is an inseparable part of his right to a fair trial."[15]

In France, the reforms of 1993 and 2000 reflect a similar high point of procedural fairness, in which equality of arms and the rights of the accused were also strengthened.[16] The French procedural tradition is different from that in England and Wales, resting on the principle of judicial rather than party-led investigation, and so a different allocation of roles and responsibilities among legal actors. The ways in which procedural fairness might be strengthened, therefore, are also different. Although resembling the due process principles found in

[11] See *R v. McIlkenny (Richard) and others* (1991) 93 Crim. App. R. 287. Paddy Hill, Richard McIlkenny, Johnny Walker, Billy Power, Hugh Callaghan, and Gerry Hunter were convicted in 1975 of the murder of twenty-one people in two pub bombings in Birmingham in 1974. In 1991, after sixteen years of imprisonment and two unsuccessful appeals, the Court of Appeal quashed their convictions; it found that the two main pieces of evidence against the men (forensic and confession evidence) were discredited. See also Belloni and Hodgson (2000: 6–14, 126–128) for a discussion of other high-profile miscarriages of justice around this time.

[12] *McIlkenny* (1991) 93 Crim. App. R. at 312.

[13] "Unused material" is understood to mean any information that has some bearing on the case, such as witness statements, that is not included in the committal bundles.

[14] See the "Guinness Advice" issued by the Director of Public Prosecutions (DPP) of England and Wales in 1992, reprinted in Walker and Starmer (1999: 123–127). As applied in *R v. Ward (Judith Theresa)* (1993) 96 Crim. App. R. 1.

[15] Per Lord Justice Steyn in *R v. Brown (Winston)* (1994) 1 W.L.R. 1599, 1606. In this line of cases, the force of the judicial argument was strengthened by the assertion of the right to a fair trial as a common-law right, rather than one depending on the ECHR. The court also made clear that the accused's right to a fair trial is linked to its own ability to reach the correct decision. Without proper disclosure, the court, as well as the accused, was deprived of all the relevant facts.

[16] For more detailed discussion, see Hodgson (2005: chap. 2). Also Colson and Field (2011).

England and Wales (a procedure considered alien and, to some extent, inferior to that of France), these new safeguards were considered more palatable by being drawn from the ECHR, which already occupied an established place in French legal discourse.[17] Following the 1991 criminal justice and human rights commission report chaired by Mireille Delmas-Marty,[18] France introduced a number of new procedural protections that, while retaining the inquisitorial framework of judicial supervision,[19] were expressly inspired by the ECHR and the principle of equality of arms.

Like PACE, the 1993 legislation sought to regulate better the period of police detention of suspects (the *garde à vue*), requiring for the first time that the public prosecutor, the procureur, be informed of, and authorize, all detentions and that suspects be permitted to inform someone of their detention, see a doctor, and most radically of all, see a lawyer. Strengthening the role of the procureur in overseeing the police detention of suspects safeguards the liberties of the suspect through judicial supervision as the prosecutor is also a *magistrat* and so a judicial officer. The presence of this protection, however, means that the role of the lawyer is considered less important. Suspects were permitted a thirty-minute consultation with their lawyer, twenty hours after the start of the *garde à vue*, but the lawyer was not permitted to be present during the police questioning of the suspect.[20]

Following a number of legal and political scandals in which politicians and powerful business people were implicated, and executive interference was suspected,[21] Pierre Truche, then president of the appeal court, the Cour de cassation, was asked to chair the Commission de réflexion sur la justice (1997). The commission was asked to look into reducing the costs, delays, and complexity of the criminal process, to strengthen its independence from government, and to strengthen the rights of the accused, including the presumption of innocence. Once again, progressive reforms followed, increasing the pretrial defense role, but in a way that complemented rather than challenged the dominance of judicial supervision.

The legislation in 2000 introduced a new preliminary article sitting at the head of the Code de procédure pénale (CPP), which informs French criminal

[17] This reflects France's monist constitution, in contrast to the dualist position in England and Wales, discussed in chapter 1.

[18] The Commission justice pénale et droits de l'homme, 1991.

[19] The commission's more radical proposals to separate out more clearly the investigative and prosecution functions were not taken up.

[20] The significance of this modest intrusion of the lawyer onto police territory and into space regulated by the *procureur* was apparent from the very strong resistance exhibited by police and *magistrats* alike—as they took to the streets and burned their codes of criminal procedure in front of the Ministry of Justice.

[21] See Godard (2002).

procedure as a whole. It expresses the importance of equality of arms, the presumption of innocence, and the right of the accused to a defense and to know the charges against her, all grounded in the principle of *contradictoire*—the right to participate and to be heard. A new judge, the *juge des libertés et de la détention*, was created, removing from the *juge d'instruction* (the judge responsible for investigating serious cases) the decision to remand in custody those investigated under the *instruction* process.[22] Suspects were allowed access to legal advice from the start of the *garde à vue*,[23] and for the first time, the police were required to inform the suspect of her right to silence. The suspect's rights to participate in the *instruction* were also improved, allowing her to request acts of investigation in the same way as the procureur. The rhetoric of this reform was positive and, once again, clearly inspired by the ECHR and the belief that fair-trial principles apply across all procedural traditions. In presenting her reform project, then-justice minister Elisabeth Guigou highlighted the importance of the rights of the defense in any fair and equitable criminal process—quite a radical proposition in a procedure dominated by a philosophy of judicial supervision and the judicial protection of the rights of the individual.

However, the promotion of fairness as a procedural value was soon to be displaced by security and crime control concerns. The gains made in 2000 were pulled back as then-minister of interior Nicolas Sarkozy, undercut Justice Ministry reforms, portraying them as being soft on crime. He introduced legislation removing suspects' rights, expanding police powers and criminalization, providing for more rapid trial procedures and draconian sentencing powers, and exhibiting a growing preoccupation with security over process rights. As the French newspaper *Le Monde* put it: in the government's war on crime, it is Sarkozy who prepared the battle plan.[24]

In Britain, too, due process gains were to be reversed, but not through the ideologies of competing ministries. While miscarriages of justice resulted in the judicial strengthening of a fair-trial model promoting equality of arms, ironically, they also led to a Royal Commission report whose recommendations led to the removal of core adversarial principles and the imposition of new obligations on the defense, based on a preoccupation with efficiency and misunderstandings of inquisitorialism.[25] The judicial culture of fair-trial protections was displaced

[22] France had been condemned for the length of time suspects were kept in pretrial custody during the *instruction*. For example, in *Tomasi v. France* (12850/87) 27 August 1992, a detention period of five and a half years before being eventually acquitted was held to be unjustified. Eighty percent of those in prison were in pretrial detention and half of those on the order of the *juge d'instruction*.

[23] The justice minister told the Sénat on 15 June 1999 that only 10 percent of suspects had been able to access custodial legal advice under existing arrangements.

[24] *Le Monde*, 17 July 2002.

[25] See the rich seam of scholarship that emerged in response to the RCCJ's recommendations, including Field and Thomas (1994); McConville and Bridges (1994); Walker and Starmer (1999).

by a legislative program set in train by the Conservative administration in 1994 and which, though opposed by Labour when in opposition, was then taken up enthusiastically when Labour came to power in 1997.[26]

In both jurisdictions, these changes were heralded as ways of modernizing and simplifying criminal justice, avoiding the delays of lengthy and complex procedures. This invocation of system efficiency in purely positive terms masks the more ideologically driven desire to remove due process safeguards that protect fundamental rights and which ensure some degree of equality of arms.[27] Procedures are simplified to enable police and prosecutors to exercise greater powers while being subject to weaker judicial checks, but the process is not simplified for the accused, who experiences only the removal of rights and protections. Furthermore, we might expect efficiency reforms to generate financial savings, but as procedural protections were being eroded, spending on the criminal justice system increased through the 1990s and early 2000s,[28] and prison numbers doubled.[29] The rationalizing of procedures was not motivated by savings of time or money, but instead reflected an agenda of securitization and crime control and a significant increase in criminalization.

The changing portrayal of criminal justice and its larger place within political discourse and policy is an important factor in the shifts in criminal justice that took place in the late twentieth and early twenty-first centuries both in Britain and in France and in the "almost hyperactive legislative behaviour" that ensued.[30] The right-wing politics of France and Britain in the 1980s led to a more punitive turn in criminal justice, to law-and-order politics and a macho rhetoric around being tough on crime and on the causes of crime.[31] Criminal justice was at the forefront of electoral politics, "with the emergence of an emotive, populist and avowedly anti-liberal political discourse that deliberately sets . . . ordinary people against the remote liberal sentiments of professional or special interest groups,

[26] See, e.g., McLaughlin, Muncie, and Hughes (2001).

[27] Colson and Field characterize this as "repressive efficacy" (2011: 26).

[28] Spending on policing rose by around 50 percent from 1998/99 to 2008/9. See the report produced by the Centre for Crime and Justice Studies, H. Mills, A. Silvestri, and R. Grimshaw (2010), *Police Expenditure, 1999–2009*, available at https://www.crimeandjustice.org.uk/sites/crimeandjustice.org.uk/files/Police%20expenditure%201999-2009.pdf.

[29] From over forty thousand in 1993 to over eighty thousand in 2018 (and for several years prior). More people were given custodial sentences; sentences were longer; and the provisions for recalls has increased, resulting in a steep increase in the number of those recalled after release, from 150 in 1995 to 6,600 in 2016. See, e.g., Ministry of Justice (2016) *Story of the Prison Population, 1993–2016, England and Wales*. Available at https://assets.publishing.service.gov.uk/government/uploads/system/uploads/attachment_data/file/541667/prison-population-story-1993-2016.pdf.

[30] The description of one civil servant interviewed by Ian Loader. See Loader (2006: 578).

[31] See Colson and Field (2011) for an account of France, in particular; see Loader (2006) for an analysis (based on interviews with civil servants and penal reformers) of the hardening of attitudes in the governance of crime, in which the liberal elites were no longer valued, as we witnessed what he terms the fall of the "platonic guardians."

most notably those of lawyers, journalists, civil libertarians, penal reformers and criminologists."[32] Zero tolerance was the mantra of both jurisdictions, and the right to security (rather than freedom) took prominence within what might be described as the politics of fear and the "heightened language of menace."[33] Justice for victims replaced justice for the accused, and insecurity became the dominant paradigm, used to justify greater police powers and intrusive forms of surveillance.[34]

B. The Rise of System Efficiency and the Eclipse of Procedural Protections

Many of the British landmark judgments condemning the police and prosecution withholding of material and reinforcing the prosecution obligation to disclose to the defense evidence helpful to its case concerned the stream of miscarriages of justice that started to emerge within five years of PACE. Many of them related to the Irish Republican Army (IRA) bombings in the 1970s in which scores of civilians were murdered—discussed further in later chapters.[35] On the day that the Birmingham Six were released, the government announced the establishment of the Royal Commission on Criminal Justice (RCCJ). Against the background of miscarriages of justice, the then home secretary explained that the aim of the RCCJ was "to minimise so far as possible the likelihood of such events happening again."[36] However, the commission was entrusted with a broader task than this and was asked to "examine the effectiveness of the criminal justice system in England and Wales in securing the conviction of those guilty of criminal offences and the acquittal of those who are innocent, having regard to the efficient use of resources."[37] It is significant that the commission was asked to consider the conviction of the guilty as well as, and indeed before, the acquittal of the innocent. The RCCJ's error of judgment was in treating these two objectives

[32] Loader (2006: 579). As Tony Blair put it, this brought about "the end of the 1960s liberal consensus on law and order" (*The Guardian*, 21 July 2004).

[33] Colson and Field (2016: 53). See also Simon (2007) for an account of what he calls the culture of fear in the United States, growing out of the political shift to governance through crime from the mid-twentieth century onward. Lacey (2008: 26–29) challenges the portrayal of penal populism as universal (in accounts such as Garland's [2001], who uses as his unit of analysis "late modern society"), citing examples of jurisdictions facing the same economic and social challenges, but which respond in less punitive ways.

[34] See, e.g., Danet (2003); Hodgson (2005).

[35] As terrorism cases, these are not typical of the routine work of the criminal courts. The pressure on the police to obtain convictions is much greater. On the other hand, these cases also demonstrate the routine practices of police culture that characterized many police-citizen interactions and the environment in which these types of malpractice were able to flourish. See Belloni and Hodgson (2000).

[36] HC Debates *Hansard* 14 March 1991 Col 1109.

[37] RCCJ (1993: i).

as being of equal importance and as being inextricably bound together.[38] In this way, the RCCJ redefined miscarriages of justice to include wrongful acquittals, and efficiency (rather than justice) became a clear system goal.

> [T]here is no longer a primary emphasis on suspects' rights in an adversarial system. Suspects' rights are displaced by system rights. Justice becomes a matter of just knowledge production for the efficient risk management of suspect populations . . . crime control and suspects' rights are on the way out . . . surveillance and system rights are taking their place.[39]

The miscarriages of justice that had given rise to the establishment of the RCCJ were characterized by malpractice and, in particular, by nondisclosure by the police, prosecution, and their experts of evidence that proved key to the defense case. In this sense, they revealed the police and prosecution to be, at best, excessively adversarial in the construction and presentation of their case, while preventing the defense from playing its properly adversarial role.[40] Yet the recommendations of the RCCJ were the reverse of what might have been expected: lessening the disclosure requirements for the prosecution and, for the first time, imposing a burden of disclosure on the defense—failure to comply with which could result in adverse inferences being drawn at trial.[41] For many, this was a clear betrayal of the presumption of innocence,[42] but this, the commission asserted, would streamline the process and avoid "ambush defences" being used by the accused.[43] In fact, so-called ambush defenses were rare, and the new disclosure regime was far more complex than the former practice of simply allowing those defense lawyers who asked to look through unused material.[44] Although now simplified, disclosure remains a problematic issue, with a 2017 joint inspection report noting "widespread failures across the board by both police and prosecutors."[45] There continues to be a strong culture of police

[38] These two things are not of equal concern. Wrongful acquittal and wrongful conviction both harm the interests of the victim, who does not see the offender brought to justice. Wrongful conviction produces a far greater harm, however, as the power of the state is used wrongly to convict and sentence an individual. The damage done to those wrongly imprisoned is only beginning to be understood. For an overview, see Justice (2018). Neither are they inextricably linked. Ensuring that only the guilty are convicted necessitates the acquittal of the innocent; but acquittal of the innocent does not require the conviction of the guilty.

[39] Ericson (1994: 139–140).

[40] There are, of course, more deep-seated causes underlying these, such as the policing of "suspect" communities, the social disciplinary effect of law, engrained occupational cultures, and so on. My focus here is on the shift in legislation and, to some extent, in official discourse.

[41] RCCJ (1993: chap. 6).

[42] See Zander's dissent (as a member of the commission) to this part of the RCCJ report.

[43] Belloni and Hodgson (2000: 132).

[44] Belloni and Hodgson (2000: 130–141).

[45] HMCPSI, HMIC (2017). The joint inspection found that the police simply listed items with no explanation of their contents to assist the prosecutor; had a poor understanding of the nature

withholding evidence that they do not want disclosed, with some officers being trained to list evidence incorrectly as sensitive, in order to avoid its disclosure to the defense. Neither prosecutors nor judges express confidence in the police's ability or willingness to disclose material that might undermine their case.[46] The Criminal Cases Review Commission (CCRC) has also highlighted the fact that nondisclosure continues to be a major cause of wrongful convictions.[47] While the earlier judgments of the Court of Appeal recognized the inbuilt imbalance within the adversarial procedure and sought to strengthen the principle of equality of arms, the commission's recommendations undercut this at a stroke, permitting a continued culture of nondisclosure and, potentially, wrongful convictions.

A second strike at adversarial principles was the commission's recommendation that the court be permitted to draw adverse inferences at trial from the suspect's silence in police interrogation and in the courtroom.[48] Again, this proposal ran counter to the empirical studies commissioned by the RCCJ, which found that silence was exercised only rarely by suspects,[49] was often not maintained, and had little or no effect on the investigation.[50] The right to silence is generally regarded as the expression of the accused's right not to incriminate herself. Although used infrequently, the right has an important symbolic value in preventing the police from mandating the suspect to answer questions, requiring the investigation of other evidence and the production of proof besides an admission. It also has a practical value in enabling the suspect to resist police pressure to speak and to make an admission.[51] This can prevent suspects from being drawn into inaccurate statements when the accusations against them are unclear and the nature of the evidence gathered has yet to be disclosed.[52] The removal or

of sensitive and nonsensitive data; produced deficient disclosure schedules; and lacked confidence in understanding and carrying out their role. Prosecutors simply endorsed, rather than checked, schedules, leading to poorly managed and chaotic disclosure practices. Judges expressed a lack of confidence in the CPS's ability to manage disclosure.

46 Further detail of what the inspectorate found was obtained through a request by the Centre for Criminal Appeals under the Freedom of Information Act. Available at http://www.criminalappeals.org.uk/news/2018/4/3/documents-obtained-by-centre-reveal-extent-of-disclosure-crisis and reported in *The Times* on 3 April 2018.

47 CCRC *Annual Report* 2016/17, p. 3. Examples such as the case of Sam Hallam contain all the hallmarks of twentieth-century miscarriages.

48 RCCJ (1993: chap. 4).

49 McConville and Hodgson (1993).

50 Leng (1993).

51 For a review of some of the literature around this time, see Quirk (2017: 15–20).

52 Although the availability of legal assistance is a welcome advance in this respect, the vulnerability of suspects detained in police custody is such that the risk of false confessions remains, aside from the fact that a suspect is not obliged to incriminate herself. On the inherent vulnerability of all detainees, see Hodgson (1994). On current practices of phased disclosure see Sukumar, Hodgson, and Wade (2016a, 2016b); Sukumar, Wade, and Hodgson (2016, 2018).

attenuation of such a fundamental defense right on the part of a commission that was set up in response to miscarriages of justice caused by abuses in police investigation and interrogation is troubling—and all the more so given the absence of any evidence that the use of silence was either frequent or problematic.

Third, the commission put forward proposals to encourage defendants to plead guilty at the earliest possible moment—the earlier the admission, the greater the sentence discount.[53] Once again, this measure was designed to reduce the (costly and time-consuming) opportunity for adversarial conflict.[54] As discussed in the previous chapter, plea bargaining had long been a feature of criminal justice,[55] but this recommendation and the subsequent legislation placed it on a formal footing.[56] The RCCJ characterized late plea changes (or "cracked trials") as a feature of defendants' behavior.[57] However, research suggests that it is defense counsel who press for a guilty plea (often contrary to the defendant's wishes)[58] and prosecutors who benefit from the conversion of a weak case into a guilty plea.[59] The commission's agenda for system efficiency was clear. It acknowledged that "it would be naïve to suppose that innocent persons never plead guilty because of the prospect of the sentence discount," but "[a]gainst the risk . . . must be weighed the benefits to the system and to defendants of encouraging those who are in fact guilty to plead guilty."[60]

These recommendations represented a significant shift away from adversarial values, but without substituting any coherent alternative. Rather than maintaining the burden of proof clearly on the prosecution, the accused is required to participate in the construction of the case against her and to promote the wider system goal of efficiency—in some instances, with the penalty of adverse inference for noncompliance.[61] The recommendations were taken up

53 RCCJ (1993: chap. 7, paras. 41–58).

54 RCCJ (1993: chap. 7, para. 41).

55 See, e.g., Baldwin and McConville (1977).

56 Criminal Justice and Public Order Act 1994.

57 RCCJ (1993: chap. 7, paras. 41–58).

58 McConville et al. (1994).

59 Zander and Henderson (1993) reported that of 483 "cracked trials," the prosecution believed the defendant had a "Good" chance and a "Fairly good" chance of acquittal in 8 percent and in 18 percent of the cases, respectively. They concluded (at 157): "If these figures are 'grossed up' on an annual basis it would mean that there are over 600 Crown Court defendants a year pleading guilty when the CPS believe they have 'Good' chances of an acquittal and another 2,000 or so who plead guilty when their chances of an acquittal are deemed 'Fairly good.' "

60 RCCJ (1993: chap. 7, paras. 42–45).

61 Michael Zander, wrote a strongly worded Note of Dissent from the defense disclosure recommendation: "The most important objection to defense disclosure is that it is contrary to principle for the defendant to be made to respond to the prosecution's case until it has been presented at the trial. The defendant should be required to respond to the case the prosecution makes, not to the case it says it is going to make. They are often significantly different. The fundamental issue at stake is that the burden of proof lies throughout on the prosecution. . . . [I]t is wrong to require the defendant to be helpful by giving advance notice of his defence and to penalise him by adverse comment if he fails to do so" (RCCJ [1993: 221]).

enthusiastically and legislated shortly after the commission's 1993 report: the Criminal Justice and Public Order Act 1994 attenuated the right to silence and introduced sentence discounts for guilty pleas; the Criminal Procedure and Investigations Act 1996 introduced the new defense disclosure regime. Subsequent reforms limited further the adversarial nature of the defense—relaxing aspects of the rule against admitting hearsay as evidence and requiring the defense to give notice and details of all witnesses it intends to call. Were recommendations such as those on disclosure and silence evidence of a shift to a more inquisitorial approach? The commission rejected a wholesale reform of this nature, but it did make a number of proposals that it claimed sought explicitly to move in an inquisitorial direction.[62] Was this another instance of system borrowing, again responding to the social and political pressures of miscarriages of justice?

Inquisitorialism is sometimes thought of as adopting a more "cards on the table" approach, and these provisions certainly involve the defense disclosing more of its case.[63] But in many ways this is a misunderstanding. While inquisitorial procedure adopts a more centralized pretrial enquiry, resulting in the inclusion in the dossier of evidence or information that might be helpful to the defense (provided through the participation, or at the suggestion, of the defense, or simply the result of a more neutral approach to the enquiry), this is a long way from the provisions now in place in England and Wales. Modern inquisitorial-type procedures, such as those in France, neither require defense disclosure and participation nor attach penalties for the accused's failure to do so. Furthermore, while England and Wales may require the defense to put its cards on the table, the same does not apply to the CPS, which faces no penalty for failing to disclose evidence to the defense, despite the fact that this is a far greater threat to justice than defense nondisclosure. Neither are these provisions accompanied by any measure of pretrial judicial oversight of the procedure. Placing a more onerous burden on the defense sits within neither the adversarial nor the inquisitorial model.

What is perhaps appealing about a more inquisitorial procedure is its perceived efficiency. The focus of case disposition in the adversarial model is the lengthy and therefore expensive trial, with opportunities to challenge live evidence; inquisitorialism avoids the "duplication" of evidence provision by allowing the admission in court of written evidence gathered by a judicial officer during the pretrial investigation. "From this standpoint, the inquisitorial system is cheaper and quicker as it solves the issues of guilt with a single

[62] RCCJ (1993: chap. 1, paras. 3–4).

[63] The Criminal Procedure Rules (discussed subsequently) are described as requiring a "cards on the table approach." See *R v. Newell* [2012] EWCA Crim. 650.

investigative effort."[64] Criminal justice reform in England and Wales has sought to diminish the centrality of the trial by dissuading and preventing the accused from exercising her right to trial,[65] but also to shift the weight of the proceedings and of case disposition to the pretrial phase. This trend has continued apace in the twenty-first century. However, this exemplifies the dangers of "pick and mix" borrowings and transplants, with no regard to the wider legal procedural context into which they are placed. While the "trial by dossier" procedure in countries such as France relies upon written evidence produced by a judge or by police who are, at least in theory, supervised by a judicial officer, the guilty plea in England and Wales does not. It is a finding of guilt based on a police-constructed accusation, with no external supervision or control.[66]

The trend to co-opt the defense into the system's managerialist objectives has been given further impetus by the Criminal Procedure Rules, which provide that the parties must actively assist the court in its management of the case.[67] Active case management includes the early identification of the issues in the case, ensuring that evidence is agreed where possible and presented as concisely as possible, discouraging delay and encouraging the parties to cooperate in the progression of the case.[68] In actively managing a case, the court has a number of powers, including giving directions and requiring that issues in the case be identified in writing. It may impose sanctions for failure to comply, including making a costs order. In short, the rules seek to reduce or eliminate, where possible, any conflict. This restricts the adversarial role of the lawyer and brings the judge down from her role as umpire on the bench and into the active management of litigation—not in the sense of the inquisitorial judge who participates in the investigation and exposition of evidence, as well as the review of state actors, but rather, in the administration and management of the case toward a rapid disposition. The judge's powers are wide-ranging, from the imposition of timetables, to requiring written rather than oral arguments and limiting cross-examination and the calling of defense witnesses.[69] Lord Phillips has claimed that the Criminal Procedure Rules uphold a "robust adversarial process,"[70] but

[64] Illuminati (2005: 578). In contrast, Germany, a jurisdiction from the inquisitorial tradition, does not (in principle) admit the introduction of the contents of the pretrial dossier at the trial (§ 250 German Code of Criminal Procedure).

[65] The RCCJ introduced further confusion by recommending the judge adopt a more (inquisitorial) interventionist stance at trial, but without thinking how this might fit within an overall adversarial structure.

[66] The accused will usually be legally represented, making the defense lawyer's role crucial, as the only real check on the prosecution case.

[67] For similar procedures in Scotland, see Duff (2004).

[68] Criminal Procedure Rules 3.2.

[69] *K and Others* (2006) EWCA Crim. 835; *Lee* (2007) EWCA Crim. 764.

[70] Lord Phillips, CJ, *The Objectives and Content of the First Criminal Procedure Rules*, March 2005, cited by McEwan (2011: 530).

along with the other changes following the RCCJ and later the Auld Review, they represent a surrender to the court of elements of party control of the case.[71]

It is in the interests of victims, defendants, and witnesses that cases are dealt with speedily, and the court is well placed to ensure matters progress without compromising justice. However, while emphasis is often put on the defense duty to progress the case and avoid adjournments, with the threat of a costs order representing a very real sanction, the prosecution does not appear to experience this pressure to the same extent. Disclosure is rarely provided in good time, and the extensive delegation of work to assistant prosecutors with no authority to alter or discontinue charges leads to unnecessary delay.[72]

The case management form epitomizes this "active management" nonadversarial approach.[73] It must be filled out by the defendant at her first appearance in the magistrates' court, if the charges are to be contested. Tellingly, the first question to be completed asks if the defendant understands that she will receive credit for a guilty plea—that is, that a guilty plea may affect sentence and costs. It then goes on to ask what can be agreed (presence at the scene, participation in the offense, lawful arrest, nature of the injury, forensic evidence, police interview, etc.) and if not, what is in dispute, before asking the defendant to set out the disputed issues of fact or law for trial, in addition to those already identified. This information is required before the defendant has received full disclosure and so without knowing the nature of the case against her. This militates against an adversarial defense or putting the prosecution to proof, both of which are seen as costly in terms of time and money. The antipathy shown toward this adversarial defense behavior (and the presumption of innocence) is demonstrated in the statement of the defense duty in *Malcolm v. DPP* [2007] EWHC 363 (Admin) at paragraph 31:

> In my judgment, [the defense] submissions, which emphasised the obligation of the prosecution to prove its case in its entirety before closing its case, and certainly before end of the final speech for the defence, had an anachronistic, and obsolete, ring. Criminal trials are no longer to be treated as a game, in which each move is final and any omission by the prosecution leads to its failure. It is the duty of the defence to make its defence and the issues it raises clear to the prosecution and to the court at an early stage. That duty is implicit in rule 3.3 of the Criminal Procedure Rules, which requires the parties actively to assist the exercise by the court of its case management powers, the exercise of which

71 See McEwan (2011: 530).

72 See further Soubise (2017).

73 See also *R v. Newell* for comment on the same form used in the Crown Court (the Plea and Case Management Form) and the prosecution's attempts to use statements made on the form as "inconsistent statements" of the accused, to be used against him at trial.

> requires early identification of the *real* issues. Even in a relatively straightforward trial . . . it is the duty of the defence to make the real issues clear *at the latest* before the prosecution closes its case.

The punitive regulation of defense obligations to assist the court stands in contrast to the unsanctioned practices of nondisclosure by the police and prosecution, turning adversarialism and equality of arms on their head.

A further way in which managerial and efficiency concerns have impacted on the criminal justice systems of both Britain and France is through a systematic reduction in the reliance on procedures reserved for the most serious offences. Trial by a jury of one's peers is perhaps one of the oldest and most iconic features of adversarial justice, understood to provide a core lay element of adjudication and democratic participation in the criminal justice process. Although the majority of defendants are tried in the magistrates' court, the right to jury trial continues to be regarded as a hallmark of British justice. Its significance has diminished in recent decades, however, with fewer cases triable only in the Crown Court and reduced opportunities for the accused to elect jury trial, including on the recommendation of the RCCJ. In France, the tenacity of the *juge d'instruction* has long been a thorn in the side of politicians. The investigating judge (the *juge d'instruction*) is responsible for the criminal enquiry in the most serious and complex cases (rather than a police investigation overseen by the prosecutor), and trial is in the *cour d'assises* before a mixed jury of three judges and six lay jurors, rather than in the middle-ranking court, the *tribunal correctionnel*, in front of three professional judges.[74] In both jurisdictions, these "Rolls Royce" procedures have been under attack as too costly and inefficient.[75]

In France, then-president Sarkozy made clear his desire to abolish the *instruction* investigation procedure and shift criminal investigations to the procureur (the public prosecutor) when, in 2009, he appointed the criminal justice commission chaired by Philippe Léger.[76] When the Léger Commission reported

[74] Around 17.5 percent of cases are dealt with in the Crown Court in England and Wales (88,205 cases were dealt with by the Crown Court, compared with 499,816 in the magistrates' court in 2016–17). Source: *Crown Prosecution Service Annual Report and Accounts, 2016–17* (Annex D, Tables 1 and 5). Of the 595,592 cases proceeded with in France, fewer than 3 percent (16,946) were investigated by the *juge d'instruction*. Source: Ministère de la justice et des libertés, 2017, *Activité des parquets en 2016*.

[75] There are currently discussions to create a new *tribunal criminel* without a jury to try offenses carrying up to ten years' imprisonment. The *cour d'assises* tries cases carrying a maximum sentence of ten years or more. In the Netherlands too, legislation in 1999 shifted investigative power from the investigating judge to the prosecutor. The Act on Revision of the Preliminary Judicial Investigation, Wet GVO herziening, 27 May 1999. In 2013, judge-led investigations were abolished, and the investigating judge's role was reduced to overseeing the investigation and the decisions of the prosecutor.

[76] The principal reason why many politicians are thought to oppose the *juge d'instruction* is that, unlike the *procureur*, who is under the political hierarchy of the minister of justice, the *juge d'instruction* has no political master to constrain the scope of her enquiries. During the 1990s, *juges*

in September 2009, it duly recommended the abolition of the politically independent *juge d'instruction* role so that all investigations become the responsibility of the procureur, who is hierarchically accountable to the minister of justice.[77] While the more serious cases currently investigated by the *juge d'instruction* would continue to enjoy similar safeguards when under the supervision of the procureur, the mass of ordinary cases would not. In effect, the proposals replicated the current two-tier structure (thus failing to rationalize and simplify as it was asked to do) but with both levels of investigation headed up by the procureur. This reform has, for the time being, been abandoned as a result of the ECtHR's ruling that the procureur lacks the qualities of a judicial officer, as she is one of the parties to the case and is not independent of the executive.[78] However, this has not prevented the broader trend of shifting power away from the more independent *juge d'instruction* to the procureur,[79] with the result that the criminal process is seen to be organized increasingly around the managerialist concerns of the executive, on whom the procureur depends, rather than the judicial protection of the liberties of the individual and the values of fair trial.

In England and Wales, even prior to the RCCJ, efforts were made in 1988 to reduce the number of cases tried by the Crown Court by reclassifying a number of offenses as summary only.[80] Then, in 1990, magistrates were issued with guidelines suggesting that they operate with a presumption that either-way offenses be tried summarily. These changes resulted in a reduction of the Crown Court's caseload but only by some 6 percent. Something more drastic was required to reduce both caseload and costs[81]—or as the RCCJ put it, to achieve "a more rational distribution of cases between the higher and lower courts" as well as "significant benefits for the overall efficiency of the criminal justice system."[82] Although no research was commissioned into the nature and quality

d'instruction conducted a number of controversial and high-profile investigations into politicians and business people on matters of political corruption and fraud. See Hodgson (2005: 79–85).

77 Predictably, because President Sarkozy announced in January 2010, somewhat prematurely, that the *juge d'instruction* would go. This triggered resignations from some commission members, who were under the impression that it was for them to determine the conclusions and recommendations of this supposedly independent commission.

78 In *Medvedyev v. France* (3394/03) 29 March 2010, and then *Moulin v. France* (37104/06) 23 November 2010, discussed further in later chapters and in Hodgson (2010). Belgium has proposed limiting or even abolishing its *juge d'instruction* role, but at a meeting of the association of French *juges d'instruction* in Paris in 2015, the French Justice Ministry confirmed that it did not plan to do so. However, abolition is never far from the French political agenda. In 2016, Nicolas Sarkozy again raised the issue as a part of his presidential campaign.

79 With oversight or authorization from the *juge des libertés et de la détention* in some instances, who as a *magistrat du siège* enjoys the same level of independence as the *juge d'instruction*.

80 Common assault; driving while disqualified; taking a car without the owner's consent; under £5,000 of criminal damage to property.

81 Crown Court cases cost significantly more than magistrates' court cases.

82 RCCJ (1993: chap. 6, para. 19).

of summary justice (and in particular, into the reliability of the very high number of guilty pleas) or the reasons why both defendants and magistrates might choose the Crown Court as a trial or sentencing venue, the commission nevertheless recommended that the defendant be denied any free choice to elect jury trial in either-way offenses; unless agreement could be reached between the prosecution and defense, this was to be wholly within the discretion of the magistrates.

A less draconian version of this proposal was enacted in the Criminal Procedure and Investigations Act 1996 (CPIA), whereby defendants pleading not guilty continue to enjoy the right to elect jury trial, but those indicating that they intend to plead guilty do not.[83] The accused can choose to be tried in the Crown Court, but cannot choose to be sentenced there on a plea of guilty. The commission relied simply on the fact that in 62 percent of cases sent to the Crown Court, the sentence was within the powers of the magistrates. However, the reform failed to provide the anticipated efficiency savings. In the years following the reform, magistrates continued to commit over half of all either-way cases for jury trial, and while more cases were tried summarily, the numbers committed to the Crown Court for sentence more than tripled. The Ministry of Justice reported that in the ten years since the "plea before venue" provisions were introduced, trials for either-way offenses decreased, but committals for sentence doubled.[84]

In France too, the high point of procedural protections achieved in the 2000 reform was undercut by a slew of legislation that no longer promoted procedural fairness or equality of arms, but pursued a clear agenda of crime control, reducing the rights of the accused both directly and by incentivizing various forms of rapid case disposition and diminishing the scope of judicial protections. In order to speed up the trial process, a new form of lay judge was introduced (the *juge de proximité*) to relieve the ordinary courts;[85] a form of guilty plea was introduced; and the existing rapid trial procedure of *comparution immédiate* was extended to offenses punishable by up to ten years imprisonment. Police powers were increased in a variety of ways, and broadly defined new offenses were introduced that appeared to target marginal populations and the young.[86] The regime

[83] S.49 CPIA 1996 amending s.17 Magistrates' Court Act 1980.

[84] Ministry of Justice (2008). Committals for sentence have remained stable at around 7 percent of either-way offenses dealt with in the magistrates' court. Between 2011/12 and 2016/17, the number of cases prosecuted fell, but the proportion of indictable offenses did not. And while 11.5 percent of defendants tried for either-way offenses in the Crown Court had elected to be tried there in 2011/12, this had dropped to only 2 percent in 2016/17. The value of trying cases in the magistrates' court remains a Ministry of Justice concern, it would seem: the National Audit Office (2016) estimated that hearing either-way offenses in the Crown Court costs an additional £36.1 million.

[85] This office was abolished in July 2017 and replaced with a lay judge (rather like the English magistrate) in the *tribunal d'instance*.

[86] The *flagrance* procedure, which provides the police with greater powers in the case of "recently committed" offenses, was extended to include investigations within fifteen days of the offense (rather than eight, as was previously the case). New police powers to conduct nighttime searches were provided, and powers formerly exercised only by the *juge d'instruction* were allocated to the *procureur*

in which suspects held in police custody for questioning for up to ninety-six hours in relation to drug trafficking and terrorism was extended to other forms of serious and organized crime, in which access to a lawyer could also be delayed for between forty-eight and seventy-two hours. But perhaps most astonishingly of all, having only been introduced in 2000, the requirement for the police to inform suspects of their right to silence was removed in legislation just three years later.[87]

The nature of these reforms and their inability to save time or money suggests that efficiency has been used as a proxy for the dismantling of fundamental rights and protections in both procedural traditions. However, the rhetoric of efficiency has continued within the broader trend of managerialism, which has taken hold not only in the reform of criminal justice, but across the public sector as a whole.

C. Managerialism and Efficiency

The criminal justice process has exhibited a fading preoccupation with the principles and values of a coherent procedural system, while demonstrating far greater concern with the efficient management of criminalization. Efficiency is a key objective of contemporary criminal justice policy, alongside related concerns with austerity and cost-effectiveness, risk management, reductions in delay, and a more general productivity-driven managerialism. Half a century ago, Herbert Packer theorized two competing models of criminal justice: the due process model, characterized as something of an obstacle course with procedural safeguards in place to ensure the filtering out of weak or uncertain cases; and the crime control model, concerned with the repression of crime, the processing of a high volume of offenders and a high conviction rate. These models, or ideal types, are selective in what they highlight and limited in their application. They cannot explain, for example, why crime control policing operates to discriminate between those the police consider to be deserving and undeserving suspects and witnesses.[88] However, although conceptualized at a high level of abstraction, these models continue to

with oversight from the *juge des libertés et de la détention*. Offenses relating to threatening or hostile gatherings were seen to target the young and those at the margins of society. Opposition was in terms similar to that in the UK around the Criminal Justice and Public Order Act 1994, also seen as criminalizing particular lifestyles and the young.

[87] This meant that suspects were only informed of this right at the point when they saw a lawyer, or by the *juge d'instruction* if the case was dealt with through the *instruction* procedure. In most instances, this is too late: it is in the first hours that the suspect is most vulnerable to confession and to confess unreliably. It was another eight years before the obligation to inform suspects of their right to silence was finally placed back in the CPP.

[88] For a discussion of some of the primary criticisms of Packer's models, see Macdonald (2008: 263–269). McBarnett, for example, noting the permissive nature of law and so its reflection in practices that appear to be an abuse of discretion, argues that "the law in action is only too close

serve a purpose in analyzing aspects of contemporary processes of criminal justice and the ways in which procedures and practices are weighted toward the protection of the liberties of the accused or toward their conviction.[89]

The swift disposal of cases, informal procedures, and discretionary decision-making of the crime control model characterize many of the features of modern criminal justice in Britain, France, and elsewhere in Europe and North America. As will be discussed in subsequent chapters, this tendency manifests itself in a move away from judicial procedures that provide safeguards around the exercise of state power and protect individual liberties, to be replaced by more speedy and informal procedures (often in the hands of prosecutors rather than judges) whose principal aim is the rapid disposition of cases.[90] The defense lawyer's role is limited procedurally and in resource terms, serving to legitimate the efficient processing of accused persons as much as to protect their interests. This has the effect of undermining justice and distorting the roles of legal actors tasked with privileging efficiency over the more costly and time-consuming traditional values of justice for victims and accused persons.[91]

Justice is not unique in being subject to the imperatives of efficiency and productivity. From the 1980s onward, the managerialist discourse of the commercial world began to permeate virtually all aspects of public administration in England and Wales.[92] This brought about huge transformations in the running

a parallel to the law in books; due process is for crime control" (McBarnett [1978: 31] quoted in Macdonald [2008: 265]). Macdonald himself argues that "Packer's exposition of the crime control and due process models is infested by a failure to appreciate the way that competing policies are constructed and assessed" (2008: 305).

[89] "Labels are beguiling; what Packer is in fact offering us are not two models of the criminal process. Rather . . . a stimulating depiction, rich in implications, of two clashing inner tendencies: the tendency toward efficiency and the tendency toward protecting the rights of the defendant . . . the inner tension is part and parcel of the dialectics of *any* criminal process." Damaška (1973: 576).

[90] This trend peaked in England and Wales in 2007, when more cases were disposed of outside the courtroom than in it. According to Ministry of Justice statistics, around half of all "offences brought to justice" in 2007 (722,000 out of 1,456,000) were the result of a conviction; around one-quarter (383,000) the result of police cautions; the rest offenses taken into consideration by the court (108,000), police penalty notices for disorder (144,000), and police formal warnings for cannabis possession (98,000). In France too, power is moving toward the principal pretrial actors—the prosecutor and police—and the number of cases not prosecuted, but disposed of by way of *composition pénale* or alternatives, has risen steadily (37 percent in 2008, 44 percent in 2012) and is now at 42.5 percent (Ministère de la justice et des libertés [2017]) . The numbers dealt with by the guilty plea procedure and *ordonnace pénal* are also increasing, and those sent to the *juge d'instruction* continue to decline. In the Netherlands, the target number of cases to be dealt with out of court, at the police station, is a staggering 70 percent. See Blackstock et al. (2014: 100–101).

[91] See also Edwards (2016), who argues that efficiency completely overshadows the other stated aims of the criminal justice system in dealing with cases "justly," such as acquitting the innocent and convicting the guilty; recognizing the rights of the defendant, particularly those under Article 6 of the ECHR; and ensuring that appropriate information is available to the court when bail and sentence are considered.

[92] See Stewart and Walsh (1992).

of our public services: National Health Service trusts, private finance initiative (PFI) building projects for schools and hospitals, and the contracting out of public services to private contractors by competitive tendering in areas such as policing, health, and social security. This has been accompanied by a plethora of targets, performance indicators, and league tables in order to audit everything from the academic performance of nursery school children to police arrests. This new managerialism recasts the citizen as consumer and elevates efficiency and value for money as the primary goals of the public sector. The administration of criminal justice has been no exception to this transformation.[93] This brand of managerialism can be seen in the privatization of parts of the police and prison service; in the endless tendering and contracting processes in criminal legal aid; and in the multiagency cooperation, target setting, and output measures of policing,[94] prosecution, and the courts.[95]

Resources are finite, and efficiency and value for money will always, quite properly, be factors in determining how best to deliver justice. But they cannot become ends in themselves, or even the principal guarantors in the delivery of a quality criminal justice system that must also encompass the fair treatment of accused persons as well as victims. Yet this is just what they have become, ends in themselves,[96] depoliticized as a "technocratic question of optimal resource allocation,"[97] what Feeley and Simon (1994) have described as actuarial justice, or what Ritzer (2004) has characterized as the McDonaldization of society.[98] Although presented in neutral and objective terms, these tools of management and accountability are ideologically driven, masking the increased punitiveness of criminal justice in both jurisdictions. The emphasis on legal actors as

[93] See, e.g., Lacey (1994) discussing the sentencing provisions of the Criminal Justice Act 1991. Neither the police and CPS nor the French *procureur* and *juge* are measured by the quality of their investigation or prosecution, but by outputs and performance targets, while judges are measured by the rates of case adjournments and case completion—by the National Audit Office.

[94] The Home Office has made crime reduction firmly the responsibility of the police, with "power to the people" through accountability structures at the local level (such as through the election of police and crime commissioners—a process that was a resounding failure, with a pitiful turnout of 15 percent from the electorate when introduced in 2012), as well as publishing crime data and encouraging community involvement and that of business and the voluntary sector. There is, however, limited commitment from government in the form of interventions to tackle risk factors leading to crime. There is no mention of fair or effective processes in Home Office rhetoric, only cutting red tape in a kind of mass decentralization of responsibility and increasing the discipline of punishment.

[95] E.g., the government's annual policing plan established under the Police Reform Act 2002, which required local police authorities to establish a three-year strategy in line with national priorities.

[96] Productivity and low cost become the ultimate goal. See also Alt and Le Theule (2011).

[97] Tickell (2015: 206), referring to the ECtHR's attempts to reduce its docket.

[98] Ritzer argues that society is increasingly governed by the same principles that drive the fast-food industry: efficiency (often through managerialism), calculability (quantitative measures over qualitative judgments), predictability and standardization (routinized work for consistent output), and control. These describe many of the trends and values in criminal justice. See also Bohm (2006) for a discussion of this in relation to US criminal justice.

managers of justice also influences the mindset and behavior of those working within the criminal process.[99]

Garapon notes the detrimental impact of this orientation on the professional identity of the French judiciary, for example, who must think and respond in economic rather than judicial terms.[100] The procureur is also seeing the judicial nature of her role ebbing away as she is increasingly required to implement hierarchical and ministerial policies, acting less as an independent judicial officer than as a manager whose performance is audited and accounted for. This occurs at the same time as judicial powers and functions traditionally reserved for the *juge d'instruction* are being shifted across to the procureur, and the Parquet is calling for its judicial status to be strengthened through greater independence from the minister of justice.[101] A new article in the CPP sets out the prosecutor's role in terms similar to that of the *juge d'instruction*,[102] but in the absence of reforming her status, hierarchical accountability to the executive, and appointment process, this is unlikely to do more than pay lip service to the Strasbourg jurisprudence on judicial independence.[103] In terms of evaluating these judicial roles, the criteria of success for the criminal process is not whether justice has been done, but whether the caseload has been managed effectively.[104] In government's drive for speed, efficiency, and value for money, it has redefined justice in quantitative terms, in a way that all but excludes the protection of due process rights and the importance of convicting only the guilty.

In England and Wales, the politicization of criminal justice has resulted in a plethora of strategy documents, reviews, and action plans for criminal justice, in which the rhetoric of efficiency and managerialism is ever present. Each year seems to bring a new promise to "transform" justice and to make it "simple, speedy and summary," "swift and sure," and "rebalanced in favour of the (decent) law-abiding majority."[105] While procedural fairness is absent as a concern, the documents are replete with visions, targets, planning frameworks and nationally

[99] de Gaulejac (2009: 105–196). Desrosières (2008: 12) argues that once this process of quantification becomes engrained and routinized in our practices, its results become "the reality" and in turn influence our behavior.

[100] Garapon (2013: 70). The productivity of each judge can now be measured by her outputs.

[101] While the *procureur* is a *magistrat*, she is hierarchically accountable to the executive through the minister of justice and so lacks the independence of the so-called sitting judiciary—the *juge d'instruction, juge des libertés et de la détention*, and trial judge, who are all *magistrats du siège* and cannot be given instructions by the minister, nor moved to another post. See discussion in chapters 1 and 3.

[102] The new Artice 39, line 3, is similar to Article 81 setting out the responsibility of the *juge d'instruction*.

[103] Perrier (2016).

[104] Garapon (2010: 55–56).

[105] See, e.g., Auld (2001); Department of Constitutional Affairs (2006); Gross (2011); Gross and Treacy (2012); Ministry of Justice (2012, 2013); Gross, Kinch, and Riddle (2014); Leveson (2015); Lord Chief Justice (2016).

driven programs and initiatives,[106] and promises to bring offenders to justice "within days, sometimes even hours."[107] Challenging evidence credibility is expensive and time-consuming, and even the judiciary has set about establishing means of minimizing unnecessary conflict, as the trial has come to be seen.[108] The importance of a fair and proportionate process producing a just outcome is conspicuous by its absence in these documents.

The 2015 Leveson Review of the efficiency of criminal courts stands a little apart from other reviews in pointing out the false economies of some of the government's short-term fixes.[109] Prepared in consultation with a range of criminal justice professionals, from police and defense lawyers through to those in the National Offender Management Service, this is very much a practical report, evaluating current measures and pilots and seeking to make key procedures more effective. While supporting the ambition of effectiveness, it points up some of the weaknesses in the practical implementation of proposals such as those set out in the 2012 White Paper "Swift and Sure Justice."[110] Technology needs to work well to be effective; court hearings must ensure that they retain their gravitas even with defendants present only on a screen. Prosecution and defense cooperation requires clear case ownership, rather than disjointed and discontinuous representation. The principles underpinning the criminal justice process are again absent, but the context is clear:

> Given that the origin of the Review has been a crisis over remuneration for legal professionals, however, it must be borne in mind that a criminal justice system that is professionally staffed and effective is critical to our democratic society.[111]

Efficiency here is not only about saving time and money; inaccurate verdicts may ultimately produce miscarriages of justice, which are inefficient as well as unjust.[112]

[106] For example, the 2008–2011 strategic plan contained four aims: to be more effective in bringing offenders to justice; to engage the public and inspire confidence; to put the needs of victims at its heart; and to have simple and efficient processes. Any mention of fairness relates only to public confidence in policing and the sanctioning process, and defendants merit only a single mention, at p. 18. As users of the criminal justice system, we are told that we would find it more efficient, fair, and effective. This was followed up by references to addressing "race disproportionality" (p. 35) in different parts of the criminal justice system. Office for Criminal Justice Reform (2007).

[107] Ministry of Justice (2012).

[108] Judiciary of England and Wales (2018).

[109] See also the 2013 Ministry of Justice "Transforming the Criminal Justice System Strategy and Action" and the 2014 *Disclosure Review* (Gross, Kinch, and Riddle [2014]).

[110] Ministry of Justice (2012).

[111] Leveson (2015: para. 11).

[112] Quoting his own recent judgment in *R v. Crawley* [2014] EWCA Crim. 1028 at para. 57, Leveson notes the importance of high-quality advocates in order to identify key issues and to assist the court in reaching accurate verdicts while working expeditiously and so avoiding miscarriages of justice. He also emphasizes (at para. 11) the role of court advocacy in training the judges of the future.

Making explicit the danger that an underfunded criminal justice system might produce wrongful convictions is a welcome corrective to the exclusive focus in government rhetoric on the speed at which offenders can be brought to justice, but ultimately the report's recommendations continue the theme of co-opting the defense to work alongside the prosecution toward the efficient management of cases.[113]

However, attempts to reform the criminal justice process in ways that ensure more coordinated and streamlined functioning seem doomed to continue to fail.

> [T]he criminal justice system is not, in reality a single system: the police, the CPS, the defence community, HMCTS, the judiciary, the probation service and NOMS (to say nothing of the Ministry of Justice . . . and the Home Office) all have different priorities and different financial imperatives with performance indicators (where they exist) that are not aligned.[114]

Added to this, those in the criminal justice system are experiencing what Leveson has termed "transformation exhaustion"[115] from being subjected to the vast array of pilots, initiatives, and schemes for new systems operating across the country,[116] alongside the thousands of new offenses that have been added to the statute book.[117] There is a continuous process of change, with no attempt at principled evaluation or design.

In France, too, commentators point to the growing incoherence of criminal law and procedure. As in England and Wales, procedures are adapted and expanded and new criminal offenses are added, without any trimming, restructuring, or rationalization of the criminal codes.[118] This makes the system increasingly unworkable in practice. As the number of offenses and procedures multiplies, procureurs report feeling concerned that they may trip up and initiate the wrong case pathway or policy. At the same time, they are subjected to circulars from the Justice Ministry requiring them to prioritize the prosecution

[113] E.g., the defense role in identifying issues for dispute and in advising early guilty pleas (para. 99).

[114] Leveson (2015: para. 5). HMCTS is Her Majesty's Court and Tribunals Service; NOMS is the National Offender Management System (now called Her Majesty's Prison and Probation Service).

[115] Leveson (2015: para. 14).

[116] At the time of reporting, there were around a dozen such pilots, initiatives, and schemes, including the Early Guilty Plea Scheme, Transforming Summary Justice, and the CJS Efficiency Programme. Leveson (2015: para. 12).

[117] Between 1989 and 2009 more than four thousand offenses were added to the statute book (an average of two hundred new offenses each year). Law Commission Consultation Paper (2010), para. 1.17.

[118] This legislative inflation (substantive legislation introduced each year increased from twenty reforms a year in the 1990s to thirty a year since 2002) has increased the rights of victims but has promoted a security agenda that has been in place since the 2002 presidential campaign.

of certain offenses, to the extent that 80 percent of criminal cases are now classed as priority areas.[119]

In addition to an excess of reform and review activity, which risks complicating unduly the work of those administering the criminal process, some commentators question the real nature of the measures designed to promote greater efficiency. Police powers such as those to caution or issue fixed penalties are seen as efficient ways of diverting offenders out of the criminal process of prosecution and trial, saving both time and money.[120] However, aside from concerns about the ways in which this undercuts the rights of the accused, there is evidence that diversion, especially when carried out against a backdrop of police external performance scrutiny, such as statutory performance indicators, results in the criminalization of more (not less) people, by delivering sanctions in cases that would otherwise have no action taken.[121] The same observations have been made repeatedly in France too. Rather than diverting cases out of the system or into simpler and faster procedures, the greater capacity for case disposal results in the increased criminalization of minor offenses that would not otherwise have come into the system. This appears to produce a higher rate of response, higher productivity, and an increased clear-up rate, but the successes are minor offenses and easy wins, leaving the more serious crimes unaffected.[122]

Brown (2014) also argues that cheaper adjudication, such as plea bargaining, can trigger more demand in the form of more cases entering the criminal justice system—especially when both supply and demand are controlled by public officials. In commercial terms, production efficiency may not only lower resource consumption and unit cost, but also increase production. Given the complexities of discretionary law enforcement, prosecution, and adjudication, he questions whether efficiency gains address, or in fact create, rising caseloads:

> More efficient adjudication lowers the cost of convictions and makes criminal law enforcement cheaper and more tempting to use. In this way, it contributes to the greater use of criminal law and punishment.[123]

If efficiency were the primary motivation for reform, we might also expect costs to reduce, but as noted earlier, criminal justice spending increased in the late twentieth and early twenty-first centuries, and prison numbers rocketed, with

[119] Milburn et al. (2010: 90–92).

[120] England and Wales reached a point when more cases were dealt with outside court than in it. Bridges (2010).

[121] See Hodgson and Roberts (2010) and, e.g., the Home Office's (2004) own pilot study of penalty notices for disorder, which suggests that over half of the cases would not have been cautioned or prosecuted.

[122] Discussed in more detail in chapter 5.

[123] Brown (2014: 138).

little impact on rates of crime.[124] The political space between the Left and the Right has diminished in the face of a form of punitiveness arms race, or what one civil servant described as "an auction to see whose knuckles can brush the ground hardest."[125] Legal actors are required to replace motivations of justice and fairness with concerns around the effective management of case disposal, and the accused is increasingly worse off, with fewer rights and a diminished capacity to access justice. Efficiency, managerialism, and modernization appear as a thinly veiled proxy for increased criminalization and punishment.[126]

[124] See, e.g., Lacey (2008: 16–19). In France, minimum sentences were introduced with claims that this would increase certainty and so deterrence, but levels of offending did not reduce, nor did recidivism. The main impact was to increase the severity of sentences. See Herzog-Evans (2007) and, more generally, Hodgson and Soubise (2016b).

[125] Loader (2006: 579).

[126] The politicization of criminal justice remains at the heart of this. The state's rhetoric is that security is achieved through criminalization, a form of penal populism designed to portray government as effective and so electable. See also Garland (2001); Simon (2007).

3

Terrorism, Security, and the Management of Risk

This chapter focuses on criminal justice's preoccupation with prevention, security, and the management of risk, and its particular manifestation in Britain and in France through the laws and procedures driving the investigation and prosecution of terrorism. Across both jurisdictions, discourses of precaution and security permeate twenty-first-century criminal justice and, increasingly, trump the procedural values of a fair trial, as well as criminal law principles designed to ensure that the innocent are not criminalized through premature intervention and sanction. The concept of security has been broadened and elevated, and the tools of preventive justice and risk management are called in its aid in the approach to offenses ranging from knife crime, public order, and antisocial behavior to terrorism. Criminal law and procedure have been adapted to operate prospectively and predictively, and new forms of civil and hybrid preventive orders have been introduced to provide greater flexibility. Blurring the boundaries between criminal, civil, and administrative law in this way, however, creates confusion in the allocation of legal and constitutional functions, responsibilities, and safeguards, producing what one French writer has described as a "legal cacophony" resulting in the "denaturing of criminal law and procedure."[1]

While there has been a kind of securitization of criminal justice more generally,[2] as an attack on the state's authority and a challenge to its monopoly on the use of violence, terrorism is treated as the ultimate threat to security, and so the greatest risk to be managed.[3] In addition to changes to the structure of investigations and the growing importance of intelligence, exceptional counterterrorism measures have been enacted in both Britain and France, providing for

[1] Jeanclos (2016). See also the comment of the senior procureur quoted in Hodgson (2005: 33): "My personal opinion is that we have added so much [to our criminal procedure] that we have lost the essence."

[2] For a more thoroughgoing and detailed account of security and criminal law and justice, see Zedner (2009).

[3] Empirically, terrorism does not pose the biggest threat to life—more people are killed in road traffic accidents or even accidents in the home, but the political nature of the threat and what it is understood to represent cause states to resource counterterrorism to a far greater extent than, say, gang violence or knife crime. The majority of deaths due to terrorism in the UK occurred in the 1970s and 1980s, with far fewer since the late 1990s. See Allen and Dempsey (2018: 5).

The Metamorphosis of Criminal Justice. Jacqueline S. Hodgson, Oxford University Press (2020).

DOI: 10.1093/oso/9780199981427.001.0001

additional powers of policing and surveillance, with weaker due process and judicial safeguards; lower thresholds of suspicion justifying the infringement of individual liberties; and the lengthy detention of those believed suspicious or dangerous. Over time, some of these exceptional powers have been used in more ordinary and routine ways against nonterrorist suspects, and some have gone on to be "normalized" through the ordinary common law, in what has been termed in the French context a kind of "administrativization" of coercive measures.[4] In this way, we have seen a further weakening of the position of the accused and of the presumption of innocence.

This has occurred in two principal ways. The first is through an expanded program of criminalization, in which the offense elements to be proved are so broad and vague that they are easily satisfied. But more controversial is the second, also through exceptional measures such as preventive detention, control orders, and Terrorism Prevention and Investigation Measures (TPIMs), all of which operate in a precriminal space. However, while TPIMs lack the safeguards of criminal investigation and trial, they are very few in number (there are less than ten in operation at any one time), are focused on high-risk individuals, and are subject to legal and political oversight. The expanded menu of terrorist-related criminal offenses, on the other hand, applies to large numbers of people, many of whom have little or no connection to terrorism. It gives the appearance of due process through trial and investigation, but undermines the presumption of innocence by requiring little in the way of proof. The French *association de malfaiteurs* offense[5] and similar offenses introduced in England and Wales have had a much greater impact on the liberties of citizens, therefore, than the more controversial preventive measures, as they are used much more widely, are not subject to the same degree of oversight, and allow not only prosecution and conviction, but also police powers of stop, search, arrest, and detention on a wide scale.[6] In the recent French "Tarnac Affair," the eight people prosecuted following a ten-year investigation were acquitted of any terrorist involvement, and the court described the case against them as a fiction. This illustrates how, without resort

4 Originating in the temporary and exceptional state of emergency following the terrorist attacks in France in 2015, this favors a regime of administrative judges over the usual responsibility of the criminal judge to oversee individual rights and liberties across the investigation, prosecution, and trial phases. Boucoboza and Girard (2016).

5 This offense is "the participation in any group formed or association established with a view to the preparation, marked by one or more material actions, of any of the acts of terrorism provided for under the previous articles [of the criminal code]."

6 There have been on average 254 terrorism arrests each year from 2002 to 2018, but the number of stops and searches is, of course, very much higher. See generally Home Office (2018). See also Tadros (2007: 665), who argues that "[t]he direct extension of investigatory powers . . . operates in conjunction with this broadened criminal law, permitting raids of premises and stop and search of individuals where the conduct of those individuals is only suspected to be at the very furthest margins of terrorist activity."

to any exceptional measures, individuals can have their freedom restricted or removed over a period of years, without any concrete evidence or suspicion.[7]

However, while there are clear similarities across both jurisdictions in the extension of police powers, the criminalization of behavior at the pre-*actus reus* stage, and the centralization of counterterrorism expertise, the ways in which the two legal systems respond institutionally to these new challenges also reflect something of their core values, as well as legal, institutional, and constitutional cultures.[8]

A. Security, Prevention, and the Management of Risk

Discourses of prevention, security, and the management of risk are pervasive both in criminal law and in the wider criminal process. In the late twentieth century in England and Wales they centered on issues such as offender recidivism, especially concerning sex offenders and the control of offenses such as knife crime. Post-9/11 this has been seen more forcefully through the expanding security agenda, with counterterrorism measures and the related criminalization of migration.[9] It is also present more broadly in the criminal process through a range of preventive criminal offenses and police powers, as well as precautionary sentences in which individuals are imprisoned not to punish, but in an attempt to manage the risk of future offending. The preoccupation with prevention and the use of noncriminal measures designed to prevent criminal behavior has made the boundary between civil and criminal law less clear. A range of civil preventive orders were introduced, such as the antisocial behavior order (ASBO, now replaced by civil injunctions and community protection notices, CPNs) and the sexual offenses preventive order,[10] which do not require the subject of the order

[7] Arrested by some 150 police officers, armed and wearing balaclavas, the eight accused were initially suspected of major terrorist plots. The information relied on was found to be of dubious value, the key statement obtained by police pressure, and after seven years, the terrorist elements of the case were dropped. The eight accused were finally brought to trial after ten years and were acquitted. See Angelique Chrisafis, "Leftwing 'Anarchist Terror Cell' Is Fiction, French Judges Rule," *The Guardian*, 13 April 2018. For a discussion of the sometimes absurd results of terrorism prosecutions, see Hodgson and Tadros (2009) and of the very broad ways in which terrorism is defined, see Hodgson and Tadros (2013).

[8] See also Foley (2009) for an account of police and intelligence organizational reform.

[9] Eighty-four new immigration-related offenses were introduced under Labour in 1997–2010 (compared with just ninety-one offenses between 1905 and 1996). The introduction of a new offense of failing to produce a passport resulted in a 54 percent increase in immigration-related charges in the magistrates' court between 2004 and 2005. Aliverti (2014: 50).

[10] ASBOs were introduced by section 1 of the Crime and Disorder Act 1998. That act has since been amended by the Police Reform Act 2002, the Anti-social Behaviour Act 2003, and the Serious Organised Crime and Police Act 2005. The guidance for the CPS stated that "ASBOs are civil orders to protect the public from behaviour that causes or is likely to cause harassment, alarm or distress. An order contains conditions prohibiting an individual from carrying out specific anti-social acts or (for example) from entering defined areas. The orders are not criminal sanctions and are not intended to

to be convicted of a criminal offense, though breach of the order is punishable by imprisonment.[11] The police have also been provided with a range of powers aimed at prevention and disruption, such as dispersal orders, which empower the police to disperse people from a particular area.[12] Crawford comments:

> Both collectively and individually, many of the new modes of control represent a shifting orientation towards forms of governance and behavioural regulation that focus less on knowing and accounting for past incidences than disrupting, reordering and steering possible futures.[13]

This confusion of concepts is epitomized by the UK's Prevent agenda, a strategy that utilizes a noncriminal preventive approach to identify and report people who are vulnerable to the risk of being drawn into terrorism through radicalization.[14] There is a general statutory duty on a wide range of bodies from councils, prisons, probation services, and health and social care providers, to universities, schools, and even nurseries, "to have due regard to the need to prevent people from being drawn into terrorism."[15] This is a procedure that sits

punish the individual. They are designed to be preventative, not punitive." They could also be ordered on conviction of a relevant offense if considered necessary by the court. http://www.cps.gov.uk/legal/a_to_c/anti_social_behaviour_guidance/. Like the ASBO, a Sexual Offences Prevention Order (SOPO) may be attached to a conviction for a relevant offense; or it may be requested by the chief officer of police laying a complaint in a magistrates' court if the person is a "qualifying offender," has acted in such a way as to give reasonable cause to believe that it is necessary for an order to be made, and the order is necessary for the purpose of protecting the public or any particular members of the public from serious sexual harm from the person. The relevant powers are contained in sections 104–113 of the Sexual Offences Act 2003.

[11] Civil injunctions can be imposed for up to twelve months on children aged ten and over, breach of which is punishable by a three-month detention order if under eighteen years of age, or two years' imprisonment if aged eighteen or over; a CPN can be imposed for an unlimited period on those aged sixteen or over, and breach carries a fine of up to £2,500. The Criminal Behaviour Order (CBO) can be imposed for up to three years on a convicted person aged ten or over, and breach is punishable by a two-year detention order for those under eighteen and up to five years' imprisonment and/or an unlimited fine for those over eighteen.

[12] Section 30 of the Anti-social Behaviour Act 2003 introduced police power to disperse groups of two or more people from designated areas where there is believed to be significant and persistent antisocial behavior and problems with groups of people causing intimidation. Section 27 of the Violent Crime Reduction Act 2006 permits an officer to require a person to leave a locality for up to forty-eight hours if she believes that the presence of that person is likely to cause or contribute to alcohol-related crime or disorder.

[13] Crawford (2008: 754), commenting on the increasing number of discretionary and dispositive police powers.

[14] The term "radicalization" is relatively new in this context. It was used much more frequently after 2006, as policymakers and the media increasingly required something to explain why British citizens would attack their own country. Sedgwick (2010).

[15] Section 26 of the Counter-Terrorism and Security Act 2015. The list of specified authorities to whom the duty applies is set out in Schedule 6 of the act. The impact of the duty is wide-ranging. See, for example, the Report of the Joint Committee on Human Rights, *Freedom of Speech in Universities*, March 2018, HC 589, HL Paper 111, which describes the chilling effect the duty is reported to have on freedom of speech. They have called for an independent review of the duty and, in particular, its impact on Muslim students.

outside the criminal process in a "pre-criminal space,"[16] operating only when there is no criminal investigation ongoing.[17] By recasting this reporting duty in the more paternalistic terms of safeguarding, the interventions of health workers, educators, and those charged with protecting the interests of those in their care appear more acceptable.[18] In the contexts of grooming or elder abuse, for example, safeguarding is a means of providing care and support for those lacking capacity or agency to prevent them from being harmed. The incorporation of a duty to report signs of radicalization (however understood) seems to equate vulnerability with suspicion in what is described as the securitization of safeguarding.[19]

Many have argued that these various innovations represent a "preventive turn" in criminal law and the emergence of the preventive state.[20] Ashworth and Zedner, while not disputing the recent expansion of preventive justice, note its longer history within criminal justice institutions and, in particular, the extent to which prevention underpinned the establishment of nineteenth-century policing.[21] This is true of France too, though French policing grew out of a surveillance-based intelligence-gathering function on behalf of the monarch, and later the state, and it was for this reason that it was resisted initially in England and Wales.[22] A preventive role for the police enjoyed some support in England, but in the more direct sense of officers taking precautions to prevent crime at the local level. The police introduced in Paris in 1829 were also resisted

[16] Goldberg (2017). Precrime investigation and surveillance has become common place within criminal justice and procedure as part of the process of securitization. See also Zedner (2009: chap. 4).

[17] In 2015/16, 7,631 individuals were subject to referral under this policy. Thirty-six percent left the process requiring no further action; 50 percent were signposted to alternative services; 14 percent were deemed suitable for the program. Fifty-six percent were aged twenty or under and 78 percent were male. Young men made up an even greater proportion of those deemed suitable for support. Of the 7,631 referrals, 33 percent came from the education sector and 31 percent the police. Sixty-five percent concerned Islamist extremism and 10 percent right-wing extremism. One-quarter were from London. Home Office (2017).

[18] The UK is unique in delivering part of its counterterrorism strategy through education, health, and social care as a form of safeguarding. Heath-Kelly and Straus (2018: 10).

[19] McKendrick and Finch (2017). Conceptualizing the duty to prevent crime as a form of safeguarding also introduces a conflict of interest into the medic-patient relationship, employing the language of surveillance rather than safeguarding. See Heath-Kelly and Strausz (2018).

[20] While there are historical examples of the ways that preventive justice is embedded within our criminal justice institutions, what is perhaps new is the expansive and all-encompassing nature of prevention as an ideology. Steiker argued some time ago in relation to the United States that proper consideration of the protections and policy limits of preventive state action is hindered by the fact that "[n]ot only do courts and commentators often trivialize objections to actions of a 'merely' preventive (as opposed to punitive) state, they also do not tend to see the various preventive policies and practices . . . as part of a unified problem" (1998: 778).

[21] For a comprehensive analysis of preventive justice see Ashworth and Zedner (2014). For a different engagement with the "preventive turn in criminal law" and its relationship to the liberal model of criminal law, see Carvalho (2017).

[22] See Hodgson (2005: 85–88).

as the political tools of those in authority, and their gradual acceptance was inspired by the success of Robert Peel's beat officers in England.[23] This dualism is retained in the modern French police role, which includes an administrative role of information gathering and surveillance with officers accountable to the minister of interior via superior officers, and a criminal investigation role with accountability to the minister of justice via the oversight of the local judiciary. Sometimes, the line between intelligence gathering and criminal investigation is unclear, a factor that has been exploited in the development of French counter-terrorism powers, as discussed subsequently.

Concerns with the management of risk have also extended to forms of preventive or precautionary detention, sometimes indefinitely, on the grounds of dangerousness.[24] Aimed at preventing future risks rather than punishing past behavior,[25] the Imprisonment for Public Protection (IPP) order became a major feature of those sentenced for violent and sexual offenses in England and Wales,[26] placing prisoners under an indefinite sentence of imprisonment on the grounds of "dangerousness."[27] However, imprisonment is no less a denial of liberty by labeling it preventive rather than punitive. In effect, the order employed the criminal sanction as a precautionary measure to punish future risk. The practical, as well as ideological, consequences of the IPP were huge. In addition to driving up the prison population, the requirement to demonstrate that offenders no longer posed a risk to society placed enormous pressure on prison and parole services.[28] With no resources for the provision of offender behavior courses, IPP prisoners were unable to demonstrate any reduction in risk, resulting in their

[23] Emsley (1999: 36). Although different in nature, police roles were introduced in Paris around the same time as in London.

[24] Risk may also form part of ordinary criminal sentencing. In the United States, for example, Virginia was the first state to incorporate risk assessment within its sentencing guidelines and to permit alternative sentences for lower-risk offenders. The reliability of these risk assessment instruments and the extent to which they have predictive validity or simply reinforce existing bias in criminal justice, however, is questionable. We know little of how much judges understand risk predictors or how they use them in practice. The consequences for accused persons are that this may potentially result in arbitrary decision-making and so a breach of due process. See discussion in Garrett and Monahan (2018).

[25] See *R v. Johnson* [2006] EWCA Crim. 2486.

[26] Introduced under the Criminal Justice Act 2003, an IPP order has been received by over 6,000 people since the procedure was implemented in 2005, and in January 2010 there were 5,828 IPP prisoners in custody, some 2,500 of whom had already served a sentence beyond their minimum term in custody (Jacobson and Hough [2010]). The 2008 legislation removed the mandatory requirement to make an IPP in certain cases, as this resulted in many more orders than the Home Office had envisaged. IPPs were repealed in 2012, at which point there were over 6,000 IPP prisoners. In June 2017, there were still around 3,350 prisoners serving IPPs (Beard [2017]).

[27] An offender is dangerous if "the court is of the opinion that there is a significant risk to members of the public of serious harm occasioned by the commission by him of further specified offences." The court in *R v. Lang* [2005] EWCA Crim. 2864 held that "significant" means noteworthy.

[28] See HMIP (2008) and (2016). Also the Criminal Justice Joint Inspection (2010) Jacobson and Hough (2010) also question the ability of the courts and the parole board to predict risk and reductions in risk, and so the basic fairness of the procedure.

continued imprisonment. The secretary of state was held to have acted unlawfully and to have systematically breached his public law duty by introducing IPPs without first ensuring that resources were in place to enable the scheme to function as intended.[29] Furthermore, the state's failure to provide the means by which prisoners could demonstrate that they were no longer a risk to the public and so could have their IPP discharged made their detention arbitrary and unlawful under Article 5(1) ECHR.[30] Although the IPP order was repealed in 2012, there were still 3,350 prisoners serving IPP orders at the end of June 2017.[31]

The use of criminal sanctions for precautionary reasons and without corresponding criminal law safeguards is controversial.[32] This is not punishment for unlawful behavior, administered after a public trial with recognized due process safeguards. It is detention as a form of precautionary risk management, ordered many years after the original trial and sentence.[33] In place of criminal law concepts of punishment and blame based on freedom of choice and individual responsibility, we see a philosophy of determinism or even predeterminism.[34]

Preventive detention on the grounds of "dangerousness" is not unique to Britain. While detention is employed in a number of European countries, the criteria and risk thresholds differ, as does the point at which such detention might be imposed: it may follow conviction, as with the IPP, or be purely precautionary in that it is imposed even before any offense has been committed. Preventive detention is lawful through a derogation from the guarantees set out in Article 5 ECHR if there is a clear public emergency threatening the life of the nation, as

[29] In *Secretary of State for Justice v. Walker and James* [2008] EWCA Civ. 30, although not holding the applicants' detention to be unlawful (both had been given IPPs), the Court of Appeal found that the secretary of state had acted unlawfully, because "he has not provided the resources needed to give effect to the policy that would ordinarily have given IPP prisoners a fair chance of demonstrating to the Parole Board . . . that they were no longer dangerous. . . . We are satisfied that his conduct has been in breach of his public law duty because its direct and natural consequence is to make it likely that a proportion of IPP prisoners will, avoidably, be kept in prison for longer than necessary either for punishment or for protection of the public, contrary to the intention of Parliament" (at para. 40).

[30] In *James, Wells and Lee v. UK* (25119/09, 57715/09, 57877/09) 18 September 2012, the court held that the failure to provide an opportunity to prisoners on IPPs to complete the instructional courses that the parole board considered necessary to demonstrate rehabilitation resulted in their detention being arbitrary and so unlawful and in breach of Article 5(1) ECHR.

[31] Beard (2017). The numbers continue to decrease, but slowly. There were around twenty-five hundred prisoners serving IPP orders at the end of 2018. The order was repealed under the Legal Aid, Sentencing and Punishment of Offenders Act 2012, which also put in place new provisions for life sentences to be imposed on conviction for a second serious offense and a new provision for extended sentences. See the provisions set out in Chapter 5 of the 2012 act.

[32] See further the discussion in the ECtHR case *M v. Germany* ECtHR (19359/04) 17 December 2009, re the distinctions made between penalties and preventive measures.

[33] "After conviction" means that the detention "must result from, follow and depend upon or occur by virtue of the 'conviction.'" *M v. Germany*, para. 88. See also *Jendrowiak v. Germany* (30060/04) 14 April 2011.

[34] Delmas-Marty criticizes this idea of predetermined behavior as a dangerous form of dehumanization. See Anne Chemin and Jean-Baptise Jacquin, "Loi antiterroriste: 'Nous sommes passés de l'Etat de droit à l'Etat de surveillance,'" *Le Monde*, 11 October 2017.

might be claimed to justify some counterterrorism measures, as discussed subsequently. But many of these orders concern the ordinary criminal law and often disproportionately include the young and the mentally disordered, as well as recidivists, especially in crimes of sexual violence.

In Belgium, like the IPP, preventive measures may be imposed after sentence for offenders considered dangerous,[35] or likely to commit further offenses because of a mental disorder.[36] In Switzerland too, dangerous offenders can be imprisoned, and sexual or violent offenders considered to be very dangerous and untreatable may be imprisoned for life on the basis of testimony from two experts. In France, those who are convicted of the most serious crimes, have a serious mental disorder,[37] and are sentenced to fifteen years' imprisonment or more can be placed in preventive detention under a security order (*rétention de sûreté*) for one year, renewable indefinitely. The order is imposed by a criminal judge, based on the perceived dangerousness of the individual in the opinion of a committee of experts.[38] Although it is described as an "exceptional" measure, the types of offenders eligible for this assessment have already been expanded.[39] The order has been criticized as confusing the responses of punishment and treatment, by confusing criminal responsibility and mental illness.[40]

B. Countering the Risk of Terrorism

Existing criminal justice narratives of security, dangerousness, and the management of risk paved the way for the preventive and precautionary approaches deemed necessary to address what was characterized as the new and different threat posed by twenty-first-century terrorism. By framing terrorism as exceptional, the state's powers to interfere with the liberty of individuals have been extended, enabling it to do more, for longer, and with less justification. This is evidenced through different, often preventive, modes of criminalization; the

[35] That is, where there is a risk that the offender will repeat serious offenses harming the physical or mental integrity of a person and there is no way to contain that risk through release under parole.

[36] See, e.g., Mary et al. (2011).

[37] Article 706-53-13 CPP.

[38] The French Conseil constitutionnel has considered whether the *rétention de sûreté* is a criminal or a security measure (in determining the permissibility of retrospective application) but has reached no clear conclusion. Decision No. 2008-562 DC, 21 February 2008. While holding that it is neither a punishment nor a penalty resembling a punishment, the Conseil inferred that the principle of nonretroactivity did not apply. However, it then went on to say that because preventive detention is a deprivation of liberty that may last for a person's lifetime and is ordered after criminal conviction, the measure should not be applied retrospectively.

[39] For further discussion of this and the sentencing process in France, see Hodgson and Soubise (2016b).

[40] Wyvekens (2010); Herzog-Evans (2011).

provision of new investigative and surveillance powers with lower thresholds of suspicion; the weakening of legal and judicial safeguards; and a greater reliance on intelligence in the development of law and policy, as well as in the operational policing of terrorism.[41] In both jurisdictions, the boundaries between the criminal and administrative have been dismantled by counterterrorism measures that challenge criminal procedural values as well as the institutional allocation of power and responsibility. Although Britain and France share common aims and objectives in the treatment of terrorism, the different ways in which they have effected legal and procedural reform reflect differences in their legal, institutional, and constitutional cultures as well as in the core values that shape their processes of law and criminal justice.

For example, at the heart of French terrorism investigations is a close collaboration between the judiciary and the intelligence services, in a way that would be alien to criminal justice actors in England and Wales. Faced with an unprecedented caseload following the wave of Basque and Corsican separatist terrorist attacks in the 1990s, this practice developed at the initiative of the judiciary, made possible by the existing legal structures of judicial supervision, in which police and judicial functions work cooperatively. No formal legal or procedural change was required. The judges responsible for the investigation, the *juges d'instruction*, simply adapted existing procedure in order to have the intelligence services, as well as police, at their disposal.[42] Several other factors ensured the success of this initiative. First, the predominant place of the judiciary within French legal culture means that *magistrats* are able to shape and influence criminal justice in a way that might be deemed inappropriate within the model in England and Wales, where judicial independence requires a greater separation from the executive and the development of law and policy.[43]

Second, a very broad definition of terrorism was provided for in the offense of *association de malfaiteurs*: "the participation in any group formed or association established with a view to the preparation, marked by one or more material actions, of any of the acts of terrorism provided for under the previous articles [of the criminal code]."[44] Described by the French government as "the

[41] Investigation and evidence gathering places greater emphasis on preventive intelligence gathering, integrating it more closely within the law enforcement function See, e.g., CONTEST in the UK, the counterterrorism strategy governing the organization intelligence agencies and counterterrorism policing.

[42] The intelligence agency, the DST (Direction de la surveillance du territoire), had previously operated only under the authority of the interior minister. See further Hodgson (2006a).

[43] A *magistrat* is the general French term for a judge or judicial officer, collectively known as the *magistrature*. A *juge* tends to refer to trial judges and the investigating judge (the *juge d'instruction*) and related roles that form part of sitting judiciary. These judges are independent of the executive and cannot be moved to a different post. The procureur, on the other hand, is under the hierarchy of the minister of justice and can be moved.

[44] In its 1999 report "France: Paving the Way for Arbitrary Justice," the Fédération internationale des droits de l'homme criticized the arbitrary and open-ended nature of the offense and the fact that

cornerstone of the system" of its counterterrorist work,[45] this allows the *juge* to open investigations into those involved with terrorist organizations (within and outside France) before any terrorist act has taken place.[46] The offense pushes back the boundary of criminality, enabling the judge to act very much earlier, when no criminal act has been committed but when the "suspect" is buying materials, is in the very early stages of preparation for a terrorist act, or is simply associating with a group established to prepare acts of terrorism—even when the judge is unable to identify a specific date or terrorist target to which these activities are linked.[47] This poses real challenges for the defense to try to unpick long and complex investigations built on an idea or a movement, rather than on the individual accused.[48]

The third key to the success of this investigative collaboration is the evidential use that can be made of information sourced from intelligence services, enabled by a model of pretrial judicial scrutiny understood to ensure the reliability and credibility of information presented as evidence. This reflects the different approach to the testing of evidence in French criminal procedure. In this more centralized, truth-seeking process, the emphasis is less on procedural standards of proof, with more latitude given to judicial fact-finding. There is an obvious tension, however, between the ECHR fair-trial right of the accused to confront and have examined witnesses against her and the reliance, in part, on a judicial officer to do this.[49] This is not an investigative response that is likely to develop

"the investigating and prosecuting authorities . . . are statutorily absolved from any duty to link the alleged participation with any actual execution of a terrorist offense or even a verifiable plan for the execution of such a plan. . . . That failure to concretize the alleged object of the association or conspiracy inevitably allows almost any kind of 'evidence' however trivial to be invested with significance" (FIDH [1999: 9–10]).

[45] Villepin (2006: 53).

[46] The law is very flexible concerning territoriality. This offense applies to those within and outside France, and to targets within and outside France. See, e.g., the arrest in June 2003 of Christian Ganczarski, a German national suspected by the French authorities of helping to organize the bombing of a synagogue in Djerba, Tunisia, killing twenty-one people. When the German authorities indicated that they lacked sufficient evidence to arrest him, the Saudi authorities deporting Ganczarski placed him on a flight via Paris, where he was arrested—the French claiming jurisdiction because French nationals were among the casualties in the Tunisia attack. Craig Whitlock, "French Push Limits in Fight on Terrorism," *Washington Post Foreign Service*, 2 November 2004.

[47] See also the excellent report and analysis of Human Rights Watch (2008).

[48] Defense lawyer Dominique Tricaud, as reported in Human Rights Watch (2008). Another defense lawyer, Henri de Beauregard, also explained: "There are 7.5 meters of case file, 78 volumes . . . 325 kilos of paper. That represents 541 hours of reading time, in other words three and a half months. The lawyer's fee for Mr. Charouali [his client] is 450 euro. So when you do the math, I have the right to 75 cents per hour to guarantee his defense. And I didn't have two to three months to prepare my case like the prosecutor did, but one-and-a-half months. The defense lawyer cannot do his job." Human Rights Watch (2008: 17).

[49] The principle of *contradictoire* is designed to bridge this procedural gap in a way that fits with more inquisitorial practices, but France has a poor record in enforcing the accused's right to examine witnesses, relying on written statements in place of oral testimony. See Weigend (2019) and the cases listed in note 147.

in England and Wales, however, where there is a very differently defined judicial function and the police enjoy exclusive authority over the pretrial investigation. Within an adversarial model of procedure, the greater focus on the trial and the testing of evidence through live testimony and cross-examination restricts the use that can be made of intelligence, including that obtained through intercept.[50]

However, recognizing the potential value of intelligence to terrorism prosecutions, some have given thought to the possibility of developing a French-inspired approach to enable the courts to admit intercept material as evidence in the criminal trial in England and Wales.[51] Using a judge to conduct a pretrial sift of the intelligence to be admitted as evidence, the Home Office carried out a pilot study, but concluded that this would not provide a suitable model.[52] There remained a "reliability gap" between evidence and intelligence, as the usual tests of credibility could not be applied: witnesses could not be cross-examined to determine the reliability of their evidence, and juries would be unable to assess the reliability of facts that were unsourced.[53]

While France is content to rely upon the "judicialization" of intelligence (the process of transforming intelligence into evidence through the vehicle of the judicial investigation), without proper opportunity for the defense to test out the intelligence evidence through cross-examination, this is not acceptable within more adversarial procedures. However, the government's concern with due process and respect for adversarial safeguards in this context is nevertheless surprising, given its willingness to weaken protections elsewhere.[54] A stronger motivation for the rejection of the pilot procedure was more likely to be concern over the obligations to disclose unused material once such evidence entered the

50 This has prevented prosecution in some cases where the primary evidence has been obtained by intercept and, some would argue, has been a factor in necessitating TPIMs and, before them, control orders.

51 See further discussion in Joint Committee on Human Rights (2006).

52 This would provide for a closed pretrial hearing in which sensitive material would be examined with a view to producing a statement of open evidence and conclusions from the closed material. A special advocate would represent the defendant. At trial, the defense could challenge the statement, but would have no right to go behind it to examine the material upon which it was based. The jury would be told of the process that had led to the production of the statement and would be able to consider it as they would a witness statement. The report of this pilot was provided to me by the Home Office when commissioning my 2006 report (Hodgson [2006a]. It is also referenced in the Joint Committee on Human Rights (2006: para. 75).

53 The study concluded that the intelligence material was inherently incapable of being properly tested and so could not be relied upon—a problem exacerbated when the intelligence source was outside the UK. The court cannot know the agent's motives, the circumstances in which the information was obtained, or whether the agent has been misled.

54 See, e.g., the UK government's willingness to accept evidence obtained through torture, provided the UK was not itself implicated in the act of torture in *A and Others v. Secretary of State for the Home Department (No. 2)* [2004] EWCA Civ. 1123. This was accepted by the Court of Appeal but then overruled by the House of Lords—see *A and Others v. Secretary of State for the Home Department (No. 2)* [2005] UKHL 71. For discussion of the use of evidence obtained by torture in terrorism cases, see Gasper (2005).

trial arena, which the government feared might pose an additional risk of compromising sources or methods.

Despite the claims of judicial supervision as a means of ensuring investigative oversight and pretrial scrutiny of evidence, it is unclear that it is able to offer the necessary guarantees implied by Article 6 ECHR, such as the right to confront and to challenge witnesses and evidence. The French model of pretrial judicial oversight does not interrogate either the nature or the basis of intelligence in the ways that the defense would wish. The *juge d'instruction* does not scrutinize intelligence as she might other forms of evidence. Like much of French criminal justice, this relies on the relationship of trust between the police and the judiciary.[55] A leading counterterrorism *juge d'instruction* explained the judiciary's total reliance on police:

> They're the ones who do the interfacing [with other intelligence services], and they don't tell us where they got the information. . . . We don't know whether the methods used were human or technical, or [even whether] the information comes from a third country.[56]

The result is the use of unsourced intelligence, produced by unknown persons in unknown conditions, which lacks credibility and poses real risks to those who are its subjects.[57] Of particular concern here is the use in criminal proceedings of information from third countries, which may have been obtained through torture or ill-treatment, and which is dignified as "evidence" despite the absence of any real judicial or defense scrutiny.

Although the legal procedural values, cultures, and structures in place in England and Wales would not permit such a radical transformation in working practices and accountability as seen in France, nonetheless, the framework and procedure of pretrial investigation have been adapted significantly in terrorism

[55] See generally Hodgson (2005); Mouhanna (2001).

[56] Former counterterrorism *juge d'instruction* M. Brugière, explaining to Human Rights Watch (2008) that judges only received evidence from the DST.

[57] The case of Hassan Diab, a Canadian citizen of Lebanese origin extradited by Canada to France for the bombing of a synagogue in 1980, demonstrates many of the dangers of relying on unsourced intelligence, as well as different evidential thresholds. Unknown intelligence sources claimed to point to Diab's involvement, but once in court, the handwriting "expert" who concluded that Diab's writing matched that of the suspected bomber was found to have used a sample of his wife's handwriting. An additional expert was called, and although the Canadian court had reservations as to the expert's reliability, this report tipped the balance to extradition. See *France v. Diab*, 2014 ONCA 374. The case was then investigated in France and the *juge d'instruction* concluded that there was insufficient evidence to go to trial. Diab's release was ordered eight times by four different judges, but overturned on appeal each time. http://www.lemonde.fr/societe/article/2017/11/08/nouvel-examen-de-la-demande-de-remise-en-liberte-du-principal-suspect-de-l-attentat-de-la-rue-copernic_5212133_3224.html. After spending three years in prison, Diab was finally returned to Canada in January 2018. See Segal (2019).

cases there too. The successful collaboration between police and prosecutors in the CPS Counter Terrorism Division contrasts sharply with the structural separation of police and prosecution functions in ordinary crime, and (unconsciously) reflects something of the French model of judicial supervision through cooperation during the investigation phase. Now merged into the Special Crime and Counter Terrorism Division, prosecuting lawyers work closely with investigating officers as well as with the Director of Public Prosecutions (DPP). They are responsible for advising the police in all terrorism cases and are frequently consulted during the evidence-gathering phase, as well as making all charging decisions. In this way they work alongside, rather than after, the police investigation. This seems also to engender a more positive professional culture of co-operation, in contrast to the resentment sometimes felt by officers toward the CPS role in ordinary investigations.[58] The nature of this collaboration is limited, however, by the institutional structures of police and prosecution in England and Wales compared with those in France: unlike the procureur (public prosecutor) or the *juge d'instruction*, crown prosecutors have no direct authority over the police, nor any originating powers of investigation.

(i) Ordinary and Exceptional?

The importance of counterterrorism responses grounded in criminal law and fair trial rights[59]—rather than using, for example, the kinds of special jurisdiction employed by France during the Algerian conflict[60]—is often emphasized. However, terrorism is also considered to be qualitatively different from other types of crime in its scope, in the nature of the harm that it causes, and in the threat that it poses to legal and political security. In this sense, it is characterized as exceptional. What might loosely be termed contemporary Islamist terrorism is understood to be different again, taking place in less organized and systematic ways,[61] often involving the suicide of perpetrators, and lacking the clear political

[58] See discussion in the following chapter.

[59] See e.g., Directive (EU) 2017/541 of 15 March 2017 on combatting terrorism and replacing Council Framework Decision 2002/475/JHA and amending Council Decision 2005/671/JHA. Also Galli and Weyembergh (2012).

[60] A state security court (*cour de sûreté de l'état*) was charged with investigating, prosecuting, and trying offenses against the internal and external security of the state. It sat in secret and was composed partly of military officers. It was seen ultimately as a tool of political oppression and was dismantled in 1981 when Mitterand took power. Hodgson (2006a).

[61] See further Phythian (2005). Kepel (2004: 6) describes al-Qaeda as "less of a military base of operations than a database that connected jihadists all over the world via the Internet. . . . Even as bin Laden disappeared into the valleys and caves of the Afghan-Pakistan border, he reappeared in cyberspace to claim responsibility for deadly attacks as far away as Indonesia."

objectives of those carrying out earlier forms of terrorist attacks.[62] The nature of the harm is described variously as a threat to the values of Western societies, to "our way of life," or to "the fundamentals of our democracy"[63] and even as motivated by a "hatred of our very existence."[64] Uncertainty is its key feature, and so surveillance, intelligence, mass data gathering and prevention are central,[65] underwritten in part by the EU.[66] This new mode of terrorism is understood to require, and so to justify, exceptional responses different from those of the ordinary criminal law.[67]

In both Britain and France, as a result, we have witnessed voluminous and complex legislation introduced at great speed, through emergency procedures and with little oversight. Exceptional forms of police and administrative detention and questioning are permitted, and new preventive and even precautionary criminal offenses, drafted in vague and contingent terms, criminalize behavior (or the risk of criminal behavior) at an early stage.[68] Administrative authorities are empowered to exercise criminal-type powers, restricting the liberty and freedoms of individuals considered dangerous in some form, while safeguards over the exercise of these powers, especially when used routinely and at street level, have been weakened or removed altogether.[69]

62 In the French white paper "Prevailing against Terrorism," Villepin (2006: 10) characterizes the threat as coming from "global Islamist-inspired terrorism. . . . It is distinguished by its ability to borrow from globalization the very tools that have enabled globalization to succeed. It manages to combine very personal individual concerns with lofty international perspectives; it shows a preference for people-to-people networks; it uses electronic means; it places a premium on publicity; and it shows a capacity for permanent evolution, even advance planning."

63 Then-home secretary Charles Clarke, in response to a question from the Home Affairs Select Committee, Minutes of Evidence, 8 February 2005, answer to Q5.

64 Then-chancellor Gordon Brown said of al-Qaeda, "Let us be clear: we face enemies that not only have a hatred of the policies we pursue, but a hatred of our very existence." 13 February 2006, speech at Royal United Services Institute.

65 These intrusions into individual privacy, without any criminal suspicion, are conducted without informing the individual under observation (Roach [2004: 522]), in a way that is more akin to intelligence gathering than criminal investigation.

66 The European Data Retention Directive (2006) requires member states to retain communications data relating to the traffic between individuals and organizations.

67 See discussion in Hodgson and Tadros (2013), who argue that the definition of terrorism is unclear and leaves an overbroad discretion to prosecutors and ministers. The same view was expressed by David Anderson, then independent reviewer of terrorism legislation in part 10 of his 2014 annual report and in subsequent years. See also Weigend (2006b); Marret (2003); Walker (2007). The lack of clarity is also problematic for the courts. See, e.g., *R (Miranda) v. Secretary of State for the Home Department and Commissioner for the Metropolitan Police* [2016] EWCA 6 concerning detention and seizing of journalistic material under terrorism powers. The Court of Appeal read a mens rea requirement into the definition of terrorism under the 2000 Terrorism Act, but the home secretary declined to amend the statute accordingly.

68 By contingent I mean that there are not fixed parameters or conditions for commission of the offense, but a series of possibilities.

69 This has happened through France's state of emergency (extended police powers to search bags and to conduct house searches at night; administrative police powers to detain a person for questioning for four hours without a lawyer) and then in both France (legislating many of the "emergency" powers) and the UK (new criminal offenses and police powers) as part of the ordinary criminal law.

Underpinning this exceptionalism is a precautionary approach based on the possibility of harm, through which governments seek to expand investigative powers, often claiming reliance on intelligence sources.[70] This was seen in the fixation on increased periods of detention for terrorist suspects in England and Wales, which gave rise to concerns about the lawfulness of what seemed to be a de facto strategy of prevention and disruption, given that "the criminal law has not traditionally been a preventive tool in the UK."[71] Although Article 5(1) ECHR prohibits detention for the purposes of disruption or prevention, in 2006, the Home Affairs Committee reported that this was in fact its primary use and suggested, further, that preventive detention should be included as a statutory ground for detention. This was swiftly rejected by the Joint Committee on Human Rights (2006), which pointed out that this would require a derogation from Article 5(1), something the committee did not believe to be necessary.[72] The proposals to extend detention and questioning yet further from twenty-eight to forty-two days in terrorism cases also lacked the kinds of safeguards necessary to oversee the police exercise of such power and could not even be said to be a properly judicial procedure. Made on the order of the home secretary, it would be a decision of the executive. Furthermore, the extended detention and questioning of terrorist suspects became increasingly symbolic of a political discourse emphasizing fear of the unknown from which the public could be protected, rather than a legal necessity. Despite claims of the increasingly complex nature of terrorism investigations and the race against time to search computers domestically and internationally, the impetus for extending detention came from the government, rather than those working in counterterrorism cases. The Crown Prosecution Service opposed the extension to forty-two days, the government itself did not contend that the twenty-eight-day limit had proved inadequate, and the home secretary admitted that the security service had not directly requested a longer detention period.

[70] For example, in 2007, the day before the government announced proposals to extend precharge detention and questioning of terrorist suspects in police custody from twenty-eight to forty-two days, the head of M15 announced that there were two thousand active terrorists in Britain with a strategy of "methodically and intentionally targeting young people and children in this country" (Jonathon Evans, the head of M15, 5 November, 2007). Government claims that investigations would be hampered without longer periods of precharge detention were unsubstantiated, and the proposal was defeated in the Lords. In 2012, the detention period was reduced to fourteen days under the Protection of Freedoms Act, with provision for emergency legislation allowing twenty-eight-day detention in exceptional cases.

[71] Joint Committee on Human Rights (2006: para. 12).

[72] The government continued to argue that twenty-eight days was insufficient but there was no evidence that the terrorist threat had increased since the twenty-eight-day limit was set, nor that the complexity of terrorist investigations had increased. Home Affairs Select Committee (2007); Joint Committee on Human Rights (2007, 2008).

The political, rather than legal, character of these debates is borne out by the figures for the detention of terrorist suspects, which suggest that the reduction in 2011 to fourteen days was never likely to hamper investigations: of the 1,558 terrorist suspects detained in the decade since 11 September 2001, only 11 were held for longer than fourteen days.[73] However, the attenuation of due process safeguards remains. Two weeks is still considerably longer than detention in nonterrorist cases, and while the figures suggest that terrorist suspects are not being held for weeks at a time, much is left to investigative discretion, and more than half of all suspects held are released without charge.[74] There are grounds additional to those in nonterrorist cases, on which access to legal advice and informing a third party of the suspect's detention may be delayed, as well as financial sanctions and restrictions on movement after the sentence has been served.[75]

In France too, the detention of terrorist suspects has been extended to six days. As with other serious crimes such as organized crime and drug trafficking, detention beyond forty-eight hours requires the authorization of the *juge des libertés et de la détention*. As a member of the "sitting" judiciary, she is independent of the executive and so regarded as a stronger judicial authority than the procureur (who authorizes detention up to forty-eight hours), able to sanction greater infringements of liberty and more intrusive police measures. However, this period of detention relates only to police questioning. If the case then passes to the *juge d'instruction* for investigation, as all terrorism cases will, detention will continue to be reviewed by the *juge des libertés et de la détention*, but the

[73] Home Office (2011), Table 1.03; 517 suspects were charged, 906 released, and 135 cautioned under nonterrorist legislation or dealt with under immigration or mental health legislation. Of these suspects, 694 were held for less than one day, a further 292 for up to two days, a further 411 for under seven days, and a further 150 for under fourteen days. Figures from more recent reports from the independent reviewer of terrorism legislation suggest that nearly all suspects are detained for less than a week and around one-quarter for less than two days (after which time a warrant for further detention is required from the court).

[74] The Terrorism Act 2000, section 41, also provides for a special power of arrest that does not require the officer to have a specific offense in mind—it is enough that there is reasonable suspicion that a person is or has been concerned in the commission, preparation, or instigation of acts of terrorism. This power is used around fifty times each year. Most terrorism-related arrests are under PACE rather than terrorism legislation (see Independent Reviewer of Terrorism Legislation, Annual Report 2015, section 8).

[75] Section 8 of Schedule 8 of the Terrorism Act 2000. Section 9 of Schedule 8 also permits legal advice to take place within the sight and hearing of a police officer in some circumstances. The greater reach of state powers extends to asset freezing. There are provisions in section 2 of the Terrorist Asset Freezing etc. Act 2010 to freeze the assets of those that the Treasury reasonably believes to be involved in the commission, preparation, or instigation of acts of terrorism, or those supporting or facilitating others in such involvement. The government has made it clear that this does not require proof even on the balance of probabilities. (See Joint Committee on Human Rights [2010]). Part IV of the Counter-Terrorism Act 2008 imposes a requirement on those convicted of terrorist offenses for a period of ten years to keep the police informed of their name, address, date of birth, and national insurance number and, in some instances, of any intention to leave the country, including destination and proposed dates.

suspect may be held in custody for up to four years.[76] It is of course possible that at the end of this period, no prosecution will be brought.[77] This lengthy and substantial infringement of liberty has been held to be proportionate by the Conseil constitutionnel and not to violate individual freedom excessively.

In both jurisdictions, offenses relating to terrorism are drafted in contingent terms—criminalizing the possession of information that is "likely to be useful" to a person preparing an act of terrorism,[78] or articles possessed "in circumstances which give rise to a reasonable suspicion" that possession is "for a purpose connected with the commission, preparation or instigation of acts of terrorism"[79] and even criminalizing the failure of individuals and organizations to report their suspicions. These offenses are extremely broad, with little or no mens rea requirement, lacking the precision that we expect and require of the criminal law.[80] Under the Terrorism Act 2006, for example, sections 1 and 2 create new offenses of the encouragement of terrorism and the dissemination of terrorist publications (both punishable by up to seven years' imprisonment), described by some commentators as part of the "new global McCarthyism."[81] They have been criticized as being vague in their definition and scope, and an unnecessary extension of the current criminal prohibitions on incitement to violence.[82] Although these provisions were presented as the enactment of the Council of Europe Convention on the Prevention of Terrorism 2005,[83] the Joint Committee on Human Rights concluded that the offense of encouraging or glorifying terrorism does not comply with the permitted restrictions to the right to freedom of expression under Article 10 ECHR.[84]

[76] Article 145-2 CPP. Where there is an exceptional security risk if the person were to be released, the *chambre de l'instruction* may extend detention for four months, renewable once, making an additional eight months in total.

[77] There is a statutory right to compensation in such cases, but the fact remains that this is detention for investigation, not while awaiting trial.

[78] Section 57 Terrorism Act 2000.

[79] Section 58 Terrorism Act 2000.

[80] See Hodgson and Tadros (2009, 2013).

[81] See, e.g., Johnson (2005). George Clooney's film on McCarthyism, *Goodnight and Good Luck* (2005), captures well the ease with which, within a climate of fear, a creeping enemy is created, despite the absence of hard fact or evidence.

[82] See further Hunt (2007).

[83] While the Convention expressly requires that there is a specific intention to incite the commission of a terrorist offense, the *mens rea* for the section 1 offense includes reckless as well as intentional encouragement. The second restriction that the Convention places on the definition of the offense is that there must be danger that someone will be encouraged to commit an act of terrorism (in order to guard against undue interference with freedom of expression, particularly in "indirect encouragement" cases), but the UK statute does not include this. Terrorism Act 2006 section 1(5)(b). See Hunt (2007: 457), who argues that section 3 Human Rights Act 1998 requires that the danger element be read into the statute to comply with the proportionality requirements of Article 10 ECHR.

[84] The "glorification" requirement is too vague, the definition of terrorism too broad, and the offense may be committed with no awareness that the defendant's statement is likely to encourage the commission of a terrorist act—objective recklessness will suffice. This was changed from subjective to objective recklessness at the report stage of the bill. Showing remarkably little faith in the jury's

In England and Wales, one of the most controversial new offenses was that of acts preparatory to terrorism, created under section 5 of the Terrorism Act 2006. While the ordinary criminal law defines an attempt as an act that is "more than merely preparatory" and requires an intention to commit an offense,[85] the new offense criminalizes conduct in preparation for giving effect to an intention to commit or assist in acts of terrorism, that is, activity that is "merely preparatory." Thus, the prosecution must show that there is an intention to commit an act of terrorism or to assist another to do so, and some act that works toward giving effect to that intention. In this highly precautionary approach, the individual is criminalized at a very early stage, and much rests on the exercise of prosecutorial discretion. Similar to the French *association de malfaiteurs*, the offense is celebrated for its flexibility in allowing for the intervention of criminal investigation powers in a more preventive intelligence-gathering fashion.

Lending further weight to the discourse of exceptionalism and the urgency of taking action has been the rhetoric of the "war on terror" seen most strongly in the first decade following 9/11.[86] Rejecting rule-of-law considerations such as accountability and proportionality, casting the subject of the criminal law as an enemy to be controlled, politicians resorted to the politics of fear to justify measures that would otherwise be impermissible, "opportunistic changes that would not have been sustained outside a period of crisis,"[87] in what Kostakopoulou describes as a siege mode of democracy.[88] Furthermore, once in place, such reforms provided an alibi for a more general expansion of police and executive power.[89] For example, the former Labour administration sought to introduce an identity card scheme, claiming that "the scheme will help the security services in their investigations into organised crime and terrorist activities and

ability to assess the evidence at trial, Hazel Blears, MP, said, "If we have only a subjective test, people will be able to say that they did not realise what the effect of their actions would be. We would then find it incredibly difficult to prosecute people who genuinely were encouraging other people, indirectly, to commit terrorist acts." House of Commons Debate, *Hansard* 9 November 2005, col. 390.

[85] Section 1(1) Criminal Attempts Act 1981: "If, with intent to commit an offence to which this section applies, a person does an act which is more than merely preparatory to the commission of the offence, he is guilty of attempting to commit the offence." See, e.g., *Geddes* (1996) Crim. LR 894 (CA).

[86] See, e.g., Sassòli (2006); Marret (2003: 10). The attack on the World Trade Center was quickly compared in the United States to the attack on Pearl Harbor. Even President Obama, in his inauguration speech, continued to talk of America being at war. Governments have also declared a war on drugs, on organized crime, and so on, perhaps denoting their determination to deal with the issue, but these are harms that can be reduced, not wars that can be won.

[87] Walker (2006: 1143).

[88] One that supplants the rights model of democracy: "Under such circumstances, officials invoke the existence of an emergency in order to protect the life of the nation and are willing to apply the national security exception even to areas where clearly national security is not at issue." Kostakopoulou (2008: 321).

[89] See, e.g., Cahn (2009: 469).

help protect the UK against threats to national security."[90] It seems unlikely that an identity card requirement would assist the counterterrorism effort, and the subsequent coalition government abandoned the proposal. In France, immediately following the death of Mohamed Merah, the man responsible for killing seven people in Toulouse in 2012, President Sarkozy announced that anybody regularly consulting websites apologizing for terrorism or violence would be held criminally liable, as would those responsible for the propagation of terrorist ideology.[91] Yet Merah had been under surveillance by the Direction centrale du renseignement intérieur (Central Directorate of Domestic Intelligence), which described him as a lone wolf, and there was nothing to suggest that he had been radicalized through such sites.[92]

The rhetoric has now changed in some quarters.[93] President Obama officially rejected the narrative of the war on terror, though he continued to speak of a war against al-Qaeda,[94] and arguably, there is a shift away from the politics of fear, of the Muslim "other,"[95] a strategy that inevitably failed to win the confidence of the communities whose support governments needed.[96] The UK's counterterrorism strategy continues to emphasize prevention, focusing on infrastructure

[90] "Benefits to Society" Identity and Passport Service, Home Office at www.identitycards.gov.uk/benefits-society-terrorism.asp.

[91] Being an apologist for terrorism is broadly conceived. A "militant vegan" was placed under investigation in France in March 2018 for posting on Facebook that there was some justice in a butcher (himself a killer) being killed by a terrorist.

[92] Yves Bordenave and Laurent Borredon, "Questions sur la surveillance de Mohamed Merah par la DCRI," *Le Monde*, 22 March 2012. Also controversial were the arrests of twenty or more suspected Islamists within a week of Merah's death.

[93] On 7 December 2017, the UK foreign secretary, Boris Johnson, speaking of the defeat of Daesh in Raqqa, spoke of "prosecuting the struggle" and the need to change the metaphor to one of disease and contagion. "How Global Britain Is Helping to Win the Struggle against Islamist Terror," speech delivered on 7 December 2017 by Boris Johnson, available at https://www.gov.uk/government/speeches/how-global-britain-is-helping-to-win-the-struggle-against-islamist-terror. The British government's 2011 "Review of Counter-Terrorism and Security Powers," for example, purported to offer a corrective in favor of liberty.

[94] Introducing his May 2010 National Security Strategy (pp. ii–iii), he announced: "Our long-term security will come not from our ability to instill fear in other peoples, but through our capacity to speak to their hopes." The strategy (Barack Obama, 2010: 19–20) talks of "waging a global campaign against al-Qa'ida and its terrorist affiliates . . . pursuing a strategy that . . . builds positive partnerships with Muslim communities around the world. . . . We will always seek to delegitimize the use of terrorism and to isolate those who carry it out. Yet this is not a global war against a tactic—terrorism or a religion—Islam. We are at war with a specific network, al-Qa'ida, and its affiliates who support efforts to attack the United States, our allies, and partners."

[95] As Croft (2007: 319) notes: "Prior to 9/11, no-one spoke of the category: 'British Muslim.' It is a category entirely created by those attacks, by government, media and broader community responses."

[96] See, e.g., in the UK, the evidence of the former head of MI5 Eliza Manningham-Buller, to the Chilcot inquiry into the Iraq war. She told the inquiry: "Our involvement in Iraq radicalised, for want of a better word, a whole generation of young people—not a whole generation, a few among a generation—who saw our involvement in Iraq and Afghanistan as being an attack upon Islam." She also stated that it substantially exacerbated the threat to Britain of international terrorism. "Former MI5 Chief Delivers Damning Verdict on Iraq Invasion," *The Guardian*, 20 July 2010.

resilience and identifying and working to prevent radicalization,[97] with intelligence remaining a key plank in government policy. France, however, has suffered major attacks on its own soil and has responded by continuing to legislate. Following the 2015 Paris attacks, a state of emergency was declared that lasted two years, bringing in new exceptional powers that ultimately became a part of the ordinary common law.

(ii) Prevention without Criminalization

In addition to using the ordinary criminal law in exceptional ways, an important strand of counterterrorism strategy both in Britain and in France has been to utilize means other than the criminal law to search, question, investigate, and detain individuals. By employing powers and measures located within immigration and administrative structures, the due process protections of the criminal process could be avoided. In England and Wales, preventive detention and restrictions to freedom of movement have been employed in order to manage the perceived risk of mainly foreign nationals considered a danger to national security.[98] These measures represent a kind of securitization of immigration procedures in what has come to be known as a process of "crimmigration."[99] The Anti-Terrorism, Crime and Security Act (ATCSA) 2001 put in place a form of preventive detention that, while clearly coercive and involving a significant (and indefinite) deprivation of liberty of foreign nationals, was characterized as an immigration, rather than criminal, procedure. The detainees were held in Belmarsh high-security prison and could not be deported because of the ill-treatment they were likely to suffer in their home country, nor could they be prosecuted because of the sensitive nature of the intelligence against them. While concern to protect sources and operational methods is quite legitimate, perhaps more surprising are the terms in which the then-head of M15 explained the difficulties in bringing a criminal prosecution in these instances: "We may be *confident* that an individual or group is planning an attack but that *confidence* comes from the sort of intelligence I described earlier, *patchy* and *fragmentary* and *uncertain*, to be interpreted and assessed."[100]

97 The Prevent strategy focuses on the prevention of radicalization and is part of the wider counterterrorist policy CONTEST.

98 Though interestingly, when control orders were introduced in 2005, replacing preventive detention in Belmarsh, all those subject to the orders were foreign nationals. When they were replaced by a new form of order, the TPIM (Terrorism Prevention and Investigation Measure), all were British citizens.

99 A term coined by Stumpf (2006).

100 Eliza Manningham-Buller, director general of the Security Service (head of M15), speech at the Ridderzaal, Binnehof, The Hague, Netherlands, to commemorate the sixtieth anniversary of the Dutch security service, the AIVD; my emphasis.

Detainees were not permitted to know the full extent of the accusations against them, and special advocates were appointed to examine and challenge the secret evidence. The value of this was limited by the fact that special advocates could not discuss the "closed" information with the detainees and so could not take any specific instructions that might enable them to challenge the veracity of the material. National security trumped the usual adversarial guarantees that would be required were this to be classed as a criminal matter, and this was criticized as turning the Special Immigration Appeals Commission (SIAC) "from a specialist immigration tribunal to a de facto counter-terrorism court."[101]

This controversial regime was brought to an end in *A v. Secretary of State for the Home Department* [2004] UKHL 56. The court declared the detention of foreign nationals under section 23 of ATCSA incompatible with Article 5 of the ECHR, rejecting the derogation argument.[102] It was a disproportionate response in Convention terms. It failed to resolve the problem it claimed to address: foreign nationals could choose deportation and so "export" terrorism, and UK citizens suspected of terrorism remained at large. Lord Hoffman argued that it was not necessary to decide whether the nonapplication of the legislation to UK citizens was fatal, as, in his view, there was no threat to the life of the nation and so derogation was not permissible. The government's response was the enactment of the Prevention of Terrorism Act 2005, section 2 of which allowed the home secretary to place individuals under a control order if she suspects terrorist involvement and considers the order necessary to protect the public from a risk of terrorism. The control order mirrored the kinds of bail conditions imposed by SIAC on those not subjected to the Belmarsh prison detention regime, but unlike the Belmarsh regime, they could also be used against British citizens.[103]

Control orders and their successor, the TPIM (Terrorism Prevention and Investigation Measure), are further examples of preventive justice. Although this authority is not part of the criminal law, the individual may have her liberty restricted in various ways if the home secretary (approved by the High Court) considers this necessary to protect the public from a risk of terrorism.[104] Typically, this will require residence at a specified address, a curfew, and restrictions on travel and movement, on financial and property transactions, on

[101] Justice evidence to Select Committee quoted in Boon and Nash (2006: n. 34).

[102] Under Article 5 ECHR, detention is permissible while action is being taken to deport a person, but not to hold a person indefinitely on security grounds.

[103] See the description of the bail conditions of G, one of the appellants in *A v. Secretary of State for the Home Department* [2004] UKHL 56, described at para. 35.

[104] Under the Terrorism Prevention and Investigation Measures Act 2011, section 3, the home secretary must be satisfied on the balance of probabilities that the individual is, or has been, involved in terrorism-related activity, some or all of which must be new terrorism-related activity. The restriction must be necessary to protect the public and restrict the person's involvement in terrorist activity.

electronic communications, and on association and communication. Initially, the TPIM lasts for up to two years, but on new evidence it can be renewed for a further two years and so on, indefinitely. These are significant preventive measures to impose on a person who has not been tried and convicted in a criminal court, with the attendant procedural and evidential safeguards. Like detention under the ATCSA and control orders, TPIMs will be made on the basis of secret evidence examined in closed proceedings, using special advocates; neither the subject of the TPIM nor her lawyer is permitted to be present.[105] Special advocates have reported the excessive use of closed evidence. In all cases, they have been able to point to material that was available from an open source, but which the government unnecessarily placed as closed material.[106]

In practice, although the impact on the individual's freedom is great, these preventive orders have been made against a small number of people, in contrast to the thousands of individuals impacted by extended police powers and new terrorism offenses. However, despite their limited use, preventive orders have been important as a display of executive power in response to a perceived threat and in pushing the boundaries of procedures and processes that would not ordinarily be tolerated—the use of closed evidence and secret hearings so that evidence cannot be challenged and trials are not public, and a denial of proper legal representation through the special advocate scheme.[107] Once in place, these exceptional procedures have spread to other types of hearing as a model to be copied.[108]

In France, the existing preventive/investigative dualism inherent in the police function, which had proved so useful to the judiciary in recruiting the aid of the intelligence services, this time provided the framework for placing counter-terrorism measures outside, rather than within, the criminal law. Following the November 2015 attacks in Paris, a three-month state of emergency was imposed (ultimately extended to two years), under which France introduced a variety of

[105] TPIMs are resource intensive and have been the subject of much controversy. There are now fewer than ten in operation in the UK, and they are applied overwhelmingly to British citizens, rather than foreign nationals.

[106] See, e.g., the Justice report *Secret Evidence* (2009: paras. 432–437); JCHR (2007a: paras. 195–199); and the oral evidence of Nick Blake, QC, to the committee. He gave an example of material dealt with in closed evidence that appeared to be from a senior al-Qaeda suspect, but which it emerged (when a Security Service witness was questioned) had been published on the internet by the Iraqi government the previous year. It should have been within the open evidence, but since most barristers are not Arabic linguists, they had no way of verifying this.

[107] Special advocates cannot advocate for the person they represent in the way that is required within the professional lawyer-client relationship. Disclosure of the "gist" of matters that are to be kept secret is not enough, and the system of closed hearings and special advocates "is, self evidently and admittedly, a distinctly second best attempt to secure a just outcome to proceedings. . . . It should never be regarded as an acceptable substitute for the compromise of a fundamental right such as is at stake in this case." *Al Rawi v. Security Service* [2011] UKSC 34 at para. 94.

[108] See, e.g., Justice and Security Act 2013. As well as in SIAC and for TPIMs, these procedures are used in Asset Freezing Orders, Employment Tribunals.

exceptional police powers and preventive measures that sit outside the traditional regime of judicial procedural protections. Characterized as powers designed to prevent rather than investigate terrorism, they are exercised by officers in their administrative rather than criminal function. Therefore, rather than being accountable to an independent judicial authority, officers are able to operate under the administrative authority of the préfet—the representative of state authority in the region and head of the local political administration.[109]

The measures put in place included broad discretionary powers allowing the administrative police to search people's homes, including at night, without the usual judicial authorization that would be constitutionally required if these same powers were carried out as part of a criminal investigation.[110] In this way, powers infringing the rights of the individual, usually requiring reasonable suspicion of criminal activity and exercised under judicial control, were assigned to the political administration, requiring only weak justificatory grounds that depended on vague concepts of dangerousness.[111] The very broad criteria for such searches tend toward a permissive, rather than a cautious, approach,[112] and evidence suggests that officers abused this discretion. Independent oversight bodies report that the police and gendarmes exercised their powers in discriminatory and disproportionate ways.[113] Those subject to searches were treated violently, their property damaged, and actions were targeted at them as Muslims rather than being motivated by any ground for legal suspicion.[114] There were also reports that these exceptional powers were used for purposes unconnected to the state of

[109] The préfet enjoys the powers of the administrative police and is responsible for public order. The direct representative of the prime minister, she is named by the Council of Ministers, by presidential decree on the advice of the prime minister and the interior minister. She has a range of responsibilities including organizing elections, being responsible for issuing identity cards and driver's licenses, promoting the social economic and cultural life of the region, and managing the emergency services.

[110] In the first ten weeks of the state of emergency regime, 3,242 searches were carried out, according to the Ministry of Interior. Amnesty International (2016: 10).

[111] The administrative police are required simply to have serious grounds to think the person is a threat to public order. This is in addition to the wider powers already extended to the police to conduct identity checks; to conduct searches of vehicles and dwellings without the owner's consent; to engage in undercover surveillance by placing cameras in dwellings and in vehicles and to infiltrate organizations; to intercept communications; and to interview witnesses and suspects abroad. Legislation in 2006 allowed (and even required) the use of video surveillance cameras in airports, train stations, on public transport, and wherever acts of terrorism may be carried out, and in the interests of fighting terrorism, the many databases held by the police and gendarmes have been formalized and centralized.

[112] Searches of any premises are permitted if there are serious reasons to believe the location is frequented by a person whose behavior constitutes a threat to public order and security. Article 11 of Law No. 55-385 of 3 April 1955 regarding the state of emergency, amended on 21 November 2015. Under Article 6, assigned residence can be ordered on the same grounds, authorized by the Ministry of Interior.

[113] France has two policing bodies or functions: the national police, working under the interior minister, and the gendarmes who are part of the army.

[114] Amnesty International (2016); Défenseur des droits (2016).

emergency, for example, placing climate change activists under house arrest.[115] Reporting to the French parliament in February 2016, the *défenseur des droits*, Jacques Toubon, noted complaints relating to police behavior during searches,[116] but also other measures connected to the state of emergency in which individuals had been mistreated and discriminated against for wearing a veil, having a beard, or wearing a headscarf, for example.[117]

Although not placing people in preventive detention as allowed in Britain under the ATCSA 2001, the temporary emergency regime also permitted the préfet to place individuals under house arrest and to impose conditions on their movements and communications,[118] in a way similar to the TPIM, as well as to detain individuals for up to four hours if there are serious reasons to think they might be linked to terrorist activity. The measures were controversial, and, reporting on their implementation, Amnesty found evidence that they were exercised in a way that was disproportionate and discriminatory. Turning to the no-suspicion stop-and-search powers provided to police in England and Wales under the 2000 Terrorism Act, in both jurisdictions we observe that the precautionary approach to terrorism has produced exceptional powers, widely drawn, with weak justification thresholds and little or no independent oversight, and those powers come to be exercised routinely and disproportionately, to the point where they are no longer considered exceptional.

(iii) Normalizing the Exceptional

Without stringent processes of accountability, there is always the fear that powers and procedures justified as exceptional will be used for nonexceptional purposes and ultimately will find their way into the ordinary law, especially when other nonterrorist forms of criminality are added to the mix. This was seen in the United States as fourteen of the sixteen temporary powers contained in the 2001 USA Patriot Act (itself legislated with no opportunity for anything more than a thumbs up or down) were made permanent, and the 2006 USA Patriot Improvement Act expanded counterterrorist powers and attached unrelated antidrug measures.[119]

115 Amnesty International (2016).

116 For example, a search conducted from midnight until 4:00 a.m., searching the children's bedrooms without their parents being present, requiring the children to place their hands in the air.

117 Avis du Défenseur des droits No. 16-06, available at https://ipcan.org/fr/publications-fr/defenseur-des-droits-avis-n16-06-du-26-fevrier-2016.

118 By the end of January 2015, more than 350 people were subject to assigned residence orders. Amnesty International (2016: 6).

119 Donoghue (2008: 2).

In France, terrorism powers are often extended to drug trafficking and organized crime, permitting longer detention in police custody, for example. However, in 2006, substantially greater investigative powers, including covert surveillance in people's homes, were provided for in terrorism investigations and so more generally in the investigation of organized crime.[120] In practice, this has widened police powers in the nonterrorism context considerably, as organized crime is not limited to the most serious forms of criminal activity, but is defined in very broad terms: there are eighteen types of offenses in this category ranging from murder to theft,[121] which constitute organized, rather than ordinary, crime when committed by "any group formed or any association established for the preparation of one or more offenses, characterised by one or more material acts."[122] This means that two children who steal the pencil case of their classmate have engaged in organized crime.

In England and Wales, like the broad administrative powers provided under the state of emergency in France, wide police powers were legislated, but with insufficient oversight and accountability to ensure they were not used in the policing of nonexceptional and nonterrorist matters. Sections 44 and 45 of the Terrorism Act 2000 gave the police in England and Wales the power to stop vehicles and pedestrians at random and to search for articles that might be used in connection with terrorism—but without the need for any grounds for suspecting the presence of such articles. As an exceptional power (in both its breadth and imprecision), authorization for a maximum period of twenty-eight days was required to carry out such searches within a specified area if it was considered "expedient" for the prevention of acts of terrorism.[123] However, the power was not used in an exceptional way: uninterrupted authorizations in the Metropolitan Police District were made from the moment the law came into force on 19 February 2001 and continued for nearly a decade.[124]

Both Lord Carlile (then independent reviewer of counterterrorism legislation) and the Joint Committee on Human Rights expressed deep concern at

[120] In order to combat terrorism and other forms of organized crime, the police now enjoy wider powers to conduct identity checks; to conduct searches of vehicles and dwellings without the owner's consent; to engage in undercover surveillance by placing cameras in dwellings and in vehicles and to infiltrate organizations; to intercept communications; and to interview witnesses and suspects abroad.

[121] Articles 706-773 and 706-674 CPP.

[122] Article 132-171 *code pénal*, the French penal code.

[123] As the ECtHR pointed out in *Gillan and Quinton v. UK* (4158/04) 12 January 2010, at para. 80, " '[E]xpedient' means no more than 'advantageous' or 'helpful.' There is no requirement at the authorisation stage that the stop and search power be considered 'necessary' and therefore no requirement of any assessment of the proportionality of the measure."

[124] Areas with strikingly similar risk profiles did not use the powers in this way, and the then-independent reviewer of UK terrorism legislation, Lord Carlile, noted that existing ordinary police powers were found to be adequate in policing the G8 summit in Scotland in 2005, for example.

the excessive and inappropriate use of section 44.[125] The power was used disproportionately against black and Asian people, and there are ample examples of protestors and journalists being stopped and searched under the terrorist legislation.[126] When the powers were challenged in the courts, the House of Lords considered legal controls on the police use of discretion to be adequate, but the ECtHR in *Gillan v. UK* found the powers to breach Article 8 ECHR: "[T]he safeguards provided by domestic law have not been demonstrated to constitute a real curb on the wide powers afforded the executive so as to offer the individual adequate protection against arbitrary interference."[127] At this time (2010), 117,278 people were being searched each year under section 44, yet no terrorism conviction ever resulted. As a result of the government review following the *Gillan* judgment, the powers were repealed by the Protection of Freedoms Act 2012.[128]

The path of France's state of emergency has also led to the regularization of powers originally justified as exceptional, despite evidence of their discriminatory and disproportionate use.[129] Just one month into the emergency powers regime, the government sought to introduce some of these temporary powers onto the statute book permanently—ironically, inserting them into an existing bill to strengthen procedural safeguards for suspects.[130] The permanent granting of criminal-type powers to the administrative police, acting within the institutional framework of the local political administration under the préfet, has been criticized by lawyers and *magistrats* as a further weakening of judicial protection and an encroachment on the independence of the judiciary and their constitutional role as guarantors of citizens' rights and freedoms, including from arbitrary detention. Placing powers of search and detention in the hands of the executive adds to an already complicated legislative framework, creating a confusion of

[125] As the court noted at para. 84: "[I]n his 2008 report Lord Carlile noted that examples of poor and unnecessary use of section 44 abounded, there being evidence of cases where the person stopped was so obviously far from any known terrorism profile that, realistically, there was not the slightest possibility of him/her being a terrorist, and no other feature to justify the stop."

[126] See, e.g., Joint Committee on Human Rights (2009).

[127] *Gillan v. UK*, para. 79.

[128] Section 43 of the Terrorism Act 2000 as amended still allows the stop and search of a person an officer reasonably suspects to be a terrorist, and section 43A allows the search of a vehicle an officer reasonably believes is being used for the purposes of terrorism. In the Metropolitan Police District 483 searches were conducted under these sections in 2016.

[129] Delmas-Marty describes society as being anesthetized into accepting the exceptional as commonplace. She anticipates a state of "soft despotism" along the lines anticipated by the French political philosopher Alexis de Tocqueville, in which the sovereign power stupefies society before reducing it to a flock of timid and industrious sheep, shepherded by government. See Anne Chemin and Jean-Baptise Jacquin "Loi antiterroriste: 'Nous sommes passés de l'Etat de droit à l'Etat de surveillance,'" *Le Monde*, 11 October 2017.

[130] This was also opposed by senior members of the Parquet such as the *procureur général* of Paris, Jean-Claude Marin.

roles and responsibilities, while also failing to respect the separation of powers by permitting infringements of liberty with no judicial oversight.

On 1 November 2017, after being renewed on five occasions, the state of emergency came to an end, with many of the measures remaining in force on a permanent basis, as part of the criminal code. On the one hand, this was received as a positive step, lifting the cloud of "emergency measures" and signaling a return to normality. On the other hand, it is seen by some as legislating a permanent state of emergency, with exceptional powers of search, detention, and the restriction of citizens' movements now at the disposal of the police under the authority of the state through the préfet. This reflects the broader trend away from the judicial to the executive in criminal justice matters. Officers charged with preventive policing are now exercising repressive powers, and the infringement of individual liberties is being authorized by administrative rather than criminal judges.[131] While terrorism is the latest incarnation and a powerful justification, administrative and criminal functions are being fused more generally around concepts of dangerousness, prevention, and precautionary justice.

(iv) Liberty and Security

In both jurisdictions, there is a familiar narrative in which certain rights or liberties are traded for greater security.[132] The meaning of security here is unclear—what precisely is being offered as justification for the weakening or derogation from fundamental rights and freedoms? Is this what Zedner (2005) describes as objective security (our personal safety and protection from harm) or a more subjective notion of a sense of security, a kind of reassurance? It is often this latter sense that is invoked, but this provides only weak justification for rights-infringing measures, as reassurance and public confidence are not linked to any objective measure of effectiveness and, in fact, might be achieved by purely symbolic actions.[133]

There can be no doubt that the wide powers of investigation and surveillance available to *magistrats* and to the UK and French police result in the production

[131] Although still independent as judges, there are significant differences. Criminal judges are recruited and trained through the national judicial training school (École nationale de la magistrature, ENM), whereas administrative judges are trained through the national administrative college (École national de l'administration, ENA), which is designed explicitly to inculcate strong links with government: many top politicians and virtually every French president bar Nicolas Sarkozy has studied at the ENA.

[132] Existing discourses around the security of victims have made this right-to-security (Ramsay [2012: 3–5]) narrative all the more easy to employ in the terrorism context.

[133] Public confidence in policing, for example, might be linked to the reassurance of police visibility, rather than to rates of crime. This is just what we found in a recent study of preventive policing. Hodgson et al. (2018).

of valuable information in the investigation, prosecution, and prevention of terrorism. What, of course, is less clear is the price paid by citizens in terms of surrendering their privacy and even their liberty.[134] Security can never be satisfied, in that there will always be threats of some kind, and so there are continuing demands for more state powers, and more collection, retention, and sharing of data—never for the greater protection of liberties. The surveillance, detention, and questioning of individuals is an infringement of individual freedom that, even in cases as grave as suspected terrorism, can only be justified domestically and within Articles 5 and 6 ECHR, when based on clear legal grounds. With offenses as broad as *association des malfaiteurs* and the use of intelligence as evidence in France, the extent to which individuals are subjected to speculative enquiry or effective targeting is also unknown. French police have rounded up citizens with little thought of arrest and charge, but rather to disrupt and so, hopefully, prevent and deter.[135] Hundreds of French citizens have been detained and then released after days, months, and even years in custody while investigations are ongoing.[136] The laws originating from France's state of emergency now further permit police searches of homes at night, with children present, with only the most basic suspicion of criminal activity and no effective judicial oversight.

In the UK, too, police powers of investigation and surveillance have led commentators to warn that we are sleepwalking into a surveillance society, in which we unwittingly surrender our privacy.[137] On the other hand, such is the continuing preoccupation with the management (even eradication) of risk, that after every terrorist attack, there are questions asked as to why the police or intelligence services failed to spot the danger. Why was the attack not prevented? It seems there is no shortage of information being gathered, but there is a question mark over how effectively it is shared and used. In December 2017, the then-home secretary, Amber Rudd, told Parliament that MI5 and counterterrorism policing were reported to be running more than five hundred live operations involving around three thousand "subjects of interest." She also told

[134] Although expressed as a balancing exercise, the security-versus-liberty dichotomy is experienced in neither a universal nor a balanced way. Powers are often exercised in discriminatory ways, and in the name of protecting the security of the many, it is generally the liberties of a few that are traded off. See Waldron (2003: 210), who concludes: "We should be cautious about giving up our civil liberties. We should be even more cautious about giving up our commitment to the civil liberties of a minority, so that we can enjoy *our* liberties in greater security. We should be worried about the enhanced power of the state (and we should reject as magical thinking the idea that the risk from that power goes down as the risk from terrorism goes up)."

[135] The word *rafle* has been used, evoking the roundup of Jews in German-occupied France. See further Hodgson (2006a).

[136] One journalist reports that Juge Bruguière has ordered the arrest of over five hundred people on suspicion of conspiracy in relation to terrorism. Craig Whitlock, "French Push Limits in Fight on Terrorism," *Washington Post Foreign Service*, 2 November 2004.

[137] The routine and systematic search of phones belonging to suspects, arrestees, and even complainants in sexual assault cases is the latest practice to attract attention, discussed subsequently.

the House that twenty-two Islamist terrorist plots had been disrupted since the murder of Lee Rigby in May 2013, including nine since the Westminster attack in March 2017.[138] However, despite this, those responsible for the Westminster and Manchester attacks in 2017 were among more than twenty thousand "closed subjects of interest" who had been investigated previously and might again pose a threat, but who were not under active investigation.[139] Khuram Butt, responsible for the London Bridge attack in June 2017, had been an active subject of interest since mid-2015.[140] While all terrorist attacks cannot be prevented, no matter how wide the powers,[141] reviews of these recent UK terror attacks recommend better sharing of intelligence from MI5 with other agencies, including neighborhood policing, and more effective approaches by the police and MI5 to the acquisition, sharing, and analysis of data, regardless of ideology.[142]

Digital information is posing new challenges in striking the balance between security and liberty—not only in the context of terrorism or serious crime, but across all forms of criminality.[143] We leave a digital footprint in most aspects of our daily lives: the websites we visit, our engagement with social media, the things that we buy, and the places that we go. This data is collected routinely by private organizations, as well as in the course of intelligence gathering and

[138] Amber Rudd's speech is available at https://www.gov.uk/government/speeches/statement-on-reviews-into-the-attacks-in-manchester-and-london. David Anderson, QC, in his independent review of the attacks of 2017, reported that ten life sentences had been handed down in relation to the seven plots that had so far come to trial. Anderson (2017).

[139] Khalid Massod was responsible for the Westminster attack in March 2017, which killed five people and injured forty-nine. He drove a car into pedestrians on the bridge and then went on to stab PC Keith Palmer who was on duty outside the Houses of Parliament. He had been known to the security services since 2004 and was a subject of interest in 2009. Salman Abedi was responsible for the Manchester attack in May 2017 in which twenty-two people were killed (ten of them under twenty, the youngest being eight years old) and five hundred injured. He detonated an explosive charge in Manchester Arena at the end of a concert attended by thousands of children. See Anderson (2017).

[140] The London Bridge attack in June 2017 killed eight people and injured forty-eight. Butt drove a car into pedestrians on London Bridge. The attack in Finsbury Park in which one person was killed and ten were injured was carried out by Darren Osborne, who was unknown to the security services. He drove a car into worshippers outside Finsbury Park Islamic Centre.

[141] The key question is perhaps what is acceptable? How much surveillance or detention powers are proportionate to prevent terrorist attacks committed by perhaps a tiny proportion of those deemed to be of interest? Is this the most effective use of resources (alongside programs designed to prevent people being "radicalized")?

[142] Reviews were conducted internally and the former independent reviewer of terrorism legislation, David Anderson, QC, reviewed and reported on nine classified reports from MI5 and Counter-Terrorism Policing on the 2017 attacks. It should also be remembered that the use of intelligence is not unproblematic. "In the best-known cases of intelligence failure, the most crucial mistakes have seldom been made by collectors of raw information, occasionally by professionals who produce finished analyses, but most often by the decision makers who consume the products of intelligence services. . . . Intelligence failure is political and psychological more often than organizational." R. K. Betts (1978), "Analysis, War and Decision: Why Intelligence Failure Are Inevitable," 31(1) *World Politics* 61–89 at 61, cited by Phythian (2005: 362).

[143] For discussion of issues around security and digital evidence from a variety of disciplinary perspectives see generally *Les cahiers du numérique* (2003) 4(3), and in particular, Eric Freyssinet, "La prevue numérique," 205–217.

non-terrorism-related criminal investigation, and much of it is captured and shared using our mobile phones. In England and Wales, the police routinely extract and download information from the mobile phones of suspects, arrestees, and witnesses, often without their knowledge or consent, providing access to material that would normally need a search warrant.[144] This does not target information relevant to an enquiry, but rather, extracts data en masse in what police describe as unavoidable collateral intrusion.[145] While the digital sphere offers seemingly limitless information for crime prevention (or prediction) through automated forms of risk management, the gathering of information through algorithms and digital technologies is of concern, not only as another form of surveillance and privacy intrusion, but also because these data sources and the conclusions they produce are hard to interrogate and challenge.[146] Rather like the use of intelligence as evidence, where the sources of data are unclear or unknown, they risk reproducing an existing criminal justice bias,[147] especially where data sets are merged or repurposed to produce something new, outside of the original context.[148] Equality of arms requires both parties to have the opportunity to test out the reliability of evidence, but if the data is unknown, or the algorithm producing the information cannot be revealed for the sake of future investigations, this becomes impossible. This produces an asymmetry of knowledge and an inequality of arms between the parties. Yet the automated nature of the evidence may make it appear more scientific and less subjective—and so more reliable.[149]

In France, this "liberty versus security" dichotomy is reflected in political debate around *sûreté* (inspired by the right of habeas corpus, the freedom from arbitrary arrest or detention, established in the 1789 Déclaration des droits de l'homme et du citoyen) and the more contemporary theme championed by the Right—*sécurité*, which is declared a fundamental right and a condition for the exercise of individual and collective freedoms.[150] In the UK, the Joint Committee on Human Rights has rejected this liberty-versus-security narrative, agreeing

[144] See *The Guardian*, 13 January 2017, "Police Should Need Warrants to Search Mobile Phones, Say Campaigners," available at https://www.theguardian.com/uk-news/2017/jan/13/police-warrant-search-mobile-phones-campaigners-privacy-international.

[145] See Hayley Dixon, "Police Rolling Out Technology Which Allows Them to Raid Victims [*sic*] Phones without a Warrant," *The Telegraph*, 31 March 2018, available at https://www.telegraph.co.uk/news/2018/03/31/police-rolling-technology-allows-raid-victims-phones-without/.

[146] Governments have called for online social media platforms to use their algorithms to identify potential terrorists (Rifkind [2014]; Toor [2016]), and some platforms are already doing this to identify accounts generating extremist content.

[147] Council of Europe Study (2017: 11).

[148] Council of Europe Study (2017: 13–16).

[149] Fingerprint and DNA evidence were once thought unassailable as proof when first introduced into the criminal trial.

[150] In Italy too, new constitutional principles recognize security as a right in and of itself rather than simply as a pre-condition for enjoying other rights.

with the Venice Commission that "[s]tate security and fundamental rights are not competitive values: they are each other's precondition."[151] In 2004, holding as unlawful the indefinite detention of foreign nationals thought to be a risk to national security, Lord Hoffman stated:

> The real threat to the life of the nation, in the sense of a people living in accordance with its traditional laws and political values, comes not from terrorism but from laws such as these. That is the true measure of what terrorism may achieve.[152]

In France, the exercise of counterterrorism powers has been criticized sharply. The treatment of suspects held in police custody has been condemned repeatedly by the ECtHR and the Council of Europe's European Committee for the Prevention of Torture and Inhuman or Degrading Treatment or Punishment, and in this the counterterrorism police have been marked out for particular criticism. The actions of the counterterrorism *juges d'instruction* have been seen as heavy-handed by human rights organizations and the roundups have been described as arbitrary.[153] The powers exercised under the state of emergency, and now placed on a permanent footing, have been criticized as being exercised in disproportionate and discriminatory ways. The elevation of *sécurité* as a value, although used increasingly interchangeably with *sûreté*, in practice threatens to undermine the individual's right to *sûreté*. The recent Tarnac Affair, in which more than a hundred masked police officers, accompanied by the press, stormed the village of Tarnac in 2008 to arrest fifteen people accused of terrorist plots, is yet another example of the dangers of the very broad powers that can be exercised on the basis of little or no evidence, resulting in unwarranted infringements of individual liberties. In the case of what was described initially as an extreme left or anarchist organization carrying out major disruption of the transport system, seven years into the investigation the *juge d'instruction* reclassified the case as nonterrorist, and in 2018, ten years after the initial arrests, the eight accused were cleared of all charges.[154]

[151] Joint Committee on Human Rights (2006: 13).

[152] *A v. Secretary of State for the Home Department*, para. 97.

[153] Discussed in Hodgson (2006a: 41–48; 2013b).

[154] The trial took place in the lower-ranking court, the *tribunal correctionnel*, rather than the *cour d'assises*, which hears more serious cases and all terrorism trials. There were only convictions for minor offenses of refusing to consent to DNA samples, handling stolen goods, and attempting to falsify documents. See "C'est quoi l'affaire Tarnac?," *franceinfo*, 13 March 2018 available at https://www.francetvinfo.fr/faits-divers/justice-proces/affaire-tarnac/c-est-quoi-l-affaire-tarnac-on-vous-resume-le-dossier-qui-s-est-beaucoup-degonfle-au-fil-des-annees_2654340.html; Angelique Chrisafis, "Leftwing 'Anarchist Terror Cell' Is Fiction, French Judges Rule," *The Guardian*, 13 April 2018; the account in English by Franck Richard, for Statewatch, available at http://www.statewatch.org/analyses/no-328-france-tarnac-affair.pdf.

Across jurisdictions, the "war on terror" has had profound implications for the ways in which we respond to the threat of harm, but also in shaping criminal law and justice in more permanent ways. As a 2010 European Parliament briefing paper described it:

> [T]he scale of the damage done to international human rights law, and to the practical protection of human rights, by the "war on terror" should not be underestimated, and concerted efforts will be needed to reverse it. . . . At a national level, in both EU and non-EU states, the past eight years have seen the growth of administrative counter-terrorism measures, including administrative detention, control orders and measures based on immigration law, and many of these remain in place, displacing the primacy of the criminal justice system and providing insufficient protection for human rights.[155]

The way in which the threat of terrorism has been portrayed has resulted not only in disproportionate infringements of individual liberties through wide powers and sanctions, but also in expenditure, as security becomes an end but also a means—both legislative and technological. While the rhetoric of efficiency and managerialism is used to diminish the rights of the individual, that of security is employed to justify huge increases in resources. Despite the large number of stops and searches under terrorism powers, there have been relatively few terrorism-related arrests, and even fewer charges and convictions.[156] It might be argued that the relatively low number of lives lost through UK terrorism since 11 September 2001 is evidence of the success of preventive measures,[157] but the need for exceptional powers such as those of detention and preventive orders is not borne out in the very small numbers of those held.[158] And while global deaths through terrorism have declined, it is now far-right terrorism that is on the rise in Western Europe and the United States—often motivated by anti-Muslim sentiments.

155 Pillay (2010: 3).

156 Allen and Dempsey (2018). Arrests rose by 58 percent in 2017 to 412, following the Westminster Bridge, Manchester, and London Bridge attacks as well as the Finsbury Park mosque and Parsons Green tube attacks; 110 terrorism-related charges were brought. Alan Travis, "UK Terror-Related Arrests Rose Almost 60% to Record High in 2017," *The Guardian*, 8 March 2018.

157 Fifty-four people died between 11 September 2001 and 31 March 2016, compared with 3,208 between 1970 and 2001. See Allen and Dempsey (2018: 5). This number has subsequently increased by thirty-six after the murder of Jo Cox and the London and Manchester attacks. Higher numbers are reported elsewhere. See Ashley Kirk, "How Many People Are Killed by Terrorist Attacks in the UK?," *The Telegraph*, 17 October 2017.

158 There are currently 7 TPIMs in force and there were never more than 20 control orders at any one time. Of the 1,983 people arrested under s.41 of the Terrorism Act 2000 since 11 September 2001, 38 percent were detained for less than one day; 50 percent for between 1 and 7 days; and just 11 people were detained for more than 14 days (10 people in 2006/07 and 1 in 2007/08). 6 people were detained for 28 days in 2006/07. Allen and Dempsey (2018: 20).

PART 2
PROSECUTION

4

The Role and Status of the Prosecutor

In France and in England and Wales, prosecutors play a pivotal role at the heart of the criminal justice process, preparing and prosecuting criminal matters, managing the flux of cases, and, increasingly, disposing of cases through alternatives to prosecution.[1] Although they are public prosecutors in both jurisdictions, there are important differences in their professional status, in the scope of their function, and in their relationships with other legal and political actors. They have emerged from very different histories and continue to evolve in response to a range of factors, both from outside the prosecution service and from within. By situating these two types of prosecutor, one a lawyer, one a judicial officer, within the broader legal cultural traditions in which they operate, this chapter compares the nature of the prosecutors' role and functions in the two jurisdictions, their relationship with the investigation, and the different ways in which prosecutors' independence and accountability are structured and understood.

In both jurisdictions, the prosecutor is more than just a criminal justice actor—she is also a public representation of state power, whose role and decisions have implications for the rights and freedoms of the individual as well as local criminal justice policy. This requires her to be independent and to apply the law with fairness and impartiality, but also to be accountable in some way to the democratic institutions in whose name she acts. Such accountability may be achieved in a variety of ways depending on the wider legal and political landscape—the professional status of the prosecutor, the scope of her function, and the constitutional relationship between judges, prosecutors, and government.[2] Within the adversarial tradition, the status of the prosecutor in England and Wales broadly mirrors that of the defense lawyer: she is the legal representative of a party to the case, a lawyer, not a judicial officer. The judicial role is entirely separate, focused primarily on adjudication rather than investigation or prosecution, and is independent of any executive control. Within the constitutional relationship of the

[1] For a discussion of the variety of prosecution roles across European jurisdictions, see the recommendation adopted by the Council of Europe, Committee of Ministers (2000), *The Role of the Public Prosecution in the Criminal Justice System*.

[2] In North America, for example, prosecutors are elected in the locality within which they serve. In theory, this looks to provide strong democratic input into law enforcement, but in practice, the process of periodic election represents a very weak form of accountability for the wide powers exercised. See Tonry (2012); the contributions in Langer and Slansky (2017).

The Metamorphosis of Criminal Justice. Jacqueline S. Hodgson, Oxford University Press (2020).

DOI: 10.1093/oso/9780199981427.001.0001

separation of powers, the judiciary has an important role in ensuring that executive action does not exceed the limits that the law has set.

In France, the position is more complex. Prosecutors are part of the trained judicial corps of career *magistrats*, and so in one sense, as judicial officers with a public-interest-oriented ideology, they enjoy greater independence than their English and Welsh counterparts. However, the structure of authority within which they operate reflects their subordination to executive power through their professional hierarchy, which is headed by the minister of justice, a political appointment. This is understood to provide democratic accountability to the prosecution function as, under the republican tradition, the legal and moral authority of the state derives from its status in representing the sovereign will of the people. As an unelected body acting in the name of the state and so the people, the prosecution arm of the judiciary (the Parquet) is held to democratic account, therefore, through its hierarchical accountability to the political power of the executive.[3] The constitutional relationship between the executive and the judiciary is therefore more intertwined than in England and Wales, where anything other than a clear separation of powers would be regarded with mistrust. This vertical model of authority sits more comfortably within the more centralized inquisitorial French tradition, but to those more familiar with the horizontal cross-checks of party-based adversarialism, this privileging of the state over the judiciary raises the threat of political interference rather than the promise of independence. Underlining the importance of judicial independence from the executive and the parties, the European Court of Human Rights (ECtHR) has also questioned the status of the prosecutor as an independent judicial officer in *Medvedyev v. France*, discussed subsequently.[4]

The different status of prosecutors in France and England and Wales, and their relationship to judicial and political authority, are important factors in how we understand and evaluate the functions of the prosecutor, the rights and responsibilities of other legal actors, and the legitimacy of the expanding prosecution role. The configuration of the prosecution function has consequences that are felt across the criminal process, including the protection of the accused, the structures of police investigative accountability, relationships with defense lawyers, and the nature of the trial. The next chapter develops this analysis, considering the extent to which prosecutors' core functions are changing, as the

[3] See Hodgson (2005: 75–85; 2017). It should also be noted that there is no longer equality between the three constitutional functions. In order to acknowledge the sovereign will of the people as the basis for the exercise of state power, in 1958 the judiciary was demoted from a power (*pouvoir*), to an authority (*autorité*).

[4] (3394/03) 29 March 2010. See also the Bordeaux Declaration and (extensive) explanatory note adopted by the Consultative Councils of the European Judges and European Prosecutors in 2009, available at https://rm.coe.int/1680747391.

emphasis of criminal justice moves from the trial to the pretrial, and correspondingly, responsibility shifts from the judge to the prosecutor. By focusing on the changing role that is assigned to the prosecutor in each jurisdiction, we see the ways in which two processes of criminal justice facing similar pressures and policy drivers, but with contrasting histories and procedural traditions, adapt and develop in different ways.

A. The Role of the Prosecutor

The prosecutorial function embraces a range of possible roles, from investigative supervision to prosecutorial sanctions. The different legal procedural and cultural contexts in which prosecutors operate, together with their different histories, mean that although there is some degree of functional equivalence between the public prosecutor in England and Wales and in France, there is also a great deal of difference. Both the French prosecutor, the procureur, and in England and Wales the crown prosecutor are responsible for the decision whether to prosecute or to institute some other form of proceedings or disposal, and both prosecute the case in court; this much is similar. But there are also important differences that inform their role, professional status, and relationships with other legal actors, as well as the nature of their independence from the investigation, their relationship with the executive, and the scope of their function and responsibilities.

The French prosecutor sits at the heart of the criminal process, involved in all aspects from investigation through to sentence. She is responsible for the investigation and prosecution of crime, including authorizing and overseeing the period of police detention and questioning; she can require that acts of investigation be carried out; she decides whether to open an *information* and pass the case to the *juge d'instruction* for further investigation;[5] she may request that the *juge d'instruction* carry out certain enquiries during the investigation; she determines whether to prosecute and with which offense; she may propose a lesser sentence in exchange for a guilty plea; she may propose mediation and other alternative measures; she liaises with the victim; she prosecutes and recommends a sentence to the court. Hierarchically accountable through the prosecution body, the Parquet, she is also responsible for the implementation of government policy as expressed through Justice Ministry circulars. In addition, her role requires her to contribute to the development of local penal policy in collaboration with police

[5] The *juge d'instruction* is a judicial officer responsible for investigating the most serious criminal cases. This is done through a procedure initiated by the prosecutor, called opening the *information*, the enquiry.

and members of the local political administration. The breadth of her function gives her enormous power and influence at each stage of the criminal process, from shaping local policy through to case disposition and sentence.

The role of the crown prosecutor is more limited and premised upon separation from, rather than responsibility for, the police investigation. While the procureur enjoys legal authority over criminal investigations as well as prosecutions, the essence of the crown prosecutor's role is to ensure the independence of the prosecution from the precharge phase. The definition of the crown prosecutor's role in these terms is the inevitable product of a history in which the public prosecution function was created in order to replace the inconsistency of a police-dominated and regional system of prosecutions, with a central independent agency.[6]

Prior to the establishment of the Crown Prosecution Service (CPS) the police were responsible for the investigation and prosecution of crime. Following the recommendations of the Royal Commission on the Police (1962) that the employment of police advocates was to be deplored, larger forces employed in-house lawyers to deal with the increased volume of work and for complex cases.[7] However, as employed advocates with the police as their clients, prosecuting solicitors operated within a lawyer-client relationship and were unable to do anything more than offer advice to the officers instructing them. With forty-three independent police forces, each making its own arrangements, there were no central prosecution policies or guidelines, and the Royal Commission on Criminal Procedure (RCCP, 1981) found a lack of consistency and uniformity at the national level in decisions to prosecute and in the use of cautions. It also found that the police were proceeding with too many weak cases, often against the advice of their own lawyers. Following the recommendations of the RCCP, the CPS was established to ensure a clear separation between the functions of investigation and prosecution, removing the prosecution function from the police. In order to ensure this separation, and in stark contrast to the procureur, the crown prosecutor enjoys no authority or power of direction over the police, and has no responsibility for the pretrial investigation other than in an advisory capacity in some instances.[8]

The procureur enjoys a different relationship with investigators than her English counterpart. Historically, the functions of investigation, prosecution, and adjudication all rested with the seventeenth-century office of the *lieutenant criminel*, before the investigation and prosecution roles were separated

[6] On the earlier practices of private and state prosecution, see Brants and Ringsnalda (2010: 29–34).

[7] Around three-quarters of police forces had their own prosecuting solicitors. Statement of Home Secretary William Whitelaw HC Deb, 20 November 20 1981, vol. 13, c532.

[8] This legal and functional separation between investigation and prosecution is known as the Philips principle, after the chair of the RCCP, Sir Cyril Philips.

out and vested in the procureur.[9] The modern Parquet role has evolved hand in hand with that of the police,[10] ensuring the continued unity of the investigation and prosecution functions and a degree of mutual trust and common working objectives between police and procureur. In contrast, the more recently created crown prosecutor role depends on separation from, rather than cooperation with, the police in order to ensure the independence of the prosecution function. These historically different structures of authority pose different challenges for prosecutorial independence. In England and Wales this has centered on the crown prosecutor's relationship with the police; in France on the Parquet's judicial status and its relationship to government and political influence. There is, however, also a tension in the nature of the procureur's role of pretrial investigative supervision—both in her relationship with the police and in the implications for the rights of the defense.

Although under the authority of the minister of justice through the hierarchy of the Parquet, and so enjoying less freedom and independence than the *juge d'instruction* or the trial judge, the procureur understands herself as a judicial officer acting in the public interest, performing both an investigative and a judicial function in the search for the truth, while safeguarding individual liberties.[11] Historically, this judicial status and ideology of the procureur qua *magistrat* has been understood as the primary guarantee of the suspect's rights and liberty, justifying the relatively diminished role of the criminal defense lawyer. However, there is a tension both in how these roles are structured within legal procedure and in how they are understood in practice. The procureur is dependent upon the police to carry out the investigation for which she is responsible and so must retain some close involvement; but as a *magistrat*, she must retain some distance, overseeing, and if necessary challenging, operations, as, ultimately, her supervisory role as a *magistrat* will lend the investigation the legitimacy of a judicial enquiry. Furthermore, the limited supervision that she is able (or indeed willing) to provide in practice means that the success of this arrangement rests on trust rather than judicial oversight.[12] Both procureurs and police recognize this.

[9] See Esmein (1913); Salas (2002).

[10] The procureur's contemporary role and form developed over the course of the twentieth century alongside that of the police and the practice of official police enquiries that came to be known as the *garde à vue* (GAV). The GAV was developed as a means of avoiding the safeguards provided for during the *instruction* from 1897, from which time suspects were informed of their right to silence and allowed legal assistance, and their lawyers had access to the dossier before each judicial interrogation. See Lévy (1993).

[11] For an account of the different status of the "standing judiciary" (the Parquet) and the "sitting judiciary" (the trial judge, *juge d'instruction, juge des libertés et de la détention*) see Hodgson (2005: 66–68).

[12] See Hodgson (2005: 156–161).

> There is a part of [the police's] work that I cannot evaluate. I can only talk of their role in the legal procedure, how they report on the telephone. We inhabit different worlds. They do not know the world of judges, and I do not know the world of nightclubs. (Procureur, D2)
>
> Our work is different. They are in their offices and we are outside on the ground. (Senior police officer, D5)[13]

The procureur describes herself as a judicial officer but, in practice comes to identify less with judicial values of due process than with policing priorities, redefining her role of searching for the truth as seeking a confession.[14]

The procureur also enjoys a broad discretion to determine how cases are investigated, including whether to trigger the *instruction* process with its enhanced defense rights,[15] or to retain the case under her own supervision, with none of these benefits. *Crimes*, the most serious offenses, must be investigated by the *juge d'instruction*, but the treatment of *délits* and *contraventions* is entirely within the discretion of the procureur,[16] as is the characterization of offending behaviors as a *crime* (such as rape) or a *délit* (such as sexual assault). There are no guidelines concerning which cases the procureur should pass on or retain, and on what grounds. In practice, local court resourcing is likely to determine the caseload of the *juge d'instruction*, and this is the origin of the widespread practice of *correctionalisation*, whereby *crimes* are downgraded to *délits* and tried in the *tribunal correctionnel*, rather than the more resource-intensive *cour d'assises* in front of a judge and jury.[17] However, the procureur is not required to give reasons nor to account for her choices; the broad scope of her discretion is a function of

[13] Quoted in Hodgson (2005: 160). This echoes the respondents in Mouhanna's (2001) study, such as the senior police officer who explained: "I think that there are two separate worlds—that of the police officer and that of the *magistrat*. Trust is at the point of contact of these two worlds. In his work, the *magistrat* can take refuge behind his *code*, behind the law . . . and they [*magistrats*] must not dirty their hands or they will lose their credibility. . . . They must be respected, but they must also understand that a police officer is not a *magistrat*, that we are confronted with social situations for which there is little or no legal provision. The reality that they see is a pre-digested legal reality" (Mouhanna 2001: 125–126).

[14] See the discussion in Hodgson (2005: chap. 5).

[15] During an *instruction*, the investigation, and the questioning of the suspect in particular, is conducted by an independent judge (the *juge d'instruction*, who, unlike the procureur, is not accountable to a hierarchy or to the justice minister) and the suspect is afforded access to the dossier, a lawyer, and opportunities to participate in the enquiry and request that certain investigative acts be carried out.

[16] *Délits* are middle-ranking offenses, and *contraventions* are minor offenses.

[17] This is sometimes incorrectly described as plea bargaining, but there is no bargain with the accused; it is a unilateral, resource-based decision. The practice is employed to reduce the cost and delay of having cases investigated by the *juge d'instruction* and tried by a jury in the *cour d'assises*. However, it began life in the nineteenth century as a way of reducing the number of cases tried by juries, who were perceived as too lenient and too prone to acquitting defendants. See Donovan (1999: 388–402).

the trust placed in her as a judicial officer. There is nothing, therefore, to prevent her from refraining from sending a case to the *juge d'instruction* in order, for example, to avoid the greater due process safeguards that are in place during the *instruction*. Although this seems contrary to the interests of the suspect, as well as to the judicial ideology of the *magistrat*, the French courts have held that this reasoning does not prejudice the rights of the accused, as these safeguards will be available at trial.[18] It seems disingenuous, however, to suggest that the timing of rights has no impact on their effectiveness: the ability to request acts of investigation, have access to counsel, and have access to the case file is of far greater value at the pretrial stage.[19]

The nature of the procureur's independence as a *magistrat* and the extent to which she can guarantee the rights of the accused have, however, been called into question by the ECtHR, on the grounds that she is not a judicial officer for the purposes of Article 5 ECHR. In *Medvedyev v. France*, the ECtHR emphasized the qualities required of a judicial authority: "The judicial officer must offer the requisite guarantees of independence from the executive and the parties, which precludes his subsequent intervention in criminal proceedings on behalf of the prosecuting authority."[20] This in turn suggests a potentially greater role for the defense within the French pretrial, in order to fill the gap in protection left by the absence of a neutral and public-interest-oriented judicial figure, an argument lent further weight by the ECtHR decisions following *Salduz* requiring the presence of a lawyer in police questioning,[21] and wider European Union (EU) measures put in place to strengthen procedural protections for accused persons.[22] Procureurs, however, are resistant to increasing pretrial defense rights during the police investigation, as they (and indeed French politicians) understand it as part of a wider European shift toward an accusatorial model of criminal justice, and so a radical departure from the defining principles of French criminal

[18] The courts have been inconsistent on this point. Overturning the decision of the trial court, the Cour de cassation in 2013 upheld the procureur's decision to retain control over an investigation in order that the suspect did not benefit from the rights available during *instruction*. It found that this did not infringe the suspect's right to fair trial nor disadvantage them in any way, as these rights would be available once at trial.

[19] See also Quentin (2013); Maréchal (2013).

[20] *Medvedyev v. France* (3394/03) 29 March 2010. For more detailed discussion of the case, see Hodgson (2010). The case follows a line of decisions in which independence from the executive and the parties has been held to be a crucial characteristic of a judicial officer. It contradicted, however, the jurisprudence of the French Conseil constitutionnel, which has held that procureurs (*magistrats du parquet*) as well as investigating and trial judges (*magistrats du siège*) were judicial officers. Conseil constitutionnel decision No. 93-326 DC 11 August 1993, JO 11599. This was affirmed again, Conseil constitutionnel decision No. 2011-125 QPC, 6 May 2011.

[21] *Salduz v. Turkey* (36391/02) 27 November 2008, which held for the first time that a confession would not be admissible if obtained in denial of custodial legal advice before and during police questioning.

[22] These include the right to custodial legal advice and the right to translation and interpretation, and are discussed in detail in chapter 6.

procedure.[23] Furthermore, prosecutors fear that this will result in a corresponding decline in the independence of the prosecution function, relegating it, from one of judicial supervision of the investigation and prosecution, to one of simple accusation in which the prosecutor is understood as a party to the case.[24]

In practice, there seems little threat to the prosecutor's role. Growth in the rights of the defense during the pretrial phase in France has been modest, and the scope of the defense lawyer's role remains constrained to some extent by what is permitted by the police and procureur.[25] While France has committed to respecting the principle of *contradictoire* throughout the criminal process, which implies stronger defense rights, this remains almost entirely absent during the procureur-supervised investigation.[26] There is an asymmetry between the rights of the accused during the *instruction* (the formal investigation of serious cases, overseen or conducted by the *juge d'instruction*), where the accused has the right to a lawyer, has access to the case file, and can request acts of investigation, and the preliminary police enquiry, in which the suspect has no right to a lawyer outside the *garde à vue*,[27] no access to the case file, and no way of participating in the investigation. In principle, Article 6 ECHR fair-trial rights apply to all suspects, but this form of due process legal regime is largely absent in the 97 percent of criminal matters dealt with by the police under the authority of the procureur, even though the evidence at trial will depend almost entirely on the results of this police enquiry.

In England and Wales, the prosecutor has no pretrial oversight of the investigation or the treatment of the suspect. The defense is able to intervene from the point of arrest and detention, and her role is understood in less passive terms than that of the French lawyer (*avocat*). She is there to ensure more than simply fair play: her role is to represent the interests of the accused and to build the defense case. Within this more adversarial tradition and in the absence of non-police-based oversight, this is a necessary counterbalance to, and check upon, police power. However, this model is also under enormous strain. The opportunities for proactive and adversarial defense lawyering are restricted in practice, not by the actions of police or prosecutors, but through limited access to legal aid

[23] The decision in *Medvedyev* was criticized as undermining the principles of the French procedural tradition and "seeking to impose, without any mandate, an Anglo-Saxon model of accusatorial justice across the whole continent." Renucci (2009: 601).

[24] See Beaume (2014); Milburn et al. (2010).

[25] See chapter 7 for more detailed discussion of how European standards have been transposed into national law.

[26] The principle of *contradictoire* refers to the requirement that the accused should have the opportunity to know of, and to respond to, the accusations against her—not only at trial, but during the investigation, bail hearings, etc. It also incorporates the notion of equality of arms. However, the model of judicial supervision is understood to obviate the need for strong defense rights during the pretrial phase, and access to the dossier, for example, is linked to the rights of the defense at trial.

[27] *Garde à vue* is the period of police detention and questioning of the suspect.

and systemic constraints that compel the defense lawyer to assist in the management of cases toward a guilty plea. Unlike France, the crown prosecutor has no role in the pretrial investigation; she enjoys limited professional independence and autonomy from the police and has no authority to check on the conditions of detention or to direct the investigation. The investigation therefore remains a police-dominated exercise with no input or oversight from the prosecutor, and a defense role that has been weakened severely in recent years such that it risks legitimating the police investigation, rather than protecting the rights of the accused.

B. The Crown Prosecutor and the Police

The professional training and status of the prosecutor is of importance in understanding structures of prosecutorial independence and accountability and in thinking about the implications of current reforms to the prosecution function. In England and Wales the prosecutor is a lawyer of the same training and professional standing as the defense lawyer, reflecting their respective roles as parties to the case.[28] She is not part of a separate profession, nor has she been vocationally trained as a prosecutor or judicial officer. The judicial function remains separate from both the prosecutor and the defense, part of a professional elite drawn from the ranks of experienced members of prosecution and defense lawyers. There is no professional affinity between the judge and the prosecutor, as, in contrast to the French judge, they do not share a common vocational training that is separate from the defense lawyer.[29]

As salaried lawyers, under the Director of Public Prosecutions (DPP) and the superintendence of the attorney general, it was hoped by some that crown prosecutors might perform something of a Ministry of Justice role in a fashion similar to that of public prosecutors in much of the rest of Europe, rather than that of a more adversarial partisan prosecutor, as had been the case when acting on the instructions of the police. However, the structure and role of the organization, as well as its dependent relationship upon the police, militate against this.[30] The police retain sole responsibility for the investigation of crime and, in

[28] The geography of the courtroom and its participants also reflect their status. In England and Wales, prosecution and defense are side by side, facing the judges, who sit on a raised platform. In France, the procureur used to sit alongside the trial judges. She now sits apart, but is separate from the defense lawyer.

[29] While there is no special affinity between judge and prosecutor, there is some shared professional culture between defense and prosecution barristers and judges more generally, through the common training and socializing of the bar and working in sets of chambers.

[30] Although formally a new body, the inculcation of a whole new ethos was problematic. The new CPS required over fifteen hundred lawyers, and it made sense to recruit many of these from the

most instances, for the decision whether or not to initiate proceedings through the process of charging a suspect. Although the role of the CPS is defined in terms broader than simply to prosecute and to obtain a conviction, crucially, it has no authority over the investigation. The prosecutor has no control over the gathering of evidence, no power to require further investigation, and so no duty to gather exculpatory evidence. Instead, the CPS remains wholly dependent upon the police file of evidence in making the decision whether or not to charge or prosecute.[31] She is unable to test the strength or credibility of the evidence presented, or to challenge the construction of information designed to secure a conviction.[32] This creates a tension between the prosecutor's independence from the police and the need to look beyond the parameters of the police investigation in order to come to an informed decision that does not simply replicate that of the pretrial enquiry.[33] This also reflects the inherent conflict contained within the prosecution function. The prosecutor is not the mirror image of the defense advocate; she must prosecute the case while at the same time retaining a quasi-judicial degree of objectivity, ensuring that the evidence is reliable, credible, and presented fairly.

The crown prosecutor is different, therefore, from many continental European public prosecutors. Her position in a more adversarial party-centered procedure, together with her functional dependency on the police, makes it unlikely that she will ever come to play a more central Ministry of Justice–type role, where she enjoys greater power or responsibility for investigation as well as prosecution. While this potential conflict is addressed, in theory at least, in the professional construction of the French procureur as a *magistrat*, the ethical dimension of the crown prosecutor role is less developed. In addition to the structure of the process within which she operates, the prosecutor is not trained to play this kind of role. The French prosecutor's vocational training as *magistrat* reflects the centralized judicial officer role that she is expected to play; the crown prosecutor's training, in contrast, is the same as that of the defense lawyer, mirroring their respective roles as parties to the case, albeit within an "officer of the court" framework.

existing prosecuting solicitors—giving the impression in some places that little had changed, other than the nameplate above the office door.

31 The police remain, in effect, the gatekeepers to criminal prosecution. Sanders (2016) has described the CPS as decision-reversers, rather than decision-makers.

32 For an account of the police investigation as the construction of a case against the accused, see McConville et al. (1991).

33 In the US context, Medwed (2012) has noted the institutional and cognitive impediments to the prosecutor acting as a neutral decision-maker. American Bar Association Model Rule 3.8, in which she is cast as having a minister-of-justice role, is a long way from the conveyor belt processing of guilty pleas that can be observed in the courts.

The operation of the CPS is therefore something of a paradox in which it remains structurally dependent upon officers, but is forced to operate at a distance, preventing the development of a culture that would enable the CPS to reap the benefits of working closely with the police, without the disadvantage of being dominated by them.[34] A former DPP prosecutor described the CPS's early insistence on a rigid separation from the police: "Suddenly a steel curtain came down between the two services and this went a bit too far. People in both services, both the police force and ourselves, felt that we must keep our distance, we must not talk to each other, we must not communicate."[35]

In the early years, the CPS lacked a strong independent professional occupational culture that would enable its prosecutors to stand apart from the police on equal terms. This was not helped by the fact that in many instances, the same lawyers that had been employed as police prosecuting solicitors became part of the new CPS. This arrangement had the advantage of prosecution experience, but the disadvantage of failing to establish a clear break with old working relationships and expectations.[36] Prosecutors are required to review the evidence produced by the police investigation, to filter out weak cases, and to determine whether or not any prosecution is warranted; but the police often resent the downgrading or discontinuance of charges that officers have instigated and thus consider justified.[37]

Early initiatives for closer liaison between the police and the CPS were not hugely successful,[38] the police resenting the loss of their prosecution decision-making power to the CPS. More formal arrangements were then put in place under the statutory charging scheme introduced under the Criminal Justice Act 2003, whereby the DPP determines which charges are to be brought by the police and which by the CPS.[39] Prosecutors were located at the police station to begin with, but this has since been abandoned, and most decisions are made through a central point of contact, CPS Direct. Police officers telephone the CPS, and files are now transmitted and decisions recorded digitally.[40] The CPS is responsible

[34] In the early years of the CPS, informal communications between police and prosecutors were not permitted—contact was to be through official memoranda (Sanders [2016]).

[35] Sir Allan Green, speaking in 1989, quoted in Glidewell (1998: 37).

[36] Lawyers were paid less as crown prosecutors than they had been as privately instructed solicitors. The low status and remuneration of those in the CPS made it a difficult beginning.

[37] Offenses of sexual violence may be an exception to this, as the greatest attrition occurs between reporting and prosecution.

[38] The RCCJ (1993) recommended closer consultation to reduce the number of weak cases prosecuted. The CPS (1995: 24) reported that its advice was sought in only 5 percent of cases, and a Home Office study found that rates of advice varied regionally from 1 to 14 percent (Crisp and Moxon [1994: chap. 4]).

[39] The CPS does not have a monopoly over case disposal, however. For example, the police are able to issue a penalty notice for disorder (PND) on their own authority.

[40] There are plans to expand the digitization of all case files from investigation through to trial. See Lord Chief Justice of England and Wales and Senior President of Tribunals (2016).

for framing the charge at the close of police detention and questioning in serious and complex cases, and officers are required to seek early investigative advice (EIA) in these instances, but the police remain the decision-makers on charging in 72 percent of cases.[41] These arrangements have the potential to close the gap between investigators and the CPS,[42] but a recent Joint Inspectorate Report found that there is still some way to go in making this an effective working relationship.[43] While EIA practices are well established in the specialist CPS headquarters units, such as counterterrorism, they are underutilized in local areas. The Joint Inspectorate found that only two out of thirteen rape cases and one out of twenty-one cases involving other serious sexual offenses in their sample had sought EIA.[44]

Crown prosecutors are playing a greater role in the development and implementation of criminal justice policy as well as in case building, witness care, and the prosecution and disposition of cases. They are also working with the police in criminal justice units, preparing "fast track" cases—those that can be ready for disposal following detention. In counterterrorism cases, while they are unable to direct or require officers to carry out investigations, crown prosecutors are working with police investigators to ensure the gathering of relevant and reliable evidence; and where an application is made before a High Court judge for the continued police detention of terrorism suspects for up to fourteen days, this may, and in practice will, be made by the CPS.[45] Some of these initiatives have the potential to impose a clearer legal orientation on the police case early on—a positive development given the high number of judge-ordered and judge-directed acquittals seen in recent years. However, what seems clear is that effective working relationships are forged within specialist units such as the counterterrorism division, where officers and prosecutors know one another, are likely to share common objectives, and are able to work together over a prolonged period of time, but in the ordinary run of cases with a highly centralized structure, this kind of mutual trust is harder to establish. The challenge will be to establish productive working relationships in a way that does not see the CPS's independence from the police threatened.

[41] This information was previously available on the CPS website at https://www.cps.gov.uk/about/charging.html.

[42] Indeed this was the objective of recommendations made by Lord Justice Auld in his review of the criminal justice process. See Auld (2001).

[43] In one-third of charges brought by the police, this should have been the decision of the CPS; one-tenth of cases dismissed by the CPS should have been handled by the police; and the police decision to charge was incorrect in 8 percent of cases. HMCPSI and HMIC (2015: para. 1.12).

[44] HMCPSI and HMIC (2015: paras. 6.5–6.7).

[45] In this respect it is noteworthy that the arrests in August 2006 of the suspected "liquid bombers" were followed not by two separate announcements to the media, as is the usual practice, but by a joint police-CPS press statement.

C. The Procureur as *Magistrat*

In France, together with the *juge d'instruction* and the trial judge, the procureur is a *magistrat* and so part of the judiciary.[46] *Magistrats* are trained together at a national judicial training school in Bordeaux[47] and then specialize in one of the three principal functions. A distinction is made between the sitting judiciary (the investigating and trial judges), who enjoy complete independence in their appointment and subsequent career, and the standing judiciary (the Parquet, the public prosecution service), which is hierarchically dependent on the minister of justice.[48] They inhabit the same building in most instances and enjoy frequent contact in the course of their working day. As *magistrats* they are also understood to share a common ideology—their role is to apply the law, to protect the rights of the individual, and to act in the public interest. In this way, the procureur's status as a *magistrat* defines her role and guarantees her independence.

The defense lawyer, in contrast, as an *avocat*, is very much a professional outsider; she has neither the professional status nor the ideology of the *magistrat*. While the procureur and the *juge d'instruction* are said to act in the public interest, the lawyer acts in the interests of her client, the accused. In this way, that which binds together the prosecutor, investigator, and trial judge also sets them apart from the defense lawyer. This is of enormous significance in a criminal procedure that places great emphasis on evidence gathered during the pretrial phase. However, a *juge d'instruction* reflected on how this judicial status and common training also blurs the distinction between the different roles and phases of the criminal process and impacts on the independence of the various functions:

> [There is] the unity of a single corps, which includes the functions of prosecution, of investigation and of judgment. We are the same, we come out of the same school, we know each other. That is the real problem. . . . I am often shocked by the way in which people talk about certain cases before and after the court hearing. That is already an encroachment on the independence of each. . . . Our problem is based on having multiple functions coming out of the same school. . . . Even I question myself: Do I work as a judge, investigator, or partner of the police and *gendarmerie*? I do not know. (B1)[49]

[46] This is also the position in, e.g., Italy where prosecutors and judges are both *magistrati*.

[47] The École nationale de la magistrature, known as the ENM.

[48] As well as in matters of policy, as discussed later, the ministry also controls the career postings of the procureur. Moving a prosecutor to another post in another region can be an indirect way of disciplining noncompliant members of the Parquet.

[49] This *magistrat* is quoted in Hodgson (2005: 70). Compare Samet's (2000: 33) description of whether the *juge d'instruction* is Solomon or Maigret.

The person contrasted this with the nature of prosecutorial independence in England and Wales:

> What I think is of value in the English system is this total division between the people who sit in judgment and those who prosecute. Total division. They are not friends, they do not know each other and they have different interests and different backgrounds. The negative effect is that in your country, the judge is very often somebody of note, with his total lack of understanding of the social system in which he started out. He defends a social order and not an idea of justice. (B1)

This blurring of judicial roles, emphasizing the unity of the *magistrature*, is not a new phenomenon. For jurors in the nineteenth-century *cour d'assises*, the architecture of the court together with the costume of the *magistrats* may well have given the impression of the inseparability of the procureur from the *président* of the bench.[50] The prosecutor sat on a raised dais to the side of the trial judges, while the defense lawyer stood on the floor alongside the accused; and in contrast to the black gown of the defense lawyer, the prosecutor and judges wore the same judicial red robes.[51] This symbolic unity was given more concrete form in the prosecution bias demonstrated by the judge, both in her *résumé* at the close of the trial, and in the interrogation of the accused. Armed with the dossier, the judge's questioning of the defendant sought to demonstrate the guilt of the accused, and the summing up was in effect a final address by the prosecution, delivered from the bench, with no opportunity for the accused to reply.[52] Summing up the evidence at the close of proceedings was part of the procedure borrowed from England, but while the English judge took no part in the case and so was better able to maintain a neutral position, the implication of the French judge in the trial process meant that the *président* of the *cour d'assises* played a role that was far from neutral. This *résumé* power was finally removed by the Republicans in 1881 (indeed, it was expressly forbidden on pain of nullity of the proceedings), but the judge continued to assert her support for the prosecution through the *interrogatoire* of the accused.[53]

Doubtless reacting against this conviction bias and operating with few rules of evidence to guide them, juries showed themselves to be independently minded,

[50] This "carpenter's mistake" of placing the prosecutor on the same level as the trial judges continues. See Cohen (2017).

[51] Hodgson (2006c).

[52] "[T]he English respect for the impartiality of the judge has never gained a foothold in France" (Garner [1916: 271]). See also discussion in Donovan (1999) of the jury's perception of the judge's prosecution bias as reported in the French literature.

[53] The judicial questioning of the accused. Garner (1916); Donovan (1999).

willing to question the prosecution case and more likely to acquit than the judges in the *tribunal correctionnel*.[54] The response of the judiciary was to weaken the power of the jury in two principal ways, while maintaining the appearance of democratic decision-making. First, from the mid-nineteenth century, cases were removed from the jury through the practice of *correctionalisation*, whereby offenses are downgraded in order that they might be tried by professional judges in the *tribunal correctionnel*, rather than by a jury in the *cour d'assises*.[55] This practice continues today, employed primarily as a bureaucratic tool to manage caseloads and resources.

Second, the judiciary sought to dilute and control the jury through *échevinage*—referring to a jury composed both of laypeople and professional *magistrats*. Mixed juries were first proposed in 1882, "aimed at reducing acquittals and increasing magistrates' influence over juries."[56] Premised "on the assumption that juries were too incompetent to render justice without strict supervision, *échevinage* was promoted" but was not taken up until the political climate had changed after World War I.[57] In the meantime, judges made some inroads into working with juries on their decision-making. A practice had developed whereby the president of the bench went into the jury room during deliberations to explain points of law and to discuss sentencing.[58] This, of course, provided further opportunity to raise points that the defense could not address.[59] Judges and jurors also determined sentence together from 1932. This might be seen as a reduction in the judge's power (she alone had determined sentence until this time), but it was aimed at increasing the jury's willingness to convict, as there was concern that many acquittals were to avoid the harsh sentence imposed by the judge.[60] Eventually, under the authoritarian Vichy regime in 1941, *magistrats* were added to sit alongside lay jurors and so keep them in check, while also reducing the number of lay jurors from twelve to six.[61]

[54] Garçon (1995). Garner (1916: 278) notes that juries acquitted some 33 percent of cases, compared with 9 percent in the *tribunal correctionnel*, and the difference was especially pronounced in Paris. There were reports of scandalous affairs and juries being swayed by sentiment and the morals of the day, rather than the letter of the law. After the introduction of *échevinage*, conviction rates in the *cour d'assises* increased to 90 percent.

[55] Donovan (1999: 388–402). Parliament also legislated to downgrade some *crimes* to *délits*, thus removing them from the scope of mandatory jury trial.

[56] Critics claimed that the jury's undue lenience and the inability of laypeople to evaluate expert testimony were also reasons to impose constraints on their role. See Donovan (1999: 402–420). Hostility grew as the jury was democratized, with compensation for lost wages and the admission of ordinary working people to sit as jurors alongside the bourgeoisie.

[57] Donovan (1999: 409). The same happened in Germany, where juries were merged into mixed courts in 1924.

[58] Donovan (1999: 409–410).

[59] Garçon (1995: 470–471).

[60] Donovan (1999: 411).

[61] This was later increased to nine lay jurors with three *magistrats* but has again been reduced to six lay jurors, nine in an appeal case. This shared decision-making is called *échevinage*. Furthermore,

Some French commentators have been highly critical of the reform and its implementation: "In servile imitation of the dictatorships, the government of Vichy struck a fatal blow against a jury guilty of being independent, of protecting citizens from arbitrariness, and of yielding poorly to suggested convictions."[62] Jews, Freemasons, and those deemed politically unreliable were excluded, and jury selection was removed from mixed commissions of judges and local politicians, entrusted purely to the judiciary from 1872. After the downfall of the Vichy regime in 1944, most repressive measures were repealed, but the mixed jury remained, and the conviction rate in the *cour d'assises* continued to rise. However, others have argued that it would be wrong to attribute this reform simply to the authoritarian Vichy regime. The reform had been under discussion for some time, favored by the judiciary, and it was the proposals developed between 1934 and 1938 by a government-appointed commission headed up by Paul Matter, the *procureur général* of the *cour de cassation*, that led to the introduction of *échevinage*. Although the inquisitorial model of procedure had failed to guarantee the judicial impartiality that is at the core of its rationale, the presumed benefits of this model were the very reason why some, such as Vouin, favored restrictions on the jury. He shared the concerns of others that the jury was unreliable and incompetent,[63] but more fundamentally, he asserted the superiority of safeguards offered by an inquisitorial procedure governed by judges rather than laypeople.[64]

In this way, through the processes of *correctionalisation* and *échevinage*, the jury and its challenge to the pro-prosecution bias of the judge was neutralized without completely destroying what was seen as an important gain of the Revolution. Significantly, it was the *magistrats* themselves who ensured that "an important democratic institution—trial by jury—was gradually reduced to insignificance in France."[65] In the same way that the *juges d'instruction* were able to reshape counterterrorism investigations in the late twentieth century by involving intelligence officers as investigators (described in chapter 3), this provides an earlier example of the power of the French judiciary in shaping criminal process.

Returning to the blurring of different *magistrat* roles in the French criminal process, this was identified as a major concern in reports on the Outreau affair, a case in which accusations of widespread child sexual abuse were made by a

critics characterized the jury as incompetent and unable to evaluate expert testimony. See Donovan (1999: 402–407).

[62] Garçon (1995: 469).

[63] The admission of women to the jury in 1944 made the expert guidance of the judiciary yet more important, according to Vouin, "for women are easily carried to extremes and it is dangerous to leave to its own impressions and lights a feminine jury." Vouin (1955: 506).

[64] Vouin (1956: 4–7).

[65] Donovan (1999: 380).

number of children and adults in the town of Outreau in northern France, but in which testimony was ultimately withdrawn as false, leading to the collapse of the prosecution case.[66] The various reports and enquiries criticized the ways in which the functionally separate roles of the procureur and *juge d'instruction* overlap considerably in practice. They also noted the general absence of reflexivity among the judiciary: although the case passed through the hands of some sixty different *magistrats*, none of them challenged either the central case thesis or the methods of investigation.[67] Checks are carried out, the decisions of *magistrats* monitored, but by other *magistrats* concerned to affirm rather than to challenge their colleagues' work; the professional ethics of judicial officers proved to be insufficiently independent in practice. As we see time and again, it is the occupational cultures based on shared working practices that govern the behavior of criminal justice actors, not legal procedural rules.[68]

In order to strengthen the prosecution role and prevent this confusion of functions, the Outreau report recommended that the Parquet have a career path and standing that is different from the sitting judiciary, creating a greater degree of separation between the two functions of the *magistrature*. This has been contested by procureurs who insist on the importance of their status as *magistrats*, as guarantors of individual rights and freedoms, and oppose fiercely changes that, in their view, will reduce them to the status of *fonctionnaires* or bureaucrats.[69] Instead, the direction of reforms has been in the other direction, to strengthen further the independence of the procureur's judicial status—in appearance at least. The Parquet's hierarchical accountability to executive power has been weakened—since 2013, the minister of justice may no longer give instructions in individual cases—and the duty of the procureur to investigate exculpatory as well as inculpatory evidence has been written explicitly into the Code de procédure pénale (CPP). However, ministerial authority continues to be exercised, but in different ways, by, for example, procureurs being summoned to the ministry to account for failing to respect national policies; or being subject to an urgent inspection following a high-profile affair; or even being moved to a different post when government expectations have not been met.[70] Executive interference has been most evident in the appointment and work of the post of

[66] See chapter 8 for more detailed discussion of this case and its aftermath.

[67] Vallini (2006: 276).

[68] Hodgson and Mou (2019).

[69] See, e.g., Jean-Louis Nadal (*procureur général* of the Cour de cassation), "Un risque pour notre justice et nos libertés," *Le Monde*, 2 June 2006, 18; Renucci (2009).

[70] Milburn and Mouhanna (2010: 15). The Truche Commission (1997) noted that the culture of hierarchy and subordination to the authority of the Justice Ministry is hard to break in practice, especially given the minister's influence on the career of the procureur. I was also told that requests were made in subtle and indirect ways also—asking the procureur to place a dossier at the bottom of the pile of cases to be dealt with, for example.

procureur de Paris, who works closely with the executive, dealing with sensitive political cases as well as terrorism. Despite expressing a desire to strengthen the independence of the Parquet nomination process, President Macron was accused of meddling in the appointment of the *procureur de Paris* in 2018, rejecting the three candidates selected by the justice minister and opening the way to nominate his own candidate, Rémy Heitz, who went on to be appointed.[71]

Prosecutors have called for the removal of any executive interference in the appointment of procureurs. This would retain the hierarchical link with the minister of justice,[72] thus ensuring the uniform application of penal policy, but move responsibility for nomination, discipline, and career progression to the professional regulating body for the judiciary, the Conseil supérieure de la magistrature (CSM),[73] as is currently the case with the *magistrature du siège*. The appointment and promotion of prosecutors would then be a professional rather than a political decision. Without the overwhelming support of politicians, however, such a reform continues to seem unlikely, as it require a three-fifths majority in both parliamentary chambers.

D. Independence, Discretion, and the Public Interest

There is a tension between the institutional status of the prosecutor, especially in the case of the procureur as judicial officer, and her functional role. The difficulty in expecting the person acting for the state in prosecuting its case to also retain a form of judicial independence is apparent in miscarriage-of-justice cases such as Outreau, and the now infamous cases in England and Wales in the 1980 and 1990s, such as the Birmingham Six and the Cardiff Three.[74] It is part of what Medwed has characterized as the prosecutor's "ongoing schizophrenia,"[75] the conflicting expectations we have of prosecutors as "zealous advocates and impartial reviewers of the facts, crime fighters and instruments of mercy, law enforcement leaders and officers of the court, loyal public servants and independent professionals, champions of community values and defenders of the rule of law."[76] The risk is that these conflicting roles cannot be maintained.

[71] This was seen as a cynical move by the *magistrature*, and one that undermined the independence of the process. See M. Bloch, "Quand Emmanuel Macron s'immisce dans la procédure de nomination du procureur de Paris," *Le Journal du Dimanche*, 26 September 2018.

[72] Several official enquiries and commissions have concluded that the appointment of a professional public prosecutor at the head of the public prosecution service would lack the necessary legitimacy. See Delmas-Marty (1991); Truche (1997); Nadal (2013).

[73] The opinion of the CSM is only advisory and is often ignored. Milburn and Mouhanna (2010: 15).

[74] These cases are discussed in detail in chapter 9.

[75] Medwed (2012: 3).

[76] Slansky (2016: 477).

Police tunnel vision can become prosecution tunnel vision, and weaknesses in a case can be explained away as poor police work, rather than weak evidence because there is no strong evidence. As the prosecution case gathers momentum, the prosecutor's instinct can be to bolster, rather than to challenge, the case, especially if she is implicated early in the investigation, as in the French model.[77] It is interesting to compare how this inherent tension is dealt with in the two jurisdictions. In France, the prosecutor's judicial status, training, and neutral, public-interest-centered ideology is thought to ensure independence within the framework of a broadly inquisitorial procedure. The written dossier of evidence and hierarchical accountability to the minister of justice represent further potential checks on her role, and her ability to require that certain investigations be carried out allows her to shape the enquiry beyond that determined by the police. The crown prosecutor, on the other hand, has no vocational training, no involvement in the investigation, and acts more explicitly as a party to the case. Yet these very different features of the crown prosecutor's role are understood to guarantee her independence, just as the procureur's judicial status and authority over the police are seen to guarantee hers.

In addition to independence from the narrow interests of the police investigation, the prosecutor must balance her independence from political influence with the requirement for some form of democratic accountability. Di Frederico characterizes this dilemma as having to accommodate two conflicting operational imperatives.

> On the one hand, there is awareness that public prosecution contributes substantially to the definition and implementation of criminal policy. This requires that mechanisms be devised to ensure that the active role played in that crucial area be somehow directed and controlled in the context of the democratic process. On the other hand, the need to guarantee that public prosecution be exercised with rigour, consistency and fairness makes it necessary to ensure that too close a tie with the political process be not unduly used by the existing majority to influence the conduct (actively or by omission) of public prosecution for partisan purposes; more generally to ensure that citizens be treated equally.[78]

In the United States, prosecutors are elected in the locality where they serve, understood as an important element of democratic accountability.[79] However, this

[77] See also O'Brien (2009a), who discusses the systemic features of the criminal process that encourage confirmation bias in American prosecutors.

[78] Di Federico (1998).

[79] There is some evidence that the behavior of prosecutors alters in the run-up to their election, for example, their being more likely to go to trial rather than plea bargaining. McCannon (2018) notes similar patterns among public defenders up for re-election.

populist model is criticized by some, such as Tonry, as being ineffective and in fact, "lawless" because prosecutors "exercise their enormous power over citizens' lives without being accountable to anyone but the electorate."[80] More fundamentally, despite its self-image of democracy and constitutionalism, the United States' extreme culture of penal populism, within which prosecutors play a key part, has led to the mass incarceration of young black men in particular, in a way that has attracted functional comparisons with slavery.[81] In their enthusiastic implementation of government policy, prosecutors have not shown themselves to be independent or fair in their application of law.

Italy has adopted the opposite approach in defining prosecutors' relationship with the executive. Anxious to avoid the political discrimination experienced during World War II and the Fascist period, prosecutors operate under a principle of mandatory prosecution with no accountability either to the electorate or to a political authority. This was designed to avoid the arbitrary or political exercise of power, but instead has given prosecutors a mandate to exercise discretion in a way that reflects personal and local preferences, rather than equal treatment before the law or any form of democratic accountability.[82] Although the principle of legality remains, in the thirty years since the Italian reforms toward a more accusatorial procedure the prosecutor's role has been strengthened further

[80] Tonry (2012). Simon (2007) considers the changing locus of democratic accountability. Courts enjoyed a legal and social policymaking role in the first half of the twentieth century, before then switching to a model of authority "based on popular sentiment and deference to private ordering" that made interventionist approaches less legitimate (2007: 137). He argues that

> American courts have been hobbled by the unique challenges posed by framing street crime as a fundamental political problem to be solved by government, including courts, and the resulting "war on crime" from the 1960s through the end of the twentieth century. . . . The very virtues that made courts an attractive solution to many twentieth-century governance problems—their relative autonomy from normal political and market pressures; the role of argumentation, deliberation and interpretation in shaping judicial decisions; and the ability to consider different voices and many kinds of information—have come to be seen as flaws that bespeak a lack of alignment between judicial judgment and the common good.

This favoring of the government's power to punish has been achieved through the valorization of police, prosecutors, and victims (2007: 137–138). The counterpart to the government's rise in authority has been the decline of that of the judiciary, most notably in their criminal justice role, where they are seen as "dangerous power holders, prone to acting against the interest of ordinary citizens." Simon (2007: 139).

[81] See Lacey (2008: 29–32) and references therein.

[82] Di Frederico quotes (1998: 380) Giovanni Falcone, the judge who prosecuted, and was assassinated by, the Mafia in 1992: "How can it be conceivable that in a liberal democratic regime we do not yet have a judicial policy, and everything is left to the *absolutely irresponsible decisions* of the various prosecutors' offices and often even to the personal decisions of their members? In the absence of institutional controls on the activities of public prosecutors, [there is] the peril that informal influences and hidden connections with hidden *loci* of power might influence their activities. It seems to me that the time has come to rationalise and co-ordinate the activities of public prosecutors rendered de facto unaccountable by a fetishistic conception of the principle of mandatory criminal prosecution." Falcone (1994: 173–174).

as a result of the growing importance of the pretrial phase, where the prosecutor enjoys broad discretion.[83]

In England and Wales and France too, the independence and accountability of the prosecutor are understood differently, reflecting different structures of political authority.[84] The attorney general's role in relation to the CPS provides a line of accountability and, in theory, the possibility of government interference, but in practice, by constitutional convention control over the prosecution is exercised sparingly. The AG's functions include acting as legal adviser to Parliament, as well as prosecution and civil litigation.[85] In many ways she epitomizes the tension in the prosecution function—although a minister, she is a lawyer, required to be impartial, to be independent of government and politics, and, above all, to act in the public interest. This role has been described as one of "independent aloofness" and of "intimate but independent involvement."[86] Debates around the AG's status mirror those of the French prosecutor. Former AG Lord Shawcross called for the AG to be "wholly outside the political arena and enjoying in the task of law enforcement the status and independence of a judge," in order to ensure "not only the reality (which I hope it still has) but also the appearance (which it lacks) of complete detachment from party politics."[87] Others, as with the French prosecution function, emphasize the importance of democratic accountability to Parliament.[88] Concern has been expressed at the exercise of the AG's functions in a number of high-profile cases, and in the advice to the government on the legality of Britain's entry into the Iraq war.[89] In 2007, the House of Commons Constitutional Affairs Select Committee proposed reforming the office of the AG by separating out the political and nonpolitical functions,[90] but this was rejected by the government, arguing that correcting misunderstandings of the AG role was preferable to structural reform.[91] Retaining a lawyer at the heart of government is considered an important constitutional safeguard, and conferring ministerial status ensures both authority within the cabinet and clear lines of accountability to Parliament.

83 Caianiello (2016).

84 Perrodet (2002: 417–425) describes the prosecution role in England and Wales as characterized by institutional dependence and functional autonomy, and the French as one of institutional dependence and functional subordination.

85 Walker (1999).

86 Edwards (1984).

87 Lord Shawcross, Letter to the Editor (*The Times*, 3 August 1977).

88 See further Appleby (2016).

89 Appleby (2016).

90 Constitutional Affairs Committee, *Inquiry into the Constitutional Role of the Attorney General*, House of Commons, July 2007.

91 Samuels (2014: 610) has argued for the abolition of the AG, redistributing her tasks and making her accountable to Parliament. However, this risks recreating the same conflict of interest in an office that is closer to the daily practice of the prosecution than the AG and so, arguably, is in more danger of compromising prosecutorial independence.

In France, hierarchical structures of policy implementation and accountability are typical of those associated with inquisitorial procedure and are much stronger than in England and Wales.[92] The Parquet is headed up by the minister of justice, with a chain of authority through the *procureur général* and the *procureur de la république* down to the individual *substitut du procureur*. In addition to the issuing of instructions from the Ministry of Justice, since 2007 *procureurs généraux* have been given the task of coordinating policy and overseeing the work of the Parquet at the appeal court level. They must also report annually to the minister on the work and organization of the Parquet, and how the law has been applied,[93] which for some prosecutors is experienced as a constant pressure to account for their actions.[94] This hierarchical culture of instruction and subordination also impacts on the procureur's career. Evaluation for promotion includes her "capacity to implement penal policies" and "to be part of the hierarchical relationship"; loyalty and conformity are rewarded, while independence is penalized.[95] In the French republican tradition, accountability to a democratically elected politician is seen to provide legitimacy to the prosecution role, though numerous political scandals have revealed the threat to prosecutorial independence that is posed by this relationship.[96] Together with the hierarchy's influence over the career of the procureur, and the limited nature of her status as a judicial officer, the independence of the French prosecutor is complex and contingent.[97]

Prosecutors in both jurisdictions are considered independent, albeit structured in different ways, and both are charged with acting in the public interest as part of their professional and ethical framework. But how are we to understand what is the public interest?[98] We might instinctively perceive it as a good thing—it is in, rather than against, the interest of the public; it serves the public, rather than private interests; yet it is a creature of discretion and so is hard to define. Grounded in the eighteenth-century ideology of the Enlightenment (and the Revolution), in republican France the state is understood to represent the public interest, but "Common law countries . . . regard the public interest as an interest

[92] Hodgson (2002c).
[93] Article 35 CPP.
[94] Milburn et al. (2010: 107).
[95] Cohen (2017).
[96] See, for example, the investigation and, ultimately, the conviction in 2011 of former president Jacques Chirac, discussed in Hodgson (2010). More recently, a former minister of justice, Jean-Jacques Urvoas, was investigated for breaching professional secrecy by informing a politician, Thierry Solère, about a criminal enquiry into Solère. See http://www.ledauphine.com/france-monde/2017/12/13/affaire-urvoas-la-responsabilite-penale-de-l-ex-garde-des-sceaux-engagee.
[97] For example, while the practice of issuing instructions to prosecutors in individual cases has ceased, the influence of the Ministry of Justice over the career of the procureur makes it difficult to resist more informal requests. Truche (1997); Hodgson (2005).
[98] See further the discussion in Hodgson (2017).

separate from that of the state—moreover, an interest which is often in direct conflict with the interest represented by the government."[99] Dominic Grieve, QC, at the time the attorney general, described it as "this shape without form, this shade without colour."[100] In practice, this might mean refraining from prosecution when it is not deemed to be in the public interest—defined by the policy framework within which the prosecutor exercises her discretion.

Prosecutorial discretion should also be exercised as part of a duty to prosecute effectively, but not to obtain a conviction at any cost. The decision to prosecute requires a belief in the likelihood of conviction, and prosecutors may believe in the guilt of the accused, but they are not advocates for the victim. They must also retain a "minister of justice" detachment, able to question information that appears to inculpate the accused, to accept that evidence at trial may present a different picture from that on paper, or simply to recognize that the case does not come up to proof. This represents a point of tension for prosecutors in both procedural traditions: they may believe in the guilt of the accused at the point of prosecution, but the accused and the public must trust in the fairness and professionalism of the prosecutor not to act as a simple partisan advocate whose sole aim is the obtaining of a conviction, even where the evidence not support it.[101]

Where there are structural incentives to plead guilty, the risk of prosecuting weak cases without proper scrutiny of the evidence is even greater. The contrasting ways in which prosecutors understand their responsibilities in guilty plea cases illuminates the significance of their different roles and professional status. In England and Wales, the majority of cases are disposed of by way of a guilty plea, assisted by the offer of a sentence discount. Neither crown prosecutors nor the courts look behind a guilty plea, taking the accused's plea at face value and relying on the defense lawyer to ensure evidential sufficiency. This is a kind of laissez-faire model of free choice of the parties. In France, the broader responsibility of the procureur as *magistrat* results in a different approach, one in which the prosecutor is concerned to satisfy herself that there is sufficient evidence and that the accused has made a clear admission. If this is not the case, the procureur does not attempt any tactics of persuasion or bargaining—the accused is simply referred back to court for trial.[102] The treatment of a case as a guilty plea is the decision of the prosecutor, not of the accused; it is simply an abbreviated procedure to sentence.

99 Langer (1988: 279–280).

100 Grieve (2013).

101 See discussion of the prosecutor's conviction psychology in Burke (2013: 707–711). Psychologists have found that role definition is important: those charged with investigating one side of a case in preparation for prosecution were found to be more partisan in their work than those who were told that they were the sole investigator for the case. See O'Brien (2009a); Simon et al. (2009, 2015).

102 Soubise (2016); Hodgson and Soubise (2016b).

This might be regarded as a question of professional ethics as well as of law and evidence. In November 2009, the DPP issued a "Statement of Ethical Principles for the Public Prosecutor,"[103] paragraph 3.2 of which sets out the need to take account of these issues.

> 3.2 Prosecutors must perform their duties without fear, favour or prejudice. They must:
>
> 1. take decisions based upon an impartial and professional assessment of the available evidence, independently and with objectivity within the framework laid down by the law, the [crown prosecutors'] Code, all departmental policies currently in force and all guidance issued by or on behalf of the Attorney General; and
> 2. take into account all relevant circumstances, irrespective of whether they are to the advantage or disadvantage of the defendant.

The French prosecutor is also required to act according to the Ministry of Justice's criminal justice policy and to follow the instructions of her superiors (in writing if not in the development of arguments at court), and as a *magistrat* she must act in the public interest. The expression of this judicial ideology has been strengthened in the way that the procureur's duty is inscribed in the CPP. Since the law of June 2016, her role in directing police investigations is described as to seek out the truth by ensuring that both inculpating and exculpating evidence is sought out, at the same time as ensuring respect for the interests of all parties.[104] This echoes the duty of the *juge d'instruction*, who as a *juge du siège* has a more independent status and role.[105] However, it seems unlikely that the simple addition of this phrasing will have any real impact beyond preparing the ground for the further transfer of power from the *juge d'instruction* to the procureur by attempting to elide the differences in their professional status and ideology. The function of the procureur as a public prosecutor, rather than a judicial officer with the independence that status requires, is deeply engrained in the structure of her role, as demonstrated by the ECtHR cases of *Medvedyev* and *Moulin*.[106]

[103] Available at http://www.cps.gov.uk/legal/s_to_u/statment_of_ethical_principles_for_the_public_prosecutor/.

[104] Article 39-3 CPP created by Loi No. 2016-731, 3 June 2016.

[105] These are the so-called sitting judiciary (trial judges, *juges d'instruction, juges des libertés et de la détention*) who are not under the hierarchy of the minister of justice and cannot be moved from their post.

[106] *Medvedyev v. France* (3394/03) 29 March 2010; *Moulin v. France* (37104/06) 23 November 2010. The role of the procureur as a party to the case was emphasized in these cases. These decisions effectively put a stop to the Léger Commission proposals to place all investigations under the authority of the Parquet, albeit retaining a two-tier structure in which greater due process protections were provided to those facing more serious charges. This was claimed as a simplification and rationalization of criminal procedure. However, although there would be a single authority in the form of the

The prosecutor's ability to sustain this "minister of justice" role will depend in part on her relationship with those assembling the evidence in the case, determining which leads to follow and which to leave unexplored;[107] it will depend on the policy framework within which she exercises her discretion; but it will also depend on her professional ideology as a prosecutor. As one senior French prosecutor explained it to me:

> What is the role of the *parquet*? Is it to immerse yourself completely in the direction of the investigation, or is it to maintain a quasi-Olympian detachment, waiting for it to happen, for it to deliver the results ready-made? Of course, I think, it is something between the two.[108]

Procureurs often describe their role in neutral terms, emphasizing the judicial quality of their status, and the importance of avoiding a presumption of guilt.[109] In practice, however, the procureur's interpretation of the public interest can be problematic, and far from being neutral, equates a confession with the truth.[110]

In addition to the nature of the prosecutor's independence, training, status, and professional ideology, the way in which prosecutorial discretion is structured, regulated, and exercised shapes the construction of the public interest. Despite the model of hierarchical instruction and written documentation, French prosecutors enjoy a great deal of individual discretion compared with their counterparts in England and Wales, whose decision-making is closely regulated. Crown prosecutors are subject to clear national guidelines: an overarching code for crown prosecutors, a raft of prosecution policy guidance for specific offenses, and a segmented work process in which tasks are separated out and closely circumscribed. The procureur on the other hand operates within broad policy mandates; her decision-making is more affected by local resourcing and the workload of the court. The factors to be taken into account in deciding whether to prosecute and with which offenses are not set out in a national code (though they may be part of local resource-driven policy developed by the Parquet with other local actors), leaving the procureur with a comparatively

procureur, the proposal was to retain two separate procedural regimes of rights: the *régime simple* was to be essentially the same as that currently in place for procureur-supervised investigations; and the *régime renforcé* would provide the suspect with the rights currently available during the *instruction*. In this way, one duality was replaced with another.

107 Historically, even the trial judge's independence has been found wanting. Her summing up of the evidence (the *résumé*), a procedure borrowed from the English in 1808, was found to be weighted too much in favor of the prosecution and so was abolished in 1881 (Garner [1916: 271]).

108 Prosecutor A6 in Hodgson (2005: 170).

109 One senior prosecutor (E4) referred to the Dreyfus affair when describing to me the importance of keeping an open mind.

110 Hodgson (2005).

wide discretion in what she does and why. Although their hierarchy and status as *magistrats* binds them together in some respects, procureurs also described themselves as "an individualist corps" with "freedom of action" and "a significant amount of leeway" in their treatment of cases.[111]

> Standardisation, for sure, that does not exist. Even within the same jurisdiction, depending on training, there are differences in jurisprudence. That is at the same time the variety, the strength and the weakness of the justice system. . . . Myself, I prefer a justice system without uniformity, but with freedom of action. (A6)[112]

This individualized decision-making is further accommodated by the French notion of *adaptation*, whereby the criminal response is adapted in order to deal more effectively with specific offenses, the offender, and the impact of their offending. This might result in a local policy of nonprosecution of drug possession in cities, or at the individual level, the substitution of a noncustodial sentence to enable the convicted person to continue to work.[113]

> Of course there are problems of standardisation . . . you cannot follow the same *politique pénale* everywhere because the cases are different, the populations are different, the problems are different. . . . In one instance you will prosecute far more offenders than in another, because there is less delinquency. . . . A uniform system of justice, which is delivered in the same way everywhere and so which does not take account of differences, would effectively be a non-democratic system of justice. (A6)[114]

However, this was more likely to be resource driven than to be motivated by a sense of contextual fairness.

> There is a problem in the way that the justice system is organized. There are 180 *procureurs* and they must not all be acting differently. This is partly because of resources—here, we are not as well off as smaller court regions so we cannot prosecute all of the more minor cases, which only 20km away, they may do. (D4)[115]

111 Hodgson (2005: 233–234; see generally 232–243).
112 Hodgson (2005: 234).
113 Hodgson and Soubise (2016a).
114 Hodgson (2005: 230).
115 Hodgson (2005: 231).

The existence of this broad sphere of action enables the development of local policy, but it also allows individual prosecutors to implement their own preferences—taking a harder or softer approach to certain offenses, for example.[116] This can also present difficulties for the police who work with the procureur during the investigation, preparing the case for prosecution.

> The policies or decisions of certain *magistrats* are, in identical circumstances but in different places, often different. The differences in treatment are sometimes surprising, at the heart of the same jurisdiction. The personal involvement of some *magistrats* is difficult to manage. This subjectivity, without basis, is experienced quite negatively by police personnel. (Police questionnaire respondent 5)[117]

The breadth of the procureur's discretion in practice and the trust in her role as a professional contrasts with the more closely defined contours of the crown prosecutor's decision-making and the stronger audit culture within which she is called to account. Inspectorates, reviews, and managers evaluate the work of the CPS, encompassing not only their decision to charge and prosecute, but also the speed with which they review cases and their adherence to national procedures. While the French procedural model appears more normative and hierarchical, in practice the procureur enjoys a more permissive and autonomous role than her counterpart in England and Wales.

[116] This was criticized by prosecutors in Mouhanna and Bastard's research (2010: 38–40, 43).
[117] Hodgson (2005: 234).

5
The Changing Prosecution Role

Across most Western European legal systems, the preoccupation with the efficient management of caseloads within the criminal process has led to the development of procedures that avoid contested trial and even prosecution, shifting the center of gravity away from the trial to the pretrial phase and so drawing power away from the judiciary toward the public prosecutor and, in some instances, the police. In Britain and in France, in different ways, this has reconfigured both the allocation of authority over case disposition and the locus of responsibility for protecting the rights of the accused. As the key legal actor managing criminal cases before and at trial, the prosecutor in particular has seen the nature of her role alter in order to accommodate these system demands, requiring her to act as sentencer, casework manager, policymaker, negotiator, and adjudicator, alongside her more established functions of court prosecutor and in the case of France, investigative supervisor. However, while alternatives to the fully contested trial are increasingly the norm, this has not been achieved through a strategy of decriminalization, or a turn away from punitiveness. Rather, we see a kind of banalization of criminal justice, in which some form of admission, rapidly obtained, has become the norm, with scant attention paid to the evidential basis justifying the resulting punishment. Furthermore, the growing electoral importance of criminal justice in recent decades has added to this pressure to process large numbers of cases as quickly as possible, as politicians employ a "tough on crime" rhetoric that values increased criminalization and punishment more than principles of fairness and due process.

In order to satisfy these competing objectives to process cases more efficiently, and to be (or appear to be) tough on crime, this banalization of criminal justice has spawned new and rapid ways of sanctioning greater numbers of offenders. In addition to the dominance of the guilty plea in England and Wales, now formally incentivized through a sentence reduction, in both jurisdictions relatively minor offenses are treated routinely and automatically, sanctioned through fines and community orders, without the opportunity to test the accusation or advance a defense. Through its "third way" of alternative responses,[1] France has sought actively to reduce the number of dismissals, increasing the number of cases dealt

[1] These are neither a formal prosecution nor a dismissal, but something in between.

The Metamorphosis of Criminal Justice. Jacqueline S. Hodgson, Oxford University Press (2020).

DOI: 10.1093/oso/9780199981427.001.0001

with through a variety of informal measures, but resulting in a disproportionate focus on minor offenses.

In both jurisdictions, the more rapid and routine treatment of cases has increased the scope of the prosecution function, but ironically, this has been achieved in part through a process of deprofessionalization, in which procedures for the treatment of cases are simplified, becoming almost automatic, and work is delegated to a variety of adjuncts and caseworkers. Success is measured in the cost, speed, and quantity, rather than the quality, of prosecution work. The contrasting status, role, and training of the two types of prosecutors means that change is played out differently within the two criminal justice procedural traditions, but in both jurisdictions, these shifts in the prosecution function are often experienced as conflicting imperatives. Increasingly responsible for the disposition as well as the prosecution of offenses, prosecutors have seen the scope of their role and responsibility increase, while at the same time, their status and professional autonomy are reduced through the use of predetermined and standardized forms of treatment. Prosecution relationships with other legal actors are also impacted in ways that undermine the prosecutor's professional and structural independence, values that are core to the prosecutor's own understanding of her role. In France, the more lengthy and costly investigation process of *instruction* is becoming increasingly rare, as cases are downgraded and powers are shifted to the procureur. This may streamline the system, easing resources and improving case flows, but it also raises concerns as to the independence of the legal process if the role of the independent *juge d'instruction* is marginalized and criminal justice matters are under the ultimate authority of the executive, given the evidence of political interference in high-profile cases and prosecutorial appointments.[2]

The drivers that are reshaping the prosecution service in both jurisdictions rest on neither adversarial nor inquisitorial procedural values, nor on broader concerns with fair trial, but have as their objective the processing of large numbers of cases with the minimum of cost and delay in order to demonstrate the effectiveness of criminal justice responses to crime. This recasting of the prosecution function has implications for the independence of the prosecutor, for her autonomy and professional standing, and for the balance of legal and constitutional power in the criminal process. The increased regulation and delegation of prosecution tasks produces a more standardized criminal process, the objectives and hallmarks of which are no longer procedural fairness, or the protection of the rights of victims and accused persons, but administrative efficiency.

[2] At the same time, the role of the préfet, a local political actor, is also increasing in ways that restrict the liberties of the individual and which many critics see as being properly within the sphere of criminal (rather than administrative) judicial oversight.

These features are captured in what Ritzer has described as the McDonaldization of society,[3] in which the principles of the fast-food industry have been adopted in our models of business and public service.[4] Criminal justice is routinized in order to produce predictable and standardized outputs that can be quantified in order to measure and to demonstrate efficiency. This is done through deskilling, delegation, and the removal of judicial procedures and safeguards that prevent the rapid processing of cases, replaced by less time-consuming administrative checks and controls. However, as discussed in preceding chapters, this "actuarial justice" model that measures success in managerial terms,[5] rather than those of fair trial, due process, or the prevention of reoffending, provides only the illusion of efficiency.[6]

A. The Implications of the Shift to a Pretrial System of Justice

In most jurisdictions, there is a clear trend toward expanding the role of the prosecutor as a primary measure to improve the efficient processing of cases and so reduce delays in case disposition and the courts' docket.[7] This may be through avoiding altogether the courtroom disposition of cases,[8] as with the dispositive powers of the CPS in issuing conditional cautions, or the mass policy of Dutch prosecutors issuing penal orders for offenses punishable by up to six years' imprisonment.[9] Or it may be by encouraging defendants to accept abbreviated trial procedures, such as the French guilty plea procedure,[10] or the immediate trial hearing;[11] the Italian sentence bargain,[12] or trial on the basis of the case file;[13]

[3] Ritzer (2004). This also resembles Packer's (1968) assembly line model of justice in some respects.

[4] Bohm (2006) has termed this "McJustice" in the criminal law context.

[5] Feeley and Simon (1992, 1994).

[6] Ritzer calls this the rationality of irrationality, in which rational systems come to look unreasonable, as instrumental values such as law and order are promoted over traditional legal values of justice and freedom.

[7] As discussed in chapter 2, efficiency measures may reduce the time and cost of prosecution, but not necessarily the caseload. Indeed, it may become a way of meeting increased demand when government has simultaneously pursued a policy of increased criminalization: one hundred criminal justice bills have added more than four thousand offenses to the statute book in England and Wales between 1989 and 2009. See Leveson (2015: 5, para. 13).

[8] For a discussion of the various types of case disposal in six European countries, see Wade (2008).

[9] Van de Bunt and van Gelder (2012). This legal power dates back to 2008, may also be administered by the police in cases of shoplifting or traffic offenses, and is understood as a criminal punishment. For an account of Dutch criminal justice trends, see Blackstock et al. (2014: 98–102).

[10] The *comparution sur reconnaissance préalable de culpabilité.*

[11] The *comparution immédiate.*

[12] The *patteggiamento.*

[13] The *giudizio abbreviato.*

or the long-standing practice in England and Wales and the United States of charge and sentence bargaining in exchange for a guilty plea. Or it may be by funneling cases toward the lower courts, avoiding the costs and delay of a more complex jury trial, as with the French process of *correctionalisation*, which allows cases to be tried by the *tribunal correctionnel*, avoiding the more lengthy *instruction* and trial in the *cour d'assises*; or procedures in England and Wales that encourage magistrates and prosecutors to keep cases in the lower magistrates' courts, especially where a plea of guilty is indicated. In France, prosecutors are also central in the decision to pursue alternatives to trial, such as penal orders or mediation. What these various measures and procedures have in common is a broad shift away from the public judicial disposition of cases, with associated fair-trial rights for the defense, to more rapid and so more standardized procedures, as well as an increasingly adjudicative and less public role for the prosecutor.

As the contested trial becomes the exception, most cases are disposed of without any public legal challenge. The facts of the case and the charges to be prosecuted are negotiated and agreed upon outside court.[14] Even the sanction is determined in advance where an alternative to trial, such as the *comparution sur reconnaissance préalable de culpabilité* (CRPC, the French guilty plea procedure), is used, or where an alternative to prosecution, such as the *composition pénale* (a form of prosecutorial sanction), is preferred.[15] This process is choreographed by criminal justice professionals, themselves guided by policy imperatives and targets; the participatory power of the accused is weakened by incentives to forgo any contest of the charges, and she risks being deprived of basic fair-trial rights. The role of the judge in the testing, oversight, and disposition of cases is also sidelined,[16] raising questions concerning the extent to which this due process deficit is made good either by the quasi-judicial status of the prosecutor or, more likely, through a pretrial defense role grounded in fair-trial rights and so, arguably, an accusatorial procedure. Overall, the disappearance of the contested trial and the reduced opportunities for the defense to test the prosecution case shift

[14] As a procureur in a medium-sized office told Milburn et al. (2010: 46): "The court is no longer the key moment, that is all finished . . . the trial is just a stage of a process that we control much more than the *juges du siège*."

[15] In the Netherlands, as well as in France, prosecutors can attach conditions even when the decision is to close the case. No admission is required in these conditional dismissals, but the prosecutor considers that guilt is proven. These conditions are designed to rehabilitate rather than to punish, but they infringe the liberty of the person to whom they apply in significant ways. For example, the person may be required to pay compensation, to undergo treatment, or to refrain from visiting certain areas. Penal orders are an important part of the government's drive toward the efficient disposal of cases. In the Netherlands, the aim is that 70 percent of minor offenses (those punishable by up to six years' imprisonment) are dealt with by the prosecutor imposition of a penal order while the accused is still in police custody.

[16] See further Viennot (2012).

the focus of fair-trial rights such as equality of arms toward the pretrial phase.[17] Yet there is hostility to rights and procedures once considered fundamental to a fair trial, but which are now seen as barriers to an effective justice process.

The disclosure of evidence is one such example. The right to know, and so respond to, the case against you is an essential component of a fair trial—not just at court, but in preparing the defense case and, increasingly, in deciding whether to go to trial. The significance of statements and decisions made prior to trial, in determining the fate of the accused and the possibility for alternative case disposal, makes this all the more important. Yet the necessity for the state to disclose its evidence prior to a plea of guilty, including some exculpatory evidence, is being questioned.[18] This is most evident in the strongly plea bargain-oriented culture of American criminal justice, where the prosecution obligation to disclose exculpatory material is rarely enforced and some plea bargains waive the right to this material.[19] In England and Wales, the Leveson Review of criminal justice efficiency (2015) favors early guilty pleas to avoid "unnecessary" file preparation, but this is in effect a pressure toward less disclosure. A fair, accurate, and informed plea requires knowledge of the evidence, including any exculpatory material, given the defense's lack of independent investigative resources.[20] Failure to disclose material can and does lead to miscarriages of justice,[21] including in

[17] This is, of course, also recognized through the jurisprudence of the ECtHR and EU directives on procedural rights for suspects as well as accused persons. The French Conseil constitutionnel accepted this in its decision concerning the suspect's right to legal assistance from the first police interrogation, for example. In England and Wales too, the attenuation of the right to silence and the presence of the lawyer at the police station have led courts to understand the trial process as a continuum beginning from initial questioning.

[18] In relation to pre-plea discovery in the United States, see *United States v. Ruiz* 536 U.S. 622 (2002), which held that the government was not constitutionally required to disclose impeachment evidence prior to a guilty plea.

[19] Medwed (2012); Capers (2016). A great deal of trust is placed in prosecutors in this process, despite the inequality of bargaining power with the defense and, in contrast to the judicial scrutiny of defense counsel's actions, the absence of professional regulation of prosecution behavior. American Bar Association Model Rule 3.8 describes prosecutors as having "the responsibility of a minister of justice," but Medwed (2012) argues that the ethical duties of the prosecutor should be more concretely defined and better enforced. It is assumed that as lawyers and professionals, prosecutors are above the kinds of tactics used by police to obtain a confession, but in practice, the absence of scrutiny allows prosecutors to use the same kinds of tactics as officers pressuring defendants into guilty pleas. Capers (2016).

[20] In the 1990s, the Court of Appeal made clear that, given the superior resources and powers of the state, the prosecution's duty of disclosure in an adversarial procedure is one way of ensuring equality of arms—discussed in chapter 2.

[21] See, e.g., the cases of Sam Hallam and John Kamara, wrongly convicted and imprisoned for seven and twenty years respectively, discussed in the Justice report *Supporting Exonerees* (2018). Sam Hallam's phone, examined after conviction and his first appeal, was key to overturning his conviction; John Kamara's innocence was demonstrated by 201 witness statements not disclosed by the police. This continues to be problematic and has been highlighted in the report by HMCPSI, *Disclosure—Thematic Review* (2008: para. 9.11), and by the CCRC in its annual report 2015/16, as well as in many of their previous reports. See also the nondisclosure revealed in *Barkshire* (2011) EWCA Crim. 1885. In January 2018 a number of cases collapsed when the existence of evidence casting doubt on the prosecution case, but which had not been disclosed to the defense as it should have been, came to

guilty plea cases,[22] and early disclosure will often facilitate an admission and early case disposition.[23] The logic of a shift away from trial and toward earlier case disposition based on some agreed outcome is to have earlier and fuller disclosure, rather than less.

In addition to weaker legal requirements, the ability of the CPS to provide full disclosure in the way required to ensure equality of arms is also problematic. Evidence disclosure is a CPS responsibility. As prosecuting lawyers, it is for them to judge which evidence is relevant, might assist the defense, and so should be disclosed. However, crown prosecutors are entirely dependent on the police investigation and presentation of evidence and are often aware only of the nature, not the content, of witness statements, observation logs, and so on.[24] For their part, the police are not subject to any oversight or direction in the way that the French procureur may order additional investigations to be carried out. If consulted for precharge advice, the CPS may suggest further enquiries be made, but the police are not obliged to comply. Neither is there any check on unconscious bias in case building. The forensic science regulator has highlighted difficulties in ensuring transparency when practitioners are not given original evidence for testing (for example, testing DNA from a swab, rather than from the item from which the swab was taken) or are not informed sufficiently of the manner in which evidence is seized and stored. By controlling the evidence provided to the forensic scientist, the police are limiting the nature of the investigation.[25]

Disclosure practices have been criticized by various inspectorates and were flagged in the system as a risk and a failure that needed to be addressed, leading to the attorney general commissioning a joint police and CPS inspectorate report in 2017,[26] described as a critical milestone triggering a substantive and serious change in attitude.[27] A Freedom of Information Act request to HMCPSI revealed

light. The BBC reported that, following a Freedom of Information request enquiring as to the number of cases dropped because the rules had not been followed, 916 prosecutions were dropped in 2017, compared with 537 in 2016. (Reported on BBC Radio 4 *Today*, 24 January 2018,) See the cases of Oliver Mears, Samson Makele, and Liam Allan, for example.

[22] Turner (2016) notes that in the United States, for example, 210 of the 1,575 wrongful convictions listed in the National Registry of Exonerations (13 percent) resulted from guilty pleas.

[23] Blackstock et al. (2014).

[24] The police also act as a first filter, omitting from the schedule items they consider irrelevant or unimportant.

[25] Dr. Gillian Tully, the forensic science regulator, in her written evidence to the Justice Select Committee on evidence disclosed in criminal cases. She suggested that accreditation was one guarantee of quality. Available at http://data.parliament.uk/writtenevidence/committeeevidence.svc/evidencedocument/justice-committee/disclosure-of-evidence-in-criminal-cases/written/83257.html.

[26] HMCPSI and HMIC (2017).

[27] See evidence of the minister for policing and the fire service, Nick Hurd, to the Justice Select Committee on disclosure of evidence in criminal cases, available at https://www.parliament.uk/

the extent to which the police engage in the systematic avoidance of disclosure to the defense, simply by listing evidence within the sensitive unused material schedule.[28] Senior police officers condoned this practice, and CPS lawyers were unable to look behind generic document descriptions to uncover the deliberate mis-scheduling of evidence.[29] In February 2018, the Justice Select Committee launched an enquiry into the disclosure of evidence in criminal cases, and evidence from a variety of witnesses confirmed the inability of the CPS to provide an independent check on police decision-making regarding disclosure and the failure to provide the defense with material that is key to its case. This seems likely to result in further detailed regulation of the relationship between police and CPS,[30] but the problem has not altered since its airing in the courts in the 1990s.[31] For disclosure to be fair and effective within an adversarial setting, control needs to be in the hands of someone independent—not those responsible for investigation and prosecution.

The culture of disclosure in more inquisitorial procedures is different, as, historically, the legal site of fact-finding has been the investigation, rather than the trial. The judiciary (including the court) has a duty to investigate, and the defense may request that specific investigative acts be carried out, both for fear of being seen to "interfere" with witnesses and for the practical reason that it lacks the resources to conduct its own investigations.[32] Thus, inquisitorially rooted procedure implies a greater need for early disclosure to facilitate the effective participation that modern fair-trial standards require. However, this model of defense participation and pretrial judicial fact-finding exists only in the very few cases dealt with through the *instruction* procedure: in the more than 97 percent of matters overseen by the procureur, there is little or no opportunity for investigative supervision or for defense involvement.[33] In practice, therefore, as in

business/committees/committees-a-z/commons-select/justice-committee/inquiries/parliament-2017/disclosure-criminal-cases-17-19/publications/.

[28] This request was made by the Centre for Criminal Appeals. It obtained notes from focus groups with police, prosecutors, and judges, as well as survey responses from prosecutors. Full details and copies of the documents received are available at http://www.criminalappeals.org.uk/news/2018/4/3/documents-obtained-by-centre-reveal-extent-of-disclosure-crisis.

[29] Even though prosecutors said that they could not rely on the descriptions given by the police in evidence schedules.

[30] One response has been to pilot a new form of disclosure management in Rape and Serious Sexual Offences Unit (RASSO) and Complex Case Unit (CCU) cases, which requires the police to set out what it considers reasonable lines of enquiry, in order that the CPS can review and report on this.

[31] Discussed in chapter 2.

[32] The reform in France in 2000, permitting the defense to request that acts of investigation be carried out, sought to strengthen the principle of equality of arms and so might be seen as a dilution or adaptation of the inquisitorial approach.

[33] See further the discussion in chapter 2 and Schemmel, Corell, and Richter (2014) re the doubts expressed both by judges and by defense lawyers in Germany, concerning the factual basis on which plea bargains were offered and agreed.

England and Wales, evidence disclosure and decisions as to plea occur after the police investigation is complete.

One area where fair-trial rights have been strengthened is through the ECtHR and the EU, both of which have recognized that the fairness of any trial will depend in part on the fairness of the pretrial.[34] However, as a jurisdiction with an inquisitorially rooted criminal justice process that depends upon the constitutional guarantees of judicial supervision, rather than the more party-centered approach of defense guarantees, France regards the rights-based approach of European measures as ill-suited to its own procedural tradition. While acknowledging that investigations overseen by the procureur are less faithful to the promise of judicial investigation aspired to by the *instruction*, and so reflect insufficiently the principle of *contradictoire*, France is nonetheless critical of this European approach in what it sees as the "Anglo-Saxon" trend toward the requirement to adopt more accusatorial procedures.[35] Access to a lawyer is now built into the detention and questioning of suspects, as well as new procedures such as the guilty plea, but its value is more symbolic than real, satisfying the minimal requirement that these procedures be *contradictoire*. A stronger role is resisted as unnecessary given the prosecutor's status as judicial guarantor of the liberties of the accused. In this way, the function of the defense in France is inextricably linked to that of the prosecutor. This model of criminal justice is increasingly challenged, however, by European norms that act to strengthen defense safeguards throughout the criminal process,[36] while at the same time challenging the status of the procureur as a judicial officer and so as a guarantor of due process protections.[37]

Whichever way a system seeks to protect the interests of the accused during this initial phase, in neither jurisdiction can these various pretrial procedures and safeguards offer the same guarantees as the trial. Prosecutorial and police oversight is limited, and the suspect is further hampered by a weak evidence disclosure regime during and after custodial interrogation, by systemic and police

[34] *Imbroscia v. Switzerland* (13972/88) 24 November 1993; *Salduz v. Turkey* (36391/02) 27 November 2008. Discussed further in chapters 6 and 7.

[35] For example, the Beaume Report (2014: 22) considered that the rights of the individual should be protected in the course of the enquiry, but it was not appropriate that the principle of *contradictoire* should apply from the start of the investigation. It opposed a more active defense role, but recommended that the defense might request additional investigative acts when necessary to search for the truth and prevent any miscarriage of justice (p. 71).

[36] The EU directives (discussed in chapter 6) designed to strengthen procedural protections for suspects and accused persons include measures on the provision of translation and interpretation; information for suspects on their rights while in police custody; information for suspects on their right to see a lawyer during police detention and questioning; and availability of effective legal assistance, paid for by legal aid where needed.

[37] *Medvedyev v. France* (3394/03) 29 March 2010; *Moulin v. France* (37104/06) 23 November 2010, both discussed in the preceding chapter.

pressures to make an admission, and by inconsistency in the provision and quality of legal assistance.[38] The defense and prosecution are at the heart of the process, but there is tension in their roles—in the resistance to attempts to define them at the European level, and as they are maneuvered away from their traditional, professional roles into carrying out the managerial objectives of the criminal justice system. I turn now to some of the consequences for the prosecutor's role of this shift toward pretrial forms of justice.

B. The Prosecutor as Manager

The imperative to process cases more speedily so that greater numbers can be dealt with at lower financial cost has changed the prosecution function in a variety of ways. Prosecutors in both jurisdictions have been required to adjust their practices, developing new modes of working with police and others, and innovative means of disposing of cases. This has placed greater responsibility on prosecutors and has increased prosecutorial discretion in some regards. On the face of it, this enlarges prosecutorial power, as the locus of criminal justice moves away from the trial to the pretrial phase. In France, the shift of power away from the *juge d'instruction*, as well as from the trial judge, also strengthens the power of the executive in the criminal process, through the procureur's hierarchical accountability to the minister of justice. However, it is important to contextualize the nature of this increase in power in order not to overstate the autonomy of the prosecutor. The delegation of what are effectively dispositive as well as prosecutorial powers, to police, prosecution associates, and assistants of various kinds, occurs on a large scale, enabled by standardized procedures that mandate action and, ultimately, restrict discretion. In this way, the prosecutor is responsible for the outcome of cases, and decisions are made in her name, but in practice, her power and discretion are limited through forms of standardization and routinization, by locally and nationally defined policy, and by the availability of resources.[39]

The diversion of cases away from prosecution and trial, often administered by police or some delegated form of prosecutorial authority, is common to both jurisdictions as a mode of responding to the demand to manage a greater

[38] The effectiveness of legal advice to suspects detained and questioned in police custody is discussed extensively in the following two chapters.

[39] The experience of Italy, a jurisdiction that has moved to a more accusatorial procedure while retaining many of its inquisitorial features, is a little different. Prosecutors enjoy a level of independence similar to that judges and are not bound by codes of practice or guidelines. However, this type of independence can also give rise to an absence of accountability. See Montana (2009); Di Frederico (1998).

throughput of cases at less cost. The ways in which these practices are structured, however, reflect the differences in prosecutorial power and authority, the status and organization of the public prosecutor, and different structures of institutional accountability. As an authority over the police, with responsibility for the investigation as well as prosecution of cases, the procureur is in charge of the pretrial phase and so better placed than the CPS to manage, influence, and structure alternatives to prosecution.[40] In both jurisdictions, these shifts in the prosecution role have also raised the possibility of broader changes to the nature of the prosecution function, such as increasing the authority of the crown prosecutor over the police or creating a distinct career path for the procureur. However, many prosecutors are wary of changes in their role and status, fearing an attack on the core values of their function in ways that risk compromising their independence from the police and from politics.

Recognizing the electoral importance of crime and security, governments are anxious to demonstrate how seriously they take the needs of victims by adopting a tough stance on all forms of criminal offending. Performance measurement as a key metric in this has increased in both jurisdictions, but is more prevalent in England and Wales than in France. Unlike England and Wales, France does not have multiple targets, audits, reviews, or inspectorates reporting on the work of legal actors, including the Parquet. Statistics have, however, become important. The principal measure against which prosecutors are judged is the *taux de réponse*, which compares the number of cases where sufficient evidence exists to prosecute, with those that go to court or are dealt with through alternatives to prosecution. This was introduced as a criminal justice performance indicator in 2001, in an attempt to reduce the number of dismissals by prosecutors; and by requiring the Parquet to give reasons when cases are discontinued, it creates an expectation of prosecution or some other response. The strategy appears to have been successful: dismissals have been reduced quite dramatically.[41] Yet, as a driver of efficiency, it is perhaps less effective: it has not sought to deal with cases more rapidly so that resources are freed up to deal with more serious or complex investigations. By focusing on cases that would otherwise have been dismissed, it brings more people into the criminal justice process, placing more pressure on resources to deal with cases in order to avoid delays. The net result is a greater throughput of minor crime, resulting in increased punitiveness, as more individuals are criminalized. This in turn creates recidivists (who are treated very much

[40] Her role in contributing to the formulation of local criminal justice policy and practices also gives her some influence in the structuring of prosecution and diversion norms governing police practices.

[41] The *taux de réponse* rose from 64.9 percent in 1998, to 80.4 per cent in 2006 and 93.9 per cent in 2010, from which point it has remained fairly constant, being at 92.8 per cent in 2018. (Ministère de la justice et des libertés [1999, 2007, 2011, 2019]).

more harshly) out of those with several minor convictions, rather than career criminals.[42]

Both jurisdictions have also seen a rapid increase in criminal legislation, guidelines, and policy directives. This can make it hard to keep up to date, creating some insecurity around the exercise of the prosecutor's professional functions. DPP guidelines require CPS lawyers to follow set procedures in a range of offense types, and their decisions are audited locally by their own hierarchy and nationally through inspectorates. French prosecutors expressed concern that the situation had become unworkable, with policies and guidelines being issued at such a rate that they were not always sure to have followed the correct procedure. Ministry of Justice circulars addressing priority issues were now so frequent that they were of little value: some 80 percent of the procureur's work now fell within these "priority areas."[43] Increasingly they are also coupled with circulars from the minister of interior (who is not an authority over *magistrats* but who increasingly interferes in justice matters), representing a further intrusion of security politics into the justice arena.

(i) France's Third Way

The growth in managerialism as an organizing feature of French criminal justice has its roots in the 1990s, when concerns that justice was too slow, ineffective, and distanced from the communities it served resulted in various measures to provide faster and more flexible responses as alternatives to prosecution for minor offenses, often referred to as "third way" responses.[44] These include restorative and therapeutic measures such as the *rappel à la loi, mediation pénale, injonction thérapeutique*, and *composition pénale*.[45] These provide quicker and

[42] Lenoir and Gautron (2014) found that recidivism tripled between 2000 and 2009, and instead of offenders with a long criminal career, this pattern now consisted of those with several traffic offenses.

[43] Milburn et al. (2010: 90–92). In England and Wales, Leveson (2015) also highlights the enormous increase in criminal procedural rules and in criminal law, such that the review encountered "transformation exhaustion" (1.3).

[44] This itself built on the growth in minor and mid-level offending that led to a more security-driven criminal justice agenda and increased punitiveness. See Aubert (2010); Milburn (2008). As neither convictions nor dismissals, but something in between, these are referred to as "third way" measures.

[45] Greatest use is made of the *rappel à la loi*, envisaged as a reprimand provided by the procureur, designed to caution the recipient against the consequences of offending. In practice, this can be administered by a simple written warning sent by registered post. This is the preferred response in around half of all third-way procedures—Lenoir and Gautron (2014: 597). The other responses are, respectively, mediation, treatment order, and a form of prosecution-ordered sanction. The French system has three levels of criminal record reporting. The third is for nonminor convictions and criminal penalties and is seen by the subject of these penalties. The second is reserved for certain employers and contains minor offenses also, and the first is the most complete record and is restricted to the justice system. These alternative measures are not recorded on the suspect's criminal record,

cheaper means of disposing of cases, often in noncourt spaces (*maisons de la justice et du droit*), where lay officers (*délégués du procureur*), who are typically retired public servants such as former police officers or gendarmes, administer decisions.[46] Along with the French guilty plea procedure (the CRPC), the significance, as well as the number, of these procedures has grown. They apply to increasingly serious offenses; they represent one-quarter of all simplified procedure cases; the police can propose a *composition pénale* to a suspect in GAV (originally rejected as placing the suspect at risk of pressure to confess); and it can be confirmed in either the *tribunal correctionnel* or for more minor offenses, the *tribunal de police*. This reduces the work of the court, whose role becomes one of validation, but increases that of the procureur in administrative terms.[47]

The Parquet has been instrumental in the development of many of these alternative procedures and approaches, the most celebrated of which is perhaps the real-time procedure (*traitement en temps réel*, or TTR) developed locally but now national practice since the early 2000s. By requiring prosecutors to deal with cases immediately over the phone, rather than providing written instructions on the dossier several months later, this procedure is meant to speed up the treatment of cases being investigated by the police and to reduce the number of dismissals.[48] Key to the success of TTR is the greater use made of "third way" measures and the ability to trigger these responses through standardized procedures that rely on basic offense characteristics and thresholds of gravity. In practice, the bulk of low-level offending is dealt with in this way. Permanent directives are issued by the local Parquet, setting out a standardized response to common offenses such as cannabis possession, shoplifting, or driving with excess alcohol.[49] Further threshold distinctions are made, such as the value of the property, whether the person has any previous convictions, or whether the goods were returned or paid for, to determine which response is most suitable.[50] In this way, cases are handled directly by the police, who then send them on to be dealt with by the *délégués du procureur* without the need for any further involvement on the part of the Parquet or the court.

other than the *composition pénale*, which is recorded on the first level of reporting. For more information see https://www.service-public.fr/particuliers/vosdroits/F14710.

46 Aubert (2008). See also the description in Soubise (2018).

47 Milburn et al. (2010: 84). Although others do the main work, these are cases that would otherwise have been dismissed and that must now be processed through the system.

48 Previously, case files were transmitted by post, resulting in long delays. TTR also allows police to inform the accused of their court date immediately.

49 These are issued with the agreement of judges and will vary from region to region. See Danet et al. (2013: 83–112).

50 Typically, a *rappel à la loi* or a *composition pénale* or an *ordonnance pénale*.

The focus is on managing the flux of cases as available court time diminishes, and providing a response as quickly as possible, thus ensuring a high *taux de réponse*. The availability of this range of new measures might suggest that prosecutors enjoy greater power and discretion in the treatment of cases,[51] but the fixed nature of policies triggering these third-way responses means that individual prosecutors have a very narrow margin of maneuver. These cases pass through the office of the procureur in formal terms (as she is responsible for the investigation and prosecution of crime) and so may appear as a system of structured delegation permitting the Parquet to triage cases as suitable for treatment by alternative means, but they are perhaps better understood as the mass and automatic assignment of cases to police and lay adjudicators, a form of autoprosecution dispensing with the procedural safeguard of prosecution oversight in favor of speed and so a favorable *taux de réponse*. Furthermore, as the product of local policy, they may provide locally uniform responses, but nationally, the picture is less homogenous. Aubert (2010) has shown the different use that might be made of alternatives to prosecution, depending on local crime demographics, the policy of the court area, and the nature of the personnel involved in the delivery of the various measures.

In her research period, 1999–2003, in Bobigny (Paris) Aubert found that third-way responses were used to alleviate the pressure on court time, with alternative measures rising by 46.5 percent and prosecutions falling by 9.1 percent.[52] The majority of cases following this route were dealt with by *délégués du procureur*, whose role as laypeople is to deal with straightforward cases that require no negotiation or judgment, simply the execution of the measure.[53] However, the work of *délégués* here was neither straightforward nor automatic. They were required to deal with quite serious offenses, such as sexual assaults, which would not normally be handled in this rapid way by individuals without any professional training. Furthermore, in most juvenile cases and in one-third of adult cases, the appropriate measure was left to the *délégué* to select, requiring them to enter into the details of the case and hear evidence from the parties. This degree of involvement and judgment by a non-*magistrat* exceeds what was anticipated.

In Bordeaux, third-way measures also increased, rising by 30 percent in the same period, but prosecutions declined only slightly, by 1.7 percent. The story here was less about managing the flux of cases and more about providing a response in cases that would otherwise have been dismissed. In Bordeaux, greater reliance was placed on trained individuals,[54] who had been involved in reparation

[51] Alternatives to prosecution and *ordonnances pénales* make up over half of prosecutor decisions. Ministère de la justice et des libertés (2017).

[52] Aubert (2010: 22).

[53] Ninety-one percent of third-way cases in Bobigny. Aubert (2010: 25).

[54] *Délégués* dealt with some 49 percent of third-way cases in Bordeaux.

and mediation since the 1980s, long before the establishment of the *délégués* and the *maisons de la justice*. In contrast to Bobigny, the *délégués* enjoyed little autonomy, confined to executing the precise instructions of the Parquet. Those with professional training, on the other hand, enjoyed a broad margin of discretion in selecting the most appropriate response and putting it into action.

(ii) The Impact of Managerialism on the Procureur Function

The widespread adoption of these procedures for case disposition is part of a broader set of changes that have ushered in a more managerial system of criminal justice and which now sees the procureur responsible for the final decision in half of all criminal matters.[55] However, these changes have repercussions for the nature and function of the Parquet, routinizing their work in ways that diminish rather than strengthen their professional autonomy and independence as *magistrats*.[56] They have also altered the procureur's relationship with the police. There is less scope for advice and direction, for professional dialogue or reflection. Instead their relationship is characterized by orders around standardized procedures and the rapid disposal of minor offending.

As already noted, the primary purpose of these alternatives to trial is to reduce the number of dismissals in order to increase the *taux de réponse*. This satisfies Ministry of Justice demands for a high rate of productivity within the Parquet as the number of cases dealt with has increased, but many of these, by definition, are cases that would otherwise not have been pursued formally. This has had the effect of reducing the discretion of the procureur, deskilling her work by privileging the treatment of minor crime to the detriment of serious and complex offenses.[57] The third way diverts cases into, rather than away from the criminal process, favoring purely quantitative measures over those concerned with quality or offense gravity. Rewarding these kinds of outcomes changes prosecutor behavior in unintended ways, encouraging "easy wins." One procureur explained his reasoning for the issuing of a *rappel à la loi*: it counts for the *taux de réponse* and is effectively a "free" gain, as the work passes to the police or a *délégué du procureur*, avoiding a dismissal, which would entail the procureur writing to

[55] Discussed in the submission of Christine Lazerges, president of the National Human Rights Advisory Commission (Commission nationale consultative des droits de l'homme) to the Beaume Commission (2014: Annex 5, p. 6). The same claim has been made of the Dutch prosecutor (van de Bunt and Gelder [2012: 126]).

[56] Although the Parquet contributes to the development of these case pathway policies, the result is to restrict the discretion exercised by individual prosecutors.

[57] Such is the pressure on the Parquet that some will manipulate the nature of their response and the reasons given when cases are dismissed, in order to produce the most favorable statistics, reaching a *taux de réponse* of 98 percent in some places. Lenoir and Gautron (2014: 601–604).

the victim and recording reasons for not prosecuting.[58] This creates a perverse kind of efficiency, where it is easier to bring some form of proceedings against a person than to dismiss the case.[59]

This trivialization of a core part of the prosecutor's work also impacts on those with whom she works most closely—the police. The police-procureur relationship is characterized in law as a form of judicial oversight of the criminal investigation, but has been criticized as being distant, retrospective, and bureaucratic, based on trust rather than any form of check or control.[60] Under the TTR procedure, the prosecutor is in frequent contact with the police, and some procureurs believe that this enables them to provide more effective supervision of the investigation and subsequent case disposition.[61] But this rapid-response model does not situate the procureur as a judicial officer, whose legal expertise and public interest ideology make her, in theory, a respected authority over the police. Instead, the rapid nature of this verbal exchange means that decisions are made very quickly, little or nothing is recorded on file, and prosecutors depend to a great extent on the views of police officers.[62] With no opportunity to test out the scope or the strength of the evidence, prosecutors replicate the police view, resulting in higher levels of prosecution.[63] The procureur's role as a check on police power has become less plausible as her work increasingly mirrors the priorities and working methods of the police,[64] and as the professional distance between police and procureur disappears.[65]

This shift in the procureur-police relationship is also experienced negatively by officers on the ground. Officers resented the prosecutor's constant intrusion into minor matters through TTR,[66] and were demotivated by the sense of simply following orders, discouraging any meaningful discussion of elements of the case that stray beyond the identification of basic thresholds that enable a rapid triaging of offenses,[67] and with no real investigative autonomy.[68] Officers expressed some

58 Lenoir and Gautron (2014: 598).

59 A powerful demonstration of Ritzer's (2004) account of how the irrational comes to be regarded as rational, because it serves the wider system goals of quantifiable efficiency.

60 Hodgson (2005). Also Mouhanna (2001).

61 Mouhanna and Bastard (2010: 41).

62 Mouhanna and Bastard (2010: 46) report that police views are likely to draw heavily on police files and criminal records. This was also a concern of a parliamentary report into rapid procedures for dealing with criminal cases. Zocchetto (2005).

63 Bastard and Mouhanna (2007).

64 Like those across all parts of the criminal process, the police have also been placed under pressure to produce results (Matelly and Mouhanna [2007]) and are in some senses passing these demands on to the Parquet.

65 The Beaume Report (2014: 30) proposed that the procureur no longer enjoy the same powers as the police in order to separate the two functions more clearly.

66 Long waits on the phone to obtain authorization from the procureur are now also a constant feature of police work and a constant irritation.

67 This downgrades the role of the prosecutor, turning her into what Beaume (2014: 28) has described as a form of supercop—a superior police officer, rather than an independent judicial authority.

68 Beaume (2014: 28).

deference to the judicial authority under which the law places them, but they did not feel themselves to be under the direction of the procureur who, increasingly dependent on officers' account of evidence, tended to support their requests, not to challenge them.[69] More successful in building good working relationships is the oversight that takes place at the institutional level. The Parquet organizes monthly meetings with the police to discuss policy and the nature of local criminality, as well as some individual cases; this also allows the two organizations to build trust and understanding of their respective roles.[70] As reported in earlier research, this relationship is necessarily much closer in small court centers where police and prosecutors speak more frequently and there are fewer personnel.[71]

This trend toward managerialism also undercuts core aspects of the prosecutor's role and identity as an independent, professional *magistrat*. The constant reporting requirements and the production of statistics, together with the classification of what are largely administrative procedures as part of the judicial response, means that procureurs experience *taux de réponse* as a means of managing the Parquet itself.[72] More fundamentally, autonomy, once at the heart of the Parquet's self-image and professional status, has receded as a core value. Productivity rates, demonstrated by the management of the mass of low-level cases, are how the prosecutor's value is measured. Reflection on the nature of the prosecution function, the treatment of cases, the consequences of different decisions, and the need to ensure that the criminal response is adapted to the individual (not just to local resources) has been replaced by rapid, standardized, and automatic responses.[73] The professional expertise and ethics of the procureur are underused and undervalued through this systematic routinization of work that places emphasis on minor cases in order to satisfy managerial demands, reducing, rather than freeing up, time for the Parquet to deal with serious and complex criminal investigations.[74]

Some prosecutors have expressed regret at this shift toward an occupational culture, which in their view rejects individual responsibility along with autonomy, in favor of a kind of collective approach as expressed through uniform policies mandating particular responses. The nature of their work has become more routine, less important, and, ultimately, less rewarding.[75] However,

[69] This is unsurprising as TTR is structured to produce an immediate result. It represents a kind of "template justice" with standardized and predetermined responses.

[70] Milburn et al. (2010: 114).

[71] See Milburn et al. (2010: 115); Hodgson (2005).

[72] Milburn et al. (2010: 94–99). In 2016, procureurs rebelled against the growing pressure to produce annual statistics that were not easily available, refusing to engage in external partnerships that were concerned with operational rather than policy and security matters. Jean-Baptiste Jacquin, "La colère chez les procureurs sous pression," *Le Monde*, 27 January 2016.

[73] These aspects are similar to the McDonaldization theory of assembly line justice, rather like Packer's crime control model. Ritzer (2004); Bohm (2006).

[74] Beaume (2014: 29–30).

[75] Milburn et al. (2010: 84–85).

Mouhanna and Bastard found that others preferred this more standardized approach, as it allowed them to act quickly and confidently. They favored the collegial responsibility of predetermined policies over the more individualist approach, which they saw as arbitrary and dysfunctional.[76]

Although required to implement the *politique pénale* of the executive through her own professional hierarchy, the procureur is also increasingly implicated in the development and application of local criminal justice policy. As already discussed, the practice of *correctionalisation* is used by prosecutors to keep cases in the lower court, where they can be dealt with more quickly and cheaply, avoiding the *instruction* process and trial by jury in the *cour d'assises*.[77] The extent to which the Parquet is required to "correctionalize" cases will depend on local priorities and the resources of the court and so will differ between regions. In contrast to the detailed audits of CPS work, however, there is no real accountability for these decisions, as no reasons are required to be given or recorded.

Other policies are the product of more local interagency cooperation, involving police, social workers, customs and border police, local politicians, and the préfet, with the procureur at the center. In the 1990s this began with the *groupes locaux de traitement de la délinquance*, leading to a key plank of the 1997 government's policy on security, the *contrats locaux de sécurité*. The aim is to ensure the judiciary is represented within the local administration and to produce a more coordinated response that takes account of the local context—and the experiences of policing on the ground. In this way, the Parquet has become the face of justice within civil society and local political life. Formerly, involvement in local public policy was seen to be incompatible with the independence of the procureur, as this requires her to work alongside the préfet, the government's representative in the regions. This "secularization" of justice has established itself over the last twenty-five years and is welcomed by procureurs, as it makes the role of justice more visible to the public and has asserted the place of the Parquet as a different but equal actor at the local criminal justice table.

However, there is also an ambiguity in this new professional identity and the way in which the prosecutor's judicial status is understood within it. On the one hand, it is the judicial character of the procureur that makes her so valuable in working with local political and criminal justice actors and that then enables what is understood to be a more locally adapted judicial response, through measures such as diversion and alternatives to prosecution.[78] On the other, her role in these initiatives distances the procureur from her more traditional "*magistrat*"

[76] Mouhanna and Bastard (2010: 38–40, 43). One can imagine that it is the younger, less confident and experienced prosecutors who have embraced this new way of working.

[77] Although the practice has existed for over a century, it was placed on a statutory footing only in 2004.

[78] Milburn et al. (2010: 136).

role in the courts and risks the dilution of her judicial character in the eyes of her colleagues in the *magistrature du siège*,[79] who frown upon such close ties with executive power, and describe the *préfectoralisation* of the prosecution function.[80]

There is also a wider tension surrounding the precarity of the procureur's judicial status, which taps into core aspects of her role. At the national level, the procureur acts as a form of relay between the political world of policy and the judicial institutions, applying the government's criminal justice policy through the daily practices of charge, prosecution, and diversion. This democratic accountability is understood to provide the prosecutor with legitimacy, but the judicial character of her function is also essential to this equation. The procureur resists strongly any weakening of her judicial status, or the creation of a separate career path that would place her more firmly under the control of the Ministry of Justice, or worse still, the Ministry of Interior.[81] Contributing to this fear that the Parquet might be cast out of the *magistrature* and assigned a different and inferior "*fonctionnarisé*" or "*préfectoralisé*" status is the perception that lawyers, judges, and parliament support a shift toward a more accusatorial procedure, which would reduce the procureur's role to that of a mere party, to a role of accusation alone. This would narrow the prosecution function, excluding the ways in which the procureur, as a judicial officer, is understood to ensure the independence of the investigation and prosecution and the protection of the rights of the individual.

In practice, the expansion of alternatives to trial and prosecution does not undercut the judicial status of the procureur, but is in fact reliant on her status as *magistrat*, albeit in problematic ways. These procedures are part of a broader transfer of decision-making power to the procureur (in name at least), thereby implicating the prosecutor in the sanctioning process and marginalizing the role of the *juges du siège*, weakening the independence of safeguards for the accused and the *contradictoire* nature of French criminal justice.[82] The last decade has seen a huge expansion of simplified prosecutions (CRPCs and *ordonnances*

[79] These are the trial judges, *juges d'instruction*, JLDs, etc.—those performing an adjudicative judicial function more akin to the judicial ideal as understood within more adversarial systems, who are not under the hierarchy of the minister of justice and so enjoy greater independence.

[80] Milburn et al. (2010: 135–137); Beaume (2014: 27–30).

[81] Milburn et al. (2010: 146–155). The Parquet favors strengthening her independence from the executive, not by removing altogether accountability to the minister of justice, but by assigning responsibility for her nomination and career promotion exclusively to the Conseil supérieur de la magistrature with no executive involvement, as is the case for the investigating and trial judges. The Nadal Report (2013) also recommended that the unity of the judicial corps be written into the constitution and senior prosecutors be appointed exclusively by the Conseil supérieure de la magistrature.

[82] Perrocheau (2010: 70) argues that in agreeing the levels of sanctions in advance, the *juges du siège* now encroach on the role of the Parquet by contributing to the *politique pénale*, or local criminal justice policy.

pénales) and alternatives to prosecution such as *compositions pénales*.[83] Decisions are made on the prosecution papers, with no defense input, and so they are effectively prosecutor adjudications of guilt. They also reduce the role of the victim, as there is no place for the *partie civile* in these more rapid alternative procedures: the victim's ability to participate and be heard comes to be defined by the Parquet's exercise of prosecutorial discretion or by predetermined policies of auto-prosecution.[84] Crucially, it is the prosecutor's status as *magistrat* that is understood to justify this concentration of power, and it is her professional ideology as a judicial officer that is relied upon to ensure that the rights and interests of the accused and of the victim are protected. Yet this new model of managerial justice relies on the prosecutor's judicial characteristics at the same time as it emasculates them through standardized ways of working. Managerialism has moved beyond a driver for the development of new practices and initiatives. It is engrained in the world of the *magistrat*. It has become the unending pursuit of increased productivity and reduced delay, fueled by the Ministry of Justice. Bastard et al. describe the system as having become a machine in constant acceleration, which is less and less concerned with the quality of what it does, or the practical consequences of its decisions.[85]

(iii) Delegation and Standardization in the CPS

In England and Wales, delegation and standardization are also the preferred modes of ensuring the rapid processing of cases through to court or some alternative form of case disposition. This is achieved through an increasingly centralized system of charging advice, case preparation, and prosecution, at the same time separating out responsibility for these discrete phases between different prosecution staff.[86] However, while the structure of the French prosecution

[83] From 2004 to 2013, CRPCs have risen from 2,187 each year to 65,100; *ordonnances pénales* from 58,822 to 145,066; *compositions pénales* from 25,777 to 73,723; and other alternatives from 388,944 to 493,089. (Ministère de la justice, *Statistiques: Activité des parquets des TGI*). See discussion in Hodgson and Soubise (2016a).

[84] See further Grunvald (2014). These procedures in which the prosecutor proposes a sentence or a sanction, which, if accepted, is agreed by a single judge—as it is in some 96 percent of cases, according to Perrocheau (2010: 67)—might be understood as a more contractual model of justice, governed by resources rather than by the interests of justice. The 2007 LOLF (Loi organique relative aux lois de finances) has underlined the centrality of resource efficiency across the criminal process. See also Milburn et al. (2010: 84–85).

[85] Bastard et al. (2015: 277). Again, this seems to echo the arguments of the McDonaldization of society and of justice.

[86] In England and Wales, the separation between the police investigation and the CPS prosecution is reflected in their different decisions. At the close of the investigation, the police may decide there is insufficient evidence to proceed, the case is discontinued, and the CPS is never involved. Or they may charge the suspect and the CPS will then decide whether to continue proceedings through

function means that all cases must pass through the Parquet and the procureur remains responsible for the choice of case pathway, in England and Wales, responsibility for charging has been returned to the police in the majority of cases. This is important in two respects. Politically, it is significant that this was not a CPS decision to devolve responsibility from its officers to those of the police, originating with neither the DPP nor the minister of justice. It was Theresa May, at that time the home secretary, who announced in 2011 that charging decisions would be removed from the CPS and handed to the police in 80 percent of cases, in order to reduce bureaucracy.[87] Second, it also runs counter to the trend of police and prosecution working together from an earlier stage to ensure effective case preparation.[88] The DPP issues guidance on which offenses should be charged by the police, and which require the authorization of a prosecutor in order to charge.[89] Initially, it was anticipated that prosecutors would take the decision to charge in the majority of cases, ensuring greater uniformity and independence of decision-making, but this has been reversed, and they currently do so only in around one-quarter of cases. The police also exercise significant power over case disposal. Their broad discretion to administer a simple caution, for example, means that they have a role in defining public policy, determining which cases are dealt with by the CPS and the courts, and which can be disposed of more informally.

In France, localized interagency cooperation and practices have been an important part of the transformation of the Parquet, and in England and Wales, the introduction of police and crime commissioners has been explained as part of a move to reconnect police with communities and to set local policing priorities. However, this localization is not carried through to prosecution structures or practices. Rather, centralization, through, for example, charging practices and

prosecution or to discontinue the case. Where charging advice is provided by the CPS, this effectively merges the decision to charge with that of prosecution.

87 See Catherine Baksi, "Charging Powers Passed from CPS to Police," *Law Society Gazette*, 9 May 2011, available at https://www.lawgazette.co.uk/news/charging-powers-passed-from-cps-to-police/60359.fullarticle. She described the move as "a watershed moment in policing. They show that we really mean business in busting bureaucracy." A CPS spokesperson said that the change was in response to an identified need to reduce police bureaucracy and it would also save the CPS £1.5 million a year.

88 The Narey Review (1997) recommended police and CPS cooperation through police administrative support units (ASUs), to facilitate the swifter disposal of prospective guilty plea cases, as well as a broader role for CPS caseworkers. The use of caseworkers to deal with summary guilty pleas cases was endorsed a year later in the 1998 Glidewell review of the CPS. Police-CPS cooperation was also promoted, but through criminal justice units (CJUs) under the power and control of the CPS, rather than the police.

89 The police make the decision to charge in all summary cases whatever the anticipated plea and in either-way offenses where a guilty plea is anticipated, other than in a specified list of offense types (those involving death, terrorism, violent disorder, offenses against the person, domestic abuse, hate crime, and some sexual and licensing offenses). They also deal with charging youths, unless an out-of-court disposal is not possible.

prosecution guidelines across a wide range of offense types, has been an important means of standardizing prosecution work. In matters where the police do not themselves determine charge, charging advice is dealt with centrally by CPS Direct for the most part, with area crown prosecutors involved in some early investigative advice and charging. CPS Direct is contacted directly by the police through a national telephone number, and officers simply speak to the next available prosecutor. Discussion of the case takes place over the telephone, but the evidence is transmitted electronically, as are decisions, providing an accessible case record from the outset. Consultation with the CPS is mandatory in serious and complex cases, but the police are free to consult a crown prosecutor in any case.[90] In theory, this provides prosecutors with a better opportunity for oversight and brings them closer to police officers in case building and in advising on charge and evidence. However, a recent joint inspectorate report suggests that there is still some way to go in making this an effective working relationship.[91] The inspectorate found that one-third of the cases in which the police brought charges should have been dealt with by the CPS; one-tenth of the cases dismissed by the CPS should have been decided by the police; and the police decision to charge was incorrect in 8 percent of cases.[92]

Although the CPS has seen charging powers returned to the police in the majority of cases under section 37A(1) PACE, suggesting greater police autonomy from prosecutors, the DPP now has the power to issue guidance to police custody officers on how to facilitate the crown prosecutor's charge decision. Crown prosecutors now direct (rather than advise) officers on formal cautions, warnings, and reprimands, and CPS guidance requires decisions to be based on a review of the evidence, not on an oral report. Historically, the structure of CPS independence has maintained a clear separation between the prosecution and the police investigation, with crown prosecutors able only to advise officers without being a legal authority over them. The power to direct the police in some matters therefore represents a significant shift in roles, an increase in prosecutorial authority and, crucially, a departure from the principles of constabulary independence set out in ex parte *Blackburn*.[93]

[90] CPS, *Director's Guidance*, para. 7 states that early investigative advice (EIA) may be provided in serious, sensitive, or complex cases and it should always be utilized in cases involving death, rape, or other serious sexual offenses. HMCPSI and HMIC (2015: para. 6.4) found that EIA is well established in the CPS headquarter units (such as counterterrorism), but not in local areas. Officers were uncertain as to what was available, and the joint inspectorate found that only two out of thirteen rape cases and one out of twenty-one cases involving other serious sexual offenses in their sample had sought EIA (paras. 6.5–6.7).

[91] HMCPSI and HMIC (2015), a report carried out jointly by Her Majesty's CPS Inspectorate and Her Majesty's Inspectorate of Constabulary.

[92] HMCPSI and HMIC (2015: para. 1.12). A charging decision was described as correct when the Code for Crown Prosecutors had been applied correctly.

[93] The attorney general and the DPP regard this shift in roles as the most significant change in the relatively brief history of the CPS, expanding the CPS role and limiting constabulary independence

In addition to issuing guidance to custody officers and being responsible for charging decisions in a quarter of cases, crown prosecutors are now also empowered to issue conditional cautions with punitive (rather than rehabilitative or reparative) conditions attached.[94] Although a relatively minor measure and used infrequently,[95] this represents a transfer of power from the judiciary to the CPS. The attorney general has described this as the offender's choice, with the benefit of legal advice, but this is a weak notion of consent in a criminal process that makes guilty pleas the norm, enforced through a series of systematic and institutional pressures. Neither can basic constitutional principles be traded off for efficiency. This is a punishment (rather than a prosecution diversionary measure), and its administration by a prosecutor (lacking even the basic judicial status of the French procureur) does not offer Article 6 ECHR fair-trial guarantees. This increased power in the criminal process, and in the disposition of cases in particular, places accountability for the prosecutor's exercise of her discretion further under the spotlight.

The CPS does not receive national circulars or local directives aimed at prioritizing particular areas of criminal activity in the way French prosecutors experience within the structure of their accountability. Instead, CPS policy is set by the DPP through the Code for Crown Prosecutors; charging standards designed to help clarify which charge to prefer when there is a "ladder" of offenses (such as assaults); and legal guidance extending to a wide range of offenses. A practice of public consultation around CPS policies has also been instituted, with the results being published on the CPS website.[96] In this way, the DPP provides guidance on what constitutes prosecution in the public interest

as set out in *R v. Commissioner of Police of the Metropolis*, ex parte *Blackburn* [1968] 2 QBD 118, in which Lord Denning stated that while all police officers are under a duty to enforce the law of the land, they are wholly independent of the executive and not subject to the orders of the secretary of state: "The responsibility for law enforcement lies on him. He is answerable to the law and to the law alone" (769 *per* Lord Denning, M.R.). That case referred to the range of police powers regarding law enforcement and predates the establishment of the CPS.

[94] A similar provision exists in Germany under § 153a of the German Code of Criminal Procedure.

[95] Out-of-court disposals issued by the CPS at the precharge stage (a simple caution, conditional caution, reprimand, final warning, or offense to be taken into consideration) accounted for 0.5 percent of the five hundred thousand cases prosecuted in 2018/10 (CPS, 2019). The numbers have declined, but were never more than 2.4 percent in 2008/09, (CPS, *CPS Annual Report and Resource Accounts 2010/11*, Annex B (London, 2015), https://www.cps.gov.uk/publications/reports/2010/annex_b.html). Recorded crime has declined steadily over the last decade from around six million instances in 2004 to around four million in 2014, a decrease of one-third; see Office for National Statistics, *Crime in England and Wales: Year Ending December 2015* (London, 2015), Figure 1, http://www.ons.gov.uk/peoplepopulationandcommunity/crimeandjustice/bulletins/crimeinenglandandwales/yearendingdecember2015. Prosecutions have halved in the same period from over one million to five hundred thousand.

[96] See "Consultations," Crown Prosecution Service, http://www.cps.gov.uk/consultations/index.html.

generally, as well as for specified offense types. This would not be regarded as legitimate in France, where, as a republic, the state represents the interests of its citizens and the public interest is understood as something different from the sum of publicly expressed citizen opinion.[97] For the CPS in England and Wales, however, some see these forms of public consultation as providing legitimacy: "[T]he frequency with which the public's views are sought provides some assurance that the current public interest factors carry with them their acceptance and support."[98] However, there is no explanation or justification for the rationale of accepting some views over others when shaping policy.[99] The public nature of the consultation (in contrast to the closed process of policy creation) provides the appearance of some transparency, but these are, ultimately, political choices.

A consequence of organizing charge and prosecution in this way is that the process is more closely regulated in ways that require compliance with centrally determined procedures and with measurable results. In addition to national arrangements for charging and guidance on cautions and other measures, standardization is also achieved through the increased regulation and scrutiny of prosecution work through inspectorates and reporting requirements designed to measure crown prosecutor efficiency in throughput terms. Performance is monitored locally through line managers and nationally through reporting and inspections. Prosecutors must also demonstrate compliance at all stages of case processing with the various guidelines issued by the DPP, such as when to apply the Full Code Test, or the Threshold Test to charging decisions,[100] and when to characterize offenses within certain categories such as homophobic violence or domestic abuse, and so follow the charging guidance on these and other offenses.[101] Although designed to ensure a degree of uniformity in the treatment of certain offenses, the guidance also has the effect of reducing individual professional discretion. Instead, prosecutors are required to justify their decisions and their application of specific criteria through detailed record-keeping that is subject to later review. In this way, although the internal hierarchy of the CPS is

[97] See Soubise (2016: 131).

[98] Daw and Solomon (2010).

[99] Sanders (2016).

[100] The Threshold Test may be applied where the suspect "presents a substantial bail risk if released and not all the evidence is available at the time when he or she must be released from custody unless charged. The Threshold Test may be used to charge a suspect who may be justifiably detained in custody to allow evidence to be gathered to meet the Full Code Test realistic prospect of conviction evidential standard." CPS, *Director's Guidance*, para. 11.

[101] CPS, *Domestic Abuse Guidelines for Prosecutors*, issued by the DPP http://www.cps.gov.uk/legal/d_to_g/domestic_abuse_guidelines_for_prosecutors/; CPS, *Guidance on Prosecuting Cases of Homophobic and Transphobic Crime*, issued by the DPP, http://www.cps.gov.uk/legal/h_to_k/homophobic_and_transphobic_hate_crime/. For the full range of legal guidance issued to the CPS, see http://www.cps.gov.uk/legal/.

less rigid than that of the Parquet, in practice, crown prosecutors are subject to greater levels of scrutiny and direction in their daily work.

A further feature of the modern CPS is the rigid separation of the preparation and prosecution of cases into discrete stages—charging advice, case preparation, magistrates' court, Crown Court, serious sexual offenses, trials, and so on. Prosecutors work within a team, which means that a case will pass through several pairs of hands before it is finally disposed of by the court. In theory, this looks to provide additional guarantees through a series of horizontal checks and balances, as different personnel review the case file and the earlier decisions of their colleagues. In practice, the opposite is true. The process of case preparation and prosecution is fragmented, with no case ownership, and so no clear point of responsibility.[102] Other than in serious, complex, and sensitive cases where early investigative advice (EIA) should be sought, no single crown prosecutor is responsible for a case.[103] Although there is no client as such, this is a form of discontinuous representation, where decisions are not taken in the right way in the expectation that any difficulties can be remedied by the next person who picks up the file. Case ownership has also been identified in the Leveson Review and the *Better Case Management Handbook* (2018) as essential for the effective management of cases and engagement between the parties toward a speedy resolution.[104]

This fragmentation is further aggravated by the systematic delegation to associate prosecutors (APs) of pretrial preparation tasks as well as substantial amounts of court work.[105] Under section 7A of the Prosecution of Offences Act 1985, the DPP may designate individuals who are not crown prosecutors to conduct bail hearings and noncontested magistrates' court work. The DPP is also empowered to determine the selection criteria and required training. A significant proportion of prosecution work, including bail decisions and guilty pleas, is now carried out at court by APs. Typically, these are experienced former administrators within the CPS who have undergone one week's training on criminal law and one week on criminal procedure.[106] Although they are under the authority of a crown prosecutor, the dynamic nature of court work means that in practice they will often take decisions on amending the charge or the factual

[102] For an account of typical teams and case pathways, see Soubise (2016: 142–145). Teams are made up of crown prosecutors, associate prosecutors, and paralegals.

[103] There should be "continuity of prosecutor" where the CPS has provided EIA. CPS, *Director's Guidance on Charging*, para. 7.

[104] Leveson (2015: 2.2, 2.3); Judiciary of England and Wales (2018). Furthermore, Leveson (2015: 5.1.2) identifies the need for a change in professional culture in order that engagement can take place prior to as well as at court.

[105] See Soubise (2017).

[106] For further detail and the selection and training of APs see CPS, *CPS Annual Report and Accounts 2014-15*, Annex E (London, 2015), http://www.cps.gov.uk/publications/docs/annual_report_2014_15.pdf.

basis of prosecution, rather than risk incurring the anger of the court while they halt proceedings in order to obtain crown prosecutor authorization. This means that in practice, it is an AP, rather than a legally qualified crown prosecutor, who determines whether to accept a plea of guilty and to what charges. Delegation on this scale is often problematic, as processes become routinized and work is assigned systematically, rather than being actively reviewed and delegated. The role of the AP seems set only to grow, as it is a CPS performance target to increase the number of cases dealt with by APs.[107] Furthermore, it is APs themselves who determine whether a case requires the attention of a crown prosecutor, and even where a review does take place, the crown prosecutor is unlikely to read the file, relying instead on the account provided by the AP.[108] The arrival of the AP creates a tier of CPS staff who are formally overseen by crown prosecutors, but who in practice are removed from the usual lines of accountability.

This also impacts on the protection of the defendant at court. With the mass processing of cases through guilty pleas, in which even those legally represented are unlikely to have the strength of evidence against them assessed in anything like a robust fashion, the professionalism of the prosecutor is understood as some guarantee of the credibility and reliability of the evidence, as well as the appropriateness of the level of charges brought. By placing these hearings and some of the decision-making around them in the hands of unqualified "associates," lacking the legal and professional training of lawyers, we see the real McDonaldization of criminal justice. There is a growing gap between the rhetoric of the professional prosecution role and the way that this functions in practice, as cases are simply moved along in standardized ways.

More generally, CPS work is organized as a kind of factory assembly line model.[109] The case passes through each separate stage, determined by centralized and standardized procedures that tend to routinize work in order that it can be carried out by non-crown prosecution staff. This model attaches little value to professional discretion and discourages any sense of case ownership.[110] This mass centralization can also be a barrier to effective police-prosecution working relationships. It does not promote shared working goals and objectives, and there is little place for local concerns or priorities, such as the need to address particular types of criminality that might be increasing in the area. It is interesting to contrast this with the more specialist serious crime and counterterrorism

[107] Soubise (2017: 852).

[108] Soubise (2017).

[109] Marsh (2016) describes magistrates' court disposal of cases as a rapid assembly line approach, and Soubise (2017) applies the same analogy to the micro-decisions made by CPS staff. This is also how Herbert Packer described his crime control model.

[110] Like the French model, this reflects aspects of what has been described as the McDonaldization of justice. See Bohm (2006) and Ritzer (2004).

division of the CPS, in which prosecutors do not work above or below the police, intervening before or after the police investigation. Rather, they work together on investigations, with crown prosecutors advising the police, but within a more cooperative relationship that avoids the tensions and resentments that have characterized police-CPS relations since the service was established in 1986.

Rather than a legal or political model of prosecution legitimacy, increasingly, legitimacy and accountability are bureaucratic concerns, in which effectiveness must be demonstrated so that it can be measured. This can run counter to efficiency. In France, the preoccupation with the satisfaction of the *taux de réponse* overshadows the procureur's decision-making and tends to produce outcomes that are skewed toward trivial cases, leaving fewer resources to devote to more serious and complex cases where the prosecutor's expertise is most required. In England and Wales, the crown prosecutor must demonstrate the value she adds to the case, and so a dismissal is seen as a negative outcome, just as in France, and requires explanation. This creates a presumption of prosecution in which weak cases are taken to court—but with little risk of being challenged given the systemic incentives to plead guilty, and the limited opportunities for defense scrutiny, with legal aid provision at an all-time low.

C. Concluding Comments

The prosecution function in France and in England and Wales has emerged from different histories as well as legal cultural traditions. The scope of their roles and their status in relation to other legal and political actors defines them differently in the range of tasks they perform and the ways in which they perform them. The office of public prosecutor in England and Wales was established just thirty years ago, following the recommendations of a Royal Commission and with the specific objective of ensuring that the decision to prosecute was made independently of the investigation. While the Crown Prosecution Service has made strides in establishing its place as a leading criminal justice actor, the relationship with police investigators continues to be characterized by ambivalence. The crown prosecutor is understood to be independent of the police through the principle of the separation of investigation and prosecution, yet she depends on officers to investigate and produce the evidence on which she must base her decision, with no legal authority or power to direct that additional investigations be carried out. In this sense, the prosecutor's independence is limited: decisions around case disposition are made with no opportunity to go beyond, or to test out, the case asserted by the initial police investigation. Recent changes have made the police more accountable to the prosecutor, and there are various ways in which the two bodies are required to cooperate, but the lack of any real prosecutorial authority over officers and the occupational culture of mistrust on the part of the police, together with the importance crown prosecutors place on the separation of investigation and prosecution as an overarching professional value, have limited the value of these developments in practice.

Like the crown prosecutor, the French public prosecutor, the procureur, depends on the police to gather the information necessary for prosecution, but unlike her English counterpart, the procureur is responsible for the investigation as well as the prosecution of crime. In this way, she works more closely with officers, but she is also an authority over them and has the power to instigate alternative lines of enquiry, which, together with her judicial status and the emphasis on the written dossier, is understood to provide her with sufficient distance to ensure her independence. In practice, however, supervision is light touch, distant, bureaucratic, and largely retrospective, concerned with the form rather than the content of the inquiry.[111] Earlier research has documented the importance of trust in making this relationship work; even when resources permit greater involvement, prosecutors understand supervision as a system of reporting and authorization, rather than of surveillance and direction.[112] In contrast to England and Wales, however, it is the very proximity of this professional relationship that threatens the French prosecutor's independence, aggravated by increasing requirements to manage investigations within fixed time periods, toward narrow and often predetermined outcomes.

Political independence is not generally considered problematic for crown prosecutors. Their discretion is closely regulated within the CPS hierarchy, despite the appearance of a broad discretion around charge and prosecution. The procureur's judicial status as a *magistrat* is understood to ensure a public-interest-centered approach to the investigation and prosecution of cases, as well as a guarantee of the protection of the rights of the suspect, and accountability to the minister of justice through the hierarchy of the Parquet is seen to provide democratic legitimacy to the prosecution function. The nature of this control has been softened over time, moving away from a culture of instruction and interference. However, political interference continues to be evident in key appointments and high-profile cases.

In both jurisdictions, we are seeing the reshaping of the prosecution function—not to strengthen the fairness or reliability of the criminal process for those who become its subjects, but to shift power away from the independent judiciary and the trial, to respond to more cases, faster, and to save money. This is presented as a more efficient and effective approach, but seems only to move the focus of criminalization to more minor offenses that can be dealt with easily. This

[111] Hodgson (2001; 2005, esp. chap. 6).
[112] Mouhanna (2001); Hodgson (2005).

in turn depends on a degree of routinization and systematic delegation of work to a variety of associates and paralegals. It also impacts on the independence of the criminal justice process more broadly, not only by placing more decisions in the hands of prosecutors and their staff, rather than judges, and so shifting the terrain where due process protections are needed most, but, in France, by strengthening the hand of the executive to the detriment of the judiciary. Despite the impoverished due process protections available to those investigated under the authority of the procureur, across all stages of the criminal investigation power has shifted away from the trial judge and the *juge d'instruction* (both of whom enjoy greater judicial independence than the Parquet) to the public prosecutor who is hierarchically accountable to the executive through the minister of justice.[113] This represents a greater concentration of power in the hands of the prosecutor, as well undermining the independence of the criminal justice system by placing a large portion of the criminal process under executive, rather than judicial, authority.

The changes in roles and procedures experienced in both jurisdictions are part of a constant and piecemeal reform process driven in large part by the political rhetoric and penal populism of successive governments.[114] There is little concern to structure change in order to maintain a balance of safeguards in keeping with the broader procedural tradition of each jurisdiction. In France, these reforms have been added on to the existing codes without any fundamental reappraisal of the overall functioning or integrity of the criminal process, including the role of the prosecutor.[115] A variety of commissions and enquiries have been established to address the increasing incoherence of the French criminal process,

[113] Legislation stemming from the state of emergency following the November 2015 attacks in Paris has been no exception to this trend of "dejudicialization" and growing executive power. Under these provisions, the police have wider search powers; suspects may be detained for four hours without a lawyer in some circumstances; individuals suspected of returning from training in Syria and Iraq may be placed under house arrest; and the rules on the use of armed police officers have been relaxed.

[114] Even the notion of *politique pénale*, which used to refer to prosecutorial discretion, now encapsulates a raft of policies, initiatives, and measurements. Milburn and Mouhanna (2010: 13) describe it as the will of the state to provide a judicial response to the state's security-driven policies.

[115] When establishing the Beaume Commission, the justice minister, Christine Taubira, wrote that the French criminal justice process was seriously weakened by having failed to adapt to change in a way that was sufficiently coherent and strategic and that anticipated European standards and their development. In the absence of structural reforms, the system has not developed in a planned way, but through changes imposed by the need to transpose European directives, or decisions of the ECtHR, the Cour de cassation, or the Conseil constitutionnel. The reforms to the *juge d'instruction* legislated in 2000 and those following the Outreau enquiry are the exception. They have enhanced the *contradictoire* quality of the investigation and established the role of the *juge des libertés et de la détention*. However, it is the 97 percent of cases dealt with by the procureur, where there is no *contradictoire* element to the investigation, that is of concern. Lawyers and police are unhappy with the current situation, and it is the courts that are enforcing compliance with European norms, creating judicial insecurity as cases are dismissed (Beaume [2014: Annex 1]).

and to assess the prosecution function and the prospects for reform.[116] The recent legislative project, addressing organized crime and procedural protections for accused persons, again noted the growing complexity of criminal procedure as a result of successive reforms required by European and constitutional decisions as well as measures to improve domestic security.[117] In particular, it noted the difficulties in reconciling the role of the procureur with recent calls to strengthen the *contradictoire* quality of the investigation phase. This reflects the tension between the inquisitorial tradition and European requirements to temper this through more accusatorial procedures of open debate. The principle of *contradictoire* is increasingly important, however, given the marginalization of judicial protections. It offers the possibility of going at least some way to counter the growing concentration of power in the hands of the procureur and the trend toward the administrativization of coercive measures, especially in relation to counterterrorism measures that allow police to search and detain individuals without reasonable suspicion, on the authority of the préfet, with no prior judicial authorization.[118] Placing powers formerly exercised by criminal judges into the hands of administrative judges confuses judicial and political roles and responsibilities and so infringes the separation of powers.[119]

In England and Wales, the lack of coherence and certainty in the prosecution role as a result of piecemeal reforms has also been of concern. The House of Commons Justice Committee (2009) concluded:

> The prosecution plays a pivotal role in the criminal justice system. This role has become too important to continue to be vulnerable to piecemeal amendment in response to events. We expect the Attorney General and the Director of Public Prosecutions to show clear leadership in defining the role of the prosecutor in the criminal justice system. Specific changes to the operation of the prosecution system should be made in the light of an awareness of how they affect and contribute to this clear role and to the criminal justice system as a whole.[120]

Changes have been affected, which have in theory placed prosecutors at the heart of pretrial decision-making. Yet the increasingly bureaucratic nature of

[116] For example, Beaume (2014); Garapon et al. (2013); Nadal (2103); Milburn et al. (2010). Earlier commissions include the Delmas-Marty Commission in 1990 and the Truche Commission in 1997.

[117] Loi no. 2016-731 du 3 juin 2016 renforçant la lutte contre le crime organisé, le terrorisme et leur financement, et améliorant l'efficacité et les garanties de la procédure pénale.

[118] Loi No. 2017-1510 du 30 octobre 2017 renforçant la sécurité intérieure et la lutte contre le terrorisme. See further discussion in chapter 3

[119] These two types of *juge* are very different: administrative judges are trained in the national school of administration (the ENA, École nationale d'administration) and are not governed by the same professional ethics as the fully independent *magistrats* who are trained at the national judicial school (the ENM, École nationale de la magistrature).

[120] House of Commons Justice Committee, 2009, para. 7.

the prosecution function has run counter to the leadership and professionalism identified as so essential by the Justice Committee.

These current reforms bring to the fore, once again, the question of the French prosecutor's independence. While we might not wish an independent prosecutor to reflect narrow political interests, we may expect some form of democratic connection between prosecution and wider criminal justice policy. In this way, prosecutorial independence and accountability are inextricably connected. Although structured in different ways, the independence of the prosecutor is a defining feature in both France and England and Wales. As prosecution roles change and prosecutors are invested with broader powers during the pretrial and the disposition of cases, the nature of prosecutorial independence and accountability grows more important. The increasingly close relationship between the police and prosecution functions in Britain, and the decline in the role of the *juge d'instruction* in favor of the prosecutor in France, raise new questions around where the checks and balances lie. Traditional models are being adjusted to meet the challenges of modern criminal justice procedures and a conception of fair trial shaped partly by European norms and partly by populist policies.

PART 3
DEFENSE

6

European Influences on the Pretrial Defense Role

This chapter examines the changing ways in which the role of the criminal defense lawyer is structured and understood within different procedural traditions, and the challenges posed to individual legal cultures and practices by the growing influence of the ECtHR and the EU.[1] It focuses on the earliest stages of the pretrial defense role, in part because of the determinative importance for the case of the initial police detention and questioning of the suspect, but also because this is where some of the most radical challenges to procedural values and shifts in role expectations have taken place, especially within inquisitorial-type procedures. England and Wales introduced a statutory right to custodial legal advice in 1984 as part of a wider reform of the investigation and prosecution process, but for many European jurisdictions, the defense lawyer has been less visible at the pretrial stage. The jurisprudence of the ECtHR, together with an expanding body of EU measures, has to some extent cut through the differing conceptions of procedural differences by shifting attention away from the specifics of how roles and responsibilities are allocated and shared out differently in jurisdictions, focusing instead on effective defense as a fundamental part of the right to a fair trial and an essential component of the privilege against self-incrimination. This raises the question of the extent to which European norms are contributing to the development of a more universal pan-European pretrial criminal defense role, and one that promotes a more proactive model of defense that recognizes the shrinking space between the phases of investigation and trial.[2] Although rooted in and reflecting Article 6 standards and protections that states understand themselves to respect and to apply in their own procedures, many jurisdictions are resistant to

[1] All major human rights treaties and conventions set out the right to a fair trial, e.g., International Covenant on Civil and Political Rights (Art. 14); Universal Declaration of Human Rights (Arts. 10 and 11); American Convention on Human Rights (Art. 8); African Charter on Human Rights and Peoples Rights (Art. 7).

[2] In the case of Switzerland, for example, Jackson and Summers (2013: 127) argue that although Swiss courts have traditionally been reluctant to follow ECtHR jurisprudence, the clear principles set out in *Salduz* have produced a positive response from the Swiss courts, allowing lawyers to be present during initial police hearings and overturning convictions where this has been denied. It would seem, however, that some of the clarity in its underlying principles has been lost in decisions such as *Ibrahim and others v. UK* (50541/08, 50571/08, 50573/08, 40351/09) 13 September 2016.

The Metamorphosis of Criminal Justice. Jacqueline S. Hodgson, Oxford University Press (2020).

DOI: 10.1093/oso/9780199981427.001.0001

this degree of detailed prescription. And although states themselves participate in, and are the authors of, ECtHR judgments and EU instruments, the distance between national and European norms means that the latter are inevitably perceived as externally driven and imposed from without, creating tensions between domestic and transnational understandings of the proper role of the defense.[3]

A. Introduction

The role of the defense is growing in some respects while receding in others. Procedural safeguards during the pretrial phase have been strengthened, but the defense ability to investigate and challenge the prosecution case has been undercut by the decline in legal aid in England and Wales,[4] and in both jurisdictions, by court rules and procedures designed to dispose of cases as quickly as possible and without any opportunity to contest the charges. In England and Wales, despite the lawyer's responsibility to investigate, present, and test out the prosecution case, there has been a gradual decline of adversarial values, with defendants being required to enter a plea at their first hearing and adjournments to take instructions being frowned upon. The contesting of criminal charges is actively discouraged through sentence discounts, and the process is regulated through defense disclosure and case management requirements administered by the judge, designed to eliminate conflict and promote consensus between accuser and accused.[5] Everything seems to militate against the accused's right to contest the charges against her, or to put the prosecution to proof.[6] Having improved the quality of criminal defense provision and inculcated adversarial values into lawyers' training for custodial legal advice in response to the research findings of the 1990s,[7] the financial and procedural reforms that followed, moved in the opposite direction.

In France too, although defense rights were progressively strengthened during the 1990s and in 2000 as more accusatorial elements were incorporated

[3] See further Hodgson (2011, 2012).

[4] Flynn and Hodgson (2017).

[5] A desire for case resolution through admissions is not new. By 1900 around 40 percent of jury trials were guilty pleas, compared with 2 to 5 percent in 1835. This does not include summary cases. See Feeley (1997). Guilty pleas may be seen as the ultimate expression of the party control that characterizes adversarialism (as well as ushering in a greater degree of complexity and lawyering), or its negation through pressure to avoid the promises of adversarial scrutiny through a public oral process of testimony and judgment. See the discussion of plea bargaining in chapter 1 and, in particular, Langbein (1979, 2003); Feeley (1982); McConville and Marsh (2014).

[6] For discussion of the meaning and significance of guilt in England and Wales, see Horne (2017). On the disappearance of the trial in the United States, see, e.g., Burns (2009); Kritzer (2004).

[7] See summary in Cape (2004) of the response to the findings of McConville and Hodgson (1993), McConville et al. (1994), and Bridges and Choongh (1998) in terms of changes to the profession.

into criminal procedure,[8] there has been a growing preoccupation with managerialist imperatives and the efficient disposal of cases through various alternatives to trial,[9] which appear more palatable when presented alongside safeguards of what are in effect fairly cursory defense rights. *Comparution immédiate* hearings, for example, see defendants who have been arrested, charged, and brought before the court in the space of forty-eight hours, facing immediate imprisonment, with very little time for judicial examination. Defendants are represented—but usually by young and inexperienced duty lawyers who, with only minutes during which to take instructions, are unable to deliver anything more than basic mitigation. In this way, the opportunity for defense representation (no matter how minimal in practice) can claim to satisfy fair-trial requirements, without disturbing the centrality of the judicial investigation model.[10]

At the transnational level of the ECtHR and the EU, due process protections of the accused have been strengthened through the development of custodial legal assistance within the framework of the right to a fair trial. It is recognized that the defense has an important role to play during these early stages of the investigation and the lawyer's presence in police custody has an impact on due process protections more broadly, as access to legal assistance is likely to prevent abuses and ensure that other safeguards, such as the right to remain silent, are understood by suspects and respected by police.[11] In the landmark case of *Salduz v. Turkey* (2008),[12] the ECtHR ruled that suspects must have access to legal assistance from the first interrogation by the police in order to meet the fair-trial requirements set out in Article 6 ECHR: without this fundamental guarantee, the rights of the defense "will in principle be irretrievably prejudiced" if incriminating statements made in the absence of a lawyer are used for a conviction. Subsequent cases such as *Dayanan v. Turkey*[13] have gone further in finding there to be a breach of Article 6 ECHR even where no incriminating statement was

[8] Hodgson (2005).

[9] Discussed in chapter 5.

[10] In England and Wales, the growth in legal representation through the duty solicitor schemes of the 1970s facilitated the more rapid processing of cases through the courts, as unrepresented clients slow things down (Hodgson [2006c]). In the 1990s, the presence of the lawyer in police custody was used to justify the attenuation of the right to silence; and the massive reliance on guilty pleas would be impossible without lawyers to manage clients toward this end, while also appearing to represent their interests and so ensure that fair-trial requirements are met.

[11] See, for example, the "aims pursued by the right of access to a lawyer" set out in *Beuze v. Belgium* 71409/10, 9 November 2018, §§125–130. Access to a lawyer at the pretrial stage of the proceedings contributes to the prevention of miscarriages of justice and to equality of arms. It constitutes an important counterweight to the vulnerability of suspects in police custody (vulnerability that is amplified by increasingly complex legislation around the gathering and use of evidence) and provides a fundamental safeguard against coercion and ill-treatment of suspects by the police.

[12] (36391/02) 27 November 2008.

[13] (7377/03) 13 October 2009.

made and so the conviction was not based on statements made in the absence of a lawyer.

As a result of these and subsequent cases, the initial pretrial role of the criminal defense lawyer has come under the spotlight right across Europe, setting out a model of more effective defense representation that operates independently of other safeguards such as judicial or prosecutorial investigative oversight. The court has made clear that the suspect should be able to consult with her lawyer in private at the start of custody, prior to any interview if there is one. She should be able to have her lawyer physically present during police and other pretrial questioning, and the lawyer's assistance should be practical and effective, in order to ensure that the suspect's defense rights are not prejudiced. There should also be opportunity for "the whole range of services specifically associated with legal assistance: discussion of the case, organisation of the defense, collection of exculpatory evidence, preparation for questioning, support for an accused in distress, and verification of the conditions of detention."[14] However, states have been reluctant to adjust their own procedures to ensure a clear right to custodial legal advice in all cases, preferring to see this as a problem of noncompliance by countries such as Turkey and Russia, or seeking to distinguish the case from their own procedures on other grounds. Nonetheless, often through the individual and constitutional challenges brought by activist lawyers,[15] the case law has served as a driver for legal reform, providing significant new protections for suspects and a greater emphasis on defense rights (rather than judicial supervision alone) as a procedural guarantee.

Unsurprisingly, these changes have created tensions between internal and externally driven process values, raising issues around procedural convergence and harmonization, in particular the difficulties in conforming to aspects of a single procedural model, rather than a more general "fair trial" standard. The ECtHR has become more robust in its jurisprudence around procedural safeguards, focusing less on the margin-of-appreciation approach and placing more emphasis on rules that must be followed universally and in a more clearly delineated form. This allows countries less room to claim that decisions against other states do not apply to them because of the different safeguards they have in place, which they believe ensure a fair trial overall—such as a shorter detention period, the opportunity to consult with a lawyer prior to interrogation, or the judicial supervision

[14] *Beuze v. Belgium*, §136.

[15] See, for example, *Cadder v. Her Majesty's Advocate* [2010] UKSC 43, which resulted in reform in Scotland; the decision of the Conseil constitutionnel, Decision No. 2010-14/22 QPC of 30 July 2010, which set the path for reform in France. The right to custodial legal advice was recognized by the Irish Supreme Court in *DPP v. Gormley* [2014] IESC 17, but this was held not to be a constitutional right in the later case of *DPP v. Doyle* [2017] IESC 1.

of the investigation. There has been a recent countertrend of cases, however—not to permit national variations, but returning to an overall fairness approach that is less protective of the right to legal assistance and which seems to depart from the original reasoning in *Salduz*.[16] The emerging field of EU criminal justice relating to procedural safeguards is now also part of the mix, providing more normative rules enforceable directly and without the need to demonstrate an unfair trial.[17] The implications in comparative criminal justice terms are significant: there are key defense safeguards that must be in place in all systems, whatever their procedural tradition. This may conflict with national understandings of what is appropriate and necessary, not only in inquisitorially rooted countries that have traditionally resisted calls to allow the defense lawyer into the police interrogation, but also in adversarial systems where more limited access to custodial legal advice is considered sufficient.

B. The Importance of Evidence Obtained through Police Questioning

Traditionally, the defense role has been considered more important in adversarial procedure, where the accused is a party and so is responsible for gathering and presenting evidence to support her case, as well as testing out that of the prosecution. In inquisitorial procedure, the terms of the enquiry are set more broadly. The "parties" are witnesses and participants in a case that is investigated through a central and judicial procedure whose primary objective is the search for the truth. This does not obviate the role of the accused or her lawyer entirely, but it places them more at the periphery—the lawyer's role has been seen as that of an auxiliary, complementing that of the judicial investigator.[18] Procedural differences between jurisdictions continue to be important and to offer a different framework within which legal actors operate and are accountable, but the jurisprudence of the ECtHR has been especially important in reframing defense

[16] Some recent cases where access to custodial legal advice has been delayed—either because of "compelling reasons" as allowed for in *Salduz*, or in breach of legal provisions but where no incriminating statement was made—have not resulted in a finding of a breach of Article 6. *Ibrahim and others v. UK; Simeonovi v. Bulgaria* 21980/04, 12 May 2017. In *Beuze v. Belgium* the court found a violation of Article 6(3)(c), but reaffirmed the approach in *Ibrahim*, where the prejudice to the accused and the overall fairness of the trial were assessed by the court. See subsequent discussion.

[17] As the ECtHR jurisprudence continues to evolve and EU directives take effect, the relationship between these two also has the potential to add a layer of complexity, as interpretations may differ and standards may not move in the same direction. Soo (2017); Pivaty (2018). Both ECtHR cases and the EU directive are considered in the decision in *Beuze v. Belgium*.

[18] Although an auxiliary of justice, the lawyer is not a party to the process of investigation. She does not share the truth-seeking function of the *magistrat*, nor is her role to advance the enquiry. Re France, see also Hodgson (2002a); re Germany see Leigh and Zedner (1992); Weigend (2004).

rights, and the right to legal assistance in particular, in terms of the wider right to a fair trial under Article 6 ECHR.

The right to effective defense representation is perhaps less contested and more established during the trial phase, in inquisitorial as well as adversarial-type procedures.[19] Even jurisdictions with strong inquisitorial roots have a broadly accusatorial trial procedure.[20] The evidence in these jurisdictions tends to be written rather than oral, but the prosecution case is disclosed in advance and the parties can make representations and call witnesses. In practice, however, in both jurisdictions, in the overwhelming majority of cases the trial is a form of guilty plea or accelerated hearing in which the charges are not contested and the defense does not call witnesses or cross-examine those of the prosecution. The case is effectively determined on the basis of the pretrial investigation, which is in practice a police investigation. In England and Wales this is further aggravated by the poor quality and extent of prosecution disclosure,[21] with the result that the accused is encouraged to enter a guilty plea at the earliest opportunity, on the basis of little more than a police summary,[22] which is often inaccurate and incomplete.[23]

In countries with a more inquisitorial tradition, such as France, the pretrial police investigation has traditionally been regarded as preliminary and of less importance than any subsequent judicial enquiry, characterized by diminished defense rights and a weak structure of legal regulation. However, the pretrial stage of the criminal process, and the detention and questioning of suspects in particular, is now recognized as being highly determinative of case outcome.

[19] The pretrial and investigative stage is not the focus for adversarial defense protections in many systems with adversarial traditions: for example, the absence of a statutory right to custodial legal advice in Canada and the absence of lawyers during US police interrogations in practice. On the United States in comparative perspective, see Weisselberg (2017) and re the absence of lawyers despite *Miranda* see Rossman (2017).

[20] France, Germany, the Netherlands, etc., would describe their legal procedure as "mixed": the roots and many of the institutional structures of the legal process are inquisitorial, but the trial is accusatorial, incorporating Article 6 ECHR principles of equality of arms, the opportunity to question witnesses, and defense representation. France has enshrined the principle of *contradictoire* (the right to know and respond to the accusations against you) in a preliminary article to the code of criminal procedure.

[21] The CPS endorses, rather than checks, disclosure schedules, leading to chaotic and poorly managed disclosure (HMCPSI and HMIC [2017]). See also Edwards (2016). The Law Society has advised extreme caution when advising on plea with such a poor account of the evidence. (Response of the Law Society of England and Wales to the Sentencing Council consultation on the Reduction in Sentence for a Guilty Plea Guideline May 2016.) See also discussion in chapter 5.

[22] Edwards (2016: 842) notes the real danger posed to defendants in the magistrates' court, that of counsel acting without knowing the full case against her client. He welcomes the senior presiding judge's call to ensure that the CPS cannot, without leave of the court, refer to the contents of witness statements unless they have been first served to the defense.

[23] This is a systemic feature of the criminal process, commented on in 1993 by the RCCJ (1993: chap. 3, para. 75), as well as in recent joint inspection reports (HMIC [2015]); (HMCPSI and HMIC [2017]).

Although the trial is the public focus of criminal law—it is here that cases are literally played out—what we see at court is increasingly the simple affirmation of the police investigation, clothed in the authority of a judicial finding or verdict. Across jurisdictions, guilty pleas and other forms of case disposal based upon admissions have become the norm.[24] Convictions are based upon the evidence gathered by police during the investigation, without the scrutiny of the public adversarial court hearing: the "trial as contest" is the exception. This is also reflected to a degree in the judicial investigation model in inquisitorially rooted procedures such as France, where great reliance is placed on the credibility of the dossier of evidence. Although the dossier consists of evidence and statements collected almost entirely by the police, officers work under the authority of a *magistrat* (in law if not in practice), and so the dossier is understood to be the product of a judicial or judicially supervised enquiry into the truth, conducted in the public interest.[25] For this reason, it is afforded more credibility and subjected to less scrutiny than evidence or argument presented by the defense, which is considered partisan and self-interested in this respect.[26] There is a contradiction here: as a police enquiry, the pretrial has been seen as unimportant, with no need for defense involvement;[27] yet, at the same time, as an enquiry supervised by the procureur (or *juge d'instruction*), it is treated as significant and is afforded the credibility of a judicially supervised investigation.

France has displayed a strong attachment to this model of judicial investigation, considering it as superior to, and incompatible with, a more active defense role pretrial. The comments of then-justice minister Elisabeth Guigou are typical of this view:

> The adversarial system of justice is by nature unfair and unjust. It favors the strong over the weak. It accentuates social and cultural differences, favoring the rich, who are able to engage and pay for the services of one or more lawyers. Our own system is better, in terms both of efficiency and of the rights of the individual. . . . I prefer, and I want to make this quite plain, an independent judge who

[24] In the Netherlands, for example, the government target is for 70 percent of minor offenses to be dealt with through a penal order imposed by the prosecutor while the accused is still in police detention. See Blackstock et al. (2014: 100–101).

[25] Even when an *instruction* is opened, the *juge* will typically instruct the same investigating officers to continue the enquiry, thus confirming rather than interrogating the preliminary enquiries made.

[26] This is also seen in the inquisitorial traditions of the postcommunist countries. As Grozev (2012: 99) describes the Bulgarian system during the communist regime: "The investigation was the crucial stage in the development of the proceedings, with the trial acting more like a quality control check on the investigation, rather than performing a full and independent collection and analysis of the relevant evidence." Since the late 1990s, the Bulgarian system has shifted toward a more adversarial procedure with greater emphasis on the evidence at trial and the rights of the defense.

[27] Potentially, lawyers may play a much greater role in cases investigated under the authority of the *juge d'instruction*, but these account for less than 5 percent of cases.

> investigates evidence both for and against the suspect, to police officers who carry out large parts of the criminal investigation without any judicial supervision.[28]

This marginalizing of the defense lawyer role at the pretrial phase has now been challenged.[29] This includes the position of the suspect held for police questioning and the need for effective defense rights from the point at which the suspect's position is adversely affected in order to comply with Article 6. The landmark decision of *Salduz v. Turkey*[30] recognized that the detention and questioning of suspects in police custody is where the suspect is most vulnerable and, consequently, in need of legal assistance. The case asserted the suspect's right to custodial legal advice in the strongest terms:

> [I]n order for the right to a fair trial to remain sufficiently "practical and effective" article 6 § 1 requires that, as a rule, access to a lawyer should be provided as from the first interrogation of a suspect by the police, unless it is demonstrated in the light of the particular circumstances of each case that there are compelling reasons to restrict this right. . . . The rights of the defence will in principle be irretrievably prejudiced when incriminating statements made during police interrogation without access to a lawyer are used for a conviction.[31]

National jurisdictions too, have recognized the growing significance of the pretrial phase and of the period of police detention and questioning in particular. In England and Wales, arrest and detention was originally anticipated as an exceptional procedure. It is now accepted as a standard and routine means of investigating and obtaining evidence. The suspect has enjoyed access to custodial legal advice since the Police and Criminal Evidence Act 1984 (PACE), though this benefit was later used to justify the introduction of adverse inferences being drawn from the suspect's silence under the Criminal Justice and Public Order Act 1994. In this sense, what suspects do not say has become as much a part of the evidence in the case as what they do say, and the pretrial investigation is as potent a source of evidence as that presented at trial. As Lord Justice Laws described it in *Howell v. R*: "[T]he police interview and the trial are to be seen as part of a continuous process in which the suspect is engaged from the beginning."[32] Together

[28] Addressing the Sénat, 15 June 1999. These arguments continue to be made when the strengthening of defense rights is discussed.

[29] The ECtHR has recognized that unfairness at the pretrial stage is likely to prejudice the fairness of the trial—whatever the criminal procedural tradition. *Imbrioscia v. Switzerland* (13972/88) 22 November 1993; *Salduz v. Turkey* ECHR (Grand Chamber) (36391/02) 27 November 2008; *Panovits v. Cyprus* (4268/04) 11 December 2008.

[30] (36391/02) 27 November 2008.

[31] Para. 55.

[32] [2003] EWCA Crim. 1, at para. 23.

with the increasing pressure to dispose of cases at the earliest moment possible and the woeful lack of proper disclosure of the prosecution evidence, this makes the role of the lawyer at the police station yet more crucial.[33] It also challenges the traditional account of adversarial procedure, the hallmark of which is the separation of the investigation and the trial.[34] The ability of the defense to participate in a properly adversarial way, responding to the evidence presented as well as advancing the defense case, is severely limited if the defendant is required to act without knowing the full extent of the prosecution case.

In France, when examining the lawfulness of the procedure regulating the detention and questioning of suspects in police custody, the Conseil constitutionnel recognized the huge increase in the use of custodial interrogation, and the determinative nature of evidence obtained during the period of police detention and questioning of the suspect, the *garde à vue* (GAV).[35] In the Netherlands too, while police arrest and the initial detention of up to six hours were introduced to assist the prosecutor in determining whether detention was necessary, it is now accepted as a means to interrogate the suspect and to advance the investigation. Together with the more lengthy police detention, it has become routine.

In Scotland, the 2011 Carloway Review acknowledged the importance of the police interview.[36] Over time, the investigative role in Scotland has passed from the sheriff, to the procurator fiscal, and then to the police, and "[T]he role of the police interview as both an investigative tool and a source of evidence has become enhanced."[37] The review recognized that the police interview is regarded as part of the trial in Article 6 ECHR terms and that "a significant part of the suspect's trial, in a traditional sense, is being moved in both time and location from the court room setting to that of the police station."[38] However, even with a lawyer present, there is no disclosure in the way that would be required at court and there is no judicial oversight of the process, other than retrospectively. The Carloway Review questioned the desirability of "such a general development, which involves the introduction, or perhaps reintroduction, of inquisitorial methods employed by the police (i.e. the executive), and not the judiciary, into what has become in recent years a highly adversarial trial process" and the practicability of a situation where "[t]he more the interview is perceived as part of the

[33] Tony Edwards, an experienced and respected criminal solicitor, describes the attenuation of the right to silence as doing more than anything else to increase the status of the defense lawyer (2016: 831).

[34] See also Illuminati (2005: 569).

[35] Decision No. 2010-14/22 QPC of 30 July 2010.

[36] Established to examine Scottish criminal procedure after the decision in *Cadder* and the subsequent emergency legislation put in place to provide suspects held in police custody with access to a lawyer during, as well as prior to, police interrogation.

[37] Carloway (2011: para. 6.0.9).

[38] Carloway (2011: para. 6.0.10).

trial, the more that protections, which were traditionally provided only in the context of court room proceedings, will require to be afforded at the outset of a suspect's detention."[39]

The pretrial process is key to the development of the case, but in an increasing number of instances, there is no trial at all: arrest, detention, and questioning constitute the suspect's entire experience of the criminal process. In these circumstances, in the absence of a trial in which the treatment of the accused can be contested as contrary to Article 5 or Article 6 ECHR, these rights are harder to trigger. This makes the systematic protection provided by EU measures, directly enforceable without the need to exhaust domestic proceedings and remedies, all the more significant as a means of ensuring that procedural guarantees are respected and that there is a remedy for their breach, whether or not the case goes to trial.

When thinking about the defense function as a means of ensuring that the accused receives a fair trial, one should also remember that the fair treatment of suspects is important in ways that are not tied to particular procedural models, but rather, in broader process terms. Fairness encompasses more than narrow defense interests; it also serves as a check on police and prosecution procedural compliance, and so it helps to guarantee the credibility and reliability of the evidence on which the court will base its determination of liability. It is also important simply to treat suspects fairly, even if they are not ultimately prosecuted and tried. Unfair treatment is likely to cause individuals, as citizens subjected to state power, to question the legitimacy of that power.[40]

C. The Marginal Role of the Defense in the Inquisitorial Tradition

Within adversarial procedure, the gathering, selection, and presentation of the evidence on which the court will base its verdict is the responsibility of the two opposing parties—those bringing the accusation and the defense. In this way, the defense lawyer's role is in direct opposition to that of the prosecution and carries responsibility for bringing evidence before the court that exculpates or mitigates the actions of the accused. This is an active duty without which the court would be deprived of relevant evidence—it is not a role designed simply to complement existing safeguards and procedures in the way that the defense function is often characterized in France and other inquisitorial systems. The defense also plays a

[39] Carloway (2011: para. 6.0.11).

[40] See, e.g., Tyler (1990), who has argued that this enhances people's perceptions of the legitimacy of the process, which in turn makes them more willing to obey the law and to comply with law enforcement. See also Beetham (1991) and Coicaud (2002), who discuss the nature of the legitimacy of the state as perceived by those subject to its authority.

crucial part in interrogating the credibility and reliability of the prosecution case, in order that the court does not base its finding on partial, inaccurate, or unreliable evidence. Undermining the lawyer's ability to represent the accused in this way prevents the defense case from being heard and undercuts the reliability of the court's verdict. A proactive defense role is inherent within the adversarial tradition, and with the acknowledged importance of the initial police investigation, custodial legal advice is a natural extension of the trial role.

The defense role is characterized differently in most other European countries. A judicially conducted or supervised investigation is at the heart of the criminal process model in inquisitorial-type procedures such as that in France, Belgium, and the Netherlands. The guarantees of an independent judicial enquiry, charged with investigating evidence both inculpating and exculpating any suspect, have historically been considered the most important safeguard for the accused in these systems. In Eastern Europe too, countries such as Bulgaria, Georgia, and Lithuania had a strongly (more politically driven) inquisitorial criminal procedure under the communist regime and accused persons enjoyed few defense rights.[41] Many states across Europe have been forced to reform the rights of suspects held in police custody during the criminal investigation, displacing legal procedural traditions in different ways.[42] The example of France, however, demonstrates just how entrenched the model of judicial investigation has been within criminal procedure.

In practice, French investigations are carried out by the police; most often, they are overseen by a prosecutor (the procureur, whose status is that of a judicial officer) and, in a minority of cases, by an investigating judge (*juge d'instruction*).[43] The procureur's supervision of the investigation extends to responsibility for the conduct of the detention and interrogation of suspects in GAV. This supervision is often retrospective and depends heavily on a relationship of trust with the police: operating from a separate office and receiving all information from the police by telephone, the procureur is unable and unwilling to carry out any contemporaneous control over the conditions or conduct of the GAV, including the interrogation and general treatment of the suspect.[44] This is typical of many countries: the police are legally accountable to a judicial authority, but in practice function in a largely autonomous manner.[45] The defense function is understood

41 As these states emerged out of the Soviet bloc, the strengthening of due process rights and the independence of judges and prosecutors were key reforms alongside political democratic change. See further the contributions in Cape and Namoradze (2012).

42 See, e.g., the examples reported in the Legal Aid Reformers' Network "Salduz Watch" available at http://www.legalaidreform.org/police-station-legal-advice/salduz-watch.

43 Hodgson (2001, 2002a, 2002b, 2005).

44 Hodgson (2005); Soubise (2016).

45 The Dutch public prosecutor, for example, is responsible for supervising criminal enquiries but works at a distance from the police, who carry out all investigation tasks. Judge-led investigations

as an additional check on these procedures, rather than having equal status or presenting an opposing account.

The defense role has been slow to develop in countries such as France and has tended to center on representation at court. Although it is only recently that criminal lawyers have been allowed into the GAV, they were permitted into the *instruction* process from 1897. Judicial torture had been outlawed after the French Revolution, but concern remained at the vulnerability of the suspect, who was subject to a secret and written procedure and was obliged to face the all-powerful *juge d'instruction* alone. As an additional safeguard, the lawyer was given access to the case dossier twenty-four hours before any interrogation of the suspect and had the right to be present during the questioning of her client.[46] This was a controversial reform, criticized as undermining the effectiveness of the inquisitorial process in its search for the truth.

> [B]y obliging the *juge* to warn the accused at his first formal questioning that he is free to say nothing, by imposing the presence of a lawyer at all following interrogations, by, above all, constraining the *juge* to give the case file to the defence lawyer the day before every interrogation, this law paralyses the action of the judge who can barely hope, even himself, to discover the truth.[47]

However, the practice of what we might now term "rights avoidance" appears to be a well-established one: in order to avoid the involvement of the lawyer, the procureur developed an informal procedure of enquiry (and detention) together with the police, operating outside the *instruction*. This existed outside any formal regulation until 1958, when the GAV was legally recognized and subject to some statutory control. The significance of this has increased as investigations have moved out of the hands of the *juge d'instruction* and into those of the procureur; currently less than 2 percent of investigations are carried out under the authority of the *juge d'instruction*.[48] Despite the growing importance of the GAV, the lawyer was kept firmly out of the police station until 1993. Even after this reform, her role was modest: the suspect was permitted a thirty-minute private consultation

were abolished in 2013, but the investigating judge retains a role in supervising the investigation and the decisions of the prosecutor. See Blackstock et al. (2014: 100). The judicial status of the French prosecutor for the purposes of detention under Article 5(3) ECHR has been challenged successfully in the ECtHR. See *Medvedyev v. France* (3394/03) 29 March 2010, and then *Moulin v. France* (37104/06) 23 November 2010.

46 For a detailed account of the development of the role and status of the French legal profession, see Hodgson (2005: chap. 4).

47 Lemonde (1975) *Police et justice*, 71–72, cited by Salas (1991: 249).

48 See Lévy (1993) for an account of the decline of the *juge d'instruction* and the corresponding rise in the power of the procureur and the police.

with a lawyer, twenty hours into the detention period, but she was not permitted to have her lawyer present during police questioning.[49] She was also allowed to have a friend or family member informed of her detention and to be examined by a doctor. The procureur was required to be informed at the start of the GAV of the reasons for detention. The lawyer was entitled to know the nature of the offense for which the suspect was being held, but the suspect herself had no right to be told of the offense for which she was being held, nor of her right to silence.

Although limited, the entrance of the lawyer into the GAV was controversial—among the judiciary as much as the police.[50] The second half of the reform, which would have brought forward the suspect's right to custodial legal advice to the start of detention, was swiftly abandoned. Just as with the nineteenth-century reform of the *instruction*, the presence of a lawyer during the GAV was strongly resisted as undermining judicial supervision (here, of the procureur) and the effectiveness of the enquiry.[51] It was not until 2000 that the lawyer was finally allowed into the GAV from the start of detention, though still only for a half-hour consultation, and she remained excluded from being present during the suspect's police interrogation. The justice minister made clear that this did not represent a move toward an more adversarial process—the lawyer's role was cast in terms complementary to that of the procureur: she could support her client and make sure that the GAV was properly conducted, but she had no place getting involved in the case.[52]

After the relative high point of the 2000 reform,[53] the following years saw a retreat from this, notably under the influence of Nicolas Sarkozy as interior minister and then president. The obligation of the police to inform the suspect of her right to silence, first introduced in 2000, was then removed in 2003, and police powers were extended under an agenda strongly oriented toward security. As in Britain and elsewhere, this trend continued with increased criminalization, harsher sentences (especially for repeat offenders), a pulling back of due process,[54] and

[49] This delayed-access approach is seen elsewhere. In the Netherlands, for example, until the recent *Salduz* reforms, suspects were allowed to see a lawyer only after six hours.

[50] I was beginning my research in France when this reform was implemented in 1993 and remember protests by the judiciary outside the Ministry of Justice, with *magistrats* burning the Code de procédure pénale and denouncing the reform in terms similar to the objections to the lawyer's role in the *instruction* in 1897.

[51] See the extensive quotations for observations and interviews in Hodgson (2002a).

[52] See discussion in Hodgson (2005: 26–32 and chap. 4). The Delmas-Marty Commission (1991) and that chaired by Pierre Truche (1997) set the backdrop for these reforms, as did growing pressure from the ECtHR.

[53] See discussion in chapter 2. The defense was given greater rights to participate in the *instruction* by requesting the same acts of investigation as permitted for the procureur; the *juge des libertés et de la détention* was created, separating out the judicial function from that of investigation within the office of the *juge d'instruction*; and the principle of *contradictoire* was set out as a guiding philosophy in an introductory article to the Code de procédure pénale.

[54] E.g., in a wider range of serious offenses, longer detention, and longer delays to access to legal advice.

a preoccupation with dangerousness and its control.[55] Then came the Outreau scandal in 2005, concerning the large-scale investigation of a suspected pedophile ring in the northern French town of Outreau.[56] The case collapsed at trial, and there was a great deal of concern at the lack of robust and independent investigation by the young and inexperienced *juge d'instruction*, who was overly reliant on the prosecutor and unreceptive to the defense's requests for bail and for acts of investigation to be carried out. The commissions and enquiries that followed set out proposals to strengthen both the role of the defense and the effectiveness of the pretrial judicial function of the *juge d'instruction*, in order to guard against such mistakes happening again.

However, this case also laid the ground to advance the argument for the abolition of the *juge d'instruction*, whose political independence has long been a source of inconvenience for politicians and powerful business people who have found themselves the subjects of high-profile *instruction* investigations.[57] The *juge* in the Outreau case had demonstrated the dangers of placing so much power and authority in the hands of a single person, and so before the Outreau enquiry recommendations could be put into effect, President Sarkozy established the Léger Commission (the Comité de reflexion sur la justice pénale) with the express intention of abolishing the *juge d'instruction*,[58] though its official remit was to consider measures that would restore coherence to French criminal law and procedure (the Code de procédure pénale has increased greatly in length and complexity in recent decades), as well as being effective in addressing all forms of criminality and respecting the rights of victims and the accused.

When the commission reported in September 2009, as expected, it recommended the removal of the function of *juge d'instruction*, and the establishment of the procureur as the head of all criminal investigations.[59] There were also proposals for a modest strengthening of the rights of suspects by limiting the use of the GAV, requiring that interrogations be recorded and putting in place an alternative, shorter measure of detention. As discussed in chapter 2, the terms of the recommendations, however, demonstrated that little had changed in terms of

[55] See Lazerges (2012). See also discussion in chapter 3.

[56] Discussed in detail in chapter 8, this case was a major focus of enquiry and reform. It illustrated the myth of an independent, judicial, truth-centered enquiry, as the defense was denied any opportunity to participate and contribute to the investigation and the police accounts were accepted at face value. Children were questioned with no proper safeguards, and information lacking credibility was simply incorporated into the judicial dossier as evidence, without proper testing.

[57] See Hodgson (2010).

[58] Before the commission had reported, President Sarkozy announced his intention to abolish the *juge d'instruction* in his address at the formal reopening of the Cour de cassation on 7 January 2009. This prompted the resignation of two of the commission members.

[59] This was then abandoned after the cases of *Medvedyev v. France* (3394/03) 29 March 2010 and *Moulin v. France* (37104/06) 23 November 2010, which held that the procureur was not a judicial authority for the purpose of Article 5 ECHR.

the role allotted to the defense and its inevitable subordination to the efficiency of the investigation. Instead of giving suspects in all cases the rights enjoyed by those investigated through the *instruction* procedure, the proposals were to establish a two-tier system headed by the Parquet, where the gravity of the offense would trigger a slightly enhanced regime of rights. The result was a net loss of safeguards for the accused: fuller guarantees would continue only in the more serious tier (the *régime renforcé*) and not the ordinary investigations (the *régime simple*), and the additional protection of the independent *juge d'instruction* in serious cases would be removed completely.

The commission also put forward an alternative form of detention in which those not placed in GAV could be held, but with fewer rights. For more minor offenses (including those carrying a sentence of up to five years' imprisonment), where it is necessary to take a statement from the suspect, it proposed a "judicial retention" of six hours. The suspect would have the right to legal assistance at the outset, but this was seen as a less burdensome procedure. One can imagine that this would become standard procedure for all offenses punishable by five years' imprisonment or less, reducing the rights of the suspects and easily converted into a GAV if detention beyond six hours became necessary.[60] Although less burdensome for the police, the suspect would be unlikely to experience this detention as being any less coercive than detention in GAV.

The investigation and recommendations of this comprehensive commission of enquiry such a short time before the *Salduz* and the ECtHR case law that followed, are instructive. They allow us to appreciate the extent of the shift in legal culture that was required to reverse this trend and to implement the ECtHR's ruling. The Léger Commission explicitly addressed the possibility of the presence of the defense lawyer during the police interrogation of the suspect, and rejected the idea on the ground that this would undermine the effectiveness of the enquiry, given that the early part of the investigation is often key in uncovering the truth.[61] This was, of course, the same reasoning adopted by the ECtHR in *Salduz* when considering custodial legal advice to be essential: it is because the early part of the investigation is often key that the suspect's fair-trial rights, such as legal assistance, must be engaged fully. However, while both agreed on the crucial nature of the early part of the enquiry, Léger favored

[60] This six-hour detention was apparently inspired by the Dutch experience. My recent empirical study suggests that the six-hour detention imposes no real limitation on the police, who can very easily have the period extended if necessary or even convenient. See Blackstock et al. (2013). See also discussion in the following chapter re the revelation that more than twice as many people are held and questioned as "volunteers" than are placed in GAV, in order to avoid having to activate the full GAV safeguards.

[61] Allowing the lawyer access to the dossier was also opposed for the same reason. Only if the GAV extended beyond twenty-four hours did the commission propose allowing the lawyer to be present during the police interrogation of the suspect.

privileging the effectiveness of the investigation, while the ECtHR favored the protection of due process rights in ensuring a fair trial.[62]

D. Ushering In a More Effective Defense Role: The Impact of *Salduz*

Shortly after the Léger Commission reported, a number of significant Strasbourg decisions forced the French government to take a very different direction: to abandon the abolition of the *juge d'instruction* and to strengthen the suspect's right of access to legal assistance in a far more radical way. The ECtHR cases of *Medvedyev v. France*[63] and *Moulin v. France*[64] (discussed in chapter 4) effectively put a stop to the transfer of yet more investigative and judicial power to the procureur; and *Salduz v. Turkey*[65] provided authority for greater access to custodial legal advice, setting out clear norms that members of the Council of Europe were obliged to follow. France, like many other jurisdictions, however, sought to limit the impact of *Salduz* on the defense role and on wider criminal procedure.

Salduz was a seventeen-year-old man arrested and questioned by the anti-terrorism branch of the Izmir Security Directorate in May 2001 on suspicion of having participated in an unlawful demonstration in support of an illegal organization, namely the PKK (the Workers' Party of Kurdistan) and of hanging an illegal banner from a bridge in Bornova, Turkey, on 26 April 2001. When interrogated by the police without a lawyer present, he admitted the charges against him, but immediately retracted them in his statement to the investigating judge, claiming that they were obtained under duress and that he had been beaten and insulted by the police. He was convicted in December 2001, and his appeal against conviction was dismissed in March 2002. His case before the ECtHR was that the denial of custodial legal advice violated his defense rights under Article 6(3)(c) ECHR. In its judgment of 26 April 2007, the court held that there had been no such violation. Overall, the fairness of his trial had not been prejudiced by the lack of legal assistance during police custody as the applicant had been legally represented at trial, his confession was not the sole basis for his conviction, and he had been able to challenge the prosecution case at trial under conditions that did not place him at a substantial disadvantage vis-à-vis his opponent.

62 Subsequently, the Beaume Commission (2014: 59, 70) also favored a restricted defense role and resisted the idea of the defense conducting its own investigations—believing that this would result in the resources of the accused determining the quality of the investigation.

63 ECHR (Grand Chamber) (3394/03) 29 March 2010.

64 ECHR (37104/06) 23 February 2011.

65 ECHR (Grand Chamber) (36391/02) 27 November 2008.

However, the Grand Chamber reversed this judgment, underlining the significance of the initial police investigation in shaping the case, the vulnerability of suspects at this stage in the procedure, and therefore the importance of the assistance of a lawyer "whose task it is, among other things, to help to ensure respect of the right of an accused not to incriminate himself."[66] The right was held to be of particular importance in serious charges, where the penalties are heaviest. These are, of course, the very reasons why custodial legal advice has been resisted in so many jurisdictions. The initial investigation is crucial in evidential terms, and the presence of a lawyer threatens to interfere with the police's ability to gain admissions. Furthermore, provisions generally exist to delay access to a lawyer in the most serious offense cases.

Recognizing the implications at trial and the importance of an effective remedy, the court stated that "[t]he rights of the defence will in principle be irretrievably prejudiced when incriminating statements made during police interrogation without access to a lawyer are used for a conviction."[67] The concurring judgments underlined the need for access to legal advice at the start of detention, as well as during police questioning, in order to respect Article 6 ECHR. The continuing nature of the right to custodial legal advice is important. As discussed subsequently, with limited time and resources, there is a tendency for lawyers to focus on the interrogation and immediately before it, as the only point at which suspects require legal assistance. While it is undoubtedly vital to have a lawyer present during questioning, the suspect will need legal advice far in advance of this and on other matters pertaining to detention.

The role set out for the lawyer by the court is an active one, checking detention, gathering evidence, and organizing the defense. This is also spelled out very clearly in *Dayanan v. Turkey*[68] (discussed subsequently), but the spirit of these judgments is not reflected in the various *Salduz* reforms.[69] In France, legislation permits lawyers only a passive role, denying them any opportunity to challenge questions or to intervene. In many countries, lawyers are told little about the case or the evidence against the suspect, making difficult any detailed and meaningful advice on defense strategy, or indeed any check on the legality of procedures. Consultation times have also been limited to thirty minutes (in Belgium and the Netherlands, as well as France)—hardly enough to begin organizing the defense case and gathering evidence, in addition to assessing the needs of the suspect.[70]

[66] At para. 54.

[67] At para. 55.

[68] (7377/03) 13 October 2009. See paras. 30–34.

[69] The following chapter sets out the process by which reforms in France were eventually put in place.

[70] This has changed in some countries (but not yet France). See, e.g., the Belgian Cour constitutionelle belge 14 February 2013 No. 7/2013 ruling that more than thirty minutes should be permitted when requested. The decision also reinforced the sanctions for noncompliance—a

In many ECtHR cases, the right to a fair trial is viewed globally, taking account of the procedure as a whole. Breaches of Article 6 may not result in an unfair trial if due process rights are adhered to later on in the procedure. Indeed, this was the initial approach of the court in *Salduz*. The subsequent judgment of the Grand Chamber, however, was much more robust, singling out the right to legal assistance as fundamental, a breach of which could not, in principle, be remedied subsequently. The court made clear that the initial breach of Article 6 ECHR could not be cured by subsequent legal representation: "[E]ven though the applicant had the opportunity to challenge the evidence against him at the trial and subsequently on appeal, the absence of a lawyer while he was in police custody irretrievably affected his defense rights."[71] This is important: the argument of many jurisdictions has been that the range of other safeguards in place makes custodial legal advice unnecessary.[72] The *Salduz* judgment rejects this approach in the clearest terms: legal assistance from the start of police detention and during police interrogation must be provided in all cases, whatever safeguards are provided subsequently.

In *Panovits v. Cyprus* the court again ruled that the failure to allow the applicant access to legal advice during police interrogation breached Article 6 ECHR, and this was not remedied by subsequent proceedings.[73] The court said (at para. 66):

> [T]he concept of fairness enshrined in Article 6 requires that the accused be given the benefit of the assistance of a lawyer already at the initial stages of police interrogation. The lack of legal assistance during an applicant's interrogation would constitute a restriction of his defence rights in the absence of compelling reasons that do not prejudice the overall fairness of the proceedings.

This development has been reinforced through subsequent judgments. In *Dayanan v. Turkey*[74] the court reiterated that the right to legal assistance from the start of police custody is one of the fundamental elements of a fair trial, which

conviction cannot be based on evidence obtained through interrogation without a lawyer. Suspects not under arrest should also be informed that they may leave at any time.

[71] At para. 62.

[72] As well as the more inquisitorial jurisdictions of France and the Netherlands, Ireland continued to make this argument in rejecting the fact of a constitutional right to have a lawyer present during police questioning. See *DPP v. Doyle*.

[73] *Panovits v. Cyprus* (4268/04) 11 March 2009. Panovits, aged seventeen, was questioned in relation to robbery and homicide, without the presence of a lawyer, or being informed of his right to a lawyer. He was charged with robbery and manslaughter and claimed that he had been deceived and pressured into making an admission. He was subsequently convicted and his appeal was unsuccessful.

[74] (7377/03) 13 October 2009. See paras. 30–34.

cannot be suspended, even in the most serious cases such as terrorism. In this case, the applicant had been arrested on terrorism charges and had exercised his right to silence. Under Turkish law, he was not entitled to consult with a lawyer until the end of police custody. The Turkish government argued that because the applicant had exercised his right to silence, the absence of a lawyer had not affected the observance of his defense rights under Article 6(1) and 6(3)(c) ECHR. This of course side steps the fundamental issue, that the statutory provisions denying access to a lawyer are themselves in breach of Article 6 ECHR.[75] It also suggests a restricted defense role, centering on presence during police interrogation, which while important, constitutes only part of the suspect's right to legal assistance. Finding a clear breach of Article 6 ECHR, the court rejected this narrow view of the right to legal assistance:

> [A]n accused person is entitled, as soon as he or she is taken into custody, to be assisted by a lawyer, and not only while being questioned. . . . Indeed the fairness of the proceedings requires that an accused be able to obtain the whole range of services specifically associated with legal counsel. In this regard, counsel has to be able to secure without restriction the fundamental aspects of that person's defence: discussion of the case, organisation of the defence, collection of evidence favourable to the accused, preparation for questioning, support of an accused in distress and checking of their conditions of detention.[76]

In *Pishchalnikov v. Russia*[77] the court again ruled that police interrogation of a suspect without a lawyer present breached Article 6, noting the vulnerability of suspects when questioned. In this case, the government asserted that the suspect had implicitly waived his right to legal assistance by confessing his guilt after having been warned of his right not to make self-incriminating statements. The court did not accept this, noting that

> if it is to be effective for Convention purposes, a waiver of the right [to a lawyer] must be established in an unequivocal manner and be attended by minimum standards commensurate to its importance. . . . A waiver of this right . . . must not only be voluntary, but must also constitute a knowing and intelligent relinquishment of a right. Before an accused can be said to have implicitly, through

[75] Compare also the approach of the courts in the first years after the statutory right to legal advice was introduced in England and Wales. It was argued that previous experience of custodial legal advice or the exercise of defense rights demonstrated that the suspect's interests had not been harmed by any breach in procedure. See discussion of *R v. Dunford* (1990) 91 Crim. App. R. 150 in Hodgson (1992).

[76] At para. 32.

[77] (7025/04) 24 September 2009.

> his conduct, waived an important right under Article 6, it must be shown that he could reasonably have foreseen what the consequences of his conduct would be.[78]

Underlining the importance of the lawyer in ensuring the respect of the suspect's rights, the court went on:

> [A]fter initially being advised of his rights, an accused may himself validly waive his rights and respond to interrogation. However, the Court strongly indicates that additional safeguards are necessary when the accused asks for counsel because if an accused has no lawyer, he has less chance of being informed of his rights and, as a consequence, there is less chance they will be respected.[79]

These decisions set out unequivocally, as a requirement of Article 6 ECHR, the right to legal assistance for suspects held in police custody from the start of detention and during interrogation.[80] They articulate a model of legal assistance available to all, any waiver of which must be with full knowledge of the consequences and any denial of which must be exceptional and based on compelling reasons in the particular case.

More recent case law has pulled back a little from this robust reasoning and adopted a less protective approach, by emphasizing more strongly the need to consider the fairness of the proceedings overall. *Ibrahim and others v. UK*[81] was the first case in which the court found that there were "compelling reasons" to justify restricting access to legal assistance. Three of the four applicants were suspected of carrying out the failed suicide bomb attacks in London on 21 July 2005, two weeks after the 7/7 bombings in London killed fifty-two people.[82] They were questioned in the absence of a lawyer during a safety interview, conducted immediately after they arrived at the police station, to ascertain if there was a

[78] At para. 77. See also *Panovits v. Cyprus* (4268/04) 11 March 2009, para. 68.

[79] At para. 78.

[80] See also *Brusco v. France* (1466/07) 14 October 2010 (in French only), in which France was condemned for the failure of the police to tell the suspect of his right to silence (Brusco had been treated as a witness, but the ECtHR noted that he was in fact a suspect, having been directly accused of involvement in the offense) and the failure to allow him a lawyer from the outset of detention and during his interrogation by the police.

[81] (50541/08, 50571/08, 50573/08, 40351/09) 13 September 2016.

[82] Muktar Said Ibrahim, Ramzi Mohammed, and Yassin Omar. The fourth man, Ismail Abdurahman, was suspected of having assisted a fourth bomber. He was initially questioned as a witness. The court found that when it emerged that he had assisted a fourth bomber, he should have been cautioned and dealt with as a suspect, including ensuring access to legal advice. Restricting his access to a lawyer was not justified, and a breach of Article 6 ECHR was found. However, the court found that it did not necessarily follow that Abdurahman was wrongly convicted, as the outcome of the trial, had no breach occurred, was unknown.

continuing danger to the public. Their responses were used in evidence at the trial. The court found that there were compelling reasons for the temporary restriction of their right to legal advice and that overall the proceedings were fair.

In condemning unjustified denials of legal assistance, even when no incriminating statements were made or used, earlier cases have separated out the provision of legal assistance requirement from the harm caused and the remedy to deter such practices. The question in *Ibrahim* was whether, despite the justification for refusing legal assistance, it was fair to use the resulting statements in evidence against the accused. The court decided that such statements could be used, which risks opening the door to using evidence obtained without a lawyer and appears to move away from the terms of *Salduz* and what the Council of Europe has described as "a kind of rebuttable presumption of a violation of Article 6 ECHR" where access to legal assistance is restricted.[83] *Salduz* stated quite clearly:

> Even where compelling reasons may exceptionally justify denial of access to a lawyer, such restriction—whatever its justification—must not unduly prejudice the rights of the accused under Article 6. . . . The rights of the defence will in principle be irretrievably prejudiced when incriminating statements made during police interrogation without access to a lawyer are used for a conviction.[84]

However, the court in *Ibrahim* also stated that the absence of compelling reasons did not in itself lead to a violation of Article 6. Here too, the court must (through "a very strict scrutiny") determine whether, overall, the trial was fair.[85] This represents a retreat from the more robust reasoning in earlier cases, which rejected the idea of weighing in the balance the prejudice to the accused.[86]

The following year, in the case of *Simeonovi v. Bulgaria*,[87] the court again declined to find a breach of Article 6 when the applicant had not been provided with access to a lawyer while held in police custody for three days. Because the conviction was not based on any admission made during that time, but on his

[83] *Opinion of the Secretariat on the Proposal for a Directive of the European Parliament and of the Council on "the right of access to a lawyer in criminal proceedings and on the right to communicate upon arrest,"* Council of Europe, Strasbourg, 20 September 2012, paras. 18 and 19.

[84] *Salduz v. Turkey*, para. 55.

[85] *Ibrahim and others*, para. 265.

[86] Fair Trials International has argued that the test should be whether or not the accused has been prejudiced by not having a lawyer, even if this restriction is justified. It should not look at the extent of the prejudice or attempt to assess the strength of the evidence against the accused. Written comments submitted with leave to intervene in *Beuze v. Belgium* (71409/10) 9 November 2018, heard on 20 December 2017, available at https://www.fairtrials.org/wp-content/uploads/2017/11/171020-Beuze-v-Belgium-Intervention.pdf.

[87] *Simeonovi v. Bulgaria* (21980/04) 12 May 2017.

later confession made in the presence of his lawyer,[88] as well as "a whole body of consistent evidence,"[89] which was examined at three levels of court jurisdiction, the overall fairness of the proceedings had not been irretrievably prejudiced.[90] This appears a retrograde step. Would the decision have been the same had the incriminating evidence been less strong? While no written statements were made or relied upon from the applicant's initial three-day detention, holding a person in custody without access to a lawyer is unlawful, yet carried no consequences. Nor did the court consider the purpose of holding the applicant in this way or the effect of such detention on a suspect, despite understanding the vulnerability of detainees in the first hours and days of custody.[91] Making the finding of a breach of Article 6 contingent on the effect upon the accused of breaking the rules weakens significantly the protection of the safeguard and represents a backward step from the confidence of the decision in *Salduz*.

In a third case, *Beuze v. Belgium*, Beuze was questioned five times by the police, three times by the investigating judge, and twice by the prosecutor, all without having a lawyer present.[92] Charged with several offenses, including murder, he made statements that substantially affected his position and were included in evidence.[93] He was convicted of murder. The court found a violation of Article 6(1) and (3)(c), but following the reasoning in *Ibrahim* rather than in *Salduz*, it separated out explicitly the questions of whether there were compelling reasons to restrict access to a lawyer, and whether the proceedings overall were fair. The court found that there was no compelling reason to withhold legal assistance, but this alone did not constitute a violation of Article 6. Acknowledging that this "weighs heavily in the balance when assessing the overall fairness of the criminal proceedings and may tip the balance towards finding a violation," the court held that it was still open to the government "to demonstrate convincingly why, exceptionally and in the specific circumstances of the case, the overall fairness of the criminal proceedings was not irretrievably prejudiced by the restriction on access to a lawyer."[94] It found that "the criminal

[88] Once provided with a lawyer, he remained silent during two interviews (on 6 and 12 October 1999) but then voluntarily confessed in the presence of his lawyer on 21 October 1999.

[89] This included "the statements of a large number of witnesses who had been questioned during the assessment of the case, the results of ballistic, technical and accountants' reports and medical and psychiatric opinions and also on the physical and documentary evidence gathered" (para. 142). Simeonovi was convicted of armed robbery and murder.

[90] Based on the conditions of the applicant's detention and the length and severe regime of his sentence, the court did find a breach of Article 3.

[91] See also *Krivoshey v. Ukraine* (7433/05) 23 June 2016.

[92] *Beuze v. Belgium* (71409/10) 9 November 2018.

[93] For statements to be regarded as self-incriminating it is sufficient for them to have substantially affected the accused's position. *Schmid-Laffer v. Switzerland* (41269/08) 16 June 2015, para. 37; *A. T. v. Luxembourg* (30460/13) 9 April 2015, para. 72, available at https://www.fairtrials.org/wp-content/uploads/AT-v-LUX-Intervention.pdf.

[94] At para. 145.

proceedings brought against the applicant, when considered as a whole, did not cure the procedural defects occurring at the pretrial stage."[95] In particular, the Belgian court had failed to examine how the statements had been taken, and in focusing only on police custody, had failed to consider the impact of the lawyer's absence on the wider defense rights of the accused. This takes us further away from protections of *Salduz*, introducing a much stronger emphasis on the balancing approach adopted in *Ibrahim* and so the possibility that accused persons might be convicted on the basis of evidence obtained when the suspect has wrongly been denied access to a lawyer during police detention and interrogation.

Meanwhile, at the national level, states have resisted applying the *Salduz* jurisprudence in their own legal processes. These were not decisions addressed only to the respondent state; they set out universal principles applicable to all members of the Council of Europe. Yet, because the decisions challenge the relatively diminished role allotted to the defense in most inquisitorially rooted and mixed procedures, states have attempted to distinguish their own procedures from the scope of the judgments. In addition to resistance at the judicial and executive levels, there have been practical difficulties in making the changes effective, in particular ensuring the availability of qualified and experienced advisers who are able to provide an effective defense, backed by state funding to guarantee that the right to custodial legal advice is accessible and so effective for all suspects.[96] But while reforms requiring custodial legal assistance have eventually been put in place, jurisdictions are inconsistent in their approach to the use that can be made of statements made in breach of this requirement. Some favor automatic exclusion, but many do not.[97] *Salduz* has had an enormous impact, both at national and EU levels, but this has been restricted to the scope of custodial legal advice. Wider transformation of the defense role, even during this initial investigation phase, has been resisted. In France, a stronger defense is equated with a shift to a more accusatorial procedure, which is considered undesirable and likely to result in inequalities of treatment depending on the economic resources of the accused.[98]

95 At para. 193.

96 Discussed in detail in the following chapter. See also Giannoulopoulos (2018), who reports that while Greece has fairly progressive laws in place re custodial legal advice, *Salduz* has had no real impact in moving debate on or improving the rights of suspects or the quality of defense assistance. Legal aid is also a major concern in ensuring the provision of legal assistance. For discussion of the importance of legal aid in ensuring fair trial rights through defence provision, see Flynn et al. (2016).

97 See written comments submitted by Fair Trials International with leave to intervene in *A. T. v. Luxembourg*, a. See also Soo (2017).

98 See Beaume (2014: 70). These are the same arguments advanced in the 1990s to resist any move allowing suspects access to lawyers even outside the interrogation. See Hodgson (2005: especially 131–141).

E. Consolidating Procedural Safeguards: The EU Road Map

Although drawing principally on ECHR fair-trial rights, the recent program of EU measures goes further, fleshing out what those rights mean in practice and so providing additional protection, as well as potentially stronger mechanisms of enforcement. This strengthens defense rights in new and significant ways—normative and detailed standards are set out through pan-European, top-down mechanisms, rather than broad benchmarks that are then left to individual states to implement in different ways or not at all.[99] This is both the strength of the approach and the reason why it is resisted.

A program of measures to strengthen procedural safeguards for suspects was set out in the 2009 "road map," presented by the Swedish presidency. The first, and perhaps the least controversial, measure was the right to interpretation and translation in criminal proceedings, adopted by the European Parliament in October 2010, implemented in all member states by October 2013—including the UK, which chose to opt in to this measure.[100] The second measure, also opted in to by the UK, concerned the right to information in criminal proceedings and was adopted in May 2012, implemented at the national level by June 2014.[101] This requires member states to inform suspects and accused persons of their right to legal assistance, including the conditions under which it is available free of charge; the right to be informed of the accusation; the right to interpretation and translation; and the right to remain silent. On arrest, it requires suspects to be provided with a letter of rights, setting out the right to access case materials; to have consular authorities and one person informed of their detention; to have access to urgent medical assistance; to know how long a person can be detained before being brought before a judge; and to be given information on challenging the lawfulness of arrest, on reviewing detention, and on requesting release.[102]

The third measure, adopted in October 2013, is the right to legal assistance.[103] This was the most contentious, as, although seeking only to strengthen existing principles rather than to create new rights, it nevertheless posed the greatest challenge to existing national procedures. The impact of *Salduz* served to ease its path to some extent, but as discussed in the following chapter, countries have varied in their interpretation of what this line of jurisprudence requires in terms

[99] See discussion of ECtHR and EU approaches in chapter 1. See also Hodgson (2012) for some reflections on this top-down approach.

[100] Directive 2010/64/EU.

[101] Directive 2012/13/EU.

[102] The UK also adopted other measures such as the European Protection Order, introduced by EC Directive 2011/99/EU.

[103] See also *Impact assessment accompanying the proposal for a directive of the European Parliament and of the Council on the rights of access to a lawyer and of notification of custody to a third person in criminal proceedings*. COM(2011) 326 final.

of length of consultation, the presence and role of legal assistance during police interrogation, as well as opportunities to delay access to legal advice.[104] In short, Europe was not agreed on the precise scope of the right set out in *Salduz*, making agreement on the detail and scope of an EU measure difficult to negotiate. Member states disagreed over the point at which the right to legal assistance should become available to a suspect, whether it should apply in cases of minor offenses (and what is considered "minor"),[105] the extent of the right and the remedies for any breach. Significantly, although there was criticism that the proposal failed to take account of procedural differences and the varying nature and stages of criminal proceedings, resistance did not center on these differences in procedural tradition. A group of five countries expressed shared concerns around the impact of custodial legal assistance on the effectiveness of the investigation, as well as the resource implications of greater lawyer involvement.[106] Exceptions and qualifications continued to be added to the draft directive, allowing certain features of the right to be determined according to national law. To some extent, this served to dilute the measure and to introduce greater scope for national variation—the very thing that the measure is designed to prevent.

For example, additional discretion as to how legal advice is provided has been incorporated, with the general proviso that it should not prejudice the effective exercise or essence of the right of suspects or accused persons to meet or communicate with their lawyer. However, this still allows for substantial differences in the arrangements made in different jurisdictions, as discussed in the following chapter. Advice can be provided by telephone or videoconferencing in some instances,[107] and member states are permitted to determine the length and frequency of the private consultation with the lawyer.[108] Research demonstrates that

[104] The European Commission recognized this explicitly in preparing for the new directive. See European Commission (2011: para. 3.4.2).

[105] Other than in proceedings before a criminal court, the directive does not apply to very minor offenses where deprivation of liberty cannot be imposed as a sanction (recital 17 and Art 2(4)), nor in matters where an authority other than a court is competent to impose sanctions other than deprivation of liberty (recital 16). This applies potentially to a huge number of cases. Some have argued that this is incompatible with the ECHR as demonstrated in *Jussila v. Finland* (75053/01) 23 November 2006 (Grand Chamber judgment). The German Federal Bar and the Council of Europe have drawn attention to this. In its opinion on the draft directive in September 2012, the Council of Europe expressed concern at the suggestion to exclude minor offenses not entailing a deprivation of liberty. Deprivation of liberty is not a precondition to the right to legal assistance. In order to avoid being out of step with future ECtHR jurisprudence, the Council suggested a more dynamic approach, "explicitly linking the draft Directive's scope of application and safeguards to those of Article 6 ECHR" (*Opinion of the Secretariat on the Proposal for a Directive of the European Parliament and of the Council on "the right of access to a lawyer in criminal proceedings and on the right to communicate upon arrest,"* Council of Europe, Strasbourg, 20 September 2012, para. 11).

[106] Belgium, France, Ireland, the Netherlands, and the United Kingdom were the five countries that, while accepting the importance of access to a lawyer as part of the fair-trial rights of an accused, challenged the terms of the proposed directive in a note dated 22 September 2011. 2011/0154 (COD). See discussion in Jackson (2016b).

[107] Recitals 23 and 24 of the directive.

[108] Recital 22.

lawyers attending suspects in police detention are often meeting them for the first time and with little case-related information.[109] Typically the suspect is permitted a half-hour consultation with the lawyer. This is wholly inadequate to advise the suspect of the procedures that apply, to describe her options during and after interrogation, and to gather key information for the defense. In order to work effectively, suspect and lawyer need to establish a good rapport and to build a degree of trust. This is both important and difficult, given the stressful circumstances in which their meeting takes place. Typically, it can take thirty minutes or more just for the lawyer to introduce herself; to explain why she is here, what she knows of the case, and what her professional role is; and to take down some basic biographical information from the suspect. She will then need to note down the suspect's account of the events leading up to arrest and detention. This can be quite straightforward, but often it is not, and the length of time it will take will depend on whether there is some dispute as to the alleged offense or the circumstances of the arrest, as well as the gravity and the complexity of the case, and the physical and psychological state of the suspect. If lawyers are permitted only thirty minutes, they will provide only standardized advice, and the effectiveness of the safeguard of legal assistance will be undermined.[110] They will be unable to provide the kind of defense advice anticipated by the ECtHR in *Dayanan v. Turkey*.[111]

The directive was also amended so that member states are permitted to regulate the participation of the lawyer during the police interrogation of the suspect, in accordance with procedures under national law.[112] This is a major concern in France and the Netherlands, where lawyers are present in interviews, but must remain passive throughout: any questions must be posed at the end of the interrogation. This prevents any engagement with the interrogation and makes it impossible to challenge improper questioning or to support the suspect in her articulation of events. There is also provision for temporary derogation from the right to a lawyer, including on the grounds of geographical remoteness,[113] or where there is an urgent need to avert serious adverse consequences for the life, liberty, or physical integrity of a person.[114] Other concerns center on how much

[109] McConville and Hodgson (1993); McConville et al. (1994); Blackstock et al. (2013).

[110] This mirrors some of what happens at court when duty lawyers must take on cases at short notice with only basic information about the prosecution case and a very short time in which to take instructions.

[111] 7377/03, 13 October 2009. See paras. 30–34.

[112] Recital 25—again, provided this does not prejudice the effective exercise and essence of the right concerned.

[113] Recital 30 and Article 3(5) Directive.

[114] Recital 31 and Article 3(6) Directive. This was the case in the ECtHR case *Ibrahim and others v. UK* (50541/08, 50571/08, 50573/08, 40351/09) 13 September 2016. An earlier version of the directive also included a perverse echo of the *Salduz* formulation of the importance of the right to legal assistance. Article 3(5)(b) of the draft directive allowed for temporary derogation from the right of access to a lawyer "where giving access to a lawyer or delaying the investigation would irretrievably

the police should disclose to the lawyer in order that she can advise effectively, while also respecting the need to progress the investigation.[115] In sum, the nature and scope of the defense role remain underdeveloped.

As an EU measure, there are stronger enforcement mechanisms than for the implementation of ECtHR decisions. However, the directive is based on the principle of mutual recognition, and so the extent to which it can, or indeed aims to, harmonize the laws of the member states toward uniform protections is limited.[116] For the most part it consolidates the ECtHR jurisprudence through setting minimum standards. The danger is that the repeated reference to national laws undermines the objective of harmonizing standards even in a broad sense, and of promoting consistency in implementation. And while *Salduz* set out clearly the requirement that statements made without access to a lawyer should not be used as evidence against the accused, the directive expresses this in much weaker terms: in assessing the value of such statements, the court need only take into account the rights of the accused and the fairness of the proceedings.

Where states have restrictive rules on lawyer participation, or ineffective remedies for breaches of the directive,[117] the rights and protections of suspects and accused persons will differ, undermining the objectives of the directive and weakening mutual trust and recognition. In some instances, it will enable poor practices that do not conform to the *Salduz* line of jurisprudence. As various jurisdictions interpret and apply the directive, it is also unclear whether the underlying objectives support the lawyer playing a more active role, as outlined in *Dayanan*, or whether the defense function is limited to contributing to existing procedural safeguards to ensure the legality of detention. It is well recognized that custodial legal advice promotes the effectiveness of other procedural safeguards (such as the right to silence) as well as assisting the suspect to make

prejudice an on-going investigation." One can imagine that the interpretation of this might well have depended on the prevailing legal and professional cultures and who was allowed to make this decision—the police, a prosecutor, or an independent judge. Draft directive as set out in the Council of the European Union *Progress Report*, 3 December 2012, 16521/12.

115 For discussion of police reasoning and possible consequences for the suspect, see Sukumar, Hodgson, and Wade (2016b); Sukumar, Wade, and Hodgson (2016). Permitting counsel full access to the case file was rejected in *A. T. v. Luxembourg*.

116 The idea of mutual recognition is that national measures, such as a judicial decision within a member state, are recognized in all other member states and have the same or similar effects there. This removes the need to create standard procedures that all member states would have to agree upon and work with—a requirement that would, in practice, paralyze cooperation. In this way states are able to work together effectively, but "with a minimum of procedure and formality." Ministère de la justice (1999: 89). See also Skinner (2002).

117 Article 12 of the right to counsel Directive 2013/48/EU leaves it to states to provide an effective remedy where rights are breached. Given the different procedures and traditions across Europe it is likely that this will be understood differently. For an account of the different remedies provided by member states, see Soo (2018).

key decisions affecting her defense, such as determining whether or not to respond to police questions.[118] A number of authors have argued that ECtHR case law and EU directives promote a model of defense participation that is not rooted in procedural models, but in broader fair-trial concepts, such as that of equality of arms.[119] And finally, there is an implicit assumption that tying EU measures to ECtHR jurisprudence, together with the standard nonregression clauses, will promote the development of fair-trial rights. However, if the ECtHR jurisprudence itself regresses,[120] it will be vital for national courts to uphold the autonomy of EU standards and not allow them to slip back also.

Suspects in England and Wales have enjoyed a right to legal assistance during police detention and interrogation since the mid-1980s. Yet, despite the clear influence on EU measures of the framework of safeguards in England and Wales under PACE, Britain did not opt into the directive, fearing "quite adverse and costly impacts on the ability effectively to investigate and prosecute offenders were the Commission proposal to be adopted."[121] While supporting the procedural rights in the road map and the need to "build on the rights already guaranteed by the ECHR and provide additional reassurance that the rights [are] being given practical effect in all Member States,"[122] the government has stated that it does not think there are "good practical and policy reasons" to go beyond the standards of the ECHR. Rather than opt in and negotiate over its concerns (or indeed ensure that important protections are not diluted), the UK has left this to other member states—and will probably do so on a permanent basis following Brexit.

[118] Hodgson (2016b).

[119] For further discussion of protective and participatory defense roles see Jackson and Summers (2012); Jackson (2016a); Soo (2017); Pivaty (2018).

[120] This is arguably the case re the use of evidence obtained from suspects denied legal assistance following *Ibrahim* and cases following that line of argument, discussed previously.

[121] Parliamentary Under-Secretary of State for Justice, Jonathon Djanogly, House of Commons Debate, *Hansard* 7 September 2011, col. 503.

[122] Djanogly, col. 503.

7
Custodial Legal Advice
Toward a Pan-European Model?

A. Introduction

With the gradual disappearance of the trial as a means of disposing of cases, at the same time as the scope of criminalization continues to expand, evidence gained during the suspect's detention and investigation is often determinative. It is no longer realistic to regard police questioning as an initial, preparatory, or unimportant phase of proceedings, to which minimal safeguards attach. Evidence obtained through custodial interrogation is central to case disposition, with or without trial, and so procedural protections traditionally reserved for court are increasingly required during this pretrial phase if the accused is to be dealt with according to the standards of a fair trial. This necessitates a cultural as well as legal shift in how states understand the adjudicatory phase of criminal proceedings and its backward reach to include significant aspects of the investigation.[1]

In representing the interests of her client, therefore, the lawyer has a vital role in securing the first stages of the defense case and ensuring the suspect's version of events is neither overlooked nor disregarded, as well as providing an additional check on police behavior, ensuring the proper treatment of the detainee and an appropriate outcome at the end of the custody period.[2] The degree to which she is expected to do each of these things may differ across procedural traditions according to the distribution of legal personnel and their responsibilities. She might be expected to be proactive in case building as well as process oversight within an adversarial-type procedure, whereas her role has been cast in more adjunct terms in inquisitorial traditions, where responsibility for the protection of the interests of the accused is also vested in prosecutors and judges, and the lawyer's role serves to complement rather than to challenge that of the judge and prosecutor.

[1] See also Jackson (2016a).

[2] Increasingly complex procedural rules around the gathering and use of evidence, such as detention times for serious offenses and the implications of exercising silence, amplify the vulnerability of the suspect, making the lawyer's role even more crucial, as acknowledged by the ECtHR. See, e.g., *Beuze v. Belgium* (71409/10) 9 November 2018, §127.

The Metamorphosis of Criminal Justice. Jacqueline S. Hodgson, Oxford University Press (2020).

DOI: 10.1093/oso/9780199981427.001.0001

In practice, adversarially rooted procedures do not necessarily envisage the intervention of the defense during the police interrogation of the suspect as a necessary part of the lawyer's pretrial function: England and Wales are unusual in having developed a more proactive defense role at the outset of the investigation. In the United States, for example, although ubiquitous through film and TV representations, *Miranda* rights have little impact in practice and suspects rarely receive legal assistance,[3] with suspects in Canada faring little better.[4] Suspects in Scotland had no right to have a lawyer present during police questioning prior to *Salduz*, and those in Ireland have had the right removed in 2017, just three years after suspects were first allowed legal assistance during their police interview.[5] The defense role is reflected more clearly in the later stages of the case and in the public setting of the courtroom in particular, but in the murky and uncertain reaches of police custody, the place of the defense is less established even in procedures understood to be party centered.

In establishing transnational benchmarks for pretrial defense representation as part of fair-trial standards, the ECtHR and subsequent EU directive imagine a proactive role for defense lawyers,[6] but in practice, the ability of the lawyer to act during police and judicial investigations continues to be limited: establishing a universal right to legal assistance that operates across jurisdictions and within different procedural traditions and different structures of investigative supervision poses real challenges.[7] This was seen in the process of framing the legal parameters of custodial legal advice in an EU measure in a way that would be acceptable to all member states, as discussed in the preceding chapter. But it is in the transposition of these supranational norms into domestic law and practice that we see more clearly the tensions between the aspiration toward universal standards, and the realities of entrenched procedural and legal cultural differences—not only in those aspects of practice left explicitly to member states,[8] but also in the interpretation of more general provisions. The effectiveness of legal assistance in practice will depend not only on the actions of the lawyer, but

[3] Weisselberg (2017); Skinns (2019).

[4] See, e.g., King and Snook (2009) and re Australia see Skinns (2019); Dixon and Travis (2007).

[5] In *DPP v. Gormley* [2014] IESC 17, the Irish Supreme Court extended the right to legal assistance from consultation to allowing presence in police interrogation. However, *DPP v. Doyle* [2017] IESC 1 reversed this, holding that there was no constitutional right to have a lawyer present during police questioning.

[6] Jackson (2016a: 988) argues that the ECtHR's success in promoting access to custodial legal advice "can be attributed to the court founding it upon the well-established privilege against self-incrimination. But . . . the privilege against self-incrimination does not explain the more active defence role that the court and the EU institutions would seem to envisage."

[7] See further Hodgson (2011, 2019).

[8] Such as the provision in Article 12 of the directive for "an effective remedy in national law in the event of a breach of the rights in this Directive," or arrangements to ensure the suspects can communicate with her lawyer (recitals 22 and 23) and have the lawyer "present and participate effectively when questioned by the police" (recital 25).

also on those of other legal actors, the other safeguards in place, the prevailing legal and occupational cultures, and the ways in which rights are administered to suspects. Legal advice is not a one-size-fits-all model.[9]

In order that defense rights are practical and effective, not simply theoretical or illusory,[10] in addition to a strong legal regulatory framework enforced by the courts, lawyers themselves must grasp the opportunity to provide assistance and representation and, where possible, engage with the case investigation. This active or participatory model is not as simple as it may seem. First, legal reforms must be drafted in ways that allow for proactive defense lawyering, rather than limiting the lawyer's role to that of an additional check or procedural verification.[11] Second, lawyers require additional training. Police station advice work is very different from court advocacy or advising clients in the office. It is unpredictable and requires decisions to be made quickly, often with little case-related information. In the more formal environment of the courtroom the lawyer's role is respected and her value in assisting other legal actors in the efficient processing of cases is acknowledged.[12] Police station work, on the other hand, can be confrontational, necessitating the lawyer to challenge police decisions and assert the rights of the suspect. As police territory, the police station tolerates lawyers but rarely welcomes them.[13] Neither is detention in police custody the

[9] This is also true at the level of advice provision. Aside from the offense being investigated, the needs of suspects differ, especially those with one or more vulnerabilities. The needs of a twelve-year-old are not the same as those of a seventeen-year-old; nor can all mental disorders or learning disabilities be treated in the same way. In England and Wales, children and young people, those with a mental disorder, and those with a learning disability are deemed "vulnerable." Detention and interrogation procedures are identical to those for all suspects, but with the addition of an "appropriate adult" who may be a family member, friend, health or social care professional, or volunteer. There is no training requirement, and standards of assistance vary widely. See Hodgson and Kemp (2015); Kemp and Hodgson (2016); Pierpoint (2008); Hodgson (1997). This is a narrow definition of vulnerability—there are many other ways in which young people, for example, are vulnerable and in need of additional protection, such as children in care, or recently leaving care, victims of child sexual exploitation, and so on. Neither is this a model that takes into account of overlapping vulnerabilities. Recent amendments to PACE COP C now provide more guidance on vulnerability in section 1.13(d), though still centering on the existence of a mental health condition or a mental disorder.

[10] As emphasized in ECtHR judgments such as *Imbrioscia v. Switzerland* (13972/88) 22 November 1993, at para. 38.

[11] In France, for example, the lawyer's role was until recently understood as one of moral (rather than legal) support, and so her presence in police interrogation of the suspect was not considered necessary. This is unconvincing even on its own terms: presence in interrogation would provide important moral support (to remain silent, for example) as well as legal support. The continuing ways in which the lawyer's role is stifled in countries such as France and the Netherlands is discussed in the course of this chapter.

[12] The growth of duty solicitor work in England and Wales from the 1970s was testament to this. Lawyers have professionalized the criminal process in a way that makes it run more smoothly and efficiently for other legal actors. The unrepresented defendant is like an actor with a walk-on part who has not been given her lines, while everyone else performs the same play with the same script every day. See Hodgson (2006c). On mandatory legal assistance in former Soviet bloc jurisdictions, see Cape and Namoradze (2012: 419–420).

[13] McConville et al. (1994); Skinns (2011).

ideal environment in which to take instructions. Suspects are often anxious, confused, and angry, and getting a clear account on which to base advice can be difficult.[14] Third, it requires lawyers to create new ways of working and of organizing themselves, often in collaborative ways through the local bar or duty schemes, in order to be available twenty-four hours a day, seven days a week. This poses practical challenges in balancing availability for police station advice, which might take place during the night, with office work and court advocacy. Fourth, sufficient public funding needs to be made available and administered in a way that ensures those with adequate knowledge and training are paid to attend suspects in custody.

Finally, lawyers need to understand themselves in this new, more proactive role. This can involve a significant shift in professional culture. In France, despite increased defense rights during the *instruction* phase, lawyers have been slow to break away from a culture of judicial subordination, and for more than a decade there was little pushback against the very limited right of suspects detained more than twenty hours to see a lawyer for thirty minutes, with no right to have their lawyer present during police questioning.[15] In Scotland, lawyers' decision to advise silence in nearly all cases has led them to prefer telephone advice to presence during the police interrogation of the suspect.[16] Even greater adjustments are required where professional cultures reflect and have been shaped by centralized forms of political control. In former Soviet bloc jurisdictions, the state-centered allegiance of lawyers (as well as police, prosecutors, and judges) has required a major professional cultural shift in order to embrace the more adversarial principles that accompanied the move to a more liberal democratic model.[17] In England and Wales too, despite a more adversarial culture, which might suggest an expectation of more proactive lawyering, following the enactment of the Police and Criminal Evidence Act 1984 (PACE), lawyers did not grasp the importance of their new role as custodial legal advisers, often using inexperienced and unqualified clerks to replace lawyers, with the result that suspects were poorly served.[18]

[14] See Mols (2017) for a description of a recent training initiative to "promote the development of an active, reflective and client-centred professional culture of criminal defence at the early stages of criminal proceedings" (307).

[15] Hodgson (2005: 124–128). See also Dorange and Field (2012). For their part, the *juges d'instruction* in France have also been reluctant to accept a more proactive defense role: the experience of those representing the suspects in the Outreau affair was typical of many of my own observations. In general, lawyers were submissive and did not openly challenge the *juge*; the occasional lawyer who did was treated dismissively, in a manner that left no doubt as to who was in charge of the investigation.

[16] Justice Scotland (2018); Blackstock et al. (2014).

[17] Some lawyers nevertheless collude with police to, for example, confirm their presence at an interview when they were in fact absent. Cape and Namoradze (2012: 422).

[18] McConville and Hodgson (1993); McConville et al. (1994).

Effective legal assistance depends not only on lawyers. Police officers, prosecutors, and judges must also recognize the legitimacy of a more active defense function and facilitate the suspect's exercise of her rights. Where legal actors fail to grasp the significance of legal reforms, or to accept their legitimacy, old work patterns remain, and informal practices develop to undermine the effectiveness of change. In this way, as gatekeepers to suspects' rights, police behavior, as much as any procedural model, is a strong determinant of suspects' rights, and the same kinds of rights avoidance strategies can be observed across jurisdictions in the years following significant reforms in the provision of custodial legal advice. Following PACE in England and Wales, police officers discouraged suspects from taking up legal advice by telling them that it would delay their release; or that they did not need a lawyer if they had nothing to hide; or by failing to inform them that legal advice was free at the point of delivery. Recent research in England and Wales suggests that though less widespread than previously, such ploys continue to be used.[19] The same strategies were observed in France in the 1990s and early 2000s after the suspect's right to see a lawyer was strengthened, and in the Netherlands when the so-called *Salduz* reform was introduced.[20] More difficult to shift are embedded cultures of corruption, such as those persisting in former Soviet bloc jurisdictions, where the police control which lawyers are permitted access to detainees—what one lawyer described as "pocket lawyers"—or inadmissible evidence is routinely included in the case file at court.[21] Effective defense rights are also undermined where the judicial culture is weak or insufficiently independent of police and prosecution interests to challenge improper practices such as questioning a suspect as a witness, or proceeding without formally opening an investigation in order to avoid triggering defense rights for a person who is in practice a suspect.[22]

The previous chapter discussed the role of the defense lawyer in national systems, and as constructed through the norms of ECtHR decisions and the EU directive. This chapter considers the ways in which changes to the provision

[19] Skinns (2009); Kemp (2013).

[20] Blackstock et al. (2014). At points I wondered if there was some common script that officers employed, as the forms of words across countries were almost identical. Police in the former Soviet bloc countries in Cape and Namoradze (2012) also failed to inform suspects fully of their rights.

[21] See the discussion of Bulgaria in Grozev (2012: especially 147–148).

[22] This is seen in the wake of the political authoritarianism of some former Soviet bloc countries. Failure to inform the suspect of her rights is not sanctioned, inadmissible evidence remains on file, and defense requests and motions are routinely dismissed. See, e.g., Bokhashvili's account of the criminal process in Georgia (2012: especially 191–192); Abramaviciute and Valutyte's account of Lithuania (2012: especially 253–254); Hriptievschi's account of Moldova (2012: especially 333–334); and Bushchenko and Tokarev's account of Ukraine (2012: especially 93–394). See also Cape and Namoradze (2012: 421–422). Treating suspects as witnesses or volunteers has also been a concern in French investigations as a means of both police and *juges d'instruction* avoiding formal regulatory safeguards and the presence of lawyers. See Hodgson (2005); *Brusco v. France* (1466/07) 14 October 2010 (in French only).

of custodial legal advice have been received in different jurisdictions by the courts, by review bodies, and on the ground,[23] exploring the extent to which we are seeing movement toward a pan-European model of custodial defense, or whether countervailing factors militate against harmonization beyond a set of common basic thresholds. Undertaking a legal, empirical, and comparative analysis helps us to see the complexity of this process of change as it impacts in different ways across jurisdictions, as well as illustrating the variety of daily practices and understandings that make up legal cultures and which will need to be taken account of if transnational norms are to be effective. Acceptance of, or resistance to, these developments and reforms reflects differences and similarities not only in procedural models but also in the ways that legal actors understand their role and that of the lawyer within the criminal process.

Unlike the rest of the book, this chapter goes beyond England and Wales and France, to include detailed discussion of Scotland and the Netherlands. All four jurisdictions were included in the comprehensive two-year empirical study *Inside Police Custody*, and while I could have limited discussion to two jurisdictions, the inclusion of all four enables me to draw on a wider spread of data for my overall analysis and to demonstrate a broader lesson about transnational criminal justice reform: while procedural tradition is one factor in understanding the behavior and responses of legal actors, it is often the stage of criminal justice reform toward due process and fair-trial rights that is determinative. In the early stages of introducing custodial legal advice, there is widespread resistance from police (and some politicians), and lawyers are unprepared. This gradually changes over time, as police and lawyers adapt to their roles and realize that the myths and caricatures of one another's behaviors are just that. It because custodial legal advice has been in place for thirty years in England and Wales that it is a relative success—not because it is an adversarial-type procedure. At the other end of the scale, the Netherlands has only recently allowed lawyers into the police station, and the behavior of police officers is identical to that of officers in England and Wales in the 1980s in the early days after PACE.

B. The Experience of Two Adversarial Traditions

The jurisdictions of England and Wales and of Scotland might both be thought of as sitting within a broadly adversarial tradition, though Scotland has some more inquisitorial elements, but the place of custodial interrogation and the suspect's

23 As well as my own research in France and in England and Wales, some of the empirical findings discussed here draw on the collaborative project *Inside Police Custody* (Blackstock et al. [2014]), and I gratefully acknowledge the role of my coauthors, as well as our researchers, in this.

right of access to a lawyer are very different. While England and Wales established a statutory right to custodial legal advice in 1984, it was only through litigation based on *Salduz* that Scotland finally allowed suspects to have a lawyer present during police questioning.

(i) England and Wales

When thinking about the Europeanization of the pretrial defense role, the *Salduz* decision and EU directive on access to counsel have not impacted greatly on procedure in England and Wales for two main reasons. First, under PACE, suspects in England and Wales (but not Scotland) have enjoyed the right to custodial legal advice before and during police interrogation for more than thirty years, and so *Salduz* does not require legislative changes to ensure the presence of a lawyer during questioning.[24] Second, the UK did not opt in to the directive on the right to counsel, so it is not required to make any adjustments to ensure compliance.

Nevertheless, the experience of England and Wales in legislating and implementing custodial legal advice has informed the procedures in place in other jurisdictions, the drafting of the directives on the right to counsel and on legal aid, and the work on the impact assessments for directives.[25] It has also demonstrated the importance of adequate funding if the right is to be effective,[26] and of organizing lawyer availability and training in order to ensure access to, as well as provision of, legal advice; as well as demonstrating that the presence of the lawyer does not mean the end of any useful police investigation. With more than thirty years of experience and empirical research, there has been ample time to work through many of the difficulties that we observe elsewhere, as countries come to grips with the presence of the lawyer during the detention and interrogation of suspects. Codes of practice have been adjusted to prevent the rights-avoidance strategies used by officers to discourage requesting a lawyer; lawyers' training has been put in place as well as ways of organizing the provision of custodial advice so that suspects are not left with unqualified and inexperienced advisers; and police and lawyers have, to a degree, become accustomed to their

[24] *Salduz* also states that a conviction should not rest on a confession obtained without the suspect having the opportunity to consult with a lawyer and have her present during questioning. This is unlikely in England and Wales, but exclusion of such an admission is not mandatory under section 78 PACE 1984. See also *Ibrahim v. UK* for a softening of this approach in the ECtHR, discussed in the preceding chapter.

[25] Impact assessments are carried out on a range of proposals that are expected to have a significant social, economic, or environmental impact and inform the content of legislation. See https://ec.europa.eu/info/law/law-making-process/planning-and-proposing-law/impact-assessments_en.

[26] On the impact of fixed fees (and so reduced payments) on the quality of criminal defense work in Scotland, see Tata and Stephen (2006).

respective roles. This is not to say there are not challenges remaining—around disclosure, active lawyering, reductions in legal aid provision, and some general residual hostility between police and defense lawyers.

Under section 58 of PACE 1984, suspects are entitled to receive legal assistance throughout their detention and interrogation. This must be provided in person if requested (other than for minor offenses, where only telephone advice is provided) and unlike France and the Netherlands, there is no statutory time limit to the lawyer-client consultation.[27] Although she may not speak on behalf of her client, the lawyer is not expected to be passive,[28] but may intervene during interrogation provided that she is not obstructive. Custodial legal advice is not means tested; it is free at the point of delivery. Advice is provided by solicitors in private practice, or by their accredited representatives, and is accessed through direct contact or through a duty lawyer scheme.

The way in which the criminal bar is organized at the national level is difficult to control for when developing a pan-European standard of defense assistance. The structure of the legal profession can restrict availability of suitably qualified lawyers and impact on the level of training required. In the work carried out for *Inside Police Custody*, most of the lawyers we observed in France and in the Netherlands, for example, were providing custodial legal advice on a one-off basis—that is, they were unlikely to go on to represent the suspect at court.[29] In such a one-off transaction, the lawyer had no continuing or vested interest in the client or the case. In England and Wales, however, whether attending because the suspect is an existing client, or as a duty lawyer, there is a clear expectation on both sides that the firm will continue to represent the suspect through to court and in the future, providing an incentive to provide a good standard of service.[30]

An important reason for this is that there are many more firms specializing in criminal work in England and Wales compared with countries such as France, where the criminal lawyer's role has historically been limited to court work. This means that, in theory, there are greater numbers of lawyers available and

[27] Telephone advice may be provided only for minor cases where the suspect will not be interviewed, or in exceptional cases, the reasons for which must be recorded. Legal Aid Agency, 2017 Standard Crime Contract Specification (February 2017). In a range of offenses considered minor, where the police do not need to interview the suspect, assistance is limited to telephone advice provided by the Criminal Defence Service (CDS). If held in connection with such an offense, suspects are always referred to CDS, even when they have requested a named solicitor.

[28] Lawyers were criticized for being passive and bringing no benefits to suspects in the early years following PACE. For a particularly egregious example of the dangers of passive lawyer behavior during a forceful police interrogation, see *R v. Paris, Abdullahi and Miller* (1993) 97 Crim. App. R. 99.

[29] Blackstock et al. (2014). This study observed and interviewed lawyers and police in a city and a town each in England and Wales, France, the Netherlands, and Scotland. We carried out seventy-eight weeks of observations; observed 368 cases (144 while accompanying lawyers, 224 with police); carried out ninety-four interviews (fifty with lawyers and forty-four with police).

[30] Although the firm will continue to represent the client, it is unlikely to be the same person who attended the police station, especially as this is often not a solicitor, but a police station adviser.

competing to provide custodial legal assistance. However, research showed that, in the early years following PACE, the quality of advice provided to suspects was poor, with inexperienced, untrained, and often unqualified staff being sent to the police station in place of solicitors.[31] The self-regulating nature of the profession gave solicitors sole responsibility to determine who carried out what work, free from any external control or oversight. There was neither the desire nor the resource to limit custodial legal advice to qualified and experienced solicitors, but something had to be done to improve quality as the extent of lawyers' delegation of police station work to unqualified staff became known.[32] The accreditation scheme was established to provide training in criminal law and procedure for police station advisers, and research showed that this improved significantly the quality of advice provided to suspects.[33] By making legal aid funding conditional on the qualification of the individual adviser, this ensured that only those trained and qualified to provide police station advice, either as solicitors or as their accredited representatives, provided custodial legal assistance.[34] Firms differ in how they organize police station advice, but in our most recent research, solicitors did only the minimum number of police station call-outs each year required to keep their and their firm's accreditation status; all the legal advisers we observed were accredited representatives.[35]

In contrast to the representation of suspects in the first years after PACE 1984, advisers we observed in *Inside Police Custody* were generally proactive in their dealings with the police before and during interrogation and adopted a fairly rights-based approach. They saw their role as to advance the suspects' rights during arrest and detention, to tell them about the evidence that the police had disclosed and so give them more confidence and help them to feel less pressured.[36] However, while this may be how advisers understand the role that they perform, legal assistance remains centered on presence during the interrogation and the lawyer-client consultation immediately prior to this.[37] The remainder of the suspect's time in custody—which is likely to be many hours—will

[31] McConville and Hodgson (1993).

[32] See the criticisms of the Royal Commission on Criminal Justice (1993).

[33] Bridges and Choongh (1998).

[34] It is anticipated that accredited representatives will operate under the supervision of qualified and experienced solicitors, but this safeguard has been bypassed by nonsolicitor agencies holding a legal aid agency contract and employing accredited representatives directly. See Kemp (2018).

[35] Blackstock et al. (2014).

[36] Interviews with EngCity Law2 and EngCity Law3. See Blackstock et al. (2014: 337). A large and a medium-sized site were chosen for each jurisdiction (denoted as City and Town) and interviews and observations were carried out referenced as Pol (police) and Law (lawyer). See Blackstock et al. (2014). Where quotations used here have not appeared elsewhere, I have maintained the same system of coding.

[37] See also Kemp (2018). This relies on a very small number of interviews, but is nonetheless instructive.

almost certainly be without any contact with a lawyer. Although a higher fixed fee is paid when lawyers attend in person, this is a fixed amount irrespective of the time spent at the police station or the seriousness of the offense.[38] The model of active defense preparation during the custody period, envisaged in cases such as *Pishchalnikov*, is not realized in practice.

In our observations for *Inside Police Custody*, during the police interview of the suspect, the level of intervention depended on the individual case and on the personality and approach of the adviser to some extent. Most lawyers did not challenge officers during questioning, but some were more proactive and confident in dealing with the police:

> Some solicitors are quite timid, but I'm quite bolshy. Officers have three or four times called my client a liar, and I think "hang on." Turn the tapes off and charge him if that's the case. Opinions are not allowed in the police. Police can't decide if they're guilty—that's why we have a criminal justice system in this country. Police are just there to question. The client loves it and the officer thinks "I'd better watch my step." I'm not there to be liked and I'm sure there are officers who can't stand me for the right reasons.[39]

As police are the gatekeepers to the suspect's rights during custody, effective legal assistance will depend in part on their actions. Custody and detention officers, who are, in theory, independent of the investigation and whose role is to ensure the suspect's welfare,[40] tended to accept the lawyer's role. They informed suspects of their right to legal assistance in a neutral way and seemed unlikely to try to dissuade them from exercising the right. In some instances, when suspects said they did not want a lawyer, the custody officer drew their attention to the fact that they could change their mind at any time. Perhaps unsurprisingly given the presence of both a researcher and CCTV, we did not see any evidence of police dissuading suspects from taking up legal advice, but when interviewed, some officers referred to such practices taking place: a quick chat with the investigating officer in the cell or in the car on the way to the station, away from the cameras.[41]

[38] See also Blackstock et al. (2014: chap. 7). This can have wider ramifications. For example, appropriate adults told us that they would not attend until shortly before interview, because they needed to be sure the lawyer would be present. See Kemp and Hodgson (2016). For detail on legal aid payments, see the Criminal Legal Aid (Remuneration) (Amendment) Regulations 2016 Statutory Instrument 2016 No. 313. This is a complicated system, with fixed fees for different types of work, and thresholds above which work is calculated differently.

[39] EngCity Law2. This was the lawyer's own view of the lawyer's practice, of course.

[40] This includes informing the suspect of her rights; ensuring that she is able to exercise them; conducting detention reviews; ensuring that the suspect receives appropriate food, drink, and rest; and so on. Custody officers are concerned with the procedural aspect of custody, while detention officers are more concerned with the welfare aspects. See Skinns et al. (2017).

[41] EngCity Pol3. See also Skinns (2011).

Lawyers also described situations where interviews had begun without them because they were attending another client elsewhere in the station. Officers control when the lawyer is able to speak on the phone and meet with her client, and some advisers felt that access was delayed unnecessarily.

> We get told that you can't speak to them now because they're on the intoximeter, they're still being booked in, they're having fingerprints or photograph taken, and I think they do withhold us speaking to them. Again, my gripe is in relation to sexual offenses because they need to take samples. For intimate you need permission and for non-intimate you don't. . . . They say "you can't speak to them" and the phone gets put down. We . . . don't get to speak to the client until the police have done what they need to do. . . . I would say "don't give any samples until I find out what the evidence is."[42]

As well as delaying access, lawyers also reported the police dissuading suspects from taking up their right to see a lawyer. Most commonly, this practice played on suspects' overwhelming desire to get out of custody, with police telling them, for example, that no lawyer was necessary, as they would be "in and out in five minutes." Although perhaps less common than in the past, these are tried-and-tested tactics: suspects will decline legal assistance in order to proceed with interrogation as soon as possible, in order to spend the minimum amount of time in detention;[43] others think that a lawyer will add nothing—either because they have done nothing wrong and so have nothing to hide, or because they plan on making "no comment" during an interview. Vulnerable suspects in particular may not always appreciate the importance of legal assistance.[44] The decision to waive legal advice is significant and should not be made simply in the (often unfounded) belief that it will save time. The value of legal assistance is not widely understood, and neither domestic nor European norms have addressed in concrete ways the importance of ensuring that any decision to waive legal assistance is made in a fully informed and voluntary way.[45] The importance of making an informed decision, as emphasized in ECtHR case law,[46] is only partially reflected

[42] EngCity Law2.

[43] This also motivated admissions, when the police told them they would get bail. See also Skinns (2009); Kemp (2013).

[44] "I think in some cases where the detainee has mental [health] problems or is a juvenile, they don't understand the importance of legal advice." EngCity Law3. EngCity Law4 made the same observation.

[45] Legal assistance is mandatory for vulnerable suspects such as children, in some jurisdictions.

[46] It is recognized in principle, but there are no clear requirements for action to turn this into practice. The ECtHR in *Pishchalnikov v. Russia* (7025/04) 24 September 2009, at para. 77, explained the importance of any waiver being "unequivocal" as a "knowing and intelligent relinquishment of a right" and, recognizing the pressure that suspects may be under, made clear that responding to continued police questioning did not constitute a valid waiver of legal advice. "[T]he Court does not rule out that, in a situation when his request for legal assistance by counsel has been left without adequate

in the EU directive. Any decision to waive legal assistance must be voluntary and unequivocal, based on "clear and sufficient information in simple and understandable language about the content of the right concerned and the possible consequences of waiving it."[47] However, while suspects are told that they have the right to a lawyer, they do not understand the basis on which they might take up or decline this right, nor the possible consequences of waiving it.[48] One way of ensuring that suspects make an informed decision might be to make legal advice the default position so that suspects only waive their right after having spoken with a lawyer. This is the position in Belgium, where a waiver is only valid if the suspect has first received legal advice on the matter of waiving her right to further legal assistance.[49]

Younger officers and those involved in the investigation were more likely to see the lawyer's role as opposing the interests of the investigation. Showing a surprising degree of cynicism as well as a lack of understanding of the proper role of the lawyer, one police interviewee told us:

> I don't see why they have secret consultation. They shouldn't be giving them stories of how to get out of it or false explanations. So I think an officer or independent officer should sit in on the consultations.[50]

Unsurprisingly, the police were positive about lawyers who advised the suspect to make an admission and negative about those who advised "no comment"—which officers regarded as interference with the investigation.

response, the applicant, who . . . had no previous encounters with the police, did not understand what was required to stop the interrogation. The Court is mindful that the applicant may not have had sufficient knowledge, experience, or even sufficient self-confidence to make the best choice without the advice and support of a lawyer. It is possible that he did not object to further questioning in the absence of legal assistance, seeing the confession (true or not) as the only way to end the interrogation. Given the lack of legal assistance . . . it is also unlikely that the applicant could reasonably have appreciated the consequences of his proceeding to be questioned without the assistance of legal counsel" (at para. 80).

[47] EU Directive 2013/48/EU, Article 9, para. 1(a).

[48] PACE COP C para. 11.2 provides that suspects who have waived the right to a lawyer must be reminded of the right at the start of each interrogation and informed that questioning can be delayed if they wish to exercise this right. They must also be told that they can seek telephone advice, and if they continue to waive the right, the reasons for this must be recorded in the custody record (para. 6.5).

[49] Although considered useful for vulnerable suspects, this procedure was rejected by the UK Supreme Court in *McGowan v. B* [2011] UKSC 54.

[50] EngCity Pol2. It is interesting that the officer uses the word "secret" rather than "confidential," suggesting that this degree of privacy is unwarranted.

Many officers preferred it when there was no lawyer present, simply because it enabled them to deal with the case more quickly and they felt less scrutinized in interrogation.[51] Others saw some common ground in the two roles and pointed to the benefits of a lawyer's presence in keeping the suspect calm, or in making sure that procedures were followed correctly.[52]

> I think it's an important role. I think it makes sure that we do our job correctly and I'd be quite happy to have a solicitor for every suspect if that was the case because I know that if anything seems to be going awry, they'll point it out to me and then will correct it.[53]

This was not typical of all police officers, but it is significant that some saw lawyers as engaged in a common purpose, rather than only as being in opposition to the police investigation.

Although lawyers have had an important role in police custody for thirty years, there is still a certain amount of friction between officers and advisers. Although seeing the custody record and receiving basic disclosure about the reasons for arrest and detention were both standard practice, the amount of information disclosed was ultimately within the officer's discretion, and evidence was often held back for strategic reasons—to place the suspect under pressure in the interview and to destabilize the lawyer.[54] Failure to disclose more than minimal information would often result in suspects being advised to make no comment until they knew the nature of the charges they were facing.[55] If information was brought up in interview that had not been disclosed beforehand, many advisers would comment on this and call for a break in order to discuss the new information with the client.

There are also limitations to the role that the lawyer is able to perform, in part because of the constraints of legal aid, which discourages a deeper and more lengthy engagement with the suspect and so a more active defense. The complexities of criminal procedure and the range of choices around case disposition mean that suspects require assistance beyond the confines of police interrogation, but lawyers rarely advise on anything beyond the response during questioning, nor do they remain at the police station for decisions on charge and bail.

[51] Lawyers were unlikely to delay things, other than for a short consultation prior to interrogation.

[52] French prosecutors also expressed this to me in earlier research—especially when the charges are more serious and there is more at stake.

[53] EngTown Pol6.

[54] See also Sukumar, Hodgson, and Wade (2016a, 2016b); Sukumar, Wade, and Hodgson (2016). See Kemp's (2018) suggestion for a technology-based response to the problem of disclosure.

[55] Blackstock et al. (2014); Kemp (2018).

(ii) Scotland

The Scottish legal system has a strong common-law tradition, but it also shares some features of more inquisitorial procedures, such as an established public prosecutor office that has similarities with the French procureur.[56] The Scottish procurator fiscal is responsible for the investigation and prosecution of crime and may direct the police in their investigations. In all but the most serious cases, however, the police will act independently, reporting to the procurator at the close of the investigation. And like the French minister of justice, the Lord Advocate is the head of the prosecution service, but also sits within the executive.

Until 2010, suspects held for the six-hour police detention period were permitted to have a solicitor informed of their detention,[57] but were not permitted to have a lawyer present during police questioning, nor to have any contact with a lawyer. In 2009, in the case of *Her Majesty's Advocate McLean*,[58] this aspect of Scottish criminal procedure was challenged as being contrary to Article 6 ECHR. Adopting the "overall fairness" approach that had been explicitly rejected in the decision of the ECtHR in *Salduz*, Scotland's highest court, the High Court of Justiciary, ruled by a unanimous bench of seven judges that the absence of a right to custodial legal advice in Scotland did not violate Article 6 ECHR:

> Even if, contrary to our view, the decision of the Grand Chamber in *Salduz* amounts to the expounding of a principle that Article 6 requires that access to a lawyer should be provided as from the first interrogation of a suspect by the police, we are satisfied that that principle cannot and should not be applied without qualification in this jurisdiction. In particular, if other safeguards to secure a fair trial of the kind which we have described are in place, there is, notwithstanding that a lawyer is not so provided, no violation, in our view, of Article 6.[59]

One year later, the same case came before the UK Supreme Court in *Her Majesty's Advocate v. Cadder*.[60] Overruling *McClean*, the Supreme Court held that the ECHR requires suspects held in police custody to be provided with access to a

[56] See also Blackstock et al. (2014: 118–136).
[57] Known as the right to intimation.
[58] [2009] HCJAC 97.
[59] At para. 31.
[60] [2010] UKSC 43. This was effectively an appeal against *McLean*, as Cadder had been refused leave to appeal in the Scottish courts, because his grounds of appeal were considered unarguable in the light of the seven-judge decision in *McClean*. See paras. 1–12 for a discussion of the lengths to which Cadder went in order to have his appeal heard, and the determination of the Supreme Court's jurisdiction in this matter.

lawyer, and Lord Hope stated at the outset: "It is remarkable that, until quite recently, nobody thought that there was anything wrong with this procedure."[61] Unlike the High Court of Justiciary, the Supreme Court considered that there was "no room for any escape from the *Salduz* ruling on the ground that the guarantees otherwise available under the Scottish system are sufficient to secure a fair trial . . . the ruling in para 55 of *Salduz* must be read as applicable equally in all the contracting states."[62]

Emergency legislation was passed as a result of this ruling: The Criminal Procedure (Legal Assistance, Detention and Appeals) (Scotland) Act 2010,[63] later placed on a permanent footing by the Criminal Justice (Scotland) Act 2016, which came into force on 25 January 2018. This provides suspects held for police questioning under section 14 of the Criminal Procedure (Scotland) Act 1995, as well as those attending as volunteers, with the right of access to legal assistance—either through the legal aid scheme, or a non-means-tested duty scheme. Section 44 of the 2016 act now also provides that the suspect has the right to a private consultation with a solicitor at any time.[64] The pattern of reform in Scotland has been ambitious in some respects, but cautious in others, reflecting factors such as the culture of the criminal bar and the government's decision to undertake a broader review of the criminal justice process and the promotion of fair-trial standards. For example, although the statute sets out a right for detainees to consult privately with a solicitor at any time, police guidance sounds a note of caution, underlining the limits of the new provision:

> This is not intended to mean that a person in police custody can get unlimited access to their solicitor on multiple occasions, but is intended to ensure that the person has the right to a consultation and that any initial or subsequent decline can be revisited at any time.[65]

[61] Para. 4.

[62] Para. 50. The more recent interpretation in *Beuze v. Belgium* (71409/10) 09 November 2018 suggests an approach that would require the court, where there are no compelling reasons to restrict the suspect's access to a lawyer, to determine if there were reasons that meant that the rights of the defense and the fairness of the trial were not irretrievably prejudiced.

[63] In anticipation of the *Cadder* decision, the Lord Advocate had issued "Interim Guidelines on Access to a Solicitor" in June 2010. The 2010 act was passed by Parliament the day after *Cadder*, receiving Royal Assent two days later.

[64] Subsequent to *Cadder*, the precise point at which the right to legal assistance is triggered has been discussed, with particular attention paid to the ECtHR decision of *Zaichenko v. Russia* (39660/02) 28 June 2010. In the three cases decided by the Supreme Court in *Ambrose v. Harris* [2011] UKSC 43 (see also *HM Advocate v. G* and *HM Advocate v. M*; and *HM Advocate v. P* [2011] UKSC 44), the court determined this by careful consideration of the facts of each case, and in particular, the extent to which the suspect's liberty is constrained.

[65] Police Service of Scotland, Solicitor Access, Guidance (2015), version 1.02 at 2.6.2.1.

Similarly, the act also specifies explicitly that this consultation need not be provided in person, but can be provided by telephone if considered appropriate.[66] As discussed subsequently, the "appropriate" method of consultation is not a choice that the suspect is qualified or able to make. Rather, it provides the solicitor with the option not to attend the police station in person in order to advise the suspect. On the other hand, section 32 permits the suspect to have a solicitor present while being questioned by the police,[67] and here the reform goes further than the requirements of ECtHR case law (and the more established system of custodial legal advice in neighboring England and Wales), by making mandatory the presence of a solicitor for vulnerable adults and those under sixteen.[68] However, there has also been a price to pay for bringing Scotland into line with ECHR fair-trial standards; at the same time as the rights of the suspect were strengthened, the period of detention in police custody without charge was extended from six to twelve hours,[69] as it was feared that the provision of legal assistance to suspects would prolong investigations—a fear that was not realized in practice.[70] Unfortunately, this model of rights is not uncommon: the provision of a right to custodial legal advice was cited as justification for attenuating the right to silence in England and Wales.[71]

While some jurisdictions have limited themselves to implementing European standards sufficiently to demonstrate compliance, without any broader reflection on the impact such changes might have on the wider criminal process or its future development,[72] in Scotland, Lord Carloway was appointed to lead an independent review of key elements of Scottish criminal law and practice post *Cadder*. He was asked to consider, in particular, issues relating to the right of access to legal advice, police questioning of suspects, the operation of the current system of detention, evidence (including corroboration and adverse inference), and issues arising from the 2010 act; and to recommend both legislative and procedural change and identify where new guidance may be needed. The report,

[66] Section 44(4). Perhaps tellingly, as lawyers are reluctant to attend in person, preferring to speak to clients by telephone.

[67] Lawyers are expected to attend within one hour of the police call, but this will be extended where the station is in a remote area not easily accessed.

[68] See the Carloway (2011) recommendations at para. 4.0.11 and more specifically the recommendations from part 6 of the report, summarized at pp. 222–223.

[69] This is on the authority of the custody review officer, an officer of the rank of inspector or above who is unconnected with the investigation (section 14A(7) of the amended Criminal Procedure (Scotland) Act 1995). There is also the possibility of an extension for a second twelve-hour period under section 11.

[70] See Blackstock et al. (2014: 122).

[71] The possibility of drawing adverse inferences from a suspect's exercise of her right to silence was introduced in the Criminal Justice and Public Order Act 1994.

[72] French critics have pointed to the chaotic state of French criminal procedure as a result of the myriad of reforms both domestic and European. See Jeanclos (2016) and the various reform commissions discussed in chapter 3.

published in November 2011, sought to "re-cast and modernise" aspects of the criminal justice system and to incorporate the requirements of the ECHR in a more sustained way.[73]

> In short, the Review has grasped the opportunity presented to it not just to accept the temporary, if largely effective, solutions advanced in the 2010 Act but to re-build and reinforce the system's foundations by incorporating Convention rights in larger measure and at greater depth. The thinking does not dwell upon, nor stop at, the creation of a Convention compliant set of rules. Rather it has contemplated changes that would surpass the minimum requirements dictated by the Convention jurisprudence and be capable of withstanding any predictable changes in that jurisprudence in the medium, if not longer, term.[74]

Many of the Carloway recommendations and their subsequent adoption in the 2016 act recognize not only the importance of custodial legal advice, but also the wider role that the lawyer plays beyond presence in the police interview and advising the suspect: helping to prepare her defense, ensuring her lawful detention and proper treatment (especially for young people and vulnerable adults), and assisting in the conduct of other investigative acts such as identification parades. For example, the standard caution administered to suspects outside police custody now includes information about the right to a lawyer, and access to a solicitor is available as soon as practicable after detention, regardless of whether the police intend to question the suspect.

Drawing on earlier research on custodial legal advice conducted in England and Wales,[75] which demonstrated the need for the adviser to establish a relationship of trust, to take an active interest in the suspect's welfare, and to spend sufficient time to be able to advise properly and in an informed way,[76] the report also considered how best to ensure the provision of advice that is practical and effective. It noted the importance of suitably qualified advisers, but as "there appears to be no shortage of enrolled solicitors who are willing to advise suspects, provided that the financial arrangements are satisfactory,"[77] the recommendation was that only solicitors (rather than accredited representatives as in England and Wales) should provide this advice, though the need for training was also underlined.

However, the aspirations of these recommendations and reforms have not been met in practice. Lawyers responded to the new provisions allowing suspects to

[73] Carloway (2011: para. 4.0.1).
[74] Carloway (2011: para. 4.0.3).
[75] McConville and Hodgson (1993).
[76] Carloway (2011: para. 6.1.26).
[77] Carloway (2011: para. 6.1.25).

seek legal assistance at any time during their detention in police custody by withdrawing from the duty solicitor scheme, concerned at the impact on their workload as well as inadequate funding. Six years after Carloway, solicitors are still reluctant to attend suspects in person, preferring to provide only telephone advice in the majority of cases.[78] Figures in 2018 show that only 30 percent of suspects in Scotland request a lawyer, and of those, only one-quarter receive face-to-face assistance rather than telephone advice.[79] This means that less than 10 percent of suspects held in police custody are seen by a solicitor, contrary to the guidance issued by the Law Society of Scotland.[80] Because of the corroboration rule in Scotland, as well as the lack of case-related information provided by the police, lawyers reason that the best advice is simply for the suspect to remain silent.[81]

> On virtually all occasions, I advise suspects to make no comment. I can't remember not doing that. My argument is that I can't give informed advice on the basis of the information the police give me in advance of the interview. Until we have a PACE procedure in Scotland, until the suspect knows what the allegations are and what evidence there is in advance of the interview, not under the pressure of the interview, my advice will always be to make no comment.[82]

Many consider that this advice can be just as well provided over the telephone as in person.[83]

> To advise somebody to remain silent is, to my mind, just as well done over the phone as it is face to face. At the end of the day, when we first see the accused it's through a screen anyway and you're actually speaking to them via an intercom-system and apart from actually seeing a person, you're still speaking to them via a phone line and it really doesn't make a huge deal of difference in my opinion.[84]

[78] This was overwhelmingly the case in our earlier research; see *Inside Police Custody* (Blackstock et al. [2014]).

[79] See Justice Scotland (2018: paras. 2.7–2.10). Also the Bonomy Review (2015).

[80] See Justice Scotland (2018: paras. 2.18–2.20).

[81] The corroboration rule requires that all evidence must be corroborated by a second evidential source such as a witness or forensic evidence; thus, confessions alone are never enough to convict an accused, even when made in the presence of the suspect's lawyer. The Carloway review recommended abolition of the corroboration rule, which would challenge directly lawyers' views on the wisdom of silence as a uniform strategy. Research for the Carloway review suggested that 58.5 percent of 458 serious cases discontinued in 2010 after an initial court appearance would have had a reasonable prospect of conviction (the test used by prosecutors in England and Wales) had there been no corroboration requirement. This was also true of 67 percent of the 141 sexual offense cases discontinued in the same period. Although initially attractive to the government, this proposal has now been abandoned.

[82] ScotCity Law1.

[83] There were some concerns as to the confidentiality of the telephone call.

[84] ScotTown Law2.

By providing only telephone advice, however, the suspect is left to face police questioning alone. This is entirely the lawyer's choice: the law allows for personal attendance at the police station in order to advise suspects before and during police questioning.[85] Whether or not silence is always the best strategy, advice provided over the telephone is inferior to that provided in person. It is difficult to assess the mental and emotional state of the suspect and how she is likely to perform in interview, and with little sense of the case against the suspect, the lawyer will be better informed if attending in person and certainly if present during questioning.[86] Neither can telephone advice ensure the beginnings of building the defense case. Telephone advice informs the suspect of her rights in a generalized way, but does not assist her in their exercise. In particular, it underestimates the difficulty for the suspect to remain silent in the face of police questioning. Silence is not an easy strategy to employ: suspects worry that it will make them look guilty, and they find it difficult not to respond to police accusations that they can refute.[87] Adopting this as a uniform strategy also ignores the fact that some suspects will wish to (and may be best advised to) respond to questions and to admit their involvement. Finally, the layout of police stations and the arrangements for telephone advice cannot guarantee the confidentiality of the conversations between the lawyer and her client.

Some lawyers recognized the importance of presence during the interrogation, especially in serious cases or with vulnerable suspects—to explain and reinforce earlier advice and to support suspects in the face of persistent questioning designed to prevent them from exercising their right to silence. The lawyer's role is also much more than simply advising how to respond during police questioning. As well as assessing the mental and emotional state of the suspect, the lawyer can act as a check on the conditions of detention and the suspect's treatment, and begin to organize the defense case—all of which are very difficult to do by telephone. Lawyers who attend the police station are also likely to obtain more information about the case and so can better advise their clients. However, the lawyer-client consultation is not the centerpiece of the right to legal assistance that we might expect. In practice, just as in the earlier research in England and Wales,[88] lawyers in all jurisdictions we observed spent remarkably little time

[85] One lawyer reported attending the police station in person in around forty cases each year and providing telephone advice in around three hundred.

[86] Guidance to the 2016 act notes that disclosure is not required but may make a no-comment interview less likely. Police Service of Scotland, Solicitor Access, Guidance (2015), version 1.02, at 9.1.6.

[87] McConville and Hodgson (1993). Suspects in Scotland had more success than their English and Welsh counterparts in maintaining silence, but the nature of interrogations may change as the detention period increases. Perhaps because detention was until recently limited to six hours, there appears to be less of a culture of interrogating suspects routinely in Scotland, but there is evidence of suspects feeling pressured. See Justice Scotland (2018: para. 4.20–4.34).

[88] McConville and Hodgson (1993: 53) found that half of the 180 lawyer-client consultations observed lasted under ten minutes and less than 10 percent lasted more than half an hour. In

speaking to the suspect. Lawyers in Scotland spent on average less than fifteen minutes in consultation with their client. This is a very short time to explain the procedures, gather case information, establish the trust of the client, and prepare her for interview, suggesting that lawyers understand their role as almost entirely interrogation-focused and their advice as standardized. French and Dutch lawyers did little better, spending around twenty minutes with their client, and in England and Wales, consultations lasted on average twenty-six minutes, though there were often second consultations after the police interview.[89]

In the 1980s and early 1990s, lawyers in England and Wales tended to delegate custodial legal advice work to unqualified and inexperienced staff. This was one way of maximizing their profits, but in the main, it was because they failed to grasp the significance of the police detention and questioning of suspects, and the importance of their role at this early stage in the process. Similarly, the preference among lawyers in Scotland to provide only telephone advice suggests that the profession has yet to embrace the full potential of their new role at the police station, as well as being concerned at inadequate levels of remuneration. If solicitors do start attending in person, there are practical workload considerations to be addressed: appearing in court after spending several hours at the police station during the night is not sustainable. It is for this reason that many firms in England and Wales employ accredited representatives to attend the police station to advise and represent clients. The accreditation process requires representatives to pass a law exam, but also to undertake practical training—to observe and be observed in the provision of police station advice work and to compile a reflective portfolio as a result.[90] If lawyers embrace the wider scope of their role at the police station and become more willing to attend in person, Lord Carloway may be premature in ruling out the nonsolicitor option.

The effectiveness of custodial legal advice also depends on the willingness of the police to ensure that suspects are aware of and able to exercise their rights. Officers in Scotland differed in their assessment of the suspect's right to legal advice, but as is typical of jurisdictions in the first years after lawyers make an appearance in police custody, most regarded it as problematic in one way or another, because of the laborious process of informing the suspect of her right ("It's too complex, too confusing, too time-consuming");[91] because the criminal justice system was seen generally to

22.2 percent of cases lawyers spent less than five minutes with the client; in 26.9 percent five to ten minutes; in 15.8 percent ten to fifteen minutes; and in 25.7 percent between fifteen and thirty minutes.

[89] Skinns (2011) also found that lawyers spent around an hour with suspects, spread across several consultations.

[90] See http://www.sra.org.uk/solicitors/accreditation/police-station-representatives-accreditation.page.

[91] ScotCity Officer22 (from fieldnotes).

favor the accused too much; because lawyers were considered as always advising silence; or because of the practical inconvenience of accommodating lawyers and legal consultations that slowed down the whole detention process. Some favored removing the right to legal assistance; others, conversely, suggested making the provision of legal advice the default position. Their view of lawyers was that they routinely advised silence, and so the right to a lawyer had become a paper-driven exercise. As one officer pithily commented: "Solicitors should have a voicemail: just say 'no comment.'"[92] As was the case in all four jurisdictions in our study, lawyers told us that suspects were sometimes told that requesting a lawyer would result in delays to the procedure and so, most importantly, to their release from custody.[93]

Neither did officers in Scotland generally "buy into" the idea of custodial legal advice in process terms. They saw legal advice as being for the sole benefit of the suspect or accused. Younger officers in particular did not recognize any system benefit in terms of offering a process guarantee that might also work to their advantage.[94] They had not been given any training in this area and so had little sense of a wider context of suspects' rights and how they might also strengthen the integrity of the procedure and the reliability of evidence produced for court. More experienced officers were more positive about suspects' rights (and claimed to nudge suspects toward seeking legal advice), but victims were seen to be the losers overall. The (more recent) guidance on suspects' access to lawyers, issued by the Scottish Police Service, emphasizes the legitimacy of the defense role in advancing the "legal" interests of the suspect, even where this may not assist the police investigation and underlines the need for constructive, professional relationships between officers and lawyers.[95]

Finally, most jurisdictions allow access to a lawyer to be delayed in the most serious cases, such as terrorism or drug trafficking. The *Salduz* jurisprudence notes that "it is in the face of the heaviest penalties that the right to a fair trial is to be ensured to the highest possible degree,"[96] and delaying access to a lawyer must be for compelling reasons on the facts of the particular case. However, following Lord Carloway's proposal, section 32(4) of the 2016 act allows an officer of the rank of sergeant or above, in exceptional circumstances, to interview a suspect without a lawyer being present in the interests of the investigation or prevention of crime, or the apprehension of offenders.[97] Exceptional circumstances are not defined, and there are no clear guidelines or requirements of imminence in

[92] ScotCity Pol3.

[93] See also Justice Scotland (2018: para. 2.20).

[94] Older, more experienced officers had a different view of lawyers, understanding that they would not frustrate the investigation in the way that younger officers imagined.

[95] Police Service of Scotland, Solicitor Access, Guidance (2015), version 1.02, 3.18.1–3.18.2.

[96] Para. 54, following recommendations of the Committee for the Prevention of Torture that the detainees' right to access to legal advice is a fundamental safeguard against ill-treatment.

[97] This section also applies where a person with no right of waiver (i.e., a child under sixteen) refuses the assistance of a solicitor.

relation to questioning. It is unclear how exceptional circumstances might relate to the facts of a particular case. Nor is the power exercised or overseen by a judge or the procurator fiscal. Instead, this very broad, discretionary power is vested in a senior police officer.

With custodial legal advice in its relative infancy in Scotland, a professional and cultural shift is needed on the part of lawyers and police officers to recognize the value and legitimacy of legal assistance and, in particular, of the importance of personal attendance rather than just telephone advice. The 2016 statute begins to recognize this by making personal attendance mandatory for children and vulnerable adults, but this has backfired somewhat, resulting in sections of the criminal bar withdrawing from the duty solicitor scheme, fearing the impact of this on both financial and human resources.[98]

C. The Experience of Two Inquisitorial Traditions

France and the Netherlands share many common features in the organization of their processes of criminal justice, and as broadly inquisitorial traditions, the role of the defense has been relatively limited and centered principally on the trial phase. France introduced a very limited right to custodial legal advice in 1993, allowing suspects a thirty-minute consultation with a lawyer twenty hours into their detention period. This was available from the start of detention in 2000, but it was only following *Salduz*-inspired litigation that the suspect was permitted to have her lawyer present during police questioning. In the Netherlands, *Salduz* had a greater impact, instigating legal reform that, for the first time, provided all suspects with access to legal assistance before and during police questioning. Although there had been a limited pilot procedure allowing suspects in the most serious cases access to legal advice, this represented a sudden and major shift that was resisted by police just as it had been in the first years of custodial legal advice in France and in England and Wales.

(i) France

Like Scotland and many other countries, France did not initially consider that the *Salduz* ruling required it to alter its provisions concerning suspects' access to legal assistance during the period of police custody, the *garde à vue* (GAV).[99]

[98] It is unclear why accredited representatives have not been canvassed seriously.

[99] Detention in police custody is permitted for longer than in Scotland. Suspects may be held initially for twenty-four hours, and this may be extended to forty-eight hours by the procureur. For

Following a period of litigation within the domestic courts and a ruling against France in the ECtHR, however, there was considerable judicial pressure to legislate in order to ensure conformity with the ECHR. The first key decision came in 2010 when the legal regime governing the police detention and questioning of suspects was challenged by lawyers before the Conseil constitutionnel, which ruled as unconstitutional both the absence of a right to have a lawyer present during the interrogation of the suspect,[100] and the absence of any requirement to inform the suspect of her right to silence.[101] The structure of judicial supervision by the procureur, held up for so long as the primary guarantee of individual rights, was not sufficient to obviate the need for effective custodial legal advice. However, although the *Salduz* jurisprudence provided the clear impetus for this legal challenge and influenced the reasoning of the Conseil, this was not acknowledged by the judges. Instead, the ruling was cast in terms of domestic constitutional requirements, and the need for a more effective defense role given the centrality of the GAV in the case investigation and the importance for the trial of evidence obtained through custodial interrogation.[102]

The government was given one year to effect the necessary changes, effectively allowing the constitutional breaches to continue. However, in April 2011, (when the legislation was yet to come into force), the full court of the Cour de cassation engaged directly with the impact of the ECtHR jurisprudence and ruled that *Salduz* and its application to France directly in the later case of *Brusco v. France*[103] must be given immediate effect—otherwise, France would be in breach of the ECHR. The reforms were activated immediately, effectively bringing forward the implementation of the legislation.[104] The lawyer-client consultation remained

serious and organized crime, custody may last for up to ninety-six hours and in terrorism cases, six days.

[100] See blog entry http://blogs.warwick.ac.uk/jackiehodgson/entry/reforming_the_french/.

[101] This was an astonishing omission. The obligation on police to inform the suspect of her right to silence was first introduced in legislation led by the justice minister in 2000, only to be removed three years later in a law led by the interior minister. Even during its short time of operation, the Ministry of Justice circular (10 January 2002) emphasized that the warning should not be interpreted as encouraging suspects to remain silent and that, to this end, the warning should only be given at the outset of detention, along with the suspect's other rights. It need not be repeated before questioning.

[102] While the decision was widely fêted, it applied only to the ordinary *garde à vue* regime, leaving unaltered the provisions permitting substantial delays in allowing suspects access to a lawyer in organized crime cases (forty-eight hours), drug trafficking and terrorism (seventy-two hours). This is not in line with the Strasbourg case law, which, as already noted, has made clear that any derogation from the immediate right to legal assistance should be based on the circumstances of the individual case and not applied to blanket categories of case in this way. *Salduz*, for example, made clear that any restriction on the right to legal assistance must be justified and must not, in the light of the entirety of the proceedings, deprive the accused of a fair trial (para. 52). The systematic denial of custodial legal advice in terrorism cases was therefore a breach of Article 6 (para. 56).

[103] (1466/07) 14 October 2010.

[104] See http://blogs.warwick.ac.uk/jackiehodgson/entry/storming_the_bastilleor/ and http://blogs.warwick.ac.uk/jackiehodgson/entry/lawyers_advising_suspects/.

limited to thirty minutes, but the police were required to inform the suspect of her right to silence, and for the first time, the suspect was permitted to have her lawyer present throughout the GAV, including during the police interrogation and any confrontation. In June 2016 the right to counsel was extended to presence during identity parades and crime reconstructions.

The scope and effectiveness of custodial legal advice was limited in two important ways, however. First, the right to legal assistance did not apply to those questioned as volunteers.[105] This contradicted the approach taken by the ECtHR, which emphasized that, in order to be effective, fair-trial rights (including the right to a lawyer), must come into play when the person's status is adversely affected: a volunteer under criminal suspicion clearly falls within this category. The French position was problematic, therefore, as the trigger for legal assistance was whether the person was being detained in GAV, rather than whether she was a suspect. In practice, this arrangement allowed the police to question large numbers of suspects as "volunteers," thereby avoiding the procedural safeguards in place for the protection of suspects held in GAV. This rights-avoiding strategy was widespread practice: more than twice as many individuals were questioned as volunteers each year than as formal suspects held in GAV.[106] This gap in provision remained until the more detailed and prescriptive provisions of the EU directive on legal assistance required that volunteers, as well as those arrested, were able to have their lawyer present during police questioning and to consult her privately at any time during police detention.

The second limitation has proved much harder to overcome, without the intervention of more detailed external provision. Although legislation now ensures the presence of the lawyer during police questioning, her value to the suspect is somewhat circumscribed. She is not permitted to intervene in any way, to object or to ask questions until the end of the interrogation. She is permitted to be present, to observe, but no more than that. She remains a passive presence, wholly subordinate to police authority. Asked to review criminal procedure and its future direction in the light of the various EU directives coming into force, the 2014 Beaume Report did nothing to ensure that custodial legal advice provided a real

[105] If, during questioning, the person became a formal suspect, she could be detained in *garde à vue* and benefit from the usual rights—Article 62 CPP. In its decision of 18 November 2011, the Conseil constitutionnel noted (at para. 20) that in order to respect the rights of the defense, a person cannot continue to be interviewed once she becomes a suspect and could be placed in *garde à vue*, unless she is first informed of the date and the nature of the offense of which she is suspected, and of her right to leave the police station at any time. However, if she remained of her own volition, the police could take a statement without a lawyer being present. This is especially interesting, given the context of *Brusco*, where the suspect was in fact questioned as a witness. See also the Conseil's decision of 18 June 2012.

[106] Questioning volunteers is through a procedure known as an *audition libre*. This figure was widely cited during debate around the implementation of the EU directive on the right to counsel, which closed this gap in protection. Cape and Hodgson (2014).

and effective protection to detainees. Rather, the report reinforced the historic role of the defense as an auxiliary protection to the system of judicial supervision effected in the GAV by the procureur and the *juge des libertés et de la détention*. According to the commission, legal assistance comprises a physical presence to ensure the proper conduct of the GAV and that no pressure to confess is placed upon the suspect; it is not to begin preparation of the defense case or to interfere with the conduct of the investigation, which remains the sole responsibility of the police.[107] The primary purpose of the defense lawyer is to enhance the credibility of the process, rather than to assist the accused.[108] This contradicts the ECtHR's account of the nature of the suspect's right to legal advice and assistance as part of her fair-trial protections under Article 6 ECHR:

> [A]n accused person is entitled, as soon as he or she is taken into custody, to be assisted by a lawyer, and not only while being questioned. . . . Indeed, the fairness of proceedings requires that an accused be able to obtain the whole range of services specifically associated with legal assistance. In this regard, counsel has to be able to secure without restriction the fundamental aspects of that person's defence: discussion of the case, organisation of the defence, collection of evidence favourable to the accused, preparation for questioning, support of an accused in distress and checking of the conditions of detention.[109]

Despite litigation of the *Salduz* guarantees through the highest courts in France and the adoption of the EU directive on access to a lawyer, the restrictive model of French criminal defense continues to stifle the development of the role, preventing it reaching the potential envisaged by EU legislators and the ECtHR.

In contrast to the high levels of professional autonomy enjoyed by lawyers in England and Wales and in Scotland, the independence and effectiveness of the defense role in France is limited by the narrow way it is conceived and by the fact that the police continue to have almost complete control over the extent of the lawyer's participation.[110] First, the suspect's access to legal advice can

[107] Beaume (2014: 65–66). See also discussion in Hodgson (2005: chap. 4); Field and West (2003).

[108] This has been the case since the lawyer first appeared in the *garde à vue*. Hodgson (2005); Field and West (2003); Danet (2001: 39–42).

[109] *Dayanan v. Turkey* (7377/03) 13 October 2009.

[110] There is far less professional trust between French (and Dutch) police and lawyers than in England and Wales. The facts of *François v. France* (26690/11) 23 April 2015 reveal something of the police attitude toward lawyers. In this case, François wished to place some written observations in the case dossier, recording the injuries to his juvenile client's face (which the client said were the result of police violence) and the need for a medical examination. The precise facts of whether he was permitted to make these written observations were disputed, but the lawyer was removed from the station by several officers and accused of attempting to assault the custody officer. For this offense, he was taken to a cell, had his briefcase containing his professional papers removed, told to strip and then, once naked, to bend forward and cough. He was placed in *garde à vue* for thirteen hours by the officer claiming to have been threatened with assault. No prosecution ensued. The ECtHR found the

be delayed significantly. The police can ask the procureur to delay access to a lawyer for up to twelve hours, and where the suspected offense is punishable by five years' imprisonment or more, the *juge des libertés et de la détention* can authorize a further twelve-hour delay, preventing the suspect from receiving legal advice for up to twenty-four hours.[111] The lawyer can also be prevented from seeing any statements made by the suspect during this period. While lawyers in our 2014 study did not complain that these powers were exercised with any regularity, less drastic means of undercutting the suspect's right to legal assistance were more common. Although the police must allow the lawyer two hours to attend the police station, with the agreement of the procureur, officers may begin the suspect's interrogation before the lawyer arrives if this is considered essential to the investigation. Lawyers told us that this provision was sometimes abused. For example, one *avocat* had arrived at the station within the two-hour time period, only to find that the police "had already spent 45 minutes grilling him and he had admitted everything. And this was a [homicide]."[112] Degoul also reports that officers may wait for the lawyer for the first interview, but not later ones, ensuring suspects are questioned without the presence of counsel so that they then confess.[113] More common in our study were instances of lawyers arriving at the station, having been called out, only to be told that their client had waived their right to legal advice.[114] They later learned that this was the result of persuasion by the police, telling suspects that getting a lawyer would delay things and even prolong detention—tactics all too familiar from England and Wales in the early post-PACE years and which we observed being used successfully across jurisdictions. Lawyers believed that suspects were manipulated in this way in order to enable the police to put pressure on them and to obtain a confession.[115]

Second, the lawyer must remain passive during the investigation, and if she attempts a more participatory approach, she may be excluded altogether. Article 63-4-3 of the Code de procédure pénale (code of criminal procedure, CPP) emphasizes that interrogations and confrontations are carried out under the authority of the police, who, if there is "a problem," may call a halt to them at any

lawyer's detention and treatment to be in breach of Article 5(1) ECHR. His detention, strip search, and alcohol testing had no objective justification and were neither necessary nor proportionate. It was also irregular for the custody officer herself, as the alleged victim, to place François in *garde à vue* and to oversee his treatment. The Court underlined the importance of the protection that the ECHR affords lawyers in the exercise of their function, and their central role in the administration of justice, ensuring public confidence in the work of the courts.

111 The relevant *magistrat* must provide, in writing, precise reasons as to why this is essential to the particular investigation (Art. 63-4-2 CPP).

112 FranCity Law1.

113 Degoul (2018: 32).

114 Lawyers and police in our study estimated that between half and one-third of suspects requested a lawyer. The 2013 report of the *contrôleur général des lieux de privation de liberté* also noted that fewer than half of all suspects requested a lawyer. Blackstock et al. (2014: 277).

115 Blackstock et al. (2014: 278).

point. It is clear that this "problem" may include the lawyer herself, in which case the procureur must be informed immediately, and if necessary, she must inform the head of the local bar if a replacement lawyer is required. For her part, the lawyer is only permitted to ask questions once the interrogation or the confrontation has finished, and the police may refuse to answer these if they consider that to do so would harm the smooth running of the investigation. By not being able to challenge improper or unclear questions, the lawyer's role is minimized and she is reduced to a mere presence.[116] She cannot influence the course of even improper interrogation, only observe and later comment.

This is the provision that has caused lawyers the most consternation and was raised as a concern by almost every lawyer we spoke to or observed in our research.

> We sit in the interviews but are forbidden to say a word. We're just allowed to breathe and that's it. Sometimes we even fall asleep. I'm not sure it's very useful. . . . In terms of defence rights, it's useless: we are just decorative, like a vase on the table.[117]

Other lawyers described similar experiences:

> In reality we cannot play any role. We just sit next to the suspect.[118]

> I think I am more of a moral support to the suspect. . . . I have a limited role because there is no access to the dossier.[119]

> The role of the lawyer is to remind [the suspect] of his rights.[120]

There was some resistance to this, and it was clear that some lawyers tried to be more interventionist. Those heading up the local bar in FranCity told us that they had around one letter a month complaining about lawyers exceeding their lawful role, and asking questions during interrogation. In some instances, the lawyer can help a suspect to stick to her account and prevent her from yielding to police pressure to say what officers want to hear. The desire to be released from police custody can make this very difficult. In one example, a vulnerable suspect had been implicated in several offenses by his co-accused, but admitted to only three:

> He told me, "I don't care, I'm going to say [my co-accused] is right because I can't take it anymore. I want to go home, I want to sleep, I want to eat." . . . "Tell

116 See Hodgson (2013a).
117 Law3 FranCity.
118 Law1 FranTown.
119 Law1 FranCity. See also Field and West (2003: 286–287).
120 Law2 FranCity.

me first," I said, "were you there or not?" "No, I swear I wasn't there, I only did the three I've already admitted." I said, "Look, you have to keep going, it won't go quicker if you admit to everything, they will ask you questions about how, etc. On the contrary, if you admit to it, it's precisely going to take longer, so you need to hold on." He did hold on and at the end of the confrontation the other one admitted that he lied. . . . I was glad to have been there because this young guy would have said yes to everything otherwise.[121]

Most interrogations are not recorded and an important protection that the lawyer can provide is to ensure the accuracy of the written record. These summarized accounts can often contain legally significant inaccuracies, and suspects sign without reading.[122]

I'm flabbergasted by the difference between what the suspect says and what is being written on the statements! It's not because of investigators' ill will, it's not that they want to transform what is being said. It's just that what they put on the statements is very summarised compared to what is being said. I always ask the suspect to read what is being written, because they often sign without reading it. I read it as well and I correct some things.[123]

Along with the constraints on their role during the police interrogation, lack of disclosure is perhaps French lawyers' second biggest complaint.[124]

We barely know what crime they've committed, we don't know the circumstances of the arrest or what happened. For example, if they're arrested for stealing, it's very wide, we don't know what exactly they're being suspected of. . . . Some investigators tell us a bit more about what happened, but it's a very small minority (less than one in ten).[125]

The ECtHR places great emphasis on the link between legal assistance and protection of the suspect's right not to incriminate herself[126]—a function it is difficult to fulfill without reasonable disclosure of the nature of the case against the

[121] Law1 FranCity. Law5 in FranCity also saw clear benefits of having a lawyer present: "Some lawyers think they are useless in *garde à vue* but I don't agree. Our presence puts a stop to police behaving badly. It's a start."

[122] See Hodgson (2005: 190–202).

[123] Law1 FranTown.

[124] We observed cases where even the notification of rights form was not disclosed, presumably because it had not yet been completed.

[125] Law2 FranCity.

[126] See, e.g., *Salduz* para. 54.

suspect.[127] While arguing for restricted access to the case file, the 2014 Beaume Report also linked the scope of the right of access to the dossier with the need to protect the suspect against the risk of self-incrimination and false confession. However, it recommended access to a very limited number of standard documents, leaving it to officers' discretion whether to mention in the course of the interrogation evidence already obtained.[128] Although restricted or phased disclosure of information held by the police is believed by officers to be effective in tripping up suspects or preventing them from lying, it is often not in the interests of the investigation to expect custodial legal advice to function in the context of an information deficit: it may result in suspects being less cooperative.[129] As one lawyer explained, the police never disclose evidence in advance: "They keep it as a surprise element. . . . They sometimes say in interview they have certain evidence, but I doubt it."[130] Other lawyers also said that fuller disclosure might just as likely result in advice to make an admission.[131] It was clear across all jurisdictions in our research that lawyers were more likely to advise silence when they had little information about the case against the suspect.

However, with more disclosure comes more expectation in terms of what the lawyer might achieve, and so not all lawyers argued for more information. Some were concerned that fuller disclosure would require lawyers to play a more onerous role, for which they were ill-prepared: "If we ever get access to the file, the Bar will have to be careful and make sure that lawyers do their work properly from the very start instead of sending young lawyers in *garde à vue*. We must get it right from the start."[132] Degoul (2018), in his handbook for custodial legal advice, also questions the value of consulting the dossier in practice. It will be incomplete and the lawyer is unlikely to be given sufficient time to read it thoroughly, yet the suspect will be treated differently if disclosure has occurred—in particular, it will strengthen further the presumption of guilt should the suspect remain silent. More generally, French lawyers have adopted this more cautionary approach, conscious that the opportunity to intervene will quickly become a responsibility to do so, making it difficult to challenge any irregularities later on in the procedure. Together with their historically subordinate relationship to *magistrats*, this has also resulted in a reluctance on the part of lawyers to take up

[127] See Sukumar, Hodgson, and Wade (2016a, 2016b); Sukumar, Wade, and Hodgson (2016).

[128] Beaume (2014: 57). It recommended limiting disclosure to the record evidencing that the suspect has been informed of her rights, any medical report, and any record of questioning of the suspect. Any other documents could be communicated as questioning proceeds, allowing further consultation between lawyer and client after new evidence is provided.

[129] See also Sukumar, Hodgson, and Wade (2016b); Sukumar, Wade, and Hodgson (2016).

[130] Law2 FranCity.

[131] Such as Law5 in FranCity. This was also the view of Degoul (2018: 95) in his handbook for lawyers attending the *garde à vue*.

[132] Law4 FranCity. This is precisely what research revealed to have happened in the early years of custodial legal advice in England and Wales (McConville and Hodgson [1993]).

the opportunities of a more proactive or participatory role during the pretrial phase in particular.[133] When lawyers were first permitted access to the suspect in GAV in 1993, for example, many were not enthusiastic, as they recognized that failure to challenge evidence early on may prevent them from doing so later in the proceedings when they have a better picture of the case. This places an onus on the profession to provide high-quality legal assistance; otherwise, suspects and defendants will effectively be punished for the incompetence of their lawyers. The assumption made by the courts is that legal assistance is always effective.[134]

But even where an experienced and proactive adviser attends the suspect, the procedure is structured such that the lawyer is present but can do little to influence the investigation; there is no equality of arms. The suspect gains no real benefit, but the court may assume otherwise. In effect, the lawyer's presence serves a legitimating function.

> Since we don't have access to the file, we attend police interviews but it's very risky to ask questions and later on, at court, we always get: "Come on, you've been interviewed in the presence of a lawyer." We become a kind of guarantor of what happened! It's very unpleasant! We're present but we can't do anything: it's very difficult to build a real defence. And then later on, we are guarantors that the procedure was followed properly![135]

However, in a more dossier-based procedure, there are wider fair-trial reasons why it is important that the lawyer has some knowledge of the case against the suspect and some ability to challenge or comment on it. The dossier of evidence is compiled by the police, but is technically under the supervision of the public prosecutor, who, as a *magistrat*, is understood to be a judicial officer. Oral evidence is admissible, but it is more usual for cases to be tried on the basis of the written statements in the case file. The dossier is thus central to the case, and much credibility attaches to the prosecution evidence, regarded as the product of a judicially supervised enquiry. Within the minority procedure of *instruction*, there is a more developed model of pretrial defense participation (discussed in the preceding chapter), but while procureur-supervised investigations are now the norm, there is no structured opportunity for defense participation before the decision to prosecute. With no knowledge of the police case beyond the basic

133 Lawyers were slow to make the most of the new opportunities to participate in the *instruction* after the 2000 reforms, for example. See discussion in Hodgson (2005).

134 This has been the experience of suspects in England and Wales, who have found it very difficult to challenge what takes place during detention and interrogation, if a lawyer or legal representative has been present. For an account of judicial assumptions in the first years after PACE see Hodgson (1992).

135 Lawl FranTown.

elements of the charges, nor any opportunity to challenge or contribute to it, the effectiveness of the lawyer's role even in helping to ensure the credibility of the evidence is greatly diminished.

Across jurisdictions, whatever the procedural tradition, there is resistance to the initial appearance of the defense lawyer in police custody. Police and lawyers will always have opposing interests to some extent, as one lawyer explained: "To be fair, we are there to destroy police procedures, we spend our time at court criticizing their work. So, the antagonism will always exist."[136] We saw this in England and Wales in the years following PACE, and as discussed in the next section, the Netherlands sought to limit the scope of custodial legal advice despite *Salduz*. In France too, there was resistance on the part of police and prosecutors to the introduction and then to any expansion of the right to legal assistance during the GAV, but their fears have not been realized. While officers sometimes encounter difficulties contacting lawyers and ensuring that they attend at night as well as during the day,[137] the extended presence of lawyers at the police station and their entry into the interrogation room has not paralyzed investigations, nor has it resulted in suspects refusing to speak. The number of GAVs has decreased—which was the government's desired effect—but the clear-up rate remains stable and silence is rarely exercised.[138] The police may not have welcomed lawyers with open arms, but they are certainly growing more accustomed to their presence.

The appearance of defense lawyers in the GAV, even in this relatively limited capacity, is nonetheless significant. The legal and constitutional place of the procureur, underpinned by what is understood to be the public interest-centered ideology of the *magistrature*, means that the police accept the authority of the prosecutor over the procedure much more readily than any role for the defense lawyer, who is understood to work only in the interests of the accused and so against those of the investigation.[139] Officers are accustomed to reporting to the prosecutor and do not, in general, accept the lawyer as having a legitimate role in checking on the exercise of police powers. In this way, it represents a clash between adversarial and inquisitorial values.[140]

136 Law3 FranCity.

137 Contrôleur général des lieux de privation de liberté (2015: 38). Officers encountered far greater problems contacting the procureur to inform them of the detention in *garde à vue*. As observed in earlier research (Hodgson [2005]), this was done by fax at night, but even during the day, the delay in getting through to the Parquet meant that officers telephoned at the end of the investigation, thereby excluding the possibility of any oversight by or accountability to the procureur for the lawfulness of the detention and resulting in custody being prolonged. Contrôleur général des lieux de privation de liberté (2015: 39).

138 This is demonstrated in official figures and our own observations and interviews.

139 Hodgson (2005).

140 We heard of one rather extreme response, where one of the police unions had distributed flyers at the local train station, protesting against the presence of the lawyer in GAV.

Most lawyers we spoke to thought that relations had improved with the police, as they slowly became accustomed to one another's roles. Some thought that the police still viewed lawyers in an adversarial way as "the enemy," but there was also less mistrust:

> The reception of lawyers at police stations has changed. The presence of the lawyers has become more normal. There is still a bit of mistrust because they know the lawyer is going to ask questions and make comments on the procedure but we're starting to be accepted.[141]

> I think there were some concerns when the reform came into place, from both sides. We thought going to all *gardes à vue* was going to be very complicated for us because we had to fit them in our timetables. In the end, I'm sure there are less *gardes à vue* and I don't think people always ask for a lawyer. On the whole, it works quite well.... There were some concerns as well from the investigators who imagined that we were going to be unbearable and it's not the case. We are justice auxiliaries.... The relationship between lawyer and police officer is linked to the understanding each has of the other's role.[142]

This understanding led to some softening of procedure and a willingness on the part of the police to accommodate lawyers in some instances. Lawyers told us and we observed directly, for example, that consultations sometimes took more than thirty minutes (especially in total when there were several interrogations), but the police allowed this.

Lawyers were also engaging directly with the procureur, a relationship that was entirely new at this early stage of the investigation—making representations related to the detention of a client, or discussing local arrangements. These arrangements represent, in many ways, the opposite trend to that in England and Wales, where previously lawyers could negotiate directly with the custody officer around the charge to be preferred, but the role of the crown prosecutor advising on charge has distanced the lawyer from the pretrial investigation to some degree. In France, lawyers had no presence in the pretrial police investigation. Now they are able to advise the suspect, be present during interrogation (albeit passively), and engage for the first time with the procureur in her role overseeing the conduct of the GAV.

As with consultation arrangements, there was informal liaison between the local bar, police, and the procureur over matters that arose during GAV—such as the need to be flexible in waiting for lawyers to attend, and how to organize consultations for those arrested at night but not interrogated until morning.

[141] Law2 FranCity.
[142] Law1 FranTown.

These relationships and interactions are important for the smooth running of the suspect's right to custodial legal advice, and while they do not represent a challenge to the general model of lawyers' subordination to *magistrats*, they may signal changes in the way these two legal actors regard one another and so work together in the future.

Although we generally speak of police interrogations, in France, the gendarmes also carry out criminal investigation work. The divisions between the national police (under the interior minister) and the gendarmes (part of the army and so under the defense minister) are long-standing.[143] Both carry out the same tasks, but there is a different ethos between the police and the army, which is recognized by procureurs and *juges d'instruction*: they often prefer the discipline and perseverance of the gendarmes, though their ties within the local community can make them less objective.[144] Lawyers also experienced them differently. Those in FranCity were universal in preferring to work with the gendarmes rather than the police. They were seen as more professional, more rigorous, and more helpful in setting out the details of the case. When asked if there was a difference between police and gendarmes, one lawyer explained: "Yes, a massive difference. It's like day and night. The gendarmes do their work objectively; police officers can't even spell words. The gendarmes are good and much more professional than the police."[145] This should be seen in the context of the smaller population for which the gendarmes are responsible and so the greater resources available to them, but even so, they appear to have a different working ideology and a greater acceptance of the defense role in the procedure.[146]

Finally, we have seen in the previous two jurisdictions the importance of lawyers' training and organization for their ability to provide quality legal representation to suspects at the point when it is needed.[147] Lawyers' attendance in police interrogation in France is still in its relative infancy, and the focus has been on ensuring sufficient lawyers are available to meet demand. However, while suspects will be attended by an *avocat*, there is no guarantee that this will be a lawyer with expertise or experience in the criminal law. This is a function of the way that the profession is organized, with few lawyers working solely in criminal law, and most having this as one among several areas of practice. There is no training requirement for lawyers attending the police station or

[143] See further the discussion in Hodgson (2005: chap 3).

[144] See Hodgson (2005: 88–99).

[145] Law4 FranCity.

[146] For example, Law2 and Law3 in FranCity described the gendarmes as more helpful in setting out the basic facts of the case, as well as in taking more detailed notes during interrogation and generally being more rigorous in their handling of the case.

[147] Funding is also important and the fee for attending a suspect in police custody was increased from sixty-one euros to a maximum of 300 euros once lawyers were also present in the police interrogation.

gendarmerie—this is typically organized by the local bar, and we found that the experience and expertise of lawyers attending the GAV varied greatly. This means that suspects may be advised by lawyers with little knowledge or experience of criminal work: we observed one adviser who had been qualified only one month. The advice provided prior to interview was fairly standardized, and nearly all lawyers mentioned the lower sentence that would be offered with the guilty plea procedure. There is also a belief among some *avocats* that criminal work requires the lawyer simply to sit by the client's side, a function that can just as well be carried out by the many young lawyers signed up to the duty scheme, as by an experienced criminal practitioner.

The lawyer's own conception of her role, even within the limited contours that the law allows her, is crucial in ensuring the proper treatment of the suspect. Checking on the legality of detention and challenging irregularities serves the interests of the suspect as well as helping to ensure the integrity of the process.[148] Apart from the very poor physical conditions of detention,[149] lawyers need to be able to challenge improper police behavior during interrogation and in detaining suspects. In her 2018 report, the Contrôleur général des lieux de privation de liberté (controller general of places of detention, CGLPL) expressed surprise that neither lawyers nor the procureur had challenged police practices to hold people in GAV overnight, with no intention of beginning any investigation, for no reason other than that they had been arrested after 6:00 p.m. and so could not be dealt with. In the majority of cases the procureur ordered their release the following morning after a statement had been taken by the police. The CGLPL was highly critical of this unlawful deprivation of liberty for up to fifteen hours, often for trivial offenses, because of poor police organization. Both the prosecutor and lawyers had failed to challenge this practice, accepting it as inevitable.[150] This is an interesting example of how easily roles can accommodate one another when they should be more challenging of criminal justice practices.

[148] E.g., Blackstock et al. (2014: 337–338).

[149] See, e.g., *Fakailo v. France* (2871/11) 2 October 2014, in which France was found to have breached Article 3 ECHR in holding suspects in appalling conditions. Cells were less than two meters square and less than one meter square per person in shared cells; the sleeping space only 1.45 meters × 0.5 meters with no mattress or covers; no running water, light or air circulation; no enclosed toilet that could be used out of full view. The physical environment of police custody was observed in our 2014 study to be very poor, with lawyers obliged to hold consultations in cells and spare offices, where confidentiality could not always be guaranteed. These observations have been made consistently in the annual reports of the Contrôleur général des lieux de privation de liberté, underlining the poor state of some detention rooms and serious lack of hygiene. The 2018 report notes (at p. 36) that police stations are in a very poor state, blankets provided to suspects are not cleaned, and there are no proper washing facilities. *Gendarmeries* are generally cleaner, but spartan in design, often with no heating, making them unusable for part of the year. The lack of any nighttime presence, as gendarmes sleep in another building, has also been criticized (pp. 37–38).

[150] Contrôleur général des lieux de privation de liberté (2018: 38).

Several lawyers in our research recognized the challenges posed by custodial legal advice within a police-dominated procedure:

> When we intervene in a *garde à vue,* we don't just think 24 or 48 hours ahead, we're already starting to build up a defence. That's why our role is so important and we are under pressure. That's why we need to be trained properly. It's a power struggle with the police.[151]

Reforms to custodial legal advice have been slow and incremental, demonstrating the difficulties often encountered in the implementation of supranational norms at state level, when changes are mandated from without—less a matter of governmental will than in order to do the minimum required to ensure the legality of, in this instance, police custody. Like Scotland, France established a review body in order to take a more holistic approach to the wider changes that might be necessary as a consequence of recent European-driven reforms. However, the Beaume review did not address what constitutes effective assistance, nor produce proposals for a more coherent criminal procedure.[152] As a result, the reforms represent only limited progress. The defense role remains passive, underdeveloped, and subordinate to that of the *magistrat*, with minimal access to case-related information and unable to act in a more participatory defense role in the ways anticipated both in ECtHR jurisprudence and in the EU directive. The result is that in many instances the safeguards provided are more illusory than real or effective.[153]

(ii) The Netherlands

The Netherlands has an inquisitorially rooted procedure in which the prosecutor is responsible for the oversight of criminal investigations, including the detention and questioning of suspects in police custody. She is not involved in the direction of the investigation, but like the French prosecutor, she ensures that the dossier is complete and serves as an adequate basis for decision-making.[154] She also acts as a control over the exercise of coercive powers and is understood to protect the pretrial interests of the suspect.[155] Until recently, the lawyer had very

151 FranCity Law7.

152 See Pellé (2017). Gallois (2017) also criticizes the constant cycle of reform, carried out in piecemeal fashion with insufficient attention paid to the provision of appropriate solutions.

153 Perrier (2016) describes the blind conformity to constitutional and ECHR requirements as providing protections that are simply an illusion.

154 Field et al. (1995).

155 The investigating judge no longer conducts her own investigations, but oversees the pretrial phase, including the decisions of the prosecutor.

little role in the initial stages of the police investigation: suspects were not permitted access to a lawyer until after the first interrogation, and no legal assistance was available during the first six hours of detention.

Like many other jurisdictions, the Dutch government initially took the view that the *Salduz* decision did not require changes to its regime of safeguards for suspects held in police custody, reinforced by the Dutch Supreme Court.[156] Detainees had access to a lawyer, and in addition to reliance on the integrity and professionalism of police officers, the public prosecutor oversaw the detention period, before the suspect was later brought before a judge. However, at the time of the *Salduz* decision, a pilot was already underway in Amsterdam and Rotterdam, allowing access to a lawyer during police interrogation for suspects in serious criminal cases.[157] A reform followed, which, because of the timing, became known as the *Salduz* reform, but the new legislation represented a very wide interpretation of the margin of appreciation and a very narrow view of the requirements set out by the ECtHR. From April 2010, the suspect was allowed a thirty-minute consultation with a lawyer, but was not permitted to have her present during the police interrogation, other than where the suspect was a juvenile.[158] This, in essence, reflected the position that had existed in France and which had been challenged successfully in the Conseil constitutionnel and was later judged to be in breach of Article 6 ECHR.[159] Despite the clear terms of the *Salduz* decision and subsequent jurisprudence, the different interpretations seen even as between the few jurisdictions discussed in this chapter illustrate the difficulties in translating ECtHR decisions into universal norms that can be put into practice through common standards. Different judicial cultures in the development of rights and the application of international norms, as well as domestic political will, provide contrasting answers to the same questions.[160] There was

[156] In its ruling on the consequences of *Salduz* for the Netherlands—see Brants (2011: 301–303); Mevis and Verbaan (2014: 177).

[157] This was instigated following a parliamentary inquiry into miscarriages of justice where vulnerable suspects had been subjected to questionable police interrogation tactics. Blackstock et al. (2014: 99). It also led to a decision to introduce audiovisual recordings of police interrogations. Brants (2011: 301).

[158] Consultation with a lawyer was mandatory for those suspected of serious crimes and juveniles, ensuring that these suspects understood the benefits of legal assistance and that any decision to waive the right to a lawyer is an informed decision. Those suspected of less serious crimes could not receive legal aid, but had to pay themselves. See Brants (2011: 303).

[159] The only difference was that juveniles were permitted a lawyer in interrogation, but even this was compromised by the fact that the young person could choose to have either a lawyer or a "trusted person" present, not both.

[160] Contrast the French judicial decision that *Salduz* gave rise to a right to have a lawyer present during police interrogation, without the need for domestic legislation (albeit that that legislation was soon to come into force), with the Dutch Supreme Court decision of 1 April 2014. The Dutch attorney general questioned whether the refusal to allow a lawyer to be present during police interrogation could still be justified given the EU directive that would come into force in November 2016. The Supreme Court disagreed, holding that there was no obligation to comply before that date and a

no question of the Dutch government allowing all suspects access to a lawyer during the first interrogation by the police. In line with the pilot exercise, legislation was drafted to allow some adults (those questioned in relation to serious crimes) to have a lawyer present during the police interrogation in some circumstances (provided it did not harm the interests of the investigation).[161] It was only following the more detailed and prescriptive norms of the EU directive that all suspects in the Netherlands were finally allowed to be assisted by a lawyer during police interrogation from the outset of their detention.[162]

Implementing the EU directive on access to legal counsel, legislation came into force in March 2017 permitting suspects to have their lawyer present during police questioning.[163] Like France, however, despite the significance of these changes, the lawyer's role remains limited. She is permitted to ask questions at the start and end of the interrogation and to intervene to point out if the suspect does not understand the question asked; if her physical or psychological condition prevents further questioning; or if the interrogation is coercive. The suspect or her lawyer may request a break in questioning in order to have a consultation. The extent to which the lawyer may be involved in the questioning is at the discretion of the officer. The Netherlands' implementation of the directive, just as with France, assigns a restricted and passive role to the defense, rather than ensuring that custodial legal advice is effective, as required by the directive and ECtHR jurisprudence following *Salduz*. The Dutch Association of Defence Counsel challenged the limitations of their statutory role on these grounds, but the national courts have found that the Dutch law does not impose unacceptable restrictions on the rights of the suspect.[164]

At the same time that some suspects' rights were being strengthened, others were subject to procedures that would avoid access to a lawyer completely. Following *Salduz*, the Dutch government claimed that access to custodial legal advice would slow down the processing of cases, and in order to counteract this, more measures aimed at accelerating the pretrial disposal of cases were proposed, such as the penal order dispensed by the public prosecutor.[165] And

ruling anticipating the directive's implementation into domestic law would be to exceed the judicial function. See Mervis and Verbaan (2014: 189) and Brants (2011).

161 Blackstock et al. (2014: 99–100).

162 Mevis and Verbaan (2014: 175) observe that "[d]evelopments in the field of legal assistance prior to, during, and after interrogation by the police can be perceived as the most turbulent and radical change in Dutch Criminal Proceedings of the past years."

163 The legislation is described as placing on a statutory footing the prosecutor guidelines in force since March 2016. See the news item of the Dutch government available at https://www.government.nl/latest/news/2017/02/27/legislation-access-lawyer-during-police-questioning-in-force.

164 Mols (2017: 303).

165 The prosecutor can issue a penal order for offenses punishable for up to six years' imprisonment, and may impose a variety of sanctions, but not imprisonment. See Blackstock et al. (2014: 100–101).

as the lawyer's role and presence during interrogation was placed on a statutory footing in March 2017, the time during which suspects could be held in custody increased from six to nine hours. Strangely, this is not described as a measure to aid the investigation, but the suspect; increasing the length of time during which the suspect is deprived of her liberty is "in order to enable legal counsel during questioning."[166]

The quality and availability of legal assistance is guaranteed to some extent by the legal aid provisions and those relating to qualification.[167] In all but the least serious cases, appointed lawyers are provided free at the point of delivery. Named lawyers must be paid for by the suspect, but in practice, if they are enrolled on the duty rota, they are eligible to receive legal aid and so the suspect will not have to pay. As in Scotland and France, only fully qualified lawyers (or trainees) are entitled to provide legal advice to suspects at the police station. This should offer some guarantee of quality, but in practice, inexperienced lawyers may attend, as there is little or no required training, and lawyers often fail to engage with the client and her case. Duty lawyers are available, but there are few restrictions on who can be included on the rota, and, crucially, there is no quality threshold. As well as those whose primary work is criminal, nonspecialist lawyers are listed because they find it attractive both financially and as a means of increasing their client base.[168] Lawyers in France expressed similar concerns that nonspecialists were becoming involved for these reasons. Experience in England and Wales in the years following the introduction of the statutory right to custodial legal advice taught us that along with strategies to ensure lawyer availability, some form of quality control is required, if the sharp increase in demand is to be met without placing suspects at a clear disadvantage. Detainees are unable to judge whether or not the lawyer has sufficient expertise or experience; they are reliant on the rota and the professional commitment of the lawyer.

We saw evidence of this in our own observational research. For example, a lawyer in NethCity who was not a criminal lawyer was called out to suspects held for offenses of assault and public order, but he did not know in what ways he might assist them. He told the researcher: "Perhaps a specialised criminal lawyer would know? But anyway, well, I get paid for these cases."[169] This did not inspire the confidence of clients when they were told: "I am here because it must be so." Some lawyers were more concerned with maximizing payment than with the provision of effective legal advice. One lawyer, for example, spent little of the

[166] See the news item of the Dutch government available at https://www.government.nl/latest/news/2017/02/27/legislation-access-lawyer-during-police-questioning-in-force.
[167] For rates of pay see Blackstock et al. (2014: 268).
[168] This echoes the practices of lawyers in England and Wales in the 1970s and 1980s, who saw duty lawyer schemes as a mode of expanding their client base and providing some additional income.
[169] Law3 NethCity.

consultation period ascertaining legally relevant facts or explaining the procedure to the client. He used the time to fill out the duty form and to discuss the case in very broad terms. There was no expectation of any role beyond the consultation (which was sometimes as short as eight minutes), underlined by the fact he routinely took no notes whatsoever and did not even pass on his contact details unless requested.[170]

Despite the high number of lawyers available, in both Dutch sites in our research, there was only one lawyer on duty at a time, having to cover several police stations often thirty kilometers apart and with a maximum of two hours to reach the police station. In one two-hour period, we observed a duty lawyer called to ten suspects, four of whom were juveniles, spread across three police stations. The result was a series of five-minute consultations in which suspects did not receive anything like "effective" legal assistance. This may be exceptional, but even with half these numbers, this is in many ways worse than no advice at all, as the suspect is deemed to have had the benefit of advice, but in reality has had very little. Some lawyers contacted colleagues to provide additional cover, but others effectively undermined the suspect's right to legal assistance by arranging for a "trusted person" (rather like the appropriate adult in England and Wales) to attend a juvenile suspect in place of the lawyer.

The ways in which lawyers have organized and provided custodial legal advice suggests that many do not understand themselves to have a proactive and highly skilled role in representing the interests of their clients. And while the provisions for the lawyer-client consultation are restrictive, lawyers did not seem to be pushing strongly against these restrictions. Most spent around fifteen minutes in consultation and did not seek to obtain even the disclosure to which they were legally entitled. However, we saw around a dozen consultations that exceeded thirty minutes and the police interrupted in only one of these, suggesting that there is scope for lawyers to try to develop a more proactive role. We observed a minority of lawyers, generally those with experience in criminal law practice, who adopted a more assertive stance and were more proactive in their advice and assistance. But for the most part, lawyers seemed unmotivated to spend longer with suspects, to carry out further work on the case, or to check on the conditions of detention—they were not concerned with the range of tasks that were envisaged as part of custodial legal advice in *Dayanan v. Turkey*. While a statutory right to a lawyer is the most important first step, ensuring effective legal assistance in practice requires much more than this, from the practical organization and training of the criminal bar, to more profound shifts in the occupational cultures of police, judges, and lawyers themselves.

[170] Law4 NethCity.

While lawyers need to understand themselves as active participants in the defense case, for rights to be effective those administering them also have to "buy into" those rights. The way that the police inform the suspect of her rights is crucial to whether or not she will take them up, especially as the overriding concern for the majority of suspects is to get out of the police station. This was the most frequent reason for suspects refusing legal advice—the police would often tell them that it would delay matters. Other reasons included believing that if they had been arrested in error, asking for a lawyer would make them appear to have something to hide; that the lawyer could not assist; or that they would have to pay for the lawyer. These reasons are a typical response to lawyers' first appearance in police custody and have been observed in France in the 1990s and early 2000s, and in England and Wales in the 1980s and early 1990s.

In a minority of cases, the police encouraged suspects to contact a lawyer, told them that it was free, and emphasized that this would not prolong their detention. However, most officers behaved to the contrary and their motivations were clear.

> This depends on how you tell it to [suspects]. If I say, "You can have a lawyer," all of them would tell you: "Go for it," because they think it is a good thing and it is free. But if I say, "Look, if you want a lawyer, you will have to wait for him for two hours, and if not you would be released much earlier." Then they start to think: "Yes better to be released earlier."[171]

Even assistant prosecutors (senior police officers) were seen actively to discourage the exercise of the right to a lawyer. As one assistant prosecutor told the suspect: "You should know that if you ask for a lawyer you will definitely stay here until tomorrow." In many of these cases, suspects were misled: detention would be extended whether or not a lawyer was requested.

There is little acceptance on the part of officers of a legitimate role for the defense lawyer at the police station. Lawyers are seen as their procedural adversaries and are mistrusted. Just as observed in earlier research in France, lawyers are regarded as being concerned with, and driven by, money.[172] Their role is seen as contrary to the interests of the investigation, and as promoting the interests of suspected offenders rather than of justice. There was no sense of police and lawyers being engaged together in ensuring that the investigation was properly conducted and the evidence obtained was reliable. Instead, the police feared legal scrutiny and resented the fact that lawyers might interfere with their ability to put pressure on suspects in order to obtain confessions.[173] However, the reliance

[171] Police officer NethTown.
[172] See Hodgson (2005).
[173] For similar concerns expressed in France, see Hodgson (2005: 131–141; 169–177).

placed upon the dossier of evidence and the trend toward pretrial disposal of cases that we see across jurisdictions mean that the lawyer's role is more important than ever.[174]

Although suspects may now have counsel present during police interrogations, as in France, there is little expectation that the lawyer will play an effective defense role at the police station. She is allowed only thirty minutes in consultation; she is permitted to be present in the police interrogation of her client, but her participation, like other pretrial defense rights, is controlled by police and prosecutors; she is paid a flat fee regardless of the time spent with the suspect; she is provided with little or no information about the case and will only see any case papers once the suspect is before the investigating judge with a view to pretrial detention. As observed in other jurisdictions in our and others' research, this lack of disclosure was also a reason for advising suspects to remain silent in many instances. Before the EU directive was passed and transposed into Dutch law, experimental research allowing those suspected of homicide to have a lawyer present during interrogation suggested that suspects who were allowed pre-interrogation advice only were more likely to exercise their right to silence.[175] This in turn provoked more coercive methods of questioning. This was also what we observed—suspects who did not respond were questioned repeatedly, often by two officers.

D. Concluding Comments

With the exception of England and Wales, states have acted to legislate in the wake of *Salduz*, but often only when forced to do so through litigating individual cases or constitutional challenges. The response of individual states to ECtHR decisions and the EU directive on access to a lawyer, and in particular the widespread resistance to these proposed changes, illuminates some of the underlying values of national criminal procedures and jurisdictions' reluctance to embrace a stronger model of criminal defense. There is a dissonance between, on the one hand, the broader European discourse that situates an effective pretrial defense as a key fair-trial requirement across all procedural models and, on the other, the reluctance of national systems to adapt entrenched ideologies of justice. As

[174] In 2009, already 45 percent of cases registered by the public prosecutor's office were being disposed of without a trial, and the introduction in 2011 of the penal order sought to increase this figure to 70 percent of minor offenses. Blackstock et al. (2014: 100). After five years of the policy, in July 2016 the public prosecutor estimated that around two-thirds of ordinary criminal cases are now dealt with in this way. See https://www.om.nl/onderwerpen/werkwijze-van-het-om/@95111/evaluatierapport-5/.

[175] Stevens and Verhoeven (2010), discussed in Brants (2011: 305).

criminal justice policies and practices are increasingly saturated with facets of managerialism and securitization, driven by concerns with efficiency and the management of risk, there is little space remaining for suspects' rights or the robust interrogation of the prosecution case. There is the appearance of due process, but the substance is often lacking. For example, France has incorporated the principle of *contradictoire* in its code of criminal procedure, apparently demonstrating adherence to fair-trial principles at all stages of its criminal process. Yet the principle is largely absent from the pretrial phase in the vast majority of cases—present only in the tiny minority of more serious cases handled by the *juge d'instruction*. This is surprising, given that in its ruling on the need for custodial legal assistance during, as well as prior to, the police investigation, the Conseil constitutionnel based its reasoning on the fact that a person's case is often based on the evidence gathered during GAV, and especially on any confession made. Yet the Conseil has rejected the argument that for the very same reason, the principle of *contradictoire* should apply at this stage of the proceedings. In order for the defense to take up its role as envisaged by the ECtHR in cases such as *Dayanan*, the suspect and her lawyer need greater access to the dossier, and the lawyer needs the opportunity to engage in the defense, rather than simply to observe. The current restrictions on her role mean that the GAV process does not respect the principle of *contradictoire*, despite the acknowledged importance of this first stage of the investigation to the eventual outcome of the case.

It is also important not to overemphasize the importance of procedural tradition as a determining factor in the reception of the defense lawyer at the stage of police custody. Across all jurisdictions, the police typically exhibit antipathy toward the lawyer when she is first permitted access to the custody environment, often believing that investigations will be stymied by silent suspects, or through the provision of off-the-peg defenses by corrupt lawyers. In contrast to the narratives around Article 6 ECHR, the protection of the interests of the accused is not seen positively by police or prosecutors as a guarantor of credible evidence, but as antithetical to the interests of the investigation and of achieving a successful prosecution for the victim. However, this antipathy weakens over time, as officers come to some acceptance of the defense role, realizing that the presence of the lawyer has little negative impact on the investigation and in many instances results in suspects being more cooperative.

Neither are the police neutral agents in the investigation. Acting under interior ministers (rather than justice ministers) they retain control of the investigative phase, which, in all jurisdictions, is conducted in relative secrecy. Police claims to be interested only in the "truth" foster a false sense of security and an environment in which innocent suspects have nothing to fear. Coupled with warnings that retaining a lawyer will delay proceedings and the suspect's release from custody, it is easy to see why suspects might willingly answer police questions without the benefit of legal advice. This leaves suspects at a disadvantage, where they do not know the legal significance or consequences of the answers they give and, through inadequate recall or the destabilizing effect of detention and questioning, they might incriminate themselves in error.

As custodial legal advice has gradually been introduced and expanded, lawyers have organized themselves to meet this new legal need, establishing duty rotas and some training. In order for lawyers to be effective in the provision of defense assistance, funding and training are also key factors, without which it is difficult to ensure high-quality legal advice. An adequate system of legal aid is essential to finance effective defense assistance.[176] Advisers must be competent and confident in challenging any irregularities in the police conduct of interrogations, and in detention conditions and procedures. Effective custodial legal advice requires lawyers to be proactive and to adopt a more adversarial posture, protecting the rights and interests of the suspect. This proved difficult even in England and Wales, so it is unsurprising that police and lawyers working within a more inquisitorial tradition, centered on the judicial supervision of investigations, need some time to rethink their relative roles.

There is still some way to go in ensuring uniformly effective custodial legal advice. The historic role of the prosecutor as supervisor and guarantor of the detention process in the Netherlands and France makes it especially difficult for lawyers to establish the legitimacy of their own function in assisting suspects and ensuring the proper conduct of detention and interrogation. The old inquisitorial structures that privilege the search for the truth are hard to shift. The inequality of arms between investigator and suspect and the consequences this can have for evidence reliability are somehow ignored in this truth-seeking endeavor. And with increasing reliance on pretrial forms of case disposal, ensuring effective defense as well as police input can help to produce a more credible account.

European norms can provide common standards, but custodial legal advice must also be understood in the context of the broader criminal process within which the roles of the police and lawyer are situated. Procedural traditions, professional ethics, and occupational cultures also frame the practices of legal defense. In England and Wales, the procedural framework is of adversarial trial and proof. The lawyer is a partisan representative of the accused, but also an officer of the court, and while she may represent her client's interests to the best of her ability, she may not knowingly deceive the court. In the Netherlands, by contrast, lawyers are not under the same professional ethical constraint. This means that the relationship with the client and the advice that the lawyer can give will differ

[176] As the Carloway Report has pointed out, even countries with some access to custodial legal advice, such as Germany or Hungary, often lack the legal aid infrastructure to make these provisions effective. Carloway (2011: para. 6.1.9).

in the two jurisdictions. While the Dutch lawyer can encourage the suspect to be open and tell her everything without fear that it will compromise her representation of the client later on, the lawyer in England and Wales will be more circumspect.[177]

Furthermore, all detainees must contend with officers telling them that detention will be shorter, and that things will go better for them in the long run, if they waive their right to a lawyer and simply answer all questions now. Added to this, the notion of truth can be both confusing and problematic. The police and prosecution assert an interest in finding the truth in ways that seem reasonable and straightforward, and so may be hard to resist when in the interrogation room. But this apparent simplicity masks the more complex requirements of proof and the presumption of innocence, as well as the importance of understanding the suspect's account and the nature and extent of her criminal responsibility. The police interest in truth-finding is narrowly defined and is unlikely to favor the interests of the suspect.

ECtHR case law often emphasizes the importance of the right to legal assistance in ensuring that other rights are effective, such as the right to silence. In the case of England and Wales, the possibility of adverse inferences being drawn at court from the exercise of silence at the police station makes it imperative that suspects are properly advised of the consequences of their decision whether or not to answer police questions. Lawyers may explain the right, but there is no evidence that suspects are more likely to exercise it when assisted by a lawyer. However, even when silence is advised, it is doubtful whether this is really effective if the lawyer is not also present in interrogation. Suspects find it difficult to maintain a posture of silence and will look to the lawyer for moral support. Where lawyers either choose not to attend, or are not permitted to attend, interrogations, suspects are at a serious disadvantage.

Salduz represents a radical departure for many systems of criminal justice. It challenges the participatory model of the lawyer (espoused in France right up to the Léger Commission) in which the lawyer is allied to some extent with those conducting the enquiry,[178] and replaces it with a more accusatorial role. However, this is not enough, as the variety of reforms that were apparently *Salduz* compliant demonstrates. The EU directive on the right to legal assistance seeks to provide a stronger normative role for custodial legal advice across Europe, promoting a proactive defense role that challenges as well as checks upon the investigation. But although it aims to provide a clear and uniform standard in a way that the ECtHR jurisprudence, with its margin of appreciation, cannot, the directive nevertheless leaves significant aspects of the lawyer's role to be determined at

[177] See also Hodgson (2006b) and other contributions in that issue.
[178] Discussed in the preceding chapter.

the national level, undercutting efforts to ensure a more uniform level of protection. The UK's decision not to opt in to the directive on access to counsel does not currently put it at odds with other jurisdictions, but this may change as standards evolve through case law. Brexit negotiations may be able to ensure continued co-operation through instruments such as the EAW, but this will be threatened if mutual trust is undermined through the erosion of due process safeguards as a result of the UK not keeping up with new rights and protections. Through the combination of ECtHR case law and the EU road map, Europe is moving toward a form of universal criminal defense role, the success of which will depend on the willingness of legal actors to embrace this more proactive defense model. Research, as well as miscarriages of justice, have shown us how working practices can undercut legal provisions, sometimes with disastrous consequences.

But perhaps most importantly, effective defense assistance requires legal and institutional structures that promote and support the defense role, recognizing its legitimacy in ensuring the integrity of the prosecution case. Despite the grand rights-based narratives of the two Europes, the EU and the Council of Europe, the greatest threat comes from national systems themselves, as they continue to move toward managerialist solutions that require all parties to work together toward an efficient outcome and to eliminate the trial and any contesting of the case against the accused. As the investigative and trial phases gradually fuse into one adjudicatory moment, the dividing logic of pretrial and trial protections breaks down. The elimination of conflict, like the search for the truth, may sound alluring and persuasive, but it denies the vast inequalities of arms, paying lip service to fair-trial guarantees and, ultimately, casting the defense lawyer in a role where she risks legitimating, rather than interrogating, the state's case.

PART 4

RESPONDING TO CONVICTION ERRORS

8

Miscarriages of Justice and Procedural Change

L'affaire d'Outreau

Miscarriages of justice and the malfunctions they reveal often cause us to re-assess systemic problems as well as those that are case-specific.[1] They illustrate weaknesses in processes, practices and the legal and occupational cultures of criminal justice. Just as the North American disillusionment with plea bargaining and mass guilty pleas in the 1970s and 1980s led researchers to look to Europe for better ways of doing things,[2] so too those in France, Britain, and elsewhere have looked to adapt their procedural models in the wake of miscarriages of justice.[3] This has included reforms of the processes of investigation and prosecution, but also of the mechanisms to identify and remedy wrongful convictions.[4] These adaptations do not seek to shift systems across to a different procedural model, nor are they influenced explicitly by comparative studies. Rather, they present ways to avoid some of the worst excesses or malfunctions of different processes of criminal justice. An analysis of how and why different systems break down and of the mechanisms identified to correct this provides new insights into procedural models and their limitations.

The chapters in this section reflect on the common features of miscarriages of justice across both adversarial and inquisitorial procedural traditions, noting that they have been found to malfunction in broadly similar ways in practice.

[1] The "term miscarriage of justice" is used to describe wrongful convictions. The vexed question of factual guilt or innocence is discussed separately in the following chapter. For a discussion of how the rhetoric of innocence plays out in different parts of the legal process, see Jenkins (2013), who was himself wrongly convicted and imprisoned.

[2] See, e.g., the classic debate between Langbein and Weinreb (1978) and Goldstein and Marcus (1978a, 1978b).

[3] In the Netherlands, the *Schiedammer parkmoord* (murder in Schiedam park), in which a man falsely confessed to the rape and murder of a ten-year-old girl in 2000, then retracting that confession, was a catalyst for debate around system change. See Franken (2008). In India too, the Malimath Commission considered very briefly the French criminal process. See Amnesty International (2003).

[4] Roach (2010b) discusses the role of innocence commissions in the United States, both in advocating reform to prevent future miscarriages of justice and in investigating wrongful convictions. He argues for greater clarity in distinguishing these two functions in order that commissions have the resources and expertise appropriate to their function. See also Roach (2015) for a comparison between Canadian and Australian approaches to miscarriages of justice.

The Metamorphosis of Criminal Justice. Jacqueline S. Hodgson, Oxford University Press (2020).

DOI: 10.1093/oso/9780199981427.001.0001

Neither the party-led adversarial model nor the centralized judicial enquiry of the inquisitorial model has been able to overcome the tendency to focus prematurely upon one suspect and to then set about constructing a case around this initial thesis. The presumed guilt of the suspect becomes the lens through which evidence is assembled and interpreted, with information that contradicts this being ignored or rejected as not credible. Whether under the direction of the police, prosecutor, or judge, the investigative phase becomes skewed toward this initial viewpoint, carrying over to the prosecution and trial. The defense role has also been undercut in both procedures, preventing the kinds of safeguards and cross-checking designed to test the reliability of evidence and to ensure equality of arms. In France, as a further safeguard, the concentration of power and authority in the hands of the *juge d'instruction* is understood to be tempered by a series of procedural checks and appeals adjudicated by other *magistrats*, but these typically confirm rather than challenge the investigation, lending it further credibility without scrutinizing the nature or reliability of the evidence or procedures. The reluctance of judges to contradict or to challenge the colleagues alongside whom they work and have trained is often referred to as a kind of judicial corporatism, a loyalty that is hard to break.

In seeking to address this systematic tendency toward case construction, or confirmation bias, each system has looked for new ways to provide a corrective—both during the investigation process and in reviewing possible miscarriages of justice. In so doing, procedural values are placed under the microscope as their potential within different process models is tested. In England and Wales, the establishment of the Criminal Cases Review Commission (CCRC) to investigate potential miscarriages of justice produces tensions in importing a process of inquisitorial review into a broadly adversarially structured procedure. In France, the incremental strengthening of accusatorial features seeks to challenge judicial corporatism, but in a procedure that continues to resist the strengthening of the defense role.

This chapter introduces some of the themes in miscarriages of justice across jurisdictions, before going on to focus on responses to the Outreau affair, the investigation of a pedophile ring in northern France in which the weaknesses of the *instruction* process ultimately led to the collapse of the case and to three separate commissions of enquiry, including the first ever parliamentary enquiry into a criminal case. The limited procedure for overturning convictions in France results in few miscarriage-of-justice cases, and so the high-profile Outreau affair became a touchstone for the weaknesses of the French system and the ways that it risks producing wrongful convictions, as well as for extensive discussions of ways of reform. It provides the focal point, therefore, for my analysis of how the system malfunctions and how core procedural values are strengthened, limited, or altered through proposals for reform. The following chapter examines the CCRC, an organization established in response to the major miscarriages of justice of the 1980s in England and Wales, as an example of a more radical reform—not in the investigation and trial of criminal cases, but in their postconviction review.[5] It considers in particular the nonadversarial procedural values that underpin its functioning and its status as something of a maverick institution: a broadly inquisitorial body investigating possible wrongful convictions, sandwiched between the adversarial procedures of trial and possible further appeal. Chapter 10 explores further the implications of this twin procedural approach for the would-be appellant and the representation of her interests. It analyzes the role of the defense lawyer as her status shifts from representative of "the accused" to that of "the applicant," highlighting the tensions created between intersecting adversarial and inquisitorial role expectations.

A. Introduction

Some might argue that miscarriages of justice present an atypical account of a criminal justice system, telling us only about the small number of usually very serious cases where processes or people malfunction. It is certainly true that miscarriages of justice should be read in context. In addition to the wrongdoing or poor practice of criminal justice actors, successful appeals may arise out of a change in law or advances in scientific or forensic knowledge, and they may concern issues that are limited to a specific time period, a single case, or a line of connected cases. But they also tend to reveal systemic problems, such as, typically, the subordination of defense rights; a lack of police, prosecutorial, or judicial independence during the investigation; police malpractice, poor forensic investigation, and overreliance on a single expert;[6] the withholding of evidence by the prosecution; or inadequate defense representation. And while some miscarriage cases involve isolated wrongdoing, many reflect the daily practices of criminal justice.[7] The parliamentary enquiry into the Outreau affair in France heard from lawyers and *magistrats* that the case was conducted like any other; the unity of approach between prosecutor and *juge d'instruction*, the use made of remands in custody during the investigation, and the sidelining of lawyers were

[5] Chapter 2 considers the wider criminal justice reform following these miscarriages of justice. Although the criteria for appeal were widened and a new process for investigating possible miscarriages of justice was established through the CCRC, other reforms such as new defense disclosure obligations and the attenuation of the right to silence had played no part in the miscarriage cases and weakened the position of the accused.

[6] For discussion of some of the problems of expert testimony and the approach of the courts and of the CCRC, see O'Brian (2011).

[7] Belloni and Hodgson (2000). Garrett (2011) notes that many US exonerees come to light by chance, describing them as the tip of the iceberg.

nothing unusual.[8] Legal procedures were not breached, but rather, legal discretion was exercised in ways that undermined the fairness of the investigation, the spirit of the law, and the treatment of the accused.[9]

What is perhaps less visible is the extent to which many of these same features contribute to wrongful convictions for less serious charges.[10] The mass processing of defendants through the use of plea bargains and abbreviated trial procedures can only exacerbate this and will inevitably produce wrongful convictions when justice is negotiated in order to produce the most time- and cost-efficient outcome. Courts accept guilty pleas at face value, and the accused is often ill served by her defense, lacking any real and informed understanding of the process.[11] These procedures are becoming more visible and significant as they apply to increasingly serious offenses. For example, in France in 1997, Joël Pierrot admitted committing an armed robbery, and two days later, under the rapid *comparution immédiate* procedure, he was tried, convicted, and sentenced to four years in prison, three of them suspended. His confession was never questioned, despite his claim to have used a plastic gun, in clear contradiction to the evidence of witnesses. He maintained his admission before the court, as he had been told that this would reduce his sentence. He appealed unsuccessfully in 1998. Only when he learned that two other men had confessed and had been convicted of the crime for which he too had been convicted and imprisoned was he finally successful in having his conviction overturned.

The features present in miscarriages of justice in both adversarial and inquisitorial procedures are strikingly similar, from the Irish terrorism cases in Britain in the 1970s and murder convictions in the 1980s and 1990s, to the Outreau case in France and the *Schiedammer parkmoord* (murder in Schiedam park) case in the Netherlands, to the many wrongful convictions in the United States, many of them identified through innocence commissions.[12] The classic profile is an excessively conviction-oriented investigation and prosecution, coupled with a

[8] It also received more than seven hundred letters describing cases investigated in the same ways as the Outreau affair.

[9] For discussion of the exercise of discretion as a key determinant of the functioning of processes of criminal justice from the decision to arrest, through to leave to appeal and the admissibility of evidence, see Hodgson and Mou (2019).

[10] Belloni and Hodgson (2000).

[11] See McConville et al. (1994) for a discussion of the processing of guilty pleas by defense lawyers in England and Wales; Horne (2017) for a broader discussion of the nature and implications of guilty pleas; Hodgson (2005) and (2012) for an account of the abbreviated procedures in France; Killias (2008: 150–151) for a description of wrongful convictions in Switzerland for minor offenses dealt with by a penal order (*ordonnance pénale* or *Strafbefehl*).

[12] See Garrett (2011) for a thoroughgoing analysis of US wrongful convictions. They too are characterized by "corrupted evidence, shoddy investigative practices, unsound science and poor lawyering" (7).

defense that is prevented from protecting, or is unwilling to protect, adequately the interests of the accused. A few examples from different jurisdictions serve to illustrate these similarities.

The *instruction* procedure is the strongest model of judicial investigation in French criminal procedure, where defense rights are greatest and the *magistrat* is required personally to conduct, rather than simply to oversee, the enquiry, but even this cannot prevent the potentially determinative impact of the initial police interrogation. Patrick Dils was arrested in 1987 for the murder of two eight-year-old boys in Montigny-lès-Metz. Under pressure, he confessed but withdrew his confession one month later. Dils was sixteen but with a mental age of eight. He was interrogated without a lawyer, and the *juge d'instruction* and psychiatrists later noted his suggestibility and his tendency to give the answers desired by his interrogators. They also noted the closed nature of the questions posed by the police, which were highly suggestive of the "right" answers. The same gendarme who interrogated Dils had already produced confessions to the murders from two other men—both of which had been dismissed as not being credible. Furthermore, a key witness at the scene, who reported seeing a man spattered with blood, was never asked to provide a photofit of the man he had seen. It was fifteen years before Patrick Dils's conviction was finally overturned in 2002—a reinvestigation revealed that a convicted serial killer had been working four hundred meters from the scene. He admitted to having seen the bodies but not to killing the boys. Together with the other weaknesses in the case, this was enough, however, to raise sufficient doubts about the involvement of Dils. This case is shocking not only in the wrongful conduct of police and the negligence of the judiciary, but also in its demonstration of the system's inability to recognize its own errors.[13]

France has seen a very gradual introduction of legal assistance and safeguards such as recording of interrogations, but until recently, police and gendarmes have been able to interrogate suspects unchecked. In 1998, for example, Patrice Padé was persuaded by gendarmes to confess to the rape and murder of British schoolgirl Caroline Dickinson. He was a vagrant who had been near the hostel where the girl was killed, and he had previous convictions for child sexual assault. After forty hours in *garde à vue* (GAV) he finally confessed. He later retracted his confession, and DNA evidence demonstrated that sperm found on Caroline Dickinson's body could not have been his. After eighteen days in custody, he

[13] The process of *révision* is rare, with only eleven people having their convictions quashed since 1945—six of these have been since 1999. Convicted in 2009, the former mayor of Vence, Christian Iacono, was the most recent person to have his conviction overturned, in March 2015. The Cour de révision requires a new fact or evidence that was not available to the court and which could establish innocence or cast doubt on the conviction. Since 2014 the procedure has been simplified and extended to cover cases condemned by a judgment of the ECtHR.

was released. This pattern is strikingly similar to US exoneree cases, such as that of Ronald Jones, who spent more than thirteen years in prison, before he was released after DNA testing proved that he could not have been responsible for the rape and murder of a twenty-eight-year-old woman. Homeless and an alcoholic, Jones had an IQ of 80 and confessed after many hours of interrogation, during which he alleged that he was continually assaulted. The prosecution case looked to be compelling, but the details in his statements (which only the killer would have known) were in fact provided by police investigators, and the forensic evidence was flawed and misrepresented.[14]

In the Netherlands, the *Schiedammer parkmoord* case contained all of the ingredients of a classic miscarriage of justice—a pressured confession that was retracted two days later, the suppression of exculpating forensic evidence, and a failure by the police and prosecution to take seriously the major inconsistencies in their (heavily constructed) case against the accused.[15] In 2000, a ten-year-old girl and eleven-year-old boy were sexually assaulted in Schiedam Park in the Netherlands. The boy was seriously injured, but the girl was killed. Another man, CB, saw the boy and called the police. Although he did not fit the boy's description of the attacker, CB became the prime suspect—principally because he was also a known pedophile. Under pressure, he confessed, but withdrew his confession two days later. The police (backed by a child psychologist) subjected the boy victim to further interrogation to try to force him to admit that his description of the attacker was a fabrication. He stuck to his story, but was ultimately ignored by the court. DNA found on the girl's body and on the murder weapon was from an unknown third person. Doubts about CB's guilt were expressed by the forensic scientists,[16] but the prosecution ignored these, withheld evidence of the DNA on the murder weapon, and interpreted the absence of the suspect's DNA on the body as evidence of his guilt—claiming that he had been careful to leave no traces.

Despite the weak and contradictory evidence, CB was convicted and was unsuccessful in both the Court of Appeal and the Supreme Court. Although there was widespread criticism of the case, the Supreme Court refused leave to review it as there was no new factual evidence—a new argument based on the existing

[14] In his analysis of 250 exoneree cases, Garrett (2011) found that 40 (16 percent) made full confessions, all but two of them including details that only the killer or rapist would have known. These were most likely improperly disclosed to the suspect by the police. More than half of the exonerees were juveniles or had some mental impairment; 76 percent were misidentified by an eyewitness (many of whom were pressured by the police and then expressed their lack of certainty at trial); 61 percent of the cases contained invalid forensic evidence, with few benefiting from defense experts to challenge them; 21 percent included claims from informants, cellmates who said that they had overheard admissions; and many exonerees received poor representation.

[15] See Brants (2008: 175–177); Franken (2008).

[16] These were expressed to the trial and appeal prosecutors, but were not in their final report.

case file was insufficient.[17] In 2004, another man confessed to the murder. His DNA matched that found at the scene and CB was released.

In England and Wales, between 1989 and 1991, the Court of Appeal quashed the convictions of a number of those serving sentences for terrorist-related offenses, including murder, in the 1970s.[18] The police were found to have fabricated the notes of interview in the Birmingham Six and Guildford Four cases, and the scientific evidence was found to be unreliable, as it was in the Maguire Seven case. The scale of the wrongdoing on the part of those charged with investigating terrorism and serious crime triggered a response that went beyond the appeal courts, and a Royal Commission on Criminal Justice (RCCJ) was established to address (some might say appease) the crisis of public confidence in criminal justice at that time.[19] Although these high-profile miscarriages of justice concerned some of the most serious cases, it does not necessarily follow that malpractice was limited to these. The cases were not isolated and atypical but, rather, exemplified the broader culture of policing as demonstrated through research, including that carried out for the commission itself: an overly broad discretion at all stages; a "canteen culture" based on individualized concepts of law and order and social discipline; and a tunnel vision approach to investigations in which cases are "constructed" against those identified as suspects early on in the process. Many also demonstrated serious failures in the conduct of both the prosecution and the defense cases at trial.[20]

More than thirty people were also wrongly convicted as a result of the nefarious activities of Birmingham's West Midlands Serious Crime Squad, which operated

[17] As a result of this case, new legislation in force from 1 October 2012 broadens the grounds of appeal. A new expert report will allow for the opening of a review, as will a new source of evidence if it reveals a serious suspicion that the accused would not have been convicted if the information had been presented to the judge. However, a parallel law has been introduced that would allow an acquittal on a serious charge (e.g., murder, manslaughter, rape) to be overturned if it appears that there is new evidence to prove guilt.

[18] Paul Hill, Gerry Conlon, Patrick Armstrong, and Carole Richardson, the so-called Guildford Four, were convicted in 1975 of the murders of five people in pub bombings in Guildford in 1974. Their convictions were quashed in 1989 when the police were found to have fabricated notes of interviews. The Maguire Seven, Anne Maguire (Gerry Conlon's aunt), her husband Patrick Maguire, two of her sons Vincent and Patrick, her brother William Smyth, her brother-in-law Patrick "Giuseppe" Conlon, and a family friend, Patrick O'Neill, were all convicted of possessing explosive substances in 1976. Their convictions were also overturned when the scientific evidence (the mainstay of the case) was found to be wholly unreliable. Prime Minister Tony Blair issued a public apology for the injustice that both the Guildford Four and the Maguire Seven had suffered. The so-called Birmingham Six served sixteen years in prison and had their two earlier appeals dismissed, before their convictions were finally quashed in 1991. The police had fabricated interview notes, and the scientific evidence was again unreliable. The six, Paddy Hill, Richard McIlkenny, Johnny Walker, Billy Power, Hugh Callaghan, and Gerry Hunter, had been convicted in 1975 of the murder of twenty-one people in two pub bombings in Birmingham in 1974.

[19] On the crisis in public confidence in criminal justice, see generally McConville and Bridges (1994); Field and Thomas (1994); Walker and Starmer (1999).

[20] See discussion of cases such as Ivan Fergus, Stefan Kiszko, and the Cardiff Three in Belloni and Hodgson (2000: chap. 1).

between 1974 and 1989, including the Birmingham Six, the Bridgewater Four,[21] and Derek Treadaway.[22] The squad fabricated evidence and, it was alleged, tortured suspects in order to obtain confessions.[23]

Miscarriages of justice were not limited to terrorist cases, nor to those investigated prior to the enactment of PACE with its attendant safeguards such as the recording of police interrogations and the right of suspects to have a defense lawyer present before and during police questioning. Yusef Abdullahi, Stephen Miller, and Anthony Paris (known as the Cardiff Three) were convicted in 1990 of the murder of Lynette White. One of the accused, Stephen Miller, was interrogated for thirteen hours over five days in police custody. After denying involvement more than three hundred times, he finally broke down and confessed. After hearing part of the confession, the trial judge was satisfied that it was voluntary and admitted it in evidence. The Court of Appeal took a very different view and concluded that the confession had been obtained by oppression and so unlawfully, despite the presence of Miller's solicitor. The Court of Appeal judges were clearly shocked at the treatment of Miller at the hands of the police.

> We are bound to say that on hearing tape 7, each member of this Court was horrified. Miller was bullied and hectored. The officers . . . were not questioning him so much as shouting at him what they wanted him to say. Short of physical violence, it is hard to conceive of a more hostile and intimidating approach by officers to a suspect. It is impossible to convey on the printed page the pace, force and menace of the officer's delivery . . . although we do not know what instructions he had, the solicitor appears to have been gravely at fault for sitting passively through this travesty of an interview. . . . It is clear on listening to the tapes that for extended periods, Miller was crying and sobbing, yet he was not given any respite. . . . The context was that he was being led to believe the officers were seeking to eliminate him from participation in the attack and he wanted to get to the end of the questioning.[24]

[21] See I. Burrell and J. Bennetto, "Police Unit to Blame for 'Dozens More Injustices': Miscarriages of Justice Emerge 10 Years after Break-Up of Group That Tortured Suspects," *The Independent*, 11 November 1999, 8. Michael Hickey, Vincent Hickey, James Robinson, and Patrick Molloy were wrongly convicted in 1979 of the murder of schoolboy Carl Bridgewater. Patrick Molloy died in prison in 1981; the other three men spent seventeen years in prison before their convictions were quashed.

[22] Derek Treadaway was jailed in 1983 but had his robbery conviction overturned and went on to successfully sue West Midlands police for his treatment at the hands of the West Midlands Serious Crime Squad.

[23] Kaye (1991: 50–56). The number of those found to have been wrongly convicted as a result of the squad's activities continues to grow, while the conviction of officers concerned has proved impossible—other than one former officer, Lawrence Shaw, who was jailed for twelve years for armed robberies in 2001 (http://www.telegraph.co.uk/news/uknews/1311129/Ex-detective-who-turned-to-crime-jailed-for-12-years.html) and then again for eleven years in 2010 (http://www.bbc.co.uk/news/uk-england-12053559).

[24] *Paris, Abdullahi and Miller* (1993) 97 Crim. App. R. 99, 103–105.

As with so many miscarriages of justice, it is not during the visible and public setting of the trial that things tend to go wrong—though the trial judge's failure to recognize the oppressive nature of the interrogation practices in *Paris, Abdullahi and Miller* is to be deplored. Rather, across jurisdictions, it is in the gathering of evidence, in the overly narrow focus of the investigation during which there is no opportunity for defense (or even prosecution) lawyers to challenge the case thesis or encourage an alternative perspective. This is further aggravated by failures to disclose evidence, especially relating to forensic and other expert witnesses. In the absence of any formal or effective mechanism to exercise a check on the police construction of a case against the suspect, the evidence produced risks being tainted by confirmation bias and the police investigation exists as an inquisitorial enquiry in England and Wales as well as in jurisdictions such as France or the Netherlands.

The production and nondisclosure of expert evidence, as described in the *Schiedammer parkmoord* case, can raise further problems. Not only does the presumed objectivity of the appointed expert mean that more credibility is likely to attach to her testimony than that of other witnesses,[25] but also, as those first on the scene, the evidence of prosecution experts is often relied on by those working for the defense.[26] The now-discredited tests of Dr. Frank Skuse contributed to the wrongful convictions of the Birmingham Six and the Maguire Seven. More recently, the assertions of Professor Sir Roy Meadow formed a central plank in the tragic case of Sally Clark, who was wrongly convicted of murdering her two baby sons. Meadow testified that the chances of two babies dying from cot death in the same family were seventy-three million to one—an assertion that was subsequently discredited and should never have gone before the jury.[27] This proved to be doubly misleading, as there was evidence of infection in relation to one of the children, Harry, which raised the possibility of death by natural causes. Although known to the prosecution's pathologist, Dr. Williams, this was not disclosed to other police, lawyers, or medical witnesses, nor was it mentioned at trial. This new evidence was passed to the CCRC, which referred the case back to the Court of Appeal. Experts providing evidence on appeal found it "astonishing"[28] and "a

[25] The objectivity of expert evidence, as well as juries' ability to make good judgments as to their reliability where there may be genuine disagreements on the science, is contested. See Redmayne (2001: 116–139). In relation to the CCRC's approach and the value of a third expert to assist in evaluating the competing arguments, see O'Brian (2011: 20).

[26] In the Sally Clark case, criticizing the Crown's pathologist for failing to disclose information about important and relevant tests that he had carried out, Professor Berry, a pediatric pathologist, explained that it was best practice to include all test results "to provide a complete record for anyone else who might need to interpret the post mortem report later. . . . Defence experts are completely dependent on the original pathologist and the Crown to supply all relevant results and materials." *R v. Sally Clark* [2003] EWCA Crim. 1020, para. 148.

[27] *R v. Sally Clark*, paras. 172–180.

[28] Professor Morris, a consultant pathologist with particular expertise in the role of bacteria and bacterial toxins in SIDS—sudden infant death syndrome. *R v. Sally Clark*, para. 150.

matter of great concern that this wealth of laboratory data was not disclosed."[29] The conviction was quashed after Sally Clark had spent three years in prison, but she never recovered from her ordeal and was found dead four years later.[30]

Failure to investigate the case objectively and to disclose evidence relevant to the defense case continues to result in wrongful convictions. Sam Hallam was one of the youngest victims of a miscarriage of justice, released at the age of twenty-four, having serving more than seven years in prison after his wrongful conviction for the murder of Essayas Kassahun. The evidence against him was from two witnesses, one of whom gave varying accounts and the other who retracted his evidence at trial. There was no forensic evidence linking him to the killing, and when an outside police force reviewed the case for the CCRC, they found that the witness evidence was so manifestly unreliable that it should never have been put before a jury. There was also evidence from his mobile phone that Hallam was in the pub with his father at the time of the murder. The police have a legal duty to pursue reasonable lines of enquiry that point away from the suspect's guilt as well as toward it, but this did not happen.[31] Instead, the enquiry was characterized by tunnel vision, ignoring fourteen witnesses who supported Hallam's account, including the intended victim. The police investigation was flawed, convicting an innocent man and leaving the real killer free: Hallam was "the victim of a serious miscarriage of justice brought about by a combination of manifestly unreliable identification evidence . . . failure by police properly to investigate his alibi and non-disclosure by the prosecution of material that could have supported his case."[32]

These high-profile appeals also tell us something about the institutional culture of criminal justice at particular moments in time, including the nature of legal and political trust.[33] A small number of appeals against conviction may just as likely be an indicator of a closed and nonreflexive system, as of a well-functioning one. Dongois concludes that the small number of convictions overturned in France, for example, is the result of the very limited procedure for challenging convictions, rather than the inherent reliability of the French

[29] Professor David, a consultant pediatrician instructed by the Family Court as an independent expert. *R v. Sally Clark*, para. 149.

[30] A member of her defense team described her wrongful conviction and imprisonment for the deaths of her own children as "state-sponsored torture." See Thair Shaikh, "Sally Clark, Mother Wrongly Convicted of Killing Her Sons, Found Dead at Home," *The Guardian*, 17 March 2007, available at https://www.theguardian.com/society/2007/mar/17/childrensservices.uknews.

[31] Section 23(1) Criminal Procedure and Investigations Act 1996 and Code of Practice 3.5.

[32] Henry Blaxland, QC, quoted in Sandra Laville, "Sam Hallam Released after Seven Years in Prison," *The Guardian*, 17 May 2012.

[33] Trust tells us much about the design and function of criminal justice systems and the structures of accountability. See Nelken (1994). The tensions around prosecutorial independence and accountability to the executive discussed in chapters 4 and 5 also reflect this. See, e.g., Guarnieri (1997) re low levels of trust in the executive and the strengthened independence of the Italian prosecutor.

criminal justice process.[34] Brants argues that a significant obstacle in achieving justice in the *Schiedammer parkmoord* case was the fact that the trust enjoyed by criminal justice professionals prevented them from contemplating their own fallibility and that of the system itself.[35] The Dutch system remains reluctant to open up to external scrutiny, or to contemplate anything that challenges the internal hierarchical systems of review.[36] In France too, the failure of *magistrats* (who occupy different judicial positions but have trained together and share a strong common identity) to contradict their colleagues is often seen as a form of judicial corporatism. And in England and Wales, it should not be forgotten that despite the horrendous scale of wrongdoing that was finally uncovered, the earlier appeals of the Birmingham Six and others were turned down in the most definitive terms and it took a decade and a half before their convictions were finally overturned.[37] Despite the experience of the high-profile miscarriages of justice in the 1980s and 1990s, the culture of adversarial investigation and prosecution

[34] Dongois (2008). New procedures were introduced in 2001, allowing for appeals from the *cour d'assises*. The convicted person or the procureur may appeal. Between 2003 and 2005, 95 percent of convictions appealed were upheld, but only 43 percent of acquittals that were appealed. Over the three-year period of the study, 10,478 people were convicted in the *cour d'assises*; 1,262 appealed their conviction and 64 people were successful in having their conviction overturned. Of the 652 acquitted at trial, the procureur appealed the decision in 76 cases, and 43 people were then convicted on appeal. (See *Le Monde*, 21 June 2001.) The procedures for re-examining and revising convictions was simplified and expanded slightly in 2014. A conviction that has already been appealed may be overturned if there is new evidence that suggests innocence or casts doubt on the guilt of the person convicted. New investigations can be conducted by the Commission de révision des condamnations pénales, or, at the request of the convicted person prior to bringing the case to the commission, by the procureur. Christian Iacono was only the eleventh person since 1945 to have his conviction overturned and his innocence confirmed under this procedure. His conviction for the rape of his grandson was quashed in March 2015, two years after his grandson admitted to having lied and fabricated the accusations. He had served sixteen months in prison on remand at various times, and it took fifteen years for him to clear his name. Other relatively recent *réhabilitations* are those of Abdelkader Azzimani and Abderrahim El-Jabri in 2013 after serving twenty years for the murder of a drug dealer; Marc Machin in 2012 after another man admitted to the murder for which Machin had been convicted; Loïc Sécher in 2010 after serving seven and a half years in prison, after the woman he was alleged to have raped admitted to having lied; Patrick Dils, sentenced to life imprisonment at the age of nineteen, was finally released some twelve years later; and Rida Daalouche was finally acquitted of the murder of a drug dealer in 1999 after being convicted in 1994. (See *Le Monde*, 25 March 2015.)

[35] Brants (2008: 179).

[36] Brants and Field (2016: 284).

[37] The self-protecting nature of the criminal justice system was nowhere more evident than in the comments of Lord Denning, then Master of the Rolls. In rejecting the Birmingham Six's civil action against the police for assault in 1980, he said: "If the six men win, it will mean that the police were guilty of perjury, that they were guilty of violence and threats and that the convictions were erroneous. That would mean that the Home Secretary would have to recommend they should be pardoned or remit the case to the Court of Appeal. This is such an appalling vista that every person in the land would say: 'It cannot be right that these actions should go any further.' " McIlkenny v Chief Constable of the West Midlands [1980] 2 WLR 689 at 706. He went further still in an interview for the *Spectator* magazine, arguing that it would have been better if the Birmingham Six had been hanged, so as to avoid all the damaging campaigns in support of guilty men and against the criminal justice system.

remains problematic, with nondisclosure in particular continuing to be a major cause of wrongful convictions.[38]

B. The Outreau Affair: The Familiar Hallmarks of a Miscarriage

The so-called Outreau affair concerns a major investigation into accusations of child sexual abuse made by a number of children and adults in the town of Outreau in Northern France. When the case came to trial in July 2004, two of the accused retracted their statements against their co-accused and, as a result, a large part of the prosecution case collapsed. Four of the seventeen accused were sentenced to between fifteen and twenty years in prison for offenses of sexual violence against their own and their neighbors' children,[39] but the remaining thirteen defendants were acquitted, seven by the *cour d'assises*, and a further six by the *cour d'appel* the following year. While this was not a classic case of wrongful conviction, the length of the investigation meant that those accused had spent several years in pretrial detention: between them, the defendants had served almost twenty-six years in *détention provisoire* while the *juge d'instruction* carried out his investigation. One suspect, François Mourmand, committed suicide while in custody.[40] The repercussions of the case were enormous, resulting in three major commissions of enquiry: an investigation by the Ministry of Justice,[41] one by the Inspection générale des services judiciaires

[38] See, e.g., House of Commons Justice Committee, *Disclosure of Evidence in Criminal Cases* (2018); CCRC Annual Report 2016/17, p. 3. The commission also notes that decreasing police resource aggravates this further, as officers lack the time to check material thoroughly. See also, e.g., the case of Warren Blackwell, who spent more than three years in prison for a sexual assault conviction. The police failed to disclose crucial information about the unreliability of the complainant, including previous false allegations similar to that made against Blackwell. The CCRC's written evidence to the House of Commons Justice Committee (13 December 2018, paras. 41–42) lists the "disappointingly familiar" causes of miscarriages in the cases it reviews as instances of nondisclosure of material to the defense, police tunnel vision, failure to make adequate background checks on witnesses, and new understandings of scientific evidence. Offenses relating to the nondocumentation of refugees and asylum seekers have also produced a seam of cases.

[39] The offenses against children aged between four and fourteen years took place at the offenders' home and were filmed. The couple Myriam Badaoui and Thierry Delay abused and prostituted their own children as well as those of their friends and neighbors (there were twelve victims recognized in the case). Another couple, David Delplanque and Aurélie Grenon, were also convicted. The locality is characterized by economic and social deprivation, many residents being unable to name the French president, for example. See blog post http://anti-ogre.over-blog.com/2016/05/les-victimes-de-l-affaire-d-outreau.html.

[40] The true extent of the abuse remains in doubt in the eyes of some. See, e.g., "Innocents ou coupables? Outreau, le poison du doute," *Le Nouvel Observateur*, 9 May 2011.

[41] Viout (2005). The minister of justice instructed this working party to examine what lessons could be learned from the judiciary's handling of the case and to make appropriate recommendations.

(IGSJ),[42] and the first-ever parliamentary enquiry into a criminal case, the Vallini Commission.[43]

The gravity of the accusations in the Outreau case meant that, rather than a police enquiry overseen by the public prosecutor (the procureur), it was investigated through the more rigorous *instruction*, carried out under the direction of the more independent *juge d'instruction*, who has wide powers to question witnesses and to instruct experts. The role of the *juge d'instruction* is to investigate the case (not the person), and her function is defined in statute: she must follow both inculpating and exculpating lines of enquiry, that is, work *à charge* and *à décharge*. The defense also enjoys greater rights to participate in the enquiry than is the case in the 97 percent of cases that are overseen by the procureur: the suspect may have her lawyer present during all significant acts of investigation, including when questioned by the *juge*; the lawyer has access to the case dossier; and the defense may challenge evidence and propose new lines of enquiry, including investigative acts and the commissioning of experts. The prosecutor and the victim enjoy the same rights to participate, and the victim may be legally represented. If the *juge d'instruction* refuses a request to undertake a particular act of investigation, appeal lies to the *chambre de l'instruction*. Thus, although the *juge d'instruction* is the locus of power, the defense, victim, and prosecutor have the right to participate in the investigation, and they can challenge decisions of the *juge*, triggering review by a hierarchy of *magistrats* independent of the enquiry. This is understood to act as a set of checks and balances on the conduct and scope of the enquiry.

However, the parliamentary report (the most detailed of the three, with the testimony of those called televised nationally) was critical of the single case viewpoint offered by the procureur and *juge d'instruction* (whose roles are, in theory, quite separate and distinct) and the absence of reflexivity among *magistrats*: although the case passed through the hands of some sixty different *magistrats*, none challenged either the central case thesis or the methods of investigation.[44] This is described as a form of judicial corporatism, in which there is insufficient distance between what are supposed to be different and even competing judicial functions. The parliamentary enquiry found that the procureur dominated the investigation rather than acting as any form of check, and both he

42 Raysseguier (2006). The minister of justice instructed the inspectorate to carry out an administrative enquiry: to examine all of the conditions and circumstances in which the case was handled by the judiciary; to investigate the impact on the case of the malfunctioning of the justice system and the professional errors of individual *magistrats* at each stage of the procedure; to propose reforms that would prove to be helpful.

43 Vallini (2006). This commission of enquiry was required to investigate the cause of the malfunctions of the justice system in the Outreau affair, and to formulate recommendations to avoid their recurrence.

44 Vallini (2006: 276).

and the *juge d'instruction* adopted a wholly prosecution-oriented perspective to the case—they worked only *à charge*. Even the suspects' declarations of innocence were seen as justifying repressive measures; the commission of enquiry was shocked to hear that such assertions were considered good reason to keep suspects in detention during the investigation.[45] The proximity of the procureur and the *juge d'instruction* meant that they were able to discuss the case frequently and the procureur was able to influence the enquiry informally and so invisibly: investigations carried out on the prosecutor's suggestion appeared to be on the *juge*'s own initiative and so to be more "neutral" and the result of judicial consideration. The unity of perspective of the *juge d'instruction* and the prosecutor was underlined by the fact that the final case conclusions communicated to the *cour d'assises* were simply copied and pasted by the *juge d'instruction* from those prepared by the procureur.[46]

In all this the defense was systematically prevented from participating in the enquiry and so from challenging the findings and methods of the *juge d'instruction* and stimulating investigation *à décharge* in the way envisaged by the text of the law. Statements were taken from the children making the accusations in ways that produced unreliable evidence, but the defense was not permitted to examine these witnesses on the grounds that it might traumatize the children further.[47] There were major contradictions between the findings of the various experts, but every defense request to instruct a new psychologist or psychiatrist, or to obtain additional information or clarification, was refused first by the *juge d'instruction* and again by the *chambre de l'instruction*. The defense was prevented from introducing any element of *contradictoire* into this part of the investigation.[48] The quality of the expert evidence was judged by the *juge d'instruction* alone, with no testing of what proved to be unreliable and inconsistent assertions on the part of experts through the instruction of additional witnesses.

We might expect some degree of partisanship from police investigators, but the behavior of the *juge d'instruction* in excluding the defence is perhaps more surprising. After related accusations of murder connected with a pedophile ring

[45] Vallini (2006: 333).

[46] Like many cases of plagiarism, this included factual and typographic errors (Vallini [2006: 148]).

[47] Vallini (2006: 98–112). The proximity in time of this investigation and the Belgian pedophile case of Marc Dutroux meant that public feeling around such cases was running high, and the word of a child accuser was unlikely to be challenged. Julian Licourt, "Outreau, l séisme qui aurait dû bouleverser la justice," *Le Figaro*, 24 August 2018.

[48] Psychologists and psychiatrists differed significantly in their assessment of the traits of sexual abusers, for example. The commission noted the determination of the *juge d'instruction* to block any defense request—even interpreting requests for a new expert as requests for clarification, thus enabling him to refuse them as being out of time. There were also delays of up to a year in making reports available, preventing the accused from knowing the extent of the evidence being built up against them, or from challenging the findings in a timely manner. Vallini (2006: 186–189).

in Belgium were discovered to be without foundation, the testimony of those witnesses who had lied was simply cut from the main dossier, and their overall credibility in relation to the other evidence does not seem to have been put in doubt. By removing their false testimony from the dossier, the defense was placed outside the procedure and deprived of any opportunity to question the witnesses' character. The *cour d'assises* was also deprived of important evidence. Yet, as a simple administrative measure, this action was not subject to appeal. This deception was agreed by both the Parquet and the *juge d'instruction*.[49]

In other instances, the *juge* overplayed his hand, implying that he was in possession of evidence that he was not and instructing the police to question a suspect on this basis.[50] Instead of being corrected, these problems were compounded by the pretrial appeal court, the *chambre de l'instruction*, which conducted only paper reviews and demonstrated a clear tendency to reinforce the position taken by the *juge* and the Parquet.[51] Quite simply, the defense lawyer was described as an unwelcome outsider whose counterarguments were not well received by the investigating judge.[52]

This case demonstrates the array of systemic problems in concentrating power in the hands of one individual during the investigation—especially a judicial officer whose findings are afforded considerable credibility as the product of a judicial investigation—and in a system of checks that fail to scrutinize and challenge, rather than confirm, the exercise of this power. Just as the police have been shown to focus prematurely upon a suspect and then to construct a case against her, evidence was filtered by the *juge* in order to exclude that which cast doubt on the case he had constructed against the accused. Procedures were not followed, and key investigations were not carried out that might have challenged this case construction. At least one accused was first placed in GAV in order that he could be interrogated by the police (at that point without the presence of a lawyer), when, as the Vallini Commission noted, he should have been *mis en examen* in the instruction and questioned by the *juge* with the safeguard of legal representation.[53] Contradictions in the evidence of witnesses were not followed up, and rather than the *juge* investigating *à décharge*, as he is legally required to do, it was left to the defense to try to uncover crucial gaps. Key witnesses, including the

49 Vallini (2006: 149–151).

50 Vallini (2006: 194). The report was also critical of the *juge*'s decision to have the police question the individual as a mere suspect, when there was clearly enough evidence to make him *mise en examen* and so subject to the rights and protections of being an accused within the *instruction* (2006: 195).

51 See similar observations in Hodgson (2006a).

52 Vallini (2006: 191).

53 Vallini (2006: 195). See also Hodgson (2005: 223–224) for accounts of how the *juge d'instruction* sought to keep information from the defense.

police officer heading up the enquiry, were not called, as their evidence did not confirm the *juge*'s own case thesis.[54]

The findings of the Outreau review bodies also call into question the effectiveness of recent reforms and the ability of the defense to pierce the culture of judicial corporatism. In the 1990s and notably in 2000, a variety of due process safeguards were introduced into French criminal procedure, strengthening the role of the defense and introducing greater debate and transparency into the criminal process. In particular, provision is made for defense lawyers to participate in the *instruction* enquiry and for key acts and measures to be debated. This is further enshrined in the principle of *contradictoire* set out in the preliminary article of the code of criminal procedure, which opens: "Criminal procedure must be fair and accusatorial and it must ensure equality of arms." The Outreau case therefore, in theory, offered the opportunity for the defense to participate, to challenge acts of judicial investigation, to request that specific enquiries be made and experts instructed, and to have the defense case considered during the investigation. However, the enquiry documented the overwhelming dominance of the prosecution perspective of the *magistrats* in the criminal investigation and the marginalization of the defense at all stages, leading them ultimately to question whether, given the negative experiences of defense lawyers and their treatment by *magistrats*, it can really be said that French criminal justice is either *contradictoire* or fair, as anticipated by the procedural code.[55]

The excessive amounts of time spent in custody by those under investigation was also highlighted in the parliamentary report. The 2000 reform had introduced a new procedure, whereby the *juge d'instruction* can release a suspect on bail, but detention of the *mise en examen* can only be decided by the *juge des libertés et de la détention* (JLD) after the parties have had an opportunity to make representations. Until that time, the *juge d'instruction* was empowered to remand in custody those she was investigating. The hope was that this new procedure would reduce the number of suspects held in custody, as well as respect better the phases of investigation and judgment, but in practice it made little difference, with 90 percent of detention requests being granted by the JLD.[56] Although the idea was to have the decision made by someone more objective and distanced from the investigation, ironically, lawyers in the Outreau case were critical of the JLD's lack of knowledge of the case and so inability to engage with the arguments

[54] Vallini (2006: 141–142).

[55] Vallini (2006: 191). Resources were also identified as undermining the effectiveness of the defense. Obtaining copies of the dossier was difficult, and the poor rates of pay were also found to have made more difficult the availability of lawyers.

[56] It may be, of course, that this is not any form of malfunction, but that the *juge d'instruction* requests are, on the whole, well grounded.

of the defense.[57] Four of the accused were kept in custody for two and a half years, and three others for more than three years before the case was sent to trial.

In their reports on the investigation of the Outreau case, all three bodies of enquiry identified the kinds of role malfunctioning and external pressures that are often present in miscarriage cases whatever the procedural tradition—notably a failure to collect evidence in reliable ways; an uncritical reliance on (ultimately discredited) expert evidence; a culture of disbelieving the defense; a failure of system checks and balances; and pressure from the media.[58] However, the fault here lay not only with overly conviction-oriented police officers, or even the prosecutors who were too dependent on them, but more significantly, with judicial officers who are understood to act in the public interest, protect the rights of the accused, and maintain a neutral stance in their conduct of the investigation. This might cause us to interrogate our understanding of the strengths of different models of procedure. When wrongful convictions are overturned in England and Wales, some have called for more inquisitorial procedures such as the *instruction*, as a means of avoiding the premature narrowing of suspicion by the police and the resulting construction of a case against an accused identified early in the investigation. Yet we see similar dangers in both procedural models—a confirmation bias that extends across police, prosecutors, and judicial investigators.[59] Neither the professional ideology of the *magistrat* nor the checks and balances of judicial colleagues and lawyers are sufficient to ensure that the *juge* avoids being captive to the most plausible view of the case and investigates properly the evidence that points away from the suspect's guilt.

L'affaire d'Outreau had a profound impact on the legal system, in parliament, and across French society. This was not the result of technical legal error or reasonable, but ultimately unproved, accusation. Neither was it the product of rogue police officers or incompetent lawyers. The case went to the heart of the inquisitorial ideal, the functioning of the judicial investigation through the iconic *instruction*. It also recognized a new category of "victims of the judicial system"—a system that was acknowledged to be at fault, to have ruined the lives of innocent citizens, and for which judges and politicians alike apologized in the strongest of terms.[60] The case demonstrated the deep fault lines running through inquisitorial

[57] Vallini (2006: 223–227). The JLD noted that lawyers failed to make full written arguments as required. The rather vague ground of *trouble à l'ordre public*—maintaining public order—was also found to have been used in this case and, more generally, too frequently and as a means of avoiding properly evidenced and reasoned decisions to remand in custody. Vallini (2006: 255–256).

[58] On miscarriages of justice, see, e.g., Hodgson (2005: 181–185); Belloni and Hodgson (2000); Walker and Starmer (1999); McConville and Bridges (1994).

[59] On confirmation bias see Nickerson (1998). In relation to criminal investigations, see Kassin et al. (2003); O'Brien (2009a, 2009b); Judson (2017).

[60] Besnier and Salas (2008). The parliamentary enquiry was hugely oversubscribed, with four applicants per place, and nearly half of the group were from a legal background. In some respects the harm suffered by the child victims was overshadowed by the shock that such an injustice could have happened in France.

procedure: the enormous discretion vested in the judiciary and how, without exceeding the limits of the law, they were able to present a case built on lies and unreliable accounts as an objective judicial investigation uncovering the truth. The experience of those accused in the Outreau cases was not unusual: one-third of those in French prisons at that time were held in *détention provisoire* and one-tenth of those were likely to be found innocent of all charges.[61] It was as if the everyday practices of criminal justice were being exposed for the first time.[62]

C. Reforming Inquisitorial Procedure

After six months' work, during which over two hundred witnesses were interviewed, the parliamentary enquiry produced a six-hundred-page report, containing eighty recommendations for major reforms across French criminal procedure. The failings of the criminal process and their catastrophic consequences for those placed under investigation were acknowledged throughout the report, as each phase of the *instruction* was examined. The proposals for change touched most aspects of the pretrial process, from police detention and questioning to the role of the *chambre de l'instruction* in overseeing the conduct of the *instruction*.[63] The recommendations sought to dilute the worst excesses of inquisitorial procedure by making it less secret, more accountable, and more accusatorial—taking more seriously the principle of *contradictoire* as an organizing feature of the criminal process.

The commission proposed stronger defense rights throughout the criminal process and during the GAV in particular, including allowing the suspect's lawyer to be present during interrogations and to have access to the dossier when police detention is prolonged beyond twenty-four hours, as well as video recording of all interrogations. It proposed introducing more *contradictoire* features into the mass of investigations overseen by the procureur, and more collegiality of

[61] Parliamentary report (Vallini [2006: *avant-propos* by André Vallini]). This compared with a pretrial detention rate of 19 percent in Germany and England and Wales and 20 percent in the United States.

[62] This was also the case for those engaged with the criminal process. One psychology expert expressed surprise at the weight attached to his opinion and that a decision to detain a suspect in custody might be based on something that he had said, taken out of context.

[63] The reforms included stronger safeguards during the GAV; making the procureur-supervised enquiry more *contradictoire*; limiting the length and grounds of detention during investigation; making the *instruction* collegial, rather than conducted by a single judge; removing the secrecy of the *instruction* at the defense's request; strengthening defense rights throughout the investigation, including access to the dossier; reforming the *chambre de l'instruction*; improving the quality of expert evidence; protecting the interests and improving the evidence of children; reforming the training of *magistrats* and the professional ethics of judges and the media; increasing parliamentary accountability for criminal justice police; and, finally, making sufficient resources available to bring about the necessary reforms.

decision-making to address the isolation of the *magistrat*. Decisions to place those *mis en examen* in custody would shift from the JLD to a group of three judges, as would the process of *instruction*. This was commendable in its recognition of systemic problems, rather than attributing fault to isolated errors of human judgment. Yet adding some checks and balances to what remained a *magistrat*-controlled enquiry fell short of the kind of root-and-branch reform needed, and the basic structures of the criminal investigation were left unchanged.

Of the eighty recommendations, only a small number were taken forward by the minister, and even fewer have resulted in any concrete change. The judiciary has shown itself to be open to change, and the training of *magistrats* has been adapted to take account of some of the lessons of Outreau. Judges must now spend a period of time at the start of their career working alongside defense lawyers to ensure that they understand the importance of this perspective within the justice process, and the professional training and recruitment of *magistrats* takes more seriously the human and psychological dimension of being an investigator and the need for good social skills, as well as technical legal competence. However, recommendations that have required legislation and which challenge the centrality of the police and judicial investigation have proved much more difficult to implement.

(i) Strengthening the Principle of *Contradictoire*

Many of the proposals following the review of the Outreau affair addressed the broader dysfunctional working cultures and underlying systemic problems demonstrated through individual error or wrongdoing. The driving rationale of these proposed reforms was to strengthen the accusatorial nature of French criminal procedure, to decentralize roles, and to introduce more checks and balances—in Damaška's terms, moving further away from the vertical model of hierarchical control and authority toward features of the coordinate horizontal model of cross-checks and balances.[64] The reforms of the 1990s and 2000 had gradually increased the role of the defense lawyer by including her within the structure of criminal procedure and the conduct of the most serious investigations. However,

[64] See Damaška (1975). The vertical model is typified by inquisitorial procedures, where legitimacy resides in the hierarchical structure of authority, such as that of the Parquet headed up by the minister of justice. In contrast, the horizontal model, typified by adversarial systems, is a coordinate structure of checks and balances, rather than the concentration of authority in a single office or function. Damaška argued that these structures of legal authority tended to reflect the structures and cultures of political authority. For a discussion of the models in an empirical, French context, see Hodgson (2001).

there was resistance to increasing defense rights, even in these relatively modest ways: the defense role was seen as the antithesis to an effective investigation and so particularly inapt within an inquisitorially rooted procedure. Mistrusted within the professional and legal cultures of French inquisitorialism, the role of lawyers continued to be sidelined in practice.

However, building on the principle of *contradictoire*, the parliamentary proposals sought to allow the defense to play a more effective role and to be involved earlier on in the investigation process. The recommendations are interesting in several respects. First, they recognize the limited impact of these earlier reforms in practice, which allowed the continuing dominance of the police and procureur and the resistance to defense engagement in the investigation on the part of both police and *magistrats*. Second, they recognize the determining influence of the pretrial phase and the various ways that the concentration of investigative power, even in the hands of a judicial officer, leads not to a neutral enquiry but risks confirmation bias and so to the construction of a case against the accused.[65] In particular, they take much more seriously the importance of the GAV in shaping the case investigation, rather than seeing it as simply a preliminary police enquiry. Without proper information provided to the suspect and the possibility for the defense to provide assistance, the case quickly becomes constructed around a single prosecution perspective. Third, they recognize the centrality of the procureur in all criminal cases—including those passed to the *juge d'instruction*. It is interesting to see how these themes are repeated in later reviews of the criminal process, in decisions of the Conseil constitutionnel, and in the transnational principles developed through the ECtHR and EU legislation.

The traditional approach to the production of evidence within French criminal justice is to maximize the information available on the grounds that this assists in the discovery of the truth (the overarching objective of the criminal process), and to trust in the *magistrat*, as a public-interest-centered judicial officer, to investigate, scrutinize, and assess the reliability of evidence to this end, that is, to investigate evidence pointing toward and away from the guilt of the suspect—*à charge* and *à décharge*. This, of course, becomes a dangerous exercise if narrowed to evidence gathering that points only to the guilt of the suspect and is not subject to robust evaluation in terms of its credibility and relative weight within the enquiry. These risks were all too apparent in the Outreau affair: suspects were processed through the GAV, with little opportunity to contest the accusations against them, a task that became all the more difficult as the enquiry gained momentum and accusations were repeated in the *instruction*. Neither the procureur nor the *juge d'instruction* was concerned to test out the

[65] The various commissions made clear that the difficulties and malfunctioning in this case were rooted firmly in the conduct of the investigation, e.g., Viout (2005: 140).

credibility of the evidence gained during police detention and interrogation. The duty to investigate *à décharge* was ignored, and the field of evidence gathered was narrowed prematurely in the process of constructing a case against those considered suspects.

The recommendations of the parliamentary enquiry sought to address this bias by providing the suspect and defense lawyer with more case-related information and a greater role during the GAV. It recommended that more information be provided to suspects, setting out the precise detail of the charges; that a higher threshold of suspicion be required before placing someone in GAV; and that, from the extension of detention after twenty-four hours, the lawyer be present and have access to the dossier.

Although stemming from the malfunctions revealed in the Outreau affair, these recommendations foreshadowed the eventual, more far-reaching reforms that were required in order to comply with ECHR requirements, notably the right to effective custodial legal assistance following the landmark case of *Salduz v. Turkey*, discussed in preceding chapters. Similar proposals were also put forward by the Léger Commission report in 2009. Set up at the behest of President Nicolas Sarkozy, the Léger Commission was charged with examining the French criminal process and proposing ways of making it more coherent, while ensuring that it was responsive to increasing the effectiveness of crime fighting and provided greater rights to accused persons and to victims. The proposed abolition of the *juge d'instruction* was the commission's headline recommendation, but it also proposed that more information be provided to suspects and that the lawyer be able to intervene after twelve hours of GAV and be permitted access to any statements made by the suspect at this time. If the GAV was extended for a second twenty-four hours, the commission also proposed allowing the lawyer to be present in the suspect's interrogation by the police.

Although an improvement, the role of the lawyer envisaged in both these recommendations and those of the various Outreau commissions was still somewhat marginal to the police investigation—suspects would continue to have no lawyer present during the police interrogation in the first twelve or twenty-four hours of detention, and even when a lawyer was present, there were no plans to allow her to participate in any meaningful way. This was a tinkering at the edges, rather than confronting the shortcomings and dysfunction of what purports to be a procedure of judicially supervised investigation.

A second strand of recommendations designed to strengthen the principle of *contradictoire*, following Outreau, sought to enlarge the role of the defense lawyer in challenging the pretrial investigation and so to weaken the procedural reliance on police and *magistrats* alone. At the time of the Outreau recommendations, the lawyer was allowed only a thirty-minute consultation with the suspect, and even now, although she may also be present during the police interrogation of the suspect, she still has no role beyond the GAV in cases overseen by the procureur. As a result, more than 95 percent of cases proceed without the opportunity for any defense participation or any element that might be termed *contradictoire*. This has implications beyond those cases dealt with only by the procureur. Even in the tiny minority of cases passed to the *juge d'instruction*, crucial initial investigations will have been carried out, including questioning of witnesses and the suspect. The Outreau case, as well as earlier miscarriages of justice, demonstrates the extent to which the initial imprint of the case provided by the procureur-supervised police investigation can influence the subsequent enquiry.[66]

In order to provide greater opportunity for cross-checking and challenging the direction of the enquiry, the parliamentary enquiry recommended that, where possible, the defense have the opportunity to participate in cases supervised by the procureur in a fashion similar to those dealt with under *instruction*—that the defense be able to consult the dossier, make observations, and request that specific further investigations be carried out. The commission recognized, however, that this would have a limited impact, as there would not be sufficient time for this to happen in many cases where the accused is sent straight to court.

This is not to say that the defense role during the *instruction* is unproblematic. In theory, the defense lawyer is able to participate in the *instruction* investigation, making her own investigative requests as well as monitoring those of the enquiry. In practice, however, the Outreau case demonstrated how this role can be frustrated by the *juge* and then compounded by those responsible for investigative review, the *chambre de l'instruction*, whose tendency is to confirm, rather than to challenge, the decisions of fellow *magistrats*.[67] This goes to the heart of what underlies miscarriages of justice—the absence of any effective mechanism for testing out the evidence or challenging the case theory during the investigative stage. The trial stage (if indeed there is a trial) is too late—this is about processes that determine which evidence is brought before the court or others determining the outcome of the case, ensuring that relevant leads are pursued and important evidence is not omitted.[68] A major flaw in the inquisitorial model is entrusting the discovery of the truth to a procedure that is conducted or dominated by the public prosecutor—which in many ways is not dissimilar to England and

[66] For example, cases such as that of Patrick Dils, described at the start of this chapter, where the suspect's false confession to the police was impossible to displace even when before the *juge d'instruction*.

[67] The Vallini review characterized the *chambre de l'instruction* as the *chambre de confirmation*.

[68] That is not to say that the trial can never influence the pretrial in, for example, setting procedural standards of fairness, such that investigations are conducted in the shadow of evidence admissibility rules should the case be contested and go to trial.

Wales and the investigative monopoly of the police and prosecution, other than the greater impact of (the more numerous and detailed) rules of evidence that govern investigations and the admissibility of evidence in adversarial procedure. The procureur's judicial status means that there is an assumption that evidence is reliable, without the need for scrutiny of the process of evidence gathering. Post Outreau, this has been shown not to be the case, and the various commissions of enquiry recognized that a major cultural shift was required not only to enable the lawyer to carry out the role assigned to her, but also to strengthen her function as a check on the investigation.

The problem of judicial corporatism during the *instruction* was also recognized by the reviews. They sought to address this by strengthening opportunities for the defense to contribute to and to challenge the investigation, from the outset through to the decision on how to proceed at the close of the *instruction*—what Brants and Field describe as the necessity for a culture of institutionalized dialogue.[69] For example, the IGSJ review proposed allowing the defense to challenge the accused's status as *mise en examen* throughout the *instruction*, rather than just at the outset, in order to maintain an ongoing review of the evidence against her. And where a challenge is brought to the *chambre de l'instruction*, it recommended that the accused be permitted to appear in person: currently the procedure is a paper exercise. The parliamentary commission heard that lawyers had only obtained copies of the case dossier after protesting to the head of the court circuit, and so in order to enable them to work more effectively, it advocated for better resourcing to make copies available to the defense. It also recommended allowing the defence lawyer to be present for all witness statements and confrontations as well as introducing the possibility of challenge in the selection of experts and the framing of their instructions.

In order to ensure the adoption of a more *contradictoire* approach to the *instruction*, a change in the approach and mindset of the *juge* is also needed. The commission recommended that the *juge d'instruction* be required to sum up the evidence that had been examined over the course of the enquiry both for and against the suspect—*à charge* and *à décharge*—in order to make explicit how this duty had been fulfilled. Once the parties have had a chance to respond, the commission also recommended that any decision, whether to discontinue the case or send it to trial, should first be debated by all parties in public. While this last recommendation has not been taken up, Article 184 CPP now requires the *juge d'instruction* to invite comments from the parties on her final decision, and to specify the evidence for and against the accused. This was effective for a short time, but gradually judges reverted to their previous habits, and the legislation

[69] Brants and Field (2016).

has been undermined by the courts' decision not to enforce the requirements of Article 184 CPP.[70]

(ii) Regulating the Conduct and Recording of Interviews

As an inquisitorial-type process, the place of written rather than oral evidence is often emphasized as a feature of French criminal procedure. This is perhaps most evident during the *instruction* and the *juge* is assisted in this by a professional legal secretary, the *greffier*, who helps to administer the procedure and records witness statements taken by the *juge*. However, much of the evidence is gathered by the police—either in the first days of the investigation, or once the *instruction* is opened, through the delegated powers of the *commission rogatoire*. The taking and recording of evidence by the police has not been well regulated. Failing to recognize the centrality of evidence gathered at this early stage, the statements of witnesses and suspects, until very recently, have not been tape-recorded, nor written down verbatim, but recorded as a formal statement, lacking the spontaneity and so the authenticity of the interviewee's own voice.[71] With no guarantees as to the circumstances in which individuals are questioned, nor of the accuracy of the interview record, the weight attached to these statements once incorporated into the dossier and so "judicialized" seems misplaced.[72]

These dangers are amplified when those questioned are children and so more vulnerable. In 1998, a requirement to videorecord the testimony of child victims was introduced in cases of sexual assault and other serious offenses, and this was extended to child suspects in 2000.[73] However, in the Outreau affair this was ignored, sometimes because of lack of resources, sometimes because this was the child's preference: only seven of the one hundred interviews conducted were videorecorded. Those reviewing the conduct of the case found that it was impossible to evaluate the credibility of the children's accounts,

[70] Julian Licourt, "Outreau, le séisme qui aurait dû bouleverser la justice," *Le Figaro*, 24 August 2018.

[71] Hodgson (2004, 2005).

[72] Treating the contents of the *instruction* dossier as the product of a judicial investigation is problematic when statements have been taken by the police or others prior to the judge's involvement. This is especially pointed in terrorism investigations, where unsourced intelligence becomes evidence once "judicialized" and placed in the dossier. See Hodgson (2006a).

[73] The vulnerability of children to sexual violence and exploitation had been highlighted in cases such as the Dutroux case in Belgium in the mid-1990s, as well as through a number of international conventions such as the United Nations Convention on the Rights of the Child and the European Convention on the Exercise of Children's Rights. The success of video recording children's testimony in England and Wales was also cited in support of the reform. The law does not apply to all child witnesses, only to victims.

when some had been interviewed seven times and up to ten years after the events were alleged to have taken place. The written accounts appeared unrealistic with names and dates reeled off and no indication as to the questions posed, nor whether information was spontaneously provided. The number of accused grew as the children exchanged information among themselves, and those responsible for the children's protection appeared to bolster and encourage their accounts. This was described as a proliferation of increasingly fantastical accusations: children accused those they saw at the police station while in the waiting room, in a sports shop, in a cafe, and each time, social workers made a report and passed these to the procureur.

Another focus of post-Outreau reform, therefore, was to improve the reliability of children's evidence: ensuring that the accounts of children were taken in an appropriate setting and by officers and social workers who were properly trained. Recommendations were made to ensure that the testimony of children is always videorecorded, providing as complete an account as possible, enabling observation of the child's behavior, and avoiding the child having to repeat the account.[74] Perhaps unsurprisingly, just as with the introduction of tape recording in England and Wales, evidence suggests that these recordings are rarely watched. This may be an indication that there is little to contest (indeed suspects' interviews may only be consulted if there is a challenge) or the result of inadequate resources—though evidence suggests child interviews tend to be no more than thirty minutes in order to accommodate children's difficulty in concentrating for longer periods of time.[75]

The concerns of the Outreau enquiry went beyond the difficulties in obtaining reliable testimony from children, however, and the commission recommended the audiovisual recording of all interrogations conducted during the GAV. The eventual reform, however, extended only to those suspects questioned by the police or by the *juge d'instruction*, when under investigation for the most serious offenses, *crimes*. This means that the overwhelming majority of suspects questioned will have neither video nor audio recording; the interrogation will be recorded only in writing. The commission's reforms sought to bring real improvements to the process of police detention and interrogation: to provide suspects with legal assistance; to provide details of the case against them; to record all interrogations; to strengthen the oversight of the procureur; and to improve the material conditions of detention. Yet little has changed. Suspects have no access to the dossier of evidence, the procureur

[74] Having to retell their story also risks giving the impression that the child is not believed, or that what the child says is unimportant because the adults have already forgotten it and need to hear it again.

[75] Report of the Défenseur des droits (2013: 66).

does not exercise any greater control over the GAV, and just a small minority of suspects have their interrogation recorded. Lawyers are now present during the GAV, but this was not a response to the Outreau recommendations, but rather the result of France's hand being forced by the ECtHR—and even then the lawyer's role has been tightly circumscribed by legislation. And finally, the *contrôleur général des lieux de privation de liberté* (the inspector of places of detention) continues to highlight the appalling conditions in which those placed in GAV are held. Despite the commissions and reports and the public emotion following the "judicial fiasco" of Outreau, the failure to recognize the importance of ensuring the credibility and reliability of evidence gathered by the police continues; defense rights are still weakest where the suspect is most vulnerable—during police, rather than judicial, detention and interrogation.

(iii) Dispersing the Pretrial Power of the *Magistrat*

In addition to strengthening accusatorial measures and regulating the conduct and recording of testimony from suspects and witnesses, the commissions of enquiry suggested a range of measures that dilute the inquisitorial nature of the pretrial investigation by dispersing the power of the *juge d'instruction*. The Outreau case demonstrated how isolated both the *juge d'instruction* and the *juge des libertés et de la détention* are in their operation, and this was considered a major factor in the dysfunctional nature of their decisions in the case. The Vallini Commission in particular considered the abolition of the *juge d'instruction*, but rejected such a radical reform. Unlike the Léger Commission that followed, the Vallini review recognized that simply shifting power to the police and prosecutor would not have produced a better outcome. The abolition of the *juge* would require, as the Delmas-Marty Commission set out comprehensively fifteen years before, strengthening both the investigative power and the independence of the procureur. The commission decided that a reform on this scale was both unnecessary and unlikely to resolve the issues before it.

While wishing to avoid the worst excesses of inquisitorialism, a principal concern of the commission was that abandoning the model of pretrial judicial investigation would require accused persons to conduct their own investigations, the quality of which would depend on the financial resources available to them. This is a familiar argument. The adversarial model of defense participation as a party to the case, supplanting the judicial enquirer during the pretrial, is generally regarded as weakening rather than strengthening the equality of arms, as well as undermining equal treatment. The uniform competence of the *magistrat* is assumed, while the performance of the defense lawyer is seen to depend on access to resources.[76] Instead, the commission proposed maintaining the *juge*, but reducing her isolation by making the role more collegial. By working with others, young *juges* would in effect be mentored, and in all instances there would be less opportunity for highly individualistic or inappropriate approaches to investigation.[77] Sharing responsibility for the investigation (rather than just its review) would encourage a more objective and evidence-based approach, as reasoning would be open to discussion and challenge in the normal course of decision-making.

This proposal looked unlikely to make it to the statute book after the subsequent Léger Commission's recommendation to abolish the *juge d'instruction* role completely.[78] However, the Léger proposal was not adopted, in part because the corresponding shifting of investigative judicial authority to the procureur that this would require became untenable after the ECtHR questioned the judicial status of the procureur.[79] In 2007, a law was passed to introduce collegial decision-making in the *instruction*, with three judges working on each case, but without the corresponding budget required to recruit the additional 314 *magistrats* needed to implement the reform. The legislation was a lame duck. The number of *magistrat* posts continued to fall, and the reform was delayed repeatedly until May 2017, when it was finally abandoned before it had ever been implemented. Informally, *magistrats* have reacted by increasing the practice of *co-saisine*, so that there are two judges in a case to share information and decision-making. However, because no extra resource has ever been placed into this initiative, there are insufficient personnel to truly share the work, and one *magistrat* will effectively take charge.[80]

Rather than focus on strengthening the defense role or separating out the functions of the *juge d'instruction*, the IGSJ recommendations tend toward ensuring the proper functioning of structures already in place. For example, many of the errors in Outreau might have been avoided if the procureur had been encouraged to work more proactively in the *instruction*, challenging weak

[76] See discussion in Hodgson (2005: 28–29). An effective defense will require equal access to resources, but the professional ideology of legal actors is also important. No matter how well resourced, if the *juge* (or indeed the defense lawyer) maintains a conviction orientation, the accused's interests will be ignored and relevant evidence not put before the court.

[77] The *juge d'instruction* in the Outreau investigation was twenty-nine years old and inexperienced in such a serious, complex, and large enquiry.

[78] See discussion in Hodgson (2010). Given the centrality of the *juge d'instruction* to the Outreau enquiries, it was ironic that their long and considered recommendations were swept aside and contrary proposals put forward by the Léger Commission. It is widely accepted that this was one of the main objectives in establishing the Léger Commission; Nicolas Sarkozy made no secret of his desire to abolish the *juge d'instruction* and transfer all pretrial investigative power to the procureur.

[79] *Medvedyev v. France* (3394/03) 29 March 2010.

[80] Julian Licourt, "Outreau, le séisme qui aurait dû bouleverser la justice," *Le Figaro*, 24 August 2018.

evidence and protecting the public interest by ensuring that excessive charges were not brought. The IGSJ also recommended greater cooperation between the Parquet and the *juges du siège* in cases involving juveniles and sexual offenses, in order to maximize experience and expertise.[81] These proposals are unlikely to be successful, however, without parallel changes addressing the professional culture of judicial corporatism in which as fellow *magistrats*, the prosecutor, *juge d'instruction*, JLD, and judges in the *chamber de l'instruction* are aligned.

The excessive use made of *détention provisoire* was also a concern of the parliamentary commission, given the lengthy periods of time suspects spent in custody during the *instruction*. The recommendation was for *détention provisoire* to be determined by a bench of three judges, rather than a single JLD, and that it be used only exceptionally and on clear grounds of necessity. It proposed placing limits on the time that a person under investigation could be held in custody, but this was rejected, and instead, a system of reviews every six months was put in place. The number of those detained dropped initially following this reform, but it has now risen again to the levels it was prior to Outreau, and lawyers complain that nothing has changed and that their procedural challenges continue to be rejected systematically.

D. Conclusion

The extent of the response to the Outreau affair suggests that it struck at the core of French criminal justice. Cherished at home as a truth-seeking investigator whose judicial status and ideology ensure the protection of individual rights and freedoms, the *juge d'instruction* is admired abroad as a model of enquiry that avoids the tunnel vision and confirmation bias of police investigations. Yet three separate commissions of enquiry into the Outreau affair showed the many dangers of concentrating investigating power in the hands of a single legal actor and of placing unswerving trust in the actions and ideology of that person. The response was a tempering of the inquisitorial ideal, in some respects continuing the trend to make French criminal procedure more *contradictoire*. The recommendations touched on many features of the pretrial process, but neither the proposals nor their limited implementation posed any radical challenge to the centrality of a model of investigation understood to be carried out under the authority and oversight of a judicial officer. The participation of lawyers and the means of questioning and recording witnesses and suspects changed little. This is a long way from any procedural turn, but it is perhaps a gradual acceptance

[81] Viout (2005: 131–133).

of the need for dialogue and evidential testing and challenge, in place of a more closed and centralized enquiry. This middle ground sits comfortably within the trajectory of recent decades, rejecting the need for root-and-branch procedural reform in favor of an analysis of procedural traditions, not as entirely separate, but as being more or less *contradictoire*.[82]

Some might argue that this is not enough, however.[83] It fails to address the central problem of dualism contained within the *instruction*, or the broader issue of judicial corporatism, which prevents the defense from playing an effective role within the pretrial process. Justice malfunctions less through outright rule breaking than through the ways that discretion is exercised and the development of working cultures that contradict the stated aims of the law. Change requires both legal and structural reform. To achieve this would require the more radical solution of separating out the training and career paths of the Parquet and the *juges du siège*, changing what it is to be a *magistrat*. There is also a risk that if a more collegial approach were to be adopted, it would fail. We have seen the inability and unwillingness of *magistrats* to challenge the decisions of their colleagues, and a committee of three may serve to reinforce decisions, as we saw with the *chambre de l'instruction*, making it harder, not easier, for the defense to engage with, and to challenge, the conduct of the enquiry. The nature of the *magistrature* means that, despite the separation of functions, there is a continuity that is hard to breach. Lawyers are poorly resourced and regarded as outsiders, unsuitable to contribute to a public-interest-centered investigation. A more effective reform might be to open up the pretrial phase to greater external scrutiny, to move away from internal debate and make the procedure more truly open and *contradictoire*.

[82] See, e.g., Létocart (2012), who suggests that the French system is a hybrid of inquisitorial (*inquisitoire*) and accusatorial (*accusatoire*), such that it might be described as "incusatoire."

[83] Besnier and Salas (2008) argue that the various proposed reforms were no more than a sticking plaster, a temporary solution that failed to go to the heart of the inquisitorial system that has failed those it has investigated.

9

Mixing Inquisitorial Functions within an Adversarial Process

The Criminal Cases Review Commission

Following an unprecedented number of miscarriages of justice in the 1980s and the 1990s in England and Wales, the Royal Commission on Criminal Justice (RCCJ) was appointed to examine the functioning of the criminal process from the initial police investigation through to appeal in order to restore public confidence in the system of criminal justice. One of the commission's core recommendations was the establishment of a body to review possible miscarriages of justice, with the power to refer them back to the Court of Appeal, thus providing a new remedy where rights of appeal had been exhausted. This led to the creation of the Criminal Cases Review Commission (CCRC), a broadly inquisitorial body provided with wide investigatory powers and tasked with reviewing cases for possible referral to the appeal court. This was a radical reform—both in its establishment of a new and independent body, but also in its preference for an organization structured in a nonadversarial way. This chapter centers on the tensions produced in this novel mixing of procedures: on the function of the commission as an inquisitorial review body, its interactions with legal actors and processes operating within the adversarial tradition, and how this illuminates the nature of our attachment to values such as truth, innocence, and justice as they operate within different procedural frameworks.

The idea of an inquisitorial review body following a criminal investigation and conviction in an adversarial process is not unique to England and Wales. It has also found favor as a response to miscarriage-of-justice cases in some states in the United States. There are a number of established innocence projects and commissions, but the North Carolina Innocence Inquiry Commission (NCIIC) is the country's first standing innocence commission reviewing possible wrongful convictions.[1] It has some similarities with the CCRC,[2] such as the

[1] It was established following several high-profile miscarriages of justice in North Carolina. For more detail on its origins and operation, see Maiatico (2007).

[2] Maiatico (2007: 1346) describes it as being "patterned" after the CCRC. The CCRC has been of interest to many jurisdictions, but none has adopted it in full. There is a Norwegian CCRC, and the Scottish CCRC and Australia and New Zealand have proposed similar bodies. There were calls for a body similar to the CCRC after the Dutch scandal of the *Schiedammer parkmoord* case. The

The Metamorphosis of Criminal Justice. Jacqueline S. Hodgson, Oxford University Press (2020).

DOI: 10.1093/oso/9780199981427.001.0001

requirement for new evidence, but it adopts a more narrowly inquisitorial approach, requiring applicants to waive their procedural safeguards and to provide full disclosure,[3] as well as going yet further in procedural terms, by reversing the burden of proof and requiring proof of factual innocence irrespective of whether there has been a procedural irregularity. For its part, the commission carries out an investigation on behalf of the applicant, with powers to compel the production of witnesses and documents in the same way as a court. In keeping with its nonpartisan role, it must also disclose any new evidence of a crime to the prosecution.[4] This is a "cards on the table" approach that requires trust in all aspects of the process of review and decision-making, in a way that is unimaginable in the context of a system characterized by party-based and partisan adversarialism. Once the review is complete, the standard for referring a case to the three-judge panel appointed by the chief justice is whether there is sufficient evidence of factual innocence to merit judicial review.[5] For the conviction to be reversed, the panel must find unanimously that the applicant has proved by "clear and convincing evidence" that she is innocent of the charges.[6]

Given the highly adversarial nature of American evidence and procedure in theory and the widely acknowledged prevalence of negotiated justice in practice, this commission stands in stark contrast to the rest of the criminal process. By comparison, the CCRC review process represents a less radical departure from adversarial procedure; it does not require proof of factual innocence, but new evidence that casts doubt on the reliability of the finding of the trial court and a belief that there is "a real possibility" that the Court of Appeal will not uphold

Commission for the Evaluation of Concluded Cases was established, but this only accepts cases referred to it through the prosecutor general.

[3] In this the SCCRC is also more inquisitorial than the CCRC: it requires applicants to waive their lawyer-client confidentiality privilege on their application form. This was precisely in response to a case where the applicant's solicitor told the SCCRC that the applicant had admitted his guilt immediately following trial. As it turned out, there was no chance of a referral, but the commission considered how this (inadmissible) information would weigh in the balance if a referral had been a possibility. See Duff (2009: 705–706). This is also the basis of one of the fictional scenarios in Duff's earlier piece (2001).

[4] The role of the lawyer in innocence cases is also very different from that of the adversarial trial lawyer, leading to the suggestion that there should be "role-differentiated standards of professional conduct." Risinger and Risinger (2014).

[5] This is by a five-to-eight majority of the voting members of the North Carolina Innocence Inquiry Commission, but must be unanimous in cases where the defendant pleaded guilty. Although such referrals are controversial with prosecutors, some of those exonerated through DNA evidence pleaded guilty at trial. Given the dominance of plea bargaining and the pressure experienced by defendants to comply, this is hardly surprising.

[6] This is a more onerous standard, reflecting the American courts' historic reluctance to interfere with the trial court's verdict even in the face of evidence of innocence. See discussion in Maiatico (2007: 1350–1354). Griffin (2009: 150–151) also argues that the US reverence for the jury as a constitutional right and the greater number of appeal rights that exist in the United States compared with the UK explain why a higher threshold is required to overturn the jury's verdict.

the conviction. Although broadly inquisitorial in its function, unlike the NCIIC, the test for CCRC referral of cases speaks directly to the standard and process of appeal in ordinary (adversarial) criminal procedure. Once a case is referred, the commission plays no further role and the appeal court will hear the case in the usual way.

While not as radical as the NCIIC, as a body of last resort, examining a small number of possible wrongful convictions where all other remedies have been exhausted, the CCRC nevertheless represents a very different model of investigation and review within criminal justice in England and Wales. Independent of all parties to the case and enjoying wide investigative powers, the commission offers the potential to uncover new or previously undisclosed evidence and so to serve as a corrective to a faulty police investigation or defense case. It may also investigate evidence that was simply unavailable at the time of trial, such as that resulting from advances in forensic science or from witnesses who did not come forward at the time of trial. It is this ability to challenge the original construction of the case and to bring forward new evidence, rather than simply review what we already know, that makes the CCRC unique within the mechanisms of appeal.

Although there are obvious differences between a pretrial investigation and a postconviction review, there are also interesting comparisons to be drawn between the role of the CCRC and the inquisitorial enquiry conducted in France by the *juge d'instruction*, which might cause us to interrogate procedural models and values in new ways. Both enjoy broad powers in the conduct of a wide-ranging review, the scope of which is determined by them in large part,[7] and both prepare the case, to some extent, to be argued by others at court. But while the *instruction* is an integrated part of an inquisitorially rooted criminal procedure with corresponding checks and safeguards, the CCRC's review occupies an interesting space in the criminal process, sitting apart, sandwiched between the trial and appeal phases of an adversarial process, introducing a quasi-truth-seeking

[7] The *juge d'instruction* has very wide investigative powers, but her enquiry cannot stray beyond the offense that is referred to her by the procureur. If evidence of an additional offense comes to light, it must be referred back to the procureur, who will decide whether it should stay with the *juge* (as part of the existing investigation or a new one) or should be looked at in a separate *instruction* by another judge. In most cases, the terms of the existing *instruction* are simply extended, but offenses may be separated off for political reasons, to ensure investigation by a more docile *juge*. Although in some cases grounds are put forward by the applicant, it is the commission as neutral investigator that determines the lines of enquiry, which investigations should be undertaken, and, ultimately, if the case is to be referred to the Court of Appeal, on which grounds. An analysis of referrals over a three-year period (2005–2007) showed that the grounds of appeal were identified by the commission, not the applicant or her representative, in 15 percent of cases. (This figure is higher for the SCCRC—fifteen out of forty-three cases were on grounds identified by the SCCRC, and in twelve cases the commission identified the sole grounds. SSRC Research Report—Referrals—2015 available at http://sccrc.org.uk/research.

function into the criminal process that is entirely different from either the investigation and prosecution, or the criminal trial and appeal.

The commission's approach is inquisitorial in the sense that it is led by a central investigator rather than by opposing parties, but it lacks the characteristics and mission traditionally associated with inquisitorial criminal processes: it is not a judicial enquiry, and the overriding objective is to determine the likely safety of the conviction, not to uncover the truth. In modern 'mixed' inquisitorial traditions such as in France, there are now limited, but legally prescribed, roles for the parties, ensuring their participation in the investigation process as a form of counterbalance to the power and authority of the judicial investigator. However, although sitting within a wider process that is broadly adversarial, there are no such requirements for the CCRC to engage with the parties in the course of the review, allowing the commission much greater latitude in defining the nature and parameters of its own processes of review and decision-making.[8] These overlapping and contrasting organizational features provide an interesting lens through which to examine the nature and limits of procedural models across different contexts, and the challenges of fusing, or at least working across, inquisitorial and adversarial methods.[9]

This chapter examines the operation of the commission and the procedural lens through which it understands the concepts of innocence, truth, and safety of conviction in the way that it structures its review and in its interpretation of what amounts to a real possibility that a conviction will be overturned. Together with the next chapter, it draws on a body of empirical work conducted at several points between 2006 and 2018, in order to understand better the decision-making and practices of the commission as an inquisitorial, nonjudicial body and the ways in which it engages with the adversarial players and processes that precede and follow its review.[10] It analyzes how the commission makes sense of an inquisitorial review, the objectives to be pursued, and the permitted roles of those to whom the case will revert following a referral to the appeal court. It also considers where the interests of the applicant lie in all of this and how they are

[8] The participation of the defense as a counterbalance is arguably more necessary in the French *instruction* given the role of the prosecutor and the delegation of the judicial investigation to the police.

[9] This is, in some ways, how jurisdictions from a more inquisitorial tradition sometimes experience the requirements to adopt procedures and safeguards originating in the adversarial tradition, such as a strengthened defense role.

[10] Fieldwork spans several work periods, from my own early research starting back in 2006, to that conducted (with Juliet Horne) for Hodgson and Horne (2009), additional observations on case-planning committees in 2010–2011 (with Juliet Horne and Laurène Soubise) for Hodgson, Horne, and Soubise (2018). In addition to observations, case file reading, and analysis of case statistics, we conducted twenty-three interviews: eleven with commissioners, five with case review managers, and seven with solicitors who work regularly with the CCRC. They are referred in citations to as CM/CRM/Sol 1, 2, 3, etc. These were conducted between 2007 and 2009.

understood and represented within the commission's more inquisitorial frame of reference.

A. The Structure and Operation of the Commission

It is perhaps useful to begin by outlining the background to the establishment of the commission, as well as its structure and basic functions.[11] The CCRC was set up in 1997 under the Criminal Appeal Act 1995, to investigate alleged miscarriages of justice and to refer these to the Court of Appeal, where there is a real possibility that the conviction will be found to be unsafe.[12] In addition to the wrongdoing of the police, prosecution, and their experts, the string of serious and high-profile miscarriages of justice that led to the establishment of the RCCJ in 1991 demonstrated the inadequacy of the mechanisms in place for uncovering such malpractice and bringing it before the court so that the safety of the conviction could be reviewed. Where an appeal had been turned down, the Court of Appeal had no jurisdiction to hear a second appeal, even where fresh evidence had emerged. The only way that an appellant with new evidence pointing to innocence, or undermining the conviction in other ways, could have her case reopened, was to persuade the home secretary to refer the case back to the Court of Appeal under section 17 of the Criminal Appeal Act 1968.[13] This power was exercised rarely: the Home Office received between seven hundred and eight hundred applications each year, but referred only four or five of these back to the court.[14] The delay in overturning some of the most high-profile miscarriage cases was attributed to the inadequacy of this procedure. Following the recommendations of the RCCJ, the Court of Appeal's jurisdiction was extended so that it can now receive new evidence and hear a new appeal.[15]

[11] For an account of the background to the CCRC's establishment, as well as an analysis of its working and decision-making processes, see also Hoyle and Sato (2019).

[12] The idea of an independent review body had been suggested at various points during the preceding twenty years.

[13] Investigations were the responsibility of the Home Office C3 division. This arrangement was considered slow, unreliable, reactive, and insufficiently independent given the home secretary's position within the executive, responsible for law and order and policing. See Belloni and Hodgson (2000: 181–184). The CCRC is funded by the Ministry of Justice, but members of the commission are appointed by the Crown and so are not answerable either to the executive or to the judiciary, underwriting the independence of its members.

[14] Between 1981 and 1988, thirty-six cases were referred back; in the period 1989–1992, twenty-eight cases were referred. RCCJ (1993: chap. 11, para. 5).

[15] Section 4 Criminal Appeal Act 1995 amends section 23 Criminal Appeal Act 1968. In determining whether to admit new evidence, the court is required (under section 23(2)) to have regard to whether the evidence is capable of belief, whether it may afford a ground for allowing the appeal, whether it would have been admissible at trial, and whether there is any reasonable explanation for not having adduced it at trial.

In addition to this, the establishment of the CCRC was designed explicitly to provide a fresh approach to the investigation of miscarriages of justice. The RCCJ considered the Home Office role in reviewing cases for appeal to be incompatible with the separation of powers between the courts and the executive, especially given the home secretary's responsibility for law and order and for the police. It was also critical of the purely reactive approach of Home Office investigators and described "a reluctance on the part of the Home Office to enquire deeply enough into the cases put to it."[16] In contrast, the CCRC was established as independent of the executive and proactive in its work, with a broad discretion to refer cases back to the Court of Appeal where it believes there is a real possibility that the conviction or sentence will not be upheld,[17] or as the RCCJ phrased it, where "there were reasons for supposing that a miscarriage of justice might have occurred."[18]

The Criminal Appeal Act sets out the independent status and membership of the commission, its powers, and the conditions for making references to the Court of Appeal. Where an appeal has been determined or refused, the commission must consider that there is a real possibility that the conviction would not be upheld because of evidence or an argument that was not raised at trial.[19] Where there is no new evidence or argument, or an appeal has not been brought, a reference may still be made "if it appears to the Commission that there are exceptional circumstances which justify making it."[20] Once the reference is made, the Court of Appeal must hear the appeal in the ordinary way—the commission has no standing once a case is referred to the Court of Appeal. Defense counsel will argue for the appellant, though the grounds of appeal are effectively set by the commission, as the court's permission is needed to argue any grounds beyond those on which the commission has referred the case.[21]

There are few stipulations on the commission concerning how it organizes its work and conducts its reviews. The statute requires the commission to have regard to representations made to it when considering referral, to provide reasons to the court for any case referred to it, to provide reasons to the parties for any referral or nonreferral,[22] and to make a decision to refer through a committee of at least three commission members. In other respects, the statute makes no

16 RCCJ (1993: chap. 11, para. 9).

17 Section 13 Criminal Appeal Act 1995.

18 RCCJ (1993: chap. 11, para. 12).

19 See section 13 Criminal Appeal Act 1995. The focus here is on criminal convictions—the CCRC also has the power to review sentence and court martial cases.

20 Section 13(2) Criminal Appeal Act 1995.

21 Section 315 of the Criminal Justice Act 2003.

22 Section 14(6) Criminal Appeal Act 1995. In practice, the commission takes account of any representations made in response to its "provisional statement of reasons not to refer." and these sometimes cause the commission to reconsider and to refer the conviction back to the court. Hodgson and Horne (2009).

stipulation on the organization regarding the review process, nor the evidential standards required. In particular, it is left to the commission to determine what amounts to a "real possibility" in practice. The way that the commission understands its role has significant consequences for the scope and possibility of any new appeal for the applicant—for the investigations that will be carried out and so the evidence that can be presented, and the grounds on which an appeal might be permitted.

Operating under the umbrella criterion of whether there is a real possibility that the Court of Appeal will find the conviction unsafe, the CCRC might understand itself as adopting an inquisitorial investigative approach that feeds into the broader adversarial process. Or it may regard itself as wholly separate from the surrounding criminal process in conducting a review in which none of the parties to the case has any role and which simply determines whether there are grounds to send the case back to the Court of Appeal. However it conceives of its role, the commission must navigate the procedural tensions inherent within its function as an inquisitorial body operating within an adversarial process and determine the value it attaches to concepts such as truth, innocence, guilt, or the safety of a conviction in determining the nature and scope of its work.

The commission receives around fifteen hundred cases each year and refers around one in thirty-six back to the Court of Appeal,[23] with an overall success rate of between 65 and 70 percent—considerably greater than the success of appeals via the ordinary route.[24] However, it has attracted criticism from those who feel that the CCRC should take more risks in the cases it refers and from those who consider that, in following too closely the approach and reasoning of the Court of Appeal when determining "real possibility," the commission attaches insufficient significance to the innocence of the applicant.[25] Others question how successful the CCRC has been in uncovering new evidence, arguing that its success reflects a series of easy wins: few of the commission's big miscarriage cases have involved innocent people in the way anticipated at the outset, with more stemming from a change in the law, minor offenses, or retrials that have ultimately resulted in conviction.[26] The referrals of those seeking asylum, convicted

[23] CCRC (2019). The 2016/17 report notes that only twelve cases were referred that year—an unusually low figure.

[24] In the five-year period 2006 to 2010, between 430 and 572 appeals against conviction were heard by the Court of Appeal each year, the conviction being quashed in around 37 percent of cases (see Ministry of Justice [2011]). The published CCRC success rate includes appeals both against conviction and against sentence. However, if we disaggregate the small number of sentence-only cases, the success rate of conviction referrals from the CCRC remains at around 67 percent.

[25] This was a criticism of Innocence UK, a loose network of innocence projects following on from the US innocent movement, but which has now been disbanded—though its existence as a coordinated group or movement has been called into question (Greenwood 2017).

[26] Bob Woffinden, an investigative journalist and campaigner for those believed to be wrongfully convicted, has described the CCRC as "an experiment that failed" and a "fig leaf" that allows ministers to deflect criticism of the criminal justice system. He challenges the commission's claims to

of entering the UK with false identification documents or with no documents at all, represent a case in point, as a new strand of "repeat" cases.[27] The referrals address a significant issue in the criminalization of immigration and asylum and have raised awareness of the law in this area—in which practitioners routinely, but incorrectly, had advised defendants to plead guilty. However, as repeat cases, the referrals are almost guaranteed to succeed and so, accounting for more than one-third of the convictions referred back to the Court of Appeal between 2014 and 2016,[28] they have also had the effect of bolstering the CCRC's referral statistics and success rates,[29] as well as improvements to their case review time.

The commission has also been free to establish its own staffing structure and its processes of review and referral, and so has shaped its operations around its own understanding of its role to a large extent. It sits within the Ministry of Justice[30] and is staffed by around eleven commission members (CMs), forty case review managers (CRMs), an investigations adviser, and a legal adviser.[31]

success, pointing to the minor nature of many of the decisions over a ten-year period, taking it further from its original remit. Bob Woffinden, "The Criminal Cases Review Commission Has Failed," *The Guardian*, 30 November 2010. https://www.theguardian.com/commentisfree/libertycentral/2010/nov/30/criminal-cases-review-commission-failed. This was reflected in the comments of some commission staff in the course of my own research, who described cases such as that concerning a parking violation as "up there in the league of pointless referrals" (CRM). However, only around 5 percent of referrals relate to magistrates' court convictions, and 2.5 percent go to retrial—around half of which result in acquittals.

[27] The treatment of these cases has also led to the development by the commission of an efficient process to identify and review these types of cases, building on expertise, repeating successful arguments, and so dealing with reviews more quickly. The Court of Appeal went on to criticize the CCRC for referring this line of cases "as a matter of routine," when applicants had not previously appealed, and as a result these cases are no longer automatically referred. See *YY v. The Queen* and *Ayad Mohammed Nori v. The Queen* [2016] EWCA Crim. 18. The CCRC changed its policy and stopped accepting these cases as exceptional circumstances and so referring them where no appeal had been made. One case was referred in 2017, as this was a guilty plea in the magistrates' court, from which there is no right of appeal. See Hodgson et al. (2018).

[28] Nine of the twenty-six convictions referred between April 2015 and March 2016 were asylum cases, and twelve of the thirty-four referred between March 2014 and April 2015. Sato et al. (2017) refer to nine out of thirty-three cases, but they fail to exclude sentence-only referrals.

[29] Sato et al. (2017: 110) report that a total of forty-three asylum convictions have been referred and, excluding the six pending and two abandoned, 91 percent have been quashed—a much higher rate than the 68 percent of nonasylum cases over the course of the CCRC's operation.

[30] It sat under the Home Office until 2007. The commission resisted strongly the loss of its own website (it sat within the .gov.uk website), which it considered an important demonstration of its independence from government. CCRC written evidence to the House of Commons Justice Committee, December 2013, para. 51. Since 2015, it has had its own website, independent of the government site.

[31] Section 8 Criminal Appeal Act 1995 stipulates that the commission shall consist of no fewer than eleven members of whom at least one-third must be legally qualified and two-thirds must have knowledge or experience of any aspect of the criminal justice system—one of these involving Northern Ireland. There have been periods with more than eleven, but as part of a program of financial savings (2011/12 was the sixth successive year in which the commission saw its budget cut) the numbers have dropped to nine CMs, including the chair, and some of these were part time. The 2016/17 report notes that the commission lost three of its most experienced CMs (including two highly experienced former practitioners (a prosecutor and defense lawyer), reducing the number once

Investigations are carried out by a CRM with oversight from a CM and input from a legal adviser when requested.[32] In addition to being able to compel any public body to provide information, it may also apply to the Crown Court for an order compelling private bodies or individuals to give the commission access to documents or materials within their possession.[33] Occasionally, investigations cannot properly be carried out by the CCRC itself, and so it also has the power to instruct a police officer to conduct investigations on its behalf. The vast majority of applications originate with those seeking to have their conviction quashed or sentence reduced, but the commission may also be asked by the Court of Appeal to carry out specific investigative work at either the appeal or leave-to-appeal stage.[34] Typically, these involve allegations of jury impropriety.[35]

The commission needs some way of prioritizing and organizing cases, and so applications are subject to an initial sift or screening process. Nearly half of all applications are quickly rejected at this stage on the grounds of ineligibility,[36] because there is no basis for review ("no reviewable grounds") or because no appeal

again to nine. Despite the commission's being nearly one-fifth under the statutory minimum, "[T]he Ministry of Justice has indicated that it is appropriate for the Commission to operate for a limited period with only nine Commissioners." CCRC (2012: 9). In 2019 there were thirteen commissioners, including the chair, but all were part time. CCRC (2019).

[32] CRMs are organized into small groups headed up by a group leader (GL) who is an experienced CRM. This is a relatively soft management structure: CRMs retain a large degree of autonomy and the GL role is principally to mentor new staff, manage caseloads, and facilitate the sharing of expertise and experience across groups, as much as to oversee the work of colleagues. During my research, there was no system for allocating cases to match skills or experience—although systems have recently been put in place to address this—and the variable quality of investigations was commented on by the House of Commons Justice Committee in its 2015 report. One solicitor also told us, "I can make two submissions and raise the same points of law in the submissions and get different interpretations from the Commission on each application. There's no consistency of approach" (Sol 2). This was also recognized by some commission staff: "[T]he quality of our work here is very variable and that places some applicants at a disadvantage whether they have a solicitor or not" (CM 11). Hoyle and Sato (2019: 92) also noted that "the differences in commissioner's perceived approaches to decision-making provide grounds for concern."

[33] The power to obtain information from private bodies was provided for by an amendment to the Criminal Appeal Act 1995 in July 2016. Prior to that the commission was only able to compel public bodies to provide information. This could be frustrating, as many functions previously exercised by public bodies (e.g., the Forensic Science Service) are now in the private domain.

[34] See sections 5 and 15 Criminal Appeal Act 1995. Some cases have also been referred to the commission by the police, especially concerning Northern Ireland.

[35] These directions are given priority over other cases by the commission, partly because the case is already at an advanced stage and perhaps partly because of the status of the Court of Appeal. As one CM put it (from field observations): "We can hardly say thank you very much, we'll fit you in, in 18 months' time." The commission received around eight cases per year in this way (see paras. 31–33 of CCRC written evidence to the House of Commons Justice Committee, December 2013), but this has declined to just one or two in recent years.

[36] Applications are not eligible for review if the commission lacks jurisdiction (applicants must have been convicted in the criminal courts of England, Wales, or Northern Ireland, or in the Court Martial or Service Civilian Court) or if it is a reapplication that does not present any new grounds. Together with cases still within the statutory appeal time limit, or which have an appeal pending, 6 percent of cases are rejected in this way by administrative staff (Hodgson et al. [2018]).

has been brought and there are no exceptional circumstances that would justify a review.[37] The remaining 45 percent or so of cases that get past these initial screening processes will be channeled into pathways, depending on their complexity and the time required to complete investigations. Once a case has been investigated, the CMs determine whether to refer the case back to the Court of Appeal. A decision not to refer is taken by a single CM; a referral, however, must be decided by three CMs, in accordance with statute.[38]

The commission enjoys considerable freedom to determine its own approach and to decide by what values or objectives the scope of its investigation should be guided. In determining the safety of an applicant's conviction, the commission could choose, for example, to invite the CPS to advance arguments as to why there is no real possibility that the conviction would be overturned, thus cutting short the investigation. Or it could itself focus investigations on matters pointing to guilt and the reliability of the conviction, again removing the need for extensive investigations on behalf of the applicant where there is no doubt around the safety of the conviction. This would not reflect the spirit in which the commission was established, however: to investigate whether there is fresh evidence that casts doubt on the safety of the conviction and to provide the opportunity of further appeal in such cases. In practice, although the commission does not understand itself as acting for the applicant in adversarial party terms, it positions itself at the outset as investigating any possible reasons why the conviction may be unsafe, such that the court might overturn it—as against reasons why it may be safe. During the review this sometimes raises difficult questions as to the direction of investigations—whether only those that might demonstrate innocence, or guilt, or either, should be pursued. The approach taken is generally that if something may demonstrate innocence, even if it also risks showing guilt, that is reason enough to follow that line of enquiry.

The commission is a non-judicial body required to investigate the process by which the case came to prosecution and trial in order to assess the safety of the conviction, but it is not making a judgment on the case itself. However, in practice, these two things can be hard to separate. So, for example, it may commission

[37] On the treatment of "no appeal" cases, see Hodgson et al. (2018). See also Hoyle and Sato (2019: chap. 6) on the ways that different types of application are triaged. In my own research, commission staff expressed concern at the inconsistent ways that cases were "screened" out. Hoyle and Sato (2019: 319–320) also found this, though there have been efforts to address this.

[38] Section 3(2) of Schedule 1 of the Criminal Appeal Act 1995. This means that if the investigation yields no grounds for referral, it will be passed to a single CM, who will either provide the applicant with a provisional statement of reasons explaining why the case is not being referred and inviting any further arguments for consideration or, if the CM believes a referral should be considered, pass it to a committee for decision on how to proceed. Those cases that are more complex, or where a referral looks more likely, will be considered by a committee of three CMs, assisted by the investigating CRM. The committee may need to meet several times before making a decision, requiring further research and investigation of the case to clarify potential points for referral.

further forensic tests in order to check the reliability of the findings presented at trial, or review the police procedures and collection of evidence over the course of the initial investigation. Or it may investigate the case in new ways by instructing experts, interviewing witnesses, or following up on leads that were unknown or not of interest to the police or the defense. Sometimes, further investigations into the case are needed in order to demonstrate that the conviction is unsafe—that it rests on partial or misleading evidence, for example. As a layperson, the applicant can assert her innocence, but may not be able to articulate this in terms of how she was wrongfully convicted: she knows that a witness lied, but not that this was because of pressure applied by the police; she may know that she was not present at the scene of the crime, but not that her lawyer failed to interview the key alibi witness. In order properly to review the case, the investigation can require the commission to go beyond the grounds raised in the initial application, as these are often peripheral to the real issues.[39] This then leads to a further predicament: how far it should go in this direction, acting on its own initiative rather than restricting itself to what is raised by the applicant.[40] A determination of the issues in the case by the applicant sits more comfortably within the rhetoric of party-based adversarialism, but is likely to hinder the discovery of evidence that will trigger a new appeal; a more inquisitorial approach would see the commission setting the parameters of the review in order to assess the safety of the conviction as required by statute and envisaged by the RCCJ. The overall approach is inquisitorial, as a review of the reliability of what has gone before, but also informed by the issues raised by the applicant—rather than based on the accusation as would be the case in the *instruction* investigation.

B. Innocence, Truth, and Safety

Focus on the safety of the conviction, rather than, say, the innocence of the appellant, is a major underlying difference between the nature of the commission's enquiry and the inquisitorial procedural tradition of criminal justice, which centres on truth. This illuminates the unusual role of the commission as an inquisitorial body that must operate within an adversarial criminal process, phases of which both precede and follow it. "Safety" reflects an emphasis on the reliability of the

[39] This is particularly true of unrepresented applicants, which currently stands at nearly 90 per cent. CCRC (2019: 10).

[40] When reviewed by management consultants, one suggestion for a more efficient and rational use of resources was to limit investigations to the issues raised in the application. This was not well received (and was not acted upon); staff were clear that it would hamstring and undermine the work of the commission. Such a model also seems implicitly to assume that the commission acts on the instructions of the applicant, which it does not.

evidence, traditionally a preoccupation of adversarial procedure: truth and innocence are largely absent from this criminal justice discourse.[41]

The historical context of the commission's establishment—the wrongful conviction of men and women widely believed to be innocent of the crimes for which they had served time in prison—makes the disregard for innocence as a formal criterion in CCRC referrals controversial in some quarters.[42] Commission staff recognized that the cases they referred tended not to be the kinds of case that had led to the setting up of the CCRC.

> I think we are finding it more difficult now to identify what you might say [is] a genuine miscarriage of justice[,] the real ones where you think somebody was genuinely convicted wrongly and it's all been a terrible tragedy. We get very many more technical miscarriages now where somebody, somewhere hasn't followed the rules, [but] there is not actually much doubt that the appellant was guilty as hell. (CM 11)[43]

The commission does not take less seriously the kinds of miscarriage cases that we saw in the 1980s and 1990s, which were characterized by wrongdoing on the part of the police and prosecution. Rather, it is that these do not make up the vast bulk of the applications the commission deals with.

> If there are police misconduct issues, they tend to relate to nondisclosure, more of that than beating a confession out of people. . . . it's always been the case that there's vastly more cockup then fit-up in what causes cases to be referred. . . . The exception in relation to that I think is interesting is Northern Ireland. (CRM 5)

> When I came to this role, I suppose I expected, like others expected, that policemen's conduct would be a very significant feature in the reasons why we received applications, and yet that wasn't the case . . . allegations around lawyer misconduct or lawyer ineptitude actually were very much on the agenda and have continued to be on the agenda. (CM 3)

> [O]f the ten most given reasons for making applications, the police figured at about number seven or eight . . . the top by far was the quality of the defense of people going for trial. (CM 8)

[41] Duff's (2001: 356) contention that "the Commission's primary function is a dispassionate search for the truth" seems to overdraw the inquisitorial nature of the two commissions.

[42] The definition of miscarriage of justice for the purpose of awarding compensation is different again. See, e.g., the discussion by the Supreme Court in *R (Adams) v. Secretary of State for Justice* [2011] UKSC 18.

[43] There is also some concern that there are occasional cases where the commission cannot rectify verdicts that appear palpably wrong. See Hoyle and Sato (2019: 315).

Regardless of the nature of the wrongful convictions that come to the attention of the CCRC, there are reasons to think that innocence is not the right criterion to govern reviews or referrals. There is much appeal in lay notions of miscarriage of justice representing innocence when we take as our example a case such as the Birmingham Six—a group of men who were completely failed by the legal system. Factual innocence here is easy to grasp. Similarly, we might find problematic a clear-cut case of factual guilt, where guilt is unequivocally proven by scientific evidence such as DNA, but which was obtained in a manner rendering it inadmissible. This is the "Dirty Harry" scenario—we *know* the person is guilty, but she walks free. However, these kinds of clear-cut cases are extremely rare away from the screen. Factual guilt and innocence are very difficult to establish, which is precisely why we have evidential rules to try to guarantee the reliability of information on which the jury will base its decision. While we would certainly not want legal tests and criteria to stand in the way of overturning the convictions of those who are factually innocent—this is what the CCRC was designed to overcome—this does not necessarily mean opposing overturning the convictions of the guilty.[44] As the commission itself has pointed out, it is important that convictions do not rest on police or executive malpractice.[45]

Then-CCRC chair Richard Foster set out the importance of the safety test in his foreword to the 2010/11 annual report:

> [U]nequivocal evidence of innocence is rare to find outside the pages of crime fiction. More common is evidence which may not prove innocence, but casts doubt on the safety of the conviction. What is at issue is the presumption of innocence and the integrity of the process. That is our strongest safeguard against miscarriages of the Birmingham Six kind and why safety, and not innocence, is the test Parliament requires the Court of Appeal—and thus us—to apply.[46]

This was echoed in the comments of one of the CRMs we interviewed.

[44] As Quirk (2007) has cautioned, the rhetoric of innocence suggests deserving and undeserving appellants, and a devaluing of the integrity of the criminal process as something to be protected.

[45] In 2006, the government considered removing the Court of Appeal's discretion to quash a conviction on the grounds of procedural irregularity, where there was clear evidence of guilt. The CCRC opposed this, arguing that while this applied only to an extremely small number of cases, it would represent a major disturbance of the current constitutional separation of powers and would prevent the commission from considering cases of abuse of executive power where there was also strong evidence of guilt. Such a change would alter the role of the Court of Appeal and ignore the importance of the courts in safeguarding due process protections and the rule of law. *Quashing Convictions: Report of a Review by the Home Secretary, Lord Chancellor and Attorney General* (2006), London: Office for Criminal Justice Reform. See also discussion in Spencer (2006).

[46] This quotation reminds us that although an accused begins with the benefit of the presumption of innocence, once her conviction is unsafe and has been overturned, that presumption is not reinstated. See further the home secretary's comments to Sam Hallam set out below.

> That's why, I think, sometimes organisations like MOJO[47] can go wrong . . . they kind of latch onto somebody's innocence as opposed to the safety of the conviction, and nobody can know if somebody is innocent or not. (CRM 3)

Although innocence is not a legal criterion in the criminal appeal, or in the CCRC's process of review, it is nevertheless applied by the Home Secretary to those wrongly convicted and imprisoned as the criterion for determining their eligibility for the compensation. The 1988 Criminal Justice Act stipulated that compensation would only be paid where it was proved, beyond reasonable doubt, that there had been a miscarriage of justice.[48] The Supreme Court in *R (Adams) v. Secretary of State for Justice* agreed on two categories of wrongful conviction that would constitute miscarriages of justice for compensation purposes: where fresh evidence shows innocence, or it so undermines the evidence against the defendant that no conviction could possibly be based upon it.[49] Parliament responded by amending the legislation to narrow the parameters of what constitutes a miscarriage of justice further still, requiring that factual innocence be demonstrated beyond reasonable doubt. The new subsection states that "there has been a miscarriage of justice in relation to a person convicted . . . if, and only if the new or newly discovered fact shows beyond reasonable doubt that the person did not commit the offence." This is a curious standard in many ways. First, factual innocence is something that no criminal court is required to address, but which a member of the executive, the home secretary, will be required to determine in deciding whether to award compensation. Second, it employs a criminal standard of proof in a way that has been challenged as incompatible with the presumption of innocence in Article 6(2) ECHR.[50] Third, it is the new

[47] The Miscarriages of Justice Organisation set up by Paddy Hill (one of the Birmingham Six) to help those wrongly convicted. MOJO is no longer involved in applications to the CCRC, according to recent correspondence between the author and the commission.

[48] Criminal Justice Act 1988, section 133(1): "When a person has been convicted of a criminal offense and when subsequently his conviction has been reversed or he has been pardoned on the ground that a new or newly discovered fact shows beyond reasonable doubt that there has been a miscarriage of justice, the Secretary of State shall pay compensation for the miscarriage of justice to the person who has suffered punishment as a result of such conviction or, if he is dead, to his personal representatives, unless the non-disclosure of the unknown fact was wholly or partly attributable to the person convicted."

[49] [2011] UKSC 18. The court did not include cases where the fresh evidence renders the conviction unsafe such that a reasonable jury would not have convicted, or where errors in the investigation or trial mean that the person should not have been convicted.

[50] The incompatibility argument was rejected by the Court of Appeal and then by the Supreme Court in *R (Hallam and Nealon) v. Secretary of State for Justice* [2019] UKSC 2. The ECtHR has held that Article 6(2) ECHR can apply to compensation claims relating to criminal proceedings, but the presumption of innocence will not be violated if compensation is refused, unless there has been an acquittal "on the merits." In *Allen v. UK* (25424/09) 12 July 2013, the applicant's conviction was overturned after evidence relating to shaken baby syndrome was discredited. No retrial was ordered, but this was not an acquittal on the merits. In *KF v. UK* (30178/09) Unreported September 3, 2013 ECtHR (cited in Bailin and Craven [2014: 514]), quashing a conviction without ordering a retrial was termed a discontinuance of criminal proceedings, "not an acquittal 'on the merits' in the true sense."

or newly discovered fact that must demonstrate innocence beyond reasonable doubt. This seems unnecessarily narrow, when it is likely that the new evidence together with the case taken as a whole may demonstrate innocence.

In practice, many of those who have been wrongly convicted and punished will not qualify for compensation.[51] To suffer a miscarriage of justice here means something different, a different kind of innocence.[52] Despite the state's error or wrongdoing in causing a person to be punished unjustly, compensation will be payable only if the home secretary determines that the person has been proved beyond reasonable doubt not to have committed the offense.[53] This is not something that either the CCRC or the appeal courts are qualified or required to do.[54] In some instances, the evidence is clear—where, for example, DNA shows conclusively that the appellant could not have committed the crime. In others, the conviction is unsafe, but this may be expressed in varying degrees—not as an indicator of innocence for the purpose of compensation, but relating to the strength of the appeal court's doubt as to the strength of the Crown's case.

Nevertheless, in making her determination for compensation under the act, the home secretary has drawn on comments made by the appeal court. In the case of Sam Hallam, the secretary of state took note of the fact that the Court of Appeal declined to make a declaration of innocence when invited to by defense counsel; in Victor Nealon's case, she relied on the Court of Appeal's comment that the fresh evidence did not "demolish" the prosecution case.[55] There is an obvious danger in taking comments framed as part of a judgment to overturn a conviction and using them in the context of a compensation decision. The appeal court judges are not required to address questions of innocence and so cannot be presumed to have done so. To do otherwise imports indirectly a new burden of proof into the criminal appeal, as appellants will need to argue and demonstrate innocence, rather than that their conviction is unsafe. If they do not, the absence of proof of innocence will be held against them, as they will be denied compensation for their wrongful conviction. Highlighting the surreal nature of the

[51] See further Justice briefing on the Bill at https://2bquk8cdew6192tsu41lay8t-wpengine.netdna-ssl.com/wp-content/uploads/2015/01/JUSTICE-and-Liberty-briefing-for-ASBCP-Bill-on-compensation.pdf. Also, Justice (2018a). In the UK, as in the United States, exonerees often receive less practical and financial support in general than released prisoners who have served their sentence. See the "Say I'm Innocent" campaign at http://sayiminnocent.com. One interesting suggestion has been to award exonerees back pay for the time served. Encarnacion (2017).

[52] See also Bailin and Craven (2014), who also consider the position where a retrial is ordered.

[53] This is an onerous burden of proof when compared with a civil claim, which would normally seek to place the claimant back in her original position, and requires proof on the balance of probabilities.

[54] The Court of Appeal made no declaration of innocence in any of the high-profile miscarriage-of-justice cases—the Birmingham Six, Guildford Four, Maguire Seven, Judith Ward, Cardiff Three, or Sally Clark.

[55] Annex to the judgment in *R (Hallam and Nealon) v. Secretary of State for Justice* [2016] EWCA Civ. 355, at para. 13.

mismatch of concepts between the findings of the Court of Appeal and those of the home secretary, the secretary of state's letter rejecting Sam Hallam's claim to compensation on the ground that there was no miscarriage of justice also stated that "Mr Hallam is presumed to be and remains innocent of the charges."[56]

In addition to principled legal objections to the imposition of this burden of proof, there are practical obstacles to appellants demonstrating their innocence. Aggravated by an inequality of resources and powers, it is often not within the defense's ability to gather the necessary evidence that will determine innocence. And where appeals are preceded by a CCRC investigation, there may be a direct clash of standards, as the commission may decline to carry out enquiries that might go to innocence because they are not necessary to challenge the safety of the conviction. A more equitable system of determining compensation is required, recognizing in particular when the state has not acted simply in error, but in bad faith. The appearance of innocence as a criterion highlights the inconsistencies and the tensions in values between different procedural phases and legal outcomes of the criminal process. The difficulty in establishing truth, especially in a party-driven process, is recognized in the legal procedural construction of guilt and the rules of evidence that seek to regulate the information before the court in the adversarial tradition. It is strange, therefore, that innocence, a related but even more elusive concept, should indirectly find a place in the criminal process in this way.

C. The Scope of the CCRC Review: Practical and Procedural Values

We have seen that although a broadly inquisitorial body, the commission's focus is on the safety of the conviction under review—a concept rooted in evidential standards—not on the truth in the case or the innocence of the applicant. Safety is a broad concept, however, and the commission must work to some further guiding principles or organizing features in determining the proper scope of its investigation. How it fashions these are within the commission's own discretion. In conducting its review, the commission is not reopening a criminal case in its entirety, nor is it acting as a court. It is required only to investigate potential

[56] Annex to the judgment in *R (Hallam and Nealon) v. Secretary of State for Justice* [2016] EWCA Civ. 355, at para. 7. This should be read in the light of *ALF v. UK* and *Adams v. UK* (70601/11 and 5908/12) Unreported November 12, 2013 ECtHR, in which the applicants challenged the compatibility of section 133 with the presumption of innocence under Article 6(2) ECHR. The ECtHR held that the determination of compensation did not require an assessment of the applicant's guilt (and such language should be avoided) and so did not call into question their innocence. Therefore, it did not violate Article 6(2) ECHR.

wrongful convictions, and once there is a real possibility that the conviction will not be upheld, it is for the court to evaluate the evidence both for and against the appellant. But how the commission articulates the relationship between its role as an investigator, and its task in referring cases to the appeal court, is crucial. As an investigative body, the commission has unparalleled powers to obtain information.

> We are, of course, an inquisitorial body and in an adversarial system . . . there is no body, no individual, no group, no organization that has the amount of quality information that we have about any named individual, any applicant . . . we get the defense papers, prosecution papers, police reports, forensic reports, CPS reports, memoranda, we get disclosure lists, we can go to all the public bodies to get information, by statute, and we can get loads of information from the private sector. . . . We can put it all together. It gives us an extraordinary amount of knowledge and quality information, which is far beyond anything that the prosecutors or the defenders ever could get or ever have got.[57] (CM 8)

The commission is described as, and understands itself to be, an inquisitorial body, but this descriptor alone is insufficient to determine or to capture its approach to investigations given its position as a non-judicial body operating within an otherwise adversarial process. As noted above, the commission can choose to pursue enquiries proposed by the applicant; or those it considers likely to yield useful information; or those that will provide information pointing clearly to guilt or to innocence; and it might also consider time and money limitations. There are no formal roles for the parties, so the initial application may be the only external input into the enquiry. The commission might also apply negative filters—investigating only evidence that will be admissible in the appeal court, or only evidence that it is sure will give rise to a real possibility that the conviction will not be upheld on appeal. Understanding how it exercises this discretion reveals something of the commission's values and objectives in carrying out its work and how it understands and interprets its inquisitorial investigation role.

For example, how closely should the commission's enquiries take account of the rules of evidence to which any appeal will ultimately be subjected? When questioned by the Home Affairs Select Committee in 2002, the then-CCRC chair, Sir Frederick Crawford, expressed the view that there is no point gathering evidence that will be inadmissible.[58] This seems an unnecessarily strict

[57] This CM told me that he thought the CCRC does the work that the defense would do if it had the powers and resources. This interview was conducted before the CCRC were given powers to obtain information from private bodies.

[58] Minutes of Evidence, April 2002, response to Qs 58 and 59.

interpretation and not one that the commission would now follow. Although the Court of Appeal is required to have regard to the question of admissibility when deciding whether to admit new evidence under section 23 of the Criminal Appeal Act 1968, this is not binding and is only one factor to be taken into account.

Others have argued that the commission should separate out enquiries into safety from the gathering of evidence that is admissible on appeal. Former member of the Scottish Criminal Cases Review Commission (SCCRC) Peter Duff makes several arguments in support of the latter view.[59] First, the fact that both the CCRC and the SCCRC must be made up of lay as well as legally qualified members suggests an intention that these bodies be distanced from the ordinary legal process. Second, in its discussion of the establishment of the CCRC and of the grounds for appeal, the RCCJ made clear that the commission should be able to take account of inadmissible evidence. At first blush, the problem is that inadmissible evidence, even if it demonstrates the applicant's innocence, will not meet the test of real possibility and so it will not result in a referral. However, the RCCJ considered that the Royal Prerogative of Mercy should still be available for exceptional cases and that "[t]he one category of case that has been drawn to our attention where this might happen is if the Court of Appeal were to regard as inadmissible evidence which seemed to the Authority to show that a miscarriage of justice might have occurred."[60] Third, there would be little point in having the CCRC and SCCRC if they operated in ways identical to the courts.

But if the commission does not follow evidential standards, how should it determine which evidence to gather and to take account of? It is inevitable that the commission will make judgments about the quality of evidence—these judgments inform all aspects of its work, from initial decisions on whether to pursue witnesses or new evidence at the investigation stage, to the evaluation of material obtained during an enquiry and, ultimately, whether the evidence supports a referral. So, for example, it may choose not to interview a witness that it considers will provide evidence that lacks any credibility—to take Duff's example: "where the applicant produces a new eye-witness to the crime, who claims that he saw little green Martians committing the offence rather than the applicant."[61] More commonly, the commission may make these judgments based on legal evidential standards—a witness will be considered wholly unreliable because of a previous conviction for perjury. Similarly, it may not instruct an expert in an area that has been discredited. The difficulty occurs when it is not clear-cut, when there is evidence at the close of the review pointing both ways.

[59] In its first report, the SCCRC made clear that it would "not preclude itself from taking account of evidence which would normally be classed as inadmissible" (quoted in Duff [2001: 350]).

[60] RCCJ (1993: chap. 11, para. 18).

[61] Duff (2001: 345).

The commission must then decide how far it is responsible for evaluating the evidence in order to determine whether to refer, and when it should leave this to the court in order not to usurp the judicial function.[62]

Duff links this argument to the debate around innocence and factual guilt, favoring an outcomes approach, rather than a system approach. This stems from his view of the commissions as inquisitorial, and therefore concerned to seek the truth. He argues that if the commission has evidence of breaches in due process safeguards that might result in the conviction being overturned, it should nevertheless exercise its discretion not to refer the case back to the Court of Appeal where it has credible but inadmissible evidence that the applicant committed the crime. Unappealing though it is to refer back to the Court of Appeal a case where the applicant's guilt seems in little doubt, and notwithstanding the desirability for the commissions to connect with popular understandings of miscarriages of justice, this approach arguably goes too far in allowing the commissions to assume the role of the court (or indeed to surpass it, by making a decision that the court could not) in the sense of making a final decision on the case outcome.

Duff's equating of an inquisitorial investigation with one that seeks out the truth raises an interesting question about the way that we understand the term "inquisitorial." At its broadest, the inquisitorial model represents an investigation by a single independent enquirer—in contrast to the adversarial notion of the parties investigating and presenting arguments at a hearing. But does this necessarily also encompass a truth-finding role, as Duff asserts? In France, the inquisitorial nature of the pretrial criminal procedure is certainly part of a wider criminal justice ideology of the search for the truth, carried out by a judicial officer, unencumbered by rules of evidence as complex as those in systems reliant on lay fact-finders—an ideology that carries through to trial. But the commission's role is different—a nonjudicial, postconviction review, feeding back into the adversarial process.

The commission's objective and broader ideology will affect how it chooses to structure an investigation. As noted earlier, it must exercise discretion in determining which lines of enquiry to pursue—whether to explore all of those that might have a bearing on the safety of the conviction (either to confirm it or to call it into question), or only those that might assist the applicant's case. There is also a difference between proactively pursuing enquiries that might confirm the correctness of the conviction, and following them only when they present

[62] O'Brian has observed that in cases hinging on expert evidence, the commission, rather than the courts, is best placed to weigh and sift the evidence. The CCRC is able in this way to identify cases where there is a genuine disagreement on the science, and in these instances, he argues, the real possibility test should be relaxed "to make clear that where the Commission is persuaded that the expert case at trial is materially at variance with the best view of the expert evidence as it appears to the Commission, it can and should refer the case" (2011: 25).

themselves. This is especially relevant given that investigations and references back to the Court of Appeal are also on the basis of grounds not raised by the applicant, but identified by the commission, in some 15 percent of referrals. There may even be choices to be made between two lines of investigation: one that might undermine the conviction and one that would tend to confirm it. The way that the commission exercises its discretion in these instances reveals something of the way that it understands its role as an independent investigator. One solicitor we interviewed considered this a limitation in the commission's role:

> You cannot be both judge and advocate, and the commission is in the role of being both judge and advocate. I know they are not judges, it's not a judicial body, but they are making a judgment at the end of something. . . . I just see that there is an absolute inherent conflict in interests. (Sol 7)

In case committees, the commission will flag up explicitly investigations that might either confirm or challenge the safety of the applicant's conviction. In these situations, it will undertake the enquiry, reminding itself that it does not act for the applicant. As one CM explained during a case-planning committee meeting, when deciding whether to order forensic tests: "It is broader than just how would this aid the applicant. It might also go to confirm his guilt—that is not *why* we do it, but it is part of the picture." In another case that we observed, the following conversation took place between a CRM and CM.

CRM: In the early days here, when work was proposed that could only prove guilt, I asked if we could justify it and the answer was yes. Is that still the case?

CM: Yes—particularly as they've asked us to do it.

CRM: And because if we do these [tests] first, and they prove guilt, then it stops other work?

CM: And if we have a case held up in public as a miscarriage of justice, then this impacts on the family of the victim, etc., then our role includes resolving that either way.

Once information is obtained, this choice is more obvious. As an inquisitorial body, the commission must place equal weight on all the evidence it obtains. It cannot ignore that which does not serve the applicant's case, as that would be acting in a partisan manner.[63] Indeed, these are the kinds of actions that give rise

[63] The commission understands its inquisitorial role in this way: "The CCRC is inquisitorial rather than adversarial and does not work for either side in a case. It is not uncommon for our enquiries to turn up some new evidence that assists the defence and some that assists the prosecution and all material will be taken into account. We will carry out whatever investigations we consider to be

to miscarriages of justice in the first place—when police and prosecutors suppress information that would assist the defense.

The commission must determine how broadly to cast its net of investigation, but also how much of its findings it should then report in the statement of reasons (SOR) to the court. Back in 2000, Leonard Leigh (then a CM) noted that there was disagreement on this within the commission. His own view was that the SOR should "contain a balanced account of the case, setting forward the reasons for making a reference, but not ignoring those reasons which militate against that course."[64] By demonstrating that it acts impartially and objectively, the commission would thereby win the strong support of the Court of Appeal. Others disagreed with him, believing that the SOR's purpose "is simply to inform the court why the commission refers the case and is not intended to canvass matters which are extraneous to that decision."[65] Duff also ponders this, reporting that when confronted with this in their very first referral, the SCCRC decided not to mention the incriminating evidence that they discovered, because it was already in the prosecution's possession (which had simply overlooked it) and it was not particularly damning. If entirely new and significant incriminating evidence had been discovered, the SCCRC agreed that would have to be disclosed.[66]

Deciding exactly how to investigate is part of a larger issue—as an inquisitorial body, who does the commission represent? The CCRC advises potential applicants:

> The CCRC is **completely independent**. We do not work for the courts, police or the prosecution. We do not work for the people who apply for a review of their cases. We stay independent of all sides so that we can investigate alleged miscarriages of justice impartially.[67]

The commission is neutral; it does not act for any of the parties. But there will come a point when acting to ensure that a wrongful conviction is referred coincides with acting in the applicant's interests. We asked CRMs whether, when they draft a referral SOR for the committee, they are in fact advocating for the applicant.

necessary to address an applicant's submissions or any issues in the case that we identify ourselves" (2015: 5).

[64] Leigh (2000: 374).
[65] Leigh (2000: 374).
[66] Duff (2009).
[67] https://s3-eu-west-2.amazonaws.com/ccrc-prod-storage-1jdn5d1f6iq1l/uploads/2015/01/CCRC-Useful-information-for-potential-applicants.pdf.

> I don't think it's being an advocate for the applicant, no. In a sense it's just doing what your job is. If it's an arguable point, then I think your duty is to put that across to the committee, as the committee can always say no, we don't agree because of X, Y, Z, or there might be issues that you've overlooked, etc. I just think it's a fairness point really, other than anything else. . . . I would never see myself as acting for the applicant. (CRM 4)
>
> As for acting as an advocate, I don't think it's the role of the CRM to do that. I think it is their role to put the best argument, but once they've reached the committee stage, to get the best decision and that means if the committee are of the view that there isn't a reference [to be made to the Court of Appeal], to be assiduous in making sure that the reasons for that are properly documented in an understandable way within the provisional that gets issued. (CRM 5)

In this way, the commission is concerned to ensure a proper and objective interrogation of the evidence to ensure that it has looked at things from all angles before coming to its decision. One CM was clear that there is a point at which the commission *is* acting in the interests of the applicant.

> I think some of my colleagues might disapprove of it but . . . if there was a case that really made you think, "Hey, this one doesn't feel right," it's perfectly proper to ring up the solicitor and say, "Hey, we have these huge powers. How do you think we could best deploy them?" rather than just simply saying, "Thank you very much for your application form—go away and we'll tell you in two years' time." . . . We should never be instructed, as it were . . . we shouldn't be the agents of the defence solicitor. . . . I mean actually once you do get involved in a case . . . and you do believe it should be a referral . . . you are actually acting on behalf of the applicant there, and . . . I think it's cloud cuckoo land to say that you're being totally neutral. (CM 9)

D. Interpreting "Real Possibility"

In its investigation of cases, the commission has very broad powers—it can set the terms of investigation as it sees fit; it is not constrained by the issues raised in the application; it may examine police, prosecution, and court files, as well as information withheld from the defense on public interest immunity grounds; CMs can commission new forensic and other expert evidence; and while it invites comment from the applicant (but not the CPS) before a final decision is made not to refer, ultimately it is for the commission alone to determine whether or not to refer the case back to the Court of Appeal.

However, it might be argued that while the commission enjoys considerably greater powers and resources than the former arrangements under the Home Office system, as well as an independent status, it is fettered to the extent that the structuring of its relationship with the Court of Appeal through the Criminal Appeal Act 1995 reflects much of the former approach of the home secretary. Although enjoying no formal restriction on the categories of cases that could be referred back, the home secretary adopted the practice of only referring cases where there was new evidence or "some other consideration of substance that was not before the trial court" and where there was a "real possibility of the Court of Appeal taking a different view than it did on the original appeal."[68]

The threshold of "real possibility" lies at the heart of the commission's operation too: a case can only be referred if the commission considers there to be a real possibility that the conviction will not be upheld.[69] This guides its work from the initial screening process through to decisions on whether to refer a case to the Court of Appeal.[70] It forms a crucial part of the procedural framework within which the commission must operate. This is different from a search for the truth, innocence, or even whether the applicant was wrongly convicted—by phrasing the test in this way, it conditions the commission's decision on the practices of the Court of Appeal, which themselves change over time. In practice, this stretches from clear grounds to overturn the conviction, to CMs having a "lurking doubt" where they think the evidence is "on the cusp" and so should give the applicant the benefit of the doubt, to cases that are "referable" even though the CMs "would be amazed if it was quashed."[71]

This contrasts with the legal framework of the *instruction* in which the *juge* is required to carry out any investigative acts that she considers will assist in finding the truth, both those incriminating and exculpating any suspect.[72] The criteria for sending the case to trial is simply whether, after investigating the case, the *juge* considers that the evidence shows that the person under investigation has committed an offense.[73] The CCRC's task is defined in more limited terms, because it is concerned to review the process by which the applicant was convicted,

[68] RCCJ (1993: chap. 11, para. 6).

[69] Criminal Appeal Act 1995, section 13.

[70] In his evidence to the House of Commons Justice Committee, the then-chair, Richard Foster, said that the test does not come into play until later: "When we start looking at a case, we don't start looking at it from the point of view of there being a test called the 'real possibility' test and whether this case might pass it or not. We start, when we look at a case, in the way that anybody ought to start looking at the case—by saying, 'Here's the case. Is there anything here that concerns us? If there is, let's investigate it' " (para. 13).

[71] These were all ways in which referral criteria were expressed in discussion in committees.

[72] CPP Art. 81.

[73] CPP Art. 176. There must be evidence of likely involvement in criminal behavior in order to place somebody under *instruction* (CPP Art. 80-1), and there are opportunities to appeal decisions of the *juge* at various stages of the procedure.

rather than making a judgment on the case itself.[74] It may consider that the applicant has been wrongly convicted, but unless there is a real possibility of that conviction being overturned, it will not refer the case back to the Court of Appeal. In this way, the CCRC's job is not to investigate whether a miscarriage of justice has taken place, as this alone will not result in a referral. In articulating the statutory referral criteria in these terms, there is, of course, an assumption that the same factors that have led the commission to believe that the applicant was wrongly convicted will persuade the Court of Appeal of the same. While this is true in most instances, there are exceptions; the commission may believe that the applicant was wrongly convicted, but if it does not consider there to be a real possibility that the Court of Appeal will overturn the conviction, it cannot refer the case. More often, the reverse is true; there is a procedural irregularity that makes the conviction unsafe and so it will be referred, but the commission does not believe that the applicant is innocent.[75]

Naughton and others involved in the (now disbanded) innocence projects in the UK have argued that in structuring the real-possibility test in this way, the CCRC fails to address the very problems it was set up to remedy:[76]

> [T]he CCRC does not attempt to determine the truth of alleged miscarriages of justice but, rather, whether convictions might be considered "unsafe" by the Court of Appeal. This disconnects the CCRC entirely from a concern with whether alleged victims of miscarriages of justice that apply to it for review are factually innocent or guilty. This is perhaps, most problematic at the extremes of the CCRC's operations when it means assisting the factually guilty to overturn convictions on abuses of process and turning a blind eye to potentially factually innocent victims who are unable to fulfil the real possibility test to the satisfaction of the CCRC.[77]

O'Brian is also critical of the CCRC's timidity: "[T]he Commission has been unduly deferential to the Court of Appeal in cases involving expert evidence and insufficiently focused on the goal of freeing actually innocent people."[78] To change this situation, however, would require a change in both the statutory test of the Court of Appeal and that of the CCRC—or even more radically, to make the CCRC a judicial decision-making body. The NCIIC, for example, is

[74] We would not expect it to mirror the *instruction* given that the commission is not a judicial body and so there is no justification for attaching the same credibility to its findings.

[75] This is the concern of those espousing the now-disbanded UK Innocence movement.

[76] See Roberts and Weathered (2009) for a more conciliatory approach to how the innocence projects might work to complement the function of the CCRC.

[77] Naughton (2012: 211).

[78] O'Brian (2011: 22).

able to operate in a strongly inquisitorial fashion in part because it does not then feed back into the adversarial process with its complex rules of evidence and procedure, but establishes a wholly separate panel empowered to overturn the conviction.

The real-possibility test links the broadly inquisitorial role of the commission into the adversarial procedure of the Court of Appeal in ways that may constrain its effectiveness as a review body. It may conduct an effective investigation and uncover significant new evidence, but if the practice of the Court of Appeal is not to overturn convictions on those grounds, the commission is unlikely to refer. Or, where a case is referred and the commission believes it is clear that the applicant was wrongfully convicted, the court may uphold the conviction—because some of the evidence is inadmissible or because, in counsel's translation of the new evidence into legal grounds of appeal, the overall picture and the force of the evidence are lost.

The interpretation of real possibility is key to the commission's role. Possibility is a lower threshold than probability or even likelihood. How much does the adjective "real" increase that threshold? The Crown Prosecution Service must be satisfied that there is a "realistic prospect of conviction" before bringing a prosecution, and this is generally understood to be more than a 51 percent chance of conviction.[79] Through the process of judicial review, the High Court has provided some judicial interpretation of the test. In *R v. Criminal Cases Review Commission* (ex parte *Pearson*), Lord Bingham stated:

> The real possibility test . . . denotes a contingency which, in the Commission's judgment, is more than an outside chance or a bare possibility, but which may be less than a probability or a likelihood or a racing certainty. The Commission must judge that there is at least a reasonable prospect of a conviction, if referred, not being upheld.[80]

The commission has consistently defended the test and its success rate in the Court of Appeal: 65 to 70 percent, it claims, represents a real possibility. However, while there was a broad consensus among those we spoke to at the commission

[79] The Code for Crown Prosecutors 4.6 explains this: "A realistic prospect of conviction is an objective test based solely upon the prosecutor's assessment of the evidence and any information that he or she has about the defence that might be put forward by the suspect. It means that an objective, impartial and reasonable jury or bench of magistrates or judge hearing a case alone, properly directed and acting in accordance with the law, is more likely than not to convict the defendant of the charge alleged. This is a different test from the one that the criminal courts themselves must apply. A court may only convict if it is sure that the defendant is guilty." In determining this, the prosecutor must assess the reliability of the evidence. For an argument that the requirement is lower than "an even chance," see the dissenting opinion of Lady Hale in *R (on the application of Gujra) (FC) v. Crown Prosecution Service* [2012] UKSC 52, at para. 126 onward.

[80] *R v. Criminal Cases Review Commission* (ex parte *Pearson*) [1999] 3 All ER 498.

that real possibility is the correct test, there was disagreement over how this might be measured.

> There have been suggestions that we should have regard to some other concept, such as a miscarriage of justice or innocence. I think that's complete rubbish! We are only a gateway. We don't decide, the Court of Appeal decides. The only rational basis is for us to . . . put ourselves in their minds and just aim off a bit, but it has to be the possibility of its not being upheld, exactly the same test that they have. . . . Real possibility gives that margin of error, so I'm not making my own mind up, I'm trying to predict if there is a possibility. . . . And we end up, it's something like 60 percent to 70 percent of our referrals they quash. . . . Feels about right, we don't really mind whether it's 50 percent or 80 percent but it's in that realm. (CM 2)
>
> If there were a different test, maybe more cases would be referred, if there were a lower threshold, but I can't for the life of me see what purpose that would serve. I don't believe any cases we reject, that if referred on any test, would lead the court to quash the conviction . . . the rate convictions were quashed on our referrals would fall from around 70 percent to 50-something percent. I don't for one moment think "real possibility" can mean that. (CM 10)

Rather than basing the referral on its own belief in whether there has been a wrongful conviction, the commission takes the view that it is obliged to mirror the Court of Appeal's approach to a large extent, that the test to be applied by the Court of Appeal and by the commission are "harnessed" together (or "shackled," as its critics prefer it).[81] One former chair of the commission described the necessary symmetry between the CCRC and the Court of Appeal: if there is a line of cases making clear that a particular argument will be rejected, the commission will not refer on the basis of that argument, as there is not a real possibility that the conviction will be quashed on that basis. When questioned by the House of Commons Home Affairs Select Committee in 2004, then-CCRC chairman Professor Graham Zellick explained:

> What is absolutely essential, it seems to me, is that, whatever statutory test Parliament—that is to say you—imposed, it has to be one that articulates with the test that the Court of Appeal itself has to apply. If you break that link and you establish an asymmetry between the two tests, you would be creating an absurd situation. It would create tension between the Court of Appeal and the Commission, it would raise expectations, it would cause confusion, and it is

[81] Zellick, in response to House of Commons Home Affairs Select Committee, January 2004, Q32; Naughton (2012: 211).

> difficult to see what possible public interest could be served by referring cases on a basis that had no relationship to the test employed by the Court itself.[82]

If the commission tries to mirror the court's reasoning, it will also have to second-guess how the court will exercise its discretion in receiving new evidence: whether the evidence is capable of belief, whether it will afford a ground of appeal, whether it is admissible, and whether there is a reasonable explanation for failing to adduce the evidence at trial.[83] These are broad criteria, and it is for the Court to determine how much weight to attach to each. This might be seen as a necessary and practical means of ensuring the symmetry between the court and the CCRC, or the commission overstepping its role and substituting itself for the Court of Appeal. It is further evidence of the tension between the commission's broad, inquisitorial, investigative role and the ways that translating the results of this into grounds for referral may import a different set of constraints and guiding values.

This approach also seems to undermine the fundamental role of the CCRC as an independent body investigating miscarriages of justice. The commission's task is not to determine whether it thinks the Court of Appeal will find the conviction to be unsafe,[84] but whether there is a real possibility that it will do so. There is a further danger that in trying to predict the outcome in the Court of Appeal, the commission ceases to look for a real possibility and in fact reverses the test: it fails to refer because it believes that the court might well uphold the conviction. That may be the case, but that is not incompatible with the existence of a real possibility that the court will overturn the conviction. For example, one CM commented in a case committee: "It would be nice to send it back, but I find it difficult to think that the Court of Appeal will find it enough," to which her colleague replied: "Not 'will' find, but is there a 'real possibility' that they will find it enough." Moreover, the commission was established with the express purpose of making it easier to get cases back in front of the Court of Appeal; replicating its reasoning carries the danger of closing down cases prematurely.

82 House of Commons HASC, January 2004, Minutes of Evidence, response to Q28.

83 Section 23 Criminal Appeal Act 1968. The RCCJ had recommended that the test for evidence should be whether it was capable of belief, rather than simply whether it was credible, as under the original 1968 act.

84 The Criminal Appeal Act 1995, as well as establishing the CCRC, amended the grounds on which the Court of Appeal could overturn a conviction, from unsafe and unsatisfactory, a wrong decision in law, or a material irregularity at trial, to simply whether the conviction was unsafe. This simplified test was intended to encompass all these categories of appeal. RCCJ (1993: chap. 10, para. 32). The former categories, including that of "lurking doubt" (where the jury verdict, in the context of other jury verdicts, defies any rational explanation) were effectively restated in *Pearson v. CCRC* [2000] 1 Crim. App. R. 141 at para. 10. This was the first judicial review of a decision by the CCRC not to refer a conviction to the Court of Appeal.

There is a further reason why we might question the commission's preoccupation with "symmetry." Following this logic, the CCRC would be obliged to replicate the worst aspects of the court. Indeed Professor Zellick has stated quite clearly that it is the commission's duty to follow and apply questionable decisions of the appeal courts, not "to assert ourselves as some rival juridical authority."[85] But it cannot be right that the commission should never challenge the approach of the court. If the commission believed that the court had erred in law, or was adopting an approach that was racist or homophobic, surely it would not want to follow that line of cases, and they should not operate as any bar to referral.[86] The commission must therefore make a judgment between the appeal court decisions it disagrees with, but by which it nonetheless feels itself to be bound, and those it is prepared to challenge in making a referral. This is the ground that lies between almost certain success and almost certain rejection—the possibility of success. Could we go further and dispense of the real-possibility test completely? If, after thoroughly investigating the case the commission believes there has been a wrongful conviction, on what basis would we argue that this should not then go back to the Court of Appeal?

Some, such as Duff, argue that the statutory tests for the CCRC and the SCCRC allow plenty of scope for both commissions to challenge the courts.[87] Zellick has also defended the CCRC's approach, arguing that it is not unduly deferential to the Court of Appeal, but, rather, it pushes at the boundaries and is "straining at the standards of the court."[88] This view is not shared by all of his colleagues. One CM told us:

> I think to push back the boundaries in terms of trying to get the Court of Appeal to go in legal directions they don't want to go is a well and truly hopeless and pointless task. (CM 7)

In his written evidence to the House of Commons Justice Committee, Glyn Maddocks, a lawyer with many years' experience of working on CCRC and Court of Appeal cases, argued:

85 Zellick (2005: 938).

86 We also observed this in a committee discussion where two CMs asked how much they should "buy into the likely approach of the Court of Appeal" and their colleague vehemently opposed this reasoning because he did not want to lend support to what he considered the flawed approach of the Court of Appeal.

87 Duff (2001, 2009). The SCCRC may refer where it believes a miscarriage of justice may have occurred and it is in the interests of justice to refer. It receives fewer cases (703 in the period 2008–2013, compared with 5,449 received by the CCRC) but refers a greater percentage than the CCRC (6 percent compared with 2 percent), with a success rate of around 50 percent for conviction referrals (88 percent for sentence, so 66 percent overall).

88 Zellick (2005: 950) agreeing with the words of Nobles and Schiff (2005: 189).

> The CCRC should take a far more robust approach to the CA and when it feels that the CA has got it wrong, which I believe has been the case on a number of occasions, it has a duty to say so, rather than adopting a position of silence and neutrality.[89]

The landscape of criminal appeals, he believes, has got worse since, or perhaps because of, the establishment of the CCRC: the Court of Appeal has become more reluctant to quash convictions on the basis that the jury reached the wrong decision.

Campbell Malone, another practitioner with considerable experience of CCRC applications and Court of Appeal cases, has gone further still. He argues that the CCRC does not operate in symmetry with the Court of Appeal (it might be better if it did), but is in fact more timid and more conservative in its approach; it underestimates the court's willingness to consider fresh evidence, especially expert evidence. While the commission is preoccupied with a narrowly constructed approach to the real-possibility test, the Court of Appeal is more willing to be persuaded by the interests of justice as the overriding consideration. Malone cites a number of cases where this has been the clear approach of the Court. While acknowledging the courage of the commission in some referrals, he considers these the exception, concluding:

> The CCRC have frequently been out of step with the approach taken by the CACD [Court of Appeal, Criminal Division] and have been overly cautious in their approach to fresh-evidence cases, particularly those involving expert witnesses.[90]

Taking a bolder approach to real possibility would require the commission to feel more empowered and to understand itself in more strongly independent and inquisitorial terms. It was not only solicitors who told us that they thought the commission too timid,[91] so did some CMs:

> This was an absolutely classic case of its time. . . . I lost a lot of sleep and I became very angry with the commission over that case because I got the response from my colleagues: "pure speculation—the Court of Appeal won't accept this—there's nothing proved against these police officers." And I took the view

[89] Para. 17, written evidence, February 2014.

[90] Malone (2009: 114).

[91] For example, solicitor 4 told us: "My only criticism, and I know that I'm certainly not alone in this, is that the threshold for the CCRC, for very understandable reasons, is high. And that means that they may not want to run the risk of damaging . . . their success statistics in circumstances where I think it would be right that they tested the case."

> that the Court of Appeal was actually quite a practical and pragmatic and quite savvy court in that it knows which end is up. . . . And that it was rather a naive view of ours not to think that the Court of Appeal would understand that. . . . But I think they [the other CMs] were taking a very purist, theoretical, legalistic, academic [line]. (CM 9)
>
> The commission is scared of the Court of Appeal. We need to be strong in the Home Office[92] so that we are financially secure and won't be undermined. Then we can be more confident in attacking the Court of Appeal. We should refer anyway and not be so hung up on what the Court of Appeal will think. (CM 6)

Among other CMs, there was real concern about the way that the commission was seen by the Court of Appeal and a reluctance to refer cases if there was a risk that they would "get egg on their face" or be criticized by the court if they referred.

In its 2015 review of the CCRC, the House of Commons Justice Committee did not find compelling arguments to alter the ground for referral to the Court of Appeal and so recommended retention of the real-possibility test. However, it accepted evidence that the test is sometimes applied in problematic ways and so recommended that the commission be less cautious in its application of the test.[93] It also acknowledged that in addition to the statute and its interpretation by the CCRC, the approach adopted by the Court of Appeal has a determinative effect on which cases are referred to it, and so this also bears some analysis.

This is not a new concern. The RCCJ commented that the Court of Appeal, since its creation in 1907, has been too heavily influenced by the jury. It noted that most successful appeals were on the grounds of errors of law—some 83 percent concerned the judge's summing up or a wrong decision to include or exclude evidence. Appeals were allowed on the grounds of fresh evidence in only around 5 percent of cases.[94] The Royal Commission expressed the view that the Court of Appeal needed to be more willing to accept jury mistakes and more willing to admit evidence that might favor the appellant, even if this had been available at the time of the trial.[95] Furthermore, "[O]nce the court has decided to receive

[92] This conversation took place before the CCRC was moved to the Ministry of Justice. This CM was also conscious that the commission was sometimes misjudged and also said: "We need to improve our external image. We are seen as being non-referral orientated, whereas in fact we think very hard about referrals."

[93] House of Commons Justice Committee Report (2015: paras. 16–20).

[94] RCCJ (1993: chap. 10, para. 35).

[95] Chap. 10, para. 3. It was also critical of the requirement that incompetent advocacy must be "flagrant" in order to result in a finding that the conviction is unsafe. "It cannot possibly be right that there should be defendants serving prison sentences for no other reason than that their lawyers made a decision which later turns out to have been mistaken. What matters is not the degree to which the lawyers were at fault but whether the particular decision, whether reasonable or unreasonable, caused a miscarriage of justice" (chap. 10, para. 59).

evidence that is relevant and capable of belief, and which could have affected the outcome of the case," it should not attempt to consider the weight of the evidence in order to determine what effect it might have had on a jury.[96] Instead, it should quash the conviction and order a retrial. The appeal courts have stated repeatedly their desire to avoid any usurping of the role of the jury. Yet attempting to assess the weight of the evidence and its impact on a jury does just this—it places the judges in the shoes of the jury.

However, in the absence of any statutory reforms to stimulate changes in the approach of the Court of Appeal in order to make it more willing to quash convictions, little has changed. The threshold for overturning the conviction remains extremely high—expressed in *Pope* as "where reasoned analysis of the evidence of the trial process, or both . . . leads to the inexorable conclusion that the conviction is unsafe."[97] The House of Commons Justice Committee has therefore recommended that the Law Commission review the Court of Appeal's grounds for allowing appeals.[98]

O'Brian has argued for a slightly different referral test in cases concerning expert testimony, reflecting his observations that the CCRC's expertise and procedures are more suited to the weighing and testing of expert evidence than those of the Court of Appeal.[99] He proposes a legislative amendment "to make clear that where the commission is persuaded that the expert case at trial is materially at variance with the best view of the expert evidence as it appears to the Commission, it can and should refer the case."[100]

The CCRC was considered one of the great successes to emerge from the recommendations of the RCCJ, establishing an independent review body with wide investigative powers to uncover new evidence and the power to refer cases back to the Court of Appeal. It was hoped that this new body, together with the reform allowing the Court of Appeal to hear new evidence on appeal, would

[96] This was the approach set out in *Stafford v. DPP* [1974] AC 878.

[97] *R v. Pope* [2012] EWCA Crim. 2241. This is a higher standard than that adopted by the CCRC in referring cases.

[98] This review should include consideration of the benefits and dangers of a statutory change to allow and encourage the Court of Appeal to quash a conviction where it has a serious doubt about the verdict, even without fresh evidence or fresh legal argument. If any such change is made, it should be accompanied by a review of its effects on the CCRC and of the continuing appropriateness of the "real possibility" test (para. 28).

[99] He argues that his "research strongly suggests that the Commission is very well suited to resolving issues of disputed expert evidence, almost certainly better than juries and likely better than courts" (2011: 2–3). While the Court of Appeal will have to rehear expert testimony and try to determine which is more persuasive, the commission will write to experts, asking them to comment on new evidence and the views of other experts, to determine if their evidence would be the same as that given at trial. In some cases, the experts will now agree, and in others, it seems, they agreed even at trial, but the presentation of the case in some ways masked this. Where there is no agreement, the commission will typically appoint its own expert to advise on the issues, and this report too will be sent to the defense and prosecution experts for comment (2011: 8).

[100] O'Brian (2011: 25).

overcome the problems that had prevented cases such as that of the Birmingham Six being brought before the appeal courts and having their convictions quashed. The commission's broad inquisitorial function allows it to gather the evidence necessary to mount an appeal, moving beyond the limits of what is possible in the ordinary adversarial process. It enjoys considerable freedom in how it organizes and structures its work, and although inquisitorial, it is not tasked with finding the truth; and while investigating miscarriages of justice, it is not required to determine innocence. It is uniquely placed to gain an understanding of the evidence (both new and existing) and the process of investigation in a way that no other criminal justice actor can. It has far greater powers and resources to gather information, including the commissioning of new forensic testing, than the applicant or her representatives.

Yet despite these strides in improving the investigation of wrongful convictions, the potentially radical function of the CCRC as an independent and more inquisitorial body is compromised by what comes after it. Although operating in ways that are outside the usual adversarial process, it must, at the same time, take account of the appeal process through which its referral will be heard. The commission's relationship with the Court of Appeal—as structured through its statutory test for referral and in its own interpretation of this test in determining the scope of reviews and in making referrals—continues to limit the commission's sphere of influence and activity. Furthermore, the commission's understanding of itself as an independent and inquisitorial body has resulted in its distancing itself from the interests of the applicant and from the applicant's lawyers, despite the obvious advantages that they may bring in terms of insights into the trial, communication with the applicant, and material relevant to the review. Although their interests coincide to an extent and it is the lawyer, not the commission, who will argue the case if referred to the Court of Appeal, the lawyer's partisan representation of the applicant's interests is seen to clash with the independent approach to the review of the case undertaken by the commission. It is perhaps here that we see most clearly the disruption of procedural models, as we move between inquisitorial review and adversarial appeal, and as the applicant's representative returns to her status as the criminal defense lawyer. This is the focus of the next and final chapter.

10

The Criminal Cases Review Commission, the Applicant, and Her Lawyer

A Disruption of Procedural Models

The role of the defense within criminal procedure is instructive as a lens through which to view the underpinning values and practices of each phase of the criminal process—how they articulate with formal models of procedural justice, how changes in the defense role contribute to the wider evolution of a criminal process, and how legislative trends in criminal justice are altering the defence function in significant ways. Earlier chapters have explored the broader place of the defense as it is understood across the two procedural traditions and the ways that it is called upon to serve the managerial interests of the criminal justice system as well as, and sometimes instead of, the interests of the accused. Discussion has also focused on the impact of reforms to the pre-trial role of the lawyer in response to European-level mandates, and the tensions this has created within different procedural models. Drawing on observations of the daily workings of the CCRC as well as interviews with defense lawyers and commission staff, this final chapter evaluates the uncertain place that is allotted to the defense within the inquisitorial CCRC review process and the implications this has for the investigation and any resulting appeal. The establishment and operation of the CCRC represents a unique combination of inquisitorial procedure inextricably connected to the adversarial process. As well as analyzing the challenges this poses for the commission, the applicant and her lawyer, the chapter also compares the CCRC's approach to engagement with the defense with the participatory model developed in the French *instruction*, offering a different form of comparison across criminal procedures.[1]

The relationship between the CCRC and the applicant's lawyer has proved difficult to negotiate during the case review process, despite the importance that will attach to the commission's investigation and the evidence it uncovers. Where a case is referred back to the appeal court, the results of the case review are likely

[1] This chapter includes much empirical material as the appropriate role of the lawyer was my key focus when observing at the commission and conducting interviews. It was also an issue on which solicitors and CCRC staff had strong but conflicting views.

The Metamorphosis of Criminal Justice. Jacqueline S. Hodgson, Oxford University Press (2020).

DOI: 10.1093/oso/9780199981427.001.0001

to have a significant impact on the nature of the defense case that is presented, and so, ultimately, on the success of the appeal. Equally, the way in which the defense chooses to argue the case may build on the evidence uncovered by the commission, or it may misunderstand, or fail to argue, some grounds identified by the CCRC as going to the safety of the conviction. Unlike the French procureur who is closely involved in the *juge d'instruction*'s investigation before going on to prosecute it in court, the defense remains an outsider in the CCRC's review process. In this way, the intersection of adversarial and inquisitorial roles and procedures disrupts traditional procedural models, creating an inherent tension between the commission and defense lawyer functions, which sometimes conflict and at other times coincide.

A. Introduction

We have seen that in the mixed and inquisitorially rooted French model, primacy continues to be given to the judicial enquiry, but space has also been made for a defense role. This is not the independent and proactive role of the adversarial defense lawyer, but a model of participation in which the lawyer plays a role complementary to that of the investigator, ensuring the conduct of a sufficiently broad-based and neutral enquiry. We might characterize this as the provision of assistance and a counterbalance, a form of dialogue rather than challenge. It dilutes the narrow inquisitorial centralization of the investigation, by allowing some cross-checking and the opportunity to shape parts of the enquiry. Tunnel vision on the part of police and prosecutors has been a common feature of wrongful convictions and one of the main criticisms of the Outreau affair was that the investigation suffered from confirmation bias in part because the defense was marginalized, with the resulting absence of sufficient horizontal (as opposed to vertical, in Damaška's terms) checks.

However, while the participatory role of the parties is clearly codified within French procedure as a way of enabling greater input into the investigation without displacing the authority of the *juge*, the role of the defense (or the applicant's lawyer as she is at this stage) within the CCRC investigation is not fixed. There is no formal mechanism to permit the applicant or her lawyer to play any part in the case between application and the close of the review. The CCRC has enjoyed the freedom to develop its own practices and its relationships with other criminal justice actors, such as the police, prosecutors and the applicant's lawyer. The roles that the commission assigns to these various actors—whether explicitly or implicitly through its behavior—are determined in part by the commission's understanding of its own role and function. Working outside the party-driven adversarial process and understanding itself to have a broadly inquisitorial function, the CCRC has interpreted its inquisitorial role as removing the need for applicants to have legal representation. This implies that the applicant does not need to have her interests represented, nor her case investigated, by anybody outside the commission—not because the CCRC will play the same role as a defense lawyer, but because the nature of the review is seen to be different from the earlier police investigation or even the kind of enquiry conducted in France by the *juge d'instruction*, because it sits to the side of the adversarial process, not within it. The lawyer's function consists of, and is defined by, more than adversarial argument, however, and research suggests that the commission's working practices and procedures can place unrepresented applicants at a disadvantage.[2] As anticipated by the RCCJ, the lawyer can play a role in translation and explanation, in order to ensure that the applicant is able to participate effectively in the review process through a well-expressed and evidenced application or in the response to commission requests for further information or statements of reasons for nonreferral.[3]

Currently the applicant or her lawyer has very limited possibilities to engage with the work of the commission. They have the opportunity to make representations in the initial application and then again at the close of the review if no referral to the appeal court is anticipated. Where a lawyer's expertise and experience are valued, there may be an ongoing dialogue around aspects of the investigation, but in other instances, contact may be minimal. In many cases, this is unproblematic and the commission is able to complete its investigation without any outside assistance. It has in-house legal and investigative expertise, as well as wide evidence-gathering powers. And although inquisitorial in its orientation, it makes use of committees for investigations of any depth, ensuring a broader input of viewpoints.

However, the CCRC may also be too narrow in its inquiry and become captive to a view of the case that fails to take account of relevant material—either because it is unaware of its existence, or fails to appreciate its significance. Lawyers' success in changing the commission's mind in 15 percent of cases where its initial decision was not to refer back to the appeal court is testimony to this. The nature and scope of the CCRC review is also increasingly important not only in determining if there are grounds to doubt the safety of the conviction, but also in framing the defense case in the Court of Appeal, and even in providing evidence of innocence. These additional roles are not set out in statute, nor are they acknowledged by the commission in the way it conducts its review, but they are the

[2] Hodgson and Horne (2009).

[3] The RCCJ specified that legal aid should be available for these very purposes. RCCJ (1993: chap. 11, para. 32).

logical result of restrictions and burdens placed upon the defense in arguing the case on appeal and in seeking compensation if the conviction is quashed.

Although the commission's approach to legal representation is mixed, the majority of staff see little benefit in the involvement of the applicant's lawyer.[4] This is not because lawyers have no useful role to play, but rather because the experience of many of those at the commission has been of poor-quality representation, which has been of little value to the applicant. Case review managers (CRMs) told me that lawyers would typically act as no more than a post box, passing correspondence in each direction. In many instances, they appeared not to understand the criteria for overturning a conviction, simply repeating the original grounds of appeal or even points of law that were palpably wrong.

However, it is clear that a good lawyer, who understands the CCRC review process, can make a strong contribution to the review process. In addition to providing additional case-related information, chasing witnesses, and drawing the commission's attention to relevant case law, lawyers are able to point out major flaws in the commission's reasoning, in some instances changing a rejection to a referral. This is important in understanding the contours of the commission's inquisitorial role and the extent to which investigations would benefit from a more structured role for the applicant's lawyer during the investigation, in addition to responding to the results of the review. More broadly, it lends support to the effectiveness of a participatory model, rather than the concentration of power in the hands of a single investigator or body.

The RCCJ anticipated that the commission would operate as a broadly inquisitorial body. It outlined three features that are clearly inquisitorial in character. First, the commission would have a neutral, inquisitorial *mentalité*, driven by the objective of investigating whether there has been a miscarriage of justice, rather than serving the narrower interests of the parties. Second, it would be wholly independent, both in the sense of not acting in the interests of any of the parties, and in being independent of government and the judiciary.[5] Third, the commission is given wide powers and a clear mandate to be proactive in searching out evidence.

However, the RCCJ also envisaged the participation of the applicant, though not in the traditional adversarial fashion. It envisaged that the applicant might be interviewed by the commission where helpful, be legally represented, and continue to be able to put her own arguments before the court should the case be referred—the CCRC was not to be a substitute for the defense case in a purely

[4] Hodgson and Horne (2009).

[5] In France, the enquirer is, of course, part of the judiciary. However, given their different places in the criminal process, it is important that the French enquirer is independent of the police and the CCRC of the judiciary, whose decisions it reviews and for whom it makes fresh recommendations.

inquisitorial way.[6] This is not a model that the commission has followed—in part for reasons of resource and in part based on its own conception of its role.[7] Subsequent changes, such as the requirement to obtain leave from the Court of Appeal if the defense wishes to argue grounds in addition to those included in the CCRC referral and, to a lesser extent, the criteria for an award of compensation, have further complicated this relationship.

In the early days, the commission appeared to be very much in favor of applicants being legally represented.[8] Former commission member (CM) Leonard Leigh explained: "The Commission prefers applicants to be legally represented; a good lawyer can help to clarify issues, identify documents and other relevant evidence, and locate witnesses."[9] This is no longer the commission's policy. The commission's advice instead is

> We can look at your case even if you are not legally represented. You do not have to have a legal representative to apply to us, but a solicitor might be able to help.[10]

Some CMs and CRMs thought that legal representation added little to the quality of the investigation.[11]

> It makes no difference whatsoever, in fact it can be counterproductive . . . some of them do engage, but in a crusading manner which adds really no life to the case. There are very few who actually can add material that we can't discover ourselves, or think through ourselves, and there can be a delay too. They say, "We're going to give you submissions, we're going to see this witness," and the months go by and nothing happens. (CM 2)

[6] RCCJ (1993: chap. 11, paras. 16, 25).

[7] The House of Commons Justice Committee (2015) also recommended greater engagement with applicants, including meeting them in person.

[8] In evidence to the House of Commons Home Affairs Select Committee from 1999/2000 through to 2003/4, the commission described its efforts to increase the rate of legal representation. In recent years it has plunged dramatically. Nearly 90 percent of applicants are now unrepresented according to the CCRC's own figures. Criminal Cases Review Commission (2019).

[9] Leigh (2000: 373).

[10] CCRC Questions and Answers available at https://ccrc.gov.uk/publications/application-guidance/. Although the CCRC does not want unrepresented applicants to be discouraged from applying, its policy is the following: "*Effective* representation, whether legal or otherwise, undoubtedly assists the CCRC and the applicant." CCRC Formal Memorandum, *Applicants' Representatives: Inappropriate Conduct* (2015), para. 2, available at https://s3-eu-west-2.amazonaws.com/ccrc-prod-storage-1jdn5d1f6iq1l/uploads/2018/11/Applicants-representatives-inappropriate-conduct-3.pdf.

[11] A group of CRMs told me, in discussion, that they would only be concerned that the defense were inadequate in cases where the person was innocent, and most cases are not in this category; it is an irregularity that makes the conviction unsafe. It was puzzling that a procedural-type irregularity should be connected to innocence in this way.

CM 8 told us: "The vast majority of the lawyers add no value whatsoever to the application. We act as better lawyers for them than their lawyers ever do." Poor legal assistance was thought to create delays to the review process and raise the expectations of applicants in unrealistic ways.[12]

On the other hand, where lawyers have a good understanding of the CCRC process, they can be of enormous value and this was also recognized. Unlike the commission, they have met with the applicant, they are often familiar with the case papers and the conduct of the trial, and they are able to prepare detailed submissions on new evidence or points of law.[13] Lawyers can be of value in keeping the applicant informed and chasing up the commission on their behalf, but also in participating in the review, using their detailed knowledge of the case to ensure that key points are investigated, and bringing material to the commission's attention. In short, while a poor lawyer is of no benefit and may even be damaging to a case if relied on, a good lawyer is of real help to the commission.

> To suggest that applicants shouldn't be legally represented because we're an independent body and we can be trusted to do a good job, I think, places too much belief in our ability, and when one considers that we're dealing with highly nuanced matters in the first place, where there may be a huge amount of uncertainty as to the law, sometimes as to the evidence, sometimes as to the science, then if you can get an informed and intelligent submission or further representations, as opposed to knee-jerk reflex reaction from an applicant, then I think that it can only be considered helpful. (CM 1)

> If people don't understand why having a good legal representative helps with an application, then they don't understand the first thing about the commission, and they don't understand what a good legal representative is about. (CM 5)

The value of lawyers in preparing a CCRC application is also recognized by the courts. The Supreme Court commented in the case of *Nunn*:

> There is no doubt that CCRC is much assisted by informed legal analysis and presentation if an application for review is made to it, and not only because its funding is not unlimited, but also because accurate legal formulation focuses

[12] We found one or two lawyers who were slow to respond, usually because they had taken on too many cases. In general, however, we saw no evidence of lawyers causing significant delays. Their response time was in parallel with other outstanding queries.

[13] If neither the CRM nor the lead CM has a legal background, early submissions on legal points can be especially useful.

> the mind correctly. Sometimes, such solicitors or others can usefully undertake enquiries of their own, respecting of course the interested third parties.[14]

Our earlier research found that legally represented applicants are more likely to have their cases reviewed (and reviewed more thoroughly), and ultimately to be referred to the Court of Appeal, than unrepresented applicants.[15] In some instances, there will not be a direct causal link: lawyers attach themselves to promising cases. But in others, it is clear that the interventions of the lawyer were crucial to the success of the case.[16] It should also be noted that lawyers perform a useful function in screening out cases,[17] though there is room for improvement here—17 percent of legally represented applicants were rejected for ineligibility or lack of previous appeal.[18]

B. Complementing the CCRC Role: Application and Decision

In order to understand whether lawyers might usefully contribute to the CCRC's investigation in the ways envisaged by the inquisitorial instruction, when interviewing commission staff, we asked them how a lawyer might add value to the review process. The assistance of a lawyer was considered most useful at the start of the process in the identification of issues, and at the end of the process, ensuring that the commission had not omitted anything. The lawyer's role was characterized as complementing that of the commission, providing additional information of which the commission may not be aware. This is precisely how it is envisaged that the lawyer will participate in the French *instruction*, adding to the enquiry rather than challenging it. The presence of an active defense role is also recognized through ECtHR jurisprudence and the various procedural safeguards enacted by the EU as a necessary part of ensuring due process rights

[14] *R (on the application of Nunn) v. Chief Constable of Suffolk Constabulary and another* [2014] UKSC 37, para. 41.

[15] Two percent of unrepresented applicants had their case referred to the Court of Appeal, as opposed to 8 percent of represented applicants; 51 percent of unrepresented applicants were rejected at the earliest stages (as opposed to 18.4 percent of represented applicants) (Hodgson and Horne [2009]).

[16] The role of legal representation in ensuring access to justice is well recognized in the context of the ordinary criminal trial process but perhaps less so in applications to appeal; in the CCRC review process; and even applications to the ECtHR, where 69 percent of applications declared inadmissible were submitted without any legal assistance. See European Court of Human Rights, "Note on Compulsory Legal Representation of Applicants," DH-GDR(2011)026.

[17] Solicitors we interviewed told us they turn away many more people than they agree to represent, because they consider they have no grounds to make an application.

[18] In our earlier research, we found that the top twenty firms who bring most cases to the CCRC had double the success rate of referral compared with all lawyers.

throughout any investigation—be it inquisitorial or adversarial in nature—and so contributing to a fair investigation. However, while the *juge* has a preliminary investigation to build on, the commission will be starting their enquiry from scratch, suggesting the potential for an even greater role for the applicant's lawyer in setting out the issues to be reviewed.

The importance of the initial application is perhaps obvious—this is what will determine if the case will progress to anything beyond a cursory review of the case papers. Many staff expressed concern to us that there was a much greater danger that unrepresented applicants would have their case rejected at the outset, because potential grounds would not be clearly pointed up.

> I suspect that a number of the cases that come [for initial screening], particularly in complex cases, might slip through the net because the applicant doesn't identify the issues and on the face of it there looks as if there's nothing new.... I would prefer it if the majority of our applicants were represented ... [The issues raised in the application] are not determinative in that we should pick up things that aren't raised by the solicitor which make the case referable, but if I'm being honest they are key to determining the question of how hard we look. (CM 5)

> I would prefer them to have ... advice ... not necessarily from a solicitor, but have help from somebody who understands the legal process a bit more, sort of to help them formulate their application in a concise and useful way, because I think too often at the commission, and I know this is a controversial view, we boot out cases too early where people are not able to express themselves. And we are dealing mostly with people who are very, very illiterate, some of them, and it's not fair for us to say, "Well, sorry ... you haven't given us any grounds for reviewing your case, so we're going to throw it out." (CRM 3)

This was a particular concern in relation to ineligible and "no reviewable grounds" cases (as they were called for many years), where commission staff thought cases were dealt with too quickly, risking missing important points. Second or third applications to the commission, though not common, also underline the extent to which crucial points can be missed. Lawyers' input can be determinative in shaping the review and in ensuring a referral.

> We've just had a case which is a [reapplication] to the commission and I've just written it up as a referral. The point that's now been raised has been raised by a solicitor ... it's to do with the defense case not being properly put in the summing up.... So I mean, there I'm sort of sitting wondering, "Well, has no one read the summing up before?" but then I'm thinking perhaps if I had that case

> before, if you're not sort of looking for a specific point, you might not see it, which is a little worrying. (CRM 4)

> I think it's very important and it would be very dangerous if solicitors were taken out of that loop and effectively just sending papers.... First time around, before we became involved [in a particular case], the commission had turned the application down. We refocused the application, pointed out the flaws in the evidence; the commission then did the right thing, went off and instructed an independent expert and agreed with us and referred the case. And that's an illustration of the problem really, that like any organization the commission can get it wrong, and so it needs that independent input. (Sol 2)[19]

Solicitors recognized the value of their input from the start, alongside their duty to the client.

> If I think there is a basis [for an application] then my role is to investigate the issues that have been raised as far as I can... so I can present the case in as full and detailed fashion as I can straight to the CCRC.... The CCRC has a significant workload.... It seems to me that at least by way of assistance to them... advocacy on the part of a solicitor... can at least guide them in the direction they need to go and therefore save them some time and therefore money. (Sol 5)

CM 5 also saw these two roles as compatible:

> I think that the role of representing a client to the commission is, when it's done properly, exactly the same role as in representing a client in a trial.... Having, therefore, a good lawyer... a solicitor or barrister, identifying good points is a help, and it will have a big influence on the direction of the application.

For many this included carrying out case preparation as they ordinarily would, such as interviewing witnesses and experts, in order to ensure that the commission's review had the best (and not the worst) points for the defense. Others thought this was for the commission—both on the ground that they are better resourced and tactically, to ensure that the testimony is not considered tainted by having been obtained by the defense. Many commission staff echoed these views, considering it better on balance for them to conduct interviews and instruct experts, as they would be doing this in any event. There was also a

[19] This is an interesting observation: the need for lawyers to be persistent produces a degree of skepticism as to the nature of the commission's role and emphasizes lawyers' understanding of their own role as somehow more independent.

concern that different investigative objectives might color the evidence obtained and that even experts might be misled into providing skewed testimony. Some were strongly opposed to lawyers taking statements,

> I wish they would stay away from trying to interview witnesses because they can do more harm than good, they can frighten people away. When a solicitor interviews a witness, we usually go and interview them again because they have either missed bits of information or it's full of hearsay . . . and sometimes it's just very damaging if somebody has been hectored by a solicitor. (CM 11)

When asked more specifically about the discovery of a new witness, CM 11 agreed that

> the difficulty comes down to the fact we have quite a long waiting list, and I think it would have to be a judgment call for the solicitor armed with the knowledge that it may be some months or in excess of a year before we can even allocate a case let alone make a decision about interviewing the witness. They might just want to secure some basic information in a witness statement . . . if the witness were to die, everything would die with them.

CMs with a defense background, on the other hand, thought it vital to take a witness statement as soon as possible: "The case will sit on a shelf . . . the witness may go missing, they may die"; "well, clearly, the solicitor has got to take a statement. . . . If you don't take a statement and the witness dies, let's be honest, it can take the commission three years to get round to this." These various comments illustrate the ways that acting in the interests of the applicant need not be understood in narrowly adversarial, partisan or negative ways. The commission is also concerned to gather relevant information and the applicant's lawyer can be invaluable in contributing to the review process, from the framing of the issues underpinning the wrongful conviction, to the conduct of legal research and the identification of new witnesses.

Once the review process has begun, it is within the discretion of commission staff whether the applicant or her lawyer has any further input into the case.[20] Some CRMs were comfortable maintaining regular contact, and some lawyers were trusted and their expertise valued across the commission. The point at

[20] In its Formal Memorandum Communicating with Applicants (2018), the commission says that it will update applicants on their case at least every three months (para. 9) and communications should usually be in writing in order to avoid misunderstanding or doubt (para. 18). The Guidance for Legal Representatives (2018) sets out the best way to approach an application in order to be helpful to the CCRC, as well as explaining how the commission conducts the review. Available at https://ccrc.gov.uk/publications/ccrc-casework-policies/. The only comment on communicating with the solicitor is to explain that the commission "will not usually meet with you unless this is necessary as part of the review." Available at https://ccrc.gov.uk/publications/application-guidance/.

which all applicants are invited to make representations is if a provisional statement of reasons (PSOR) is issued, detailing why the commission does not intend to refer the case back to the Court of Appeal. This is recognized as a key moment in which applicants need legal assistance, as these statements are worded for legal precision, rather than to be understood by the layperson.[21]

> Writing a statement of reasons is a difficult art in terms of balancing the tension between wanting to write something that is going to be comprehensible to an applicant who may well be unrepresented and may well have poor standards of English and little understanding of the criminal law, and writing a document that is legally correct and therefore invulnerable to challenge. . . . It is more important that it is right than it is understandable. . . . Yes, perhaps we ought to be saying to an unrepresented applicant . . . it is probably best if you do get legal representation to assist you at this point. (CRM 5)

> Over 50 percent of those in prison are seriously challenged in literacy terms. Then I think it would be ridiculous to expect an applicant to be able to respond to what we write to them, and from our point of view, if the expectation to write in clear and simple language runs contrary to the necessity to ensure legal exactitude in that language, it's the latter which has to be treated as the priority because, always with an eye on judicial review, we have to make sure that our decision is properly reasoned and legally correct. . . . Sometimes you have to conclude, "No, it's not possible to communicate this in language he could understand." . . . It is often clear that lawyers and judges can't understand some of the concepts . . . a presumption that an applicant should be able to respond in kind to our statements of reasons is utterly misconceived. (CM 1)

> [Applicants] are dealing with sometimes quite legalistic, formal, and frightening-looking documents, dealing with concepts that they are never going to be able to understand, and I think they are very disadvantaged in making a proper response to us generally. . . . The provisional statement of reasons stage is the one that traditionally worries me, as either you get no response at all, or you get a garbled response that doesn't address the issues that you have perhaps flagged up for them in the statement of reasons. It doesn't challenge, for example, decisions not to pursue a line of enquiry, when a solicitor might well be able to reason that out—say, "Ha! The reason why you need to go and do this, or receive that person is this." An applicant can't do that. . . . We do have cases that slip through the net, and we have had cases where solicitors have identified that and cases have been

[21] In recent correspondence with the author, the CCRC advised that recent process changes have sought to ensure greater use of plain English, rather than legalistic language.

> referred as a result . . . or which have persuaded us to reopen a case, and there has been a different result where there has been a referral. (CM 11)

Perhaps worryingly, some staff did not see this as problematic. This case review manager claimed that unrepresented applicants were not disadvantaged, yet then went on to describe the poor quality and irrelevant nature of the applicant's response.

> They can normally get across what they think of a point, and if you've written the provisional [statement of reasons] bearing in mind that they are not represented and you've tried not to use—I sound really patronizing—you've tried not to do things in too complicated a way, haven't used big long words, you haven't used "mens rea," if you've tried to explain your reasoning in a straightforward way, I've never really felt . . . that no further [representations] have been sent because they don't understand the provisional . . . you normally get quite a massive wad of a response back . . . normally all focusing on the summary of the prosecution and defense cases, mind you . . . saying, "Arrghh that's not fair! I don't agree with that." . . . Well, "Oh no, we know you don't, but that's why that was the prosecution case and that was the defense's case." But no, I can't say that it's ever particularly worried me. (CRM 3)

Lawyers also recognized the crucial role that they could play at the end of the review in turning a rejection into a referral. In most instances this was on the basis of new argument, or legal authorities of which the commission was unaware, but sometimes it was based on information already known to the commission, but which had not been picked up.[22] One lawyer referred to three cases in which her argument and submissions had changed a provisional nonreferral into a referral. She went on to say:

> The CCRC has got the resources and it's got the manpower and it's got the statutory powers to seize . . . considerable documents. But—this is obviously with due respect to everybody who works there—sometimes there are still things you can add and say, "Well, if you go in this direction, or if you write to this public body, you can seize this file and this particular document and that may help you in what you're looking for." . . . You can't just sort of sit back and let them get on with it, professionally I suppose, comfortable in the knowledge that everything will be done. And that's not a criticism, it's just, you know, the

[22] In one instance, this happened when the CCRC accidentally disclosed information to the applicant during correspondence explaining why the case would not be referred. This became the basis of new grounds argued by the lawyer, leading to a referral.

> nature of what you do, the adversarial system, you're representing somebody's interest. (Sol 3)

This points up clearly the ways that the adversarial perspective of the defense lawyer, representing the interests of the applicant, intersects with the inquisitorial review by the commission. The lawyer's objective is to ensure that the best version of the applicant's case for appeal is considered and investigated by the commission, so that the case is referred and is referred on the fullest possible grounds.[23] And while lawyers' responses to a PSOR can offer a corrective and ensure that material or case law that has been overlooked is properly considered, it is often more timely and effective if lawyers can contribute earlier on. However, for the lawyer to offer a steer in the light of what the commission has found requires the sharing of information during the course of the review—something the CCRC is very reluctant to engage in.

C. Making Room for an Adversarial Lawyer in an Inquisitorial Review

Determining the appropriate role of the lawyer during the review process illustrates the tensions present in the positioning of the CCRC review within an adversarial process from which it cannot remain insulated. The commission's primary interlocutor is the Court of Appeal, through the real-possibility test, the judgments of the court, and the symmetry between the two bodies that this is understood to impose. The applicant's lawyer, although a key player should the case be referred, is largely extraneous to the commission's task of case review. Understanding itself as a neutral and inquisitorial reviewer, the CCRC has rejected any formal role for the lawyer. It has not sought to include any checks on its process outside its own committee structure, but rather has relied on its inquisitorial function to trump any defense interests.

Leigh notes the tensions around the adversarial tradition and the expectations of defense lawyers, who may find it difficult to accept that the judgment around which matter to investigate is entirely that of the commission.[24] Commission staff often emphasized the need for lawyers to work with them, and not in an adversarial way.

> I think that is one of the problems, that the commission is an inquisitorial organization set in an adversarial system. And particularly I think where

[23] Leave from the court is required to argue additional grounds of appeal to those set out in the CCRC's reference.

[24] Leigh (2000).

> solicitors have not built up any experience of dealing with the commission . . . then they can approach it in a very adversarial fashion and not recognize that we're completely neutral. We are disinterested in the sort of proper meaning of that word, in the "outcome," and I think they can sometimes thereby approach us in a way that is not conducive to a speedy and efficient review. (CM 1)

> I think that the difficulty is that because we have a general adversarial system and because relationships between the legal profession and the previous C3 department could be quite hostile at times, so I'm told, they do see us as an adversary rather than an ally, and that comes through in the attitudes on the telephone, attitudes in writing, general remarks that they make to applicants about us that are repeated. But I do feel that over the years, those of them that deal with us regularly are now starting to understand that we have an objective role rather than being part of the adversarial process, but it's a long, slow thing trying to educate them to understand. (CM 11)

> I think that they should try and work with us rather than against us. A lot of the time they are a bit too combative, and when you get a good working relationship going with solicitors, it often works much better. (CRM 3)

The role that the lawyer can most usefully play during a CCRC review is different from her work at trial or appeal: she can act in her client's interests, but she must contribute to an enquiry, rather than leading and conducting it herself. However, it does not necessarily follow that the commission should disregard the applicant's lawyer entirely. While the commission is responsible for determining the lines of enquiry for the review and whether to refer the case to the Court of Appeal, this cannot be seen completely outside the adversarial context.

First, the lawyer may assist the commission in the objectives of its review—from discussing issues with the applicant, locating case papers and witnesses, to drawing attention to legal authorities. As we have seen in the French *instruction* model, the roles of defense lawyer and investigator can be complementary, helping to maximize the information on which the commission can base its decision. This allows the commission to benefit from the knowledge the lawyer has of the case, but it cannot be done solely on the basis of what is contained in the application. Investigations are organic and throw up new questions and lines of enquiry unanticipated at the outset, especially where the commission pursues a line of investigation different from that set out in the application. The defense might usefully contribute to or comment upon this, but the disclosure of information in the course of the review can be problematic for the commission. Much of the material it examines is effectively confidential to the commission, making difficult any kind of shared strategy.

Second, if referred, it is the defense lawyer who will be responsible for arguing the case before the court. This was recognized by the RCCJ, which did not envisage that the CCRC role would eclipse that of the defense in any way:

> [I]t should continue to be open to the appellant to raise before the Court of Appeal any matter of law or fact, or mixed law and fact, as she wishes, regardless of whether or not it was included in the papers sent to the court by the Authority [the CCRC].[25]

Furthermore, while the defense will develop the arguments around the evidence, the parameters of the case in the Court of Appeal are now effectively set by the commission. Section 315 of the Criminal Justice Act 2003 requires the defense to obtain leave before it may introduce grounds of appeal not included in the CCRC's reference. This means that the commission's statement of reasons (SOR), which is designed to demonstrate the grounds justifying referral rather than every point that might be argued, is now potentially determinative of the grounds of appeal that may be advanced by the appellant. In many instances, the defense and CCRC perspectives on the case are likely to be the same, and the work done by the commission will be of enormous benefit to the defense case.[26] However, in some instances the defense may want to rely on a wider set of possible grounds in order to maximize its chances of success.[27] The objectives of the appellant arguing within the adversarial setting of the appeal court go much further than those of the inquisitorially-framed commission, whose enquiries, while not explicitly focused on truth finding, may quite properly lead to evidence of guilt as well as of innocence. This will include, in some instances, setting out in the SOR why some grounds raised in the application, or otherwise considered in the course of the commission's review, do not form the basis of the CCRC's referral. The Court of Appeal is likely to place considerable weight on the CCRC's investigation of an issue and its conclusion that it cannot reasonably be pursued on appeal.[28] Unless the defense has some means of participating in the review process, it will be judged in the Court of Appeal, in part at least, on the work of the CCRC.

[25] RCCJ (1993: chap. 11, para.16).

[26] The CCRC has much greater powers and resources than the defense team, and the defense will naturally hope that the commission will instruct experts and obtain other forms of evidence that might assist the defense case. This is a legitimate expectation, though it is recognized that the defense team will also want to carry out their own investigations. See *R (on the application of Nunn) v. Chief Constable of Suffolk Constabulary and another* [2014] UKSC 37, paras. 39–41.

[27] Following the recent case law on compensation for miscarriages of justice, it might even want to try to demonstrate the factual innocence of the appellant. For discussion on how this engages the presumption of innocence under art. 6(2) ECHR, see a process that does not. See discussion of *R (Hallam and Nealon) v. Secretary of State for Justice* [2019] UKSC 2.

[28] See, e.g., *R v. Robotham* [2007] EWCA 2784. The appellant sought to introduce six additional grounds of appeal. In refusing leave for all six, the Court of Appeal quoted extensively from the CCRC's SOR before announcing (at para. 94) (for ground 3), "We agree with the CCRC's admirable exposition and adopt it" and (re ground 4), "We are very grateful to the CCRC for the full

The commission's response to the introduction of this section 315 requirement highlights some of the tensions in how it sees its role and that of the applicant and her representative, as well as the scope for differing individual approaches that we see across the commission's work. Some staff considered that this change in law made no difference to their approach to the review; others were more conscious of the possible implications for the defense at court.

> What we will be more explicit about [since the section 315 CJA 2003 reform] is if we're not investigating points . . . saying we haven't looked at this, we haven't come to any conclusions on these . . . to be fair to the applicant in those terms, I think. I don't think it's actually made a huge difference to us. . . . I don't think we feel the need to bottom out every single issue before we refer a case . . . we probably need to think a bit harder about whether it is right to stop at this point or whether we should in fact do a little bit more. (CRM 5)

> Well, it has made a difference because we end the statement of reasons differently by precisely stating the grounds on which we're referring and usually a paragraph or two before we usually make it clear the grounds on which we are not referring. (CM 4)

> You review it the same, exactly the same . . . refer it on the points you refer it on and then . . . well in the last few referrals I've had, the solicitors have added grounds anyway, and they've been allowed to do so, so I don't think it's particularly strictly adhered to. (CRM 3)

> I can't say I've noticed any particular change. I know that we were worried at the time that it came in whether it would change the way which we operate, whether we might feel obliged to bottom out every ground that an applicant has raised because they might not be able to pursue it themselves, but I think we quickly came to the conclusion that if we got what we think is a good reference point, then there's almost a duty on us to refer it on that basis, and as the applicant can still seek leave and as there have been cases where leave has been given to argue additional points, then they're not completely disadvantaged. (CM1)

An examination of ninety-four available judgments in cases referred by the CCRC to the Court of Appeal over the five-year period 2005–2010 found thirteen cases where the appellant sought leave to argue additional grounds

analysis of this ground and we reject the application for leave to appeal" (para. 97). The appeal was dismissed even on the grounds raised by the CCRC—whose referral was preceded by two failed applications, and after the threat of judicial review, the commission reviewed the case for a third time and referred it.

to those advanced by the commission. There was no clear pattern in terms of granting or refusing leave, or whether the convictions were subsequently quashed or upheld. In four cases leave was formally granted; the convictions were quashed on a combination of CCRC and additional grounds in two of these, and upheld in two. In a further three cases, although there was no explicit mention of permitting additional grounds, these were mentioned alongside the CCRC grounds in the court's decision to quash two of the convictions and to uphold the other.[29]

Referring to a specific example, one CM mentioned the difficulties that section 315 might now cause, by allowing the CCRC grounds to supersede the defense case.

> And this case should have been referred on two grounds, and it was drafted to be referred on two grounds, and the committee eradicated the first ground and in my view completely emasculated the referral. And because of section 315 and it being expressed in that way, that now means that the applicant and his representatives are going to have to argue ground one back in, when actually, in my view, it's complete stupidity on the part of the commission that it wasn't in, and so that's a double whammy—because previously we'd just say we're referring on this and they could argue on anything, and now they've got to get past the hurdle of a . . . commission being too stupid to say that that's the point on which they should have referred. (CM 5)

There is a more general point here about the scope of the commission's role in investigating evidence that might support the applicant's case on appeal. The CCRC's role is framed in such a way that it is not obliged to explore every possible ground on which a conviction might be unreliable. Once it has reached the point where it believes it has sufficient evidence to demonstrate that there is a real possibility that the conviction might be found unsafe, there is no reason for it to continue its investigation.[30] This may mean leaving unexplored other grounds, including those which the defense would not have the power or the resources to access. In view of the background against which the commission was created, where those wrongly convicted were prevented from bringing new evidence and argument before the Court of Appeal, any closing off of potential defense grounds must be considered with care. In practice, it seems likely that the commission would at the very least mention these potential additional grounds

[29] I am grateful to John Wagstaff at the CCRC for assisting us by providing some judgments that were not publicly available and to Jo Harwood for research assistance in collecting data and analyzing the appeal judgments.

[30] Concern over waiting times for applicants, many of whom are in custody, is also likely to make the commission reluctant to go beyond this threshold.

and the fact that they had not felt it necessary to investigate them given the other evidence undermining the safety of the conviction.

Some CMs thought the legislation was a change for the better, limiting the scope of what the defense could argue on appeal.

> Well I can understand. . . . I mean there were cases like *Bamber* which we referred on one ground to do with technical evidence . . . and when it went to the Court of Appeal, there were about one hundred other grounds. . . . It was rather strange, I think, that if we referred on one ground, then the whole thing was completely at large for the applicant to argue whatever he wanted. (CM 7)

> It was quite odd that they could come to us as the only body that could open the door to the Court of Appeal for them, but once we opened the door slightly with some grounds they were entitled to push it wide open and argue anything they wanted even with grounds that we explicitly reviewed and rejected. (CM 10)

This demonstrates a tension in the nature of the commission's role, sitting apart from the criminal process, while at the same time feeding directly back into it. In explaining the nature of its function, the commission is at pains to emphasize that it is not a judicial body, it sits outside of the ordinary adversarial criminal process, it investigates only whether there is a real possibility that the appeal court might overturn the conviction, and its role must not usurp that of the court in any way. Yet the views of these two CMs demonstrate a belief that the commission's investigation should impact the criminal process in an important way, by limiting the scope of the defense case on appeal.

Despite the requirement imposed by section 315 Criminal Justice Act 2003, many commission staff still believed that there was no real role for the lawyer once the review is underway.

> If the representations that they've made are okay in the first place, we know what it is, we understand, leave us to get on with it. Yes, by all means, you know, ring us every couple of months to say, "How's it going? Is there anything you can tell me?" but don't be on the phone saying, "I need to tell my client what's going on," . . . and don't be demanding interim disclosure of everything that's happened so far because actually that can . . . slow down the case, lead us into arguments that we don't need to have at that stage regarding the significance of particular bits of new materials, and can actively harm the interest of their client. (CRM 5)

> If they were good-quality submissions, then in an ideal world they would leave us to get on with it and we would contact them if we needed any clarification. (CM 11)

> I don't see that they have a role. We can't ask them to investigate things for us—we have to do that, we have to be responsible for our own decision, so we can't ask the solicitor to do that. (CM 5)

Solicitors were, unsurprisingly, mostly unhappy with this approach.

> One case review manager who I spoke to recently just literally asked for our file which we'd got from the trial solicitors, and he said, "Right, that's it then, I'll crack on and I'll let you know when we've finished." And I said, "How long do you reckon you'd be?" and he said, "Oh about twelve months." Thanks very much then. (Sol 3)

Others thought the lawyer's role was restricted to attending to the applicant—ensuring that she understood the process. The complexity of the legal arguments being raised and the poor literacy levels among applicants, especially those in prison, were seen as potential barriers to applicants understanding the process of their case review.

However, not all staff at the CCRC were negative about the involvement of lawyers. A number of CMs and CRMs outlined to us a more cooperative model where the commission directs the investigation, but recognizes the value of defense participation.

> The more they can give us to work with, the better it is. They have a significant role to play because after all, the defendant should know better than most whether they are the victim of a miscarriage of justice and may be well placed to put argument and evidence and material before us. . . . I'm all for as much assistance from lawyers and applicants as possible. (CM 10)

> In a case of any complexity I think the solicitor's input can be valuable. . . . A good legal representative of any kind can positively influence the way in which our review develops. . . . In particular, if they are the solicitor that's acted for the client all the way through, they know much better than we ever can know what happened at trial, and what the instructions were, what the significant evidence was, how the jury was swayed. . . . And they know the applicant much better than we ever can. So I think it would be arrogant of us to say, "We are the people that are going to investigate this case, and we don't want any input from you," and I think it would benefit the applicants . . . whether or not the case is referred. . . . We want the applicants to feel that they've had their case reviewed properly. (CRM 1)

Several commissioners thought that the involvement of defense lawyers was essential for the commission to do its job well.

> We can't do our job properly, it seems to me, within our limitations of budget and resource, without having somebody to point us in some kind of direction. The amount of effort it takes on a complex case, where you've got an applicant who is unrepresented, to unravel the issues and what the potential areas might be, that might reveal a miscarriage of justice, is huge, and if we were called upon to do it in relation to every case, without having some representation of applicants . . . I don't think we could do our jobs at all, to be perfectly honest . . . without our finances spiraling out of control and us overlooking miscarriages of justice. (CM 5)

> Well of course there is every chance of cases slipping through the net because we have to rely on . . . a sort of feel about a case, and it's not often that you get comprehensively argued grounds from the applicant. Yes, I would let a solicitor be involved in everything, to be perfectly frank, so that if we are saying that we have seen A but we didn't know about B and C, then they can tell us. I mean there is always a danger; it's human frailty. There is nothing we can do about it. (CM 6)

Solicitors described their role in fairly reactive terms once the review process had begun. They would be available to deal with CCRC queries and to keep the case under review, providing any additional information acquired or requested and, where necessary, arguing for specific investigations to be made. However, for lawyers to have any meaningful engagement with the review process requires the CCRC to share information in the course of its enquiries. This is perhaps the greatest source of tension between lawyers and the commission.[31] Solicitors were frustrated by the CCRC's failure to communicate until the close of the review, at which point a response was usually required within twenty-eight days. For a busy legal aid lawyer who may have to review a lot of new material in order to respond to the commission's points, this is a short time.

> This is my real beef with the commission. . . . If we pick up a case that the commission's had for a while because the appellant's recently come to us, we get all sorts of pressure from the commission, if it's at the stage where it wants to make a decision, to file our submissions. And we get, with respect to the commission, lectures about the need to complete cases and that it's in the interest of the appellant, but the moment we make a detailed submission, it disappears into a black hole. We never hear anything, apart from one or two very good case review managers who maintain regular dialogue, but apart from that, there is very little feedback from the commission. (Sol 2)

[31] There are also confidentiality issues to consider in investigations, which can make difficult the sharing of witness statements and other evidence.

The commission's inconsistent approach was also acknowledged by some staff.

> I think we should be more open than we are, and I certainly think we should be more consistent than we are, because there's a huge amount of inconsistency between some CRMs who disclose material to solicitors, and others who disclose nothing until the provisional statement of reasons stage. Particularly in the context of expert reports and the decision of whether or not we're going to instruct an expert, I think that that's a decision that we ought to look very carefully at doing at the earliest possible stage. (CM 5)

The debate is often framed around how the applicant's lawyer might engage with the commission in order to contribute to, or assist in, the review process, furthering the CCRC objective of determining whether there is a real possibility that the conviction will not be upheld. The defense objective, however, will inevitably be different from this. Its job is to go further and to convince the Court of Appeal to overturn the conviction. A successful appeal will require adequate preparation, and the material gathered during the CCRC's review and expressed in its SOR will to some extent determine what is presented at court. In this way, the defense might be expected to engage more vigorously with the CCRC—to work toward referral, but also to ensure the interests of the applicant are represented, in a similar way to the defense lawyer's engagement with the *instruction* process. As a neutral judicial figure pursuing the truth, rather than the interests of the parties, greater credibility attaches to the arguments presented in the dossier by the *juge d'instruction* than those at court by the defense. For this reason, the defense will try to get the *juge* to engage with the defense case as part of the *instruction*. In the same way, we might expect the grounds and reasoning set out by the CCRC to be treated by the court as more objective and more reliable than those argued by the defense, given the more inquisitorial nature of the commission's role. If this is the case, it benefits the applicant if defense arguments are also reflected in the CCRC's grounds for referral.[32] This brings us back to where we began, the source of the commission's resistance to greater lawyer involvement in the review process—does the imposition of adversarial values compromise the CCRC in its inquisitorial role, or is it an inevitable feature of a process that serves, and feeds directly into, the adversarial appeal phase?

[32] However, while it could only benefit the defense to have its arguments mirrored in the CCRC's own reasoning, the commission's function might be seen as having a different threshold of proof than that of the *instruction*, allowing the Court of Appeal to dismiss CCRC arguments within the broader context of the appeal.

D. Miscarriages of Justice across Procedural Models

While criminal procedures differ, the pressure points that give rise to miscarriages of justice are remarkably similar. Wrongful convictions tend to occur when the police and prosecution have focused prematurely upon one suspect and then sought to construct the case against her. When the evidence does not support their case theory, they either fail to act (for example, failing to disclose the inconsistent evidence, failing to follow up defense witnesses) or they act to eliminate the inconsistency (for example, pressuring witnesses to change their account, pressing the pathologist to alter the time of death). Pressures of time and resources militate against a strong focus on the presumption of innocence at the investigation stage,[33] resulting in insufficient testing of the initial case thesis.[34] The seeds of most miscarriages of justice are sown early on in the investigation.[35]

In an adversarial procedure, the defense role before and at trial is designed to ensure that any weaknesses in the prosecution case are tested, as well as allowing for the presentation of an alternative account. In inquisitorial processes, it is the role of the prosecutor or instructing judge that is central to the investigation of the case, ensuring that exculpating as well as incriminating lines of enquiry are carried out. We have seen that in both procedures, these safeguards may fail, further exacerbated by the current criminal justice climate that demands admissions and speedy case resolution. Avoiding wrongful convictions requires an open-minded and nonpartisan investigation. In practice, this will be difficult for those most closely involved. Investigations benefit from oversight by, or engagement with, someone who works at a distance from the immediate investigation and whose concern is, not just to get the right person, but also to ensure that they do not get the wrong person.

Are these models fit for purpose? Miscarriages of justice, alongside systematic pressures toward a form of administrative justice that values speed and efficiency over due process and fairness, serve to highlight the weaknesses that we observe in everyday practices. The *instruction* model is perhaps the most thorough and wide-ranging as an ideal-type, but judicial corporatism and the outsider status

33 Behavioral science also suggests that when under stress we tend to think in automated and almost unconscious ways, rather than adopting the more deliberative and considered approach that we might hope for in a criminal investigation. See Kahneman (2011) *Thinking Fast and Slow*, cited by Innes and Brookman (2013: 288).

34 The focus on admissions in a system that no longer has the time or resource to test out doubt might also result in the nonprosecution of cases where there is no clear admission of guilt. This certainly seems to be true of offenses of sexual assault.

35 Officers often told me the first twenty-four to forty-eight hours after a crime are the most important. This is also the rationale for the provision of wider powers in the investigation of recently committed offenses in France—*flagrant délits*.

of the defense lawyer weaken the system of checks and balances designed to prevent the conviction-oriented construction of a case against a suspect. More significantly, the *instruction* is close to extinction. The procureur heads up the vast majority of investigations, carried out by the police, with only a cursory defense presence. If the *instruction* sometimes struggles to resist the pressures of confirmation bias, how much more so a police enquiry with light-touch oversight from a prosecutor?

Adversarial procedures are structured in a more trial-focused way.[36] The accused's lawyer does not participate in or influence the investigation, but rather builds a separate defense case to challenge that of the prosecution. This model presumes an equality of arms that does not exist, and legal aid cuts coupled with increasing demands on the defense to assist in the efficient management of cases have seen the traditional defense role emasculated. Methodologically, the absence of any defense or nonpolice perspective in the pretrial phase means that key avenues of investigation will be missed or ignored. This cannot be remedied by answering the prosecution case at trial. Aside from the rarity of contested cases and the increasing numbers of out-of-court disposals, decisions taken early on in the investigation will frame how it moves forward and close off certain avenues of enquiry.

Should we be so skeptical of the police enquiry? The rhetoric of criminal procedure does not portray the police and prosecution case as the narrow and partisan accusation of the pure adversarial model, even in England and Wales. The police function is often understood as the investigation of exculpating as well as incriminating evidence—or as officers typically tell suspects: "We just want to find the truth."[37] However, this broad remit is a weak safeguard, neither legally prescribed nor enforced and so not entrenched within the criminal process.[38] Police occupational culture, the pressure on officers to obtain results with decreasing resources, and the flaws revealed by miscarriage-of-justice cases also suggest that we should have no more faith in the police's ability than we do in

[36] This also has consequences for the police investigation. "When investigative outcome is positioned as the key arbiter of success, account must also be taken of how products of an investigation perform in court . . . this accents the preparatory legal work . . . homicide detectives spend considerably more time preparing the case for court than identifying and charging the suspect. . . . The latter focus of the investigative process will often happen within days or weeks, whereas the former phase frequently takes up to 12 months" (Brookman and Innes [2013: 296–297]).

[37] The Royal Commission on Criminal Justice stated that "it is the duty of the police to investigate fairly and thoroughly all the relevant evidence, including that which exonerates the suspect" (1993: chap. 2, para. 1). The Criminal Procedure and Investigations Act 1996, Code of Practice, states, "In conducting an investigation, the investigator should pursue all reasonable lines of inquiry, whether these point toward or away from the suspect" (at para. 3.5). Officers are reminded of this in relation to questioning suspects, in PACE, Code of Practice C (Notes for Guidance 11B).

[38] Brants and Field (2016).

anyone else (such as a judge or a prosecutor) to perform this more objective function without some external steer.[39]

Where does the CCRC fit into this? It is a kind of maverick procedure, inquisitorially structured yet following on from, and feeding back into, adversarial procedures. It is not tasked with finding the truth in the way that traditional inquisitorial criminal investigations are. Rather, it is inquisitorial in its independence from the parties, from the executive, and from the courts, with an objective to review the case for possible success in the Court of Appeal, rather than simply to determine whether there has been a miscarriage of justice or a wrongful conviction. Partly as a product of these new procedural configurations, its relationship with the applicant and her lawyer is problematic. Excluding the lawyer from the case review process on the grounds that the commission performs an inquisitorial role ignores the coincidence of objectives between the two in the production of the best evidence. The RCCJ in its recommendations for the establishment of the commission and the courts in their judgments also recognize the value of lawyers both before and during the process of review.

The Commission has been widely criticized, and the nature of many of its referrals, together with its continued distance from defense interests, make it unlikely to make many new friends. Some commission members proposed improvements in how the CCRC might approach its work, notably, extending the participation of defense lawyers and even applicants themselves.

> So for somebody sitting in prison who has been sold down the line, even if their conviction isn't unsafe, not to at least have one of us turn up . . . and then they get a letter saying, "Sorry, we think you're talking nonsense" . . . I think it's outrageous. . . . So I think, frankly, . . . from a common-decency point of view, we bloody well ought to go and see them. . . . I think we could gain a lot of benefit to the review by going to the applicant. (CM 5)

> Possibly in an appropriate case, I think perhaps that is something we don't do often enough, is discuss with informed, proactive, reasonable solicitors what it is we want the expert to be doing. . . . It may be that they have value to add if they have a good understanding of the case and the issues. (CM 11)

> I think it's appalling that we don't [interview applicants]. . . . I'm not suggesting we see absolutely everybody, . . . but I think we should try to go out and explain

[39] In the context of homicide investigations, Brookman and Innes (2013: 297) report that investigations consider exculpating lines of enquiry as a means of "pre-empting and negating possible defences," but that these constraints are "ascribed a somewhat ambivalent and equivocal status by detectives" because of "a police belief that ultimately some cases are virtually impossible to legally 'prove' despite a known or suspected link between suspect and victim."

> what we do and how we do it to the people that matter. It does frustrate me tremendously when I read statements of reasons, that we've been to see the police officers but we never go near the applicants. (CM 6)

A more collegiate approach was also seen as a way of improving the process of decision-making. Committee decision-making is regarded as one of the strengths of the commission's organization, avoiding the concentration of power in the hands of a single individual. As one CM expressed it: "I think that the case committee is a very cornerstone of the integrity and the quality of our decision-making in the hard cases" (CM 7). Observation of committees suggests that they are valuable in testing out the issues in the case and helping to clarify difficult issues around whether or not to refer. We observed cases that went from a single CM who was uncomfortable with the decision to reject the application, to a committee of three CMs who then decided the case should be referred to the Court of Appeal.[40] However, this applies to only a small minority: most decisions are made by a single CM, and, until recently, around half of all cases were rejected at the outset in this way on the basis that there has been no appeal, or a plea of guilty, or there are "no reviewable grounds."[41] This procedure was not popular with many CRMs who expressed real concern over the procedure and its conflation of the investigation and decision-making roles, as well as its application of specific legal criteria to what may be a fairly basic application prepared by the applicant.[42]

> [What is wrong] about the "no reviewable grounds" system is that only one person ever looks at that case. . . . And there's been a well-established policy that one person does a review, another person takes a decision, so at least you've got two minds looking at that case, and it worries me. (CRM 1)

Most CMs thought that "no reviewable grounds" was a useful procedure: "They are so simple and obvious that there are no grounds and nothing to investigate. . . . There are no diamonds in this mound of mud" (CM 2). One CM was strongly opposed to the "no reviewable grounds" category, however, reflecting the view of the CRMs.

[40] Even the process of the CRM preparing the case and passing it to the CM to make the final decision not to refer can bring a second perspective, where evidence that was previously overlooked is noticed as important. This sometimes results in a decision to go to a committee with a view to refer, rather to reject.

[41] Nearly half of all applications are screened out fairly quickly. On the treatment of "No Appeal" cases, see Hodgson et al. (2018).

[42] Interestingly, the same concern was also expressed for many years in relation to the *juge d'instruction*'s role as investigator in the case, but also as judge in determining pretrial custody. The establishment of the *juge des libertés et de la détention* was designed to separate out these roles.

> They are a very cursory glance at one file. I don't agree with them . . . I think that it's unfair. I am concerned about it . . . I think that the work that is done on those cases is very reactive rather than proactive and the little bit of information that the applicant gives is the only information that's really considered, and for the less able applicant that's got to be bad. (CM 11)

This has now been modified so that CRMs are also involved in this process.[43] The value of a more collegiate approach in the investigation and of mixing lawyers and nonlawyers in a way that might change outcomes was also seen as a way of potentially improving the work done by the commission.

> We might do things differently if we were far better resourced. We've already talked about meeting and interviewing applicants. I'd like to see fewer or no cases decided by a single commissioner. . . . A single decision-maker in crucial matters when you are the body of last resort is not ideal. . . . When the RCCJ recommended that this body, the CCRC, should not just be lawyers, it was envisaged that the lawyers and nonlawyers would work together and influence each other and it wouldn't be dominated by lawyers. The laymen would inject a common-sense approach and the right answer would emerge. . . . We don't do that. We often have case committees made up entirely of lawyers. . . . I don't know what different results would emerge—it just seems slightly odd. The way we do it doesn't really make a lot of sense. . . . It doesn't seem to respect the thinking, the rationale for it. I don't know how you go about changing it now given the pressures on the body, and I have no basis for saying that it would lead to different decisions. Also, I'd quite like to see more cases where the work was done by two CRMs rather than one. That ought to be the norm for any case other than the most straightforward, but again, we can't afford to do that. (CM 10)

In both procedural traditions, a broader spread of decision-making power is seen as an effective way of avoiding the excessive or premature narrowing of issues that go to the culpability of the accused. There is less agreement on precisely how his decision-making should be shared. It might be through "more of the same," with several judges (in the *instruction*) or commission members (in the CCRC) in place of a single person, or by involving in more meaningful ways those representing the accused or the applicant in order to gain a contrasting perspective that can contribute to and challenge that of the primary decision-maker. The prospects for change, however, are not optimistic. Austerity measures and

[43] See Hoyle and Sato (2019: 100–109), though this does not take account of Hodgson et al. (2018) in relation to the treatment of "No Appeal" cases.

efficiency imperatives are everywhere stripping back the structures of criminal justice and weakening safeguards that ensure the reliability of evidence. While it seems likely that wrongful convictions are likely to increase in largely invisible ways as accused persons are shepherded toward some form of admission, with no prospect of reversing this trend, it seems unlikely that there will be the political will or the resources to devote to improving the ways that convictions are reviewed for possible appeal. There are also deep-seated concerns about the ways that the commission understands its role and so how it functions. It might be that more fundamental changes to its sphere of operation are considered before any tinkering with existing structures.

Concluding Comments

Centering on the criminal justice systems of England and Wales and France, this book has analyzed recent changes in criminal justice policy trends and process values as they have played out across the core functions of prosecution and defense, as well as how systems malfunction and seek to correct themselves in different ways. Both jurisdictions face common challenges, such as the changing terrorist threat, the constraints of public sector austerity, and the need to adapt to pan-European measures and standards of fair trial. The ways in which, through their criminal law and procedure, they resist, respond, or adapt to these challenges illuminate the legal and political values that motivate criminal justice in each jurisdiction. This in turn invites reflection on the nature and significance of the two contrasting procedural traditions within which they understand themselves to be located.

The criminal justice systems of France, and of England and Wales, are described as (and understand themselves to be) broadly inquisitorial and adversarial respectively, but criminal processes do not conform to a fixed model of criminal procedure. Accounts of procedural traditions are often partial and decontextualized, ideal types that take no account of the daily practices of law or the forces that shape them. To look at them at a fixed point in time, divorced from the political and historical contexts in which they developed, risks misunderstanding their nature and functioning—a particular danger for would-be reformers attracted to legal transplants. By comparing the ways that criminal systems are evolving, however, we can usefully identify some broad distinguishing features around the roles of legal actors and the structures of investigation and trial.

While the inquisitorial approach favors a centralized model of investigation and prosecution, weighted toward a pretrial enquiry conducted or overseen by a judicial officer, the adversarial approach maintains a separation between investigation and prosecution, weighted toward trial and with the opposing parties collecting and presenting evidence to be tested through live testimony. These are useful ways of understanding different modes of structuring investigation and trial, in theory at least. In addition, the status, training, and functions of legal personnel are an important part of this picture: the independence of the bar, the existence of a trained career judiciary, and the prosecutor's status as a lawyer or judge are key variables in how these structures might operate on the ground.

These different traditions are also expressions of different legal and political values. Both traditions would claim to respect standards of fairness, proof, and

The Metamorphosis of Criminal Justice. Jacqueline S. Hodgson, Oxford University Press (2020).

DOI: 10.1093/oso/9780199981427.001.0001

credible evidence in the pursuit of justice and some version of truth, but the emphasis is not the same across both systems, since these standards are reflected through different rules of evidence and procedure that variously seek to maximize or control the information presented to the fact-finder. While proponents of the adversarial tradition might be wary of placing so much power in the hands of a judicial figure, those favoring the inquisitorial approach point to the obvious inequality of arms where one side is heavily resourced by the state. The inquisitorial approach is perhaps more driven by an outcome of truth discovery and so less concerned with rules of evidence, the judge being trusted to separate out what is relevant and credible. The adversarial approach, on the other hand, focuses more strongly on the process by which the final outcome is achieved, with rules designed to manage the information that might be considered as evidence, especially when put before a lay fact-finder.

Procedural traditions, or versions of them, also capture the imagination as potential remedies for malfunctioning systems, as a means to instigate more radical change, and as a vehicle for reform. This is a complex process, as procedures cannot easily be disentangled from the wider legal and political structures, personnel, and occupational cultures of the variety of legal actors on whom the functioning of criminal procedures depends. As well as fixing on idealized accounts of criminal procedures, those seeking change may also struggle to relinquish their own criminal justice values and perspectives. England and Wales do not have a career judiciary, and the professional and constitutional culture of their judges centers on adjudication, ensuring a separation from the parties and their interests in the case. Yet inquisitorial procedure is discussed periodically as a possible remedy for the ills of adversarial procedure, especially in its apparent ability to ensure some independent oversight and control of the police investigation through different forms of supervision and accountability. However, this is very much an adversarial perspective, which anticipates that the investigative supervisor will have a particular function that is in some sense in opposition to the function of the police—she will check up on officers and even have some quasi-disciplinary role. This expectation colors the expectations some commentators have of French procedure, how it might be judged as successful and how it might be adopted in some form within the procedure of England and Wales. However, historically, the judicial officer within inquisitorial procedure was not introduced to supervise the police, as Anglo-American commentators assume. Rather, the police were brought in to assist the judicial investigator. Just as police-CPS tensions originated in the police's ceding of the prosecution function to the newly established public prosecutor, the introduction of an outside form of supervision or oversight would likely be resented by the police. This is not the case in France because police investigative powers originate with the procureur. This is not to say that the procureur is uninterested in overseeing police activity and the exercise of discretion, but it sheds some historical light on the culture of trust and cooperation that exists in the French system, and that would be unlikely to be replicated in a police-CPS relationship of this nature.

Adopting an innovative approach to the investigation of possible miscarriages of justice in England and Wales, the Criminal Cases Review Commission (CCRC) is an example of reform that, in some respects, borrows concepts, principles, and practices from the inquisitorial tradition. This development was not part of any wider shift to judicially supervised criminal investigations or other aspects of the inquisitorial tradition, but a response to a particular context and a key historical moment: a reaction to the slow recognition by the criminal justice system of a series of grave miscarriages of justice. In particular, it was hoped that an independent enquiry that does not rely on the usual parties—police, prosecutors, and defense lawyers—would gain a fresh perspective and avoid the pitfalls of prematurely focusing on a particular case thesis. As discussed in earlier chapters, the core mission of the CCRC, how it should understand a miscarriage of justice, and the place of concepts such as truth and innocence, given the broader adversarial context that precedes and follows the commission's work, have been the subject of much debate. However, there are also difficulties in how legal actors adapt their roles to a procedure that to them is relatively alien. For defense lawyers representing the interests of their clients, both as applicants to the CCRC and as appellants before the Court of Appeal, it is hard to conceive of a nonadversarial mode of working. This is not part of the culture within which they work, and (as is also true in the French *instruction* process) there is no adequate process allowing them to contribute to the enquiry in a nonadversarial way such that they can remain confident that the interests of their client will be adequately taken into account. This is in effect a mismatch of legal roles and cultures, asking adversarial lawyers to engage with a nonadversarial process of investigation, in preparation for an adversarial appeal. Even twenty-five years on, commissioners and lawyers continue to struggle to find an acceptable and effective working method. Neither has the commission resolved adequately the ways in which the more adversarial defence perspective in representing the interests of the applicant maps onto its own inquisitorial role as an investigator. Interestingly, in the French *instruction* too, the lawyer is prevented from participating fully in the enquiry, but for different reasons. Along with the prosecutor, the victim and the accused are permitted to request acts of investigation and to interrogate the case file, ensuring the widest possible input into the investigation. The professional ideology of the judicial investigator, however, has not shifted in line with the expanding defense role, and she continues to view the lawyer's role in subordinate terms. As an *avocat* rather than a judicial *magistrat*, the lawyer is viewed and treated as an outsider, yet this is the very reason why her participation is important, to offer a corrective to the perspective of the *juge*'s fellow *magistrat*, the prosecutor.

Procedural traditions continue to have some explanatory force in helping us to analyze the building blocks and structures of criminal processes as they continue to evolve, but when we look at criminal procedures in practice, structures of judicial supervision and party contest are not the defining features. In France, judicial supervision is mostly carried out by the public prosecutor (the procureur) and is minimal, largely retrospective, and overly aligned with the police; in England and Wales, the defense counsel is a far from equal party to the case and is required to serve the interests of court management over those of her client. Politically driven criminal justice narratives of securitization, preventive justice, and managerialism are increasingly displacing values of due process, freedom, or justice. These are posited in ways that compete with established values, such that more security comes at the price of less liberty. In contrast, EU legislation has focused on forms of police and judicial cooperation and common modes of crime fighting, but has more recently turned its attention to the rights of the accused, adopting measures firmly underpinned by fair-trial rights and a substantial body of ECtHR case law. This presents a more rights-based approach, but its impact is limited by the reluctance of states to make changes that displace existing structures, as well as the wider contexts of security, managerialism and efficiency within which criminal justice is played out. How do different systems reconcile these competing demands? As policy imperatives are refracted through different processes of criminal justice, how much explanatory force do the procedural traditions of adversarial and inquisitorial justice continue to have? Or have criminal systems metamorphosed beyond recognition?

It is clear that procedural tradition remains an important part of how criminal justice systems understand their own processes and ways of doing things in terms of the guiding principles and values that are claimed to underpin internal change and responses to externally driven imperatives. Many of the changes to the role of the French prosecutor, for example, are responses to a growing managerialism through which success is measured in purely quantitative terms, but it is understood within the domestic narrative in a way that does not displace the core organizing principle of judicial supervision. Powers of investigation and case disposition have been ceded to the procureur but in her capacity as judicial officer, while restating her professional ideology to mirror that of her more independent judicial colleagues, thus leaving the judicial model apparently intact. The principles and values asserted by procedural traditions are also used as a powerful means of resistance to external demands. The strengthening of pretrial defense rights in the terms advocated by the ECtHR and then the EU was opposed by France and others, who regarded it as the imposition of a more adversarial procedure that was inappropriate to inquisitorial traditions and so unnecessary. Ultimately, France accommodated the change by restricting the lawyer's role to that of a check upon the police enquiry (overseen by the procureur), thus preserving police and prosecution control, and arguably frustrating the European legislation's objective of ensuring that defense rights were effective in practice.

Procedural traditions are also appealed to in more cynical ways, as a means of altering the balance between crime control and due process, between repressive investigative powers and individual rights and freedoms. In England and Wales, the statutory right to custodial legal advice introduced under the Police and Criminal Evidence Act 1984 was a significant improvement to the rights of the suspect. However, it was soon used to justify the weakening of other core rights such as the presumption of innocence and the right of silence. This pattern has been repeated as pan-European measures have strengthened suspects' rights across jurisdictions, and access to legal assistance has been used to legitimate the extension of investigative powers by, for example, extending the length of time that suspects can be detained without charge. Access to counsel has also been used repeatedly to justify the introduction of a range of procedures encouraging early admissions, prosecutor-directed sanctions, and alternatives to trial.

Although we do not find convergence toward a unified system or approach to criminal procedure, we can identify a wider shift in criminal justice across both jurisdictions, reflecting a growth in penal populism and resulting in a retreat from fundamental values. The increased politicization of criminal justice has seen the promotion of policies that claim greater efficiency and cost-saving, but which seem mainly to refocus criminal justice toward the mass, standardized processing of medium and low-level offenses, producing apparently favorable statistics but with little impact on offending. Epitomized by the response to the threat of terrorism, preventive justice and the securitization of criminal law are animated by the politics of fear and claims around the management of risk. We have seen a range of exceptional measures, justified by exceptional circumstances that, it is claimed, warrant departures from established values and safeguards in the exercise of police powers and the attenuation of safeguards—yet many of these have subsequently been normalized and found their way into the ordinary, and increasingly punitive, criminal law. Looking across the two justice systems, these are not incidental or short-term changes. Police powers and sentencing guidelines may change to fit the politics of the day, but the roles of the two main protagonists, defense and prosecution, are being changed in fundamental and permanent ways. Increasingly, they are pulled away from their core professional tasks, called on to serve the wider interests and objectives of criminal justice managerialism through standardized procedures that reduce their professional autonomy, requiring them to act as managers more than as legal professionals.

Overlaying these various policy trends, the thrust of criminal justice policy and reform across both jurisdictions has been away from trial and the public disposition of cases, avoiding the opportunity for those accused to contest the accusation against them. Although retaining features of adversarial and inquisitorial procedures, and paying lip service to a human rights narrative, criminal processes are increasingly characterized by an administrative justice model that is measured by a set of managerialist outcomes more concerned with throughput than with the quality of justice. Within both systems of criminal justice there is a need for skepticism and cross-checking—not just at the trial, which is becoming a rare event, but more crucially during the investigation. The French trial might be described as the confirmation of an earlier set of data-collecting moments. It is during the investigation that the important work is done. But even where it occurs, is the trial in England and Wales very different? The evidence is rehearsed at court and is believed or rejected, but there is no truth-seeking function for the trial beyond an evaluation of the evidence that the parties have chosen to present and argue. There is little incentive to go beyond the initial, plausible case thesis. Avenues not explored during the investigation are unlikely to be revisited, and so even with the prospect of a trial, it is during the pretrial investigation that the processes of cross-checking and verification must take place. The ECtHR has emphasized the importance of fair-trial rights operating in practical and effective ways during the pretrial phase, in order to ensure the fairness of any trial that may follow. The participation of the accused is key to the notion of a fair trial, but relies on legal structures, ideologies, and resources to allow this. In England and Wales, the investigation is not fully adversarial: procedurally and as a result of the severe restrictions on legal aid, the defense has little chance to participate in, contribute to, or challenge acts of investigation. In France, the accused and her lawyer have greater rights to participate in the enquiry in the very small number of cases investigated through the *instruction* procedure, but the concentration of power in the *juge d'instruction* makes it difficult for the defense and, to an extent, the prosecutor to serve adequately as a counter-reflex during the investigation. In the overwhelming majority of cases, however, the investigation is overseen by the procureur, who is less independent that the *juge d'instruction* and mostly reliant on the police: there is no opportunity for the defense to have any part in the investigation.

In both jurisdictions, the overwhelming emphasis on the initial police investigation and its importance in the mode and result of case disposition suggests that we need to focus on reframing the pretrial stage so that an effective investigation is one that interrogates fully the initial case thesis. This would require some adjustment of professional ideologies and ethics, but could be accommodated within both systems around a mode of participation, cooperation, and cross-checking, rather than conflict and nondisclosure. However, although likely to produce more accurate results, better respecting the presumption of innocence, with finite and decreasing resources a broader investigative approach that is slower to discount weaker leads will inevitably be seen as inefficient, wasting time and money. Perhaps the most striking way in which the criminal justice system has metamorphosed is common between the two systems—from a more principled and unified system to one driven by managerialism and efficiency at the expense of justice.

References

Abramaviciute, I., and Valutyte, R. (2012). "National Approaches to Effective Criminal Defence: Lithuania." In Cape, E., and Namoradze, Z. (eds.) *Effective Criminal Defence in Eastern Europe* (Moldova: Legal Aid Reformers' Network) 197–258.

Adler-Nissen, R. (2014). *Opting Out of the European Union: Diplomacy, Sovereignty and European Integration* (Cambridge: Cambridge University Press).

Aliverti, A. (2014). *Crimes of Mobility: Criminal Law and the Regulation of Immigration* (New York: Routledge).

Allen, G., and Dempsey, N. (2018). *Terrorism in Great Britain: The Statistics*. House of Commons Library Briefing Paper No. CBP7613, 7 June.

Alt, E., and Le Theule, M.-A. (2011). "La justice aux prises avec l'éthique et la performance." 22 *Pyramides* 137–159.

Altheide, D. L. (2006). "The Mass Media, Crime and Terrorism." 4 *Journal of International Criminal Justice* 982–997.

Ambos, K. (2003). "International Criminal Procedure: 'Adversarial,' 'Inquisitorial' or Mixed?" 3(1) *International Criminal Law Review* 1–37.

Amnesty International (2016). *Upturned Lives: The Disproportionate Impact of France's State of Emergency*. Available at https://www.amnesty.org/en/documents/eur21/3364/2016/en/.

Anderson, D. (2014). *The Terrorism Acts in 2013. Report of the Independent Reviewer on the Operation of the Terrorism Act 2000 and Part 1 of the Terrorism Act 2006* (London: HMSO). Available at https://terrorismlegislationreviewer.independent.gov.uk/wp-content/uploads/2014/07/Independent-Review-of-Terrorism-Report-2014-print2.pdf.

Anderson, D. (2017). *Attacks in London and Manchester. March–June 2017. Independent Assessment of MI5 and Police Internal Reviews* (London: Home Office).

Appleby, G. (2016). "Reform of the Attorney General: Comparing Britain and Australia." *Public Law* 573–594.

Arbor, L. (1999). "The Need for an Independent and Effective Prosecutor in the Permanent International Criminal Court." 17 *Windsor Yearbook of Access to Justice* 207–220.

Arnold, R. (ed.) (2016). *The Convergence of the Fundamental Rights Protection in Europe. Ius Gentium: Comparative Perspectives on Law and Justice*, vol. 52. (Dordrecht: Springer).

Ashworth, A. J., and Zedner, L. (2008). "Defending the Criminal Law: Reflections on the Changing Character of Crime, Procedure, and Sanctions." 2 *Criminal Law and Philosophy* 21–51.

Ashworth, A. J., and Zedner, L. (2014). *Preventive Justice* (Oxford: Oxford University Press).

Aubert, L. (2008). "L'activité des délégués du procureur en France: De l'intention à la réalité des pratiques." 32(4) *Déviance et société* 473–494.

Aubert, L. (2010). "Systématisme pénale et alternatives aux poursuites en France: Une politique pénale en trompe-l'œil." 74(1) *Droit et société* 17–33.

Audrey, W. S. M. (2010). "Criminal Justice for All? Wrongful Convictions and Poverty in Singapore." 28 *Singapore Law Review* 67–97.

Auld, Rt. Hon. Justice (2001). *Review of the Criminal Courts of England and Wales* (London: HMSO).

Bahr, B., and Melum, J. (2017). "EU's 'Victims' Directive': A Legal Act for a Cultural Change?" 9(1) *International Journal for Court Administration* 16–20.

Bailin, A., and Craven, E. (2014). "Compensation for Miscarriages of Justice: Who Now Qualifies?" *Criminal Law Review* 511–517.

Baldwin, J., and McConville, M. (1977). *Negotiated Justice* (London: Martin Robertson).

Bar Standards Board. (2004). *Written Standards for the Conduct of Professional Work.* Code of Conduct (8th ed.).

Bastard, B., Delvaux, D., Mouhanna, C., and Schoenaers, F. (2015). "Vitesse ou precipitation? La question du temps dans le traitement des affaires pénales en France et en Belgique." 90(2) *Droit et société* 271–286.

Bastard, B., and Mouhanna, C. (2007). *Une justice dans l'urgence: Le traitement en temps réel des affaires pénales* (Paris: Presses universitaires de France).

Beattie, J. M. (1986). *Crime and the Courts in England, 1660–1800* (Oxford: Clarendon Press).

Beattie, J. M. (1991). "Scales of Justice: Defence Counsel and the English Criminal Trial in the Eighteenth and Nineteenth Centuries." 9 *Law and History Review* 221–267.

Beard, J. (2017). *Sentences of Imprisonment for Public Protection.* House of Commons Library Briefing Paper No. 06086, 25 October.

Beaume, J. (2014). *Rapport sur la procédure pénale* (Paris: Ministère de la justice).

Beetham, D. (1991). *The Legitimation of Power* (Basingstoke: Macmillan).

Belloni, F., and Hodgson, J. (2000). *Criminal Injustice: An Evaluation of the Criminal Justice Process in Britain* (Basingstoke: Macmillan).

Besnier, C., and Salas, D. (2008). "La crise d'Outreau: De l'emprise de l'émotion à l'ambiguïté de la réforme." 55(1) *Droit et cultures* 87–102.

Blackstock, J., Cape, E., Hodgson, J., Ogorodova, A., and Spronken, T. (2014). *Inside Police Custody* (Cambridge: Intersentia).

Body-Gendrot, S. (2011). "French Perspectives on Threats to Peace and Local Social Order." In Crawford, A. (ed.) *International and Comparative Criminal Justice and Urban Governance* (Cambridge: Cambridge University Press) 545–566.

Bohm, R. M. (2006). "'McJustice': On the McDonaldization of Criminal Justice." 23(1) *Justice Quarterly* 127–146.

Bokhashvili, B. (2012). "National Approaches to Effective Criminal Defence: Georgia." In Cape, E., and Namoradze, Z. (eds.) *Effective Criminal Defence in Eastern Europe* (Moldova: Legal Aid Reformers' Network) 153–195.

Bonner, D., and Cholewinski, R. (2007). "The Response of the United Kingdom's Legal and Constitutional Orders to the 1991 Gulf War and the Post-9/11 'War' on Terrorism." In Guild, E., and Baldaccini, A. (eds.) *Terrorism and the Foreigner: A Decade of Tension around the Rule of Law in Europe* (Leiden: Martinus Nijhoff) 123–174.

Bonomy, I. (2015). *The Post-corroboration Safeguards Review* (Edinburgh: Scottish Government).

Boon, A., and Nash, S. (2006). "Special Advocacy: Political Expediency and Legal Roles in Modern Judicial Systems." 9(1) *Legal Ethics* 101–124.

Bottomley, K., Coleman, C., Dixon, D., Gill, M., and Wall, D. (1991). *The Impact of PACE: Policing in a Northern Force* (Hull: Centre for Criminology and Criminal Justice).

Bottoms, A., and Tankebe, J. (2012). "Beyond Procedural Justice: A Dialogic Approach to Legitimacy in Criminal Justice." 102(1) *Journal of Criminal Law and Criminology* 119–170.

Boucobza, I., and Girard, C. (2016). "'Constitutionnaliser' l'état d'urgence ou comment soigner l'obsession d'inconstitutionnalité?" 9 *La revue des droits de l'homme*. Available at http://journals.openedition.org/revdh/1784.

Brandon, B. (2004). "Terrorism, Human Rights and the Rule of Law: 120 Years of the UK's Legal Response to Terrorism." *Criminal Law Review* 981–997.

Brants, C. (2008). "Vulnerability of Dutch Criminal Procedure to Wrongful Conviction." In Huff, R., and Killias, M. (eds.) *Wrongful Conviction: International Perspectives on Miscarriages of Justice* (Philadelphia: Temple University Press) 157–182.

Brants, C. (2011). "The Reluctant Dutch Response to Salduz." 15 *Edinburgh Law Review* 298–305.

Brants, C., and Field, S. (2016). "Truth-Finding, Procedural Traditions and Cultural Trust in the Netherlands and England and Wales: When Strengths Become Weaknesses." 20(4) *International Journal of Evidence and Proof* 266–288.

Brants, C., and Ringsnalda, A. (2010). *Issues of Convergence: Inquisitorial Prosecution in England and Wales?* (Nijmegen: Wolf Legal Publishers).

Bratza, N. (2011). "The Relationship between the UK Courts and Strasbourg." 5 *European Human Rights Law Review* 505–512.

Bridges, L. (2010). "Towards a Culture of Complacency: Criminal Justice under New Labour." 79 *Criminal Justice Matters* 22–24.

Bridges, L., and Choongh, S. (1998). *Improving Police Station Legal Advice: The Impact of the Accreditation Scheme for Police Station Legal Advisers* (London: Law Society and Legal Aid Board).

Brookman, F., and Innes, M. (2013). "The Problem of Success: What Is a 'Good' Homicide Investigation?" 23(3) *Policing and Society* 292–310.

Brown, D. (2014). "The Perverse Effects of Efficiency in Criminal Process." 100 *Virginia Law Review* 183–223.

Bui, D. T. (2016). "The Expansion and Fragmentation of Minor Offense Justice: A Convergence between the Common Law and the Civil Law." 19(3) *New Criminal Law Review* 382–411.

Bunt, H. van de, and van Gelder, J.-L. (2012). "The Dutch Prosecution Service." In Tonry, M. (ed.) *Prosecutors and Politics: A Comparative Perspective* (Chicago: University of Chicago Press) 117–140.

Burke, A. (2013). "Prosecution (Is) Complex." 10 *Ohio State Journal of Criminal Law* 703–718.

Burns, R. (2009). *The Death of the American Trial* (Chicago: University of Chicago Press).

Bushchenko, A., and Tokarev, G. (2012). "National Approaches to Effective Criminal Defence: Ukraine." In Cape, E., and Namoradze, Z. (eds.) *Effective Criminal Defence in Eastern Europe* (Moldova: Legal Aid Reformers' Network) 345–403.

Cahn, O. (2009). "The Fight against Terrorism and Human Rights: The French Perspective." In Wade, M., and Maljević, A. (eds.) *A War on Terror? The European Stance on a New Threat, Changing Laws and Human Rights* (New York: Springer) 467–503.

Caianiello, M. (2016). "Increasing Discretionary Prosecutors' Powers: The Pivotal Role of the Italian Prosecutor in the Pretrial Investigation Phase." *Oxford Handbooks Online: Criminology and Criminal Justice* (Oxford: Oxford University Press).

Cairns, D. J. A. (1998). *Advocacy and the Making of the Adversarial Trial, 1800–1865* (Oxford: Clarendon Press).

Cape, E. (2004). "The Rise (and Fall?) of a Criminal Defence Profession." *Criminal Law Review* 72–87.

Cape, E. and Hodgson, J. (2014). "The Right of Access to a Lawyer at Police Stations: Making the European Union Directive Work in Practice." 5 *New Journal of European Criminal Law* 450–479.

Cape, E., and Namoradze, Z. (eds.) (2012). *Effective Criminal Defence in Eastern Europe* (Moldova: Legal Aid Reformers' Network).

Capers, B. (2016). "The Prosecutor's Turn." 57(4) *William and Mary Law Review* 1277–1308.

Carloway, Lord (2011). *The Carloway Review: Report and Recommendations* (Edinburgh: Scottish Government). Available at http://www.gov.scot/Resource/Doc/925/0122808.pdf.

Carruba, C. J., Gabel, M., and Hankla, C. (2008). "Judicial Behaviour under Political Constraints: Evidence from the European Court of Justice." 102 *American Political Science Review* 435–452.

Carvalho, H. (2017). *The Preventive Turn in Criminal Law* (Oxford: Oxford University Press).

Chaussebourg, L., and Lumbroso, S. (2008). *Les décisions des cours d'assises d'appel* (Paris: Ministère de la justice).

Cohen, M. (2017). "The Carpenter's Mistake? The Prosecutor as Judge in France?" In Langer, M., and Slansky, D. (eds.) *Prosecutors and Democracy* (Cambridge: Cambridge University Press) 109–137.

Coicaud, J.-M. (2002). *Legitimacy and Politics*. Translated by David Ames Curtis. (Cambridge: Cambridge University Press).

Cole, J. (2008). "Poetic Justice: The Trial of 'Lyrical Terrorist' Samina Malik." *RUSI Homeland Security and Resilience Monitor* April 14–17.

Colson, R., and Field, S. (2011). *The Transformation of Criminal Justice: Comparing France with England and Wales* (n.p.: Harmattan).

Colson, R., and Field, S. (eds.) (2016). *Criminal Justice and the Challenges of Diversity* (Cambridge: Cambridge University Press).

Combs, N. A. (2012). "Legitimizing International Criminal Justice: The Importance of Process Control." 33 *Michigan Journal of International Law* 321–382.

Contrôleur général des lieux de privation de liberté (2015). *Rapport d'activité 2014* (Paris: Dalloz).

Contrôleur général des lieux de privation de liberté (2018). *Rapport d'activité 2017* (Paris: Dalloz).

Cooper, J. M. (2008). "Competing Legal Cultures and Legal Reform: The Battle of Chile." 29 *Michigan Journal of International Law* 501–563.

Council of Europe, Committee of Ministers (2000). *The Role of the Public Prosecution in the Criminal Justice System (Rec 19)*. Strasbourg: Council of Europe.

Council of Europe MSI-NET (2017). *Algorithms and Human Rights: Study on the Human Rights Dimension of Automated Data Processing Techniques and Possible Regulatory Implications*. Available at https://edoc.coe.int/en/internet/7589-algorithms-and-human-rights-study-on-the-human-rights-dimensions-of-automated-data-processing-techniques-and-possible-regulatory-implications.html#.

Crawford, A. (2003). "Contractual Governance of Deviant Behaviour." 30(4) *Journal of Law and Society* 479–505.

Crawford, A. (2008). "Dispersal Powers and the Symbolic Role of Anti-social Behaviour Legislation." 71(5) *Modern Law Review* 753–784.

Criminal Cases Review Commission (CRCC) (2011). *Annual Report and Accounts, 2010/11* (London: Stationery Office) HC 1225.

Criminal Cases Review Commission (CRCC) (2012). *Annual Report and Accounts, 2011/12* (London: Stationery Office) HC 390.

Criminal Cases Review Commission (CRCC) (2015). *Guidance for Legal Representatives.*

Criminal Cases Review Commission (CRCC) (2019). *Annual Report and Accounts, 2018/19* (London: Stationery Office) HC 2438.

Criminal Justice Joint Inspection (2010). *Indeterminate Sentence for Public Protection: A Joint Inspection by HMI Probation and HMI Prisons.* Available at http://www.justiceinspectorates.gov.uk/probation/wp-content/uploads/sites/5/2014/03/IPP_report_final_2-rps.pdf.

Crisp, D., and Moxon, D. (1994). *Case Screening by the Crown Prosecution Service: How and Why Cases Are Terminated.* Home Office Research Study No. 137 (London: Home Office).

Croft, S. (2007). "British Jihadis and the British War on Terror." 7(3) *Defence Studies* 317–337.

Cronin, A. (2009). *How Terrorism Ends* (Princeton, NJ: Princeton University Press).

Crown Prosecution Service (1995) *Crown Prosecution Service Annual Report 1994–1995* (London: HMSO).

Crown Prosecution Service (2019) *Crown Prosecution Service Annual Report and Accounts 2018–19.* (London: HMSO) HC 2286.

Cryer, R. (2006). "A Long Way from Home: Witnesses before International Criminal Tribunals." 4(1) *International Commentary on Evidence* Article 8.

Damaška, M. (1973). "Evidentiary Barriers to Conviction and Two Models of Criminal Procedure: A Comparative Study." 121 *University of Pennsylvania Law Review* 506–589.

Damaška, M. (1975). "Structures of Authority and Comparative Criminal Procedure." 84 *Yale Law Journal* 480–544.

Damaška, M. (1997). "The Uncertain Fate of Evidentiary Transplants: Anglo-American and Continental Experiments." 45 *American Journal of Comparative Law* 839–852.

Damaška, M. (2004). "Negotiated Justice in International Criminal Courts." 2 *Journal of International Criminal Justice* 1018–1039.

Damaška, M. (2011). "The Competing Visions of Fairness: The Basic Choice for International Criminal Tribunals." 36(2) *North Carolina Journal of International Law and Commercial Regulation* 365–387.

Danet, J. (2001). *Défendre: Pour une défense pénale critique* (Paris: Dalloz).

Danet, J. (2003). "Le droit pénal et la procédure pénale sous le paradigm de l'insécurité." 25(1) *Archives de politique criminelle* 37–69.

Danet, J. (ed.) (2013). *La réponse pénale dix ans de traitement des délits* (Rennes: Presses universitaires de Rennes).

Davidson, R. (2017). "Brexit and Criminal Justice: The Future of the UK's Cooperation Relationship with the EU." *Criminal Law Review* 379–395.

Daw, R., and Solomon, A. (2010). "Assisted Suicide and Identifying the Public Interest in the Decision to Prosecute." *Criminal Law Review* 737–743.

De la Barra Cousino, C. R. (1998). "Adversarial vs Inquisitorial Systems: The Rule of Law and Prospects for Criminal Procedure Reform in Chile." 5 *Southwestern Journal of Law and Trade in the Americas* 323–364.

Défenseur des droits (2013). *L'enfant et sa parole en justice: Rapport 2013 consacré aux droits de l'enfant* (Paris: La Documentation française).

Défenseur des droits (2016). *Avis No. 16-06 de février 2016: Suivi de l'état d'urgence.* Independent Police Complaints Authority Network.

Degoul, P. (2018). *L'intervention de l'avocat en garde à vue* (n.p.: n.p.).

Delage, J.-P. (2005). "La comparution sur reconnaissance préalable de culpabilité: Quand la pratique ramène à la théorie." 29 *Recueil Dalloz* 1970–1973.

Delmas-Marty, M. (1991). *La mise en état des affaires pénales: Rapport de la Commission justice pénale et droits de l'homme* (Paris: La Documentation française).

Delmas-Marty, M. (2007). "The Paradigm of the War on Crime." 5 *Journal of International Criminal Justice* 584–598.

Delmas-Marty, M. (2008). "Reflections on the Hybridisation of Criminal Procedure." In Jackson, J., Langer, M., and Tillers, P. (eds.) *Crime, Procedure and Evidence in a Comparative and International Context* (Oxford: Hart) 251–259.

Delmas-Marty, M., and Spencer, J. R. (eds.) (2002). *European Criminal Procedures.* Translation supervised by J. R. Spencer. (Cambridge: Cambridge University Press).

Depardon, R. (dir.) (2004) *10th District Court (10e Chambre) Koch Lorber Films.*

Department of Constitutional Affairs (2006). *Delivering Simple, Speedy Summary Justice.* DCA 37/06 (London: DCA).

Desrosières, A. (2008). *Gouverner par les nombres: L'argument statistique.* 2 vols. (Presses de l'Ecole des Mines, Coll. Sciences Sociales).

Dixon, D., Coleman, C., and Bottomley, K. (1990). "Consent and the Legal Regulation of Policing." 17(3) *Journal of Law and Society* 345–362.

Dixon, D., with Travis, G. (2007) *Interrogating Images: Audio-Visually Recorded Police Questioning of Suspects* (Sydney: University of Sydney).

Domingo, P., and Sieder, R. (eds.) (2001). *The Rule of Law in Latin America: The International Promotion of Judicial Reform* (London: University of London, Institute of Latin American Studies).

Dongois, N. (2008). "Wrongful Convictions in France: The Limits of 'Pourvoi en Révision.'" In Huff, R., and Killias, M. (eds.) *Wrongful Conviction: International Perspectives on Miscarriages of Justice* (Philadelphia: Temple University Press) 249–261.

Donohue, L. K. (2008). *The Cost of Counterterrorism* (Cambridge: Cambridge University Press).

Donovan, J. M. (1999). "Magistrates and Juries in France, 1791–1952." 22(3) *French Historical Studies* 379–420.

Dorange, A., and Field, S. (2012). "Reforming Defence Rights in French Police Custody: A Coming Together in Europe?" 16 *International Journal of Evidence and Proof* 153–174.

Drumbl, M. (2013). "The Future of International Criminal Law and Transitional Justice." In Schabas, W. A., McDermott, Y., and Hayes, N. (eds.) *The Ashgate Research Companion to International Criminal Law: Critical Perspectives* (Aldershot: Ashgate) 531–545.

Duff, P. (2001). "Criminal Cases Review Commissions and 'Deference' to the Courts: The Evaluation of Evidence and Evidentiary Rules." *Criminal Law Review* 341–362.

Duff, P. (2004). "Changing Conceptions of the Scottish Criminal Trial: The Duty to Agree Uncontroversial Evidence." In Duff, A., Farmer, L., Marshall, S., and Tadros, V. (eds.) *The Trial on Trial: Truth and Due Process* (Oxford: Hart) 29–50.

Duff, P. (2009). "Straddling Two Worlds: Reflections of a Retired Criminal Cases Review Commissioner." 72(5) *Modern Law Review* 693–722.
Eckes, C. (2013). "EU Access to the ECHR: Between Autonomy and Adaptation." 76(2) *Modern Law Review* 254–285.
Edwards, A. (2016). "The Changing Status of the Defence Solicitor." *Criminal Law Review* 830–843.
Edwards, J. L. (1984). *The Attorney General, Politics and the Public Interest* (London: Sweet and Maxwell).
Eijkman, Q., and van Ginkel, B. (2011). "Compatible or Incompatible? Intelligence and Human Rights in Terrorist Trials." 3(4) *Amsterdam Law Forum* 3–16.
Elm, D., Klein, S. R., and Remis, A. (2015). "Waiving the Criminal Justice System: An Empirical and Constitutional Analysis." 52 *American Criminal Law Review* 73–130.
Emsley, C. (1999). "A Typology of Nineteenth-Century Police." 3 *Crime History and Societies* 29–44.
Encarnacion, E. (2017). "Backpay for Exonerees." 29(2) *Yale Journal of Law and the Humanities* 245–271.
Ericson, R. V. (1994). "The Royal Commission on Criminal Justice Surveillance." In McConville, M., and Bridges, L. (eds.) *Criminal Justice in Crisis* (Aldershot: Edward Elgar) 113–140.
Esmein, A. (1913, reprinted 1968). *A History of Continental Criminal Procedure with Special Reference to France*. Translated by John Simpson. Vol. 5, *The Continental Legal History Series* (New York: Augustus M. Kelley).
European Commission (2011). *Impact Assessment accompanying the Proposal for a Directive of the European Parliament and of the Council on the Rights of Access to a Lawyer and of Notification of Custody to a Third Person in Criminal Proceedings*. June. SEC 686 final.
European Parliamentary Research Service (2017). *Procedural Rights and Detention Conditions* European Added Value Unit, EPRS.
Falcone, G. (1994). *Interventi e proposte (1982–92)* (Milan: Sansei).
Fédération internationale des droits de l'homme (FIDH) (1999). "France: Paving the Way for Arbitrary Justice." No. 271-2, March. http://www.fidh.org/IMG/pdf/271fran.pdf.
Feeley, M. (1982). "Plea Bargaining and the Structure of the Criminal Process." 7 *Justice System Journal* 338–354.
Feeley, M. (1997). "Legal Complexity and the Transformation of the Criminal Process: The Origins of Plea Bargaining." 31 *Israel Law Review* 183–222.
Feeley, M., and Simon, J. (1992). "The New Penology: Notes on the Emerging Strategy of Corrections and Its Implications." 30 *Criminology* 449–474.
Feeley, M., and Simon, J. (1994). "Actuarial Justice: The Emerging New Criminal Law." In Nelken, D. (ed.) *The Futures of Criminology* (London: Sage) 173–201.
Field, S. (2009). "Fair Trials and Procedural Tradition in Europe." 29(2) *Oxford Journal of Legal Studies* 365–387.
Field, S., Alldridge, P., and Jörg, N. (1995). "Prosecutors, Examining Judges and Control of Police Investigations." In Harding, C., et al. (eds.) *Criminal Justice in Europe: A Comparative Study* (Oxford: Clarendon Press) 227–249.
Field, S., and Thomas, P. (eds.) (1994). *Justice and Efficiency? The Royal Commission on Criminal Justice* (London: Blackwell). Also published as 1 *Journal of Law and Society*, 1994.

Field, S., and West, A. (1995). "A Tale of Two Reforms: French Defense Rights and Police Powers in Transition." 6(3) *Criminal Law Forum* 473–506.

Field, S., and West, A. (2003). "Dialogue and the Inquisitorial Tradition: French Defence Lawyers in the Pre-trial Criminal Process." 14(3) *Criminal Law Forum* 261–316.

Fischer Taylor, K. (1993). *In the Theater of Criminal Justice: The Palais de Justice in Second Empire Paris* (Princeton, NJ: Princeton University Press).

Flynn, A., and Hodgson, J. (eds.) (2017). *Access to Justice and Legal Aid: Comparative Perspectives on Unmet Legal Need* (Oxford: Hart).

Flynn, A., Hodgson, J., McCulloch, J., and Naylor, B. (2016). "Legal Aid and the Right to a Fair Trial: A Question of Human Rights." 40(1) *Melbourne University Law Review* 207–239.

Foley, F. (2009). "Reforming Counterterrorism: Institutions and Organizational Routines in Britain and in France." 18 *Security Studies* 435–478.

Franken, S. (2008). "Finding the Truth in Dutch Courtrooms; How Does One Deal with Miscarriages of Justice?" 4(4) *Utrecht Law Review* 218–226.

Di Federico, G. (1998). "Prosecutorial Independence and the Democratic Requirement of Accountability in Italy." 38 *British Journal of Criminology* 371–387.

Galli, F., and Weyembergh, A. (eds.) (2012). *EU Counter-terrorism Offences: What Impact on National Legislation and Case-Law?* (Brussels: University of Brussels).

Gallois, A. (2017). "L'atteinte au droit constitutionnel de se taire par l'exclusion légale d'une nullité de procédure pénale." *Recueil Dalloz* 395–399.

Garapon, A. (2004). "Three Challenges for International Justice." 2 *Journal of International Criminal Justice* 716–26.

Garapon, A. (2010). *La raison du moindre état* (Paris: Odile Jacob).

Garapon, A., Perdroille, S., and Bernabé, B. (2013). *La prudence et l'autorité: L'office du juge au XXIe siècle rapport de l'IHEJ* (Paris: Ministère de la justice).

Garcia, F. S. (1998). "The Nature of Judicial Reform in Latin America and Some Strategic Considerations." 13 *American University International Law Review* 1267–1325.

Garçon, M. (1995). "Faut-il modifier la composition et les attributions du jury." 35 *Revue de droit pénal et de criminologie* 455–472.

Gardner, J. A. (1980). *Legal Imperialism: American Lawyers and Foreign Aid in Latin America* (Madison: University of Wisconsin Press).

Garland, D. (2001). *The Culture of Control: Crime and Social Order in Contemporary Society* (Chicago: Chicago University Press).

Garner, J. W. (1916). "Criminal Procedure in France." 25(4) *Yale Law Journal* 255–284.

Garrett, B. (2011). *Convicting the Innocent: Where Criminal Prosecutions Go Wrong* (Cambridge, MA: Harvard University Press).

Garrett, B., and Monahan, J. (2018). "Judging Risk." Virginia Public Law and Legal Theory Research Paper No. 2018-44. Available at https://ssrn.com/abstract=3190403.

Gasper, B. (2005). "Examining the Use of Evidence Obtained under Torture: The Case of the British Detainees May Test the Resolve of the European Convention in the Era of Terrorism." 21(2) *American University International Law Review* 277–326.

Gaulejac de, V. (2009). *La société malade de la gestion* (Paris: Points Seuil).

Gearty, C. (2005). "11 September 2001, Counter-terrorism, and the Human Rights Act." 32(1) *Journal of Law and Society* 18–33.

Giannoulopoulos, D. (2016). "Strasbourg Jurisprudence, Law Reform and Comparative Law: A Tale of the Right to Custodial Legal Advice in Five Countries." 16(1) *Human Rights Law Review* 103–129.

Giannoulopoulos, D. (2018). "'Falling on Deaf Ears': Looking for the *Salduz* Jurisprudence in Greece." In Jackson, J., and Summers, S. (eds.) *Obstacles to Fairness in Criminal Proceedings* (Oxford: Hart) 155–177.

Glidewell, Iain, Rt. Hon. Sir (1998). *The Review of the Crown Prosecution Service*. Cmnd 3960 (London: Stationery Office).

Godard, J. (2002). "The French Judge and *les Affaires*." 166 *Justice of the Peace* 223–225.

Goldberg, D., Jadhav, S., and Younis, T. (2017). "Prevent: What Is Pre-Criminal Space?" 41(4) *British Journal of Psychology Bulletin* 208–211.

Goldstein, A., and Marcus, M. (1978a). "Comment on 'Continental Criminal Procedure.'" 87 *Yale Law Journal* 1570–1577.

Goldstein, A., and Marcus, M. (1978b). "The Myth of Judicial Supervision in Three 'Inquisitorial' Systems: France, Italy and Germany." 87 *Yale Law Journal* 240–283.

Goldston, J. (2010). "More Candour about Criteria: The Exercise of Discretion by the Prosecutor of the International Criminal Court." 8 *Journal of International Criminal Justice* 383–406.

Goodpaster, G. (1987). "On the Theory of American Adversary Trial." 78(1) Journal of Criminal Law and Criminology 118–154.

Goss, R. (2014). *Criminal Fair Trial Rights: Article 6 of the European Convention on Human Rights* (Oxford: Hart).

Goss, R. (2017). "Out of Many, One? Strasbourg's Ibrahim Decision on Article 6." 80(6) *Modern Law Review* 1137–1163.

Greenwood, H. (2017). *Exploring the UK Innocence Movement: Tension, Reconfiguration and Theorisation*. PhD diss., University of Cardiff.

Grieve, D. (2013). "The Case for the Prosecution: Independence and the Public Interest" (speech delivered at Queen Mary University of London, 13 March). Attorney General's Office.

Griffin, L. (2009). "Correcting Injustice: Studying How the United Kingdom and the United States Review Claims of Innocence." 41 *University of Toledo Law Review* 107–152.

Gross, L. J. (2011). *Review of Disclosure on Criminal Proceedings*. Judiciary of England and Wales.

Gross, L. J., and Treacy, L. J. (2012). *Further Review of Disclosure in Criminal Proceedings: Sanctions for Failure*. Judiciary of England and Wales.

Gross, L. J., Kinch, H. H. J., and Riddle, H. (2014). *Magistrates Court Disclosure Review*. Judiciary of England and Wales.

Grozev, Y. (2012). "National Approaches to Effective Criminal Defence: Bulgaria." In Cape, E., and Namoradze, Z. (eds.) *Effective Criminal Defence in Eastern Europe* (Moldova: Legal Aid Reformers' Network) 93–151.

Grunvald, S. (2014). "La diversification de la réponse pénale: Approche du point de vue des victimes." 88(3) *Droit et société* 649–664.

Guarnieri, C. (1997). "Prosecution in Two Civil Law Countries: France and Italy." In Nelken, D. (ed.) *Comparing Legal Cultures* (Aldershot: Ashgate) 183–193.

Hay, D. (1983). "Controlling the English Prosecutor." 21(2) *Osgoode Hall Law Journal* 165–186.

Heath-Kelly, C., and Strausz, E. (2018). *Counter-terrorism in the NHS: Evaluating the Prevent Duty Safeguarding the NHS*. Available at https://warwick.ac.uk/fac/soc/pais/research/researchcentres/irs/counterterrorisminthenhs/project_report_60pp.pdf.

Her Majesty's Crown Prosecution Service Inspectorate (HMCPSI) and HM Inspectorate of Constabulary (HMIC) (2015). *Joint Inspection of the Provision of Charging Decisions*.

HMCPSI Publications https://www.justiceinspectorates.gov.uk/hmic/wp-content/uploads/joint-inspection-of-the-provision-of-charging-decisions.pdf.

Her Majesty's Crown Prosecution Service Inspectorate (HMCPSI) and HM Inspectorate of Constabulary (HMIC) (2017). *Making It Fair: A Joint Inspection of the Disclosure of Unused Material in Volume Crown Court cases.* HMCPSI Publications http://www.justiceinspectorates.gov.uk/cjji/wp-content/uploads/sites/2/2017/07/CJJI_DSC_thm_July17_rpt.pdf.

Her Majesty's Inspectorate of Constabulary (HMIC) (2015). *Witness for the Prosecution: Identifying Victim and Witness Vulnerability in Criminal Cases.* HMIC Publications https://www.justiceinspectorates.gov.uk/hmicfrs/wp-content/uploads/vulnerability-in-criminal-case-files-wiltshire.pdf.

Her Majesty's Inspectorate of Prisons (2008). *The Indeterminate Sentence for Public Protection.* Available at https://www.justiceinspectorates.gov.uk/hmiprisons/inspections/the-indeterminate-sentence-for-public-protection/.

Her Majesty's Inspectorate of Prisons (2016). *Unintended Consequences: Finding a Way Forward for Prisoners Serving Sentences of Imprisonment for Public Protection.* Available at https://www.justiceinspectorates.gov.uk/hmiprisons/inspections/unintended-consequences-finding-a-way-forward-for-prisoners-serving-sentences-of-imprisonment- for-public-protection/.

Herzog-Evans, M. (2007). "Prévenir la récidive: Les limites de la répression pénale." *Actualité juridique pénal* 357–363.

Herzog-Evans, M. (2011). *Droit de l'exécution des peines* (Paris: Dalloz).

Hodgson, J. (1992). "Tipping the Scales of Justice: The Suspect's Right to Legal Advice." *Criminal Law Review* 854–862.

Hodgson, J. (1994). "Adding Injury to Injustice: The Suspect at the Police Station." 21(1) *Journal of Law and Society* 85–101.

Hodgson, J. (1997). "Vulnerable Suspects and the Appropriate Adult." *Criminal Law Review* 785–795.

Hodgson, J. (2001). "The Police, the Prosecutor and the *Juge d'Instruction:* Judicial Supervision in France, Theory and Practice." 41(2) *British Journal of Criminology* 342–361.

Hodgson, J. (2002a). "Constructing the Pre-trial Role of the Defence in French Criminal Procedure: An Adversarial Outsider in an Inquisitorial Process?" 6(1) *International Journal of Evidence and Proof* 1–16.

Hodgson, J. (2002b). "Suspects, Defendants and Victims in the French Criminal Process: The Context of Recent Reform." 51(4) *International and Comparative Law Quarterly* 781–816.

Hodgson, J. (2002c). "Hierarchy, Bureaucracy and Ideology in French Criminal Justice: Some Empirical Observations." 29 *Journal of Law and Society* 227–257.

Hodgson, J. (2004). "The Detention and Interrogation of Suspects Detained in Police Custody in France: A Comparative Account." 1(2) *European Journal of Criminology* 163–199.

Hodgson, J. (2005). *French Criminal Justice: A Comparative Account of the Investigation and Prosecution of Crime in France* (Oxford: Hart).

Hodgson, J. (2006a). *The Investigation and Prosecution of Terrorist Suspects in France.* Report for the Home Office.

Hodgson, J. (2006b). "The Role of the Criminal Defence Lawyer in an Inquisitorial Procedure: Legal and Ethical Constraints." 9(1) *Legal Ethics* 125–146.

Hodgson, J. (2006c). "Conceptions of the Trial in Inquisitorial and Adversarial Procedure." In Duff, A., Farmer, L., Marshall, S., and Tadros, V. (eds.) *Judgment and Calling to Account* (Oxford: Hart) 223–242.

Hodgson, J. (2010). "The French Prosecutor in Question." 67(4) *Washington & Lee Law Review* 1361–1411.

Hodgson, J. (2011). "Safeguarding Suspects' Rights in Europe: A Comparative Perspective." 14(4) *New Criminal Law Review* 611–665.

Hodgson, J. (2012). "EU Criminal Justice: Crime Control and Due Process within a Framework of Mutual Recognition." 37 *North Carolina Journal of International Law and Commercial Regulation* 307–320.

Hodgson, J. (2013a). "The Impact of *Salduz* in France: Making Custodial Legal Advice More Effective." 92 *Criminal Justice Matters* 14–15.

Hodgson, J. (2013b). "Legitimacy and State Responses to Terrorism: The UK and France." In Tankebe, J., and Liebling, A. (eds.) *Legitimacy and Criminal Justice: An International Exploration* (Oxford: Oxford University Press) 178–205.

Hodgson, J. (2015). "Plea Bargaining: A Comparative Analysis." In Wright, J. (ed.) 18 *International Encyclopedia of the Social and Behavioral Sciences* (Amsterdam: Elsevier) 226–231.

Hodgson, J. (2016a). "From the Domestic to the European: An Empirical Approach to Comparative Custodial Legal Advice." In Ross, J., and Thaman, S. (eds.) *Handbook on Comparative Criminal Procedure* (Cheltenham: Edward Elgar) 258–279.

Hodgson, J. (2016b). "Criminal Procedure in Europe's Area of Freedom, Security and Justice: The Rights of the Suspect." In Mitsilegas, V., Bergström, M., and Konstadinides, T. (eds.) *Research Handbook in EU Criminal Law* (Cheltenham: Edward Elgar) 168–188.

Hodgson, J. (2017). "The Democratic Accountability of Prosecutors in England and Wales and in France: Independence, Discretion and Managerialism." In Langer, M., and Slansky, D. (eds.) *Prosecutors and Democracy* (Cambridge: Cambridge University Press) 76–108.

Hodgson, J. (2019). "The Challenge of Universal Norms: Securing Effective Defence Rights Across Different Jurisdictions and Legal Cultures" 46 *Journal of Law and Society* S95–S114.

Hodgson, J., and Horne, J. (2009). *The Extent and Impact of Legal Representation on Applications to the CCRC.* University of Warwick. Available at http://ssrn.com/abstarct=1483721.

Hodgson, J., Horne, J., and Soubise, L. (2018). *The Criminal Cases Review Commission: Last Resort or First Appeal? An Examination of the CCRC's Discretion to Refer Cases Not Previously Appealed* (Coventry: University of Warwick, Criminal Justice Centre). Available at https://warwick.ac.uk/fac/soc/law/research/centres/cjc/news/65867_law_a4_report_1.pdf.

Hodgson, J., and Kemp, V. (2015). "Ensuring 'Appropriate' Protections for Young Suspects." In Panzavolta, M., de Vocht, D., Van Oosterhout, and M., Vanderhallen, M. (eds.) *Interrogating Young Suspects: Procedural Safeguards from a Legal Perspective* (Antwerp: Intersentia) 123–178.

Hodgson, J., and Mou, Y. (2019). "Empirical Approaches to Criminal Procedure." In Brown, D. K., Iontcheva, J., and Weisser, B. (eds.) *The Oxford Handbook of Criminal Process* (Oxford: Oxford University Press) 42–66.

Hodgson, J., and Roach, K. (2017). "Disenfranchisement as Punishment: European Court of Human Rights, UK and Canadian Responses to Prisoner Voting." *Public Law* 450–468.

Hodgson, J., and Roberts, A. (2010). "Criminal Process and Prosecution." In Cane, P., and Kritzer, B. (eds.) *Oxford Handbook of Empirical Legal Research* (Oxford: Oxford University Press) 64–95.

Hodgson, J., and Soubise, L. (2016a). "The Public Prosecutor in France." *Oxford Handbooks Online: Criminology and Criminal Justice* (Oxford: Oxford University Press).

Hodgson, J., and Soubise, L. (2016b). "Understanding the Sentencing Process in France." In Tonry, M. (ed.) *Sentencing Policies and Practices in Western Countries* (Chicago: University of Chicago Press) 221–265.

Hodgson, J., and Tadros, V. (2009). "How to Make a Terrorist out of Nothing." 72(6) *Modern Law Review* 985–999.

Hodgson, J., and Tadros, V. (2013). "The Impossibility of Defining Terrorism." 16(3) *New Criminal Law Review* 494–526.

Hodgson, J., Wade, K., Stewart, N., Hearty, K., Kyneswood, N., Quispe Torreblanca, E., and Mullett, T. (2018). *Public Confidence and Crime Reduction: The Impact of Forensic Property Marking* (University of Warwick). Available at http://wrap.warwick.ac.uk/117625/1/WRAP-public-confidence-reduction-impact-forensic-property-marking-Hodgson-2018.pdf.

Home Office (2004). *RDS Findings No. 257* (London: Home Office).

Home Office (2006). *Rebalancing the Criminal Justice System in Favour of the Law-Abiding Majority* (London: Home Office).

Home Office (2011). *Operation of Police Powers under the Terrorism Act 2000 and Subsequent Legislation: Arrests, Outcomes and Stops and Searches.* Home Office Statistical Bulletin 19/11, 15 December.

Home Office (2017). *Individuals Referred to and Supported through the Prevent Programme, April 2015 to March 2016.* Home Office: Statistical Bulletin 23/17, 9 November.

Home Office (2018). *Operation of Police Powers under the Terrorism Act 2000 and Subsequent Legislation: Arrests, Outcomes, and Stop and Search, Great Britain, Quarterly Update to September 2018.* Home Office: Statistical Bulletin 29/18, 6 December.

Horne, J. (2017). *A Plea of Convenience: An Examination of the Guilty Plea in England and Wales*. PhD diss., University of Warwick.

Houllé, R., and Vaney, G. (2017). "La comparution sur reconnaissance préalable de culpabilité, une procédure pénale de plus en plus utilisée." 157 *Bulletin d'information statistique* (Ministère de la justice). Available at http://www.inserr.fr/sites/default/files/public/media/stat_infostat_157.pdf.

House of Commons Home Affairs Committee (2006). *Terrorism Detention Powers (Fourth Report of Session 2005–06)* (London: Stationery Office).

House of Commons Home Affairs Committee (2007). *The Government's Counter-terrorism Proposals (First Report of Session 2007–08)* (London: Stationery Office).

House of Commons Justice Committee (2008). *Towards Effective Sanctioning: Twelfth Report of Session 2007–08.* HC 184 (London: Stationery Office).

House of Commons Justice Committee (2009). *The Crown Prosecution Service: Gatekeeper to the Criminal Justice System: Ninth Report of Session 2008–09* (London: Stationery Office).

House of Commons Justice Committee (2015). *The Criminal Cases Review Commission: Twelfth Report of Session 2014–15.* HC 850 (London: Stationery Office).

House of Lords European Union Committee (2016). "Brexit: Future UK-EU Security and Police Co-operation: 7th Report of Session 2016–17." HL Paper 77.

House of Commons Justice Committee (2018). *Disclosure of Evidence in Criminal Cases. Eleventh Report of Session 2017–19.* HC 859 (London: Stationery Office).

Hoyle, C., and Sato, M. (2019). *Reasons to Doubt: Wrongful Convictions and the Criminal Cases Review Commission* (Oxford: Oxford University Press).

Hriptievschi, N. (2012). "National Approaches to Effective Criminal Defence: Moldova." In Cape, E., and Namoradze, Z. (eds.) *Effective Criminal Defence in Eastern Europe* (Moldova: Legal Aid Reformers' Network) 259–343.

Huff, R., and Killias, M. (eds.) (2008). *Wrongful Conviction: International Perspectives on Miscarriages of Justice* (Philadelphia: Temple University Press).

Human Rights Watch (2007). *France. In the Name of Prevention: Insufficient Safeguards in National Security Removals* 19(3) Human Rights Watch.

Human Rights Watch (2008). *Preempting Justice: Counterterrorism Laws and Procedures in France.*

Hunt, A. (2007). "Criminal Prohibitions on Direct and Indirect Encouragement of Terrorism." *Criminal Law Review* 441–458.

Illuminati, G. (2005). "The Frustrated Turn to Adversarial Procedure in Italy." 4(3) *Washington University Global Studies Law Review* 567–581.

Illuminati, G. (2010). "The Accusatorial Process from the Italian Point of View." 35 *North Carolina Journal of International Law and Commercial Regulation* 297–318.

Innes, M., and Brookman, F. (2013). "Introduction. Helping the Police with Their Enquiries: International Perspectives on Homicide Investigation." 23(3) *Policing and Society* 285–291.

Jackson, J. (1988). "Two Methods of Proof in Criminal Procedure." 51 *Modern Law Review* 549–568.

Jackson, J. (2005). "The Effect of Human Rights on Criminal Evidentiary Processes: Towards Convergence, Divergence or Realignment?" 68(5) *Modern Law Review* 737–764.

Jackson, J. (2009). "Finding the Best Epistemic Fit for International Criminal Tribunals." 7 *Journal of International Criminal Justice* 17–39.

Jackson, J. (2016a). "Responses to Salduz: Procedural Tradition, Change and the Need for an Effective Defence." 79 *Modern Law Review* 987–1018.

Jackson, J. (2016b). "Cultural Barriers on the Road to Providing Suspects with Access to a Lawyer." In Colson, R., and Field, S. (eds.) *EU Criminal Justice and the Challenges of Diversity* (Cambridge: Cambridge University Press) 181–198.

Jackson, J., and Doran, S. (1995). *Judge without Jury* (Oxford: Clarendon Press).

Jackson, J., and Summers, S. (2012). *The Internationalisation of Criminal Evidence: Beyond the Common Law and Civil Law Traditions* (Cambridge: Cambridge University Press).

Jackson, J., and Summers, S. (2013). "Confrontation with Strasbourg: UK and Swiss Approaches to Criminal Evidence." *Criminal Law Review* 114–130.

Jacobs, L., Baglay, S., Kwok, M., Mavrikkou, M., and Tay, K. L. (2011). "The Nature of Inquisitorial Processes in Administrative Regimes: Global Perspectives Research Workshop Report." 24 *Canadian Journal of Administrative Law and Practice* 261–283.

Jacobson, J., and Hough, M. (2010). *Unjust Deserts: Imprisonment for Public Protection* (London: Prison Reform Trust).

Jasiński, W. and Kremens, K. (2019) *Criminal Law in Poland* (Wolters Kluwer International).

Jeanclos, Y. (2016). "La confusion pénale." 3 February. Available at https://www.huffingtonpost.fr/yves-jeanclos/decheance-de-nationalite-confusion-penale-professeur-de-droit_b_9148406.html.

Jenkins, S. (2013). "Miscarriages of Justice and the Discourse of Innocence: Perspectives from Appellants, Campaigners, Journalists and Legal Practitioners." 40(3) *Journal of Law and Society* 329–355.

Jensen, E., and Heller, T. (eds.) (2003). *Beyond Common Knowledge: Empirical Approaches to the Rule of Law* (Stanford, CA: Stanford University Press).

Johnson, H. (2005). *The Age of Anxiety: McCarthyism to Terrorism* (Orlando, FL: Harcourt).

Joint Committee on Human Rights (2005). *Counter-terrorism Policy and Human Rights: Terrorism Bill and Related Matters (Third Report of Session 2005–06)* (London: Stationery Office).

Joint Committee on Human Rights (2006). *Counter-terrorism Policy and Human Rights: Prosecution and Pre-charge Detention (Twenty-fourth Report of Session 2005–06)* (London: Stationery Office).

Joint Committee on Human Rights (2007a). *Counter-terrorism Policy and Human Rights: 28 Days, Intercept and Post-charge Questioning (19th Report of Session, 2006–07)* (London: Stationery Office).

Joint Committee on Human Rights (2007b). *Counter-terrorism Policy and Human Rights: 42 Days (Second Report of Session, 2007–08)* (London: Stationery Office).

Joint Committee on Human Rights (2009). *Demonstrating Respect for Rights? A Human Rights Approach to Policing Protest.* March (London: Stationery Office).

Joint Committee on Human Rights (2010). *Legislative Scrutiny: Terrorist Asset Freezing Etc. Bill (Second Report); and Other Bills.* November (London: Stationery Office).

Judiciary of England and Wales (2018). *The Better Case Management (BCM) Handbook.* Available at https://www.judiciary.uk/wp-content/uploads/2018/02/bcm-guide-for-practitioners-05032018.pdf.

Judson, K. (2017). "Bias, Subjectivity and Wrongful Conviction." 50(3) *University of Michigan Journal of Law Reform* 779–794.

Justice (2009). *Secret Evidence* (London: Justice). Available at https://2bquk8cdew6192tsu41lay8t-wpengine.netdna-ssl.com/wp-content/uploads/2015/07/Secret-Evidence-10-June-2009.pdf.

Justice (2018). *Supporting Exonerees: Ensuring Accessible, Consistent and Continuing Support* (London: Justice). Available at https://justice.org.uk/our-work/areas-of-work/criminal-justice-system/supporting-exonerees-ensuring-accessible-continuing-and-consistent-support/.

Justice Scotland (2018). *Legal Assistance in the Police Station.* Chaired by The Right Honourable Lord Eassie (London: Justice).

Karpik, L. (1999). *French Lawyers: A Study in Collective Action 1274 to 1994.* Translated by Nora Scott. (Oxford: Clarendon Press).

Kassin, S. L., Goldstein, C. C., and Savitsky, K. (2003). "Behavioral Confirmation in the Interrogation Room: On the Dangers of Presuming Guilt." 27(2) *Law and Human Behaviour* 187–203.

Kay, S. (2004). "The Move from Oral Evidence to Written Evidence." 2 *Journal of International Criminal Justice* 495–502.

Kaye, T. (1991). *Unsafe and Unsatisfactory? Report of the Independent Inquiry into the Working Practices of the West Midlands Police Serious Crime Squad* (London: Civil Liberties Trust).

Kemp, V. (2013). "'No Time for a Solicitor': Implications for Delays on the Take-Up of Legal Advice." *Criminal Law Review* 184–202.

Kemp, V. (2018). *Effective Police Station Legal Advice—Country Report 2: England and Wales.* University of Nottingham. Available at http://eprints.nottingham.ac.uk/51145/.

Kemp, V., and Hodgson, J. (2016). "England and Wales: Empirical Findings." In Vanderhallen, M., van Oosterhout, M., Panzavolta, M., and de Vocht, D. (eds.) *Interrogating Young Suspects: Procedural Safeguards from an Empirical Perspective* (Antwerp: Intersentia) 127–181.

Kepel, G. (2004). *The War for Muslim Minds: Islam and the West* (Cambridge, MA: Belknap Press of Harvard University Press).

Kahneman, D. (2011). *Thinking Fast and Slow* (London: Penguin).

Killias, M. (2008). "Wrongful Convictions in Switzerland: The Experience of a Continental Law Country." In Huff, R., and Killias, M. (eds.) *Wrongful Conviction: International Perspectives on Miscarriages of Justice* (Philadelphia: Temple University Press) 139–155.

King, J. D. (2017). "The Public Defender as International Transplant." 38(3) *University of Pennsylvania Journal of International Law* 832–893.

King, L., and Snook, B. (2009). "Peering Inside a Canadian Interrogation Room: An Examination of the Reid Model of Interrogation, Influence Tactics and Coercive Strategies." 36(7) *Criminal Justice Behavior* 674–694.

Kostakopoulou, D. (2008). "How to Do Things with Security Post 9/11." 28(2) *Oxford Journal of Legal Studies* 317–42.

Kritzer, H. H. (2004). "Disappearing Trials? A Comparative Perspective." 1 *Journal of Empirical Legal Studies* 735–754.

Kuczynska, H. (2015). *The Accusation Model before the International Criminal Court* (Cham, Switzerland: Springer).

Lacey, N. (1994). "Government as Manager, Citizen as Consumer: The Case of the Criminal Justice Act 1991." 57 *Modern Law Review* 534–554.

Lacey, N. (2008). *The Prisoners' Dilemma: Political Economy and Punishment in Contemporary Democracies* (Cambridge: Cambridge University Press).

Landsman, S. (1990). "The Rise of the Contentious Spirit: Adversary Procedure in Eighteenth Century England." 75 *Cornell Law Review* 497–606.

Langbein, J. H. (1979). "Understanding the Short History of Plea Bargaining." 14 *Law and Society Review* 261–272.

Langbein, J. H. (2003). *The Origins of Adversary Criminal Trial* (Oxford: Oxford University Press).

Langbein, J. H., and Weinreb, L. L. (1978). "Continental Criminal Procedure: 'Myth' and Reality." 87 *Yale Law Journal* 1549–1569.

Langer, M. (2004). "From Legal Transplants to Legal Translations: The Globalization of Plea Bargaining and the Americanization Thesis in Criminal Procedure." 45(1) *Harvard International Law Journal* 1–64.

Langer, M. (2005). "The Rise of Managerial Judging in International Criminal Law." 53 *American Journal of Comparative Law* 835–909.

Langer, M. (2007). "Revolution in Latin American Criminal Procedure: Diffusion of Legal Ideas from the Periphery." 55(4) *American Journal of Comparative Law* 617–676.

Langer, M. (2014). "The Long Shadow of the Adversarial and Inquisitorial Categories." In Dubber, M. D., and Höernle, T. (eds.) *Handbook of Criminal Law* (Oxford: Oxford University Press) 887–912.

Langer, M., and Doherty, J. (2009). "Managerial Judging, Court's Limited Information and Parties' Resistance: An Empirical Assessment of Why the Reforms to Expedite the Procedure of the International Criminal Tribunal for Former Yugoslavia Did Not Work." UCLA School of Law, Law & Economics Research Paper No. 09-12. http://ssrn.com/abstract=1422685.

Langer, M., and Slansky, D. (2017). *Prosecutors and Democracy* (Cambridge: Cambridge University Press).

Langer, V. (1988). "Public Interest in Civil Law, Socialist Law, and Common Law Systems: The Role of the Public Prosecutor." 36 *American Journal of Comparative Law* 279–305.

Lawyers Committee for Human Rights (2000). *Advancing Judicial Reform: An Environmental Case Study in Bolivia*. New York: Lawyers Committee for Human Rights.

Lazerges, C. (2012). "Le choix de la fuite en avant au nom de la dangerosité: Les lois 1,2,3,4,5 etc sur la prévention et la répression de la récidive." *Revue de science criminelle et de droit pénal comparé* 274–282.

Léger, P. (2009). *Rapport du Comité de réflexion sur la justice pénale* (Paris: La Documentation française).

Legrand, P. (1996). "European Legal Systems Are Not Converging." 45 *International and Comparative Law Quarterly* 52–81.

Leigh, L. H. (2000). "Correcting Miscarriages of Justice: The Role of the Criminal Cases Review Commission." 38(2) *Alberta Law Review* 365–377.

Leigh, L. H., and Zedner, L. (1992). *A Report on the Administration of Criminal Justice in France and Germany*. RCCJ Research Study No. 1 (London: HMSO).

Leng, R. (1993). *The Right to Silence in Police Interrogation: A Study of Some of the Issues Underlying the Debate*. RCCJ Research Study No. 10 (London: HMSO).

Lemonde, M. (1975). *Police et Justice* Thesis, Lyon.

Lenoir, A., and Gautron, V. (2014). "Les pratiques des parquets face à l'injonction politique de réduire le taux de classement sans suite." 88(3) *Droit et société* 591–606.

Létocart, A. (2012). "Les procedures accusatoires et le rôle du juge d'instruction." In Benillouche, M. (ed.) *Les procédures pénales accusatoires* (Paris: Presses universitaires de France) 69–81.

Leverick, F., Chalmers, J., Armstrong, S., and McNeill, F. (2009). *Scottish Criminal Cases Review Commission 10th Anniversary Research* (Scottish Centre for Crime and Justice Research).

Leveson, Brian, Sir (2015). *Review of Efficiency in Criminal Proceedings*. Judiciary of England and Wales.

Lévy, R. (1993). "Police and the Judiciary in France since the Nineteenth Century." 33(2) *British Journal of criminology* 167–186.

Loader, I. (2006). "Fall of the Platonic Guardians." 46(4) *British Journal of Criminology* 561–586.

Lord Chief Justice of England and Wales and Senior President of Tribunals (2016). *Transforming Our Justice System*. Ministry of Justice. Available at https://www.gov.uk/government/publications/transforming-our-justice-system-joint-statement.

Loveman, B. (1993). *The Constitution of Tyranny: Regimes of Exception in Spanish America* (Pittsburgh: University of Pittsburgh Press).

Macdonald, S. (2008). "Constructing a Framework for Criminal Justice Research: Learning from Packer's Mistakes." 11(2) *New Criminal Law Review* 257–311.

Madsen, M. R. (2004). "France, the UK, and the 'Boomerang' of the Internationalisation of Human Rights, 1945–2000." In Halliday, S., and Schmidt, P. (eds.) *Human Rights Brought Home: Socio-legal Perspectives on Human Rights in a National Context* (Oxford: Hart) 57–86.

Maduro, M., and Azoulai, L. (eds.) (2010). *The Past and Future of EU Law: The Classics of EU Law Revisited on the 50th Anniversary of Rome* (Oxford: Hart).

Maiatico, J. M. (2007). "All Eyes on Us: A Comparative Critique of the North Carolina Innocence Inquiry Commission." 56 *Duke Law Journal* 1345–1376.

Amnesty International. (2003). *India: Report of the Malimath Committee on Reforms of the Criminal Justice System: Some Observations* (London: International Secretariat).

Malone, C. (2009). "Only the Freshest Will Do." In Naughton, M. (ed.) *The Criminal Cases Review Commission: Hope for the Innocent?* (Basingstoke: Palgrave Macmillan) 107–117.

Marafioti, L. (2008). "Italian Criminal Procedure: A System Caught between Two Traditions." In Jackson, J., Langer, M., and Tillers, P. (eds.) *Crime, Procedure and Evidence in a Comparative and International Context* (Oxford: Hart) 81–98.

Maréchal, J.-Y. (2013). *Les droits de la defense au cours de l'enqête préliminaire: Rien à signaler!* JCP EG No. 17 du 22 avril 2013 (Cass, crim. 6 mars 2013).

Markesinis, B. (ed.) (1994). *The Gradual Convergence: Foreign Ideas, Foreign Influences and English Law on the Eve of the 21st Century* (Oxford: Clarendon Press).

Marret, J.-L. (2003). *Terrorisme: Les stratégies de communication* (Paris: Centre d'études en sciences sociales de la défense, Ministère de la défense).

Mary, P., Kaminsky, D., Maes, E., and Vanhamme, F. (2011). "Le traitement de la 'Dangerosité' en Belgique: Internement et mise à la disposition du gouvernement." *Champ pénal / Penal Field* 8. http://champpenal.revues.org.

Marsh, L. (2016). "Leveson's Narrow Pursuit of Justice." 45 *Common Law World Review* 51–67.

Matelly, J.-H., and Mouhanna, C. (2007). *Police: Des chiffres et des doutes* (Paris: Michalon).

Mather, L. M. (1979). *Plea-Bargaining or Trial: The Process of Criminal-Case Disposition* (Lexington, MA: Lexington Books).

Mattei, U. (2003). "A Theory of Imperial Law: A Study on U.S. Hegemony and the Latin Resistance." 10(1) *Indiana Journal of Global Legal Studies* 383–448.

McBarnett, D. (1978). "False Dichotomies in Criminal Justice Research." In Baldwin, J. and Bottomley, A. K. (eds.) *Criminal Justice: Selected Readings* (London: Martin Robertson) 23–34.

McCannon, B. C. (2018). "Debundling Accountability: Prosecutor and Public Defender Elections in Florida." Available at SSRN: https://ssrn.com/abstract=3204623.

McConville, M., and Bridges, L. (eds.) (1994). *Criminal Justice in Crisis* (Aldershot: Edward Elgar).

McConville, M., and Hodgson, J. (1993). *Custodial Legal Advice and the Right to Silence.* RCCJ Research Study No. 16 (London: HMSO).

McConville, M., Hodgson, J., Bridges, L., and Pavlovic, A. (1994). *Standing Accused: The Organisation and Practices of Criminal Defence Lawyers in Britain* (Oxford: Clarendon Press).

McConville, M., and Marsh, L. (2014). *Criminal Judges: Legitimacy, Courts and State-Induced Guilty Pleas in Britain* (Cheltenham: Edward Elgar).

McConville, M., and Pils, P. (2013). *Comparative Perspectives on Criminal Justice in China* (Cheltenham: Edward Elgar).

McConville, M., Sanders, A., and Leng, R. (1991). *The Case for the Prosecution* (London: Routledge).

McConville, M., et al. (2011). *Criminal Justice in China: An Empirical Inquiry* (Cheltenham: Edward Elgar).

McDermott, Y. (2013). "Rights in Reverse: A Critical Analysis of Fair Trial Rights under International Criminal Law." In Schabas, W. A., McDermott, Y., and Hayes, N. (eds.)

The Ashgate Research Companion to International Criminal Law: Critical Perspectives (Aldershot: Ashgate) 165–180.

McDermott, Y. (2016). *Fairness in International Criminal Trials* (Oxford: Oxford University Press).

McEwan, J. (2011). "From Adversarialism to Managerialism: Criminal Justice in Transition." 31(4) *Legal Studies* 519–546.

McIntyre, G. (2003). "Equality of Arms—Defining Human Rights in the Jurisprudence of the International Criminal Tribunal for the Former Yugoslavia." 16(2) *Leiden Journal of International Law* 269–320.

McKendrick, D., and Finch, J. (2017). "Downpressor Man: Securitisation, Safeguarding and Social Work." 5(3) *Critical and Radical Social Work* 287–300.

McLaughlin, E., Muncie, J., and Hughes, G. (2001). "The Permanent Revolution: New Labour, New Public Management and the Modernization of Criminal Justice." 1(3) *Criminal Justice* 301–318.

Medwed, D. S. (2012). *Prosecution Complex: America's Race to Convict and Its Impact on the Innocent* (New York: New York University Press).

Mégret, F. (2012). "Accountability and Ethics." In Reydams, L., et al. (eds.) *International Prosecutors* (Oxford: Oxford University Press) 416–487.

Mevis, P., and Verbaan, J. (2014). "Legal Assistance and Police Interrogation." 7(4) *Erasmus Law Review* 175–190.

Milburn, P. (2008). "De la frénésie de sécurité à la surpénalisation: La justice sous pression." In Mucchielli, L. (ed.) *La frénésie sécuritaire: Retour à l'ordre et nouveau contrôle social* (Paris: La Découverte) 41–51.

Milburn, P., Kostuluski, K., and Salas, D. (eds.) (2010). *Les procureurs: Entre vocation judiciaire et fonctions politiques* (Paris: Presses universitaires de France).

Milburn, P., and Mouhanna, C. (2010). "Présentation." 74(1) *Droit et société* 7–16.

Miller, M. L. (2004). "Domination and Dissatisfaction: Prosecutors as Sentencers." 56 *Stanford Law Review* 1211–1269.

Ministère de la justice (1999). *L'espace judiciaire européen: Actes du Colloque d'Avignon* (Paris: La Documentation française).

Ministère de la justice et des libertés. Various years. *Chiffres-clés de la justice* (Paris: Sous-direction de la statistique et des etudes).

Ministry of Justice (2008). *Judicial and Court Statistics 2007*. Cm 7467 (London: Stationery Office).

Ministry of Justice (2011). "Judicial and Court Statistics 2010." Available at https://www.gov.uk/government/statistics/judicial-and-court-statistics-annual-2010.

Ministry of Justice (2012). *Swift and Sure Justice: The Government's Plans for Reform of the Criminal Justice System*. Cm 8388, July (London: Stationery Office).

Ministry of Justice (2013). *Transforming the CJS: A Strategy and Action Plan to Reform the Criminal Justice System*. HM 8658, June (London: Stationery Office).

Ministry of Justice (2015). *Code of Practice for Victims of Crime* (London: Stationery Office). Available at https://assets.publishing.service.gov.uk/government/uploads/system/uploads/attachment_data/file/476900/code-of-practice-for-victims-of-crime.PDF.

Mitsilegas, V. (2016). "The Uneasy Relationship between the UK and European Criminal Law: From Opt-Outs to Brexit?" *Criminal Law Review* 519–538.

Mitsilegas, V., Carrera, S., and Eisele, K. (2014). "The End of the Transition Period for Police and Criminal Justice Measures Adopted before the Lisbon Treaty: Who

Monitors Trust in the European Criminal Justice Area?" Study for the Committee on Civil Liberties, Justice and Home Affairs (LIBE), European Parliament. Available at https://www.ceps.eu/ceps-publications/end-transitional-period-police-and-criminal-justice-measures-adopted-lisbon-treaty-who/.

Mols, V. (2017). "Bringing Directives on Procedural Rights of the EU to Police Stations: Practical Training for Criminal Defence Lawyers." 8(3) *New Journal of European Criminal Law* 300–308.

Montana, R. (2009). "Paradigms of Judicial Supervision and Coordination between Police and Prosecutors: The Italian Case in Comparative Perspective." 17(4) *European Journal of Crime, Criminal Law and Criminal Justice* 309–333.

Moody, J., and Toombs, S. (1982). *Prosecution in the Public Interest* (Edinburgh: Scottish Academic Press).

Mou, Y. (2017). "Overseeing Criminal Justice: The Supervisory Role of the Public Prosecution Service in China." 44(4) *Journal of Law and Society* 620–645.

Mou, Y. (2020). *The Construction of Guilt in China: An Empirical Account of Routine Chinese Injustice* (London: Hart Publishing).

Mouhanna, C. (2001). *Polices judiciaires et magistrats: Une affaire de confiance* (Paris: La Documentation française).

Mouhanna, C., and Bastard, B. (2010). "Procureurs et substituts: L'évolution du système de production des decisions pénales." 74(1) *Droit et société* 35–53.

Muñoz, D. P. (2011). "Criminal Procedure Reform in Chile: New Agents and the Restructuring of a Field." In Dezalay, Y., and Garth, B. G. (eds.) *Lawyers and the Rule of Law in an Era of Globalization* (New York: Routledge) 112–133.

Murray, B. M. (2016). "Prosecutorial Responsibility and Collateral Consequences." 12 *Stanford Journal of Civil Rights and Civil Liberties* 213–247.

Nadal, J.-L. (2013). *Refonder le ministère public Commission de modernisation de l'action publique* (Paris: Ministère de la justice).

Nagle, L. E. (2000). "The Cinderella of Government: Judicial Reform in Latin America." 30(2) *California Western International Law Journal* 345–379.

Narey, M. (1997). *Review of Delay in the Criminal Justice System: A Report* (London: Home Office).

National Audit Office (2016). *Efficiency in the Criminal Justice System.* HC 852 https://www.nao.org.uk/wp-content/uploads/2016/03/Efficiency-in-the-criminal-justice-system.pdf.

Naughton, M. (2012). *The Criminal Cases Review Commission: Hope for the Innocent?* (Basingstoke: Palgrave Macmillan).

Nelken, D. (1994). "Whom Can You Trust? The Future of Criminology." In Nelken, D. (ed.) *The Futures of Criminology* (London: Sage) 220–244.

Newman, D. (2013). *Legal Aid Lawyers and the Quest for Justice* (Oxford: Hart).

Nickerson, R. S. (1998). "Confirmation Bias: A Ubiquitous Phenomenon in Many Guises." 2(2) *Review of General Psychology* 175–220.

Nobles, R., and Schiff, D. (2000). *Understanding Miscarriages of Justice* (Oxford: Oxford University Press).

Nobles, R., and Schiff, D. (2005). "The Criminal Cases Review Commission: Establishing a Workable Relationship with the Court of Appeal." *Criminal Law Review* 173.

Obama, B. (2010). National Security Strategy (President of the United States) Available at http://unipd-centrodirittiumani.it/public/docs/USA_NSS_2010.pdf.

O'Brian, W. (2011). "Fresh Expert Evidence in CCRC Cases." 22(1) *Kings Law Journal* 1–26.

O'Brien, B. (2009a). "A Recipe for Bias: An Empirical Look at the Interplay between Institutional Incentives and Bounded Rationality in Prosecutorial Decision Making." 74 *Missouri Law Review* 999–1050.

O'Brien, B. (2009b). "Prime Suspect: An Examination of Factors That Aggravate and Counteract Confirmation Bias in Criminal Investigations." 15(4) *Psychology, Public Policy and Law* 315–334.

O'Brien, K. A. (2005). "France." In von Hippel, K. (ed.) *Europe Confronts Terrorism* (Basingstoke: Palgrave Macmillan) 19–42.

Office for Criminal Justice Reform (2007). *Working Together to Cut Crime and Deliver Justice.* Cm 7247 (London: Stationery Office).

Packer, H. (1968). *The Limits of the Criminal Sanction* (Stanford, CA: Stanford University Press).

Pakes, F. (2006). "The Ebb and Flow of Criminal Justice in the Netherlands." 34(3) *International Journal of the Sociology of Law* 141–156.

Patane, V. (2006). "Recent Italian Efforts to Respond to Terrorism at the Legislative Level." 4(5) *Journal of International Criminal Justice* 1166–1180.

Pellé, S. (2017). "Garde à vue et audition libre: Acte final? Bilan d'un cycle de réformes (lois 14 avril 2011, 27 mai 2014 et 3 juin 2016)." *Receuil Dalloz* 359–368.

Perrier, J.-B. (2016). "Les guaranties de la procédure pénale dans la loi du 3 juin 2016: Entre illusion(s) et désillusions(s)." *Recueil Dalloz* 21–34.

Perrocheau, V. (2010). "La composition pénale et la comparution sur reconnaissance de culpabilité: Quelles limites à l'ominipotence du parquet?" 74(1) *Droit et société* 55–71.

Perrodet, A. (2002). "The Public Prosecutor." In Delmas-Marty, M., and Spencer, J. R. (eds.), *European Criminal Procedures* (Cambridge: Cambridge University Press) 415–458.

Phythian, M. (2005). "Intelligence, Policy-Making and the 7 July London Bombings." 44 *Crime, Law and Social Change* 361–385.

Pierpoint, H. (2008). "Quickening the PACE: The Use of Volunteers as Appropriate Adults." 18(4) *Policing and Society* 397–410.

Pillay, R. (2010). *Current Challenges Regarding Respect of Human Rights in the Fight against Terrorism.* Briefing paper. (Brussels: European Parliament, Directorate-General for External Policies).

Pivaty, A. (2018). "The Right to Custodial Legal Assistance in Europe: In Search of Rationales." 26(1) *European Journal of Crime, Criminal Law and Justice* 62–98.

Pizzi, W. T. (2006). "Overcoming Logistical and Structural Barriers to Fair Trials at International Tribunals." 4(1) *International Commentary on Evidence* Article 4.

Pizzi, W. T., and Montagna, M. (2004). "The Battle to Establish an Adversarial Trial System in Italy." 25 *Michigan Journal of International Law* 429–466.

Pradel, J. (2002). *Procédure pénale* (Paris: Éditions Cujas).

Prillaman, W. C. (2000). *The Judiciary and Democratic Decay in Latin America: Declining Confidence in the Rule of Law* (Westport, CT: Praeger).

Quentin, B. (2013). *Enquête préliminaire ne rime pas toujours avec procès équitable: JCP G* 2013, doctr. 323, Mot de la semaine.

Quirk, H. (2007). "Identifying Miscarriages of Justice: Why Innocence in the UK Is Not the Answer." 70(5) *Modern Law Review* 759–777.

Quirk, H. (2017). *The Rise and Fall of the Right to Silence: Principle, Politics and Policy* (New York: Routledge).

Ramsay, P. (2012). *The Insecurity State* (Oxford: Oxford University Press).

Rauxloh, R. (2011). "Formalization of Plea Bargaining in Germany: Will the New Legislation Be Able to Square the Circle?" 34(2) *Fordham International Law Journal* 296–331.

Raysseguier, C. (2006). *Conditions du traitement judiciaire de l'affaire dite "d'Outreau": Rapport de l'Inspection générale des services judiciaires* (Paris: Ministère de la justice).

Redmayne, M. (2001). *Expert Evidence and Criminal Justice* (Oxford: Oxford University Press).

Renucci, J.-F. (2009). "Un séisme judiciaire: Pour la COUR européenne des droits de l'homme, les magistrats du parquet ne sont pas une autorité judiciaire." 9 *Recueil Dalloz* 600–601.

Riego, C. (2008). "Oral Procedures and Case Management: The Innovation of Chile's Reform." 14 *Southwestern Journal of Law and Trade in the Americas* 339–356.

Riego, C., and Vargas, J. E. (2003). *Criminal Justice Reform in Latin America: Successes and Difficulties*. Available at http:www.iadb.org/sds/doc/SGC-Panel_II_EN3.pdf.

Rifkind, M. (2014). *Report on the Intelligence Relating to the Murder of Fusilier Lee Rigby* Intelligence and Security Committee of Parliament, HC 795 (London: HMSO).

Risinger, M. D., and Risinger, L. C. (2014). "The Emerging Role of the Innocence Lawyer and the Need for Role-Differentiated Standards of Professional Conduct." In Cooper, S. *Controversies in Innocence Cases in America* (Burlington, VT: Ashgate Publishing) 123–138.

Ritzer, G. (2004). *The McDonaldization of Society* (Thousand Oaks, CA: Pine Forge Press).

Roach, K. (2004). "The World-Wide Expansion of Anti-terrorism Laws after 1 September 2001." 3 *Studi Senesi* 487–527.

Roach, K. (2010a). "Wrongful Convictions: Adversarial and Inquisitorial Themes." 35 *North Carolina Journal of International Law and Regulation* 387–446.

Roach, K. (2010b). "The Role of Innocence Commissions." 85(1) *Chicago-Kent Law Review* 89–125.

Roach, K. (2015). "Comparative Reflections on Miscarriages of Justice in Australia and Canada." 17 *Flinders Law Journal* 381–431.

Roach, K. (2017). "Exceptional Procedures to Correct Miscarriages of Justice in Common Law Systems." Available at SSRN: https://ssrn.com/abstract=3006704.

Roberts, S., and Weathered, L. (2009). "Assisting the Factually Innocent: The Contradictions and Compatibility of Innocence Projects and the Criminal Cases Review Commission." 29(1) *Oxford Journal of Legal Studies* 43–70.

Robertson, G. "General Editor's Introduction to Essays on Fairness and Evidence in War Crimes Trial." 4(1) *International Commentary on Evidence* Article 1.

Roht-Arriaza, N. (2019). "Transitional Justice in Latin America: Achievements and Limitations." In Meierhenrich, J., Hinton, A. L., and Douglas, L. (eds.) *The Oxford Handbook of Transitional Justice* (Oxford: Oxford University Press). Available at https://papers.ssrn.com/sol3/papers.cfm?abstract_id=3281991.

Rossman, D. (2017). "Resurrecting *Miranda*'s Right to Counsel." 97(3) *Boston University Law Review* 1129–1156.

Royal Commission on Criminal Justice (RCCJ) (1993). *Report*. Cmnd 2263 (London: HMSO).

Royal Commission on Criminal Procedure (1981). *Report*. Cmnd 8092 (London: HMSO).

Royal Commission on the Police (1962). *Report*. Cmnd 1728 (London: HMSO).

Ryan, A. (2014). *Towards a System of European Criminal Justice* (New York: Routledge).

Salas, D. (1991). "Note sur l'histoire de l'instruction préparatoire en France." In Delmas-Marty, M. *La mise en état des affaires pénales: Rapport de la Commission justice pénale et droits de l'homme* (Paris: La Documentation française) 241–252.

Salas, D. (2002). "The Role of the Judge." In Delmas-Marty, M., and Spencer, J. R. (eds.), *European Criminal Procedures* (Cambridge: Cambridge University Press) 488–540.

Salas, L. (2001). "From Law and Development to Rule of Law: New and Old Issues in Justice Reform in Latin America." In Domingo, P., and Sieder, R. (eds.) *The Rule of Law in Latin America: The International Promotion of Judicial Reform* (London: University of London, Institute of Latin American Studies) 17–46.

Samet, C. (2000). *Journal d'un juge d'instruction* (Paris: Presses universitaires de France).

Samuels, A. (2014). "Abolish the Office of Attorney-General." *Public Law* 609–614.

Sanders, S. (2016). "The CPS: 30 Years On." *Criminal Law Review* 82–98.

Sassòli, M. (2006). "Terrorism and War." 4 *Journal of International Criminal Justice* 959–981.

Sato, M., Hoyle, C., and Speechley, N.-E. (2017). "Wrongful Convictions of Refugees and Asylum Seekers: Responses by the Criminal Cases Review Commission." *Criminal Law Review* 106–122.

Schabas, W. (2006). "Fair Trials and National Security Evidence." 4(1) *International Commentary on Evidence* Article 9.

Schemmel, A., Corell, C., and Richter, N. (2014). "Plea Bargaining in Criminal Proceedings: Changes to Criminal Defense Counsel Practice as a Result of Constitutional Court Verdict of 19 March 2013?" 15 *German Law Journal* 44–64.

Schulhofer, S. J. (1984). "Is Plea Bargaining Inevitable?" 97 *Harvard Law Review* 1037–1107.

Scott, R. E., and Stuntz, W. J. (1992). "Plea Bargaining as Contract." 101 *Yale Law Journal* 1909–1968.

Secretary of State for the Home Department (2011). *Review of Counter-terrorism and Security Powers.* Cm 8004 (London: Stationery Office).

Sedgwick, M. (2010). "The Concept of Radicalisation as a Source of Confusion." 22(4) *Political Violence* 479–494.

Segal, M. (2019). *Independent Review of the Extradition of Dr. Hassan Diab* (Government of Canada, Department of Justice). Available at https://www.canada.ca/en/department-justice/news/2019/07/government-releases-independent-review-of-dr-hassan-diab-extradition.html.

Shapiro, J., and Suzan, B. (2003). "The French Experience of Counter-terrorism." 45(1) *Survival* 67–98.

Sieder, R., Schjolden, L., and Angell, A. (eds.) (2005). *The Judicialisation of Politics in Latin America* (New York: Palgrave Macmillan).

Sigler, J. A. (1979). "The Prosecutor: A Comparative Functional Analysis." In McDonald, W. F. (ed.) *The Prosecutor* (Beverly Hills, CA: Sage) 53–74.

Simon, D., Stenstrom, D., and Read, J. (2009). "Adversarial and Non-adversarial Investigations: An Experiment." Available at http://ssrn.com/abstract=1401723.

Simon, D., Stenstrom, D., and Read, J. (2015). "The Coherence Effect: Blending Cold and Hot Cognitions." University of Southern California Law School, Legal Studies Working Paper No. 173.

Simon, J. (2007). *Governing through Crime* (New York: Oxford University Press).

Skinner, S. (2002). "The Third Pillar Treaty Provisions on Police Cooperation: Has the EU Bitten Off More Than It Can Chew?" 8 *Columbia Journal of European Law* 203–220.

Skinns, L. (2009). "'I'm a Detainee Get Me Out of Here': Predictors of Access to Custodial Legal Advice in Public and Privatized Police Custody Areas in England and Wales." 49 *British Journal of Criminology* 399–417.

Skinns, L. (2011). *Police Custody: Governance, Legitimacy and Reform in the Criminal Justice Process* (Abingdon: Willan).

Skinns, L. (2019). *Police Powers and Citizens' Rights: Discretionary Decision-Making in Police Detention* (New York: Routledge).

Skinns, L., Sprawson, A., Sorsby, A., Smith, R., and Woof, A. (2017). "Police Custody Delivery in the Twenty-First Century in England and Wales: Current Arrangements and Their Implications for Patterns of Policing." 4(3) *European Journal of Policing Studies* 325–348.

Slansky, D. (2016). "The Nature and Function of Prosecutorial Power." 106(3) *Journal of Criminal Law and Criminology* 473–520.

Soo, A. (2017). "Divergence of European Union and Strasbourg Standards on Defence Rights in Criminal Proceedings? *Ibrahim and others v. the UK* (13th of September 2016)." 25(4) *European Journal of Crime, Criminal Law and Criminal Justice* 327–346.

Soo, A. (2018). "(Effective) Remedies for a Violation of the Right to Counsel during Criminal Proceedings in the European Union: An Empirical Study." 14(1) *Utrecht Law Review* 18–60.

Soubise, L. (2016). *Prosecutorial Discretion and Accountability: A Comparative Study of France and England and Wales*. PhD diss., University of Warwick.

Soubise, L. (2017). "Prosecuting in the Magistrates' Court in a Time of Austerity." *Criminal Law Review* 847–859.

Soubise, L. (2018). "Guilty Pleas in an Inquisitorial Setting: An Empirical Study of France." 45(3) *Journal of Law and Society* 398–426.

Spencer, J. R. (2002). "Introduction." In Delmas-Marty, M., and Spencer, J. R. (eds.), *European Criminal Procedures* (Cambridge: Cambridge University Press) 1–75.

Spencer, J. R. (2006). "Quashing Convictions and Squashing the Court of Appeal." 170 *Justice of the Peace* 790–793.

Steiker, C. (1998). "The Limits of the Preventive State." 88 *Journal of Criminal Law and Criminology* 771–808.

Stewart, J., and Walsh, K. (1992). "Change in the Management of Public Services." 70(4) *Public Administration* 499–518.

Strickland, P., and Beard, J. (2012). "Sentences of Imprisonment for Public Protection." In *Home Affairs Section Standard Note*. SN/HA/6086, House of Commons Library.

Stumpf, J. (2006). "The Crimmigration Crisis: Immigrants, Crime and Sovereign Power." 56(2) *American University Law Review* Article 3.

Sukumar, D., Hodgson, J., and Wade, K. (2016a). "Behind Closed Doors: Live Observations of Current Police Station Disclosure Practices and Lawyer-Client Consultations." *Criminal Law Review* 900–914.

Sukumar, D., Hodgson, J., and Wade, K. (2016b). "How the Timing of Police Evidence Disclosure Impacts Custodial Legal Advice." 20(3) *International Journal of Evidence and Proof* 200–216.

Sukumar, D., Wade, K., and Hodgson, J. (2016). "Strategic Disclosure of Evidence: Perspectives from Psychology and Law." 22(3) *Psychology, Public Policy, and Law* 306–313.

Sukumar, D., Wade, K. A., and Hodgson, J. (2018). "Truth-Tellers Stand the Test of Time and Contradict Evidence Less Than Liars, Even Months after a Crime." 42(2) *Law and Human Behavior* 145–155.

Summers, S. (2007). *Fair Trials: The European Criminal Procedural Tradition and the European Court of Human Rights* (Oxford: Hart).

Tadros, V. (2007). "Justice and Terrorism." 10(4) *New Criminal Law Review* 658–689.

Tata, C., and Stephen, F. (2006). "'Swings and Roundabouts': Do Changes to the Structure of Legal Aid Remuneration Make a Real Difference to Criminal Case Management and Case Outcomes?" *Criminal Law Review* 722–741.

Thaman, S. (ed.) (2010). *World Plea Bargaining: Consensual Procedures and the Avoidance of the Full Criminal Trial* (Durham: North Carolina Academic Press).

Tickell, A. (2015). "More 'efficient' Justice at the European Court of Human Rights: But at Whose Expense?" *Public Law* 206–215.

Tonry, M. (ed.) (2012). *Prosecutors and Politics: A Comparative Perspective* (Chicago: University of Chicago Press).

Toor, A. (2016). "Automated Systems Fight ISIS Propaganda, but at What Cost?" *The Verge*. Available at http://www.theverge.com/2016/9/6/12811680/isis-propaganda-algorithm-facebook—twitter-google.

Truche, P. (1997). *Rapport de la Commission de réflexion sur la justice* (Paris: La Documentation française).

Turner, J. I. (2016). "Plea Bargaining and Disclosure in Germany and the United States: Comparative Lessons." 57(4) *William and Mary Law Review* 1549–1596.

Turner, J. I. (2017). "Plea Bargaining and International Justice." 48(2) *University of the Pacific Law Review* 219–246.

Turner, J. I., and Weigend, T. (2013). "Negotiated Justice." In Sluiter, G., Friman, H., Linton, S., Vasilev, S., and Zappalà, S. (eds.) *International Criminal Procedure: Principles and Rules* (Oxford: Oxford University Press) 1377–1413.

Tyler, R. (1990). *Why People Obey the Law* (New Haven: Yale University Press).

Vallini, A. (2006). *Rapport fait au nom de la commission d'enquête chargée de rechercher les causes des dysfonctionnements de la justice dans l'affaire dite d'Outreau et de formuler des propositions pour éviter leur renouvellement* (Paris: Assemblée nationale).

Van de Bunt, H., and van Gelder, J.-L. (2012). "The Dutch Prosecution Service." In Tonry, M. (ed.) *Prosecutors and Politics: A Comparative Perspective* (Chicago: University of Chicago Press) 117–140.

Vasiliev, S. (2016). "Trial Process at the ECCC: The Rise and Fall of the Inquisitorial Paradigm in International Criminal Law?" In Meisenberg, S., and Stegmiller, I. (eds.) *The Hybrid Contributions of the Extraordinary Chambers in the Courts of Cambodia to International Criminal Law* (The Hague: Asser Press) 389–435.

Véliz, C. P. (2012). "Criminal Procedure Reform: A New Form of Criminal Justice for Chile." 80(4) *University of Cincinnati Law Review* 1363–1372.

Viennot, C. (2012). *Le process pénal accéléré: Etude des transformations du jugement pénal* (Paris: Dalloz).

Villepin, D. de (2006). *Prevailing against Terrorism: White Paper on Domestic Security against Terrorism* (Paris: La Documentation française).

Viout, J.-O. (2005). *Rapport du groupe de travail chargé de tirer les enseignements du traitement judiciaire de l'affaire dite "d'Outreau"* (Paris: Ministère de la justice).

Voeten, E. (2008). "The Impartiality of International Judges: Evidence from the European Court of Human Rights." 102 *American Political Science Review* 417–433.

Vogler, R. K. (2005). *A World View of Criminal Procedure* (Aldershot: Ashgate).

Von Hippel, K. (ed.) (2005). *Europe Confronts Terrorism* (Basingstoke: Palgrave Macmillan).

Vouin, R. (1955). "La question du jury." 20 *Revue de science criminelle et de droit pénal comparé* 503–507.
Vouin, R. (1956). "The Protection of the Accused in French Criminal Procedure." 5(1) *International and Comparative Law Quarterly* 1–25.
Wade, M. (2008). "The Januses of Justice: How Prosecutors Define the Kind of Justice Done across Europe." 16 *European Journal of Crime, Criminal Law and Criminal Justice* 433–455.
Waldron, J. (2003). "Security and Liberty: The Image of Balance." 11(2) *Journal of Political Philosophy* 191–210.
Walker, C. (2006). "Clamping Down on Terrorism in the United Kingdom." 4 *Journal of International Criminal Justice* 1137–1151.
Walker, C. (2007). "The Legal Definition of 'Terrorism' in United Kingdom Law and Beyond." *Public Law* 331–352.
Walker, C., and Starmer, K. (eds.) (1999). *Miscarriages of Justice: A Review of Justice in Error* (London: Blackstone Press).
Walker, N. (1999). "The Antinomies of the Law Officers." In Sunkin, M., and Payne, S. (eds.) *The Nature of the Crown: A Legal and Political Analysis* (Oxford: Oxford University Press) 135–169.
Weatheritt, M. (1980). *The Prosecution System: Survey of Prosecuting Solicitors' Departments*. RCCP Research Study No. 11 (London: HMSO).
Weigend, T. (2004). "The Prosecution Service in the German Administration of Criminal Justice." In Tak, J. P. (ed.) *Tasks and Powers of the Prosecution Services in the EU Member States* (Nijmegen: Wolf Legal Publishers) 203–222.
Weigend, T. (2006a). "Why Have a Trial When You Can Have a Bargain." In Duff, A., Farmer, L., Marshall, S., and Tadros, V. (eds.) *The Trial on Trial: Judgment and Calling to Account* (Oxford: Hart) 207–222.
Weigend, T. (2006b). "The Universal Terrorist." 4 *Journal of International Criminal Justice* 912–932.
Weigend, T. (2008). "The Decay of the Inquisitorial Ideal: Plea Bargaining Invades German Criminal Procedure." In Jackson, J., Langer, M., and Tillers, P. (eds.) *Crime, Procedure and Evidence in a Comparative and International Context* (Oxford: Hart) 39–64.
Weigend, T. (2011). "Should We Search for the Truth, and Who Should Do it?" 36(2) *North Carolina Journal of International Law and Commercial Regulation* 389–415.
Weigend, T. (2019). "Defense Rights in European Legal Systems under the Influence of the European Court of Human Rights." In Brown, D. K., Turner, J. I., and Weisser, B. (eds.) *Oxford Handbook of Criminal Process* (Oxford: Oxford University Press) 163–188.
Weigend, T., and Turner, J. (2014). "The Constitutionality of Negotiated Criminal Judgments in Germany." 15(1) *German Law Journal* 81–105.
Weisselberg, C. D. (2017). "Exporting and Importing *Miranda*." 97(3) *Boston University Law Review* 1235–1291.
Wyvekens, Anne. (2010). "La rétention de sûreté en France: Une défense sociale en trompe-l'oeil (ou les habits neufs de l'empereur)." 34(4) *Déviance et société* 503–525.
Zander, M., and Henderson, P. (1993). *The Crown Court Study.* RCCJ Study No. 1 (London: HMSO).
Zedner, L. (2005). "Securing Liberty in the Face of Terror: Reflections from Criminal Justice." 32(4) *Journal of Law and Society* 507–533.

Zedner, L. (2009). *Security* (New York: Routledge).

Zellick, G. (2005). "The Criminal Cases Review Commission and the Court of Appeal: The Commission's Perspective." *Criminal Law Review* 937–950.

Zocchetto, F. (2005). *Juger vite, juger mieux? Les procédures rapides de traitement des affaires pénales, état des lieux*. Sénat, rapport d'information no. 17.

Index

For the benefit of digital users, indexed terms that span two pages (e.g., 52–53) may, on occasion, appear on only one of those pages.